STUDY GUIDE

Richard O. Straub

University of Michigan, Dearborn

to accompany

PSYCHOLOGY

in Everyday Life

fourth edition

DAVID G. MYERS

Hope College
Holland, Michigan

C. NATHAN DEWALL

University of Kentucky
Lexington, Kentucky

 worth publishers
Macmillan Learning
New York

Study Guide
by Richard O. Straub
to accompany
Myers and DeWall: **Psychology in Everyday Life,** Fourth Edition

Printed in the United States of America

ISBN 13: 978-1-319-07983-3
ISBN 10: 1-319-07983-0

First printing

Worth Publishers/Macmillan

One New York Plaza
Suite 4500
New York, NY 10004-1562

STUDY GUIDE

Contents

Preface   vii

CHAPTER 1
Psychology's Roots, Big Ideas, and Critical
Thinking Tools   1

CHAPTER 2
The Biology of Mind and Consciousness   21

CHAPTER 3
Developing Through the Life Span   45

CHAPTER 4
Gender and Sexuality   69

CHAPTER 5
Sensation and Perception   85

CHAPTER 6
Learning   113

CHAPTER 7
Memory   133

CHAPTER 8
Thinking, Language, and Intelligence   153

CHAPTER 9
Motivation and Emotion   177

CHAPTER 10
Stress, Health, and Human Flourishing   197

CHAPTER 11
Social Psychology   213

CHAPTER 12
Personality   235

CHAPTER 13
Psychological Disorders   259

CHAPTER 14
Therapy   287

APPENDIX A
Statistical Reasoning in Everyday Life   311

APPENDIX B
Psychology at Work   323

Preface

This Study Guide is designed for use with *Psychology in Everyday Life,* Fourth Edition, by David G. Myers and C. Nathan DeWall. It is intended to help you to learn material in the textbook, to evaluate your understanding of that material, and then to review any problem areas. Many students will also benefit from reading "Time Management: Or, How to Be a Great Student and Still Have a Life" in the text. This essay offers proven study suggestions for useful note-taking, evaluating your exam performance, and improving your comprehension while studying from textbooks.

Features

This Study Guide offers many useful features. Each chapter begins with a Chapter Review that is organized by major text section and one or more learning objectives. Each objective is followed by a brief summary of important concepts from the text, including all key terms. Under each objective are a number of fill-in and essay-type questions, art to be labeled, and summary tables to be completed or that are already completed for you. Also included are practical study tips and applications. These tips and applications are designed to help you evaluate your understanding of the text chapter's broader concepts, and make the text material more meaningful by relating it to your own life. Following the Chapter Review is a Progress Test consisting of

multiple-choice, matching, and essay questions that focus on facts and definitions. For all questions, the correct answers are given, and explanations of why the answer is correct as well as why the other choices are incorrect. Most chapters also include at least one Summing Up concept map in the form of a flow chart. Designed to promote a deeper understanding of the conceptual relationships among chapter issues, these review charts follow the lead of the text in emphasizing the importance of viewing human behavior as a product of biological, psychological, and social-cultural influences. Some tell a story, so that you are learning the concepts as applied to real-life situations.

Acknowledgments

Special thanks are due to Betty Shapiro Probert for her extraordinary editorial contributions and to Don Probert for his skill and efficiency in the composition of this guide. I would also like to thank Won McIntosh and Sarah Segal for their dedication and energy in skillfully coordinating various aspects of production. Most important, I want to thank Jeremy, Rebecca, Melissa, and Pam for their enduring love and support.

Richard O. Straub

Psychology's Roots, Big Ideas, and Critical Thinking Tools

Chapter Overview

Chapter 1 begins by describing the basic elements of the scientific attitude. The chapter then traces modern psychology back to Wundt's first laboratory experiments and describes current perspectives and major subfields. The chapter then discusses four big ideas that penetrate psychology: the importance of critical thinking and the biopsychosocial approach, as well as the ideas that we operate with a two-track mind and that psychology explores both human strengths and challenges. The core of the chapter describes the methods of research: the case study, naturalistic observation, surveys, correlation, and experimentation. The next section answers some common questions about psychology. The chapter concludes with suggestions for improving your study habits.

Chapter Review

First, skim each text section, noting headings and bold-face items. Review the section by reading the objectives and summaries provided here, then answer the questions that follow. In some cases, STUDY TIPS explain how best to learn a difficult concept and APPLICATIONS help you to know how well you understand the material. Check your understanding of the material by consulting the answers beginning on page 15. Do not continue with the next section until you understand each answer. If you need to, review or reread the section in the textbook before continuing.

Psychology's Roots

Objective 1-1: Identify the three key elements of the scientific attitude, and explain how they support scientific inquiry.

The scientific attitude reflects a hard-headed *curiosity* to explore and understand the world without being fooled by it. The eagerness to *skeptically* scrutinize competing claims requires *humility* because it means we may have to reject our own ideas. This attitude, coupled with scientific principles for sifting reality from fantasy, helps us separate sense from nonsense, and thus makes modern science possible.

1. The scientific approach is characterized by the attitudes of _____ , _____ , and _____ .

APPLICATION:

2. In psychology, the motto that "the rat is always right" expresses a humble attitude. Explain.

_____

_____

_____

Objective 1-2: Discuss how psychology's focus has changed over time.

Wilhelm Wundt established the first psychological laboratory in 1879 in Leipzig, Germany. He sought to measure the fastest and simplest mental processes.

Psychology's pioneers came from many different disciplines and countries. Its pioneers included Russian physiologist Ivan Pavlov, Austrian personality theorist Sigmund Freud, and Swiss biologist Jean Piaget. William James, who wrote a psychology textbook in 1890, helped change psychology from an all-male discipline. He mentored Mary Whiton Calkins, the first female president of APA. Margaret Floy Washburn was the first psychology Ph.D. and the second female president of APA.

Until the 1920s, psychology was defined as the science of mental life. From the 1920s through the 1960s, American psychologists, led by John Watson and later by B. F. Skinner, both **behaviorists,** redefined psychology as the scientific study of observable behavior. In responding to Freudian psychology and behaviorism, **humanistic psychology** emphasized human growth potential and the importance of meeting our needs for love and acceptance. In the 1960s, psychology began to recapture its initial interest in mental processes; **cognitive psychology** was born as a result of this *cognitive revolution.* More recently, **cognitive neuroscience** has increased our understanding of the brain's role in mental activities. Today, **psychology** is defined as the *scientific study of behavior and mental processes.* Behavior is anything an organism does. Mental processes are the internal subjective experiences we infer from behavior, for example, perceptions, thoughts, and feelings.

3. The first psychological laboratory was founded in 1879 by Wilhelm _____ .

4. Some early psychologists included Ivan Pavlov, who pioneered the study of _____ ; the personality theorist _____ ; and Jean Piaget, who studied _____ .

5. The teacher-writer of psychology, _____ , mentored _____ , who became the first female president of the American Psychological Association. The first woman to receive a Ph.D. in psychology was _____ .

6. In its earliest years, psychology was defined as the science of _____ life. From the 1920s into the 1960s, psychology in America was redefined as the science of _____ behavior. This second major force in psychology's history was _____ .

7. As a response to Freudian psychology and to _____ , which they considered too limiting, pioneers _____ and _____ forged _____ psychology, which emphasized ways that environment can help or hinder personal _____ .

8. During the 1960s, psychology underwent a _____ revolution as it began to recapture interest in _____ processes. The study of the brain processes underlying thought is called _____ _____ .

9. Today, we define psychology as the scientific study of _____ and _____ processes.

APPLICATION: Dharma has to write a term paper on the history of psychology. As part of her paper, she notes that "psychology has been defined in various ways depending on the researchers' perspective, but today it is generally defined as the 'scientific study of behavior and mental processes.'"

10. In identifying the different definitions, Dharma explains that Wilhelm Wundt would have omitted the phrase "_____ _____" from the definition.

11. In concluding her paper, Dharma recaps by saying that
   a. psychology began as the science of mental life.
   b. from the 1920s into the 1960s, psychology was defined as the scientific study of observable behavior.
   c. contemporary psychologists study both overt behavior and covert thoughts.
   d. all of these statements are true.

Objective 1-3: Describe psychology's current perspectives, and identify some of its subfields.

Psychology's varied perspectives share a common goal: describing and explaining behavior and the mind underlying it. The *neuroscience perspective* studies how the body and brain work to create emotions, memories, and sensory experiences. The *evolutionary perspective* considers how the natural selection of traits has promoted the survival of genes. The *behavior genetics perspective* considers how genes and environment influence our individual differences. The *psychodynamic perspective* views behavior as springing from unconscious drives and conflicts. The *behavioral perspective* examines how observable responses are learned. The *cognitive perspective* studies how we encode, process, store, and retrieve information. The *social-cultural perspective* examines how behavior and thinking vary across situations and cultures.

Psychologists work in a variety of fields. *Biological psychologists* explore the link between brain and mind; *developmental psychologists* study our changing abilities from womb to tomb; *cognitive psychologists* experiment with how we perceive, think, and solve problems; *personality psychologists* investigate our persistent traits; *social psychologists* explore how we view and affect one another; *counseling psychologists* assist people with problems in living and in achieving greater well-being; *health psychologists* investigate the psychological, biological, and behavioral factors that promote or impair our health; *clinical psychologists* assess and treat people with mental, emotional, and behavior disorders; *industrial-organizational psychologists* study and advise on behavior in the workplace; and *community psychologists* work to create healthy social and physical environments.

STUDY TIP: This section describes a number of perspectives in psychology. Keep in mind that each perspective is nothing more than how certain psychologists feel behavior and mental processes should be investigated. For example, a clinical psychologist could approach the study of abnormal behavior from any of the perspectives discussed. Typically, however, psychologists work from a combination of perspectives rather than exclusively from only one. To deepen your understanding of the various perspectives, review the following chart. In the first column are listed psychology's contemporary perspectives. In the second column are listed historical roots and the pioneers who contributed to each modern-day perspective and the subfield that derives from it. As you work through the chapters, you might want to annotate this chart to include what you know about these psychologists.

Perspective	Historical Roots and Pioneers
Neuroscience	Wundt
Evolutionary	Darwin, Freud
Behavior Genetics	Darwin
Psychodynamic	Freud
Behavioral	Pavlov, Watson, Skinner
Cognitive	Wundt (quantifying mental processes), Piaget
Social-Cultural	Piaget, Rogers, Maslow

APPLICATION:

12. Match each psychological perspective and subfield with its definition or description.

Perspective or Subfield

_____ 1. neuroscience perspective
_____ 2. social-cultural perspective
_____ 3. psychiatry
_____ 4. clinical psychology
_____ 5. behavior genetics perspective
_____ 6. behavioral perspective
_____ 7. industrial-organizational psychology
_____ 8. cognitive perspective
_____ 9. personality psychology
_____ 10. developmental psychology
_____ 11. evolutionary perspective
_____ 12. psychodynamic perspective
_____ 13. counseling psychology
_____ 14. social psychology
_____ 15. health psychology

Definitions or Descriptions

a. the study of behavior in the workplace

b. how people differ as products of different environments

c. the study of how people change over the life span

d. how psychological, biological, and behavioral factors promote or impair our health

e. how the body and brain create emotions, memories, and sensations

f. how the mind encodes, processes, stores, and retrieves information

g. helping people to cope with personal and career challenges

h. how the natural selection of traits passed down through generations has promoted the survival of one's genes

i. assessing and treating troubled people

j. the medical treatment of psychological disorders

k. the disguised effects of unfulfilled wishes and childhood traumas

l. the analysis of people's persistent traits

m. how much genes and environment contribute to individual differences

n. how people affect one another

o. the mechanisms by which observable responses are learned

Four Big Ideas in Psychology

Objective 1-4: Identify four big ideas that run throughout this book.

The four big ideas of psychology that run through this text, are the following.
- *Critical thinking* is smart thinking. Critical thinkers do not blindly accept arguments and conclusions. They examine assumptions, uncover hidden values, weigh evidence, and assess conclusions.
- Behavior is a *biopsychosocial* event. To understand behavior, we need several levels of analysis—biological, psychological, and social-*cultural*. The *nature-nurture issue*—the relative contributions of genes and experience—is a major issue.
- We operate with a two-track mind (*dual processing*)—that is, information is processed both consciously and unconsciously.
- Psychology explores human strengths as well as challenges. The scientific study of human strengths is called *positive psychology.*

13. Psychology's first big idea is that _____ _____ is smart thinking. This means that this type of thinker examines _____ , uncovers hidden _____ , weighs _____ , and tests _____ .

14. Each person is a complex _____ that is part of a larger _____ _____ and at the same time composed of smaller systems. For this reason, psychologists work from three main _____ of _____ — biological , _____ , and _____ - _____ — which together form an integrated _____ approach to the study of behavior and mental processes.

15. _____ refers to the traits and behaviors we expect from a boy or girl, or a man or woman in a specific culture. _____ refers to the biological characteristics people inherit. To study gender similarities and differences, we want to know about _____ influences, but we also want to understand how the group views gender. Culture refers to the _____ _____ , _____ , _____ , _____ , and _____ shared by a large group of people that one generation passes on to the next.

16. The nature–nurture issue is the debate over the relative contributions of _____ and _____ .

The nature–nurture issue is psychology's biggest and most persistent debate. Psychologists explore the issue by asking, for example, how differences in intelligence, personality, and psychological disorders are influenced by heredity and by environment. Today, contemporary science recognizes that *nurture works on what nature provides.* Our species is graced with an enormous capacity to learn and adapt. Moreover, every psychological event is simultaneously a biological event.

APPLICATION:

17. A friend majoring in anthropology is critical of psychological research because she believes that it often ignores the influence of culture on thoughts and actions. You point out that psychologists today take a _____ approach because they are aware that nature and nurture _____ .

18. Psychology's third big idea is that information is often processed simultaneously on separate _____ and _____ tracks. This principle is called _____ _____ .

19. Psychology's fourth big idea is that psychology explores human _____ and _____ .

20. Martin Seligman called for more research on _____ _____ . The scientific study of positive _____ , positive _____ traits, and positive _____ is called _____ _____ .

Why Do Psychology?

Objective 1-5: Explain how our everyday thinking sometimes leads us to the wrong conclusion.

The **hindsight bias,** also known as the *I-knew-it-all-along phenomenon,* is the tendency to believe, after learning an outcome, that one would have foreseen it. Finding out that something has happened makes it seem inevitable. Thus, after learning the results of a study in psychology, it may seem to be obvious common sense. However, experiments have found that events seem far less obvious and predictable beforehand than in hindsight. Sometimes psychological findings even jolt our common sense.

Our everyday thinking is also limited by our tendency to think we know more than we do. Asked how sure we are of our answers to factual questions, we tend to be more confident than correct. Students' predictions of their future behaviors are similarly *overconfident.*

We also tend to perceive patterns where there are none. Even in random, unrelated data we often find order, because *random sequences often don't look random.*

21. Although human _____ is important, research shows that our gut feelings lead us astray.

22. The tendency to perceive an outcome that has occurred as being obvious and predictable is called _____ _____ . This phenomenon is _____ (rare/common). Because it is _____ (after the fact/usually wrong), this tendency makes research findings seem like mere common sense.

23. Our everyday thinking is also limited by _____ in what we think we know. Most people are _____ (better/worse/equally wrong) in predicting their social behavior.

24. In our natural eagerness to make sense of our world we often perceive _____ where they _____ (do/do not) exist.

How Do Psychologists Ask and Answer Questions?

Objective 1-6: Describe how theories advance psychological science.

A useful **theory** effectively organizes a wide range of observations and implies testable predictions, called **hypotheses.** By enabling us to test and reject or revise a particular theory, such predictions give direction to research. They specify in advance what results would support the theory and what results would lead us to revise or reject it. As a check on their biases, psychologists report their results precisely with clear **operational definitions** of concepts. Such statements of the procedures used to define research variables allow others to **replicate,** or repeat, their observations. Often, research leads to a revised theory that better organizes and predicts observable behaviors or events.

25. Psychologists use the _____ _____ to guide their study of behavior and mental processes.

26. An explanation using principles that organize observations and predict behaviors or events is a _____ . Testable predictions that allow a scientist to evaluate a theory are called _____ . These predictions give direction to _____ .

27. To prevent theoretical biases from influencing scientific observations, research must be reported precisely—using clear _____ _____ of all concepts—so that others can _____ the findings.

28. The test of a useful theory is the extent to which it effectively _____ a range of self-reports and observations and leads to clear _____ . A good theory also often leads to new _____ and a revised theory.

29. Psychologists conduct research using _____ , _____ , and _____ .

Objective 1-7: Describe how psychologists use case studies, naturalistic observations, and surveys to observe and describe behavior, and explain the importance of random sampling.

The **case study** is the method by which psychologists analyze one person or group in great depth in the hope of revealing things true of us all. While individual cases can suggest fruitful ideas, any given individual may be atypical, making the case misleading.

Naturalistic observation consists of observing and recording the behavior of organisms in their natural environment. Like the case study, this research strategy describes behavior but does not explain it.

The **survey** looks at many cases in less depth and asks people to report their behavior or opinions. Asking questions is tricky because even subtle changes in the order or wording of questions can dramatically affect responses. In everyday experience, we are tempted to generalize from a few vivid but unrepresentative cases. The survey learns the self-reported attitudes or behaviors of a **population** by questioning a *representative, random sample.*

30. The research strategy in which one individual or group is studied in depth in order to reveal universal principles of behavior is the _____ _____ .

31. Although case studies can suggest directions for further study, a potential problem with this method is that any given individual may be _____ .

32. The research method in which people or animals are directly observed in their natural environments is called _____ _____ .

33. The scope of this observational method is expanding because the new _____ involved in sites such as Facebook and Twitter provide a chance for "big data" observations.

34. Case studies and naturalistic observation do not explain behavior; they simply _____ it.

35. The method in which a group of people is questioned about their attitudes or behavior is the _____ .

36. An important factor in the validity of survey research is the _____ of questions.

37. Surveys try to obtain a _____ sample, one that will be representative of the _____ being studied. In such a sample, every person _____ (does/does not) have a chance of being included.

38. Large, representative samples _____ (are/are not) better than small ones. If the sample is not _____, even a large sample can be misleading.

APPLICATIONS:

39. Marcus has been in a car accident and has suffered brain damage. By observing his changed behavior, a psychologist might be able to learn which area of the brain is responsible for that behavior. Marcus' injury provides _____ _____ information for the psychologist.

40. Dr. Adamson is a chaperone at a high school prom and is observing the interaction of the teens as the boys and girls come together or separate in selecting dance partners. What type of research is he conducting?
    a. a case study
    b. naturalistic observation
    c. survey
    d. hypothetical

Objective 1-8: Describe positive and negative correlations, and explain how they can lead to prediction but not cause-effect explanation.

When surveys and naturalistic observations reveal that one trait or behavior accompanies another, we say the two **correlate**. A *correlation coefficient* is a statistical measure of relationship. A *positive correlation* indicates a direct relationship, meaning that two things increase together or decrease together. A *negative correlation* indicates an inverse relationship: As one thing increases, the other decreases. The correlation coefficient helps us to see the world more clearly by revealing the extent to which two things relate.

Perhaps the most irresistible thinking error is to assume that correlation proves causation. Correlation reveals how closely two things vary together and thus how well one predicts the other. However, the fact that events are correlated does not mean that one causes the other. Thus, while correlation enables prediction, it does not provide explanation.

STUDY TIP: Many students find the concept of correlation confusing. A common mistake is the belief that a negative correlation indicates a weak or absent relationship between two variables. Remember that correlation does not prove causa-

tion; rather, it indicates the degree to which you can predict changes in one variable from another. The *strength* of a correlation, indicated by a numerical value, is independent of the *direction* (positive [+] or negative [−]) of the relationship. A negative correlation simply means that two variables change in opposite directions, such as when sales of hot chocolate decrease as the average daily temperature increases.

41. When changes in one factor are accompanied by changes in another, the two factors are said to be _____, and one is thus able to _____ the other. The statistical expression of this relationship is called a _____ _____.

42. If two factors increase or decrease together, they are _____ _____. If, however, one decreases as the other increases, they are _____ _____. Another way to state the latter is that the two variables relate _____.

43. A negative correlation between two variables does not indicate the _____ or _____ of the relationship. Nor does correlation prove _____; rather, it merely indicates the possibility of a _____-_____ relationship.

44. A correlation between two events or behaviors means only that one event can be _____ from the other.

45. Because two events may both be caused by some other _____, a correlation does not mean that one _____ the other. For this reason, correlation thus does not enable _____.

APPLICATIONS:

Test your understanding of correlational research by answering these questions.

46. If your level of test anxiety goes down as your time spent studying for the exam goes up, you would say these events are _____ (positively/negatively) correlated. Explain your reasoning. _____ _____ _____

47. If eating saturated fat and the likelihood of contracting cancer are positively correlated, what could you say about the relationship between saturated fat and cancer? _____

_____

_____

48. Knowing that height and body weight are positively correlated means that as height increases, weight _____ (increases/decreases).

Objective 1-9: Describe how experiments clarify or reveal cause-effect relationships.

The *experiment* is a research method in which the investigator manipulates one or more factors to observe their effect on some behavior or mental process while controlling other factors. If a behavior changes when we vary an experimental factor, then we know the factor is having a causal effect.

In many experiments, control is achieved by *randomly assigning* people either to an *experimental group,* in which they are exposed to the treatment, or a *control group,* in which they are not exposed.

Often, the research participants are blind (uninformed) about what treatment, if any, they are receiving. One group might receive the treatment, while the other group receives a *placebo* (an inactive substance or condition). Often both the participant and the research assistant who collects the data will not know which group the participant is in (the *double-blind procedure*). The *placebo effect* is well-documented. Just thinking one is receiving treatment can lead to symptom relief.

The *independent variable* is the experimental factor that is being manipulated. It is the variable whose effect is being studied. A *confounding variable* is a factor other than the independent variable that might produce an effect. The *dependent variable* is the variable that may change in response to the manipulations of the independent variable. It is the outcome factor.

49. To isolate _____ and _____ , researchers have to simplify our complex world. They do this by using the _____ method.

50. Using this method, a researcher _____ the factor of interest while _____ _____ (controlling) other factors. By _____ assigning participants to groups, researchers are able to hold _____ all factors except the one being investigated.

51. Research studies have found that breast-fed, preterm infants _____ (do/do not) grow up with higher intelligence scores than those of infants who are bottle-fed with formula.

Experiments such as this must involve at least two groups: the _____ group, who receive the treatment (are breast-fed), and the _____ group, who do not receive the treatment (are bottle-fed).

52. To ensure that the two groups are identical, experimenters rely on the _____ _____ of individuals to the two groups.

53. Researchers sometimes give certain participants an inactive substance or treatment, called a _____ , and compare their behavior with that of participants who receive the actual treatment. When merely thinking that one is receiving a treatment produces results, a

_____ _____

is said to occur.

54. When neither the participants nor the person collecting the data knows which condition a participant is in, the researcher is making use of the

_____-_____

procedure.

55. The factor that is being manipulated in an experiment is called the _____ variable. The measurable factor that may change as a result of these manipulations is called the _____ variable. Other factors that can potentially influence the results of an experiment are called _____

_____ .

STUDY TIP: Students often confuse *independent variables* and *dependent variables.* Remember that independent variables are manipulated directly by the researcher to determine how they affect dependent variables. Dependent variables are the behaviors and mental processes that psychologists are trying to understand. In a sense, dependent variables *depend* on the actions of independent variables. When you are struggling to distinguish two variables, ask yourself, "Which of these two variables can affect the other?" Consider, for example, a researcher investigating caffeine and reaction time. After randomly assigning different students to groups that drink a highly caffeinated drink and a weakly caffeinated drink, she measures each student's speed in pushing a button in response to a signal light. Which variable is the independent variable, and which is the dependent variable? If the answer is not obvious, try the test question, "Which variable can affect the other?" Clearly, reaction time cannot affect caffeine. So in this example, the dose of caffeine is the independent variable and reaction time is the dependent variable.

56. The aim of an experiment is to _____

a(n) _____ variable,

_____ the _____

variable, and _____ all other

_____ .

Explain at least one advantage of the experiment as a research method.

STUDY TIP/APPLICATIONS: The concepts of *control* and *operational definition* are important in experimental research. In an experiment, researchers strive to hold constant (control) the possible effects of all variables on the dependent variable, except the one that is being manipulated (independent variable). Operational definitions, which were explained earlier, are like recipes for measuring a variable so that other researchers can replicate your results. They are much more precise than dictionary definitions. For example, the dictionary might define intelligence as "the capacity to reason." Because this definition is too vague for research purposes, a psychologist might create the operational definition of intelligence as "a person's answers to a specific set of IQ test questions." Test your understanding of these important concepts by completing the following exercises.

---

57. The concept of control is important in psychological research because it allows researchers to study the influence of one or two _____ variables on a _____ variable while holding other potential influences _____ .

58. Martina believes that high doses of caffeine slow a person's reaction time. To test this belief, she has five friends each drink three 8-ounce cups of coffee and then measures their reaction time on a learning task. What is wrong with Martina's research strategy?

 a. No independent variable is specified.
 b. No dependent variable is specified.
 c. There is no control group.
 d. There is no provision for replication of the findings.

59. How would you operationally define the following variables?

　　Exercise:

　　Anger:

　　Stress:

Objective 1-10: Explain how simplified laboratory conditions help us understand general principles of behavior.

The experimenter intends the laboratory experiment to be a simplified reality, one in which important features can be simulated and controlled. The experiment's pur-

pose is not to re-create the exact behaviors of everyday life but to test theoretical principles. It is the resulting principles—not the specific findings—that help explain everyday behavior.

60. In laboratory experiments, psychologists' concern is not with specific behaviors but with the underlying theoretical _____ .

61. Psychologists conduct experiments on simplified behaviors in a laboratory environment in order to gain _____ over the many variables present in the "real world." In doing so, they are able to test general _____ of behavior that also operate in the real world.

APPLICATION:

62. Your best friend criticizes psychological research for being artificial and having no relevance to behavior in real life. In defense of psychology's use of laboratory experiments you point out that

 a. psychologists make every attempt to avoid artificiality by setting up experiments that closely simulate real-world environments.
 b. psychologists who conduct basic research are not concerned with the applicability of their findings to the real world.
 c. most psychological research is not conducted in a laboratory environment.
 d. psychologists intentionally study behavior in simplified environments in order to gain greater control over variables and to test general principles that help to explain many behaviors.

Psychology's Research Ethics

Objective 1-11: Explain why psychologists study animals, and identify the ethical guidelines that safeguard human and animal research participants. Describe how personal values can influence psychologists' research and applications.

Some psychologists study animals out of an interest in animal behaviors. Others do so because knowledge of the physiological and psychological processes of animals enables them to better understand the similar processes that operate in humans.

Because psychologists follow ethical and legal guidelines, animals used in psychological experiments rarely experience pain. The debate between animal protection organizations and researchers has raised two important issues: Is it right to place the well-being of humans above that of animals, and what safeguards are in place to protect the well-being of animals in research? Many professional organizations and funding agencies have developed extensive guidelines for the humane use of animals.

Ethical principles for the treatment of human participants urge investigators to obtain *informed consent,* protect participants from harm and discomfort, treat information about individuals confidentially, and fully explain the research afterward (*debrief* them).

Psychologists' values can influence their choice of research topic, their theories and observations, their labels for behavior, and their professional advice.

Knowledge is power that can be used for good or evil. Applications of psychology's principles have so far been mostly for the good, and psychology addresses some of humanity's greatest problems and deepest longings.

63. Many psychologists study animals because they are fascinating. More important, they study animals because of the _____ (similarities/differences) between humans and other animals. These studies have led to treatments for human _____ and to a better understanding of human functioning.

64. Some people question whether experiments with animals are _____ . They wonder whether it is right to place the _____ of humans over those of animals.

65. Opposition to animal experimentation also raises the question of what _____ should protect the well-being of animals.

66. The ethics code of the _____ _____ _____ urges researchers to obtain participants' _____ _____ and fully _____ people after the research.

Describe the goals of the ethical guidelines for psychological research.

67. Psychologists' values _____ (do/do not) influence their theories, observations, and professional advice.

68. Although psychology _____ (can/cannot) be used to manipulate people, its purpose is to _____ .

Use Psychology to Become a Stronger Person—and a Better Student

Research has shown that repeated self-testing and rehearsal of previously learned material improves your ability to cement new learning (called the **testing effect**).

To master information, you must actively process it. People learn and remember material best when they put it in their own words, rehearse it, and then review and rehearse it again. An acronym for Survey, Question, Read, Retrieve, and Review, *SQ3R* is a study method that encourages active processing of new information.

Objective 1-12: Explain how psychological principles can help you learn, remember, and thrive.

69. Five suggestions for living a happy, effective, flourishing life are as follows:
   a. _____
   b. _____
   c. _____
   d. _____
   e. _____

70. Repeated _____ and _____ of previously studied material improves retention of information. This is called the _____ _____ .

71. In order to master any subject, you must _____ process it.

72. The _____ study method incorporates five steps: a. _____ ,
   b. _____ , c. _____ ,
   d. _____ , and
   e. _____ .

List four more study tips identified in the text.
   a. _____
   b. _____
   c. _____
   d. _____

APPLICATIONS:

73. Your roommate announces that her schedule permits her to devote three hours to studying for an upcoming quiz. You advise her to
   a. spend most of her time reading and rereading the text material.
   b. focus primarily on her lecture notes.
   c. space study time over several short sessions.
   d. cram for three hours just before the quiz.

74. A fraternity brother rationalizes the fact that he spends very little time studying by saying that he "doesn't want to peak too soon and have the test material become stale." You tell him that
    a. he is probably overestimating his knowledge of the material.
    b. if he devotes extra time to studying, his retention of the material will be improved.
    c. the more often students test themselves on the material, the better their exam scores.
    d. all of these statements are true.

75. Brad, who prepares for exams simply by reading the textbook assignment several times, evidently has not heard about
    a. replication.
    b. positive psychology.
    c. the testing effect.
    d. the nature–nurture issue.

Progress Test

Multiple-Choice Questions

Circle your answers to the following questions and check them with the answers beginning on page 16. If your answer is incorrect, read the explanation for why it is incorrect and then consult the text.

1. In its earliest days, *psychology* was defined as the
   a. science of mental life.
   b. study of conscious and unconscious activity.
   c. science of observable behavior.
   d. science of behavior and mental processes.

2. Who would be most likely to agree with the statement, "Psychology should investigate only behaviors that can be observed"?
   a. Wilhelm Wundt
   b. Sigmund Freud
   c. John B. Watson
   d. William James

3. Today, *psychology* is defined as the
   a. science of mental phenomena.
   b. science of conscious and unconscious activity.
   c. science of behavior.
   d. science of behavior and mental processes.

4. Who was a legendary teacher-writer of psychology?
   a. Wilhelm Wundt   c. Jean Piaget
   b. Ivan Pavlov   d. William James

5. Psychologists who study the degree to which genes influence our personality are working from the _____ perspective.
   a. behavioral   c. behavior genetics
   b. evolutionary   d. neuroscience

6. Which of the following best describes the issue of the relative importance of nature and nurture on our behavior?
   a. the issue of the relative influence of biology and experience on behavior
   b. the issue of the relative influence of rewards and punishments on behavior
   c. the debate as to the relative importance of heredity and instinct in determining behavior
   d. the debate as to whether mental processes are a legitimate area of scientific study

7. Raoul is a psychologist studying the brain's role in human emotions. Which psychological perspective is he working from?
   a. neuroscience
   b. cognitive
   c. behavioral
   d. behavior genetics

8. A psychologist who explores how Asian and North American definitions of attractiveness differ is working from the _____ perspective.
   a. behavioral   c. cognitive
   b. evolutionary   d. social-cultural

9. Manuel has had several anxiety attacks over the last month. Which type of psychologist would treat Manuel?
   a. counseling psychologist
   b. personality psychologist
   c. clinical psychologist
   d. psychiatrist

10. After detailed study of a gunshot wound victim, a psychologist concludes that the brain region destroyed is likely to be important for memory functions. Which type of research did the psychologist use to deduce this?
    a. the case study   c. correlation
    b. a survey   d. experimentation

11. In an experiment to determine the effects of loud noise on studying, the loud noise is the
    a. control condition.
    b. confounding variable.
    c. independent variable.
    d. dependent variable.

12. To determine the effects of a new drug on memory, researchers give one group of people a pill that contains the drug. A second group is given a pill that does not contain the drug. This second group constitutes the
    a. random sample.   c. control group.
    b. experimental group.   d. test group.

13. *Theories* are defined as
    a. testable propositions.
    b. factors that may change in response to manipulation.

   c. statements of the procedures used to describe research variables.

   d. principles that help to organize, predict, and explain facts.

14. A psychologist studies the play behavior of third-grade children by watching groups during recess at school. Which type of research is she using?

   a. correlation

   b. case study

   c. experimentation

   d. naturalistic observation

15. To ensure that other researchers can repeat their work, psychologists use

   a. control groups.

   b. random assignment.

   c. double-blind procedures.

   d. operational definitions.

16. The scientific attitude of skepticism is based on the belief that

   a. people are rarely candid in revealing their thoughts.

   b. mental processes can't be studied objectively.

   c. the scientist's intuition about behavior is usually correct.

   d. ideas need to be tested against observable evidence.

17. Psychologists' personal values

   a. have little influence on how their experiments are conducted.

   b. do not influence the interpretation of experimental results because of the use of statistical techniques that guard against subjective bias.

   c. can bias both scientific observation and interpretation of data.

   d. have little influence on investigative methods but a significant effect on interpretation.

18. If shoe size and IQ are negatively correlated, which of the following is true?

   a. People with large feet tend to have high IQs.

   b. People with small feet tend to have high IQs.

   c. People with small feet tend to have low IQs.

   d. IQ is unpredictable based on a person's shoe size.

19. Which of the following would be best for determining whether alcohol impairs memory?

   a. case study   **c.** survey

   b. naturalistic observation   **d.** experiment

20. Well-done surveys measure attitudes in a representative subset, or _____ , of an entire group, or _____ .

   a. population; random sample

   b. control group; experimental group

   c. experimental group; control group

   d. random sample; population

21. The first psychology laboratory was established by _____ in the year _____ .

   a. Wundt; 1879   **c.** Freud; 1900

   b. James; 1890   **d.** Watson; 1913

22. Who would be most likely to agree with the statement, "Psychology is the science of mental life"?

   a. Wilhelm Wundt

   b. John Watson

   c. Ivan Pavlov

   d. virtually any American psychologist during the 1960s

23. In psychology, *behavior* is best defined as

   a. anything a person says, does, or feels.

   b. any action we can observe and record.

   c. any action, whether observable or not.

   d. anything we can infer from a person's actions.

24. Carl Rogers and Abraham Maslow are most closely associated with

   a. cognitive psychology.

   b. behaviorism.

   c. psychodynamic theory.

   d. humanistic psychology.

25. The technology that enables sites such as Facebook and Twitter has expanded the role of _____ in psychological research.

   a. case studies

   b. experimentation

   c. naturalistic observation

   d. correlation

26. A teacher was interested in knowing whether her students' test performance could be predicted from their proximity to the front of the classroom. So she matched her students' scores on a math test with their seating position. This is an example of

   a. experimentation.

   b. correlational research.

   c. a survey.

   d. naturalistic observation.

27. The way the mind encodes, processes, stores, and retrieves information is the primary concern of the _____ perspective.

   a. neuroscience   **c.** social-cultural

   b. evolutionary   **d.** cognitive

28. Of the following, who is also a physician?

   a. clinical psychologist

   b. experimental psychologist

   c. psychiatrist

   d. biological psychologist

29. Dr. Jones is researching the relationship between changes in our thinking over the life span and changes in moral reasoning. He is most likely a

   a. clinical psychologist.

   b. personality psychologist.

   c. psychiatrist.

   d. developmental psychologist.

30. Which psychologist is most directly concerned with suggesting ways to improve worker productivity in a computer factory?
   a. clinical psychologist
   b. personality psychologist
   c. industrial-organizational psychologist
   d. psychiatrist

31. Dr. Ernst explains behavior in terms of different situations. Dr. Ernst is working from the _____ perspective.
   a. behavioral   c. social-cultural
   b. evolutionary   d. cognitive

32. Which perspective emphasizes the learning of observable responses?
   a. behavioral   c. neuroscience
   b. social-cultural   d. cognitive

33. The biopsychosocial approach emphasizes the importance of
   a. different levels of analysis in exploring behavior and mental processes.
   b. observable behavior over mental processes.
   c. the environment over heredity.
   d. having a single academic perspective to guide research.

34. To prevent the possibility that a placebo effect or researchers' expectations will influence a study's results, scientists use
   a. control groups.
   b. experimental groups.
   c. random assignment.
   d. the double-blind procedure.

35. In an experiment to determine the effects of attention on memory, memory is the
   a. control condition.
   b. confounding variable.
   c. independent variable.
   d. dependent variable.

36. Which of the following BEST describes hindsight bias?
   a. Events seem more predictable before they have occurred.
   b. Events seem more predictable after they have occurred.
   c. A person's intuition is usually correct.
   d. A person's intuition is usually not correct.

37. The procedure designed to ensure that the experimental and control groups do not differ in any way that might affect the experiment's results is called
   a. variable controlling.
   b. random assignment.
   c. representative sampling.
   d. stratification.

38. In an experiment to test the effects of a new drug on weight loss, the participants' ages would be a(n)
   a. independent variable.
   b. confounding variable.
   c. placebo effect.
   d. hypothesis.

39. Which type of research would allow you to determine whether students' college grades accurately predict later income?
   a. case study   c. experimentation
   b. naturalistic observation   d. correlation

40. In a test of the effects of air pollution, groups of students performed a reaction time task in a polluted or an unpolluted room. To what condition were students in the unpolluted room exposed?
   a. experimental   c. randomly assigned
   b. control   d. dependent

41. To study the effects of lighting on mood, Dr. Cooper had students fill out questionnaires in brightly lit or dimly lit rooms. In this study, the independent variable consisted of
   a. the number of students assigned to each group.
   b. the students' responses to the questionnaire.
   c. the room lighting.
   d. the subject matter of the questions asked.

42. You decide to test your belief that men drink more soft drinks than women by finding out whether more soft drinks are consumed per day in the men's dorm than in the women's dorm. Your belief is a(n) _____ , and your research prediction is a(n) _____ .
   a. hypothesis; theory
   b. theory; hypothesis
   c. independent variable; dependent variable
   d. dependent variable; independent variable

43. To examine assumptions, discern hidden values, evaluate evidence, and assess conclusions is to
   a. conduct a survey.
   b. develop a theory.
   c. experiment.
   d. think critically.

44. Which of the following procedures is an example of the use of a placebo?
   a. In a test of the effects of a drug on memory, a participant is led to believe that a harmless pill actually contains an active drug.
   b. A participant in an experiment is led to believe that a pill, which actually contains an active drug, is harmless.
   c. Participants in an experiment are not told which treatment condition is in effect.
   d. Neither the participants nor the experimenter knows which treatment condition is in effect.

45. The psychologist who has called for a more positive psychology is
   a. William James.   c. B. F. Skinner.
   b. Martin Seligman.   d. Sigmund Freud.

46. A major principle underlying the SQ3R study method is that
    a. people learn and remember material best when they actively process it.
    b. many students overestimate their mastery of text and lecture material.
    c. study time should be spaced over time rather than crammed into one session.
    d. overlearning disrupts efficient retention.

47. To say that we operate with a two-track mind means that we
    a. can think of several things at once.
    b. process information at conscious and unconscious levels.
    c. think both objectively and subjectively.
    d. examine assumptions and assess conclusions.

Matching Items

Match each term with its definition or description.

Terms

_____ **1.** hypothesis
_____ **2.** theory
_____ **3.** independent variable
_____ **4.** dependent variable
_____ **5.** experimental group
_____ **6.** control group
_____ **7.** case study
_____ **8.** survey
_____ **9.** replication
_____ **10.** random assignment
_____ **11.** experiment
_____ **12.** double-blind
_____ **13.** culture
_____ **14.** confounding variable

Definitions or Descriptions

a. an in-depth observational study of one person
b. the variable being manipulated in an experiment
c. the variable being measured in an experiment
d. the "treatment-absent" group in an experiment
e. an uncontrolled variable in an experiment
f. repeating an experiment to see whether the same results are obtained
g. the process in which research participants are selected by chance for different groups in an experiment
h. an explanation using an integrated set of principles that organizes observations and predicts behavior
i. the research strategy in which the effects of one or more variables on behavior are tested
j. shared ideas and behaviors passed from one generation to the next
k. the "treatment-present" group in an experiment
l. the research strategy in which a representative sample of individuals is questioned
m. experimental procedure in which neither the research participant nor the experimenter knows which condition the participant is in
n. testable proposition

Application Essay

Elio has a theory that regular exercise can improve thinking. Help him design an experiment evaluating this theory. (Use the space below to list the points you want to make, and organize them. Then write the essay on a separate piece of paper.)

Summing Up

To study increased suicide rates among teenagers, a researcher develops a hypothesis that anxiety leads to depression, which may lead to suicidal behavior. She has a variety of research methods to choose from.

She can focus on one or two extreme situations to educate herself about depression among young people, a method called the _____ _____ ,

which can

suggest _____ for further study,

but

the information generated may not be _____ of all young people.

The researcher could also study teenagers at school or at play, a method called _____ _____ .

However, like the above _____ method, this method does not _____ behavior.

Yet another alternative would be for the researcher to conduct a _____ ,

interviewing _____ (a few/many) teenagers in _____ (more/less) depth, creating questions carefully to avoid _____ effects.

If the researcher finds that these traits occur together—as anxiety increases, so does depression—she can say that they are positively _____ .

To determine whether anxiety causes depression, the researcher conducts an _____ ,

randomly assigning participants to two groups,

teens who are exposed to an anxiety-arousing movie, the _____ group,

and

teens who see a romantic movie, the _____ group.

Both groups then take a test to measure depression.

In this study, the movie is the _____ variable, the variable that is manipulated,

in order to see the effect on

the teens' level of depression, which is the _____ variable.

Terms and Concepts to Remember

Using your own words, on a separate piece of paper write a brief definition or explanation of each of the following.

1. behaviorism
2. humanistic psychology
3. cognitive psychology
4. cognitive neuroscience
5. psychology
6. critical thinking
7. biopsychosocial approach
8. culture
9. nature–nurture issue
10. dual processing
11. positive psychology
12. hindsight bias
13. theory
14. hypothesis
15. operational definition
16. replication
17. case study
18. naturalistic observation
19. survey
20. population
21. random sample
22. correlation
23. experiment
24. random assignment
25. experimental group
26. control group
27. placebo
28. double-blind procedure
29. placebo effect
30. independent variable
31. confounding variable
32. dependent variable
33. informed consent
34. debriefing
35. testing effect
36. SQ3R

Answers

Chapter Review

Psychology's Roots

1. curiosity; skepticism; humility
2. This expression suggests that if research does not support our predictions, we must revise our predic-

tions and do more research. "The rat [the research subject in many experiments] is always right [it tells us so]."

3. Wundt
4. learning; Sigmund Freud; children
5. William James; Mary Whiton Calkins; Margaret Floy Washburn
6. mental; observable; behaviorism
7. behaviorism; Carl Rogers; Abraham Maslow; humanistic; growth
8. cognitive; mental; cognitive neuroscience
9. behavior; mental
10. "behavior and." In performing the first experiment, Wundt was attempting to measure the fastest and simplest *mental processes*.
11. All of these statements about psychology's history are true, so **d.** is the answer.
12. Matching

1. e	6. o	11. h
2. b	7. a	12. k
3. j	8. f	13. g
4. i	9. l	14. n
5. m	10. c	15. d

Four Big Ideas in Psychology

13. critical thinking; assumptions; values; evidence; conclusions
14. system; social system; levels; analysis; psychological; social-cultural; biopsychosocial
15. Gender; Sex; biological; enduring behaviors; attitudes; ideas; values; traditions
16. biology; experience
17. biopsychosocial; interact
18. conscious; unconscious; dual processing
19. strengths; challenges
20. human flourishing; emotions; character; institutions; positive psychology

Why Do Psychology?

21. intuition
22. hindsight bias; common; after the fact
23. overconfidence; equally wrong
24. patterns; do not

How Do Psychologists Ask and Answer Questions?

25. scientific method
26. theory; hypotheses; research
27. operational definitions; replicate
28. organizes; predictions; research
29. description; correlation; experimentation
30. case study
31. atypical
32. naturalistic observation
33. technologies
34. describe

35. survey
36. wording
37. random; population; does
38. are; representative
39. case study
40. **b.** is the answer.
    a. In a case study, one person is studied in depth.
    c. Surveys use questionnaires or interviews to obtain the self-reported attitudes or behaviors of a large group of people.
    d. Hypothetical is not a type of research. Hypotheses are testable predictions.
41. correlated; predict; correlation coefficient
42. positively correlated; negatively correlated; inversely
43. strength; weakness; causation; cause-effect
44. predicted
45. event; caused; explanation
46. negatively. This is an example of a negative correlation. As one factor (time spent studying) increases, the other factor (anxiety level) decreases.
47. A positive correlation simply means that two factors tend to increase or decrease together; so the more saturated fat you eat, the more likely you are to contract cancer. However, eating saturated fat doesn't necessarily cause cancer; other factors may be involved.
48. increases. If height and weight are positively correlated, increased height is associated with increased weight. Thus, one can predict a person's weight from his or her height.
49. cause; effect; experimental
50. manipulates; holding constant; randomly; constant
51. do; experimental; control
52. random assignment
53. placebo; placebo effect
54. double-blind
55. independent; dependent; confounding variables
56. manipulate; independent; measure; dependent; control; variables

Experimentation has the advantage of increasing the investigator's control of both relevant and irrelevant variables that might influence behavior. Experiments also permit the investigator to go beyond observation and description to uncover cause-effect relationships in behavior.

57. independent; dependent; constant. By being able to control the variables and hold other possible factors constant, the experimenter is able to demonstrate cause and effect, rather than simply describe the situation.
58. **c.** is the answer. To determine the effects of caffeine on reaction time, Martina needs to measure reaction time in a control, or comparison, group that does not receive caffeine. Note that caffeine is the independent variable, and reaction time is the dependent variable.

59. Some possible operational definitions would be:
    Exercise: Jogging 30 minutes at a pace of 9 minutes per mile.
    Anger: Observable attack behavior, such as hitting someone.
    Stress: Number of negative life events.
60. principles
61. control; principles
62. **d.** is the answer

Psychology's Research Ethics

63. similarities; diseases
64. ethical; well-being
65. safeguards
66. American Psychological Association; informed consent; debrief

Ethical guidelines require investigators to (1) obtain informed consent of potential participants, (2) protect them from harm and discomfort, (3) treat information about participants confidentially, and (4) fully explain the research afterward.

67. do
68. can; enlighten

Use Psychology to Become a Stronger Person—and a Better Student

69. Five suggestions for living a happy, effective, flourishing life are
    a. Get a full night's sleep.
    b. Make space for exercise.
    c. Set long-term goals, with daily aims.
    d. Have a "growth mind-set."
    e. Prioritize relationships.
70. self-testing; rehearsal; testing effect
71. actively
72. SQ3R; a. survey; b. question; c. read; d. retrieve; e. review
    a. Distribute study time.
    b. Process class information actively.
    c. Overlearn material.
    d. Learn to think critically.
73. **c.** is the answer.
    a. To be effective, study must be active rather than passive in nature.
    b. Most exams are based on lecture and textbook material.
    d. Cramming hinders retention.
74. **d.** is the answer.
75. **c.** is the answer.

Progress Test

Multiple-Choice Questions

1. **a.** is the answer.
    b. Psychology has never been defined in terms of conscious and unconscious activity.
    c. From the 1920s into the 1960s, psychology was defined as the scientific study of observable behavior.

d. *Psychology* today is defined as the science of behavior and mental processes. In its earliest days, however, psychology focused exclusively on mental phenomena.

2. **c.** is the answer.
   a. Wilhelm Wundt was seeking to measure the simplest mental processes.
   b. Sigmund Freud developed an influential theory of personality that focused on unconscious processes.
   d. William James was more interested in mental phenomena than observable behavior.

3. **d.** is the answer.
   a. In its earliest days, psychology was defined as the science of mental phenomena.
   b. Psychology has never been defined in terms of conscious and unconscious activity.
   c. From the 1920s into the 1960s, psychology was defined as the scientific study of behavior.

4. **d.** is the answer.
   a. Wilhelm Wundt founded the first psychology laboratory.
   b. Ivan Pavlov pioneered the study of learning.
   c. Jean Piaget was the twentieth century's most influential observer of children.

5. **c.** is the answer.

6. **a.** is the answer. Biology and experience are internal and external influences, respectively.
   b. Rewards and punishments are both external influences on behavior.
   c. Heredity and instinct are both internal influences on behavior.
   d. The legitimacy of the study of mental processes does not relate to the internal/external issue.

7. **a.** is the answer.
   b. The cognitive perspective would be concerned with how information was encoded, processed, stored, and retrieved.
   c. The behavioral perspective studies the mechanisms by which observable responses are acquired and changed.
   d. The behavior genetics perspective focuses on the relative contributions of genes and environment to individual differences.

8. **d.** is the answer.
   a. Behavioral psychologists investigate how learned behaviors are acquired. They generally do not focus on subjective opinions, such as attractiveness.
   b. The evolutionary perspective studies how the natural selection of traits passed from one generation to the next promotes the survival of one's genes.
   c. Cognitive psychologists study the mechanisms of thinking and memory, and generally do not investigate attitudes. Also, because the question specifies that the psychologist is interested in comparing two cultures, d. is the best answer.

9. **c.** is the answer.
   a. Counseling psychologists help people cope with personal and vocational challenges.
   b. Personality psychologists study people's traits.
   d. Psychiatrists are medical doctors who can prescribe drugs.

10. **a.** is the answer. In a case study, one person or group is studied in depth.
    b. In survey research, a group of people is interviewed.
    c. Correlations identify whether two factors are related.
    d. In an experiment, an investigator manipulates one variable to observe its effect on another.

11. **c.** is the answer. The loud noise is the variable being manipulated in the experiment.
    a. A control condition for this experiment would be a group of people studying in a quiet room.
    b. A confounding variable is a variable other than those being manipulated that may influence behavior.
    d. The dependent variable is the behavior measured by the experimenter—here, the effects of loud noise.

12. **c.** is the answer. The control group is the group for which the experimental treatment (the new drug) is absent.
    a. A random sample is a subset of a population in which every person has an equal chance of being selected.
    b. The experimental group is the group for which the experimental treatment (the drug) is present.
    d. "Test group" is an ambiguous term; both the experimental and control group are tested.

13. **d.** is the answer.
    a. Hypotheses are testable propositions.
    b. Dependent variables are factors that may change in response to manipulated independent variables.
    c. This refers to an operational definition.

14. **d.** is the answer.

15. **d.** is the answer.

16. **d.** is the answer.

17. **c.** is the answer.
    a., b., & d. Psychologists' personal values can influence all of these.

18. **b.** is the answer.
    a. & c. These answers would have been correct had the question stated that there is a *positive* correlation between shoe size and IQ. Actually, there is probably no correlation at all!

19. **d.** is the answer. In an experiment, it would be possible to manipulate alcohol consumption and observe the effects, if any, on memory.
    a., b., & c. These answers are incorrect because only by directly controlling the variables of interest can a researcher uncover cause-effect relationships.

20. **d.** is the answer.
    a. A sample is a subset of a population.
    b. & c. Control and experimental groups are used in experimentation, not in survey research.

21. **a.** is the answer.

22. **a.** is the answer.
    b. & d. John Watson, like many American psychologists during his time, believed that psychology should focus on the study of observable behavior.
    c. Because he pioneered the study of learning, Pavlov focused on observable behavior and would certainly have *disagreed* with this statement.

23. **b.** is the answer.

24. **d.** is the answer.

25. **c.** is the answer.

26. **b.** is the answer.
    a. This is not an experiment because the teacher is not manipulating the independent variable (seating position); she is merely measuring whether variation in this factor predicts test performance.
    c. If the study were based entirely on students' self-reported responses, this would be a survey.
    d. This study goes beyond naturalistic observation, which merely describes behavior as it occurs, to determine if test scores can be predicted from students' seating position.

27. **d.** is the answer.
    a. The neuroscience perspective studies the biological bases for a range of psychological phenomena.
    b. The evolutionary perspective studies how the natural selection of traits passed down from one generation to the next promotes the survival of one's genes.
    c. The social-cultural perspective is concerned with variations in behavior across situations and cultures.

28. **c.** is the answer. Psychiatrists are the only ones with medical degrees.

29. **d.** is the answer. The emphasis on change during the life span indicates that Dr. Jones is most likely a developmental psychologist.
    a. Clinical psychologists assess and treat people who are psychologically troubled.
    b. Personality psychologists study our traits.
    c. Psychiatrists are medical doctors.

30. **c.** is the answer.
    a. Clinical psychologists assess and treat people with psychological disorders.
    b. & d. Personality psychologists and psychiatrists do not usually study people in work situations.

31. **c.** is the answer.
    a. Psychologists who follow the behavioral perspective emphasize observable, external influences on behavior.
    b. The evolutionary perspective studies how the natural selection of traits passed down from one generation to the next promotes the survival of one's genes.
    d. The cognitive perspective places emphasis on conscious, rather than unconscious, processes.

32. **a.** is the answer.

33. **a.** is the answer.
    b. & c. The biopsychosocial approach has nothing to do with the relative importance of basic research and applied research and is equally applicable to both.
    d. On the contrary, the biopsychosocial approach is based on the idea that single academic perspectives are often limited.

34. **d.** is the answer.
    a. & b. The double-blind procedure is one way to create experimental and control groups.

    c. Research participants are randomly assigned to either an experimental or a control group.

35. **d.** is the answer.
    a. The control condition is the comparison group, in which the experimental treatment (the treatment of interest) is absent.
    b. A confounding variable is a variable other than those being manipulated that may influence behavior.
    c. Attention is the independent variable, which is being manipulated.

36. **b.** is the answer.
    a. The phenomenon is related to hindsight rather than foresight.
    c. & d. The phenomenon doesn't involve whether or not the intuitions are correct but rather people's attitude that they had the correct intuition.

37. **b.** is the answer. If enough participants are used in an experiment and they are randomly assigned to the two groups, any differences that emerge between the groups should stem from the experiment itself.
    a., c., & d. None of these terms describes precautions taken in setting up groups for experiments.

38. **b.** is the answer.
    a. The drug would be the independent variable.
    c. The placebo effect occurs when the results of an experiment are caused by a participant's expectations about what is really going on.
    d. A hypothesis is a testable prediction.

39. **d.** is the answer. Correlations show how well one factor can be predicted from another.
    a. Because a case study focuses in great detail on the behavior of an individual, it's probably not useful in showing whether predictions are possible.
    b. Naturalistic observation is a method of describing, rather than predicting, behavior.
    c. In experimental research, the effects of manipulated independent variables on dependent variables are measured. It is not clear how an experiment could help determine whether college grades predict later income.

40. **b.** is the answer. The control condition is the one in which the treatment—in this case, pollution—is absent.
    a. Students in the polluted room would be in the experimental condition.
    c. Presumably, all students in both conditions were randomly assigned to their groups. Random assignment is a method for establishing groups, rather than a condition.
    d. The word *dependent* refers to a kind of variable in experiments; conditions are either experimental or control.

41. **c.** is the answer. The lighting is the factor being manipulated.
    a. & d. These answers are incorrect because they involve aspects of the experiment other than the variables.
    b. This answer is the dependent, not the independent, variable.

42. **b.** is the answer. A general belief such as this one is a theory; it helps organize, explain, and generate testable predictions (called hypotheses) such as "men drink more soft drinks than women."
c. & d. Independent and dependent variables are experimental treatments and behaviors, respectively. Beliefs and predictions may involve such variables, but are not themselves those variables.

43. **d.** is the answer.

44. **a.** is the answer.
b. Use of a placebo tests whether the behavior of a research participant, who mistakenly believes that a treatment (such as a drug) is in effect, is the same as it would be if the treatment were actually present.
c. & d. These are examples of *blind* and *double-blind* control procedures.

45. **b.** is the answer.
a. William James, author of an important 1890 textbook, was a philosopher and was more interested in mental phenomena than observable behavior.
c. B. F. Skinner was a behaviorist who believed that only observable behavior could be studied scientifically.
d. Sigmund Freud developed an influential theory of personality that focused on unconscious processes.

46. **a.** is the answer.
b. & c. Although each of these is true, SQ3R is based on the more general principle of active learning.
d. In fact, just the opposite is true.

47. **b.** is the answer.

Matching Items

1. n	5. k	9. f	13. j
2. h	6. d	10. g	14. e
3. b	7. a	11. i	
4. c	8. l	12. m	

Application Essay

Elio's hypothesis is that daily aerobic exercise for one month will improve memory. Exercise is the independent variable. The dependent variable is memory. Exercise could be manipulated by having people in an experimental group jog for 30 minutes each day. Memory could be measured by comparing the number of words they recall from a test list studied before the exercise experiment begins, and again afterward. A control group that does not exercise is needed so that any improvement in the experimental group's memory can be attributed to exercise, and not to some other factor, such as the passage of one month's time or familiarity with the memory test. The control group should engage in some nonexercise activity for the same amount of time each day that the experimental group exercises. The participants should be randomly selected from the population at large, and then randomly assigned to the experimental and control groups.

Summing Up

To study increased suicide rates among teenagers, a researcher develops a hypothesis that anxiety leads to depression, which may lead to suicidal behavior. She has a variety of research methods to choose from.

She can focus on one or two extreme situations to educate herself about depression among young people, a method called the *case study*, which can suggest *hypotheses* for further study, but the information generated may not be *representative* of all young people. The researcher could also study teenagers at school or online, a method called *naturalistic observation*. However, like the above *descriptive* method, this method does not *explain* behavior. Yet another alternative would be for the researcher to conduct a *survey*, interviewing *many* teenagers in *less* depth, creating questions carefully to avoid *wording* effects. If the researcher finds that these traits occur together—as anxiety increases, so does depression—she can say that they are positively *correlated*.

To determine whether anxiety *causes* depression, the researcher conducts an *experiment*, randomly assigning participants to two groups, teens who are exposed to an anxiety-arousing movie, the *experimental* group, and teens who see a romantic movie, the *control* group. Both groups then take a test to measure depression. In this study, the movie is the *independent* variable, the variable that is manipulated, in order to see the effect on the teens' level of depression, which is the *dependent* variable.

Terms and Concepts to Remember

1. **Behaviorism** is the view that psychology should be an objective science that studies behaviors without reference to mental processes.

2. **Humanistic psychology** is the branch of psychology that emphasizes human growth potential.

3. **Cognitive psychology** is the study of mental processes, such as occur when we perceive, learn, remember, think, communicate, and solve problems.

4. **Cognitive neuroscience** is the interdisciplinary study of how brain activity is linked with memory, language, and other forms of mental activity.

5. **Psychology** is the science of behavior and mental processes.

6. **Critical thinking** is careful reasoning that examines assumptions, discerns hidden values, evaluates evidence, and assesses conclusions.

7. The **biopsychosocial approach** is an integrated approach that focuses on biological, psychological, and social-cultural levels of analysis for a given behavior or mental process.

8. **Culture** is the enduring behaviors, ideas, attitudes, values, and traditions shared by a group of people and handed down from one generation to the next.

9. The **nature–nurture issue** is the controversy over the relative contributions that genes (nature) and experience (nurture) make to the development of psychological traits and behaviors.

10. **Dual processing** is the principle that we often process information at the same time on separate conscious and unconscious tracks.

11. **Positive psychology** is the scientific study of human functioning, with the goals of discovering and promoting strengths and virtues that help people and communities to thrive.

12. **Hindsight bias** refers to the tendency to believe, after learning an outcome, that one would have foreseen it; also called the *I-knew-it-all-along phenomenon*.

13. A **theory** is an explanation using an integrated set of principles that organizes observations and predicts behaviors or events.

14. A **hypothesis** is a testable prediction, often implied by a theory; testing the hypothesis helps scientists to test the theory.

    Example: To test his theory of why people conform, Solomon Asch formulated the testable **hypothesis** that an individual would be more likely to go along with the majority opinion of a large group than with that of a smaller group.

15. An **operational definition** is a precise statement of the procedures (operations) used to define research variables.

16. **Replication** is the process of repeating the essence of a research study, usually with different participants and in different situations, to see whether the basic finding generalizes to other people and circumstances.

17. The **case study** is an observation technique in which one individual or group is studied in great depth, often with the intention of revealing universal principles.

18. **Naturalistic observation** involves observing and recording behavior in naturally occurring situations without manipulating and controlling the situation.

19. The **survey** is a technique for obtaining the self-reported attitudes or behaviors of a group, usually by questioning a representative, random sample of that group.

20. A **population** consists of all the members of a group being studied.

21. A **random sample** is one that is representative because every member of the population has an equal chance of being included.

22. **Correlation** is a measure of the extent to which two factors vary together, and thus of how well either factor predicts the other. The *correlation coefficient* is a statistical measure of the relationship; it can be positive or negative.

    Example: With a positive correlation between air temperature and ice cream sales, the warmer (higher) it is, the more ice cream is sold. With a negative correlation between air temperature and sales of cocoa, the cooler (lower) it is, the more cocoa is sold.

23. An **experiment** is a research method in which a researcher manipulates one or more factors (independent variables) in order to observe their effect on some behavior or mental process (the dependent variable); experiments therefore make it possible to establish cause-effect relationships.

24. **Random assignment** is the procedure of assigning participants to the experimental and control conditions by chance in order to minimize preexisting differences between those assigned to the different groups.

25. The **experimental group** of an experiment is the one that is exposed to the independent variable being studied.

    Example: In the study of the effects of a new drug on reaction time, participants in the **experimental group** would actually receive the drug being tested.

26. The **control group** of an experiment is the one that is not exposed to the treatment of interest, or independent variable, so a comparison to the experimental condition can be made.

    Example: The **control group** for an experiment testing the effects of a new drug on reaction time would be a group of participants given a placebo (inactive drug or sugar pill) instead of the drug being tested.

27. **Placebos** are inert substances or conditions that are assumed to be active agents.

28. A **double-blind procedure** is an experimental procedure in which neither the experimenter nor the research participants are aware of which condition is in effect. It is used to prevent experimenters' and participants' expectations from influencing the results of an experiment.

29. The **placebo effect** occurs when the results of an experiment are caused by a participant's expectations about what is really going on.

30. The **independent variable** of an experiment is the factor being manipulated and tested by the investigator.

    Example: In the study of the effects of a new drug on reaction time, the drug is the **independent variable**.

31. In an experiment, a **confounding variable** is a factor other than the independent variable that might influence the results.

32. The **dependent variable** of an experiment is the factor being measured by the investigator.

    Example: In the study of the effects of a new drug on reaction time, the participants' reaction time is the **dependent variable.**

33. **Informed consent** is the ethical practice of giving research participants enough information to enable them to choose whether they wish to take part in a study.

34. **Debriefing** is the ethical practice of explaining a study, including its purpose and any deceptions, to participants after they have finished.

35. The **testing effect** (also called the *retrieval practice effect* or *test-enhanced learning*) refers to the beneficial effects on memory of actively retrieving, rather than simply reading, information.

36. **SQ3R** is a study method consisting of five steps: Survey, Question, Read, Retrieve, and Review.

The Biology of Mind and Consciousness

Chapter Overview

Chapter 2 is concerned with the functions of the brain and its component neural systems, which provide the basis for all human behavior. Under the direction of the brain, the nervous and endocrine systems coordinate a variety of voluntary and involuntary behaviors and serve as the body's mechanisms for communication with the external environment. Consciousness—our awareness of ourselves and our environment—can be experienced in various states. Chapter 2 examines normal consciousness as well as sleep and dreaming.

Chapter Review

First, skim each text section, noting headings and bold-face items. Review the section by reading the objectives and summaries provided here, then answer the questions that follow. In some cases, STUDY TIPS explain how best to learn a difficult concept and APPLICATIONS help you to know how well you understand the material. Check your understanding of the material by consulting the answers beginning on page 37. Do not continue with the next section until you understand each answer. If you need to, review or reread the section in the textbook before continuing.

The Brain: A Work in Progress

Objective 2-1: Describe how biology and experience interact.

Your brain is constantly changing, building new pathways as it adjusts to new experiences. This neural change is called *plasticity,* and it continues throughout your life. *Biological psychologists* study the links between biology and behavior. In *cognitive neuroscience,* people from many fields join forces to study the connections between brain activity and mental processes.

1. The quality of the brain that makes it possible for undamaged brain areas to take over the functions of damaged regions is known as _____ .

This quality is especially apparent in the brains of _____ (young children/adolescents/adults).

2. Researchers who study the links between biology and behavior are called _____

_____ .

3. The interdisciplinary study of brain activity linked to cognition is called _____

_____ .

STUDY TIP: Many students find the technical material in this chapter difficult to master. Not only are there many terms for you to remember, but you must also know the organization and function of the various divisions of the nervous system. Learning this material will require a great deal of rehearsal. Working the chapter review several times, drawing and labeling brain diagrams, making flash cards, answering the text Retrieve + Remember questions, and mentally reciting terms are all useful techniques for rehearsing this type of material.

APPLICATION:

4. Cite some possible areas a biological psychologist would be likely to study.

Neural Communication

Objective 2-2: Identify the parts of a neuron, and describe an *action potential.*

A *neuron* consists of a cell body and branching fibers: The *dendrite* fibers receive information from sensory receptors or other neurons and conduct them toward the cell body. The **axon** fibers pass that information along to other neurons or to muscles or glands. They do so by means of a nerve impulse, called the **action potential,** which is a brief electrical signal that travels down the axon. *Glial cells (glia)* support, nourish, and protect the nerve cells of the nervous system; they provide the *myelin* that insulates some neurons and speeds the impulse along. Glia may also play a role in learning, thinking, and memory. The junction between two neurons is called the **synapse,** and the space between neurons is the *synaptic gap.*

5. Our body's neural system is built from billions of nerve cells, or _____ .

6. The extensions of a neuron that receive messages from other neurons are the _____ .
   The extension of a neuron that transmits information to other neurons is the _____ .

7. The neural impulse, or _____ _____ , is a brief electrical charge that travels down a(n) _____ .

8. The junction between two neurons is called a _____ . The space between the sending and receiving neurons is called the _____ _____ .

9. Identify the major parts of the neuron and the activity diagrammed below:

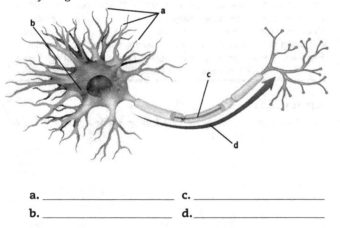

   a. _____   c. _____
   b. _____   d. _____

10. The cells in the nervous system that support, nourish, and protect neurons are the _____ _____ .

Objective 2-3: Describe how neurons communicate.

A nerve impulse fires when the neuron is stimulated by signals from sensory receptors or when triggered by chemical signals from adjacent neurons. Received signals trigger an action potential only if the excitatory signals exceed the inhibitory signals by a minimum intensity called the **threshold.** After a neuron has fired, it

needs a brief rest, called the **refractory period.** The neuron's reaction is an **all-or-none response.**

When the action potential reaches the axon's end, your neural system converts an *electrical* impulse into a *chemical* message. The action potential triggers the release of chemical messengers called **neurotransmitters,** which cross the synaptic gap. They then combine with receptor sites on neighboring neurons, thus passing on their excitatory or inhibitory messages. The sending neuron, in a process called **reuptake,** normally absorbs the excess neurotransmitter molecules in the gap.

11. To trigger an action potential, the _____ signals must exceed the _____ signals by a certain intensity, called the _____ . Increasing a stimulus above this level _____ (will/will not) increase the neural impulse's intensity. This phenomenon is called an _____ -_____ -_____ response. Instead, intensity is determined by _____ _____ .

12. The strength of a stimulus _____ (does/does not) affect the speed of a neural impulse.

STUDY TIP/APPLICATION: To understand the relationships among excitatory and inhibitory impulses, synapses, threshold, and the all-or-none response, you should think of the neuron as a simple switch that is always either "on" or "off." This "all-or-none" response is in contrast to the graded, "partially on" response of the more complex dimmer switch. Whether the all-or-none response occurs depends on whether the input to the neuron is sufficient to allow it to reach its threshold—much as a simple light switch requires a certain amount of force to operate. In the neuron's case, the "force" refers to the combination of excitatory inputs (which promote a response) and inhibitory inputs (which promote the neuron's remaining in its resting state).

13. Several shy neurons send an inhibitory message to neighboring neuron Joni. At the same time, a larger group of party-going neurons send Joni excitatory messages. What will Joni do? _____ _____ _____

14. At the synapse, the neural impulse triggers the release of chemical messengers called _____ . These chemicals cross the synaptic gap and bind to _____ sites on the receiving neuron.

15. Neurotransmitters influence neurons either by

_____ or _____

their readiness to fire. Excess neurotransmitters are
reabsorbed by the sending neuron in a process
called _____ .

Outline the sequence of reactions that occur when a
neural impulse is generated and transmitted from one
neuron to another.

Objective 2-4: Describe how neurotransmitters affect our
mood and behavior.

Different neurotransmitters have different effects on
behavior and emotion. For example, the neurotransmitter serotonin affects mood, hunger, sleep, and arousal.
Dopamine influences movement, learning, attention,
and feelings of pleasure and reward. The brain's *endorphins,* natural *opiates* released in response to pain and
vigorous exercise, explain the "runner's high" and the
painkilling effects of acupuncture.

When the brain is flooded with opiate drugs such as
heroin and morphine, it may stop producing its own natural opiates, and withdrawal of these drugs may deprive
the brain of any form of relief.

16. The neurotransmitter serotonin affects our

_____

_____ .

Dopamine influences _____

_____ .

17. Naturally occurring opiate-like neurotransmitters
that are present in the brain are called
_____ . When the brain is flooded
with drugs such as _____ or
_____ , it may stop producing these
neurotransmitters.

APPLICATIONS:

18. Lolita is feeling depressed for no particular reason. It is
possible that she has an undersupply of _____ .

19. Punjab had lunch at the local Chinese restaurant.
Afterward, he suffered a migraine, most likely caused by
an _____ of _____ .

The Nervous System

Objective 2-5: Identify the two major divisions of the
nervous system, and describe their basic functions.

Neurons communicating with other neurons form our
body's *nervous system.* The brain and spinal cord form
the *central nervous system (CNS).* The *peripheral nervous
system (PNS)* links the central nervous system with the
body's sense organs, muscles, and glands. The axons
carrying this PNS information are bundled into the electrical cables we know as *nerves.*

Sensory neurons carry information from the body's
tissues and sensory receptors inward to the brain and
spinal cord, which process the information. *Motor neurons* carry outgoing information from the central nervous
system to the body's muscles and glands. *Interneurons* in
the CNS communicate internally and intervene between
the sensory inputs and the motor outputs.

The peripheral nervous system consists of two sub-
systems. The *somatic nervous system* enables control of
our skeletal muscles. The *autonomic nervous system* is a
dual self-regulating system that influences our glands
and the muscles of our internal organs. The *sympathetic
nervous system* arouses; the *parasympathetic nervous system* calms.

In the central nervous system, the brain enables our
thinking, feeling, and acting. Its billions of neurons cluster into work groups called *neural networks.* The spinal
cord is a two-way highway connecting the PNS and the
brain. Nerve fibers carry information from the senses to
the brain, and others carry motor-control information to
body parts. The neural pathways governing our *reflexes*
illustrate the spinal cord's work.

20. Taken altogether, the neurons of the body form the

_____ _____ ,

defined as the body's speedy, _____

communication network.

21. The brain and spinal cord comprise the
_____ nervous system. The neu-
rons that link the brain and spinal cord to the body's
sense receptors, muscles, and glands form the
_____ nervous system.

22. Sensory and motor axons are bundled into electrical
cables called _____ .

23. Information arriving in the central nervous system
from the body travels in _____
neurons. The central nervous system sends instructions to the body's muscles and glands by means of
_____ neurons. The neurons that
enable internal communication within the central
nervous system are called _____ .

24. The division of the peripheral nervous system that
enables voluntary control of the skeletal muscles is
the _____ nervous system.

25. Responses of the glands and muscles of internal organs are controlled by the _____ nervous system.

26. The body is made ready for action by the _____ division of the autonomic nervous system, mobilizing its _____ . The _____ division of the autonomic nervous system calms the body, conserving its _____ .

27. The brain's neurons cluster into work groups called _____ _____ .

28. The spinal cord is a two-way highway connecting the _____ and the _____ . The spinal cord's work is illustrated by _____ , simple, automatic responses to sensory stimuli.

STUDY TIP/APPLICATION: To keep the various functions of the peripheral nervous system (PNS) straight, remember that the PNS consists of two main divisions: somatic and autonomic. The somatic ("S") division primarily regulates "S functions," such as the senses and skeletal muscles. The autonomic ("A") division regulates automatic ("A") physical systems that do not require conscious attention. These include breathing, heart rate, and digestion, to name a few.

29. You are sitting at your desk at home, studying for an exam. No one else is home, but you hear creaking floorboards. You sneak downstairs, only to discover your parents have returned home early. Describe and explain the sequence of physical reactions that occurred in your body as you felt fear and then relief.

The Endocrine System

Objective 2-6: Describe how the endocrine system transmits information, and discuss its interaction with the nervous system.

The *endocrine system*'s glands secrete *hormones,* chemical messengers produced in one tissue that travel through the bloodstream and affect other tissues, including the brain. Compared with the speed at which messages move through the nervous system, endocrine messages move more slowly but their effects are usually longer-lasting. The endocrine system's hormones influence many aspects of our lives, including growth, reproduction, metabolism, and mood, working with our nervous system to keep everything in balance while responding

to stress, exertion, and thoughts. In a moment of danger, the *adrenal glands* release the hormones *epinephrine* and *norepinephrine,* which increase heart rate, blood pressure, and blood sugar, providing us with a surge of energy known as the *fight-or-flight response.* The **pituitary gland** is the endocrine system's control center (often called the "master gland"). Under the influence of the brain's *hypothalamus,* the pituitary's secretions influence growth and the release of hormones by other endocrine glands. These may in turn influence both the brain and behavior and thus reveal the intimate connection of the nervous and endocrine systems. Among the hormones released by the pituitary is *oxytocin,* which promotes social interactions.

30. The body's chemical communication network is called the _____ _____ . This system transmits information through chemical messengers called _____ at a much _____ (faster/slower) rate than the nervous system, and its effects last _____ (a longer time/a shorter time).

31. In a moment of danger, the _____ glands release _____ and _____ , which cause increases in your _____ rate, _____ _____ , and _____ _____ , giving you a surge of energy known as the _____-_____-_____ response.

32. The control center is the _____ gland, which, under the control of an adjacent brain area called the _____ , helps regulate _____ and promotes social interactions through the release of _____ . It also sends messages for the release of hormones by other endocrine glands.

33. The feedback system linking the nervous and endocrine systems is thus:

    brain's _____ → _____ → other glands → _____ → body and brain.

APPLICATION:

34. A bodybuilder friend suddenly seems to have grown several inches in height. You suspect that your friend's growth spurt has occurred because he has been using drugs that affect the _____ gland(s).

The Brain

Objective 2-7: Describe some techniques for studying the brain.

Powerful techniques now reveal brain structures and activities in the living brain. By recording electrical activity on the brain's surface *(EEG [electroencephalograph])* and by looking inside the living brain to see its activity using the *PET (positron emission tomography) scan,* MRI *(magnetic resonance imaging),* and *fMRI (functional MRI),* neuroscientists examine the connections between brain, mind, and behavior.

35. The _____ is a recording of the electrical activity of the whole brain.

36. The technique depicting the level of activity of brain areas by measuring the brain's consumption of glucose is called the _____

    _____ .

Briefly explain the purpose of the PET scan.

37. A technique that produces clearer images of the brain (and other body parts) by using magnetic fields and radio waves is known as

    _____ .

38. By taking pictures less than a second apart, the

    _____ _____

    detects blood rushing to the part of the cortex thought to control the bodily activity being studied.

STUDY TIP/APPLICATIONS: To help keep the various research methods for studying the brain straight, think of the methods as falling into two categories: (1) those that measure ongoing electrical or metabolic brain activity in real time (EEG, PET scan, fMRI) and (2) those that merely provide a momentary picture of the brain's anatomical structure (MRI).

39. **a.** Which method would be most useful to a neurologist attempting to locate a tumor in a patient's brain?

    _____

    b. Which method would be most useful to a researcher attempting to pinpoint the area of the brain that is most critical to speaking aloud? _____

    c. What are some other instances when a researcher would be best advised to use methods that give a picture of the brain's structure?

    d. What are some other instances when a researcher would be best advised to use methods that measure brain activity?

Objective 2-8: Identify the structures that make up the brainstem, and describe the functions of the brainstem, thalamus, reticular formation, and cerebellum.

The **brainstem** is the brain's oldest and innermost region. It includes the **medulla,** which controls heartbeat and breathing; the *pons,* which helps coordinate movement and control sleep; and the **reticular formation,** which acts as a filter, relaying important information to other brain areas; it also plays an important role in controlling arousal. The brainstem is a crossover point. Atop the brainstem is the **thalamus,** the brain's sensory control center. It receives information from all the senses except smell and sends it to the brain regions that deal with seeing, hearing, tasting, and touching. The **cerebellum,** attached to the rear of the brainstem, coordinates voluntary movement and balance. It helps process and store memories that we cannot consciously recall. Like the other older brain structures, it processes most information outside of our awareness. It also helps us judge time, control our emotions, and discriminate sounds and textures.

40. The oldest and innermost region of the brain is the

    _____ .

41. At the base of the brainstem, where the spinal cord enters the skull, lies the _____ , which controls _____ and _____ . Just above this structure is the _____ , which helps coordinate movement and control _____ .

42. Nerves from each side of the brain cross over to connect with the body's opposite side in the

    _____ .

43. At the top of the brainstem sits the _____ , which serves as the brain's sensory control center, receiving information from all the senses except _____ and forwarding it to the regions dealing with those senses. These egg-shaped structures also receive replies from the higher regions, which they direct to the _____ and the _____ for processing.

44. The _____ _____ is a nerve network inside the brainstem that plays an important role in controlling _____ . Electrically stimulating this area will produce a(n) _____ animal. Severing this area from higher brain regions will cause an animal to lapse into a(n) _____ .

45. At the rear of the brainstem lies the
_____ . It helps process and store
_____ for things we cannot consciously recall, helps us judge
_____ , discriminate sounds and
_____ , control our
_____ , and coordinate movement
output and _____ .

46. The lower brain functions occur without
_____ effort, indicating that our
two-track brain processes most information
_____ (inside/outside) of our
awareness.

APPLICATIONS:

47. The part of the human brain that is most like that of a
shark is the _____ .

48. Dr. Frankenstein made a mistake during neurosurgery
on his monster. After the operation, the monster "saw"
with his ears and "heard" with his eyes. It is likely that Dr.
Frankenstein "rewired" neural connections in the
monster's _____ .

Objective 2-9: Describe the structures and functions of
the limbic system.

The **limbic system** has been
linked primarily to memory,
emotions, and drives. For
example, one of its neural
centers, the **amygdala,** influences aggression and fear.
A second, the **hypothalamus,**
has been linked to various
bodily maintenance func-
tions and to pleasurable
rewards. Its hormones influ-
ence the pituitary gland and thus it provides a major link
between the nervous and endocrine systems. A third, the
hippocampus, processes conscious (explicit) memories.

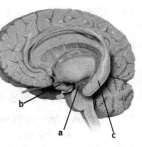

49. Between the brainstem and cerebral hemispheres is
the _____ system. Aggression or
fear will result from stimulation of different regions
of the _____ (see a in the above
drawing).

50. We must remember, however, that the brain
_____ (is/is not) neatly organized
into structures that correspond to our categories of
behavior. For example, aggressive behavior
_____ (does/does not) involve neural activity in many brain areas.

51. Below the thalamus is the _____ (b);
some neural clusters influence _____ ,

while others regulate behaviors such as
_____ , _____
_____ , and _____ .
_____ . Together, these
functions help us maintain a steady _____
state. This area also regulates behavior by secreting
_____ that enable it to control the
nearby "master" gland, the _____
gland. Olds and Milner discovered that this region
also contains _____ centers, which
organisms will work hard to have stimulated.

52. The component of this system that processes
conscious, _____ memories of
facts and events is the _____
(see c).

APPLICATIONS:

53. If Dr. Rogers wishes to conduct an experiment on the
effects of stimulating the reward centers of a rat's brain,
he should insert an electrode into the
_____ .

54. A scientist from another planet wishes to study the simplest brain mechanisms underlying emotion and memory.
You recommend that the scientist study the
_____ _____ .

Objective 2-10: Identify and locate the four lobes of the
cerebral cortex.

The **cerebral cortex,** a thin surface layer of interconnected
neural cells that covers the brain's two hemispheres
(the *cerebrum*), is our body's ultimate control and information-processing center. Each hemisphere has four
lobes. The **frontal lobes** are just behind the forehead. The
parietal lobes are at the top of the head and toward the
rear. The **occipital lobes** are at the back of the head. The
temporal lobes are just above the ears. Each lobe performs
many functions, and many functions require the cooperation of several lobes.

55. The most complex functions of human behavior are
linked to the most developed part of the brain, the
_____ _____ .

This thin layer of interconnected neural cells is the
body's ultimate control and
_____-_____
center.

56. List the four lobes of the brain.

a. _____   c. _____

b. _____   d. _____

Objective 2-11: Describe the functions of the motor cortex, somatosensory cortex, and association areas.

The *motor cortex,* an arch-shaped region at the rear of the frontal lobes, controls voluntary muscle movements on the opposite side of the body. Body parts requiring the most precise control occupy the greatest amount of cortical space. The *somatosensory cortex,* a region at the front of the parietal lobes parallel to the motor cortex, registers and processes our senses of touch and movement. The most sensitive body parts require the largest amount of space in the somatosensory cortex. Other senses send input to other parts of the cortex. Visual information goes to the occipital lobes, and sounds go to the temporal lobes. People with schizophrenia sometimes experience auditory *hallucinations* in the auditory cortex.

The *association areas* are not involved in primary motor or sensory functions. Rather, they are involved in higher mental functions, such as learning, remembering, thinking, and speaking. Association areas are found in all four lobes. For more about the association areas, see material under Objective 2-12.

Complex mental functions don't reside in any one place. Our mental experiences arise from coordinated brain activity.

57. Electrical stimulation of one side of the _____ cortex, an arch-shaped region at the back of the _____ lobe, will produce movement on the opposite side of the body. The more precise the control needed, the

_____ (smaller/ greater) amount of cortical space occupied.

58. At the front of the parietal lobes lies the _____ cortex, which, when stimulated, elicits a sensation of _____ .

59. The more sensitive a body region, the greater the area of _____ _____ devoted to it.

60. Visual information is received in the _____ lobes; auditory information is received in the _____ lobes.

61. People with schizophrenia sometimes have false sensory experiences called _____ .

62. Areas of the brain that don't receive sensory information or direct movement but, rather, integrate and interpret information received by other regions are known as _____ _____ . Such areas in the _____ lobe are involved in judging, planning, and processing of new memories. _____ lobe damage can alter personality. In the _____ lobe, these areas enable mathematical and spatial reasoning, and an area of the _____ lobe enables us to recognize faces.

APPLICATION:

63. In the diagrams to the right, the numbers refer to brain locations that have been damaged. Based on the text explanation of each area's function, match each location with its probable effect on behavior.

Location		*Behavioral Effect*
_____	1.	a. vision disorder
_____	2.	b. insensitivity to touch
_____	3.	c. motor paralysis
_____	4.	d. hearing problem
_____	5.	e. lack of coordination
_____	6.	f. abnormal hunger
_____	7.	g. sleep/arousal disorder

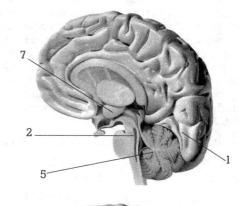

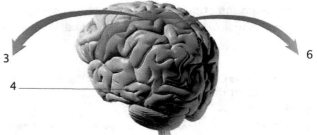

APPLICATIONS:

64. Your roommate Bruce plays the guitar and is part of a band that works at local clubs on weekends. Your musical talent is restricted to "listening to his band." You would expect that Bruce has more cortical space dedicated to "finger control" in the _____ lobes of his brain.

65. Gustav has been diagnosed with a brain tumor. To pinpoint the location of that tumor, his doctor electrically stimulated parts of his somatosensory cortex. If Gustav was conscious during the procedure, he probably experienced _____ .

Objective 2-12: Discuss whether we really use only 10 percent of our brain.

Electrically probing an association area does not produce an observable response, which leads to the myth that we use only 10 percent of our brain. However, association areas interpret, integrate, and act on sensory information and link it with stored memories.

66. When an association area is electrically probed, an observable response _____ (is/is not) produced.

67. The _____ intelligent the animal, the _____ the association areas.

Objective 2-13: Describe how the brain modifies itself after some kinds of damage.

Research indicates that some neural tissue can reorganize in response to damage. When one brain area is damaged, others may in time take over some of its function. For example, if you lose a finger, the somatosensory cortex that received its input will begin to receive input from the adjacent fingers, which become more sensitive. Evidence reveals that adult humans can also generate new brain cells in a process called **neurogenesis.** Our brains are most plastic when we are young children. In fact, children who have had an entire hemisphere removed still lead normal lives.

68. As noted earlier, our brain adapts to new situations, a phenomenon known as _____ . In some cases, brain neural tissue can _____ in response to damage. Also, the brain sometimes attempts to mend itself by producing new neurons, a process called _____ .

Objective 2-14: Define the split brain, and discuss what it reveals about the functions of our two brain hemispheres.

A **split brain** is one whose **corpus callosum,** the wide band of axon fibers that connects the two brain hemispheres, has been severed. Experiments on split-brain patients have refined our knowledge of interactions between the brain's two hemispheres, as well as each hemisphere's special functions (called *lateralization*). In the laboratory, investigators ask a split-brain patient to look at a designated spot, then send information to either the left or right hemisphere (by flashing it to the right or left visual field). Quizzing each hemisphere separately, the researchers have confirmed that the left hemisphere is more active when the person speaks or calculates and the right hemisphere excels in performing a perceptual task, making inferences, and enabling self-awareness. Studies of people with intact brains have confirmed that we have unified brains with specialized parts.

69. In treating patients with severe epilepsy, neurosurgeons separated the two hemispheres of the brain by cutting the _____ _____ . When this structure is severed, the result is referred to as a _____ _____ .

70. In a split-brain patient, only the _____ hemisphere will be aware of an unseen object held in the left hand. In this case, the person would not be able to _____ the object.

Explain why a split-brain patient would be able to read aloud the word *pencil* flashed to his or her right visual field but would be unable to identify a *pencil* by touch using only the left hand.

71. When the "two minds" of a split brain are at odds, the _____ hemisphere tries to rationalize what it doesn't understand. The _____ hemisphere is also used by deaf people to process sign language.

72. Although the _____ hemisphere is better at making quick, literal interpretations of language, the _____ hemisphere excels at making _____ . It also excels at perceptual tasks, fine-tuning our speech, and orchestrating our _____ .

APPLICATIONS:

73. A split-brain patient has a picture of a knife flashed to her left hemisphere and that of a fork to her right hemisphere. She will be able to identify the _____ with her _____ hand. She would then be able to verbally report that she had seen the

_____ .

74. Anton is applying for a technician's job with a neurosurgeon. In trying to impress his potential employer with his knowledge of the brain, he says, "After my father's stroke I knew immediately that the blood clot had affected his left cerebral hemisphere because he claimed that he could move his paralyzed left arm." Should Anton be hired? ____ Explain your answer. _____

_____

Brain States and Consciousness

Objective 2-15: Define _consciousness_, and explain how selective attention directs our perceptions.

Consciousness is a product of coordinated, brainwide activity. It enables us to exert voluntary control and to communicate our mental states to others. Using our two-track mind, we use **sequential processing** for new or complex tasks that require our full attention and **parallel processing** for more automatic functions.

Selective attention means that at any moment, awareness focuses on only a limited aspect of all that we experience. In one study, people left in a room for 28 minutes were free to surf the Internet and to control and watch a TV. Their attention between the two shifted 120 times. Selective attention limits our perception, as many stimuli will pass by unnoticed. This lack of awareness is evident in studies of **inattentional blindness**. One form of this is **change blindness**.

75. Consciousness is defined as _____
_____ .

76. When we focus our conscious awareness on a particular stimulus we are using _____
_____ .

77. When researchers told participants to press a key each time they saw a black-shirted basketball player, they displayed _____ _____
and failed to notice a gorilla-suited assistant who passed through. One form of this phenomenon, in which people don't notice a change that occurs after a brief visual interruption, is called _____
_____ .

Objective 2-16: Define the _circadian rhythm_, and identify the stages of our nightly sleep cycle.

Our 24-hour schedule of waking and sleeping is governed by an internal biological clock known as **circadian rhythm**. Our body temperature rises as morning approaches, peaks during the day, dips for a time in early afternoon, and then begins to drop again before we go to sleep. Thinking is sharpest and memory most accurate when people are at their peak in circadian arousal. Age and experience can alter our circadian rhythm.

We pass through a cycle of four sleep stages that total about 90 minutes. As we lie awake and relaxed,

before we _sleep_, our EEG shows relatively slow _alpha waves_. Stage 1 sleep (NREM-1) is characterized by fantastic images resembling hallucinations (_hypnagogic sensations_). Stage 2 sleep (NREM-2, the stage in which we spend about half the night) follows for the next 20 minutes, with its bursts of rapid, rhythmic brain-wave activity. During stage 3 slow-wave sleep (NREM-3), the brain emits large, slow _delta waves_. This slow-wave sleep stage lasts for about 30 minutes, during which we are hard to awaken. Reversing course, we retrace our path through these stages with one difference. About an hour after falling asleep, we begin approximately 10 minutes of **REM** (rapid eye movement) _sleep_ in which most dreaming occurs. In this fourth stage (also known as _paradoxical_ sleep), we are internally aroused but outwardly paralyzed. The sleep cycle repeats itself about every 90 minutes for younger adults (somewhat more frequently for older adults), with periods of deep NREM-3 sleep progressively shortening and periods of REM and NREM-2 sleep lengthening.

78. Our bodies' internal "clocks" control several
_____ _____ .

79. The sleep-waking cycle follows a 24-hour clock called the _____
_____ .

80. Body temperature _____ (rises/falls) as morning approaches and begins to _____ (rise/fall) again before we go to sleep.

81. When people are at their daily peak in circadian arousal, _____ is sharpest and _____ is most accurate.

82. Our circadian rhythm is altered by _____ and _____ . Before age 20, we tend to be _____-energized "owls"; we then become _____-loving "larks."

83. The rhythm of sleep cycles was discovered when Aserinsky noticed that, at periodic intervals during the night, the _____ of a sleeping child moved rapidly. This stage of sleep, during which _____ occur, is called _____ _____ .

84. The relatively slow brain waves of the awake but relaxed state are known as _____ waves.

85. During NREM-1 sleep, people often experience fantastic sensations similar to _____ . These are called _____ sensations and later may be incorporated into our _____ .

86. The bursts of brain-wave activity that occur during NREM-2 sleep are _____ (slow/rapid) and _____ (rhythmic/arrhythmic). During this stage a person _____ (is/is not) clearly asleep.

87. During NREM-3 sleep the brain emits large, slow _____ waves. A person in this stage of _____-_____ sleep generally will be _____ (easy/difficult) to awaken.

Describe the course of a typical sleep cycle.

Describe the bodily changes that accompany REM sleep.

88. During REM sleep, the motor cortex is _____ (active/relaxed), while the muscles are _____ (active/relaxed). For this reason, REM is often referred to as _____ sleep.

89. The rapid eye movements generally signal the beginning of a _____ , which during REM sleep is often storylike, _____ , and more richly hallucinatory.

90. The sleep cycle repeats itself about every _____ minutes. As the night progresses, NREM-3 sleep becomes _____ (longer/briefer) and REM and NREM-2 periods become _____ (longer/briefer). Approximately _____ percent of a night's sleep is spent in REM sleep.

APPLICATION:

91. Match the sleep stage with a description of that stage or an activity that occurs then.

Sleep Stage

_____ 1. NREM-1 sleep

_____ 2. NREM-2 sleep

_____ 3. NREM-3 sleep

_____ 4. REM sleep

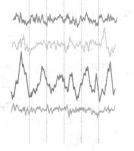

Description or Example

a. Bonita dreams that she's dancing with Justin Bieber at a grand ball.
b. Manfred feels like he's floating above the bed.
c. Rapid, rhythmic brain-wave activity indicates you are clearly asleep.
d. You are in slow-wave sleep and you do not awaken easily.

Objective 2-17: Explain how our sleep patterns differ, and discuss five theories that describe our need to sleep.

People differ in their individual sleep requirements. For example, newborns often sleep twice as much as adults. These age-related changes are rivaled by differences in the normal amount of sleep among individuals of any age. Twin studies suggest that these differences are partially genetic, but they are also influenced by individual and social-cultural forces. People in modern industrialized nations get less sleep because of modern lighting, shift work, and social diversions, for example. Bright light also can disrupt our biological clock. Light-sensitive proteins in the retina signal the *suprachiasmatic nucleus*

(SCN) to decrease production of the sleep-inducing hormone *melatonin*.

The first theory of why we sleep is that sleep may have played a protective role in keeping our distant ancestors safe during potentially dangerous times. A second theory is that sleep may help us recover, restoring and repairing brain tissue. Third, sleep restores and rebuilds our fading memories of the day's experiences. Fourth, after working on a task, then sleeping on it, people solve problems more insightfully than do those who stay awake. Finally, sleep is linked with the release of pituitary growth hormone and so may play a role in the growth process.

92. Newborns often spend _____ (how much?) of their day asleep, while adults spend no more than _____ .

93. Sleep patterns are influenced by _____ , but sleep is also influenced by _____ and _____-_____ forces, as indicated by the fact that people in industrialized nations now sleep _____ (more/less) than they did a century ago.

State five possible reasons that we need to sleep.

94. Sleep patterns are well-suited to each _____ place in nature. Those who sleep less have the greatest need to _____ and the least ability to _____ .

95. Animals that need to sleep a lot produce an abundance of chemical _____ _____ that are toxic to our _____ . Sleep also stimulates _____ thinking.

96. During sleep a growth hormone is released by the _____ gland. Adults spend _____ (more/less) time in deep sleep than children and so release _____ (more/less) growth hormone.

APPLICATIONS:

97. Arsenio is participating in a sleep experiment. While he sleeps, a PET scan of his brain reveals increased activity in the amygdala of the limbic system. This most likely indicates that Arsenio is in _____ sleep.

98. Concluding her presentation on contemporary theories of why sleep is necessary, Marilynn makes all of the following points except that
    a. sleep may have evolved because it kept our ancestors safe during potentially dangerous periods.
    b. sleep gives the brain time to heal, as it restores and repairs damaged neurons.

    c. sleep encourages growth through a hormone secreted during NREM-3.
    d. slow-wave sleep provides a "psychic safety valve" for stressful waking experiences.

Objective 2-18: Discuss how sleep loss affects us, and identify the major sleep disorders.

People today suffer from sleep patterns that thwart their having an energized feeling of well-being. Findings suggest that sleep deprivation predicts depression and puts people at risk for a depressed immune system, and slowed performance with greater vulnerability to accidents. Chronic sleep deprivation can also create conditions that may contribute to obesity, high blood pressure, and memory impairment.

Some 1 in 10 adults, and 1 in 4 older adults, complain of *insomnia,* problems in falling or staying asleep. Rarer but more severe than insomnia are the sleep disorders narcolepsy and sleep apnea. People with *narcolepsy* suffer periodic, overwhelming sleepiness, sometimes at the most inopportune times. Those who suffer *sleep apnea* (mostly obese men) repeatedly stop breathing during sleep. The effects are fatigue and depression, and obesity (especially among men). Still other sleepers, mostly children, experience *night terrors.* They sit up or walk around, talk nonsense, experience a doubling of heart and breathing rates, and appear terrified. Sleepwalking and sleeptalking are also usually childhood disorders.

99. Sleep loss has a number of effects, including predicting _____ , suppressing the _____ _____ , and tiredness. It can also make you fatter by increasing _____ , a hunger-arousing hormone, and decreasing _____ , a hunger-suppressing hormone.

100. A persistent difficulty in falling or staying asleep is characteristic of _____ . Sleeping pills and alcohol may make the problem worse because they tend to _____ (increase/ reduce) REM sleep. They also lead to _____ , a state in which increasing doses are needed to produce an effect.

101. The sleep disorder in which a person experiences uncontrollable sleep attacks is _____ . The person sometimes lapses directly into _____ _____ .

102. Individuals suffering from _____ _____ stop breathing while sleeping. An effect of this disorder is _____ , especially among men.

103. The sleep disorder characterized by extreme fright and a doubling of heart and breathing rates is called _____ _____ . These episodes usually happen during _____ sleep. The same is true of episodes of _____ and _____ . These sleep episodes are most likely to be experienced by _____ (young children/ adolescents/older adults), in whom this stage tends to be the lengthiest and deepest.

Objective 2-19: Describe what we dream about, and identify five explanations of *why* we dream.

REM *dreams* are vivid, emotional, and bizarre. Common themes are failing, being attacked and pursued, and experiencing misfortune. The story line of our dreams—what Sigmund Freud called their *manifest content*—sometimes incorporates traces of previous days' experiences and preoccupations. Only 1 in 10 dreams among young men and 1 in 30 among young women have sexual overtones. Sensory stimuli may also intrude on our dreams as our two-track mind monitors our environment.

In his wish-fulfillment theory, Freud suggested that a dream's manifest content is a censored version of its *latent content,* which gratifies our unconscious wishes. The *information-processing* perspective suggests that dreams help us process information and fix it in memory. Some physiological theories propose that REM-induced regular brain stimulation helps develop and preserve neural pathways in the brain. Another explanation is that random neural activity spreads upward from the brainstem; our brain attempts to make sense of the activity, pasting the random bits of information into a meaningful image. A final perspective maintains that dreams represent the dreamer's level of brain maturation and cognitive development. Despite their differences, most theorists agree that REM sleep and its associated dreams serve an important function, as shown by the **REM rebound** that occurs following REM deprivation.

104. Dreams experienced during _____ sleep are vivid, emotional, and bizarre.

105. For both men and women, 8 in 10 dreams are marked by _____ (positive/negative) emotions, such as fears of being _____ .

106. Freud referred to the actual content of a dream as its _____ content. Freud believed that this is a censored, symbolic version of the true meaning, or _____ content, of the dream.

107. According to Freud, most of the dreams of adults reflect _____ wishes and are the key to understanding inner wishes that cannot be expressed publicly. To Freud, dreams serve as a _____ _____ that discharges otherwise unacceptable feelings.

108. Researchers who believe that dreams serve an _____-processing function receive support from the fact that REM sleep facilitates _____ . Brain scans confirm this link.

109. Other theories propose that dreaming serves to develop and preserve _____ _____ . For example, REM sleep may give the sleeping brain a workout that helps it _____ . Such an explanation is supported by the fact that _____ (infants/adults) spend the most time in REM sleep.

110. Still other theories propose that dreams are elicited by random bursts of _____ activity originating in lower regions of the brain, such as the _____ . According to this perspective, dreams are the brain's attempt to make sense of this activity. According to another theory, dreams are a natural part of brain _____ and _____ development.

111. Researchers agree that we _____ (need/do not need) REM sleep. After being deprived of REM sleep, a person spends more time in REM sleep; this is the _____ _____ effect.

APPLICATIONS:

112. Barry has participated in a sleep study for the last four nights. He was awakened each time he entered REM sleep. Now that the experiment is over, Barry will most likely show a(n) _____ (increase/decrease) in REM sleep, a phenomenon known as _____ _____ .

113. Bahara dreams that she trips and falls as she walks up the steps to the stage to receive her college diploma. Her psychoanalyst suggests that the dream might symbolize her fear of moving on to the next stage of her life—a career. The analyst is evidently attempting to interpret the _____ content of Bahara's dream.

Progress Test

Multiple-Choice Questions

Circle your answers to the following questions and check them with the answers beginning on page 39. If your answer is incorrect, read the explanation for why it is incorrect and then consult the text.

1. Heartbeat, digestion, and other self-regulating bodily functions are governed by the
   a. voluntary nervous system.
   b. autonomic nervous system.
   c. sympathetic division of the autonomic nervous system.
   d. somatic nervous system.

2. A strong stimulus can increase the
   a. speed of the impulse the neuron fires.
   b. intensity of the impulse the neuron fires.
   c. number of times the neuron fires.
   d. threshold that must be reached before the neuron fires.

3. The pain of heroin withdrawal occurs because
   a. under the influence of heroin the brain ceases production of endorphins.
   b. under the influence of heroin the brain ceases production of all neurotransmitters.
   c. during heroin withdrawal the brain's production of all neurotransmitters is greatly increased.
   d. heroin destroys endorphin receptors in the brain.

4. The brain research technique that involves monitoring the brain's use of glucose is called the
   a. PET scan.   c. EEG.
   b. fMRI.   d. MRI.

5. Although there is no single "control center" for emotions, their regulation is primarily attributed to the brain region known as the
   a. limbic system.   c. brainstem.
   b. reticular formation.   d. cerebellum.

6. Which of the following is typically controlled by the right hemisphere?
   a. language
   b. learned voluntary movements
   c. arithmetic reasoning
   d. perceptual tasks

7. Dr. Hernandez is studying neurotransmitter abnormalities in depressed patients. She would most likely describe herself as a
   a. personality psychologist.
   b. behaviorist.
   c. psychoanalyst.
   d. biological psychologist.

8. Voluntary movements, such as writing with a pencil, are directed by the
   a. sympathetic nervous system.
   b. somatic nervous system.
   c. parasympathetic nervous system.
   d. autonomic nervous system.

9. A neuron will generate action potentials when
   a. it remains below its threshold.
   b. it receives an excitatory input.
   c. excitatory inputs exceed inhibitory inputs by a minimum intensity.
   d. it is stimulated by a neurotransmitter.

10. Which is the correct sequence in the transmission of a neural impulse?
    a. axon, dendrite, cell body, synapse
    b. dendrite, axon, cell body, synapse
    c. synapse, axon, dendrite, cell body
    d. dendrite, cell body, axon, synapse

11. Chemical messengers produced by endocrine glands are called
    a. lobes.   c. hormones.
    b. neurotransmitters.   d. enzymes.

12. Following a head injury, a person has ongoing difficulties staying awake. Most likely, the damage occurred to the
    a. thalamus.   c. reticular formation.
    b. corpus callosum.   d. cerebellum.

13. An experimenter flashes the word FLYTRAP onto a screen facing a split-brain patient so that FLY projects to her right hemisphere and TRAP to her left hemisphere. When asked what she saw, the patient will
    a. say she saw FLY.
    b. say she saw TRAP.
    c. point to FLY using her right hand.
    d. point to TRAP using her left hand.

14. Cortical areas that are NOT primarily concerned with sensory, motor, or language functions are
    a. called projection areas.
    b. called association areas.
    c. located mostly in the parietal lobe.
    d. located mostly in the temporal lobe.

15. The visual cortex is located in the
    a. occipital lobe.   c. frontal lobe.
    b. temporal lobe.   d. parietal lobe.

16. Which of the following is typically controlled by the left hemisphere?
    a. spatial reasoning
    b. word recognition
    c. the left side of the body
    d. perceptual skills

17. When Sandy scalded her toe in a tub of hot water, the pain message was carried to her spinal cord by the _____ nervous system.
    a. somatic   c. parasympathetic
    b. sympathetic   d. central

18. Melissa has just completed running a marathon. She is so elated that she feels little fatigue or discomfort. Her lack of pain is probably the result of the release of
    a. ACh.
    b. endorphins.
    c. dopamine.
    d. norepinephrine.

19. I am a relatively fast-acting chemical messenger that affects mood, hunger, sleep, and arousal. What am I?
    a. acetylcholine
    b. dopamine
    c. norepinephrine
    d. serotonin

20. The gland that regulates body growth is the
    a. adrenal.
    b. thyroid.
    c. hypothalamus.
    d. pituitary.

21. Epinephrine and norepinephrine are _____ that are released by the _____ gland.
    a. neurotransmitters; pituitary
    b. hormones; pituitary
    c. neurotransmitters; thyroid
    d. hormones; adrenal

22. Jessica experienced difficulty keeping her balance after receiving a blow to the back of her head. It is likely that she injured her
    a. medulla.
    b. thalamus.
    c. hypothalamus.
    d. cerebellum.

23. Researchers caused a cat to lapse into a coma by severing neural connections between the cortex and the
    a. reticular formation.
    b. hypothalamus.
    c. thalamus.
    d. cerebellum.

24. Research has found that the amount of representation in the motor cortex reflects the
    a. size of the body parts.
    b. degree of precise control required by each of the parts.
    c. sensitivity of the body region.
    d. area of the occipital lobe being stimulated by the environment.

25. The nerve fibers that enable communication between the right and left cerebral hemispheres and that have been severed in split-brain patients form a structure called the
    a. reticular formation.
    b. association areas.
    c. corpus callosum.
    d. parietal lobes.

26. Beginning at the front of the brain and moving toward the back of the head, then down the skull and back around to the front, which of the following is the correct order of the cortical regions?
    a. occipital lobe; temporal lobe; parietal lobe; frontal lobe
    b. temporal lobe; frontal lobe; parietal lobe; occipital lobe
    c. frontal lobe; occipital lobe; temporal lobe; parietal lobe
    d. frontal lobe; parietal lobe; occipital lobe; temporal lobe

27. Following a nail gun wound to his head, Jack became more uninhibited, irritable, dishonest, and profane. It is likely that his personality change was the result of injury to his
    a. parietal lobe.
    b. temporal lobe.
    c. occipital lobe.
    d. frontal lobe.

28. Three-year-old Marco suffered damage to the speech area of the brain's left hemisphere when he fell from a swing. Research suggests that
    a. he may never speak again.
    b. his motor abilities may improve so that he can easily use sign language.
    c. his right hemisphere may take over much of the language function.
    d. his earlier experience with speech may enable him to continue speaking.

29. Large, slow waves predominate during which stage of sleep?
    a. NREM-1
    b. NREM-2
    c. NREM-3
    d. REM sleep

30. During which stage of sleep does the body experience increased heart rate, rapid breathing, and genital arousal?
    a. NREM-1
    b. NREM-2
    c. NREM-3
    d. REM sleep

31. The sleep cycle is approximately _____ minutes.
    a. 30
    b. 50
    c. 75
    d. 90

32. The effects of chronic sleep deprivation include
    a. depression.
    b. suppressed immune system.
    c. a tendency to gain weight.
    d. all of these conditions.

33. One effect of sleeping pills is to
    a. decrease REM sleep.
    b. increase REM sleep.
    c. decrease NREM-2 sleep.
    d. increase NREM-2 sleep.

34. According to Freud, dreams are
    a. a symbolic fulfillment of erotic wishes.
    b. the result of random neural activity in the brainstem.
    c. the brain's mechanism for self-stimulation.
    d. the overt expressions of wishes we can't fulfill in public.

35. Which of the following is NOT a theory of dreaming mentioned in the text?
    a. Dreams facilitate information processing.
    b. Dreaming stimulates the developing brain.

c. Dreams result from random neural activity originating in the brainstem.
d. Dreaming is an attempt to escape from social stimulation.

36. Which of the following statements regarding REM sleep is true?
a. Adults spend more time than infants in REM sleep.
b. REM sleep deprivation results in REM rebound.
c. People deprived of REM sleep adapt easily.
d. Sleeping medications tend to increase REM sleep.

37. The perceptual error in which we fail to see an object when our attention is directed elsewhere is
a. neurogenesis.
b. inattentional blindness.
c. narcolepsy.
d. an all-or-none response.

38. A person whose EEG shows a high proportion of alpha waves is most likely
a. dreaming.
b. in NREM-2 sleep.
c. in NREM-3 sleep.
d. awake and relaxed.

39. Circadian rhythms are the
a. brain waves that occur during NREM-3 sleep.
b. muscular tremors that occur during opiate withdrawal.
c. regular body cycles that occur on a 24-hour schedule.
d. brain waves that are indicative of NREM-2 sleep.

40. Which of the following is NOT an example of a biological rhythm?
a. the circadian rhythm
b. the 90-minute sleep cycle
c. the four sleep stages
d. sudden sleep attacks during the day

41. Which of the following is characteristic of REM sleep?
a. genital arousal
b. increased muscular tension
c. night terrors
d. alpha waves

42. When we talk about the conscious part of our two-track mind, what are we referring to?
a. our mental life
b. selective attention to ongoing perceptions, thoughts, and feelings
c. information processing
d. our awareness of ourselves and our environment

Matching Items 1

Match each structure or technique with its corresponding function or description.

Structures

_____ 1. hypothalamus
_____ 2. EEG
_____ 3. fMRI
_____ 4. reticular formation
_____ 5. MRI
_____ 6. thalamus
_____ 7. corpus callosum
_____ 8. cerebellum
_____ 9. amygdala
_____ 10. medulla

Functions or Descriptions

a. amplified recording of brain waves
b. technique that uses radio waves and magnetic fields to image brain anatomy
c. serves as sensory control center
d. contains reward centers
e. technique that uses radio waves and magnetic fields to show brain function
f. helps control arousal
g. links the cerebral hemispheres
h. enables aggression and fear
i. regulates breathing and heartbeat
j. enables coordinated movement

Matching Items 2

Match each term with its appropriate definition or description.

Definitions or Descriptions

_____ **1.** surface meaning of dreams
_____ **2.** deeper meaning of dreams
_____ **3.** stage of sleep associated with delta waves
_____ **4.** stage of sleep associated with muscular relaxation
_____ **5.** sleep disorder in which breathing stops
_____ **6.** sleep disorder occurring in NREM-3 sleep
_____ **7.** twilight stage of sleep associated with imagery resembling hallucinations
_____ **8.** disorder in which sleep attacks occur

Terms

a. NREM-1 sleep
b. night terrors
c. manifest content
d. narcolepsy
e. sleep apnea
f. NREM-3 sleep
g. REM sleep
h. latent content

Application Essay

Discuss how the endocrine and nervous systems become involved when a student feels stress—such as that associated with an upcoming final exam. (Use the space below to list the points you want to make, and organize them. Then write the essay on a separate sheet of paper.)

Terms and Concepts to Remember

Using your own words, on a separate piece of paper write a brief definition or explanation of each of the following terms.

1. plasticity
2. biological psychology
3. cognitive neuroscience
4. neuron
5. dendrites
6. axon
7. action potential

8. glial cells (glia)
9. synapse
10. threshold
11. refractory period
12. all-or-none response
13. neurotransmitters
14. reuptake
15. opiate
16. endorphins
17. nervous system
18. central nervous system (CNS)
19. peripheral nervous system (PNS)
20. nerves
21. sensory neuron
22. motor neuron
23. interneuron
24. somatic nervous system
25. autonomic nervous system
26. sympathetic nervous system
27. parasympathetic nervous system
28. reflex
29. endocrine system
30. hormones
31. adrenal glands
32. pituitary gland
33. EEG (electroencephalograph)
34. PET (positron emission tomography) scan
35. MRI (magnetic resonance imaging)
36. fMRI (functional MRI)
37. brainstem
38. medulla
39. thalamus
40. reticular formation
41. cerebellum

42. limbic system
43. amygdala
44. hypothalamus
45. hippocampus
46. cerebral cortex
47. frontal lobes
48. parietal lobes
49. occipital lobes
50. temporal lobes
51. motor cortex
52. somatosensory cortex
53. hallucination
54. association areas
55. neurogenesis
56. corpus callosum
57. split brain
58. consciousness
59. sequential processing
60. parallel processing
61. selective attention
62. inattentional blindness
63. change blindness
64. circadian rhythm
65. REM sleep
66. alpha waves
67. sleep
68. delta waves
69. suprachiasmatic nucleus (SCN)
70. insomnia
71. narcolepsy
72. sleep apnea
73. dream
74. manifest content
75. latent content
76. REM rebound

Answers

Chapter Review

The Brain: A Work in Progress

1. plasticity; young children
2. biological psychologists
3. cognitive neuroscience
4. A biological psychologist might study chemical changes that accompany emotions, how muscle tension varies with facial expression, how heart rate changes as people become angry, and so on.

Neural Communication

5. neurons
6. dendrites; axon
7. action potential; axon

8. synapse; synaptic gap
9. a. dendrites
   b. cell body
   c. axon
   d. neural impulse (action potential)
10. glial cells
11. excitatory; inhibitory; threshold; will not; all-or-none; the number of neurons that fire and the frequency of firing
12. does not
13. Because she has reached her threshold, she will probably fire.
14. neurotransmitters; receptor
15. exciting; inhibiting; reuptake

A neural impulse (action potential) is generated by excitatory signals exceeding inhibitory signals by a certain threshold. The stimuli are received through the dendrites, combined in the cell body, and electrically transmitted in an all-or-none fashion down the length of the axon. When the combined signal reaches the end of the axon, chemical messengers called neurotransmitters are released into the synaptic gap between two neurons. Neurotransmitter molecules bind to receptor sites on the dendrites of neighboring neurons and have either an excitatory or inhibitory influence on that neuron's tendency to generate its own neural impulse.

16. mood, hunger, sleep, and arousal; movement, learning, attention, and feelings of pleasure and reward
17. endorphins; heroin; morphine
18. norepinephrine. An undersupply can cause depression.
19. oversupply; glutamate. Glutamate is in MSG, which is commonly used in Chinese cooking. Glutamate can cause migraines because an oversupply can overstimulate the brain.

The Nervous System

20. nervous system; electrochemical
21. central; peripheral
22. nerves
23. sensory; motor; interneurons
24. somatic
25. autonomic
26. sympathetic; energy; parasympathetic; energy
27. neural networks
28. brain; peripheral nervous system; reflexes
29. When you hear the creaking, you become afraid. The sympathetic division of your autonomic nervous system becomes aroused, causing these physiological changes: accelerated heartbeat, elevated blood sugar, dilation of arteries, slowing of digestion, and increased perspiration to cool the body. When you realize it's only your parents, your parasympathetic nervous system produces the opposite physical reactions, calming your body.

The Endocrine System

30. endocrine system; hormones; slower; a longer time

31. adrenal; epinephrine (adrenaline); norepinephrine (noradrenaline); heart; blood pressure; blood sugar; fight-or-flight

32. pituitary; hypothalamus; growth; oxytocin

33. hypothalamus → pituitary → other glands → hormones → body and brain

34. pituitary

The Brain

35. EEG (electroencephalograph)

36. PET scan

By depicting the brain's consumption of a temporarily radioactive form of glucose, the PET scan allows researchers to see which brain areas are most active as a person performs various tasks. This provides additional information on the specialized functions of various regions of the brain.

37. MRI (magnetic resonance imaging)

38. functional MRI (fMRI)

39. **a.** MRI
  b. PET scan
  c. to study developmental changes in brain structure, to compare brain anatomy in women and men
  d. to learn which areas of the brain become active during strong emotions, to determine whether brain activity is abnormal in people suffering from memory and language problems

40. brainstem

41. medulla; breathing; heartbeat; pons; sleep

42. brainstem

43. thalamus; smell; medulla; cerebellum

44. reticular formation; arousal; alert (awake); coma

45. cerebellum; memories; time; textures; emotions; balance

46. conscious; outside

47. brainstem. The brainstem is the oldest and most primitive region of the brain. It is found in lower vertebrates, such as the shark, as well as in humans and other mammals.

48. thalamus. The thalamus relays sensory messages from the eyes, ears, and other receptors to the appropriate projection areas of the cortex. "Rewiring" the thalamus, theoretically, could have the effects stated in this question.

49. limbic; amygdala

50. is not; does

51. hypothalamus; hunger; thirst; body temperature; sexual behavior; internal; hormones; pituitary; reward

52. explicit; hippocampus

53. hypothalamus. As Olds and Milner discovered, electrical stimulation of the hypothalamus is a highly reinforcing event because it is the location of the animal's reward centers.

54. limbic system. The hippocampus of the limbic system is involved in processing memory. The amygdala of the limbic system influences fear and anger.

55. cerebral cortex; information-processing

56. **a.** frontal lobe   **c.** occipital lobe
  b. parietal lobe   **d.** temporal lobe

57. motor; frontal; greater

58. somatosensory; touch

59. somatosensory cortex

69. occipital; temporal

61. hallucinations

62. association areas; prefrontal; Frontal; parietal; temporal

63. Brain Damage Diagram
  1. a   **4.** d   **7.** f
  2. g   **5.** e
  3. c   **6.** b

64. frontal. The motor cortex, which determines the precision with which various parts of the body can be moved, is located in the frontal lobes.

65. a sense of touch. Stimulation of the somatosensory cortex elicits a sense of touch, as the experiments of Wilder Penfield demonstrated.

66. is not

67. more; larger

68. plasticity; reorganize; neurogenesis

69. corpus callosum; split brain

70. right; name

The word *pencil*, when flashed to a split-brain patient's right visual field, would project only to the opposite, or left, hemisphere of the patient's brain. Because the left hemisphere contains the language control centers of the brain, the patient would be able to read the word aloud. The left hand is controlled by the right hemisphere of the brain. Because the right hemisphere would not be aware of the word, it would not be able to guide the left hand in identifying a pencil by touch.

71. left; left

72. left; right; inferences; self-awareness

73. fork; left; knife. The left hand, controlled by the right hemisphere, would be able to identify the fork, the picture of which is flashed to the right hemisphere. She would verbally report she had seen the knife because it was flashed to her left hemisphere.

74. no. The left hemisphere does not enable our self-awareness. And blood clots can form anywhere in the brain.

Brain States and Consciousness

75. our awareness of ourselves and our environment

76. selective attention

77. inattentional blindness; change blindness

78. biological rhythms

79. circadian rhythm

80. rises; fall

81. thinking; memory

82. age; experience; evening; morning

83. eyes; dreams; REM sleep

84. alpha
85. hallucinations; hypnagogic; memories
86. rapid; rhythmic; is
87. delta; slow-wave; difficult

When you first slip into sleep, you experience slowed breathing and the irregular brain waves of NREM-1 sleep. This is followed by 20 minutes of NREM-2 sleep, with its bursts of rapid, rhythmic brain waves, and then 30 minutes of slow-wave (NREM-3) sleep, characterized by delta waves. You then cycle back through these stages and finally enter REM sleep. Each cycle lasts about 90 minutes.

During REM sleep, brain waves become as rapid as those of NREM-1 sleep, heart rate and breathing become more rapid and irregular, and genital arousal and rapid eye movements occur.

88. active; relaxed; paradoxical
89. dream; emotional
90. 90; briefer; longer; 20 to 25
91. 1. b   3. d
    2. c   4. a
92. two-thirds; one-third
93. genes; psychological; social-cultural; less

Sleep may have played a protected our distant ancestors during potentially dangerous times. A second theory is that sleep may help us recuperate, restoring and repairing brain tissue. Third, sleep restores and rebuilds our fading memories of the day's experiences. Fourth, sleep promotes creative thinking. Finally, sleep may have evolved because it promotes growth.

94. species'; graze; hide
95. free radicals; neurons; creative
96. pituitary; less; less
97. REM. The amygdala is involved in emotion, and dreams during REM sleep often tend to be emotional.
98. **d.** is the answer. Freud's theory proposed that dreams, which occur during fast-wave, REM sleep, serve as a psychic safety valve.
99. depression; immune system; ghrelin; leptin
100. insomnia; reduce; tolerance
101. narcolepsy; REM sleep
102. sleep apnea; obesity
103. night terrors; NREM-3; sleepwalking; sleeptalking; young children
104. REM
105. negative; attacked, pursued, or rejected, or of experiencing misfortune
106. manifest; latent
107. erotic; safety valve
108. information; memory
109. neural pathways; develop; infants
110. neural; brainstem; maturation; cognitive
111. need; REM rebound
112. increase; REM rebound. The existence of REM rebound is evidence of our need for REM sleep.

113. latent. The analyst is evidently trying to go beyond the events in the dream and understand the dream's hidden meaning, or the dream's latent content.

Progress Test

Multiple-Choice Questions

1. **b.** is the answer. The autonomic nervous system controls internal functioning, including heartbeat, digestion, and glandular activity.
   a. The functions mentioned are all automatic, not voluntary, so this answer cannot be correct.
   c. This answer is incorrect because most organs are affected by both divisions of the ANS.
   d. The somatic nervous system monitors sensory input and triggers motor output; it also enables voluntary control of skeletal muscles.

2. **c.** is the answer. Stimulus strength can affect only the number of times a neuron fires or the number of neurons that fire.
   a., b., & d. These answers are incorrect because firing is an all-or-none response, so intensity remains the same regardless of stimulus strength. Nor can stimulus strength change the neuronal threshold or the impulse speed.

3. **a.** is the answer. Endorphins are neurotransmitters that function as natural painkillers. When the body has a supply of artificial painkillers such as heroin, endorphin production stops.
   b. The production of neurotransmitters other than endorphins does not cease.
   c. Neurotransmitter production does not increase during withdrawal.
   d. Heroin makes use of the same receptor sites as endorphins.

4. **a.** is the answer. The PET scan measures glucose consumption in different areas of the brain to determine their levels of activity.
   b. The fMRI compares MRI scans taken less than a second apart to reveal brain anatomy and function.
   c. The EEG is a measure of electrical activity in the brain.
   d. MRI uses magnetic fields and radio waves to produce computer-generated images of soft tissues of the body.

5. **a.** is the answer.
   b. The reticular formation is linked to arousal.
   c. The brainstem governs the mechanisms of basic survival—heartbeat and breathing, for example—and has many other roles.
   d. The cerebellum coordinates movement output and balance.

6. **d.** is the answer.
   a. In most persons, language is primarily a left hemisphere function.
   b. Learned movements are unrelated to hemispheric specialization.
   c. Arithmetic reasoning is generally a left hemisphere function.

7. **d.** is the answer. Biological psychologists study the

links between biology (in this case, neurotransmitters) and psychology (depression, in this example).

8. **b.** is the answer.
   a., c., & d. The autonomic nervous system, which is divided into the sympathetic and parasympathetic divisions, is concerned with regulating basic bodily maintenance functions.

9. **c.** is the answer.
   a. An action potential will occur only when the neuron's threshold is *exceeded*.
   b. An excitatory input that does not reach the neuron's threshold will not trigger an action potential.
   d. This answer is incorrect because some neurotransmitters inhibit a neuron's readiness to fire.

10. **d.** is the answer. A neuron receives incoming stimuli on its dendrites and cell body. These electrochemical signals are combined in the cell body, generating an impulse that travels down the axon, causing the release of neurotransmitter substances into the synaptic cleft or gap.

11. **c.** is the answer.
    a. Each hemisphere of the brain is divided into four lobes.
    b. Neurotransmitters are the chemicals involved in synaptic transmission in the nervous system.
    d. Enzymes are chemicals that facilitate various chemical reactions throughout the body but are not involved in communication within the endocrine system.

12. **c.** is the answer. The reticular formation plays an important role in arousal.
    a. The thalamus relays sensory input.
    b. The corpus callosum links the two cerebral hemispheres.
    d. The cerebellum is involved in coordination of movement output and balance.

13. **b.** is the answer.

14. **b.** is the answer. Association areas interpret, integrate, and act on information from other areas of the cortex.

15. **a.** is the answer. The visual cortex is located at the very back of the brain.

16. **b.** is the answer.
    a., c., & d. Spatial reasoning, perceptual skills, and the left side of the body are primarily influenced by the right hemisphere.

17. **a.** is the answer. Sensory neurons in the somatic nervous system relay such messages.
    b. & c. These divisions of the autonomic nervous system are concerned with the regulation of bodily maintenance functions such as heartbeat, digestion, and glandular activity.
    d. The spinal cord itself is part of the central nervous system, but the message is carried to the spinal cord by the somatic division of the peripheral nervous system.

18. **b.** is the answer. Endorphins are neurotransmitters that function as natural painkillers and are evidently involved in the "runner's high" and other situations in which discomfort or fatigue is expected but not experienced.

a. ACh is a neurotransmitter involved in muscular control.
c. Dopamine is a neurotransmitter involved in, among other things, motor control.
d. Norepinephrine is an adrenal hormone released to help us respond in moments of danger.

19. **d.** is the answer.

20. **d.** is the answer. The pituitary regulates body growth, and some of its secretions regulate the release of hormones from other glands.
    a. The adrenal glands are stimulated by the autonomic nervous system to release epinephrine and norepinephrine.
    b. The thyroid gland affects metabolism, among other things.
    c. The hypothalamus regulates the pituitary but does not itself directly regulate growth.

21. **d.** is the answer. Also known as adrenaline and noradrenaline, epinephrine and norepinephrine are hormones released by the adrenal glands.

22. **d.** is the answer. The cerebellum is involved in the coordination of voluntary muscular movements.
    a. The medulla regulates breathing and heartbeat.
    b. The thalamus relays sensory inputs to the appropriate higher centers of the brain.
    c. The hypothalamus is concerned with the regulation of basic drives and emotions.

23. **a.** is the answer. The reticular formation controls arousal via its connections to the cortex. Thus, separating the two produces a coma.
    b., c., & d. None of these structures controls arousal. The hypothalamus regulates hunger, thirst, sexual behavior, and other basic drives; the thalamus is a sensory control center; and the cerebellum coordinates voluntary movement.

24. **b.** is the answer.
    c. & d. These refer to the sensory cortex.

25. **c.** is the answer. The corpus callosum is a large band of neural fibers linking the right and left cerebral hemispheres. To sever the corpus callosum is in effect to split the brain.

26. **d.** is the answer. The frontal lobe is in the front of the brain. Just behind is the parietal lobe. The occipital lobe is located at the very back of the head and just below the parietal lobe. Next to the occipital lobe and toward the front of the head is the temporal lobe.

27. **d.** is the answer. As demonstrated in the case of Phineas Gage, injury to the frontal lobe may produce such changes in personality.
    a. Damage to the parietal lobe might disrupt functions involving the sensory cortex.
    b. Damage to the temporal lobe might impair hearing.
    c. Occipital damage might impair vision.

28. **c.** is the answer. Especially in young children, the brain may attempt to reorganize after damage.

29. **c.** is the answer.

a. & b. Irregular waves that resemble REM waves predominate during NREM-1, and rapid, rhythmic waves are characteristic of NREM-2.
d. Faster, nearly waking brain waves occur during REM sleep.

30. **d.** is the answer.
a., b., & c. During non-REM stages 1–3 heart rate and breathing are slow and regular and the genitals are not aroused.

31. **d.** is the answer.

32. **d.** is the answer.

33. **a.** is the answer. Like alcohol, sleeping pills carry the undesirable consequence of reducing REM sleep and may make insomnia worse in the long run.
b., c., & d. Sleeping pills do not produce these effects.

34. **a.** is the answer. Freud saw dreams as psychic safety valves that discharge unacceptable feelings that are often related to erotic wishes.
b. & c. These physiological theories of dreaming are not associated with Freud.
d. According to Freud, dreams represent the individual's conflicts and wishes but in disguised, rather than transparent, form.

35. **d.** is the answer.
a., b., & c. Each of these describes a valid theory of dreaming that was mentioned in the text.

36. **b.** is the answer. Following REM deprivation, people temporarily increase their amount of REM sleep, in a phenomenon known as REM rebound.
a. Just the opposite is true: The amount of REM sleep is greatest in infancy.
c. Deprived of REM sleep by repeated awakenings, people return more and more quickly to the REM stages after falling back to sleep. They by no means adapt easily to the deprivations.
d. Just the opposite occurs: They tend to suppress REM sleep.

37. **b.** is the answer.
a. Neurogenesis is the formation of new neurons.
c. Narcolepsy is a sleep disorder in which the person falls asleep at inopportune times.
d. The all-or-none response refers to the fact that neurons either respond or do not respond.

38. **d.** is the answer.
a. The brain waves of REM sleep (dream sleep) are more like those of NREM-1 sleepers.
b. NREM-2 is characterized by sleep spindles.
c. NREM-3 is characterized by slow, rolling delta waves.

39. **c.** is the answer.

40. **d.** is the answer.

41. **a.** is the answer.
b. During REM sleep, muscular tension is low.
c. Night terrors are associated with NREM-3 sleep.
d. Alpha waves are characteristic of the relaxed, awake state.

42. **d.** is the answer.

Matching Items 1

1.	d	**5.**	b	**9.**	h
2.	a	**6.**	c	**10.**	i
3.	e	**7.**	g		
4.	f	**8.**	j		

Matching Items 2

1.	c	**5.**	e
2.	h	**6.**	b
3.	f	**7.**	a
4.	g	**8.**	d

Application Essay

The body's response to stress is regulated by the nervous system. As the date of the exam approaches, the stressed student's cerebral cortex activates the hypothalamus, triggering the release of hormones that in turn activate the sympathetic branch of the autonomic nervous system and the endocrine system. The autonomic nervous system controls involuntary bodily responses such as breathing, heartbeat, and digestion. The endocrine system's glands secrete hormones into the bloodstream that regulate the functions of body organs.

In response to activation by the hypothalamus, the student's pituitary gland would secrete a hormone, which in turn triggers the release of epinephrine, norepinephrine, and other stress hormones from the adrenal glands. These hormones would help the student's body manage stress by making nutrients available to meet the increased demands for energy stores the body often faces in coping with stress. As these hormones activate the sympathetic division of the autonomic system, the body's fight-or-flight response occurs, including increased heart rate, breathing, and blood pressure and the suppression of digestion. After the exam date has passed, the student's body would attempt to restore its normal, pre-stress state. The parasympathetic branch of the autonomic system would slow the student's heartbeat and breathing and digestive processes would no longer be suppressed, perhaps causing the student to feel hungry.

Terms and Concepts to Remember

1. **Plasticity** is the brain's capacity for modification, as evidenced by brain reorganization following damage (especially in children).

2. **Biological psychology** is the study of the links between biology and behavior.

3. **Cognitive neuroscience** is the interdisciplinary study of the brain activity linked with cognition.

4. The **neuron**, or nerve cell, is the basic building block of the nervous system.

5. The **dendrites** of a neuron are the bushy, branching extensions that receive messages from other nerve cells and conduct impulses toward the cell body.

6. The **axon** of a neuron is the extension that sends impulses to other nerve cells or to muscles or glands.

7. An **action potential** is a neural impulse that travels down the nerve cell's axon.

8. More numerous than neurons, the **glial cells (glia)** of the nervous system guide neural connections, provide nutrients and insulating myelin, and clean up after neurons send messages to one another.

9. A **synapse** is the junction between the axon tip of the sending neuron and the dendrite or cell body of the receiving neuron. The tiny gap at this junction is called the *synaptic gap*.

10. A neuron's **threshold** is the level of stimulation that must be exceeded in order for the neuron to fire, or generate an electrical impulse.

11. **The refractory period** is the brief resting period after a neuron has fired.

12. The **all-or-none response** is a neuron's reaction of either firing (with a full-strength response) or not firing.

13. **Neurotransmitters** are chemicals that are released into synaptic gaps and so *transmit neural messages* from neuron to neuron.

14. **Reuptake** is the reabsorption by a sending neuron of a neurotransmitter.

15. An **opiate** is a chemical, such as morphine, that depresses neural activity, temporarily lessening pain and anxiety.

16. **Endorphins** are natural, opiate-like neurotransmitters linked to pain control and to pleasure.

    Memory aid: <u>End</u>orphins *end* pain.

17. The **nervous system** is the speedy, electrochemical communication system, consisting of all the nerve cells in the peripheral and central nervous systems.

18. The **central nervous system (CNS)** consists of the brain and spinal cord; it is located at the *center*, or internal core, of the body.

19. The **peripheral nervous system (PNS)** includes the sensory and motor neurons that connect the central nervous system to the body's sense receptors, muscles, and glands; it is at the *periphery* of the body relative to the brain and spinal cord.

20. **Nerves** are bundles of neural axons, which are part of the PNS, that connect the central nervous system with muscles, glands, and sense organs.

21. A **sensory neuron** carries information from the body's tissues and sensory receptors to the central nervous system for processing.

22. A **motor neuron** carries information and instructions for action from the central nervous system to muscles, glands, and sense organs.

23. An **interneuron** is a neuron of the central nervous system that links the sensory and motor neurons in the transmission of sensory inputs and motor outputs.

24. The **somatic nervous system** is the division of the peripheral nervous system that enables voluntary control of the skeletal muscles; also called the *skeletal nervous system*.

25. The **autonomic nervous system** is the division of the peripheral nervous system that controls the glands and the muscles of internal organs and thereby controls internal functioning; it regulates the *automatic* behaviors necessary for survival.

26. The **sympathetic nervous system** is the division of the autonomic nervous system that arouses the body, mobilizing its energy.

27. The **parasympathetic nervous system** is the division of the autonomic nervous system that calms the body, conserving its energy.

28. A **reflex** is a simple, automatic response to a sensory stimulus; it is governed by a very simple neural pathway.

29. The **endocrine system**, the body's "slower" chemical communication system, consists of glands that secrete hormones into the bloodstream.

30. **Hormones** are chemical messengers, mostly those manufactured by the endocrine glands, that are produced in one tissue and circulate through the bloodstream to their target tissues, on which they have specific effects.

31. The **adrenal glands** produce epinephrine and norepinephrine, hormones that prepare the body to deal with emergencies or stress.

32. The **pituitary gland**, under the influence of the hypothalamus, regulates growth and controls other endocrine glands; sometimes called the "master" gland.

33. An **EEG (electroencephalograph)** is an apparatus, using electrodes placed on the scalp, that records waves of electrical activity that sweep across the brain's surface. *Encephalo* comes from a Greek word meaning "related to the brain."

34. The **PET (positron emission tomography) scan** measures the levels of activity of different areas of the brain by tracing their consumption of a radioactive form of glucose, the brain's fuel.

35. **MRI (magnetic resonance imaging)** uses magnetic fields and radio waves to produce computer-generated images that show brain structures more clearly.

36. In a **fMRI (functional MRI),** MRI scans taken less than a second apart are compared to reveal bloodflow and, therefore, brain anatomy and function.

37. The **brainstem**, the oldest and innermost region of the brain, is an extension of the spinal cord and is the central core of the brain; its structures direct automatic survival functions.

38. Located in the brainstem, the **medulla** controls breathing and heartbeat.

39. Located atop the brainstem, the **thalamus** routes incoming messages to the appropriate cortical centers and transmits replies to the medulla and cerebellum.

40. Running through the brainstem and extending into the thalamus, the **reticular formation** is a nerve network that plays an important role in controlling arousal.

41. The **cerebellum** processes sensory input and coordinates movement output and balance; also involved in learning and memory.

42. The **limbic system** is the neural system associated with emotions such as fear and aggression and basic physiological drives.

    Memory aid: Its name comes from the Latin word *limbus*, meaning "border"; the **limbic system** is at the border of the brainstem and cerebral hemispheres.

43. The **amygdala** is part of the limbic system and influences the emotions of fear and aggression.

44. Also part of the limbic system, the **hypothalamus** regulates hunger, thirst, body temperature, and sex; helps govern the endocrine system via the pituitary gland; and contains the so-called reward centers of the brain.

45. The **hippocampus** is a neural center in the limbic system that helps process explicit memories of facts and events for storage.

46. The **cerebral cortex** is a thin intricate covering of interconnected neural cells atop the cerebral hemispheres. The seat of information processing, the cortex is responsible for those complex functions that make us distinctively human.

    Memory aid: Cortex in Latin means "bark." As bark covers a tree, the **cerebral cortex** is the "bark of the brain."

47. Located at the front of the brain, just behind the forehead, the **frontal lobes** are involved in speaking and muscle movements and in making plans and judgments.

48. Situated between the frontal and occipital lobes, the **parietal lobes** contain the sensory cortex.

49. Located at the back and base of the brain, the **occipital lobes** contain the visual cortex, which receives information from the eyes.

50. Located on the sides of the brain, the **temporal lobes** contain the auditory areas, which receive information from the ears.

    Memory aid: The **temporal lobes** are located near the *temples.*

51. Located at the back of the frontal lobe, the **motor cortex** controls voluntary movement.

52. The **somatosensory cortex** is located at the front of the parietal lobes, just behind the motor cortex. It registers and processes body touch and movement sensations.

53. A **hallucination** is a false sensory experience that occurs without any sensory stimulus.

54. Located throughout the cortex, **association areas** of the brain are involved in higher mental functions, such as learning, remembering, and abstract thinking.

    Memory aid: Among their other functions, **association areas** of the cortex are involved in integrating, or *associating,* information from different areas of the brain.

55. **Neurogenesis** is the formation of new neurons.

56. The **corpus callosum** is the large band of neural fibers that links the right and left cerebral hemispheres. Without this band of nerve fibers, the two hemispheres could not interact.

57. **Split brain** is a condition in which the major connections between the two cerebral hemispheres (the corpus callosum) are severed, literally resulting in a split brain.

58. For most psychologists, **consciousness** is our awareness of ourselves and our environment.

59. **Sequential processing** refers to the processing of one aspect of a problem at a time; used for new or complex tasks.

60. **Parallel processing** is the processing of many aspects of a problem at the same time; used for many common functions.

61. **Selective attention** is the focusing of our awareness on a particular stimulus.

62. **Inattentional blindness** is a perceptual error in which we fail to see a visible object when our attention is directed elsewhere.

63. **Change blindness** is a perceptual error in which we fail to notice a change in the environment

64. A **circadian rhythm** is any regular bodily rhythm, such as body temperature and sleep-wakefulness, that follows a 24-hour cycle.

    Memory aid: In Latin, *circa* means "about" and *dies* means "day." A **circadian rhythm** is one that is about a day, or 24 hours, in duration.

65. **REM** (rapid eye movement) **sleep** is the sleep stage in which the brain and eyes are active, the muscles are relaxed, and vivid dreaming occurs; also known as *paradoxical sleep.*

    Memory aid: **REM** is an acronym for rapid eye movement, the distinguishing feature of this sleep stage that led to its discovery.

66. **Alpha waves** are the relatively slow brain waves characteristic of an awake, relaxed state.

67. **Sleep** is the natural, periodic, reversible loss of consciousness, on which the body and mind depend for healthy functioning.

68. **Delta waves** are the large, slow brain waves that occur during deep sleep.

69. The **suprachiasmatic nucleus (SCN)** is a pair of cell clusters in the hypothalamus that controls the circadian rhythm. With bright light, the SCN decreases production of melatonin.

70. **Insomnia** is a sleep disorder in which the person regularly has difficulty in falling or staying asleep.

71. **Narcolepsy** is a sleep disorder in which the victim suffers sudden, uncontrollable sleep attacks, sometimes characterized by entry directly into REM.

72. **Sleep apnea** is a sleep disorder in which the person repeatedly ceases breathing while asleep.

73. **Dreams** are vivid sequences of images, emotions, and thoughts, the most vivid of which occur during REM sleep.

74. In Freud's theory of dreaming, the **manifest content** is the remembered story line.

75. In Freud's theory of dreaming, the **latent content** is the underlying but censored meaning of a dream.

Memory aids for 74 and 75: *Manifest* means "clearly apparent, obvious"; *latent* means "hidden, concealed." A dream's **manifest content** is that which is obvious; its **latent content** remains hidden until its symbolism is interpreted.

76. **REM rebound** is the tendency for REM sleep to increase following REM sleep deprivation.

Developing Through the Life Span

Chapter Overview

Developmental psychologists study the life cycle, from conception to death. Chapter 3 covers physical, cognitive, and social development over the life span and introduces three major issues in developmental psychology: (1) how our genetic heritage, or nature, interacts with our individual experiences, or nurture, to shape who we are; (2) whether development is best described as gradual and continuous or as a discontinuous sequence of stages; and (3) whether the individual's personality remains stable or changes over the life span.

Chapter Review

First, skim each text section, noting headings and bold-face items. Review the section by reading the objectives and summaries provided here, then answer the questions that follow. In some cases, STUDY TIPS explain how best to learn a difficult concept and APPLICATIONS help you to know how well you understand the material. Check your understanding of the material by consulting the answers beginning on page 60. Do not continue with the next section until you understand each answer. If you need to, review or reread the section in the textbook before continuing.

Developmental Psychology's Major Issues

Objective 3-1: Identify the three major issues studied by developmental psychologists.

Developmental psychologists study physical, cognitive, and social changes throughout the life cycle. Three issues pervade this study: (1) the relative impact of genes and experience on behavior *(nature and nurture),* (2) whether development is best described as gradual and continuous or as a sequence of separate stages *(continuity and stages),* and (3) whether personality traits remain stable or change over the life span *(stability and change).*

1. Scientists who study physical, cognitive, and social changes throughout the life span are called

   _____ _____ .

2. One of the major issues in developmental psychology concerns how our genes interact with our experience to influence our development; this is the issue of _____ and _____ . Because neither acts alone, we are formed by the interaction of _____ , _____ , and _____- _____ forces.

3. A second developmental issue concerns whether developmental changes are gradual or abrupt; this is the issue of _____ or _____ .

4. A third controversial issue concerns the consistency of personality and whether development is characterized more by _____ over time or by change. Developmental psychologists' research shows that we _____ (do/do not) experience both stability and change. Some of our characteristics, such as _____ (emotional excitability), are very stable.

Prenatal Development and the Newborn

Objective 3-2: Describe conception, define *chromosomes, DNA, genes,* and the *genome,* and explain how genes and the environment interact.

A total of 250 million or more sperm deposited during intercourse approach the egg 85,000 times their own size. The few that make it to the egg release digestive enzymes that eat away the egg's protective coating, allowing a sperm to penetrate. The egg's surface blocks out all others and within a half day, the egg nucleus and the sperm nucleus fuse.

Every cell contains the genetic master code for the body. Within each cell are **chromosomes,** threadlike structures composed of molecules called **DNA (deoxyribonucleic acid).** *Genes* are DNA segments that, when "turned on," guide your development. These elements make up your **heredity.** The *genome* provides the complete instructions for making an organism, consisting of all the genetic material in the organism's chromosomes. Variations at particular gene sites in the DNA define each person's uniqueness. Human traits are influenced by many genes *interacting* with the *environment*. The field of *epigenetics* explores environmental influences on gene expression.

5. Conception begins when a woman's

    _____ releases a mature

    _____ .

6. The few _____ from the man that reach the egg release digestive _____ that eat away the egg's protective covering. As soon as one sperm penetrates the egg, the egg's surface _____ all other sperm. The egg and sperm _____ then fuse and become one.

7. The master plans for development are stored in the _____ . Each is composed of molecules of _____ .

8. The biochemical units that influence development are called _____ . Together, these are the elements of _____ .

9. The complete instructions for making an organism are referred to as the human _____ .

STUDY TIP: To keep the various elements of heredity (chromosomes, genes, and DNA) straight, you might find it helpful to think of a metaphor. The chromosomes would be the "books" of heredity, with the "words" that make each of us a distinctive human being the genes, and the "letters," the DNA. You can also keep the relationship among genes, DNA, and chromosomes straight by thinking visually. Chromosomes are the largest of the units. They are made of up genes, which are in turn made up of DNA. Test your understanding by identifying the elements of heredity in the drawing below. Note that c. is the unit that contains the code for proteins, and d. is the spiraling, complex molecule.

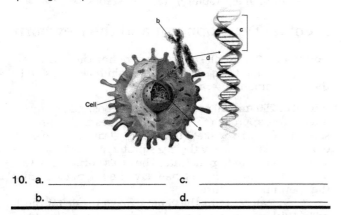

10. a. _____   c. _____
    b. _____   d. _____

---

11. Human differences are also shaped by external influences in the _____ . In psychology, an _____ occurs when the effect of one factor (such as _____)

depends on another factor (such as

_____).

12. The field of _____ studies how the environment influences the _____ of genes. The molecules that trigger or block genetic expression are called _____

    _____ .

13. Which of the following is an example of an interaction?
    a. Swimmers swim fastest during competition against other swimmers.
    b. Swimmers with certain personality traits swim fastest during competition, while those with other personality traits swim fastest during solo time trials.
    c. As the average daily temperature increases, sales of ice cream decrease.
    d. As the average daily temperature increases, sales of lemonade increase.

Objective 3-3: Describe how life develops before birth, and explain how *teratogens* put prenatal development at risk.

The fertilized egg is called a **zygote.** Fewer than half of these zygotes survive beyond 2 weeks. In the first week, cell division produces a zygote of some 100 identical cells, which then begin to specialize. About 10 days after conception, the zygote attaches to the wall of the mother's uterus. Many of the outer cells become the *placenta* through which nourishment and oxygen passes. The inner cells become the *embryo.*

By 9 weeks after conception, the embryo looks unmistakably human and is now a *fetus.* During the sixth month, organs have developed enough to allow a prematurely born fetus a chance of survival. At each prenatal stage, genetic and environmental factors affect development. Along with nutrients and oxygen, *teratogens* ingested by the mother can reach the developing child and place it at risk. If the mother drinks heavily, the effects may be visible as *fetal alcohol syndrome (FAS).*

14. Fertilized human eggs are called _____ . After the first week, the cells in this cluster begin to _____ . The outer part of the fertilized egg forms the _____ .

15. From about 2 until 8 weeks of age the developing human, formed from the inner cells of the fertilized egg, is called a(n) _____ .

16. During the final stage of prenatal development, the developing human is called a(n)

    _____ .

17. Along with nutrients and oxygen, a range of harmful substances known as _____ can pass through the placenta.

18. If a woman drinks during pregnancy, the alcohol enters her and her fetus' bloodstream, depressing activity in both their _____ nervous systems. If a mother drinks heavily, her baby is at risk for the birth defects and mental retardation that accompany _____

_____ _____ .

Objective 3-4: Describe some of the newborn's abilities and traits.

Newborns are surprisingly competent. They are born with sensory equipment and *reflexes* that facilitate their interacting with adults and securing nourishment. Touched on its cheek, a baby opens its mouth and *roots* for a nipple. Finding one, it begins *sucking*. Other reflexes that helped our ancestors survive include the *startle* reflex and the surprisingly strong *grasping* reflex. Newborns turn their heads toward human voices and gaze longer at a drawing of a face-like image. They prefer to look at objects 8 to 12 inches away, the approximate distance between a nursing infant's eyes and the mother's. Within days after birth, the newborn distinguishes its mother's odor.

Similar as newborns are, they also differ. This difference is **temperament**, or emotional excitability. Temperament, which helps form our enduring personality, seems to be rooted in our biology.

19. Newborns come equipped with automatic _____ responses suited to their survival. When an infant's cheek is touched, for example, it will vigorously _____ for a nipple.

Give some evidence supporting the claim that a newborn's sensory equipment is biologically prewired to facilitate social responsiveness.

20. The term that refers to the inborn personality, especially the child's emotional excitability, is _____ , which _____ (does/does not) endure over time.

21. From the first weeks of life, some babies are difficult; they are _____ , _____ , and _____ . Other babies are easy— _____ , _____ , and _____ in feeding and sleeping.

22. Faced with a new or strange situation, anxious, inhibited infants become _____ (more/less) physiologically aroused than less excitable infants.

APPLICATION:

23. Despite growing up in the same home environment, Karen and her brother John have personalities as different from each other as two people selected randomly from the population. This is because of the _____ of their individual _____ and nonshared _____ .

Objective 3-5: Explain how twin and adoption studies help us understand the effects of nature and nurture.

Comparisons of identical twins and fraternal twins help research tease apart the effects of heredity and environment. **Identical *(monozygotic)* twins** develop from a single fertilized egg. **Fraternal *(dizygotic)* twins** develop from separate fertilized eggs. Findings indicate that identical twins are much more similar than fraternals in abilities, personality traits, and even interests. The discovery that identical twins separated at birth show remarkable similarities also suggests genetic influence. Indeed, separated fraternal twins do not exhibit similarities comparable with those of separated identical twins. Adoption studies enable comparisons with both genetic and environmental relatives. Adoptees' traits bear more similarities to their biological parents than to their caregiving adoptive parents.

24. To study the power and limits of genetic influences on behavior, researchers use _____ and _____ studies.

25. Twins who developed from a single fertilized egg are genetically _____ (monozygotic). Twins who developed from different fertilized eggs are no more genetically alike than siblings and are called _____ (dizygotic) twins.

26. In terms of abilities, personal traits, and interests, identical twins are _____ (more/no more) alike than are fraternal twins.

27. Through research on identical twins raised apart, psychologists are able to study the influence of the _____ .

28. Studies tend to show that the personalities of adopted children _____ (do/do not) closely resemble those of their adoptive parents. In traits such as _____ and _____ , they are more similar to their biological parents.

APPLICATION:

29. Dr. Gonzalez is conducting research on whether people who do well in school can thank their genes or their environment for their success. To distinguish how much genetic and environmental factors affect school success, Dr. Gonzalez should compare children with _____ (the same/different) genes and _____ (the same/different) environments.

Infancy and Childhood

Objective 3-6: Describe how the brain and motor abilities develop during infancy and childhood.

Maturation, the biological growth processes that enable orderly changes in behavior, sets the basic course of development; experience adjusts it. Maturation accounts for commonalities, such as standing before walking. Within the brain, nerve cells form before birth. After birth, the neural networks that enable us to walk, talk, and remember have a wild growth spurt. From ages 3 to 6, growth occurs most rapidly in the frontal lobes, which enable reasoning and planning. The association areas linked with thinking, memory, and language are the last cortical areas to develop. The neural pathways supporting language and agility grow rapidly into puberty, when a *pruning process* takes place. Your genes laid down the basic design of your brain; experience fills in the details.

Nature and nurture interact to sculpt our synapses. During early childhood—while excess connections are still on call—youngsters can most easily master another language. We seem to have a **critical period** for some skills.

As the infant's muscles and nervous system mature, ever more complicated skills emerge. The sequence is universal; the timing varies. Babies roll over before they sit unsupported, and they crawl before they walk. Genes play a major role. Identical twins typically begin sitting up and walking on nearly the same day. Experience has a limited effect for other physical skills as well, including those that enable bowel and bladder control.

Although we consciously recall little from before age 4 (*infantile amnesia*), our brain was processing and storing information during that time. Experiments do show, however, that infants can retain learning over time. For example, Rovee-Collier's 2-month-old who learned to propel a mobile by moving his legs retained the association for at least a month. Studies of adults indicate that sometimes what the conscious mind cannot recall in words from the earliest years, the nervous system and our two-track mind somehow remember.

30. Biological growth processes that enable orderly changes in behavior are called _____ .

31. The developing brain _____ (over/under) produces neurons. At birth, the human nervous system _____ (is/is not) fully mature.

32. Between 3 and 6 years of age, the brain is developing most rapidly in the _____ lobes, which enable _____ and _____ . The last cortical areas to develop are the _____ _____ .

33. After puberty, a process of _____ shuts down some neural connections and strengthens others. For some skills there is a _____ _____ during which exposure to certain experiences is needed for normal development to occur.

34. Infants pass the milestones of _____ development at different rates, but the basic _____ of stages is fixed. For example, they crawl before they _____ .

35. Heredity plays a _____ (major/minor) role in motor development.

36. Until the necessary muscular and neural maturation is complete, including the rapid development of the brain's _____ , experience has a _____ (large/small) effect on behavior.

37. Although we cannot consciously recall experiences before age 4, called _____ , we are capable of _____ as early as 2 months of age.

APPLICATION:

38. Calvin, who is trying to impress his psychology professor with his knowledge of infant motor development, asks why some infants learn to roll over before they lift their heads from a prone position, while others develop these skills in the opposite order. What should Calvin's professor conclude from this question?
    a. Calvin clearly understands that the sequence of motor development is not the same for all infants.
    b. Calvin doesn't know what he's talking about. Although some infants reach these developmental milestones ahead of others, the order is the same for all infants.
    c. Calvin needs to be reminded that rolling over is an inherited reflex, not a learned skill.
    d. Calvin understands an important principle: Motor development is unpredictable.

Objective 3-7: Describe how a child's mind develops from the perspectives of Piaget, Vygotsky, and today's researchers.

Cognition refers to all the mental activities associated with thinking, knowing, remembering, and communicating. Thanks partly to Jean Piaget's pioneering work, we now understand that the mind of the child is not a miniature model of the adult's. Piaget theorized that the mind tries to make sense of experience by forming *schemas*, concepts or frameworks that organize and interpret information. We *assimilate* new experiences, that is, interpret them in terms of our current understandings. But we also sometimes adjust, or *accommodate*, our current understanding to incorporate new information.

During the *sensorimotor stage* (birth to nearly age 2) of cognitive development, children experience the world through their senses and actions. By about 8 months, an infant exhibits *object permanence*, an awareness that things still exist even when they are out of sight. Today's researchers believe that object permanence unfolds gradually, and they view development as more continuous than Piaget did.

Piaget maintained that up to about age 6 or 7, children are in a *preoperational stage*—too young to perform mental operations. They are *egocentric*, that is, they cannot perceive things from another's point of view and lack a *theory of mind*. (*Autism spectrum disorder* [*ASD*, formerly referred to as "autism"] is also marked by impaired ability to infer others' mental states. ASD has different levels of severity.) Piaget thought that at about age 6 or 7, children become capable of performing *concrete operations*, for example, those required to understand the principle of *conservation*. They think logically about concrete events and understand reversing mathematical operations. By age 12, reasoning expands from the purely concrete to encompass abstract thinking, which Piaget called *formal operational thinking*. At about the same time as Piaget was developing his theory, Lev Vygotsky proposed that children learn in part by talking to themselves and from *scaffolding* by parents.

Today's research shows that young children are more capable and their development more continuous than Piaget believed. Nonetheless, studies support his idea that human cognition unfolds basically in the sequence he proposed.

39. *Cognition* refers to all the mental activities associated with _____ , _____ , _____ , and _____ .

40. The first researcher to show that the thought processes of adults and children are very different was _____ . He believed that children are _____ thinkers as they try to make sense of their experiences.

41. To organize and interpret his or her experiences, the developing child constructs concepts or mental molds called _____ .

42. The interpretation of new experiences in terms of existing ideas is called _____ . The adaptation of existing ideas to fit new experiences is called _____ .

43. In Piaget's first stage of development, the _____ stage, children experience the world through their motor and sensory interactions with objects.

44. The awareness that things continue to exist even when they are removed from view is called _____ _____ .

45. Developmental researchers have found that Piaget and his followers _____ (overestimated/underestimated) young children's competence and that development is more _____ than Piaget believed.

46. The principle that the quantity of a substance remains the same even when the shape of its container changes is called _____ . Piaget believed that preschoolers, who are in the _____ stage, _____ (have/have not) developed this concept. When a child becomes capable of performing mental operations such as this one, he or she can think in _____ and thus enjoy _____ _____ .

47. Preschoolers have difficulty perceiving things from another person's point of view. This inability is called _____ .

48. The child's growing ability to take another's perspective is evidence that the child is acquiring a _____ _____ . Between about 3 and 4½, children come to realize that others may hold _____ _____ .

49. The group of disorders characterized by deficient _____ and _____ interaction and an impaired _____ _____ _____ , as well as fixated interests and _____ behaviors, is referred to as _____ _____ _____ . Biological factors, including _____ influences and abnormal _____ development, contribute to ASD. Baron-Cohen believes that ASD represents an extreme male brain; boys are better _____ , whereas girls are better _____ .

50. Piaget believed that children acquire the mental abilities needed to understand simple math and conservation by about _____ years of age. At this time, they enter the _____ _____ stage.

51. In Piaget's final stage, the _____
_____ stage, reasoning expands
from the purely concrete to encompass
_____ thinking.

52. Russian psychologist _____ noted
that by age _____ children stop
thinking aloud and instead rely on
_____ _____ .
When parents give children words, they provide,
according to this theorist, a _____
upon which the child can build higher-level
thinking.

53. Piaget identified significant milestones in cognitive
development; his emphasis was less on the
_____ at which children typically
reach these milestones than on their
_____ .

STUDY TIP/APPLICATION: Jean Piaget was the first
major theorist to realize that each stage of life has its own
characteristic way of thinking. To deepen your understanding of Jean Piaget's stages of cognitive development, fill in
the blanks in the chart below. Do as much as you can without
reviewing the text. To get you started, the first stage has been
completed.

54. Typical Age Range	Stage	New Developments	Test to Determine If Someone Is in This Stage
Birth to nearly 2 years	Sensorimotor	Stranger anxiety Object permanence	Have the child's mother leave the room Hide a toy under a blanket
2 to _____	_____		
	Concrete _____		
About 12 through _____	_____		

APPLICATIONS:

55. Compared with when he was younger, 4-year-old Antonio
is better able to empathize with his friend's feelings. This
growing ability to take another's perspective indicates that
Antonio is acquiring a _____
_____ .

56. As 8-year-old Gabriella observes, liquid is transferred
from a tall, thin tube into a short, wide jar. She is asked
if there is now less liquid in order to determine if she has
mastered the concept of _____ .

57. Caleb is 14 months old and he behaves as though "out of
sight is out of existence." He is in Piaget's
_____ stage of cognitive development.

58. Makayla is 3 years old, can use language, and has trouble
taking another person's perspective. She is in Piaget's
_____ stage of cognitive development.

59. Four-year-old Jamail has a younger sister. When asked if
he has a sister, he is likely to answer _____
(yes/no); when asked if his sister has a brother, Jamail is
likely to answer _____ (yes/no).

Objective 3-8: Describe how attachment bonds form
between caregivers and infants.

Stranger anxiety is the fear of unfamiliar faces that
infants commonly display, beginning by about 8 months
of age (soon after object permanence emerges). They
greet strangers by crying and reaching for their familiar
caregivers. *The brain, mind, and social-emotional behavior
develop together.*
   The *attachment* bond is a survival impulse that keeps
infants close to their caregivers. The Harlows found that
infant monkeys became attached to "mothers" that provided contact comfort rather than nourishment. Human
infants also become attached to their parents or primary
caregivers not simply because they gratify biological
needs (nourishment) but because they provide body
contact that is soft and warm. The human parent also

provides a safe haven for a troubled child and a secure base from which to explore.

60. Soon after _____ _____ emerges and children become mobile, a new fear, called _____ _____ , emerges. This fear emerges at about age _____ .

61. The development of a strong emotional bond between infant and parent is called _____ .

62. The Harlows' studies of monkeys have shown that mother-infant attachment does not depend on the mother providing nourishment as much as it does on her providing _____ _____ .

63. Human attachment involves one person providing another with a _____ _____ when distressed and a _____ _____ from which to explore.

Objective 3-9: Explain why secure and insecure attachments matter, and describe how an infant's ability to develop basic trust affects later relationships.

When placed in a *strange situation* such as a laboratory playroom, about 60 percent of children display *secure attachment*; they play comfortably in their mother's presence, are distressed when she leaves, and seek contact when she returns. Other infants, who are *insecurely attached,* are less likely to explore their surroundings and, when their mother leaves, cry loudly and remain upset or seem indifferent to her going and returning. Sensitive, responsive parents tend to have securely attached children. Insensitive, unresponsive parents have infants who often become insecurely attached. Although genetically influenced *temperament* may elicit responsive parenting, parental sensitivity has been taught and does increase secure attachment to some extent. Erik Erikson attributed the child's development of **basic trust**—a sense that the world is predictable and reliable—to sensitive, loving caregivers. Adult relationships tend to reflect the attachment styles of early childhood.

Infants who experience abuse or extreme neglect often become withdrawn, frightened, even speechless. Young monkeys who are deprived of attachment may, as adults, cower in fright or lash out in aggression when placed with other monkeys their age. In humans, too, the unloved sometimes become the unloving. But children are *resilient* and can go on to a better life.

Severe and prolonged abuse places children at increased risk for nightmares, depression, and an adolescence troubled by substance abuse, binge eating, and aggression.

64. Placed in a research setting called the _____ _____ ,

children show one of two patterns of attachment: _____ attachment or _____ attachment, marked by either anxiety or _____ of trusting relationships.

Contrast the responses of securely and insecurely attached infants to strange situations.

Discuss the impact of responsive parenting on infant attachment.

65. Attachment style _____ (is/is not) entirely the result of parenting. Equally important is the infant's inborn _____ .

66. Separation anxiety peaks in infants around _____ months, then _____ (gradually declines/remains constant for about a year). This is true of children _____ (in North America/throughout the world).

67. According to Erikson, securely attached infants approach life with a sense of _____ _____ .

68. Abuse victims have a doubled risk of later _____ , especially if they carry a gene variation that spurs _____-_____ production. Although abused children _____ (are/are not) at risk for various problems, some abused children show great _____ and go on to lead better lives.

APPLICATION:

69. Layla and Christian Bishop have a 13-month-old boy. According to Erikson, the Bishops' sensitive, loving care of their child contributes to the child's _____ _____ .

Objective 3-10: Describe the four main parenting styles.

Authoritarian parents impose rules and expect obedience. *Permissive* parents submit to their children's desires, make few demands, and use little punishment. *Negligent* parents are uninvolved. *Authoritative* parents are both demanding and responsive. Child-raising practices reflect cultural values. The Westernized culture of the United States today favors independence. Many Asian and African cultures place less value on independence and more on a strong sense of family self.

70. Parents who impose rules and expect obedience are exhibiting a(n) _____ style of parenting. Parents who make few demands of their children and tend to submit to their children's desires are identified as _____ parents. Parents who are uninvolved are said to be _____ .

71. Setting and enforcing standards after discussion with their children is the approach taken by _____ parents.

72. Remember that culture refers to the set of _____ , _____ , _____ , and _____ shared by a group of people and transmitted from one _____ to the next. Westernized culture prefers children who are _____ , while many Asian and African cultures place more value on a strong sense of _____ _____ .

Objective 3-11: Describe the outcomes associated with each parenting style.

Children with the highest self-esteem, self-reliance, and social competence generally have warm, concerned, authoritative parents. However, other forces, such as *culture*, are also factors in how parents raise their children.

73. Authoritarian parents have children who have less _____ _____ and _____ . Permissive parents have children who are more _____ and _____ . Children of negligent parents have poor _____ and social outcomes.

74. Studies have shown that children with high self-esteem, self-restraint, and social competence tend to have _____ parents.

75. Note that correlational studies _____ (do/do not) prove causation.

Adolescence

Objective 3-12: Define *adolescence,* and identify the major physical changes during this period.

Adolescence, the transition period from childhood to adulthood, typically begins at **puberty** with the onset of rapid growth and developing sexual maturity. As in earlier life stages, the *sequence* of physical changes is more predictable than the *timing* (for example, breast buds and visible pubic hair appear before *menarche,* the first menstrual period). Early maturation has mixed effects for boys; early-maturing boys are more popular, self-assured, and independent but also more at risk for alcohol use, delinquency, and premature sexual activity. Early maturation may be a challenge for girls.

Frontal lobe maturation that improves judgment and impulse control lags the emotional limbic system. The pubertal hormonal surge, early development of the emotional limbic system, and later maturation of the frontal lobe help explain teens' occasional impulsiveness, risky behaviors, and emotional storms.

76. *Adolescence* is defined as the transition period between _____ and _____ .

77. Adolescence begins with the time of developing sexual maturity known as _____ .

78. The first menstrual period is called _____ .

79. The _____ (timing/sequence) of pubertal changes is more predictable than their _____ (timing/sequence).

Briefly describe the effects of early maturation on boys and girls.

80. Teens' occasional impulsiveness and risky behaviors may be due, in part, to the fact that development in the brain's _____ _____ lags behind that of the _____ _____ .

Objective 3-13: Describe adolescent cognitive and moral development, according to Piaget, Kohlberg, and later researchers.

During the early teen years, reasoning is often self-focused. Adolescents may think their private experiences are unique. Gradually, adolescents develop the capacity for what Piaget called *formal operations,* the capacity to reason abstractly. This includes the ability to spot hypocrisy and detect inconsistencies in others' reasoning. The new reasoning power is evident in adolescents' pondering and debating such abstract topics as human nature, good and evil, and truth and justice.

Lawrence Kohlberg contended that moral thinking likewise proceeds through a series of stages, from a *preconventional* morality of self-interest, to a *conventional morality* that cares for others and upholds laws and rules, to (in some people) a *postconventional* morality of agreed-upon rights or basic ethical principles. Kohlberg's critics argue that the postconventional level is culturally limited, appearing mostly among people who prize individualism. Jonathan Haidt's *moral intuitionist* explanation is that moral feelings precede moral reasoning, and so moral judgment involves quick gut feelings. Character-education programs focus both on moral reasoning and on *doing* the right thing. These programs also teach teens to *delay gratification*.

81. During the early teen years, reasoning is often _____ , as adolescents often feel their experiences are unique.

82. Piaget's final stage of cognitive development is the stage of _____ _____ . The adolescent in this stage is capable of thinking logically about _____ as well as concrete propositions. This enables them to detect _____ in others' reasoning and to spot hypocrisy.

83. The theorist who proposed that moral thought progresses through stages is _____ . These stages are divided into three basic levels: _____ , _____ , and _____ .

84. In the preconventional stages of morality, characteristic of children, the emphasis is on obeying rules in order to avoid _____ or gain _____ .

85. Conventional morality usually emerges by early _____ . The emphasis is on gaining social _____ or upholding the social _____ .

86. Individuals who base moral judgments on their own perceptions of basic ethical principles are said by Kohlberg to employ _____ morality.

87. Critics of Kohlberg's theory argue that the _____ level is found mostly among people who prize _____ . His theory is biased against _____ societies.

88. The idea that moral feelings precede moral reasoning is expressed in Haidt's moral _____ view of morality. Research studies using _____ support the idea that moral judgment involves more than merely thinking; it is also gut-level feeling.

89. Morality involves doing the right thing. Today's _____-_____ _____ focus on moral issues and doing the right thing. Teens who participate in these programs have experienced an increased sense of _____ and a desire to serve.

90. Children who learn to delay _____ become more socially responsible, _____ successful, and productive.

APPLICATIONS:

91. Jake, a junior in high school, regularly attends church because his family and friends think he should. Jake is in Kohlberg's _____ stage of moral reasoning.

92. In Jada's country, people believe in family togetherness above all else. Because her culture does not give priority to _____ , Kohlberg would say that she is not at his highest level of moral reasoning, the _____ level.

Objective 3-14: Describe the social tasks and challenges of adolescence.

Erik Erikson theorized eight stages of life, each with its own *psychosocial* task. In infancy (the first year), the issue is *trust* versus mistrust. In toddlerhood (the second year), the challenge is *autonomy* versus shame and doubt. Preschoolers (age 3 to 5) learn *initiative* or guilt, and elementary school children (age 6 to puberty) develop *competence* or inferiority. A chief task of adolescence is to solidify one's sense of self—one's **identity**. Part of this self-concept is adolescents' **social identity,** their sense of group membership. Adolescents in Western cultures usually try out different "selves" in different situations. Most adolescents eventually unify the various selves into a consistent and comfortable sense of themselves. For young adults (twenties to early forties) the issue is **intimacy,** the ability to form emotionally close relationships, versus isolation, and for middle-aged adults (forties to sixties), generativity versus stagnation. Late adulthood's (late sixties and older) challenge is integrity versus despair.

93. To refine their sense of identity, adolescents in Western cultures experiment with different _____ in different situations. The result may be role _____ , which is resolved by forming a self-definition, or _____ . The aspect of people's self-concept that forms around their group membership is their _____ _____ .

94. Some adolescents forge their identity early, simply by _____ their parents' values and

expectations. Others may adopt the identity of a particular _____ _____ .

95. Cultures that inform adolescents about who they are, rather than letting them decide on their own, are traditional, more _____ cultures that place less value on _____ .

96. During the early to mid-teen years, self-esteem generally _____ (rises/falls/remains stable). During the late teens and twenties, self-image generally _____ (rises/falls/remains stable). _____ and _____ _____ also increase during late adolescence.

97. Erikson saw the formation of identity as a prerequisite for the development of _____ in young adulthood.

STUDY TIP: Summary tables can help clarify all the stages of a theory such as Erikson's. Complete the missing information in the following table of Erikson's stages of psychosocial development and use it as a study guide.

Group Age	Psychosocial Stage
Infancy	_____
_____	Autonomy vs. shame and doubt
Preschooler	_____
_____	Competence vs. inferiority
Adolescence	_____
_____	Intimacy vs. isolation
Middle adulthood	_____
_____	Integrity vs. despair

Objective 3-15: Contrast parental and peer influences during adolescence.

As adolescents in Western cultures form their own identities, they become increasingly independent of their parents. Nonetheless, researchers have found that most teenagers relate to their parents reasonably well. Positive relations with parents support positive peer relations. Teens are herd animals, and they talk, dress, and act more like their peers than their parents. Although adolescence is a time of increasing peer influence, parents continue to influence teens in shaping their religious faith, as well as college and career choices.

Although parents do not determine their children's personality, they do influence their attitudes, values, manners, faith, and politics. Child neglect, abuse, and parental divorce are rare in adoptive homes. And adopted children tend to be more self-giving than average.

98. Adolescence is typically a time of increasing influence from one's _____ and decreasing influence from _____ .

99. Peer influence is primarily a result of the desire to fit in, and similarities among peers may result from a _____ _____ , as kids seek out peers with similar attitudes and interests.

100. Most adolescents report that they usually _____ (do/do not) get along with their parents. They see their parents as having the most influence in shaping their _____ _____ and in thinking about _____ and _____ choices.

101. Research on social relationships between parents and their adolescent children shows that high school girls who have the most _____ relationships with their mothers tend to enjoy the most _____ friendships with girlfriends.

102. Teens who are excluded or bullied may suffer in silence or _____ . The pain of exclusion _____ (does/does not) persist. In one large study, those who were bullied as children showed poorer _____ health and greater _____ distress 40 years later.

103. In personality measures, shared environmental influences account for less than _____ percent of children's differences.

104. Adoption studies show that parenting _____ (does/does not) matter. For example, many adopted children score _____ (higher/lower) than their biological parents on intelligence tests.

105. Parents influence their children's attitudes, values, manners, _____ , and _____ .

Objective 3-16: Describe emerging adulthood.

Clearly, the graduation from adolescence to adulthood is now taking longer. In the United States, since 1960 fewer than half of 30-year-old women and one-third of 30-year-old men have left home, married, and had a child. The time from 18 to the mid-twenties is an increasingly not-yet-settled phase of life, which is now called *emerging adulthood*. During this time, many young people attend college or work but continue to live with their parents.

106. At earlier times, and in other parts of the world today, shortly after _____ _____ , teens would assume adult responsibilities and _____ . The event might be celebrated with an elaborate initiation, a public _____

_____ _____ .

107. Adolescents today are taking _____ (more/less) time to establish their independence as adults. At the same time, puberty is beginning _____ (earlier/later) than in the past.

108. Because the time from 18 to the mid-twenties is increasingly a not-yet-settled phase of life, some psychologists refer to this period as a time of

_____ _____ .

Adulthood

Objective 3-17: Describe how our bodies and sensory abilities change from early to late adulthood.

Muscular strength, reaction time, sensory keenness, and cardiac output crest by the mid-twenties and then slowly begin to decline. These barely perceptible physical declines of early adulthood begin to accelerate during middle adulthood. For women, a significant physical change of adult life is *menopause,* the end of the menstrual cycle. Men experience no equivalent of menopause and no sharp drop in sex hormones. After middle age, most men and women remain capable of satisfying sexual activity.

In later life, vision, muscle strength, reaction time, stamina, hearing, smell, and distance perception diminish. Short-term ailments are fewer, but a weakened immune system makes life-threatening ailments more likely.

109. Adulthood may be divided into three stages:

Early adulthood: _____

Middle adulthood: _____

Late adulthood: _____

110. During adulthood, age _____ (is/is not) a very good predictor of people's traits.

111. The mid-twenties are the peak years for

_____ _____ ,

_____ _____ ,

_____ _____ ,

and _____ _____ .

112. During early and middle adulthood, physical vigor has less to do with _____ than with a person's _____ and _____ habits.

113. The end of the menstrual cycle, known as _____ , occurs within a few years of _____ .

114. Although men do not go through any kind of menopause, they do experience a more gradual decline in _____ count, level of the hormone _____ , and speed of erection and ejaculation during later life.

115. With age, the eye's pupil _____ (shrinks/enlarges) and its lens becomes cloudy. As a result, the amount of light that reaches the retina is _____ (increased/reduced).

116. Aging causes a gradual loss of _____ _____ and _____ (slows/speeds/has no effect on) neural processing. The brain regions that shrink during aging are the areas important to _____ . In addition, the _____ lobes, which restrain _____ , shrink with age.

117. Physical exercise stimulates _____ _____ development and _____ connections and promotes _____ , the birth of new nerve cells, in the hippocampus.

118. With age, the tips of our chromosomes, called _____ , shorten. However, they can be maintained by _____ .

119. Although older adults are _____ (more/less) susceptible to life-threatening ailments, they suffer from short-term ailments such as flu _____ (more/less) often than younger adults.

Objective 3-18: Describe how memory changes with age.

As the years pass, recognition memory remains strong, although recall begins to decline, especially for meaningless information. Older adults may take longer than younger adults to produce the words and things they know. Exercising the body feeds the brain and helps compensate for the loss of brain cells.

Cross-sectional studies, in which people of different ages are compared with one another, and *longitudinal studies,* in which the same people are restudied and retested over a long period, have identified mental abilities that do and do not change as we age. Especially in the last three or four years of life, cognitive decline typically accelerates. Researchers call this near-death drop *terminal decline.*

120. Studies of developmental changes in learning and memory show that during adulthood there is a decline in the ability to _____ (recall/recognize) new information but not in the ability to _____ (recall/recognize) such information. One factor that influences memory in older people is the _____ of material.

121. A research study in which people of various ages are compared with one another is called a _____-_____ study.

122. A research study in which the same people are retested over a period of years is called a _____ study.

123. Whether brain-exercise programs can improve cognitive fitness _____ (has/has not) been demonstrated by research. While brain-exercise programs have improved the practiced skills; they _____ (have/have not) boost overall cognitive fitness.

APPLICATION:

124. Which statement illustrates cognitive development during the course of adult life?
    a. Forty-three-year-old Sophia has better recognition memory than 72-year-old Kylie.
    b. Both Sophia and Kylie have strong recall and recognition memory.
    c. Kylie's recognition memory decreased sharply at age 50.
    d. Forty-three-year-old Sophia has better recall memory than 72-year-old Kylie.

Objective 3-19: Identify adulthood's two primary commitments, and explain how chance events and the social clock influence us.

Two basic aspects of our lives dominate adulthood. Erik Erikson called them *intimacy* (forming close relationships) and *generativity* (being productive and supporting future generations). Evolutionary psychologists suggest that marriage had survival value for our ancestors in that parents who cooperated to nurture their children to maturity were more likely to have their gene-carrying children survive and reproduce. Compared with their counterparts of 30 years ago, people in Western countries are better educated and marrying later. These trends may help explain why the American divorce rate, which surged from 1960 to 1980, has since leveled off and even slightly declined in some areas. And marriage is a predictor of happiness, sexual satisfaction, income, and mental health. Often, love bears children. Most parents are happy to see their children grow up, leave home, marry, and have careers.

For adults, a large part of the answer to "Who are you?" is the answer to "What do you do?" Choosing a career path is difficult, especially during bad economic times. Although chance events may alter our course, the *social clock* still defines the best time to leave home, get a job, marry, and so on.

125. According to Erikson, the two basic tasks of adulthood are achieving _____ and _____ . According to Freud, the healthy adult is one who can _____ and _____ .

126. One factor that promotes lasting bonds of love in couples is _____ , which refers to the willingness to reveal intimate aspects of oneself to others. The chances of a marriage lasting increase when couples marry after age _____ and are well _____ .

127. Over the last 30 years, the American divorce rate has _____ (increased/decreased), while standards have a _____ (increased/decreased). Couples who live together before marriage have a _____ (higher/lower) divorce rate than those who do not.

128. Marriage is a predictor of _____ , _____ _____ , _____ , and _____ .

129. For most couples, the children's leaving home produces a(n) _____ (increase/decrease) in marital satisfaction.

130. For men and women, happiness is having work that fits their interests and provides them with a sense of _____ and _____ .

131. The term used to refer to the culturally preferred timing for leaving home, getting a job, marrying, and so on is the _____ _____ . Today, the timing of such life events is becoming _____ (more/less) predictable.

APPLICATION:

132. After a series of unfulfilling relationships, 30-year-old Carlos tells a friend that he doesn't want to marry because he is afraid of losing his freedom and independence. Erikson would say that Carlos is having difficulty with the psychosocial task of
    a. trust versus mistrust.
    b. autonomy versus doubt.
    c. intimacy versus isolation.
    d. identity versus role confusion.

Objective 3-20: Identify the factors that affect our well-being in later life.

People of all ages report similar feelings of happiness and satisfaction with life. If anything, positive feelings grow after midlife and negative feelings subside.

Moreover, the bad feelings we associate with negative events fade faster than do the good feelings we associate with positive events.

133. From the teens to midlife, people typically experience a strengthening sense of

_____ , _____ , and _____ .

134. According to studies, older people _____ (do/do not) report as much happiness and satisfaction with life as younger people do.

135. After midlife, _____ (positive/ negative) feelings tend to grow and _____ (positive/negative) feelings decline, in part because of our greater _____ control. Older adults experience _____ (more/ fewer) problems in their relationships.

APPLICATION:

136. The text discusses well-being across the life span. Which of the following people is likely to report the greatest life satisfaction?
  a. Billy, a 7-year-old second-grader
  b. Kathy, a 17-year-old high-school senior
  c. Mildred, a 70-year-old retired teacher
  d. too little information to tell

Objective 3-21: Explain how people vary in their responses to a loved one's death.

Usually, the most difficult separation is from one's spouse or partner. Grief is especially severe when the death of a loved one comes before its expected time on the social clock. The normal range of reactions to a loved one's death is wider than most people suppose. Some cultures encourage public weeping and wailing; others hide grief. Within any culture, some individuals grieve more intensely and openly. Research discounts the popular idea that terminally ill and bereaved people go through predictable stages. Life itself can be affirmed even at death, especially if one's life has been meaningful and worthwhile, what Erikson called a sense of *integrity*.

137. Grief over a loved one's death is especially severe when it comes _____ .

138. Reactions to a loved one's death _____ (do/do not) vary according to cultural norms. Those who express the strongest grief immediately _____ (do/do not) purge their grief more quickly.

139. Terminally ill and grief-stricken people _____ (do/do not) go through identical stages.

Progress Test

Multiple-Choice Questions

Circle your answers to the following questions and check them with the answers beginning on page 64. If your answer is incorrect, read the explanation for why it is incorrect and then consult the text.

1. Of the following, the best way to separate the effects of genes and environment in research is to study
  a. fraternal twins.
  b. identical twins.
  c. adopted children and their adoptive parents.
  d. identical twins raised in different environments.

2. Unlike _____ twins, who develop from a single fertilized egg, _____ twins develop from separate fertilized eggs.
  a. fraternal; identical
  b. identical; fraternal
  c. placental; nonplacental
  d. nonplacental; placental

3. Temperament refers to a person's characteristic
  a. emotional reactivity and intensity.
  b. attitudes.
  c. behaviors.
  d. role-related traits.

4. Physiological tests reveal that anxious, inhibited infants
  a. become less physically aroused when facing new situations.
  b. have slow, steady heart rates.
  c. have high and variable heart rates.
  d. have underreactive nervous systems.

5. The human genome is best defined as
  a. a complex molecule containing genetic information that makes up the chromosomes.
  b. a segment of DNA.
  c. the complete instructions for making an organism.
  d. the inner cells of the zygote.

6. Most human traits are
  a. learned.
  b. determined by a single gene.
  c. influenced by many genes acting together.
  d. unpredictable.

7. Several studies of long-separated identical twins have found that these twins
  a. have little in common, due to the different environments in which they were raised.
  b. have many similarities, in everything from medical histories to personalities.
  c. have similar personalities, but very different likes, dislikes, and lifestyles.
  d. are no more similar than are fraternal twins reared apart.

8. Adoption studies show that the personalities of adopted children
   a. closely match those of their adoptive parents.
   b. are more similar to their biological parents than to their adoptive parents.
   c. closely match those of the biological children of their adoptive parents.
   d. closely match those of other children reared in the same home, whether or not they are biologically related.

9. Chromosomes are composed of small segments of
   a. DNA called genes.
   b. DNA called neurotransmitters.
   c. DNA called endorphins.
   d. DNA called enzymes.

10. When the effect of one factor (such as environment) depends on another (such as heredity), we say there is a(n) _____ between the two factors.
    a. attachment
    b. positive correlation
    c. negative correlation
    d. interaction

11. Dr. Joan Goodman is studying how memory changes as people get older. She is most likely a(n) _____ psychologist.
    a. social   c. developmental
    b. cognitive   d. experimental

12. In Piaget's concrete operational stage, the child is able to understand the principle of
    a. conservation.   c. attachment.
    b. schemas.   d. object permanence.

13. Piaget held that egocentrism is characteristic of the
    a. sensorimotor stage.
    b. preoperational stage.
    c. concrete operational stage.
    d. formal operational stage.

14. During which stage of cognitive development do children begin to show object permanence?
    a. sensorimotor   c. concrete operational
    b. preoperational   d. formal operational

15. Babies will vigorously root for a nipple when
    a. their foot is tickled.
    b. their cheek is touched.
    c. they hear a loud noise.
    d. they make eye contact with their caregiver.

16. The Harlows' studies of attachment in monkeys showed that
    a. nourishment was the single most important factor motivating attachment.
    b. a cloth mother produced the greatest attachment response.
    c. whether a cloth or wire mother was present mattered less than the presence or absence of other infants.
    d. attachment in monkeys is based on stability.

17. When psychologists discuss maturation, they are referring to stages of growth that are NOT influenced by
    a. conservation.   c. nurture.
    b. nature.   d. continuity.

18. The developmental theorist who suggested that securely attached children develop an attitude of basic trust is
    a. Piaget.   c. Vygotsky.
    b. Harlow.   d. Erikson.

19. Research findings on infant motor development are consistent with the idea that
    a. cognitive development lags behind motor skills development.
    b. maturation of physical skills is relatively unaffected by experience.
    c. motor-skill development is slowed down by lack of useful experience.
    d. in humans, the process of maturation may be significantly altered by cultural factors.

20. According to Erikson, the central psychological challenges related to adolescence, young adulthood, and middle age, respectively, are
    a. identity formation, intimacy, generativity.
    b. intimacy, identity formation, generativity.
    c. generativity, intimacy, identity formation.
    d. intimacy, generativity, identity formation.

21. In preconventional morality, the person
    a. obeys out of a sense of social duty.
    b. conforms to gain social approval.
    c. obeys to avoid punishment or to gain concrete rewards.
    d. follows his or her conscience.

22. Among the hallmarks of growing up is a girl's first menstrual period, which also is called
    a. puberty.   c. menarche.
    b. menopause.   d. generativity.

23. An older person who can remember his or her life with a sense of satisfaction and completion has attained Erikson's stage of
    a. generativity.   c. isolation.
    b. intimacy.   d. integrity.

24. According to Piaget, the ability to reason abstractly is characteristic of the stage of
    a. preoperational thought.
    b. concrete operations.
    c. formal operations.
    d. conventional morality.

25. The cognitive ability that has been shown to decline during adulthood is the ability to
    a. recall new information.
    b. recognize new information.
    c. learn meaningful new material.
    d. use judgment in dealing with daily life problems.

26. Which of the following statements concerning the effects of aging is true?
    a. Aging will probably lead to total memory failure if an individual lives long enough.
    b. Aging increases susceptibility to short-term ailments such as the flu.
    c. Significant increases in life satisfaction are associated with aging.
    d. The aging process can be significantly affected by the individual's activity patterns.

27. Adolescence is marked by the onset of
    a. an identity crisis.
    b. parent-child conflict.
    c. the concrete operational stage.
    d. puberty.

28. The end of menstruation is called
    a. menarche.   c. genome.
    b. menopause.   d. generativity.

29. The idea that terminally ill and grief-stricken people go through identical stages, such as denial before anger,
    a. is widely supported by research.
    b. more accurately describes grieving in some cultures than others.
    c. is true of women but not men.
    d. is not supported by research studies.

30. Stranger anxiety develops soon after
    a. the concept of conservation.
    b. egocentrism.
    c. a theory of mind.
    d. the concept of object permanence.

31. Before Piaget, people were more likely to believe that
    a. the child's mind is a miniature model of the adult's.
    b. children think about the world in radically different ways from adults.
    c. the child's mind develops through a series of stages.
    d. children interpret their experiences in terms of their current understandings.

32. Which is the correct sequence of stages in Piaget's theory of cognitive development?
    a. sensorimotor, preoperational, concrete operational, formal operational
    b. sensorimotor, preoperational, formal operational, concrete operational
    c. preoperational, sensorimotor, concrete operational, formal operational
    d. preoperational, sensorimotor, formal operational, concrete operational

33. A child whose mother drank heavily when she was pregnant is at heightened risk of
    a. being emotionally excitable during childhood.
    b. becoming insecurely attached.
    c. being born with the physical and cognitive abnormalities of fetal alcohol syndrome.
    d. addiction to a range of drugs throughout life.

34. Which is the correct order of stages of prenatal development?
    a. zygote, fetus, embryo
    b. zygote, embryo, fetus
    c. embryo, zygote, fetus
    d. embryo, fetus, zygote

35. The term *critical period* refers to
    a. prenatal development.
    b. the initial 2 hours after a child's birth.
    c. the preoperational stage.
    d. a restricted time for learning.

36. Which of the following was NOT found by the Harlows in socially deprived monkeys?
    a. They had difficulty mating.
    b. They showed extreme fear or aggression when first seeing other monkeys.
    c. They showed abnormal physical development.
    d. The females were abusive mothers.

37. Insecurely attached infants who are left by their mothers in an unfamiliar setting often will
    a. hold fast to their mothers on their return.
    b. explore the new surroundings confidently.
    c. be indifferent toward their mothers on their return.
    d. display little emotion at any time.

38. Whose stage theory of moral development was based on how people reasoned about ethical dilemmas?
    a. Erikson   c. Harlow
    b. Piaget   d. Kohlberg

39. The *social clock* refers to
    a. an individual or society's distribution of work and leisure time.
    b. adulthood responsibilities.
    c. typical ages for starting a career, marrying, and so on.
    d. age-related changes in one's circle of friends.

40. At which of Kohlberg's levels is moral reasoning based on the existence of fundamental human rights?
    a. preconventional morality
    b. conventional morality
    c. postconventional morality
    d. generative morality

41. In Erikson's theory, individuals generally focus on developing _____ during adolescence and then _____ during young adulthood.
    a. identity; intimacy
    b. intimacy; identity
    c. basic trust; identity
    d. identity; basic trust

42. After their grown children have left home, most couples experience
    a. distress because the "nest is empty."
    b. increased strain in their marital relationship.
    c. the desire to start another family.
    d. happiness and enjoyment in their relationship.

43. Psychologists Jonathan Haidt believes that much of our moral reasoning is rooted in our
    a. genes.
    b. cultural norms.
    c. cognitive development.
    d. moral intuitions.

44. Stage theories have been criticized because they fail to consider that development may be significantly affected by
    a. variations in the social clock.
    b. each individual's experiences.
    c. each individual's historical and cultural setting.
    d. all of these factors.

Application Essay

Sheryl is a 12-year-old living in the United States. She is in the sixth grade. Describe the developmental changes she is likely to be experiencing according to Piaget, Kohlberg, and Erikson. (Use the space below to list the points you want to make, and organize them. Then write the essay on a separate sheet of paper.)

Summing Up

See the next page.

Terms and Concepts to Remember

Using your own words, on a piece of paper write a brief definition or explanation of each of the following terms.

1. developmental psychology
2. chromosomes
3. DNA (deoxyribonucleic acid)
4. genes

5. heredity
6. genome
7. environment
8. interaction
9. epigenetics
10. zygote
11. embryo
12. fetus
13. teratogen
14. fetal alcohol syndrome (FAS)
15. reflex
16. temperament
17. identical (monozygotic) twins
18. fraternal (dizygotic) twins
19. maturation
20. critical period
21. cognition
22. schema
23. assimilation
24. accommodation
25. sensorimotor stage
26. object permanence
27. preoperational stage
28. conservation
29. egocentrism
30. theory of mind
31. autism spectrum disorder
32. concrete operational stage
33. formal operational stage
34. stranger anxiety
35. attachment
36. basic trust
37. adolescence
38. puberty
39. identity
40. social identity
41. intimacy
42. emerging adulthood
43. menopause
44. cross-sectional study
45. longitudinal study
46. social clock

Answers

Chapter Review

Developmental Psychology's Major Issues

1. developmental psychologists
2. nature; nurture; biological; psychological; social-cultural

Summing Up

Jorge and Sonya Nuñez have conceived a male child, whom they will name Felipe.

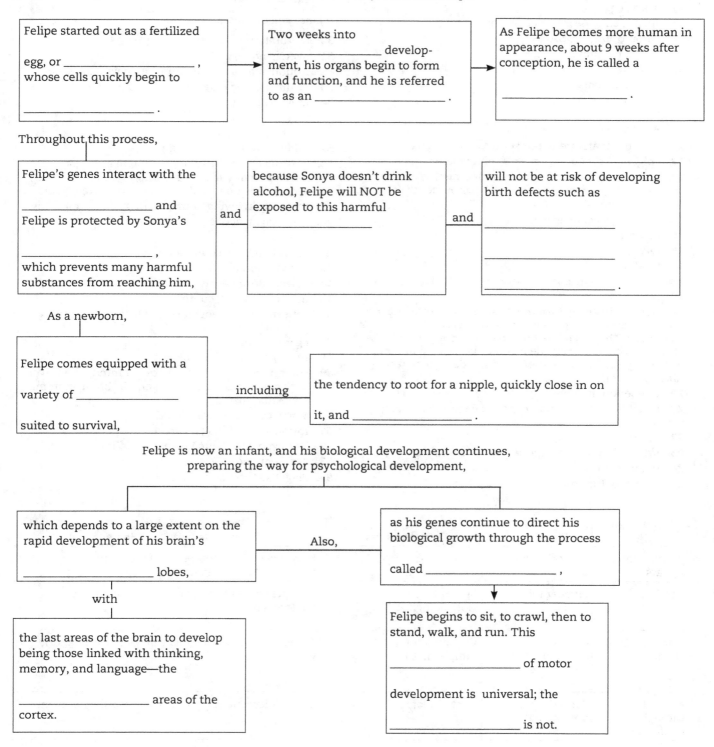

Felipe started out as a fertilized egg, or _____ , whose cells quickly begin to _____ .

Two weeks into _____ development, his organs begin to form and function, and he is referred to as an _____ .

As Felipe becomes more human in appearance, about 9 weeks after conception, he is called a _____ .

Throughout this process,

Felipe's genes interact with the _____ and Felipe is protected by Sonya's _____ , which prevents many harmful substances from reaching him,

and

because Sonya doesn't drink alcohol, Felipe will NOT be exposed to this harmful _____

and

will not be at risk of developing birth defects such as _____ _____ _____ .

As a newborn,

Felipe comes equipped with a variety of _____ suited to survival,

including

the tendency to root for a nipple, quickly close in on it, and _____ .

Felipe is now an infant, and his biological development continues, preparing the way for psychological development,

which depends to a large extent on the rapid development of his brain's _____ lobes,

Also,

as his genes continue to direct his biological growth through the process called _____ ,

with

the last areas of the brain to develop being those linked with thinking, memory, and language—the _____ areas of the cortex.

Felipe begins to sit, to crawl, then to stand, walk, and run. This _____ of motor development is universal; the _____ is not.

3. continuity; stages
4. stability; do; temperament

Prenatal Development and the Newborn

5. ovary; egg
6. sperm; enzymes; blocks; nuclei
7. chromosomes; DNA
8. genes; heredity
9. genome
10. **a.** cell nucleus
    b. chromosome
    c. gene
    d. DNA
11. environment; interaction; environment; heredity
12. epigenetics; expression; epigenetic marks
13. **b.** is the answer. It describes an interaction between heredity (personality trait) and environment (swim competition).
14. zygotes; specialize; placenta
15. embryo
16. fetus
17. teratogens
18. central; fetal alcohol syndrome
19. reflex; root
Newborns reflexively turn their heads in the direction of human voices. They gaze longer at a drawing of a face-like image. They focus best on objects about 8 to 12 inches away, which is about the distance between a nursing infant's eyes and the mother's. Within days, they recognize their mother's smell.
20. temperament; does
21. irritable; intense; unpredictable; cheerful; relaxed; predictable
22. more
23. interaction; genes; experiences (environment)
24. twin; adoption
25. identical; fraternal

26. more
27. environment
28. do not; outgoingness; agreeableness
29. same; different

Infancy and Childhood

30. maturation
31. over; is not
32. frontal; reasoning; planning; association areas
33. pruning; critical period
34. motor; sequence; walk
35. major
36. cerebellum; small
37. infantile amnesia; learning
38. **b.** is the answer. Although the rate of motor development varies from child to child, the basic sequence is universal and, therefore, predictable.
39. thinking; knowing; remembering; communicating
40. Jean Piaget; active
41. schemas
42. assimilation; accommodation
43. sensorimotor
44. object permanence
45. underestimated; continuous
46. conservation; preoperational; have not; symbols; pretend play
47. egocentrism
48. theory of mind; false beliefs
49. communication; social; theory of mind; repetitive; autism spectrum disorder; genetic; brain; systemizers; empathizers
50. 6 or 7; concrete operational
51. formal operational; abstract
52. Lev Vygotsky; 7; inner speech; scaffold
53. age; sequence
54. Piaget's stages summarized

Typical Age Range	Stage	New Developments	Test to Determine If Someone Is in This Stage
Birth to nearly 2 years	Sensorimotor	Stranger anxiety Object permanence	Have the child's mother leave the room Hide a toy under a blanket
2 to 6 or 7 years	Preoperational	Egocentrism Not yet logical	Ask questions to determine child's ability to take another's perspective
6 or 7 to 11 years	Concrete operational	Conservation Simple math	Transfer liquid from a tall, thin glass into a short, wide glass
About 12 through adulthood	Formal operational	Abstract logic	Give adolescent a hypothetical reasoning problem

55. theory of mind
56. conservation
57. sensorimotor
58. preoperational
59. yes; no
60. object permanence; stranger anxiety; 8 months
61. attachment
62. contact comfort
63. safe haven; secure base
64. strange situation; secure; insecure; avoidance

Placed in a strange situation, securely attached infants play comfortably, happily exploring their new environment. In contrast, insecurely attached infants are less likely to explore their surroundings and may even cling to their mothers. When separated from their mothers, insecurely attached infants are much more distressed than securely attached infants. When reunited with their mothers, insecurely attached infants may be indifferent.

Research studies conducted by Mary Ainsworth have revealed that sensitive, responsive mothers tend to have securely attached infants, whereas insensitive, unresponsive mothers often have insecurely attached infants. Other studies have found that temperamentally difficult infants whose mothers receive training in responsive parenting are more likely to become securely attached than are control infants.

65. is not; temperament
66. 13; gradually declines; throughout the world
67. basic trust
68. depression; stress-hormone; are; resilience
69. basic trust
70. authoritarian; permissive; negligent
71. authoritative
72. behaviors; attitudes; values; traditions; generation; independence; family self
73. social skill; self-esteem; aggressive; immature; academic
74. authoritative
75. do not

Adolescence

76. childhood; adulthood
77. puberty
78. menarche
79. sequence; timing

For boys, early maturation has mixed effects. Teen boys who are stronger and more athletic tend to be more popular, self-assured, and independent, though also more at risk for alcohol use, delinquency, and premature sexual activity. For a girl, early maturation can be a challenge. She may search out older teens or may suffer teasing or sexual harassment.

80. frontal lobe; limbic system
81. self-focused
82. formal operations; abstract; inconsistencies
83. Lawrence Kohlberg; preconventional; conventional; postconventional

84. punishment; rewards
85. adolescence; approval; order
86. postconventional
87. postconventional; individualism; collectivist
88. intuitionist; moral paradoxes
89. character-education programs; competences
90. gratification; academically
91. preconventional
92. individualism; postconventional
93. selves; confusion; identity; social identity
94. adopting; peer group
95. collectivist; individualism
96. falls; rises; agreeableness; emotional stability
97. intimacy

Erikson's stages of psychosocial development

Group Age	Psychosocial Stage
Infancy	Trust vs. mistrust
Toddlerhood	Autonomy vs. shame and doubt
Preschooler	Initiative vs. guilt
Elementary school	Competence vs. inferiority
Adolescence	Identity vs. role confusion
Young adulthood	Intimacy vs. isolation
Middle adulthood	Generativity vs. stagnation
Late adulthood	Integrity vs. despair

98. peers; parents
99. selection effect
100. do; religious faith; college; career
101. affectionate; intimate
102. act out in violence against their classmates; physical; psychological
103. 10
104. does; higher
105. faith; politics
106. sexual maturity; status; rite of passage
107. more; earlier
108. emerging adulthood

Adulthood

109. Early adulthood: roughly twenties and thirties
Middle adulthood: to age 65
Late adulthood: the years after 65
110. is not
111. muscular strength; reaction time; sensory keenness; cardiac output
112. age; health; exercise
113. menopause; 50
114. sperm; testosterone
115. shrinks; reduced
116. brain cells; slows; memory; frontal; impulsivity
117. brain cell; neural; neurogenesis
118. telomeres; exercise

119. more; less
120. recall; recognize; meaningfulness
121. cross-sectional
122. longitudinal
123. has not; have not
124. **d.** is the answer. In tests of recognition memory, the performance of older persons shows little decline. The ability to recall material, especially meaningless material, declines with age.
125. intimacy; generativity; love; work
126. self-disclosure; 20; educated
127. decreased; increased; higher
128. happiness; sexual satisfaction; income; mental health
129. increase
130. competence; accomplishment
131. social clock; less
132. **c.** is the answer. Carlos' age and struggle to form a close relationship place him squarely in this stage.

    a. Trust versus mistrust is the psychosocial task of infancy.

    b. Autonomy versus doubt is the psychosocial task of toddlerhood.

    d. Identity versus role confusion is the psychosocial task of adolescence.
133. identity; confidence; self-esteem
134. do
135. positive; negative; emotional; fewer
136. **d.** is the answer. Research has not uncovered a tendency for people of any particular age group to report greater feelings of satisfaction or well-being.
137. suddenly and before its expected time
138. do; do not
139. do not

Progress Test

Multiple-Choice Questions

1. **d.** is the answer.
2. **b.** is the answer.

   c. & d. There are no such things as "placental" or "nonplacental" twins. All twins have a placenta during prenatal development.
3. **a.** is the answer.
4. **c.** is the answer.

   a., b., & d. The reactions of these infants are the opposite of what these choices describe.
5. **c.** is the answer.

   a. This defines DNA.
   b. This is a gene.
   d. These become the embryo.
6. **c.** is the answer.
7. **b.** is the answer.

   a., c., & d. Despite being raised in different environments, long-separated identical twins often have much in common, including likes, dislikes, and lifestyles. This indicates the significant heritability of many traits.
8. **b.** is the answer.

   a., c., & d. The personalities of adopted children do not much resemble those of their adoptive parents (therefore, not a.) or other children raised in the same home (therefore, not c. or d.).
9. **a.** is the answer.

   b. Neurotransmitters are the chemicals involved in synaptic transmission in the nervous system.
   c. Endorphins are the brain's naturally occurring opiate-like neurotransmitters that are responsible for the "runner's high," for example.
   d. Enzymes are chemicals that facilitate various chemical reactions throughout the body but are not involved in heredity.
10. **d.** is the answer.

    a. Attachment is an emotional tie between two people.
    b. & c. When two factors are correlated, it means either that increases in one factor are accompanied by increases in the other (positive correlation) or that increases in one factor are accompanied by decreases in the other (negative correlation).
11. **c.** is the answer. Developmental psychologists study physical, cognitive (memory, in this example), and social change throughout the life span.

    a. Social psychologists study how people influence and are influenced by others.
    b. Cognitive psychologists *do* study memory; because Dr. Goodman is interested in life-span *changes* in memory, she is more likely a developmental psychologist.
    d. Experimental psychologists study physiology, sensation, perception, learning, and other aspects of behavior. Only developmental psychologists focus on developmental changes.
12. **a.** is the answer.

    b. Schemas are mental concepts or frameworks that organize and interpret information.
    c. Piaget's theory is not concerned with attachment.
    d. Attaining object permanence is the hallmark of sensorimotor thought.
13. **b.** is the answer. The preoperational child sees the world from his or her own viewpoint.

    a. As immature as egocentrism is, it represents a significant cognitive advance over the sensorimotor child, who knows the world only through senses and actions. Even simple self-awareness takes a while to develop.
    c. & d. As children attain the operational stages, they become more able to see the world through the eyes of others.
14. **a.** is the answer. Before object permanence is attained, "out of sight" is truly "out of mind."

    b., c., & d. Developments during the preoperational, concrete operational, and formal operational stages include the use of language, conservation, and abstract reasoning, respectively.

15. **b.** is the answer. The infant turns its head and begins sucking when its cheek is stroked.
a., c., & d. These stimuli produce other reflexes in the newborn.

16. **b.** is the answer.
a. When given the choice between a wire mother with a bottle and a cloth mother without, the monkeys preferred the cloth mother.
c. The presence of other infants made no difference.
d. Stability was not a factor in this experiment.

17. **c.** is the answer. Through maturation—an orderly sequence of biological growth processes that are relatively unaffected by experience—all humans develop.
a. Conservation is the cognitive awareness that objects do not change with changes in shape.
b. The forces of nature *are* those that direct maturation.
d. The continuity-stages debate has to do with whether development is a gradual and continuous process or a distinct stagelike process. Those who emphasize maturation see development as occurring in stages, not continuously.

18. **d.** is the answer. Erikson proposed that development occurs in a series of stages. During the first stage the child develops an attitude of either basic trust or mistrust.
a. Piaget's theory is concerned with cognitive development.
b. Harlow conducted research on attachment.
c. Vygotsky focused on the influence of social factors on cognitive development.

19. **b.** is the answer.

20. **a.** is the answer.

21. **c.** is the answer. At the preconventional level, moral reasoning centers on self-interest, whether this means obtaining rewards or avoiding punishment.
a. & b. Moral reasoning based on a sense of social duty or a desire to gain social approval is associated with the conventional level of moral development.
d. Reasoning based on ethical principles is characteristic of the postconventional level of moral development.

22. **c.** is the answer.
a. Puberty refers to the early adolescent period during which accelerated growth and sexual maturation occur, not to the first menstrual period.
b. Menopause is the cessation of menstruation, which typically occurs in the early fifties.
d. In Erikson's theory, generativity, or the sense of contributing and being productive, is the task of middle adulthood.

23. **d.** is the answer.
a. Generativity is associated with middle adulthood.
b. & c. Intimacy and isolation are associated with young adulthood.

24. **c.** is the answer. Once formal operational thought has been attained, thinking is no longer limited to concrete events.

a. & b. Preoperational thought and concrete operational thought emerge before, and do not include, the ability to think logically about abstractions.
d. Conventional morality is one of Kohlberg's stages, which begins in early adolescence.

25. **a.** is the answer.
b., c., & d. These cognitive abilities remain essentially unchanged as the person ages.

26. **d.** is the answer. We are more likely to rust from disuse than to wear out from overuse. Fit bodies support fit minds.
a. Most older people suffer some memory loss but remember some events very well.
b. Although older adults are more subject to long-term ailments than younger adults, they actually suffer fewer short-term ailments.
c. People of all ages report equal happiness or satisfaction with life.

27. **d.** is the answer. The physical changes of puberty mark the onset of adolescence.
a. & b. An identity crisis or parent-child conflict may or may not occur during adolescence; neither of these formally marks its onset.
c. Formal operational thought, rather than concrete reasoning, typically develops in adolescence.

28. **b.** is the answer.
a. Menarche refers to the onset of menstruation.
c. The human genome is the complete genetic instructions for making an organism.
d. Generativity is Erikson's term for productivity during middle adulthood.

29. **d.** is the answer.

30. **d.** is the answer. With object permanence, a child develops schemas for familiar objects, including faces, and may become upset by a stranger who does not fit any of these schemas.
a. The concept of conservation develops during the concrete operational stage, whereas stranger anxiety develops during the sensorimotor stage.
b. & c. Egocentrism and a theory of mind both develop during the preoperational stage. This follows the sensorimotor stage, when stranger anxiety develops.

31. **a.** is the answer.
b., c., & d. Each of these is an understanding developed by Piaget.

32. **a.** is the answer.

33. **c.** is the answer.
a., b., & d. A child's emotional temperament, attachment, and addiction have not been linked to the mother's drinking while pregnant.

34. **b.** is the answer.

35. **d.** is the answer. A critical period is a restricted time during which an organism must be exposed to certain influences or experiences for a particular kind of learning to occur.
a. Critical periods refer to developmental periods after birth.
b. Critical periods vary from behavior to behavior, but they are not confined to the hours following birth.
c. Critical periods are not specifically associated with the preoperational period.

36. **c.** is the answer. Deprived monkeys were impaired in their social behaviors but not in their physical development.

    a., b., & d. Each of these was found in socially deprived monkeys.

37. **c.** is the answer.

    a. Insecurely attached infants often cling to their mothers when placed in a new situation; yet, when the mother returns after an absence, the infant's reaction tends to be one of indifference.

    b. These behaviors are characteristic of securely attached infants.

    d. Insecurely attached infants in unfamiliar surroundings will often exhibit a range of emotional behaviors.

38. **d.** is the answer.

    a. Erikson studied psychosocial development.

    b. Piaget studied cognitive development.

    c. Harlow is known for his studies of attachment in infant monkeys.

39. **c.** is the answer. Different societies and eras have somewhat different ideas about the age at which major life events should ideally occur.

40. **c.** is the answer.

    a. Preconventional morality is based on avoiding punishment and obtaining rewards.

    b. Conventional morality is based on gaining the approval of others and/or on following the law and social convention.

    d. There is no such thing as generative morality.

41. **a.** is the answer.

    b. According to Erikson, identity develops before intimacy.

    c. & d. Forming basic trust is the task of infancy.

42. **d.** is the answer.

    a., b., & c. Most couples do not feel a loss of purpose or marital strain following the departure of grown children.

43. **d.** is the answer.

44. **d.** is the answer.

Application Essay

Sheryl's age would place her at the beginning of Piaget's stage of formal operations. Although her thinking is probably still somewhat self-focused, Sheryl is becoming capable of abstract, logical thought. Because her logical thinking also enables her to detect inconsistencies in others' reasoning and between their ideals and actions, Sheryl and her parents may be having some heated debates about now.

According to Kohlberg, Sheryl is probably at the beginning of postconventional morality. When she was younger, Sheryl probably abided by rules to gain social approval, or simply because "rules are rules" (conventional morality). Now that she is older, Sheryl's moral reasoning will increasingly be based on her own personal code of ethics and an affirmation of people's agreed-upon rights.

According to Erikson, psychosocial development occurs in eight stages, each of which focuses on a particular task. As an adolescent, Sheryl's psychosocial task is to develop a sense of self by testing roles, then integrating them to form a single identity. Erikson called this stage "identity versus role confusion."

Summing Up

Jorge and Sonya Nuñez have conceived a male child, whom they will name Felipe. Felipe begins his life as a fertilized egg, or *zygote*, whose cells quickly begin to *divide*. Two weeks into *prenatal* development, his organs begin to form and function, and he is referred to as an *embryo*. As Felipe becomes more human, about 9 weeks after conception, he is called a *fetus*.

Throughout this process, Felipe's genes interact with the *environment*, and Felipe is protected by Sonya's *placenta*, which prevents many harmful substances from reaching him, and because Sonya doesn't drink alcohol, Felipe will NOT be exposed to this harmful *teratogen* and will not be at risk of developing birth defects such as *fetal alcohol syndrome*.

As a newborn, Felipe comes equipped with a variety of *reflexes* suited to survival, including the tendency to root for a nipple, quickly close in on it, and *suck*.

Felipe is now an infant, and his biological development continues, preparing the way for psychological development, which depends to a large extent on the rapid development of his brain's *frontal lobes*, with the last areas of the brain to develop being those linked with thinking, memory, and language—the *association* areas of the cortex. Also, as his genes continue to direct his biological growth through the process called *maturation*, Felipe begins to sit, to crawl, then to stand, walk, and run. This *sequence* of motor development is universal; the *timing* is not.

Terms and Concepts to Remember

1. **Developmental psychology** is the branch of psychology concerned with physical, cognitive, and social change throughout the life span.

2. **Chromosomes** are threadlike structures made of DNA molecules, which contain the genes. In conception, the 23 chromosomes in the egg are paired with the 23 chromosomes in the sperm.

3. **DNA** (*deoxyribonucleic acid*) is a complex molecule containing the genetic information that makes up the chromosomes.

4. **Genes** are the biochemical units of heredity that make up the chromosomes; they are segments of the DNA molecules capable of synthesizing a protein.

5. **Heredity** is the genetic transfer of characteristics from parents to offspring.

6. A **genome** is the complete genetic instructions for making an organism.

7. **Environment** is every external influence, from prenatal nutrition to social support in later life.

8. An **interaction** occurs when the effects of one factor (such as environment) depend on another factor (such as heredity).

    Example: Because the way people react to us (an environmental factor) depends on our genetically influenced temperament (a genetic factor), there is an **interaction** between environment and heredity.

9. **Epigenetics** is the scientific study of environmental influences on gene expression.

10. The **zygote** (a term derived from the Greek word for "joint") is the fertilized egg, that is, the cluster of cells formed during conception by the union of sperm and egg.

11. The **embryo** is the developing prenatal organism from about 2 weeks through 2 months after conception.

12. The **fetus** is the developing prenatal human from 9 weeks after conception to birth.

13. **Teratogens** (literally, poisons) are any chemicals and viruses that cross the mother's placenta and can harm the developing embryo or fetus.

14. **Fetal alcohol syndrome (FAS)** refers to the physical and cognitive abnormalities that heavy drinking by a pregnant woman may cause in the developing child.

15. A **reflex** is an unlearned and automatic response to a sensory stimulus.

16. **Temperament** refers to a person's characteristic emotional reactivity and intensity.

17. **Identical (monozygotic) twins** develop from a single fertilized egg that splits in two, creating two genetically identical siblings.

18. **Fraternal (dizygotic) twins** develop from two separate eggs fertilized by different sperm and therefore are no more genetically similar than ordinary siblings.

19. **Maturation** refers to the biological growth processes that enable orderly changes in behavior, relatively uninfluenced by experience or other environmental factors.

    Example: The ability to walk depends on a certain level of neural and muscular **maturation**. For this reason, until the toddler's body is physically ready to walk, practice "walking" has little effect.

20. A **critical period** is a limited time early in life during which an organism must be exposed to certain stimuli or experiences if it is to develop properly.

21. **Cognition** refers to all the mental processes associated with thinking, knowing, remembering, and communicating.

22. In Piaget's theory of cognitive development, **schemas** are mental concepts or frameworks that organize and interpret information.

23. In Piaget's theory, **assimilation** refers to interpreting a new experience in terms of an existing schema.

24. In Piaget's theory, **accommodation** refers to changing an existing schema to incorporate new information that cannot be assimilated.

25. In Piaget's theory of cognitive stages, the **sensorimotor stage** lasts from birth to about age 2. During this stage, infants gain knowledge of the world through their senses and their motor activities.

26. **Object permanence,** which develops during the sensorimotor stage, is the awareness that things do not cease to exist when not perceived.

27. In Piaget's theory, the **preoperational stage** lasts from about 2 to 6 or 7 years of age. During this stage, language development is rapid, but the child is unable to understand the mental operations of concrete logic.

28. **Conservation** is the principle that properties such as number, volume, and mass remain constant despite changes in the forms of objects; it is acquired during the concrete operational stage.

29. In Piaget's theory, **egocentrism** refers to the difficulty that preoperational children have in considering another's viewpoint. *Ego* means "self," and *centrism* indicates "in the center"; the preoperational child is "self-centered."

30. Our ideas about our own and others' thoughts, feelings, and perceptions and the behaviors these might predict constitute our **theory of mind**.

31. **Autism spectrum disorder** is a group of disorders, including *autistic disorder* and *Asperger's disorder,* that appears in childhood and is marked by deficient communication and social interaction, and by fixated interests and repetitive behaviors.

32. During the **concrete operational stage,** lasting from about ages 6 or 7 to 11, children can think logically about concrete events and objects.

33. In Piaget's theory, the **formal operational stage** normally begins about age 12. During this stage people begin to think logically about abstract concepts.

    Memory aid: To help differentiate Piaget's stages remember that "operations" are mental transformations. *Pre*operational children, who lack the ability to perform transformations, are "before" this developmental milestone. Concrete operational children can operate on real, or concrete, objects. Formal operational children can perform logical transformations on abstract concepts.

34. **Stranger anxiety** is the fear of strangers that infants begin to display by about 8 months of age.

35. **Attachment** is an emotional tie with another person, shown in young children by their seeking closeness to a caregiver and showing distress on separation.

36. According to Erikson, **basic trust** is a sense that the world is predictable and trustworthy—a concept that infants form if their needs are met by responsive caregiving.

37. **Adolescence** refers to the life stage from puberty to independent adulthood.

38. **Puberty** is the early adolescent period of sexual maturation, during which a person becomes capable of reproduction.

39. In Erikson's theory, establishing an **identity,** or a sense of self, is the primary task of adolescence.

40. **Social identity** is our sense of who we are that comes from the groups to which we belong.

41. In Erikson's theory, **intimacy,** or the ability to establish close, loving relationships, is the primary task of early adulthood.

42. **Emerging adulthood** refers to the period between age 18 and the mid-twenties, when many in Western cultures are no longer adolescents but have not yet achieved full independence as adults.

43. **Menopause** is the natural end of menstruation and typically occurs in the early fifties. It also can mean the biological transition a woman experiences from before to after the end of menstruation.

44. In a **cross-sectional study,** people of different ages are compared with one another.

45. In a **longitudinal study,** the same people are restudied and retested over a long period.

46. The **social clock** refers to the culturally preferred timing of social events, such as leaving home, marrying, having children, and retiring.

Sex, Gender, and Sexuality

Chapter Overview

Chapter 4 is concerned with sex, gender, and sexuality. The first section explores how genes and environment interact to shape both the biological and social aspects of our gender. In the end, the message is clear: Our genes and our experience together form who we are.

The next section discusses human sexuality, including how hormones influence sexual motivation, the sexual response cycle, and the impact of external and imagined stimuli on sexual arousal. Sexually transmitted infections and adolescents' use of contraceptives are also explored. Sexual motivation in men and women is triggered less by physiological factors and more by external incentives. Even so, research studies demonstrate that sexual orientation is neither willfully chosen nor easily changed.

The third section explores an evolutionary explanation of gender differences and mating preferences. The chapter concludes with a discussion of the social significance of sex and reflections on nature–nurture interactions in sex, gender, and sexuality.

Chapter Review

First, skim each text section, noting headings and bold-face items. Review the section by reading the objectives and summaries provided here, then answer the questions that follow. In some cases, STUDY TIPS explain how best to learn a difficult concept and THINK ABOUT IT and APPLICATIONS help you to know how well you understand the material. Check your understanding of the material by consulting the answers beginning on page 80. Do not continue with the next section until you understand each answer. If you need to, review or reread the section in the textbook before continuing.

Gender Development

Objective 4-1: Explain the difference between the meaning of *gender* and the meaning of *sex*.

Sex refers to the biologically influenced characteristics by which people define *male* and *female*. **Gender** refers to the biologically and socially influenced roles and characteristics by which members of a culture define *male* and *female*.

1. Sex refers to the _____ influenced characteristics by which people define *male* and *female*. The roles and characteristics by which cultures define *male* and *female* constitute a person's

_____ .

Objective 4-2: Discuss some ways in which males and females tend to be alike and to differ.

Although males and females are similar in most ways, they differ in the age at which they enter puberty and life expectancy. Women are more vulnerable to depression, anxiety, and eating disorders. In contrast, men are more likely to commit suicide and develop alcohol use disorder. They are also much more likely to be diagnosed with autism spectrum disorder, color-deficient vision, attention-deficit/hyperactivity disorder as children, and antisocial personality disorder as adults.

Men generally admit to more **aggression** than do women, and experiments confirm that men tend to behave more aggressively, such as by blasting people with what they believed was intense and prolonged noise. The same difference is reflected in violent crime rates. The gender gap in physical aggression appears worldwide. Women are slightly more likely than men to commit acts of **relational aggression.**

Around the world, men place more importance on power and achievement and are socially dominant.

In comparison to men, who tend to be *independent*, women are more *interdependent*. This gender difference surfaces early, in children's play. As teens, girls spend more time with friends and on social networking sites and less time alone. Women emphasize caring, often assuming responsibility for the very young and very old. Both men and women indicate that their friendships with women tend to be more intimate, enjoyable, and nurturing.

2. Among your _____ (how many?) chromosomes, _____ (how many?) are unisex.

3. Compared with boys, girls enter puberty _____ (earlier/later). A woman's life span is_____ (longer/shorter), and women express emotions _____ (more/less) freely. Women

are more likely than men to suffer from
_____ , _____ ,
and _____ _____ .

4. Compared with women, men are more likely to
commit _____ and to develop
_____ _____ dis-
order. They are also more likely to be diagnosed
with _____ _____
_____ , _____ -
_____ _____ ,
_____ - _____ /
_____ disorder, and
_____ _____
disorder.

5. *Aggression* is defined as any act that is
_____ to hurt someone
_____ or _____ .
An act of aggression intended to harm a person's
relationship or social standing is called
_____ _____ .

6. Worldwide, men are more likely than women to
engage in _____ ,
_____ , _____ ,
and _____ _____ .

7. Compared with women, in most societies men place
more importance on _____ and
_____ and are socially
_____ .

8. In satisfying their need to _____ ,
males tend to be _____ and females
to be more _____ . This difference is
noticeable in how children _____ ,
and it continues throughout the teen and adult
years. Girls play in groups that are
_____ and less _____
than boys' groups.

9. Because they are more _____ , women
are likely to use conversation to _____
_____ , while men are likely to use
conversation to _____
_____ . In coping with stress, women
are more likely to turn to others for support. They
are said to _____ _____
_____ .

10. Gender differences in power and social connected-
ness generally peak during _____ |
_____ and _____
_____ and then gradually_
_____ (increase/decrease) as we age.

APPLICATION:

11. Mackenzie and Zachary live next door to Ella and Michael.
They've become good friends, and every Sunday they get
together for dinner. Zachary and Michael discuss the best
way to clean their roofs, demonstrating the male tendency
to _____ ..
Mackenzie and Ella talk about how to make their new
neighbors feel welcome, demonstrating the female tendency to _____ .

Objective 4-3: Identify the factors that contribute to gender bias in the workplace.

Several factors contribute to gender bias in the workplace, including differences in perception (among politicians who seem power-hungry, women are seen as
aggressive and men are seen as take-charge) , compen-
sation, child-care responsibilities, social norms, everyday behaviors, and leadership and interaction styles. In
groups, leadership tends to go to males, and men tend
to be more *directive*, while women are more *democratic*. In
everyday behavior, men are more likely to talk assertively, to interrupt, to initiate touching, to smile and apologize less, and to stare.

12. Among politicians who seem power-hungry,
_____ (men/women) are more successful. In medicine, _____ (men/women)
receive higher salaries. In academia,
_____ (men/women) have been less
likely to be funded.

13. When groups form, leadership _____
(does/does not) tend to go to males. As leaders, men
tend to be more _____ , while women
are more _____ .

14. When interacting, men have been more likely to
offer _____ , women to express
_____ .

15. In everyday behavior, men talk assertively,
_____ , initiate
_____ , and _____ .
And they smile and _____ less.

16. Gender roles _____ (do/do not) vary
widely across place and time. Gender differences in
both social connectedness and power are greatest in
_____ _____ and

_____ _____ . By age 50, most parenting-related gender differences _____ . Men become less domineering and more _____ . Women—especially those with paid employment—become more assertive and _____ .

Objective 4-4: Describe how sex hormones influence prenatal and adolescent development, and define an *intersex* condition.

Biological sex is determined by the twenty-third pair of chromosomes, the two sex chromosomes. The member of the pair inherited from the mother is an **X chromosome.** The X (female) or Y (male) chromosome that comes from the father determines the child's sex. The **Y chromosome** triggers the production of the principal male sex hormone, **testosterone,** which in turn triggers the development of male sex organs.

During the fourth and fifth prenatal months, the sex hormones will tilt the brain's wiring toward male or female patterns.

Adolescence typically begins at **puberty** with the onset of rapid growth and developing sexual maturity. A surge of hormones triggers a two-year period of growth that begins in girls at about age 11 and in boys at about age 12. During the growth spurt, the reproductive organs and external genitalia, or **primary sex characteristics,** develop dramatically. So do the **secondary sex characteristics,** such as the breasts and hips in girls, facial hair and a deepened voice in boys, and pubic and underarm hair in both sexes. The landmarks of puberty are the first ejaculation (**spermarche**) in boys, which usually occurs by about age 14, and the first menstrual period (**menarche**) in girls, usually within a year of age 12½.

17. Biology influences gender _____ (the sex chromosomes) and _____ (the sex hormones).

18. The twenty-third pair of chromosomes determines the developing person's _____ .
    The mother always contributes a(n) _____ chromosome. When the father contributes a(n) _____ chromosome, the testes begin producing the hormone _____ . In about the _____ week, this hormone initiates the development of male sex organs.

19. Adolescence begins with the time of developing sexual maturity known as _____ . A two-year period of rapid physical development begins in girls at about the age of _____ and in boys at about the age of _____ . This growth spurt is marked by the development of the reproductive organs and external genitalia, or _____ _____ characteristics, as well as by the development of breasts

and larger hips in girls and facial hair in boys. These nonreproductive traits are known as _____ _____ characteristics.

20. The first ejaculation is called _____ . The first menstrual period is called _____ .

21. Individuals who are born with combinations of male and female physical features are said to be _____ .

Objective 4-5: Explain how gender roles and gender identity differ.

Although biology influences our gender, gender is also socially constructed. Culture shapes our **roles.** For example, *gender roles*—the social expectations that guide our behavior as men and women—shift over time and they differ from place to place. In just a thin slice of history, gender roles have undergone an extreme makeover, worldwide. The modern economy has produced jobs that rely not on brute strength but on social intelligence, open communication, and the ability to sit still and focus.

Society assigns each of us to the social category of male and female. The result is our **gender identity,** our sense of being male or female. **Social learning theory** assumes that children learn gender-linked behaviors by observing and imitating others and by being rewarded and punished. To varying degrees, we also undergo **gender typing,** acquiring a traditional male or female role. Some children organize themselves into "boy worlds" and "girl worlds." Others seem to prefer **androgyny.** Thinking also matters. As children, we form *gender schemas,* frameworks for organizing boy-girl characteristics. In every culture, people communicate their gender in many ways. Their *gender expression* drops hints not only in their language but also in their clothes, toys, books, media, and games. For **transgender** people, gender identity or expression differs from the behaviors or traits considered typical for their biological sex.

22. The social expectations about the way people in a certain social position should behave defines their _____ . Our culture defines how men and women should behave as their _____ _____ .

23. Gender roles _____ (are/are not) rigidly fixed, as evidenced by the fact that they vary across _____ and over _____ and _____ .

24. Our individual sense of being male or female is called our _____ _____ . The degree to which we exhibit traditionally male or female roles is called _____ _____ .

25. According to _____
    _____ theory, children learn
    gender-linked behaviors by observing and imitating
    others and being rewarded or punished. Even when
    their families discourage traditional gender typing,
    children _____ (do/do not) orga-
    nize themselves into "boy worlds" and "girl worlds."
    A blend of masculine and feminine psychological
    characteristics is called _____ .

26. As young children, we formed _____
    that helped us make sense of the world. To organize
    boy-girl characteristics, we formed a
    _____ _____ ,
    which became a gender lens through which we
    viewed our experiences.

27. People whose gender identity or expression differs
    from that associated with their birth sex are said to
    be _____ . Some of these people
    are also _____ .

APPLICATIONS:

28. Rod has always felt pressure to be the driver when travel-
    ing in a car with Sue because he learned that this was
    expected of men. Rod's feelings illustrate the influence of
    _____ _____ .

29. Pat and Alex have been married for about 10 years.
    During that time, Alex is the one most likely to spend less
    time at work, more time with household chores, and more
    time caring for the very young and the very old. Alex is
    most likely _____ (male/female).

30. When his son cries because another child has taken his
    favorite toy, Brandon admonishes him by saying, "Big
    boys don't cry." Evidently, Brandon is an advocate of
    _____ _____ theory
    in accounting for the development of gender-linked
    behaviors.

31. Three-year-old Caleb shares a toy chest with his
    18-month-old sister Elena. Caleb has put all cars, trucks,
    and superheroes to his side of the chest and all the dolls,
    stuffed animals, and miniature furniture to Elena's side.
    Caleb has clearly formed a _____
    _____ about gender-linked behaviors.

32. Rufus has always felt like a woman in a man's body; he
    would be referred to as a _____ . After
    sex-reassignment surgery, Rufus became Ruth and would
    be defined as a _____ .

Human Sexuality

For all but the tiny fraction of us considered *asexual,* dating and mating become a high priority from puberty on.

Objective 4-6: Explain how hormones influence human
sexual motivation.

The sex hormones direct the physical development of
male and female sex characteristics and, especially in
nonhuman animals, activate sexual behavior. The main
male sex hormone is *testosterone*. The main female sex
hormones are the *estrogens* such as *estradiol*.
    In humans, the hormones influence sexual behav-
iors more loosely than in most mammals. Large hormonal shifts, such as occur at puberty, have a greater effect.
Also, in later life, as sex hormones decline, the frequency
of sexual fantasies and intercourse also declines. Chance
events, such as surgery or drugs, may cause hormonal
shifts that affect sexual behavior.

33. A person who does not experience sexual attraction
    to others is said to be _____ .

34. In most mammals, females are sexually receptive
    during ovulation, when the female sex hormones,
    the _____ , such as
    _____ , peak.

35. The importance of the hormone
    _____ to male sexual arousal
    is confirmed by the fact that sexual interest declines
    in animals if their _____ are
    surgically removed. In women, low levels of the
    hormone _____ may cause a
    waning of sexual interest.

36. Normal hormonal fluctuations in humans have
    _____ (little/significant) effect
    on sexual motivation—except at two predictable
    points in the life span. During _____ ,
    a surge in _____ hormones
    triggers the development of _____
    _____ and interests. In later
    life, levels of the hormones _____
    and _____ fall, and the fre-
    quency of sexual fantasies and
    _____ declines as well.

37. A third possibility is that hormonal shifts may
    be caused by _____ or
    drugs, resulting in a(n) _____
    (increase/ decrease) in the sex drive as
    _____ levels decline.

Objective 4-7: Describe the *human sexual response cycle,* and explain how sexual dysfunctions can interfere with this cycle.

The human **sexual response cycle** normally follows a pattern of *excitement, plateau, orgasm* (which seems to involve similar feelings and brain activity in males and females), and *resolution,* followed in males by a **refractory period,** during which renewed arousal and orgasm are not possible.

 Sexual dysfunctions are problems that consistently impair sexual arousal or functioning. *Premature ejaculation* and **female orgasmic disorder** can often be treated by therapy. **Erectile disorder** is routinely treated by taking a pill. Some modestly effective drug treatments for *female sexual interest/arousal disorder* are also available.

38. The two researchers who identified a four-stage sexual response cycle are _____ and _____ . In order, the stages of the cycle are the _____ phase, the _____ phase, _____ , and the _____ phase.

39. During resolution, males experience a _____ _____ , during which they are incapable of another orgasm.

40. Problems that consistently impair sexual functioning are called _____ _____ . Examples of such problems in men include _____ _____ and _____ _____ ; and in women, _____ _____ _____ .

Objective 4-8: Describe how sexually transmitted infections can be prevented.

Unprotected sex has led to increased rates of *sexually transmitted infections (STIs),* including **AIDS.** Teenage girls, because of their less mature anatomy and lower levels of protective antibodies, seem especially vulnerable to STIs. Although condoms do not protect against all STIs, they are 80 percent effective in preventing the transmission of *HIV (human immunodeficiency virus),* the virusts that causes **AIDS—acquired immune deficiency syndrome.** Oral sex is linked to STIs, such as the *human papillomavirus (HPV),* and risks rise with the number of sexual partners.

41. Especially in people under 25, _____ _____ _____ have ballooned in recent years. Teen girls, because of their lower levels of protective _____ , may be especially vulnerable to STIs.

42. Condom use is effective in preventing the transmission of _____ , the virus that causes _____ . This virus is passed more often from _____ (male to female/female to male) than from _____ (male to female/female to male).

43. There is a significant link between oral sex and STIs, such as the _____ _____ _____ .

Objective 4-9: Discuss how external and imagined stimuli contribute to sexual arousal.

External stimuli, such as sexually explicit materials, can trigger arousal in both men and women. Sexually coercive material tends to increase viewers' acceptance of rape and violence toward women. Images of sexually attractive men and women may lead people to be less satisfied with their own partners. With repeated exposure to a particular erotic stimulus, we may *habituate.* Our imaginations also influence sexual motivation.

 Wide-awake people become sexually aroused both by memories of prior sexual activities and by fantasies. About 95 percent of both men and women say they have had sexual fantasies.

44. Research has shown that erotic stimuli _____ (are/are not) as arousing for women as for men. In men more than in women, _____ of sexual arousal closely mirror their (more obvious) physical genital responses

45. With repeated exposure, the emotional response to an erotic stimulus often _____ .

Explain some of the possible harmful consequences of sexually explicit material.

46. Most women and men _____ (have/do not have) sexual fantasies. Compared with women's fantasies, men's sexual fantasies are more _____ .

Objective 4-10: Identify the factors that influence teenagers' sexual behavior and use of contraceptives.

American teens have higher pregnancy rates than European teens. Reasons for this include passion overwhelming intentions; minimal communication about birth control, as many teenagers are uncomfortable discussing contraception with either parents or partners; alcohol use, which can break down normal restraints; and the popular media helping to write the *social scripts* that shape our views of how to act.

Teens with high intelligence more often delay sex. Religious engagement, father presence, and participation in service learning programs are also predictors of sexual restraint.

47. Compared with European teens, American teens have _____ (higher/lower) rates of teen pregnancy.

State four factors that contribute to the high rate of unprotected sex among teenagers.

State several predictors of sexual restraint (delayed sexuality).

APPLICATION:

48. Which of the following teens is most likely to delay the initiation of sex?
    a. Jack, who has below-average intelligence
    b. Jason, who is not religiously active
    c. Ron, who regularly volunteers his time in community service
    d. It is impossible to predict.

Sexual Orientation

Objective 4-11: Describe what research has taught us about sexual orientation.

Sexual orientation is our enduring sexual attraction toward members of either our own sex (*homosexual*), the other sex (*heterosexual*), or both sexes (*bisexual*). About 3 or 4 percent of men and 2 percent of women are exclusively homosexual. Less than 1 percent are actively bisexual.

Sexual orientation is neither willfully chosen nor willfully changed. Women's sexual orientation tends to be less strongly felt and more variable than men's.

Although we are still unsure why one person becomes homosexual and another heterosexual, it

is beginning to look as though biological factors are involved. No links have been found between homosexuality and a child's relationships with parents, fear or hatred of people of the other gender, childhood sexual experience, or sex hormone levels currently in the blood. On the other hand, biological influences are evident in studies of same-sex relations in several hundred species; straight-gay differences in brain characteristics and traits; genetic studies of family members, twins, and fruit flies; and the effect of exposure to certain hormones during critical periods of prenatal development.

49. A person's sexual attraction toward members of a particular gender is referred to as _____ _____ .

50. Historically, _____ (all/a slight majority) of the world's cultures have been predominantly heterosexual.

51. Estimates indicate that approximately _____ percent of men and _____ percent of women are exclusively homosexual. Fewer than 1 percent report being actively _____ .

52. A person's sexual orientation _____ (does/does not) appear to be voluntarily chosen. Several research studies reveal that sexual orientation among _____ (women/men) tends to be less strongly felt and more variable than among the other gender.

53. Gays and lesbians, especially during adolescence, suffer increased rates of anxiety and _____ and risk of _____ attempts, but this may result from lack of social support.

54. Children's relationships with parents _____ (are/are not) important factors in determining a person's sexual orientation.

55. Homosexuality _____ (does/does not) involve a fear or hatred of the other gender that leads people to direct their sexual desires toward members of their own gender.

56. Sex hormone levels _____ (do/do not) predict sexual orientation.

57. As children, most homosexuals _____ (were/were not) sexually victimized.

58. Same-sex attraction _____ (does/does not) occur among many species.

59. Researcher Simon LeVay discovered a cluster of cells in the _____ that is larger in _____ men than in all others.

60. In fruit fly studies, altering a single _____ has changed the fly's sexual orientation.

61. Studies of families and twins suggest that genes probably _____ (do/do not) play a role in homosexuality. Research has confirmed that homosexuality is often transmitted through the _____ (mother's/father's) side of the family. Also, identical twins _____ (are/are not) somewhat more likely than fraternal twins to share a homosexual orientation.

62. In animals and some rare human cases, sexual orientation has been altered by abnormal _____ conditions during prenatal development. In humans, prenatal exposure to hormone levels typical of _____, particularly during the _____ _____, may predispose an attraction to males.

63. Men who have older brothers are somewhat _____ (more/less) likely to be gay. This phenomenon, which has been called the _____-_____ _____, may represent a defensive maternal _____ response to substances produced by _____ (male/ female) fetuses.

64. There are several behavioral and biological traits on which homosexuals appear to fall midway between _____ females and males. These include _____ _____.

An Evolutionary Explanation of Human Sexuality

Objective 4-12: Discuss how an evolutionary psychologist might explain male-female differences in sexuality and mating preferences.

Evolutionary psychologists use the principles of *natural selection* to understand human behavior and mental processes. They explain how natural selection favors behavioral tendencies that contributed to the survival and spread of our genes. The principle helps us understand gender differences and similarities and important aspects of human sexuality.

In comparison to women, men think more about sex, masturbate more often, are more likely to initiate sex, and view more pornography.

Evolutionary psychologists apply the principle of natural selection to explain why our natural yearnings are our genes' way of reproducing themselves. Women have more at stake and are limited in the number of

children they can have between puberty and menopause. Women increase their own and children's chances of survival by searching for mates who offer their offspring support and protection, that is, men who are mature, dominant, bold, and wealthy. Being attracted to healthy, fertile-appearing partners increases men's chances of spreading their genes widely.

65. Researchers who use natural selection to explain the adaptive nature of human behavior are called _____ _____.

66. According to the principle of _____ _____, traits that contribute to _____ and _____ will be most likely to be passed on to succeeding generations.

67. According to this view, men who were most likely to pass on their genes were attracted to women with features that implied _____ and _____.

68. According to the evolutionary perspective, women prefer partners who will offer their offspring support and protection, and so often feel attracted to men who are _____, _____, _____, and _____.

69. One evolutionary explanation of why "gay genes" might persist is the _____ _____ theory. According to this theory, women in a homosexual man's family tended to have families that are _____ (smaller/larger) than normal.

THINK ABOUT IT: A key concept closely related to the principle of natural selection is fitness. We've all heard about "survival of the fittest," but the phrase is often misunderstood. It is not always true that "only the strong survive." From the standpoint of evolutionary psychology, "fitness" most directly refers to reproductive success. Traits and behaviors that have a genetic basis obviously cannot be passed on to succeeding generations if individuals do not have offspring. As you think about gender issues and sexuality, it may be helpful to consider the question, "How might this trait or behavior have promoted reproductive success over evolutionary time?"

Objective 4-13: Summarize the key criticisms of evolutionary explanations of human sexuality, and describe how evolutionary psychologists respond.

Critics argue that evolutionary psychologists start with an effect (e.g., gender sexuality difference) and work backward to propose an explanation. Other critics ask why we should try to explain today's behavior based on decisions our ancestors made thousands of years ago. In addition, much of who we are is not hard-wired. Cultural expectations can bend the genders. Still others suggest that evolutionary explanations may undercut moral responsibility for sexual behavior. In response, evolutionary psychologists point to the explanatory power of their theoretical principles, especially those offering testable predictions. They also note that understanding what we are capable of doing can help us become better people.

State several criticisms of evolutionary psychology.

APPLICATION:

70. Responding to the argument that gender differences are often products of a culture's social and family structures, an evolutionary psychologist is most likely to point to our great human capacity to _____ and to _____ and to survive.

Social Influences on Human Sexuality

Objective 4-14: Describe the role that social factors play in our sexuality.

Intimacy expresses our social nature. Most people find greater satisfaction after intercourse and orgasm with their loved one. Sex at its human best is life uniting and love renewing.

71. Sex is a _____ significant act.

72. One study of 2035 married people found that couples who reported being in a deeply committed relationship before having sex also reported greater relationship _____ and _____ —and better sex than those who had sex very early in their relation.

Reflections on the Nature and Nurture of Sex, Gender, and Sexuality

Objective 4-15: Explain how nature, nurture, and our own choices influence gender roles and sexuality.

Our genes form us. But our culture and experiences also shape us. In many modern cultures, gender roles are merging. Brute strength is becoming less and less important for power and status. We are the product of nature and nurture, but we're also an open system. Genes are all-pervasive but not all-powerful. People may reject their evolutionary role as transmitters of genes and choose not to reproduce. Culture, too, is all-pervasive but not all-powerful.

73. We are the product of our _____ and _____ , but we are also a system that is _____ .

Progress Test

Multiple-Choice Questions

Circle your answers to the following questions and check them with the answers beginning on page 81. If your answer is incorrect, read the explanation for why it is incorrect and then consult the text.

1. Dr. Ross believes that principles of natural selection help explain why infants come to fear strangers about the time they become mobile. Dr. Ross is most likely a(n)
   a. behavior geneticist.
   b. behaviorist.
   c. evolutionary psychologist.
   d. biologist.

2. Through natural selection, the traits that are most likely to be passed on to succeeding generations are those that contribute to
   a. reproduction.   c. aggressiveness.
   b. power.   d. connectedness.

3. Which of the following is NOT true regarding gender and sexuality?
   a. Men are more likely than women to masturbate.
   b. Women are more likely than men to cite affection as a reason for first intercourse.
   c. Men are more likely than women to initiate sexual activity.
   d. Gender differences in sexuality are noticeably absent among gay men and lesbian women.

4. Evolutionary psychologists attribute gender differences in sexuality to the fact that women have
   a. greater reproductive potential than do men.
   b. lower reproductive potential than do men.
   c. weaker sex drives than men.
   d. stronger sex drives than men.

5. According to evolutionary psychology, men are drawn sexually to women who seem _____ , while women are attracted to men who seem _____ .
   a. nurturing; youthful
   b. youthful and fertile; mature and wealthy
   c. slender; muscular
   d. exciting; dominant

6. Gender refers to
   a. the social characteristics by which people define male and female.
   b. the biological definition of male and female.
   c. our sense of being male or female.
   d. the extent to which we exhibit traditionally male or female traits.

7. The fertilized egg will develop into a boy if, at conception,
   a. the sperm contributes an X chromosome.
   b. the sperm contributes a Y chromosome.
   c. the egg contributes an X chromosome.
   d. the egg contributes a Y chromosome.

8. An androgynous child is one who
   a. acquires a traditional masculine or feminine role.
   b. possesses biological sexual characteristics of both sexes.
   c. has a gender identity that differs from his or her birth sex.
   d. displays traditional masculine and feminine psychological characteristics.

9. The hormone testosterone
   a. is found only in females.
   b. determines the sex of the developing person.
   c. stimulates growth of the female sex organs.
   d. stimulates growth of the male sex organs.

10. Each cell of the human body has a total of
    a. 23 chromosomes.   c. 46 chromosomes.
    b. 23 genes.   d. 46 genes.

11. Evolutionary explanations of gender differences in sexuality have been criticized because
    a. they offer "after-the-fact" explanations.
    b. they seem to excuse men's sexual aggression.
    c. they underestimate cultural influences on sexuality.
    d. of all of these reasons.

12. Children raised by parents who discourage traditional gender typing
    a. are less likely to display gender-typed behaviors themselves.
    b. often become confused and develop an ambiguous gender identity.
    c. nevertheless often organize themselves into "girl worlds" and "boy worlds."
    d. display excessively masculine and feminine traits as adults.

13. The correct order of the stages of Masters and Johnson's sexual response cycle is
    a. plateau; excitement; orgasm; resolution.
    b. excitement; plateau; orgasm; resolution.
    c. excitement; orgasm; resolution; refractory.
    d. plateau; excitement; orgasm; refractory.

14. Which of the following is NOT true regarding sexual orientation?
    a. Sexual orientation is neither willfully chosen nor willfully changed.
    b. All cultures in all times have been predominantly heterosexual.
    c. Men's sexual orientation is potentially more fluid and changeable than women's.
    d. Women, regardless of sexual orientation, respond to both female and male erotic stimuli.

15. Surgically removing the testes of male hamsters results in
    a. reduced testosterone and sexual interest.
    b. reduced testosterone, but no change in sexual interest.
    c. reduced estrogen and sexual interest.
    d. reduced estrogen, but no change in sexual interest.

16. Exposing a fetus to the hormones typical of females during the _____ may predispose the developing human to become attracted to males.
    a. first trimester   c. third trimester
    b. second trimester   d. entire pregnancy

17. Which of the following statements concerning homosexuality is true?
    a. Homosexuals have abnormal hormone levels.
    b. As children, most homosexuals were molested by an adult homosexual.
    c. Homosexuals had a domineering opposite-sex parent.
    d. Research strongly supports a biological explanation for sexual orientation.

18. Sexual orientation refers to
    a. a person's tendency to display behaviors typical of males or females.
    b. a person's sense of identity as a male or female.
    c. a person's enduring sexual attraction toward others
    d. characteristics defined by society as male or female.

19. According to Masters and Johnson, the sexual response of males is most likely to differ from that of females during
    a. the excitement phase.
    b. the plateau phase.
    c. orgasm.
    d. the resolution phase.

20. Which of the following was NOT identified as a contributing factor in the high rate of teen pregnancy?
    a. alcohol use
    b. thrill-seeking
    c. mass media sexual norms
    d. ignorance

21. The older-brother effect refers to the fact that
    a. men who have younger brothers are somewhat more likely to be gay.
    b. men who have older brothers are somewhat more likely to be gay.
    c. men who are fraternal twins are somewhat more likely to be gay.
    d. adopted men with younger brothers are somewhat more likely to be gay.

22. Some scientific evidence makes a preliminary link between homosexuality and
    a. late sexual maturation.
    b. the age of an individual's first erotic experience.
    c. atypical prenatal hormones.
    d. early problems in relationships with parents.

23. Among the hallmarks of growing up are a girl's first menstrual period and a boy's first ejaculation, which is also called
    a. puberty.
    b. menopause.
    c. menarche.
    d. spermarche.

24. People whose gender identity differs from that associated with their birth sex are said to be
    a. asexual.
    b. gender-typed.
    c. androgynous.
    d. transgender.

25. Secondary sex characteristics relate to _____; primary sex characteristics relate to _____.
    a. nonreproductive traits; reproductive organs
    b. testes and ovaries; facial and underarm hair
    c. menarche; spermarche
    d. gender orientation; gender expression

26. Which of the following is an example of relational aggression?
    a. slapping someone
    b. passing along hurtful gossip about someone
    c. slamming a door after a frustrating meeting with the boss
    d. punching a wall out of anger

27. An intersex person is someone
    a. born with combinations of male and female physical features.
    b. who does not experience sexual arousal.
    c. who displays both traditional feminine and masculine characteristics.
    d. whose gender expression differs from that associated with his or her birth sex.

28. Which of the following factors has been shown to contribute to unplanned teen pregnancies?
    a. higher intelligence
    b. alcohol use
    c. father presence.
    d. religious engagement

Application Essay

Lakia's new boyfriend has been pressuring her to become more sexually intimate than she wants to at this early stage in their relationship. Strongly gender-typed and "macho" in attitude, Jerome is becoming increasingly frustrated with Lakia's hesitation, while Lakia is starting to wonder if a long-term relationship with this type of man is what she really wants. In light of your understanding of the evolutionary explanation of gender differences in sexuality, explain why the tension between Lakia and Jerome would be considered understandable. (Use the space below to list points you want to make, and organize them. Then write the essay on a separate piece of paper.)

Summing Up

See the next page.

Terms and Concepts to Remember

Using your own words, on a piece of paper write a brief definition or explanation of each of the following terms.

1. sex

2. gender

3. aggression

4. relational aggression

5. X chromosome

6. Y chromosome

7. testosterone

8. puberty

9. primary sex characteristics

Summing Up

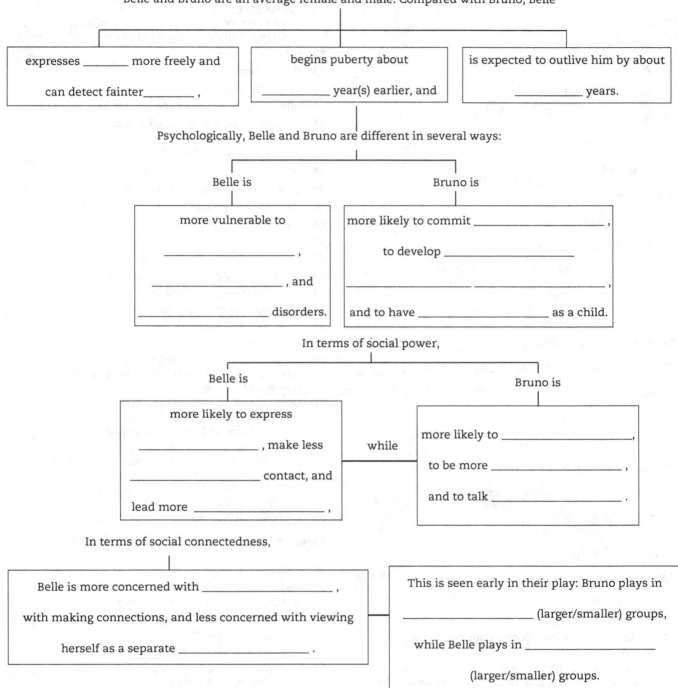

10. secondary sex characteristics

11. spermarche

12. menarche

13. intersex

14. role

15. gender role

16. gender identity

17. social learning theory

18. gender typing

19. androgyny

20. transgender

21. asexual

22. estrogens

23. sexual response cycle

24. refractory period

25. sexual dysfunction

26. erectile disorder

27. female orgasmic disorder

28. AIDS (acquired immune deficiency syndrome)

29. social script

30. sexual orientation

31. evolutionary psychology

32. natural selection

Answers

Chapter Review

Gender Development

1. biologically; gender

2. 46; 45

3. earlier; longer; more; depression; anxiety; eating disorders

4. suicide; alcohol use; autism spectrum disorder, color-deficient vision, attention-deficit/hyperactivity, antisocial personality

5. intended; physically; emotionally; relational aggression

6. hunting; fighting; warring; supporting war

7. power; achievement; dominant

8. belong; independent; interdependent; play; smaller; competitive

9. interdependent; explore relationships; find solutions; tend and befriend

10. late adolescence; early adulthood; decrease

11. talk with others to find solutions; talk with others to explore relationships. Men prefer working with things and women prefer working with people, such as trying to make a new neighbor feel welcome.

12. men; men; women

13. does; directive; democratic

14. opinions; support

15. interrupt; touches; staring; apologize

16. do; late adolescence and early adulthood; decrease; empathic; self-confident

17. genetically; physiologically

18. sex; X; Y; testosterone; seventh

19. puberty; 11; 12; primary sex; secondary sex

20. spermarche; menarche

21. intersex

22. roles; gender role

23. are not; cultures; time; place

24. gender identity; gender typing

25. social learning; do; androgyny

26. schemas; gender schema

27. transgender; transsexual

28. gender roles

29. female. Males such as Pat are more likely to spend more time at work and less time at home doing household chores.

30. social learning. Following social learning theory, Brandon is using verbal punishment to discourage what he believes to be an inappropriate gender-linked behavior in his son.

31. gender schema. Even when parents raise children in a gender-neutral environment, the children often automatically divide things into a "girls' world" and a "boys' world."

32. transgender; transsexual

Human Sexuality

33. asexual

34. estrogens; estradiol

35. testosterone; testes; testosterone

36. little; puberty; sex; sex characteristics; testosterone; estrogen; intercourse

37. surgery; decrease; testosterone

38. William Masters; Virginia Johnson; excitement; plateau; orgasm; resolution

39. refractory period

40. sexual dysfunctions; erectile disorder; premature ejaculation; female orgasmic disorder

41. sexually transmitted infections (STIs); antibodies

42. HIV; AIDS; male to female; female to male

43. human papilloma virus

44. are; feelings

45. habituates

Erotic material may increase the viewer's acceptance of the false idea that women enjoy rape, may increase men's willingness to hurt women, may lead people to devalue their partners, and may diminish people's satisfaction with their own sexual partners.

46. have; frequent, physical, and less romantic

47. higher

Among the factors that contribute to teen pregnancy are (1) minimal communication about birth control, (2) passion overwhelming self-control, (3) alcohol use, and (4) mass media norms of unprotected promiscuity.

High intelligence, religious engagement, father presence, and participation in service learning programs predict sexual restraint in teens.

48. c. is the answer. Teens with high intelligence (therefore, not a.) and those who are religiously active (therefore, not b.) are most likely to delay sex.

Sexual Orientation

49. sexual orientation

50. all

51. 3 or 4; 2; bisexual

52. does not; women

53. depression; suicide

54. are not

55. does not

56. do not

57. were not

58. does

59. hypothalamus; heterosexual

60. gene

61. do; mother's; are

62. hormone; females; second trimester

63. more; older-brother effect; immune; male

64. heterosexual; spatial abilities, fingerprint ridge counts, handedness, and gender nonconformity (See text Table 4.1 for more traits.)

An Evolutionary Explanation of Human Sexuality

65. evolutionary psychologists

66. natural selection; survival; reproduction

67. health; fertility

68. mature, dominant, bold, wealthy

69. fertile females; larger

Evolutionary psychology has been criticized for starting with an effect and working backward, for ignoring the impact of culture, and for implying that because genes are destiny men don't need to take responsibility for their sexual behaviors.

70. adapt; learn

Social Influences on Human Sexuality

71. socially

72. satisfaction; stability

Reflections on the Nature and Nurture of Sex, Gender, and Sexuality

73. nature; nurture; open

Progress Test

Multiple-Choice Questions

1. c. is the answer.

2. a. is the answer.
b., c., & d. Natural selection favors traits that send one's genes into the future, such as surviving longer and reproducing more often. Aggression, power, and connectedness do not necessarily promote either.

3. d. is the answer. Such gender differences characterize both heterosexual and homosexual people.

4. b. is the answer. Most women incubate and nurse only one infant at a time.
c. & d. The text does not suggest that there is a gender difference in the strength of the sex drive.

5. b. is the answer.
a. According to this perspective, women prefer mates with the potential for long-term nurturing investment in their joint offspring.
c. Men are drawn to women who suggest fertility, which is not necessarily a slender body.
d. Excitement was not mentioned as a criterion for mating.

6. a. is the answer.
b. This definition is incomplete.
c. This defines gender identity.
d. This defines gender typing.

7. b. is the answer.
a. In this case, a female would develop.
c. & d. The egg can contribute only an X chromosome. Thus, the sex of the child is determined by which chromosome the sperm contributes.

8. d. is the answer.
a. This is gender-typed.
b. This is an intersex person.
c. This is a transgender person.

9. d. is the answer.
a. Although testosterone is the principal male hormone, it is present in both females and males.
b. This is determined by the sex chromosomes.
c. In the absence of testosterone, female sex organs will develop.

10. c. is the answer.
b. & d. Each cell of the human body contains hundreds of genes.

11. d. is the answer.

12. c. is the answer.
b. & d. There is no evidence that being raised in a "gender neutral" home confuses children or fosters a backlash of excessive gender typing.

13. **b.** is the answer.

14. **c.** is the answer. Research studies suggest that women's sexual orientation is potentially more fluid and changeable than men's.

15. **a.** is the answer.

    c. & d. Surgically removing the testes, which produce testosterone, does not alter estrogen levels.

16. **b.** is the answer. A fetus (either male or female) exposed to typical female hormone levels during this period may be attracted to males in later life.

17. **d.** is the answer. Researchers have not been able to find any clear differences, psychological or otherwise, between homosexuals and heterosexuals. Thus, the basis for sexual orientation remains unknown, although recent evidence points more to a biological basis.

18. **c.** is the answer.

19. **d.** is the answer. During the resolution phase males experience a refractory period.

    a., b., & c. The male and female responses are very similar in each of these phases.

20. **b.** is the answer.

21. **b.** is the answer.

22. **c.** is the answer.
    a., b., & d. None of these is linked to homosexuality.

23. **d.** is the answer.

24. **d.** is the answer.

25. **a.** is the answer.

26. **b.** is the answer.
    a., c., & d. These are examples of aggression, but not relational aggression, which is intended to harm a person's social standing or relationships with others.

27. **a.** is the answer.
    b. This describes someone who is asexual.
    c. This describes androgyny.
    d. This describes someone who is transgender.

28. **b.** is the answer.

Application Essay

Evolutionary psychologists would not be surprised by the tension between Lakia and Jerome and would see it as a reflection of women's and men's differing approaches to sex. Women prefer mates who will be committed to caring for their joint offspring. According to this perspective, this may be why Lakia is not in a hurry to become sexually intimate with Jerome. Men, on the other hand, are selected for behaving in a way that will maximize the spreading of their genes. This is especially true of men like Jerome, who have traditional masculine attitudes.

Summing Up

Belle and Bruno are an average female and male. Compared with Bruno, Belle expresses *emotions* more freely and can detect fainter *odors*, begins puberty about *one*

year earlier, and is expected to outlive him by about 5 years.

Psychologically, Belle and Bruno are different in several ways: Belle is more vulnerable to *depression, anxiety,* and *eating disorders.* Bruno is more likely to commit suicide, to develop *alcohol use disorder,* and to have *ADHD* as a child.

In terms of social power, Belle is more likely to express *support,* make less *eye* contact, and lead *democratically,* while Bruno is more likely to *dominate,* to be more *directive,* and to talk *assertively.*

In terms of social connectedness, Belle is more concerned with *relationships,* with making connections, and less concerned with viewing herself as a separate *individual.* This is seen early in their play: Bruno plays in *larger* groups, while Belle plays in *smaller* groups.

Terms and Concepts to Remember

1. In psychology, **sex** is the biologically influenced characteristics by which people define *male* and *female.*

2. In psychology, **gender** refers to the socially influenced characteristics by which people define *male* and *female.*

3. **Aggression** is any act intended to hurt someone physically or emotionally.

4. **Relational aggression** is physical or verbal aggression intended to harm a person's relationship or social standing.

5. The **X chromosome** is the sex chromosome found in both men and women. Females inherit an X chromosome from each parent.

6. The **Y chromosome** is the sex chromosome found only in men. Males inherit an X chromosome from their mothers and a Y chromosome from their fathers.

7. **Testosterone** is the principal male sex hormone. During prenatal development, testosterone stimulates the development of the external male sex organs.

8. **Puberty** is the period of sexual maturation during which sexual reproduction becomes possible.

9. **Primary sex characteristics** refer to the bodily structures that make sexual reproduction possible.

10. **Secondary sex characteristics** are the nonreproductive sexual traits, such as female breasts and male body hair.

11. **Spermarche** is the first ejaculation.

12. **Menarche** is the first menstrual period.

13. **Intersex** refers to the condition of possessing biological sexual characteristics of both sexes.

14. A **role** is a cluster of prescribed behaviors expected of those who occupy a particular social position.

15. A **gender role** is a set of expected behaviors for males or for females.

16. **Gender identity** is our sense of being male or female.

17. According to **social learning theory**, people learn social behavior (such as gender roles) by observing and imitating and by being rewarded or punished.

18. **Gender typing** is the acquisition of a traditional feminine or masculine role.

19. **Androgyny** refers to the display of both traditional masculine and feminine psychological characteristics.

20. **Transgender** describes people whose gender identity or expression differs from that of their birth sex.

21. **Asexual** is the absence of sexual attraction to others.

22. **Estrogens** are sex hormones secreted in greater amounts by females than by males. In mammals other than humans, estrogen levels peak during ovulation and trigger sexual receptivity.

23. The **sexual response cycle** described by Masters and Johnson consists of four stages of bodily reaction: excitement, plateau, orgasm, and resolution.

24. The **refractory period** is a resting period after orgasm, during which a male cannot be aroused to another orgasm.

25. **Sexual dysfunctions** are problems that consistently impair sexual arousal or functioning.

26. **Erectile disorder** is the inability to develop or maintain an erection due to insufficient bloodflow to the penis.

27. **Female orgasmic disorder** is distress over having infrequent or no orgasms.

28. **AIDS (acquired immune deficiency syndrome)** is the life-threatening, sexually transmitted infection caused by the *human immunodeficiency virus* (HIV).

29. A **social script** is a culturally influenced guide for how to act in different situations.

30. **Sexual orientation** refers to an enduring attraction to members of one's own sex, the other sex, or both sexes.

31. **Evolutionary psychology** is the study of how our behavior and mind have changed in adaptive ways over time due to natural selection.

32. **Natural selection** is the principle that, among the range of inherited trait variations, those that lead to increased reproduction and survival will most likely be passed on to succeeding generations.

Sensation and Perception

5

Chapter Overview

Chapter 5 explores the processes by which our sense receptors and nervous system represent our external environment (sensation), as well as how we mentally organize and interpret this information (perception). The senses of vision, hearing, taste, touch, smell, and body position and movement are described, along with the ways in which we organize the stimuli reaching these senses to perceive form; depth; and constant color, shape, and size. To enhance your understanding of these processes, the chapter also discusses research findings from studies of subliminal stimulation, sensory restriction, recovery from blindness, adaptation to distorted environments, perceptual set, and extrasensory perception.

Chapter Review

First, skim each section, noting headings and boldface items. After you have read the section, review each objective by answering the fill-in and essay-type questions that follow it. STUDY TIPS explain how best to learn a difficult concept and APPLICATIONS help you to know how well you understand the material. As you proceed, evaluate your performance by consulting the answers beginning on page 103. Do not continue with the next section until you understand each answer. If you need to, review or reread the section in the textbook before continuing.

Basic Concepts of Sensation and Perception

Objective 5-1: Define *sensation* and *perception,* and explain what we mean by *bottom-up processing* and *top-down processing.*

Sensation is the process by which we take in stimulus energy from our environment. **Perception** is the process by which our brain organizes and interprets sensory information, enabling us to recognize meaningful objects and events.

1. The perceptual disorder in which a person has lost the ability to recognize familiar faces is

    _____ .

2. The process by which our sensory receptors and nervous system receive and represent stimulus energies from the environment and transmit them to our brain is _____ . The process by which our brain organizes and interprets sensory information is _____ .

3. Sensory analysis, which starts at the entry level and works up, is called _____-

    _____ _____ .

    Perceptual analysis, which works from our experience and expectations, is called

    _____-_____

    _____ .

STUDY TIP: An excellent way to study all the technical material in this chapter is to organize it into a chart. For each sense you need to know several facts, including the nature of the stimulus input, the type of receptor that transmits the stimulus energy, and how the information is processed in the brain. To help you review your understanding of sensation and perception, refer often to the summary chart on the next page.

Sense	Stimulus Input	Receptors	Notes
Vision	Visible electromagnetic energy	Rods and cones	Wavelength = hue; intensity = brightness; rods = black and white; cones = color
Hearing	Sound waves of moving air molecules	Hair cells in the cochlea	Wavelength = pitch; amplitude = loudness
Touch	Pressure, warmth, cold, pain	Specialized nerve endings	Cold + pressure = wetness; side-by-side pressure = tickle
Pain	No one type of stimulus	No special receptors (nociceptors)	Natural endorphins relieve pain; hypnosis used for treating pain
Taste	Chemical molecules corresponding to sweet, salty, sour, bitter, and umami	Hair cells in the taste pores	Sensory interaction: smell influences; taste; smell + texture = taste = flavor
Smell	Airborne chemical molecules	Olfactory receptor cells in the nasal cavity	The brain's circuitry for smell connects with areas involved in memory storage
Position and movement	Changes in body's position (kinesthesia) Changes in the head's (and thus the body's position (vestibular sense)	Sensors in muscles, tendons, and joints Hair-like receptors in the ear's semicircular canals and vestibular sacs of the inner ear	Millions of position and motion sensors Messages sent to the brain's cerebellum

APPLICATIONS:

4. Sensation is to _____ as perception is to_____ .

   a. recognizing a stimulus; interpreting a stimulus
   b. detecting a stimulus; recognizing a stimulus
   c. interpreting a stimulus; detecting a stimulus
   d. seeing; hearing

5. Superman's eyes used _____ , while his brain used _____ .

   a. perception; sensation
   b. top-down processing; bottom-up processing
   c. bottom-up processing; top-down processing

6. Concluding her presentation on sensation and perception, Kelly notes that

   a. perception is bottom-up processing.
   b. sensation is top-down processing.
   c. without sensation there is no perception.
   d. sensation and perception blend into one continuous process.

Objective 5-2: Identify the three steps that are basic to all our sensory systems.

All sensory systems must receive stimulation, transform it into neural impulses (called *transduction*), and deliver the information to our brain.

7. All our senses perform three basic steps; they _____ sensory information, _____ that stimulation into neural impulses that our brain can use, and _____ that neural information to our brain.

8. The process of converting one form of energy into another that your brain can use is called _____ .

Objective 5-3: Distinguish between *absolute thresholds* and *difference thresholds,* and explain Weber's law.

An **absolute threshold** is the minimum stimulation needed to detect a particular stimulus 50 percent of the time. Stimuli you cannot detect 50 percent of the time are **subliminal**, that is, below your absolute threshold.

   A **difference threshold** is the minimum difference between two stimuli that a person can detect 50 percent of the time (a *just noticeable difference [jnd]*). In humans, the stimuli must differ by a constant minimum proportion, not a constant amount. This principle is known as *Weber's law.*

9. The _____ _____ refers to the minimum stimulation necessary for a stimulus to be detected _____ percent of the time.

10. Stimuli you cannot detect 50 percent of the time are "below threshold," or _____ .

11. The minimum difference required to distinguish two stimuli 50 percent of the time is called the

    _____ _____ .

    Another term for this value is the

    _____ _____

    _____ .

12. The principle that the difference threshold is not a constant amount, but a constant minimum percentage, is known as _____

    _____ .The proportion depends on the _____ .

STUDY TIP: The concept of threshold can be confusing. Since you can count on at least one exam question on this topic, be sure you understand the concept: "Below threshold" means the stimulus is undetectable; "above threshold" means the stimulus is strong enough to be detected.

APPLICATIONS:

13. While you are outside with your friends, you see a dog that appears to be howling but you can't hear any sound coming from the dog. The dog's howling is below your _____ _____ .

14. In shopping for a new stereo, you discover that you cannot differentiate between the sounds of models X and Y. The difference between X and Y is below your
    a. absolute threshold.
    b. subliminal threshold.
    c. receptor threshold.
    d. difference threshold.

Objective 5-4: Discuss how we are affected by subliminal stimuli.

Although we can be affected by subliminal stimuli some of the time, advertising claims of subliminal persuasion are not true. Researchers use *priming* to activate unconscious associations. The effect of subliminal stimuli is subtle and fleeting, with no powerful enduring influence on behavior.

15. Under certain conditions, an invisible image or word can _____ a person's response to a later question. This illustrates that much of our information processing occurs outside _____ awareness. This is another illustration of our _____-_____ mind.

16. Research indicated that we cannot be _____ by subliminal stimuli. These stimuli _____ (did/did not) have powerful, enduring influences.

17. Subliminal recordings to lose weight or stop smoking, for example, did not help more than a _____ .

Objective 5-5: Explain the function of sensory adaptation.

Sensory adaptation refers to the diminished sensitivity that is a consequence of constant stimulation. Constant, unchanging images on the eye's inner surface fade and then reappear. The phenomenon of sensory adaptation enables us to focus our attention on informative changes in our environment without being distracted by the uninformative, constant stimulation of garments, odors, and street noise, for example.

18. After constant exposure to an unchanging stimulus, the receptor cells of our senses begin to fire less vigorously; this phenomenon is called _____ _____ .

19. This phenomenon illustrates that sensation is designed to focus on _____ changes in the environment.

APPLICATION:

20. Calvin usually runs his fingertips over a cloth's surface when trying to decide whether the texture is right for what he wants. By moving his fingers over the cloth, he prevents the occurrence of _____ _____ to the feel.

Objective 5-6: Explain how our expectations, contexts, motivations, and emotions influence our perceptions.

Clear evidence that perception is influenced by our experiences—our learned assumptions and beliefs—as well as by sensory input comes from the many demonstrations of *perceptual set,* a mental predisposition to perceive one thing and not another. Perceptual set can influence what we hear, taste, feel, and see.
   A given stimulus may trigger radically different perceptions because of the immediate context. Motivation and emotion also influence our perceptions.

21. A mental predisposition to perceive one thing and not another is called a _____ _____ .

22. How a stimulus is perceived depends on our perceptual _____ and the _____ in which it is experienced.

23. The context of a stimulus creates a _____ (top-down/bottom-up) expectation that influences our perception as we match our _____ (top-down/bottom-up) signal against it.

24. Our perceptions are also influenced, top-down, by our _____ . For example, a water bottle appears closer if we are _____ . _____ can similarly shove our _____ in one direction or another.

APPLICATION:

25. Although carpenter Smith perceived a briefly viewed object as a screwdriver, police officer Wesson perceived the same object as a knife. This illustrates that perception is guided by
    a. bottom-up processing.   c. transduction.
    b. sensory adaptation.   d. perceptual set.

Vision: Sensory and Perceptual Processing

Objective 5-7: Identify the characteristics of the energy we see as visible light, and describe the structures in the eye that help focus that energy.

The energies we experience as visible light are a thin slice from the wide spectrum of electromagnetic energy. Our sensory experience of light is determined largely by the light energy's *wavelength,* which determines the **hue** of a color (and the *pitch* of sound), and its **intensity** (determined by a wave's *amplitude,* or height), which influences *brightness* (and *loudness* in sound).

After light enters the eye through the *pupil,* whose size is regulated by the *iris,* the *lens* focuses the rays by changing its curvature. The light-sensitive surface of the **retina** contains receptors that begin the processing of visual information.

26. The visible spectrum of light is a small portion of the wide spectrum of _____ energy.

27. The distance from one light wave peak to the next is called _____ . This value determines the wave's color, or _____ . The amount of energy in light waves, or _____ , determined by a wave's _____ , or height, influences the _____ of a light.

28. Light enters the eye through the _____ , then passes through a small opening called the _____ ; the size of this opening is controlled by the colored _____ .

29. The curve and thickness of the _____ change in order to focus the image of an object onto the _____ , the light-sensitive inner surface of the eye.

STUDY TIP/APPLICATION: The stimulus energy for both vision and hearing can be described as a traveling wave that varies in wavelength and amplitude. The wavelength of a visual or auditory stimulus is measured as the distance from the peak of one wave to the next—the shorter the distance, the greater the frequency of the waves. Short, high frequency waves produce "cool" or bluish colors for visual stimuli. They produce high-pitched sounds for auditory stimuli. Long, low frequency waves produce "warm" or reddish colors and low-pitched sounds.

The wave's amplitude is measured as the distance from the top of its peak to the bottom. High amplitude waves produce bright colors and loud sounds, while low amplitude waves produce dull colors and soft sounds.

To test your understanding, take a look at the two waves at the top of the next column.

30. **a.** Assuming that these two waves were light energy, would they differ in appearance? How so?

   b. Assuming that these two waves were sound energy, would they sound the same? If not, how would they differ?

APPLICATION:

31. In comparing the human eye to a camera, the film would be located in the eye's
   a. pupil.   **c.** cornea.
   b. lens.   **d.** retina.

Objective 5-8: Explain how the rods and cones process information, and describe the path information takes from the eye to the brain..

The light energy triggers chemical changes in the retina's **rods** and **cones** (most of which are clustered around the *fovea,* the retina's area of central focus). That chemical reaction sparks neural signals in the nearby bipolar cells, which in turn activate neighboring *ganglion* cells, whose axons converge to form the **optic nerve** that carries information to the brain's *thalamus,* which distributes it to higher-level regions. Where the optic nerve leaves the eye, there are no receptor cells—creating a **blind spot**. The cones enable vision of color and fine detail. The rods enable black-and-white vision, remain sensitive in dim light, and are necessary for peripheral vision.

32. The retina's receptor cells are the _____ and _____ .

33. Chemical reactions in the rods and cones activate neural signals in the neighboring _____ cells, which then activate a network of _____ cells.

34. The axons of ganglion cells converge to form the _____ _____ , which carries the visual information first to the _____ , and then on to its final destination, the _____ .

35. Where this nerve leaves the eye, there are no receptor cells; thus, the area is called the

_____ _____ .

36. Most cones are clustered around the retina's

_____ , its area of central focus, whereas the rods are concentrated in more

_____ regions of the retina. Many cones have their own hotline to communicate with the visual cortex. Rods _____ (do/do not) have direct links.

37. It is the _____ (rods/cones) of the eye that permit the perception of color, whereas

_____ (rods/cones) enable black-and-white vision.

38. Unlike cones, in dim light the rods are

_____ (sensitive/insensitive).

APPLICATIONS:

39. To maximize your sensitivity to fine visual detail you should
   a. stare off to one side of the object you are attempting to see.
   b. close one eye.
   c. decrease the intensity of the light falling upon the object.
   d. stare directly at the object.

40. Which of the following is true of cones?
   a. Cones enable color vision.
   b. Cones are highly concentrated in the central region of the retina.
   c. Cones have a higher absolute threshold for brightness than rods.
   d. All of these statements are true.

41. Assuming that the visual systems of humans and other mammals function similarly, you would expect that the retina of a nocturnal mammal (one active only at night) would contain
   a. mostly cones.
   b. mostly rods.
   c. an equal number of rods and cones.
   d. more bipolar cells than an animal active only during the day.

42. As the football game continued into the night, LeVar noticed that he was having difficulty distinguishing the colors of the players' uniforms. This is because the _____ , which enable color vision, have a _____ absolute threshold for brightness than the available light intensity.
   a. rods; higher
   b. cones; higher
   c. rods; lower
   d. cones; lower

Objective 5-9: Describe how we perceive color in the world around us.

The earliest theory of color vision, the **Young-Helmholtz trichromatic (three-color) theory** states that the retina has three types of color receptors, each type especially sensitive to the wavelengths of one of three colors: red, green, and blue. When light stimulates combinations of these cones, we see other colors. Ewald Hering noted that the trichromatic theory leaves some parts of the color vision mystery unsolved. Based on his knowledge of *afterimages*, Hering proposed the **opponent-process theory** that color vision depends on three pairs of opponent retinal processes—red-green, yellow-blue, and white-black. Current understanding is that color vision occurs in two stages, first as Young and Helmholtz predicted and second as Hering proposed.

43. An object appears to be red in color because it _____ the long wavelengths of red and because of our mental _____ of the color.

44. One out of every 50 people has color-deficient vision; this is usually a male because the defect is genetically _____ _____ .

45. According to the _____ - _____ _____ theory, the eyes have three types of color receptors: one reacts most strongly to _____ , one to _____ , and one to _____ .

46. After staring at a green square for a while and then looking at a white sheet of paper, you will see the color red, its _____ color, as an _____ .

47. Hering's theory of color vision is called the _____ - _____ theory. According to this theory, after visual information leaves the receptors it is analyzed in terms of pairs of opposing colors: _____ versus _____ , _____ versus _____ , and _____ versus _____ .

Summarize the two stages of color processing.

APPLICATIONS:

48. I am a cell in the thalamus that is excited by red and inhibited by green. I am a(n)
    a. ganglion cell.
    b. cone.
    c. bipolar cell.
    d. opponent-process cell.

49. After staring at a very intense red stimulus for a few minutes, Carrie shifted her gaze to a beige wall and "saw" the color _____ . Carrie's experience provides support for the _____ theory.
    a. green; trichromatic
    b. blue; opponent-process
    c. green; opponent-process
    d. blue; trichromatic

Objective 5-10: Define *feature detectors,* and describe what they do.

In the cortex, individual neurons (**feature detectors**) respond to specific features of a visual stimulus— to particular edges, lines, angles, and movements. These cells pass this information along to other areas of the cortex, where teams of cells *(supercell clusters)* respond to more complex patterns, such as recognizing faces.

50. Hubel and Wiesel discovered that the neurons in the brain respond only to specific features of what is viewed. Because they respond only to particular _____ , _____ , and _____ , they called these neurons _____ _____ . These neurons pass their information to other cortical areas, where teams of cells, called _____ _____ , respond to complex patterns.

51. One brain area in the _____ _____ enables you to perceive faces and to recognize them from many viewpoints.

Objective 5-11: Explain how the brain uses parallel processing to construct visual perceptions.

Aspects of vision (color, movement, depth, and form) are processed by neural teams working separately and simultaneously, illustrating our brain's capacity for *parallel processing.* Our perceptions result from the integration of these teams working together.

52. The brain achieves its remarkable speed in visual perception by processing several subdivisions of a stimulus _____ (simultaneously/sequentially). This procedure, called _____ _____ ,

may explain why people who have suffered a stroke may lose just one aspect of vision.

Objective 5-12: Identify the main message of Gestalt psychology, and explain how figure-ground and grouping principles help us perceive forms.

Gestalt psychologists described principles by which we organize our sensations into perceptions. They provided many compelling demonstrations of how, given a cluster of sensations, the human perceiver organizes them into a *gestalt,* a German word meaning a "form" or a "whole." They further demonstrated that *the whole may exceed the sum of its parts.* Clearly, our brains do more than merely register information about the world. We are always filtering sensory information and constructing perceptions.

Our first task in perception is to perceive any object, called the *figure,* as distinct from its surroundings, called the *ground.* We must also organize the figure into a meaningful form. Gestalt principles for **grouping** that describe this process include *proximity* (we group nearby figures together), *continuity* (we perceive smooth, continuous patterns rather than discontinuous ones), and *closure* (we fill in gaps to create a whole object).

53. According to the _____ school of psychology, we tend to organize a cluster of sensations into a _____ , or form.

54. When we view a scene, we see the central object, or _____ , as distinct from surrounding stimuli, or the _____ .

55. Proximity, continuity, and closure are examples of Gestalt rules of _____ .

56. The principle that we organize stimuli into smooth, continuous patterns is called _____ . The principle that we fill in gaps to create a complete, whole object is _____ . The grouping of items that are close to each other is the principle of _____ .

APPLICATION:

57. Studying the road map before her trip, Colleen had no trouble following the route of the highway she planned to travel. Colleen's ability illustrates the principle of
    a. closure.
    b. figure-ground.
    c. continuity.
    d. proximity.

Objective 5-13: Explain how we use binocular and monocular cues to perceive the world in three dimensions, and describe how we perceive motion.

Depth perception is the ability to see objects in three dimensions although the images that strike the eye are two dimensional. Depth perception enables us to judge distance. Research on the **visual cliff** (a small cliff with a drop-off covered by sturdy glass) reveals that depth perception is partly innate. Many species perceive the world in three dimensions at, or very soon after, birth.

Binocular cues require information from both eyes. In the **retinal disparity** cue, the brain computes the relative distance of an object by comparing the slightly different images an object casts on our two retinas. The greater the difference, the greater the distance.

Monocular cues enable us to judge depth using information from only one eye. The monocular cues include *relative size* (the smaller image of two objects of the same size appears more distant), *interposition* (nearby objects partially obstruct our view of more distant objects), *relative height* (higher objects are farther away), *relative motion* (as we move, objects at different distances change their relative positions in our visual image, with those closest moving most), *linear perspective* (the converging of parallel lines indicates greater distance), and *light and shadow* (dimmer objects seem more distant).

Normally, the brain computes motion based partly on its assumption that shrinking objects are moving away (not getting smaller) and enlarging objects are approaching. Sometimes, the brain is tricked. When large and small objects move at the same speed, the large objects appear to move more slowly

58. The ability to see objects in three dimensions despite their two-dimensional representations on our retinas is called _____ _____ . It enables us to estimate _____ .

59. Gibson and Walk developed the _____ _____ to test depth perception in infants. They found that each species, by the time it is _____ , has the perceptual abilities it needs.

Summarize the results of Gibson and Walk's studies of depth perception.

For questions 60–68, identify the depth perception cue that is defined.

60. Any cue that requires both eyes: _____ .

61. The greater the difference between the images received by the two eyes, the nearer the object: _____ _____ .

3-D movies simulate this cue by photographing each scene with two cameras.

62. Any cue that requires either eye alone: _____ .

63. If two objects are presumed to be the same size, the one that casts a smaller retinal image is perceived as farther away: _____ _____ .

64. An object partially covered by another is seen as farther away: _____ .

65. Objects lower in the visual field are seen as nearer: _____ _____ .

66. As we move, objects at different distances appear to move at different rates: _____ _____ .

67. Parallel lines appear to converge in the distance: _____ _____ .

68. The dimmer of two objects seems farther away: _____ _____ _____ .

69. Partly assuming that shrinking objects are moving _____ (away/closer) and enlarging objects are moving _____ (away/closer) enables the brain to compute _____ .

STUDY TIP: Monocular depth cues are used by either eye alone to determine the distance of objects. They include relative height, size, and motion; interposition; linear perspective; and light and shadow.

70. Test your understanding of these cues by drawing a picture (in the box below) of a person on a bus or train, a fence, a house, and trees. Use each cue at least once, and in your drawing place the objects in the following order (closest to most distant): person, fence, house, and trees.

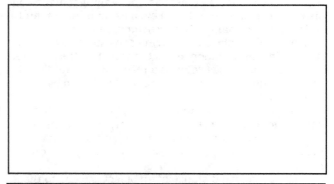

APPLICATIONS:

71. When two familiar objects of equal size cast unequal retinal images, the object that casts the smaller retinal image will be perceived as being
    a. closer than the other object.
    b. more distant than the other object.
    c. larger than the other object.
    d. smaller than the other object.

72. As her friend Milo walks toward her, Noriko perceives his size as remaining constant because his perceived distance _____ at the same time that her retinal image of him _____ .
    a. increases; decreases
    b. increases; increases
    c. decreases; decreases
    d. decreases; increases

73. How do we perceive a pole that partially covers a wall?
    a. as farther away
    b. as nearer
    c. as larger
    d. There is not enough information to determine the object's size or distance.

74. An artist paints a tree orchard so that the parallel rows of trees converge at the top of the canvas. Which cue has the artist used to convey distance?
    a. interposition
    b. retinal disparity
    c. linear perspective
    d. figure-ground

75. Objects higher in our field of vision are perceived as _____ due to the principle of _____ .
    a. nearer; relative height
    b. nearer; linear perspective
    c. farther away; relative height
    d. farther away; linear perspective

Objective 5-14: Explain how perceptual constancies help us construct meaningful perceptions.

Perceptual constancy is necessary to recognize an object. It enables us to see an object as unchanging (having consistent color, shape, and size) even as illumination and retinal images change. *Color constancy* refers to our perceiving familiar objects as having consistent color, even if changing illumination alters the wavelengths reflected by the object. We see color as a result of our brain's ability to decode the meaning of the light reflected by any object relative to its *context*.

Shape constancy is our ability to perceive familiar objects (for example, an opening door) as unchanging in shape. *Size constancy* is perceiving objects as unchanging in size, despite the changing images they cast on our retinas.

The perceived distance of an object is a cue to the object's size. The perceived relationship between distance and size is generally valid but under special cir-

cumstances can lead us astray. For example, one reason for the *Moon illusion* is that cues to objects' distances at the horizon make the Moon behind them seem farther away. Thus, the Moon on the horizon seems larger.

76. Our tendency to see objects as unchanging while the stimuli from them change in size, shape, and color is a _____-_____ process called _____ _____ .

77. The experience of color depends on the surrounding _____ in which an object is seen. In an unvarying context, a familiar object will be perceived as having consistent color, even as the illumination changes. This phenomenon is called _____ _____ .

78. We see color as a result of our brains' computations of the light _____ by any object relative to its _____ .

79. Due to shape and size constancy, familiar objects _____ (do/do not) appear to change shape or size despite changes in our _____ images of them.

80. Several illusions, including the _____ illusion, are explained by the interplay between perceived _____ and perceived _____ . When distance cues are removed, these illusions are _____ (diminished/strengthened).

APPLICATIONS:

81. In the absence of perceptual constancy
    a. objects would appear to change size as their distance from us changed.
    b. depth perception would be based exclusively on monocular cues.
    c. depth perception would be based exclusively on binocular cues.
    d. depth perception would be impossible.

82. Your friend tosses you a Frisbee. You know that it is getting closer instead of larger because of
    a. shape constancy.
    b. relative motion.
    c. size constancy.
    d. all of these factors.

Objective 5-15: Describe what research on restored vision, sensory restriction, and perceptual adaptation reveals about the effects of experience on perception.

In the classic version of the nature–nurture debate, the German philosopher Immanuel Kant maintained that knowledge comes from our innate ways of organizing sensory experiences. On the other side, the British philosopher John Locke argued that we learn to perceive the world through our experiences of it. It's now clear that different aspects of perception depend more or less on both nature and nurture.

When cataracts are removed from adults who have been blind from birth, these people remain unable to perceive the world normally. Generally, they can distinguish figure from ground and sense colors, but they are unable to visually recognize objects that were familiar by touch. In controlled experiments, kittens and infant monkeys have been raised with severely restricted visual input. When their visual exposure is returned to normal, they, too, suffer enduring visual handicaps.

Human perception is remarkably **adaptable.** Given glasses that shift the world slightly to the left or right, or even turn it upside down, people manage to adapt their movements and, with practice, to move about with ease.

83. The idea that knowledge comes from inborn ways of organizing sensory experiences was proposed by the German philosopher _____ . On the other side were philosophers who maintained that we learn to perceive the world by experiencing it. One British philosopher of this school was

_____ .

84. Studies of cases in which vision has been restored to a person who was blind from birth show that, upon seeing tactilely familiar objects for the first time, the person _____ (can/cannot) recognize them.

85. Studies of sensory restriction demonstrate that visual experiences during infancy are crucial for perceptual development. Such experiences suggest that there is a _____ _____ for normal sensory and perceptual development.

86. Humans given glasses that shift or invert the visual field _____ (will/will not) adapt to the distorted perception. This is called

_____ _____ .

Animals such as baby chicks _____ (adapt/do not adapt) to distorting lenses.

The Nonvisual Senses

Objective 5-16: Describe the characteristics of the air pressure waves that we hear as sound.

Audition, or hearing, is highly adaptive. The pressure waves we experience as sound vary in *amplitude* and *frequency* and correspondingly in perceived *loudness* and *pitch*. *Decibels* are the measuring unit for sound energy.

87. The stimulus for hearing, or _____ , is sound waves, created by the compression and expansion of _____

_____ .

88. The height, or amplitude, of a sound wave determines the sound's _____ .

89. The length, or frequency, of a sound wave determines the _____ we perceive.

90. Sound energy is measured in units called _____ , with _____ such units representing the lowest level detectable by human ears.

Objective 5-17: Explain how the ear transforms sound energy into neural messages.

Sound waves entering your *outer ear* are channeled through the *auditory canal* to the *eardrum,* a tight membrane that vibrates with the waves. Transmitted via the three tiny bones of the **middle ear** (the *hammer, anvil,* and *stirrup*) to the fluid-filled **cochlea** in the **inner ear,** these vibrations cause the *oval window* to vibrate, causing ripples that bend the *hair cells* lining the *basilar membrane*. This movement triggers impulses in nerve cells, whose axons combine to form the *auditory nerve*. These neural messages are sent (via the thalamus) to the *auditory cortex* in the brain's temporal lobe.

Damage to the hair cells or their associated nerves, called **sensorineural hearing loss** (or nerve deafness), accounts for most hearing loss. Problems with the mechanical system that conducts sound waves to the cochlea cause **conduction hearing loss.** Nerve deafness cannot be reversed. For now, the only way to restore hearing is a sort of bionic ear—a **cochlear implant.**

Sound waves strike one ear sooner and more intensely than the other ear. We localize sounds by detecting the minute differences in the intensity and timing of the sounds received by each ear.

91. The ear is divided into three main parts: the _____ ear, the _____ ear, and the _____ ear.

92. The outer ear channels sound waves toward the _____ , a tight membrane that then vibrates.

93. The middle ear transmits the vibrations through three small bones: the _____ , _____ , and _____ .

94. In the inner ear, a coiled, bony, fluid-filled tube called the _____ contains the receptor cells for hearing. The incoming vibrations

cause the _____

_____ to vibrate the fluid that fills
the tube, which causes ripples in the _____

_____ _____ ,
bending the _____ _____ that line
its surface. This movement triggers impulses in the
adjacent nerve cells. Axons of those cells converge
to form the auditory nerve, which carries the neural
messages (via the _____) to the
_____ lobe's auditory cortex.

95. Damage to the cochlea's hair cell receptors or their
associated auditory nerves can cause
_____ hearing loss. It may be
caused by disease, but more often it results from the
biological changes linked with heredity,
_____ , and prolonged exposure
to ear-splitting noise or music.

96. Problems in the mechanical system that conducts
sound waves to the cochlea may cause

_____ _____

_____ .

97. An electronic device that restores hearing among
nerve-deafened people is a _____

_____ .

98. We locate a sound by sensing differences in the
_____ and _____
with which it reaches our ears.

99. A sound that comes from directly ahead will be _
_____ (easier/harder) to locate
than a sound that comes from off to one side.

APPLICATIONS:

100. Which of the following correctly lists the order of structures through which sound travels after entering the
ear?
a. auditory canal, eardrum, middle ear, cochlea
b. eardrum, auditory canal, middle ear, cochlea
c. eardrum, middle ear, cochlea, auditory canal
d. cochlea, eardrum, middle ear, auditory canal

101. Dr. Frankenstein has forgotten to give his monster an
important part; as a result, the monster cannot transform
sound. Dr. Frankenstein omitted the
a. eardrum.
b. middle ear.
c. semicircular canals.
d. basilar membrane.

Objective 5-18: Name the four basic touch sensations,
and describe how we sense touch.

Our sense of touch is actually four senses—pressure,
warmth, cold, and pain—that combine to produce other
sensations, such as "hot." There is no simple relationship between what we feel and the type of specialized
nerve ending found there.

102. The sense of touch is a mixture of at least four
senses: _____ ,
_____ , _____ ,
and _____ . Other skin
sensations, such as tickle, itch, hot, and wetness,
are _____ of the basic ones.

Objective 5-19: Describe the biological, psychological,
and social-cultural influences that affect our experience
of pain, and explain how placebos, distraction, and hypnosis help control pain.

Pain is our body's way of telling us something is wrong.
Pain experiences vary greatly, depending on our physiology, our experiences and attention, and our culture. No
one type of stimulus triggers pain, and there are no special receptors for pain. At low intensities, the stimuli that
produce pain cause other sensations, including warmth
or coolness, smoothness or roughness.
    We have some built-in pain controls, the *endorphins.*
Other pain controls involve distraction, the tendency to
remember only the pain we felt at the end of a procedure, and **hypnosis.**

103. People born without the ability to feel pain may be
unaware of experiencing severe
_____ . More numerous are
those who live with _____ pain
in the form of persistent headaches and backaches,
for example.

104. Our feeling of pain reflects both _____
sensations and _____ cognition.

105. The pain system _____ (is/is
not) triggered by one specific type of physical
energy. The body _____ (does/
does not) have specialized receptor cells for pain.
Instead, different sensory receptors
(_____) in your skin detect
hurtful temperatures, pressure, or chemicals.

106. Pain is a _____ event. It is a
property of our _____
and our _____
_____ , as well as a product
of our _____ , _____ ,
and _____ .

107. A sensation of pain in an amputated leg is referred to as a _____ _____ sensation, illustrating that pain is mostly a function of our brain. Our brain-pain connection is also made clear by our _____ of pain, which are based on peak and end moments of pain.

108. In response to severe pain or even vigorous exercise, our body produces its own natural painkillers, the _____ . When combined with _____ , pain may go unnoticed for a time. Even _____ can help, by dampening the central nervous system's attention and responses to painful experiences.

109. One technique that has proved useful in relieving pain is _____ . One theory of how this works is that it is a form of normal _____ influences. Another theory is that it produces a split, or _____ , between normal sensations and _____ . During a hypnosis session, a clinician may give the subject a _____ _____ to be carried out after the subject is no longer hypnotized.

APPLICATIONS:

110. The phantom limb sensation indicates that
  a. pain is a purely sensory phenomenon.
  b. the central nervous system plays only a minor role in the experience of pain.
  c. pain involves the brain's interpretation of neural activity.
  d. all of these statements are true.

111. How does pain differ from other senses?
  a. It has no special receptors.
  b. It has no single stimulus.
  c. It is influenced by both physical and psychological phenomena.
  d. All of these statements are true.

Objective 5-20: Discuss how our senses of taste and smell are similar and how they differ.

Taste, a chemical sense, is a composite of sweet, sour, salty, bitter, and umami sensations and of the aromas that interact with information from the taste buds. Taste buds on the top and sides of the tongue contain taste receptor cells, which send information to an area of the temporal lobe.

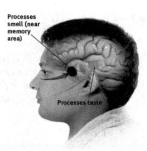

Smell is also a chemical sense, but without any basic sensations. The 20 million olfactory receptor cells recognize individual odor molecules, with some odors triggering a combination of receptors. The receptor cells send messages to the olfactory lobe. An odor's ability to spontaneously evoke memories is due in part to the close connections between brain areas that process smell and those involved in memory storage.

112. The basic taste sensations are _____ , _____ , _____ , _____ , and a meaty taste called _____ .

113. Taste, which is a _____ sense, is enabled by the 200 or more _____ on the top and sides of the tongue. Each contains a _____ with antenna-like hairs that detect information about molecules of food chemicals and carry it back to your _____ _____ .

114. Taste receptors reproduce themselves every _____ . As we age, the number of taste buds _____ (increases/decreases/remains unchanged) and our taste sensitivity _____ (increases/decreases/remains unchanged). Taste is also affected by _____ and by _____ use, and by our _____ .

115. Like taste, smell (or _____) is a _____ sense. There _____ (is/is not) a distinct receptor for each detectable odor.

116. Odors are able to evoke memories and feelings because there is a direct link between the brain area that gets information from the nose and the brain centers associated with memories and _____ .

117. Seventy-year-old Mrs. Martinez finds that she must spice her food heavily or she cannot taste it. Unfortunately, her son often finds her cooking inedible because it is so spicy. What is the likely explanation for their taste differences?
    a. Women have higher taste thresholds than men.
    b. Men have higher taste thresholds than women.
    c. Being 70 years old, Mrs. Martinez probably has fewer taste buds than her son.
    d. All of these are likely explanations.

Objective 5-21: Explain how we sense our body's position and movement.

Kinesthesia is the system for sensing the position and movement of individual body parts. Sensors in the muscles, tendons, and joints are continually providing our brain with information. A companion *vestibular sense* monitors the head's (and thus the body's) position and movement. Controls for this sense of equilibrium are in the inner ear.

118. The system for sensing the position and movement of body parts is called _____ .
    The receptors for this sense are located in the _
    _____ , _____ ,
    and _____ .

119. The sense that monitors the position and movement of the head (and thus the body) is the
    _____ _____ .
    The receptors for this sense are located in the
    _____ _____
    and _____ _____
    of the inner ear.

Sensory Interaction

Objective 5-22: Describe how sensory interaction influences our perceptions, and define embodied cognition.

Sensory interaction refers to the principle that one sense may influence another, as when the smell of food influences its taste. If our senses disagree, our brain may perceive a third sound that blends both inputs.
    The brain circuits processing our bodily sensations may sometimes interact with brain circuits responsible for cognition, with *embodied cognition* as the result.

120. When the sense of smell is blocked, as when we have a cold, foods do not taste the same; this illustrates the principle of _____
    _____ . The _____
    effect occurs when we _____
    a speaker saying one syllable while
    _____ another.

121. The influence of bodily sensations, gestures, and other states on our cognitive preferences and judgments is called _____
    _____ .

122. In a few rare individuals one sensation (such as hearing sound) produces another (such as sensing color). This is called _____ .

123. Which of the following is an example of sensory interaction?
    a. finding that despite its delicious aroma, a weird-looking meal tastes awful
    b. finding that food tastes bland when you have a bad cold
    c. finding it difficult to maintain your balance when you have an ear infection
    d. All of these are examples.

124. Tamiko hates the bitter taste of her cough syrup. Which of the following would she find most helpful in minimizing the syrup's bad taste?
    a. tasting something very sweet before taking the cough syrup
    b. keeping the syrup in her mouth for several seconds before swallowing it
    c. holding her nose while taking the cough syrup
    d. gulping the cough syrup so that it misses her tongue

ESP—Perception Without Sensation?

Objective 5-23: Identify the claims of ESP, and discuss the conclusions of most research psychologists after putting these claims to the test.

Three varieties of *extrasensory perception (ESP)* are *telepathy* (mind-to-mind communication), *clairvoyance* (perceiving remote events), and *precognition* (perceiving future events). Closely linked with these are claims of *psychokinesis,* or "mind over matter."
    Research psychologists remain skeptical because the acts of so-called psychics have typically turned out to be nothing more than the illusions of stage magicians, because checks of psychic visions have been no more accurate than guesses made by others, and because sheer chance guarantees that some stunning coincidences are sure to occur. An important reason for their skepticism, however, is the absence of a reproducible ESP result.

125. Perception outside the range of normal sensation is called _____
    _____ .

126. The form of ESP in which people claim to be capable of reading others' minds is called
    _____ . A person who "senses"

that a friend is in danger might claim to have the ESP ability of _____ .

An ability to "see" into the future is called _____ . A person who claims to be able to levitate and move objects is claiming the power of _____ .

127. Analyses of psychic visions and premonitions reveal _____ (high/chance-level) accuracy. Nevertheless, some people continue to believe in their accuracy because vague predictions often are later _____ to match events that have already occurred. In addition, people are more likely to recall or _____ dreams that seem to have come true.

128. Critics point out that a major difficulty for parapsychology is that ESP phenomena are not consistently _____ .

129. Daryl Bem, who has been skeptical of stage psychics, conducted research in which participants _____ (did/did not) accurately guess the position of an erotic scene.

APPLICATIONS:

130. Regina claims that she can bend spoons, levitate furniture, and perform many other "mind over matter" feats. Regina apparently believes she has the power of
    a. telepathy.
    b. clairvoyance.
    c. precognition.
    d. psychokinesis.

131. Which of the following is true of the predictions of leading psychics?
    a. They are often ambiguous prophecies later interpreted to match actual events.
    b. They are no more accurate than guesses made by others.
    c. They are nearly always inaccurate.
    d. All of these statements are true.

Progress Test

Multiple-Choice Questions

Circle your answers to the following questions and check them with the answers beginning on page 106. If your answer is incorrect, read the explanation for why it is incorrect and then consult the text.

1. Which of the following is true?
    a. The absolute threshold is the same for all stimuli.
    b. The absolute threshold varies depending on the stimulus (sight, sound, or touch, for example).

    c. The absolute threshold is defined as the minimum amount of stimulation necessary for a stimulus to be detected 75 percent of the time.
    d. The absolute threshold is defined as the minimum amount of stimulation necessary for a stimulus to be detected 60 percent of the time.

2. If you can just notice the difference between 10- and 11-pound weights, which of the following weights could you differentiate from a 100-pound weight?
    a. 101-pound weight
    b. 105-pound weight
    c. 110-pound weight
    d. There is no basis for prediction.

3. A decrease in sensory responsiveness accompanying an unchanging stimulus is called
    a. sensory fatigue.   c. sensory adaptation.
    b. feature detection.   d. sensory interaction.

4. The size of the pupil is controlled by the
    a. lens.   c. cornea.
    b. retina.   d. iris.

5. The receptor of the eye that functions best in dim light is the
    a. ganglion cell.   c. bipolar cell.
    b. cone.   d. rod.

6. Frequency is to pitch as _____ is to _____ .
    a. wavelength; loudness
    b. amplitude; loudness
    c. wavelength; intensity
    d. amplitude; intensity

7. Our experience of pain when we are injured depends on
    a. our biological makeup and the type of injury we have sustained.
    b. how well medical personnel deal with our injury.
    c. our senses, expectations and attention, and culture.
    b. what our culture allows us to express in terms of feelings of pain.

8. The transformation of light energy into nerve impulses takes place in the
    a. iris.   c. lens.
    b. retina.   d. optic nerve.

9. The brain breaks vision into separate dimensions such as movement, form, depth, and color, and works on each aspect simultaneously. This is called
    a. feature detection.
    b. parallel processing.
    c. the vestibular sense.
    d. sensory adaptation.

10. Kinesthesia involves
    a. the bones of the middle ear.
    b. information from the muscles, tendons, and joints.
    c. membranes within the cochlea.
    d. the body's sense of balance.

11. One light may appear reddish and another greenish if they differ in
    a. wavelength.   c. opponent processes.
    b. amplitude.   d. brightness.

12. Which of the following explains why a rose appears equally red in bright and dim light?
    a. sensory adaptation
    b. subliminal stimulation
    c. feature detection
    d. color constancy

13. Which of the following is an example of sensory adaptation?
    a. finding the cold water of a swimming pool warmer after you have been in it for a while
    b. developing an increased sensitivity to salt the more you use it in foods
    c. becoming very irritated at the continuing sound of a dripping faucet
    d. All of these are examples.

14. Most color-deficient people will probably
    a. lack functioning red- or green-sensitive cones.
    b. see the world in only black and white.
    c. also suffer from poor vision.
    d. have above-average vision to compensate for the deficit.

15. The historical movement associated with the statement "The whole may exceed the sum of its parts" is
    a. cognitive psychology.
    b. behavioral psychology.
    c. functional psychology.
    d. Gestalt psychology.

16. Figures tend to be perceived as whole, complete objects, even if spaces or gaps exist in the representation, thus demonstrating the principle of
    a. interposition.   c. continuity.
    b. retinal disparity. d. closure.

17. The figure-ground relationship has demonstrated that
    a. perception is largely innate.
    b. perception is simply a point-for-point representation of sensation.
    c. the same stimulus can trigger more than one perception.
    d. different people see different things when viewing a scene.

18. When we stare at an object, each eye receives a slightly different image, providing a depth cue known as
    a. interposition.   c. relative motion.
    b. linear perspective. d. retinal disparity.

19. As we move, viewed objects cast changing shapes on our retinas, although we do not perceive the objects as changing. This is part of the phenomenon of
    a. perceptual constancy.
    b. relative motion.
    c. linear perspective.
    d. continuity.

20. A person claiming to be able to read another's mind is claiming to have the ESP ability of
    a. psychokinesis.   c. clairvoyance.
    b. precognition.   d. telepathy.

21. Which philosopher maintained that knowledge comes from inborn ways of organizing our sensory experiences?
    a. Locke   c. Gibson
    b. Kant   d. Walk

22. Adults who are born blind but later have their vision restored
    a. are almost immediately able to recognize familiar objects.
    b. typically fail to recognize familiar objects.
    c. are unable to follow moving objects with their eyes.
    d. have excellent eye-hand coordination.

23. _____ processing refers to how the physical characteristics of stimuli influence their interpretation.
    a. Top-down   c. Behavioral
    b. Bottom-up   d. Parallel

24. Which of the following is NOT a monocular depth cue?
    a. light and shadow   c. retinal disparity
    b. relative height   d. interposition

25. The Moon illusion occurs in part because distance cues at the horizon make the Moon seem
    a. farther away and therefore larger.
    b. closer and therefore larger.
    c. farther away and therefore smaller.
    d. closer and therefore smaller.

26. Figure is to ground as _____ is to _____ .
    a. night; day   c. cloud; sky
    b. top; bottom   d. sensation; perception

27. The study of perception is primarily concerned with how we
    a. detect sights, sounds, and other stimuli.
    b. sense environmental stimuli.
    c. develop sensitivity to illusions.
    d. interpret sensory stimuli.

that a friend is in danger might claim to have the ESP ability of _____ .
An ability to "see" into the future is called _____ . A person who claims to be able to levitate and move objects is claiming the power of _____ .

127. Analyses of psychic visions and premonitions reveal _____ (high/chance-level) accuracy. Nevertheless, some people continue to believe in their accuracy because vague predictions often are later _____ to match events that have already occurred. In addition, people are more likely to recall or _____ dreams that seem to have come true.

128. Critics point out that a major difficulty for parapsychology is that ESP phenomena are not consistently _____ .

129. Daryl Bem, who has been skeptical of stage psychics, conducted research in which participants _____ (did/did not) accurately guess the position of an erotic scene.

APPLICATIONS:

130. Regina claims that she can bend spoons, levitate furniture, and perform many other "mind over matter" feats. Regina apparently believes she has the power of
    a. telepathy.
    b. clairvoyance.
    c. precognition.
    d. psychokinesis.

131. Which of the following is true of the predictions of leading psychics?
    a. They are often ambiguous prophecies later interpreted to match actual events.
    b. They are no more accurate than guesses made by others.
    c. They are nearly always inaccurate.
    d. All of these statements are true.

Progress Test

Multiple-Choice Questions

Circle your answers to the following questions and check them with the answers beginning on page 106. If your answer is incorrect, read the explanation for why it is incorrect and then consult the text.

1. Which of the following is true?
    a. The absolute threshold is the same for all stimuli.
    b. The absolute threshold varies depending on the stimulus (sight, sound, or touch, for example).
    c. The absolute threshold is defined as the minimum amount of stimulation necessary for a stimulus to be detected 75 percent of the time.
    d. The absolute threshold is defined as the minimum amount of stimulation necessary for a stimulus to be detected 60 percent of the time.

2. If you can just notice the difference between 10- and 11-pound weights, which of the following weights could you differentiate from a 100-pound weight?
    a. 101-pound weight
    b. 105-pound weight
    c. 110-pound weight
    d. There is no basis for prediction.

3. A decrease in sensory responsiveness accompanying an unchanging stimulus is called
    a. sensory fatigue.   c. sensory adaptation.
    b. feature detection.   d. sensory interaction.

4. The size of the pupil is controlled by the
    a. lens.   c. cornea.
    b. retina.   d. iris.

5. The receptor of the eye that functions best in dim light is the
    a. ganglion cell.   c. bipolar cell.
    b. cone.   d. rod.

6. Frequency is to pitch as _____ is to _____ .
    a. wavelength; loudness
    b. amplitude; loudness
    c. wavelength; intensity
    d. amplitude; intensity

7. Our experience of pain when we are injured depends on
    a. our biological makeup and the type of injury we have sustained.
    b. how well medical personnel deal with our injury.
    c. our senses, expectations and attention, and culture.
    b. what our culture allows us to express in terms of feelings of pain.

8. The transformation of light energy into nerve impulses takes place in the
    a. iris.   c. lens.
    b. retina.   d. optic nerve.

9. The brain breaks vision into separate dimensions such as movement, form, depth, and color, and works on each aspect simultaneously. This is called
    a. feature detection.
    b. parallel processing.
    c. the vestibular sense.
    d. sensory adaptation.

10. Kinesthesia involves
    a. the bones of the middle ear.
    b. information from the muscles, tendons, and joints.
    c. membranes within the cochlea.
    d. the body's sense of balance.

11. One light may appear reddish and another greenish if they differ in
    a. wavelength.
    b. amplitude.
    c. opponent processes.
    d. brightness.

12. Which of the following explains why a rose appears equally red in bright and dim light?
    a. sensory adaptation
    b. subliminal stimulation
    c. feature detection
    d. color constancy

13. Which of the following is an example of sensory adaptation?
    a. finding the cold water of a swimming pool warmer after you have been in it for a while
    b. developing an increased sensitivity to salt the more you use it in foods
    c. becoming very irritated at the continuing sound of a dripping faucet
    d. All of these are examples.

14. Most color-deficient people will probably
    a. lack functioning red- or green-sensitive cones.
    b. see the world in only black and white.
    c. also suffer from poor vision.
    d. have above-average vision to compensate for the deficit.

15. The historical movement associated with the statement "The whole may exceed the sum of its parts" is
    a. cognitive psychology.
    b. behavioral psychology.
    c. functional psychology.
    d. Gestalt psychology.

16. Figures tend to be perceived as whole, complete objects, even if spaces or gaps exist in the representation, thus demonstrating the principle of
    a. interposition.
    b. retinal disparity.
    c. continuity.
    d. closure.

17. The figure-ground relationship has demonstrated that
    a. perception is largely innate.
    b. perception is simply a point-for-point representation of sensation.
    c. the same stimulus can trigger more than one perception.
    d. different people see different things when viewing a scene.

18. When we stare at an object, each eye receives a slightly different image, providing a depth cue known as
    a. interposition.
    b. linear perspective.
    c. relative motion.
    d. retinal disparity.

19. As we move, viewed objects cast changing shapes on our retinas, although we do not perceive the objects as changing. This is part of the phenomenon of
    a. perceptual constancy.
    b. relative motion.
    c. linear perspective.
    d. continuity.

20. A person claiming to be able to read another's mind is claiming to have the ESP ability of
    a. psychokinesis.
    b. precognition.
    c. clairvoyance.
    d. telepathy.

21. Which philosopher maintained that knowledge comes from inborn ways of organizing our sensory experiences?
    a. Locke
    b. Kant
    c. Gibson
    d. Walk

22. Adults who are born blind but later have their vision restored
    a. are almost immediately able to recognize familiar objects.
    b. typically fail to recognize familiar objects.
    c. are unable to follow moving objects with their eyes.
    d. have excellent eye-hand coordination.

23. _____ processing refers to how the physical characteristics of stimuli influence their interpretation.
    a. Top-down
    b. Bottom-up
    c. Behavioral
    d. Parallel

24. Which of the following is NOT a monocular depth cue?
    a. light and shadow
    b. relative height
    c. retinal disparity
    d. interposition

25. The Moon illusion occurs in part because distance cues at the horizon make the Moon seem
    a. farther away and therefore larger.
    b. closer and therefore larger.
    c. farther away and therefore smaller.
    d. closer and therefore smaller.

26. Figure is to ground as _____ is to _____ .
    a. night; day
    b. top; bottom
    c. cloud; sky
    d. sensation; perception

27. The study of perception is primarily concerned with how we
    a. detect sights, sounds, and other stimuli.
    b. sense environmental stimuli.
    c. develop sensitivity to illusions.
    d. interpret sensory stimuli.

28. Which of the following influences perception?

  a. genes

  b. the context in which stimuli are perceived

  c. expectations

  d. All of these factors influence perception.

29. Jack claims that he often has dreams that predict future events. He claims to have the power of

  a. telepathy.   **c.** precognition.

  b. clairvoyance.   **d.** psychokinesis.

30. Which of the following is true regarding scientific investigations of precognition?

  a. A growing body of research demonstrates that some people are truly "psychic."

  b. Studies that seem to provide evidence of precognitive ability have been criticized for being badly flawed.

  c. The search for a valid test of ESP has resulted in only a handful of studies.

  d. All of these statements are true.

31. Which of the following is NOT a basic taste?

  a. sweet   **c.** umami

  b. salty   **d.** bland

32. Bottom-up processing begins with the

  a. feature detectors.   **c.** retina.

  b. cerebral cortex.   **d.** sensory receptors.

33. The process by which sensory information is converted into neural energy is

  a. sensory adaptation.   **c.** sensory interaction.

  b. feature detection.   **d.** transduction.

34. The receptors for taste are located in the

  a. taste buds.   **c.** thalamus.

  b. cochlea.   **d.** cortex.

35. The inner ear contains receptors for

  a. audition and kinesthesia.

  b. kinesthesia and the vestibular sense.

  c. audition and the vestibular sense.

  d. audition, kinesthesia, and the vestibular sense.

36. According to the opponent-process theory

  a. there are three types of color-sensitive cones.

  b. the process of color vision begins in the cortex.

  c. neurons involved in color vision are stimulated by one color's wavelength and inhibited by another's.

  d. all of these statements are true.

37. What enables you to feel yourself wiggling your toes even with your eyes closed?

  a. vestibular sense

  b. kinesthesia

  c. the skin senses

  d. sensory interaction

38. Hubel and Wiesel discovered feature detectors in the

  a. fovea.   **c.** iris.

  b. optic nerve.   **d.** cortex.

39. Weber's law states that

  a. the absolute threshold for any stimulus is a constant.

  b. the jnd for any stimulus is a constant.

  c. the absolute threshold for any stimulus is a constant percentage.

  d. the jnd for any stimulus is a constant proportion.

40. The principle that one sense may influence another is

  a. perceptual set.   **c.** Weber's law.

  b. sensory adaptation.   **d.** sensory interaction.

41. Which of the following is the correct order of the structures through which light passes after entering the eye?

  a. lens, pupil, cornea, retina

  b. pupil, cornea, lens, retina

  c. pupil, lens, cornea, retina

  d. cornea, pupil, lens, retina

42. In the opponent-process theory, the three pairs of processes are

  a. red-green, blue-yellow, black-white.

  b. red-blue, green-yellow, black-white.

  c. red-yellow, blue-green, black-white.

  d. dependent upon the individual's experience.

43. Wavelength is to _____ as _____ is to brightness.

  a. hue; intensity

  b. intensity; hue

  c. frequency; amplitude

  d. brightness; hue

44. Concerning the evidence for subliminal stimulation, which of the following is the best answer?

  a. The brain processes some information without our awareness.

  b. Stimuli too weak to cross our thresholds for awareness may trigger a response in our sense receptors.

  c. An unnoticed image or word can briefly prime our response to a later question.

  d. All of these statements are true.

45. A subliminal stimulus is one that

  a. is too weak to cross the difference threshold.

  b. is too weak to cross the absolute threshold.

  c. is too weak to cross either the difference threshold or the absolute threshold.

  d. strikes the blind spot of the eye's retina.

46. Which of the following is the most accurate description of how we process color?
- **a.** Throughout the visual system, color processing is divided into separate red, green, and blue systems.
- **b.** Red-green, blue-yellow, and black-white opponent processes operate throughout the visual system.
- **c.** Color processing occurs in two stages: (1) a three-color system in the retina and (2) opponent-process cells en route to the visual cortex.
- **d.** Color processing occurs in two stages: (1) an opponent-process system in the retina and (2) a three-color system en route to the visual cortex.

47. One reason that your ability to detect fine visual details is greatest when scenes are focused on the center of your retina is that
- **a.** there are more feature detectors in the center than in the peripheral regions of the retina.
- **b.** cones in the center are nearer to the optic nerve than those in peripheral regions of the retina.
- **c.** many rods, which are clustered in the center, have individual bipolar cells to relay their information to the cortex.
- **d.** many cones, which are clustered in the center, have individual bipolar cells to relay their information to the cortex.

48. Given normal sensory ability, a person standing atop a mountain on a dark, clear night can see a candle flame atop a mountain 30 miles away. This is a description of vision's
- **a.** difference threshold.
- **b.** jnd.
- **c.** absolute threshold.
- **d.** feature detection.

49. The tendency to organize stimuli into smooth, uninterrupted patterns is called
- **a.** closure.
- **b.** continuity.
- **c.** disparity.
- **d.** proximity.

50. Which of the following statements is consistent with the Gestalt theory of perception?
- **a.** Perception develops largely through learning.
- **b.** Perception is the product of heredity.
- **c.** The mind organizes sensations into meaningful perceptions.
- **d.** Perception results directly from sensation.

51. Experiments with distorted visual environments demonstrate that
- **a.** adaptation rarely takes place.
- **b.** animals adapt readily, but humans do not.
- **c.** humans adapt readily, while lower animals typically do not.
- **d.** adaptation is possible during a critical period in infancy but not thereafter.

52. The phenomenon that refers to the ways in which an individual's expectations influence perception is called
- **a.** perceptual set.
- **b.** retinal disparity.
- **c.** interposition.
- **d.** kinesthesia.

53. According to the philosopher _____ , we learn to perceive the world.
- **a.** Locke
- **b.** Kant
- **c.** Gibson
- **d.** Walk

54. The phenomenon of size constancy is based on the close connection between an object's perceived _____ and its perceived _____ .
- **a.** size; shape
- **b.** size; distance
- **c.** size; brightness
- **d.** shape; distance

55. Which of the following statements best describes the effects of sensory restriction?
- **a.** It produces functional blindness when experienced for any length of time at any age.
- **b.** It has greater effects on humans than on animals.
- **c.** It has more damaging effects when experienced during infancy.
- **d.** It has greater effects on adults than on children.

56. The depth cue that occurs when we watch stable objects at different distances as we are moving is
- **a.** linear perspective.
- **b.** interposition.
- **c.** relative size.
- **d.** relative motion.

57. Which of the following statements concerning ESP is true?
- **a.** Most ESP researchers are quacks.
- **b.** There have been a large number of reliable demonstrations of ESP.
- **c.** Most research psychologists are skeptical of the claims of defenders of ESP.
- **d.** There have been reliable laboratory demonstrations of ESP, but the results are no different from those that would occur by chance.

58. The term *gestalt* means
- **a.** grouping.
- **b.** sensation.
- **c.** perception.
- **d.** whole.

59. Studies of the visual cliff have provided evidence that much of depth perception is
- **a.** innate.
- **b.** learned.
- **c.** innate in lower animals, learned in humans.
- **d.** innate in humans, learned in lower animals.

60. All of the following are laws of perceptual organization EXCEPT
- **a.** proximity.
- **b.** closure.
- **c.** continuity.
- **d.** retinal disparity.

61. You probably perceive the diagram above as three sets of two lines due to the principle of
- **a.** proximity.
- **b.** continuity.
- **c.** closure.
- **d.** linear perspective.

62. Sensorineural hearing loss is caused by
   a. wax buildup in the outer ear.
   b. damage to the eardrum.
   c. blockage in the middle ear because of infection.
   d. damage to the cochlea.

63. The Young-Helmholtz theory proposes that
   a. there are three different types of color-sensitive cones.
   b. retinal cells are excited by one color and inhibited by its complementary color.
   c. there are four different types of cones.
   d. rod, not cone, vision accounts for our ability to detect fine visual detail.

Matching Items

Match each of the structures with its function or description.

Structures

_____ **1.** lens
_____ **2.** retina
_____ **3.** pupil
_____ **4.** rods
_____ **5.** cones
_____ **6.** eardrum
_____ **7.** cochlea
_____ **8.** iris
_____ **9.** hammer, anvil, and stirrup
_____ **10.** semicircular canals
_____ **11.** sensors in joints

Functions or Descriptions

a. amplifies sounds
b. vibrates from sound waves
c. vestibular sense
d. contains the rods and cones
e. controls the size of the pupil
f. transforms sound waves
g. admits light
h. vision in dim light
i. focuses light rays on the retina
j. kinesthesia
k. color vision

True–False Items

Indicate whether each statement is true or false by placing T or F in the blank next to the item.

_____ **1.** Once we perceive an item as a figure, it is impossible to see it as ground.

_____ **2.** Laboratory experiments have laid to rest all criticisms of ESP.

_____ **3.** Six-month-old infants will cross a visual cliff if their mother calls.

_____ **4.** Unlike other animals, humans have no critical period for visual stimulation.

_____ **5.** Immanuel Kant argued that experience determined how we perceive the world.

_____ **6.** It is just as easy to touch two pencil tips together with only one eye open as it is with both eyes open.

_____ **7.** After some time, humans are able to adjust to living in a world made upside down by distorting goggles.

_____ **8.** As our distance from an object changes, the object's size seems to change.

_____ **9.** Perception is influenced by psychological factors such as set and expectation as well as by physiological events.

_____ **10.** John Locke argued that perception is inborn.

Application Essays

1. A dancer in a chorus line uses many sensory cues when performing. Discuss three senses that dancers rely on, and explain why each is important. (Use the space below to list the points you want to make, and organize them. Then write the essay on a separate sheet of paper.)

2. In many movies from the 1930s, dancers performed seemingly meaningless movements which, when viewed from above, were transformed into intricate patterns and designs. Similarly, the formations of marching bands often create pictures and spell words. Identify and describe three Gestalt principles of grouping that explain the audience's perception of the images created by these types of formations. (Use the space below to list the points you want to make, and organize them. Then write the essay on a separate piece of paper.)

Summing Up

Use the diagrams to identify the parts of the eye and ear, then describe how each contributes to vision or hearing. Also, briefly explain the role of each structure.

The Eye

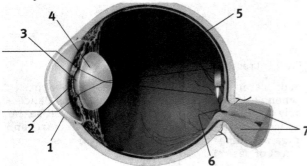

1. _____

   _____

2. _____

   _____

3. _____

   _____

4. _____

   _____

5. _____

   _____

6. _____

   _____

7. _____

   _____

The Ear

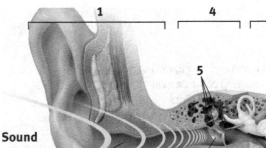
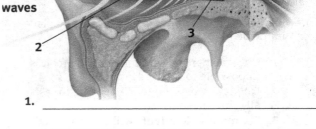

1. _____

   _____

2. _____

   _____

3. _____

   _____

4. _____

   _____

5. _____

   _____

6. _____

   _____

7. _____

   _____

8. _____

   _____

Terms and Concepts to Remember

Using your own words, on a piece of paper write a brief definition or explanation of each of the following terms.

1. sensation
2. perception
3. bottom-up processing
4. top-down processing
5. transduction
6. absolute threshold
7. subliminal
8. difference threshold
9. priming
10. Weber's law
11. sensory adaptation
12. perceptual set
13. wavelength and hue
14. intensity
15. retina
16. rods and cones
17. optic nerve
18. blind spot
19. Young-Helmholtz trichromatic (three-color) theory
20. opponent-process theory
21. feature detectors
22. parallel processing
23. gestalt
24. figure-ground
25. grouping
26. depth perception
27. visual cliff
28. binocular cue
29. retinal disparity
30. monocular cue
31. perceptual constancy
32. color constancy
33. perceptual adaptation
34. audition
35. frequency and pitch
36. middle ear
37. cochlea
38. inner ear
39. sensorineural hearing loss
40. conduction hearing loss
41. cochlear implant
42. hypnosis
43. posthypnotic suggestion
44. kinesthesia
45. vestibular sense
46. sensory interaction
47. embodied cognition
48. extrasensory perception (ESP)

Answers

Chapter Review

Basic Concepts of Sensation and Perception

1. prosopagnosia
2. sensation; perception
3. bottom-up processing; top-down processing
4. **b.** is the answer.
   a. Both recognition and interpretation are examples of perception.
   c. This answer would have been correct if the question had read, "Perception is to sensation as _____ is to _____ ."
   d. Sensation and perception are important processes in both hearing and seeing.
5. **c.** is the answer.
6. **d.** is the answer.
7. receive; transform; deliver
8. transduction
9. absolute threshold; 50
10. subliminal
11. difference threshold; just noticeable difference (jnd)
12. Weber's law; stimulus
13. absolute threshold. This is the minimum stimulation needed to detect a stimulus 50 percent of the time.
14. **d.** is the answer.
    a. The absolute threshold refers to whether a single stimulus can be detected, not to whether two stimuli can be differentiated.
    b. Subliminal refers to stimuli below the absolute threshold.
    c. A receptor threshold is a minimum amount of energy that will elicit a neural impulse in a receptor cell.
15. prime; conscious; two-track
16. persuaded; did not
17. placebo
18. sensory adaptation
19. informative

20. sensory adaptation. This occurs when we remain fixed on a stimulus. Moving his fingers prevents his sense of touch from adapting.

21. perceptual set

22. set; context

23. top-down; bottom-up

24. motivations; thirsty; Emotions; perceptions

25. **d.** is the answer. The two people interpreted a briefly perceived object in terms of their perceptual sets, or mental predispositions, in this case conditioned by their work experiences.
    a. Their different interpretations reflect top-down processing.
    b. Sensory adaptation refers to the decreased sensitivity that occurs with continued exposure to an unchanging stimulus.
    c. Transduction is the transformation of one form of energy into another.

Vision: Sensory and Perceptual Processing

26. electromagnetic

27. wavelength; hue; intensity; amplitude; brightness

28. cornea; pupil; iris

29. lens; retina

30. **a.** yes. The left-hand wave has lower amplitude and the colors would be duller. The right-hand wave has similar frequency (and therefore hue) but a higher amplitude, making it brighter.
    b. yes. The sounds have similar frequency (and therefore pitch), but the right-hand sound has higher amplitude and would therefore be louder.

31. **d.** is the answer. Just as light strikes the film of a camera, visual images entering the eye are projected onto the retina.
    a. The pupil would be analogous to the aperture of a camera, since both control the amount of light permitted to enter.
    b. The lens of the eye performs a focusing function similar to the lens of the camera.
    c. The cornea would be analogous to a camera's lens cap in that both protect delicate inner structures.

32. rods; cones

33. bipolar; ganglion

34. optic nerve; thalamus; visual cortex

35. blind spot

36. fovea; peripheral; do not

37. cones; rods

38. sensitive

39. **d.** is the answer. Greater sensitivity to fine visual detail is associated with the cones, which have their own bipolar cells to relay information to the cortex. The cones are concentrated in the fovea, the retina's point of central focus. For this reason, staring directly at an object maximizes sensitivity to fine detail.
    a. If you stare off to one side, the image falls onto peripheral regions of the retina, where rods are concentrated and sensitivity to fine visual detail is poor.

b. Sensitivity to detail is not directly influenced by whether one or both eyes are stimulated.
c. Decreasing the intensity of light would only impair the functioning of the cones, which are sensitive to visual detail but have a high threshold for light intensity.

40. **d.** is the answer.

41. **b.** is the answer. Rods and cones enable vision in dim and bright light, respectively. If an animal is active only at night, it is likely to have more rods than cones in its retinas.
    d. Bipolar cells link both cones and rods to ganglion cells. There is no reason to expect that a nocturnal mammal would have more bipolar cells than a mammal active both during the day and at night. If anything, because several rods share a single bipolar cell, whereas many cones have their own, a nocturnal animal (with a visual system consisting mostly of rods) might be expected to have fewer bipolar cells than an animal active during the day (with a visual system consisting mostly of cones).

42. **b.** is the answer.
    a. & c. It is the cones, rather than the rods, that enable color vision.
    d. If the cones' threshold were lower than the available light intensity, they would be able to function and therefore detect the colors of the players' uniforms.

43. reflects (rejects); construction

44. sex linked

45. Young-Helmholtz trichromatic; red; green; blue

46. opponent; afterimage

47. opponent-process; red; green; yellow; blue; black; white

In the first stage of color processing, the retina's red, green, and blue cones respond in varying degrees to different color stimuli, as suggested by the three-color theory. The resulting signals are then processed in the retina and in the thalamus by red-green, blue-yellow, and black-white opponent-process cells, which are "turned on" by one wavelength and "turned off" by its opponent.

48. **d.** is the answer.
    a., b., & c. Cones, bipolar cells, and ganglion cells are located in the retina. Moreover, none of them is excited by some colors and inhibited by others.

49. **c.** is the answer.
    a. The trichromatic theory cannot account for the experience of afterimages.
    b. & d. Afterimages are experienced as the complementary color of a stimulus. Green, not blue, is red's complement.

50. edges; lines; angles; feature detectors; supercell clusters

51. temporal lobe

52. simultaneously; parallel processing

53. Gestalt; whole

54. figure; ground

55. grouping

56. continuity; closure; proximity

57. **c.** is the answer. She perceives the line for the road as continuous, even though it is interrupted by lines indicating other roads.
    a. Closure refers to the perceptual filling in of gaps in a stimulus to create a complete, whole object.
    b. Figure-ground refers to organizing a scene into objects and their surroundings.
    d. Proximity is the tendency to group objects near to one another as a single unit.

58. depth perception; distance

59. visual cliff; mobile

Research on the visual cliff suggests that in many species the ability to perceive depth is present at, or very shortly after, birth. Learning is also a factor because crawling seems to increase infants' fear of heights.

60. binocular

61. retinal disparity

62. monocular

63. relative size

64. interposition

65. relative height

66. relative motion

67. linear perspective

68. light and shadow

69. away; closer; motion

70.

71. **b.** is the answer. The phenomenon described is the basis for the monocular cue of relative size.
    a. The object casting the *larger* retinal image would be perceived as closer.
    c. & d. Because of size constancy, the perceived size of familiar objects remains constant, despite changes in their retinal image size.

72. **d.** is the answer.

73. **b.** is the answer. This is an example of the principle of interposition in depth perception.
    a. The partially obscured object is perceived as farther away.
    c. The perceived size of an object is not altered when that object overlaps another.

74. **c.** is the answer.
    a. Interposition is a monocular depth cue in which an object that partially covers another is perceived as closer.
    b. Retinal disparity refers to the difference between the two images received by our eyes. which allows

us to perceive depth. It has nothing to do with the way the artist placed the trees.
    d. Figure-ground refers to the organization of the field into objects that stand out from their surroundings.

75. **c.** is the answer.
    b. & d. Linear perspective is the apparent convergence of parallel lines as a cue to distance.

76. top-down; perceptual constancy

77. context; color constancy

78. reflected; surrounding objects

79. do not; retinal

80. Moon; size; distance; diminished

81. **a.** is the answer. Because we perceive the size of a familiar object as constant even as its retinal image grows smaller, we perceive the object as being farther away.
    b. & c. Perceptual constancy is a cognitive, rather than sensory, phenomenon. Therefore, the ab-sence of perceptual constancy would not alter sensitivity to monocular or binocular cues.
    d. Although the absence of perceptual constancy would impair depth perception based on the size-distance relationship, other cues to depth, such as texture gradient, could still be used.

82. **c.** is the answer.

83. Immanuel Kant; John Locke

84. cannot

85. critical period

86. will; perceptual adaptation; do not adapt

The Nonvisual Senses

87. audition; air molecules

88. loudness

89. pitch

90. decibels; zero

91. outer; middle; inner

92. eardrum

93. hammer; anvil; stirrup

94. cochlea; oval window; basilar membrane; hair cells; thalamus; temporal

95. sensorineural; aging

96. conduction hearing loss

97. cochlear implant

98. timing; intensity

99. harder

100. **a.** is the answer.

101. **d.** is the answer. The hair cells, which transform sound energy, are located on the basilar membrane.
    a. & b. The eardrum and bones of the middle ear merely conduct sound waves to the inner ear, where they are transformed.
    c. The semicircular canals are involved in the vestibular sense, not hearing.

102. pressure; warmth; cold; pain; variations

103. injury; chronic
104. bottom-up; top-down
105. is not; does not; nociceptors
106. biopsychosocial; genes; physical characteristics; expectations; attention; culture
107. phantom limb; memories
108. endorphins; distraction; placebos
109. hypnosis; social; dissociation; conscious awareness; posthypnotic suggestion
110. c. is the answer. Because pain is felt in the limb that does not exist, the pain is simply the brain's (mis)interpretation of neural activity.
    a. If pain were a purely sensory phenomenon, phantom limb pain would not occur because the receptors are no longer present.
    b. That pain is experienced when a limb is missing indicates that the central nervous system, especially the brain, is where pain is sensed.
111. d. is the answer.
112. sweet; sour; salty; bitter; umami
113. chemical; taste buds; pore; taste receptor cells
114. week or two; decreases; decreases; smoking; alcohol; expectations
115. olfaction; chemical; is not
116. emotions
117. c. is the answer. As people age they lose taste buds and their taste thresholds increase. For this reason, Mrs. Martinez needs more concentrated tastes than her son to find food palatable.
    a. & b. There is no evidence that women and men differ in their absolute thresholds for taste.
118. kinesthesia; tendons; joints; muscles
119. vestibular sense; semicircular canals; vestibular sacs

Sensory Interaction

120. sensory interaction; McGurk; see; hearing
121. embodied cognition
122. synesthesia
123. d. is the answer. Each of these is an example of the interaction of two senses—vision and taste in the case of (a.), taste and smell in the case of (b.), and hearing and the vestibular sense in the case of (c.).
124. c. is the answer. Because of the powerful sensory interaction between taste and smell, eliminating the odor of the cough syrup should make its taste more pleasant.
    a. If anything, the contrasting tastes might make the bitter syrup even less palatable.
    b. If Tamiko keeps the syrup in her mouth for several seconds, it will ensure that her taste pores fully "catch" the stimulus, thus intensifying the bitter taste.
    d. It's probably impossible to miss the tongue completely.

ESP—Perception Without Sensation?

125. extrasensory perception
126. telepathy; clairvoyance; precognition; psychokinesis
127. chance-level; interpreted (retrofitted); reconstruct
128. reproducible
129. did
130. d. is the answer.
    a. Telepathy is the claimed ability to "read" minds.
    b. Clairvoyance refers to the claimed ability to perceive remote events.
    c. Precognition refers to the claimed ability to perceive future events.
131. d. is the answer.

Progress Test

Multiple-Choice Questions

1. b. is the answer. Psychological factors can affect the absolute threshold for a stimulus.
    a. The absolute threshold for detecting a stimulus depends not only on the strength of the stimulus but also on psychological factors such as experience, expectations, motivation, and fatigue. Thus, the threshold cannot be a constant.
    c. & d. The absolute threshold is defined as the minimum stimulus that is detected 50 percent of the time.
2. c. is the answer. According to Weber's law, the difference threshold is a constant proportion of the stimulus. There is a 10 percent difference between 10 and 11 pounds; since the difference threshold is a constant proportion, the weight closest to 100 pounds that can nonetheless be differentiated from it is 110 pounds (or 100 pounds plus 10 percent).
3. c. is the answer.
    a. "Sensory fatigue" is not a term in psychology.
    b. Feature detection explains how the brain recognizes visual images by analyzing their distinctive features of edge, line, and angle.
    d. Sensory interaction is the principle that one sense may influence another.
4. d. is the answer.
    a. The lens lies behind the pupil and focuses light on the retina.
    b. The retina is the inner surface of the eyeball and contains the rods and cones.
    c. The cornea lies in front of the pupil and is the first structure that light passes through as it enters the eye.
5. d. is the answer.
    a. The fovea is not a receptor; it is a region of the retina that contains only cones.
    b. Cones have a higher threshold for brightness than rods and therefore do not function as well in dim light.

c. Bipolar cells are not receptors; they are neurons in the retina that link rods and cones with ganglion cells, which make up the optic nerve.

6. **b.** is the answer. Just as wave frequency determines pitch, so wave amplitude determines loudness.
   a. Amplitude is the physical basis of loudness; wavelength determines frequency and thereby pitch.
   c. & d. Wavelength, amplitude, and intensity are physical aspects of light and sound. Because the question is based on a relationship between a physical property (frequency) of a stimulus and its psychological attribute (pitch), these answers are incorrect.

7. **c.** is the answer. Our experience of pain depends on our genes and physical characteristics, as well as our attention, expectations, and culture.

8. **b.** is the answer.
   a. The iris controls the diameter of the pupil.
   c. The lens changes its shape to focus images on the retina.
   d. The optic nerve carries nerve impulses from the retina to the visual cortex.

9. **b.** is the answer.
   a. Feature detection is the process by which nerve cells in the brain respond to specific visual features of a stimulus, such as movement or shape.
   c. The vestibular sense of your head's (and thus your body's) movement and position.
   d. Sensory adaptation refers to the diminished sensitivity that occurs with continued exposure to an unchanging stimulus.

10. **b.** is the answer. Kinesthesia, or the sense of the position and movement of body parts, is based on information from the tendons, joints, and muscles.
    a. & c. The ear plays no role in kinesthesia.
    d. Equilibrium, or the vestibular sense, is not involved in kinesthesia but is, rather, a companion sense.

11. **a.** is the answer. Wavelength determines hue, or color.
    b. & d. The amplitude of light determines its brightness.
    c. Opponent processes are neural systems involved in color vision, not properties of light.

12. **d.** is the answer. Color constancy is the perception that a familiar object has consistent color, even if changing illumination alters the wavelengths reflected by that object.
    a. & b. These theories explain how the visual system detects color; they do not explain why colors do not seem to change when lighting does.
    c. Feature detection explains how the brain recognizes visual images by analyzing their distinctive features of edge, line, and angle.

13. **a.** is the answer. Sensory adaptation means a diminishing sensitivity to an unchanging stimulus. Only the adjustment to cold water involves a decrease in sensitivity; the other examples involve an increase.

14. **a.** is the answer. Thus, they have difficulty discriminating these two colors.

b. Those who are color deficient are usually not "color blind" in a literal sense. Instead, they are unable to distinguish certain hues, such as red from green.
c. Failure to distinguish red and green is separate from, and does not usually affect, general visual ability.
d. Color deficiency does not enhance vision. A deficit in one sense often is compensated for by overdevelopment of another sense—for example, hearing in blind people.

15. **d.** is the answer. Gestalt psychology, which developed in Germany early in the twentieth century, was interested in how clusters of sensations are organized into "whole" perceptions.
    a. Cognitive psychology focuses on thinking, knowing, remembering, and communicating.
    b. & c. Behavioral and functional psychology developed later in the United States.

16. **d.** is the answer.
    a. Interposition is the tendency to perceive objects that partially block our view of another object as closer.
    b. Linear perspective is when parallel lines appear to meet in the distance.
    c. Continuity refers to the tendency to group stimuli into smooth, continuous patterns.

17. **c.** is the answer. Although we always differentiate a stimulus into figure and ground, those elements of the stimulus we perceive as figure and those as ground may change. In this way, the same stimulus can trigger more than one perception.
    a. The idea of a figure-ground relationship has no bearing on the issue of whether perception is innate.
    b. Perception cannot be simply a point-for-point representation of sensation, since in figure-ground relationships a single stimulus can trigger more than one perception.
    d. Figure-ground relationships demonstrate the existence of general, rather than individual, principles of perceptual organization. Significantly, even the same person can see different figure-ground relationships when viewing a scene.

18. **d.** is the answer. The greater the retinal disparity, or difference between the images, the less the distance.
    a. Interposition is the monocular distance cue in which an object that partially blocks another object is seen as closer.
    b. Linear perspective is the monocular distance cue in which parallel lines appear to converge in the distance.
    c. Relative motion is the monocular distance cue in which objects at different distances change their relative positions in our visual image, with those closest moving most.

19. **a.** is the answer. Perception of constant shape, like perception of constant size, is part of the phenomenon of perceptual constancy.
    b. Relative motion is a monocular distance cue in which objects at different distances appear to move at different rates.

c. Linear perspective is a monocular distance cue in which lines we know to be parallel converge in the distance, thus indicating depth.
d. Continuity is the perceptual tendency to group items into continuous patterns.

20. **d.** is the answer.
a. Psychokinesis refers to the claimed ability to perform acts of "mind over matter."
b. Precognition refers to the claimed ability to perceive future events.
c. Clairvoyance refers to the claimed ability to perceive remote events.

21. **b.** is the answer.
a. Locke argued that knowledge is not inborn but comes through learning.
c. & d. Gibson and Walk studied depth perception using the visual cliff; they made no claims about the source of knowledge.

22. **b.** is the answer. Because they have not had early visual experiences, these adults typically have difficulty learning to perceive objects.
a. Such patients typically could not visually recognize objects with which they were familiar by touch, and in some cases this inability persisted.
c. Being able to perceive figure-ground relationships, patients are able to follow moving objects with their eyes.
d. This answer is incorrect because eye-hand coordination is an acquired skill and requires much practice.

23. **b.** is the answer.
a. Top-down processing refers to how our knowledge and expectations influence perception.
c. Behavioral processing is not a term.
d. Parallel processing is information processing in which several aspects of a stimulus, such as light or sound, are processed simultaneously.

24. **c.** is the answer. Retinal disparity is a *binocular* cue; all the other cues mentioned are monocular.

25. **a.** is the answer. The Moon appears larger at the horizon than overhead in the sky because objects at the horizon provide distance cues that make the Moon seem farther away and therefore larger. In the open sky, of course, there are no such cues.

26. **c.** is the answer. We see a cloud as a figure against the background of sky.
a., b., & d. The figure-ground relationship refers to the organization of the visual field into objects (figures) that stand out from their surroundings (ground).

27. **d.** is the answer.
a. & b. The study of sensation is concerned with these processes.
c. Although studying illusions has helped psychologists understand ordinary perceptual mechanisms, it is not the primary focus of the field of perception.

28. **d.** is the answer.

29. **c.** is the answer.

a. This answer would be correct had Jack claimed to be able to read someone else's mind.
b. This answer would be correct had Jack claimed to be able to sense remote events, such as a friend in distress.
d. This answer would be correct had Jack claimed to be able to levitate objects or bend spoons without applying any physical force.

30. **b.** is the answer.
31. **d.** is the answer.
32. **d.** is the answer.
33. **d.** is the answer.
a. Sensory adaptation refers to the diminished sensitivity that occurs with unchanging stimulation.
b. Feature detection refers to the process by which nerve cells in the brain respond to specific aspects of visual stimuli, such as movement or shape.
c. Sensory interaction is the principle that one sense may influence another.

34. **a.** is the answer.
b. The cochlea contains receptors for hearing.
c. The thalamus is the part of the brain that directs sensory messages to the cortex.
d. The cortex is the outer layer of the brain, where information detected by the receptors is processed.

35. **c.** is the answer. The inner ear contains the receptors for audition (hearing) and the vestibular sense; those for kinesthesia are located in the tendons, joints, and muscles.

36. **c.** is the answer. After leaving the receptor cells, visual information is analyzed in terms of pairs of opponent colors; neurons stimulated by one member of a pair are inhibited by the other.
a. The idea that there are three types of color-sensitive cones is the basis of the Young-Helmholtz three-color theory.
b. According to the opponent-process theory, and all other theories of color vision, the process of color vision begins in the retina.

37. **b.** is the answer. Kinesthesia, the sense of movement of body parts, would enable you to feel your toes wiggling.
a. The vestibular sense is concerned with movement and position, or balance, of the whole body, not of its parts.
c. The skin, or tactile, senses are pressure, pain, warmth, and cold; they have nothing to do with movement of body parts.
d. Sensory interaction, the principle that the senses influence each other, does not play a role in this example, which involves only kinesthesia.

38. **d.** is the answer. Feature detectors are cortical neurons and so are located in the visual cortex.
a. The fovea contains cones.
b. The optic nerve contains neurons that relay nerve impulses from the retina to higher centers in the visual system.
c. The iris is simply a ring of muscle tissue, which controls the diameter of the pupil.

39. **d.** is the answer. Weber's law concerns the difference threshold (jnd), not the absolute threshold, and states that these are constant percentages of the stimuli, not that they remain constant.

40. **d.** is the answer.
    a. Perceptual set is the tendency to perceive one thing and not another.
    b. Sensory adaptation is diminished sensitivity to unchanging stimulation.
    c. Weber's law states that the jnd is a constant proportion of a stimulus.

41. **d.** is the answer.

42. **a.** is the answer.

43. **a.** is the answer. Wavelength determines hue, and intensity determines brightness.

44. **d.** is the answer.

45. **c.** is the answer.

46. **c.** is the answer.
    a. This answer is incorrect because separate red, green, and blue systems operate only in the retina.
    b. This answer is incorrect because opponent-process systems operate en route to the brain, after visual processing in the receptors is completed.
    d. This answer is incorrect because it reverses the correct order of the two stages of processing.

47. **d.** is the answer.
    a. Feature detectors are nerve cells located in the visual cortex, not in the fovea of the retina.
    b. The proximity of rods and cones to the optic nerve does not influence their ability to resolve fine details.
    c. Rods are concentrated in the peripheral regions of the retina, not in the fovea; moreover, several rods share a single bipolar cell.

48. **c.** is the answer. The absolute threshold is the minimum stimulation needed to detect a stimulus 50 percent of the time.
    a. & b. The difference threshold, which is also known as the jnd, is the minimum difference between two stimuli that a person can detect. In this example, there is only one stimulus—the sight of the flame.
    d. Feature detection refers to nerve cells in the brain responding to specific features of a stimulus.

49. **b.** is the answer.
    a. Closure refers to the tendency to perceptually fill in gaps in recognizable objects in the visual field.
    c. Interposition is the tendency to perceive objects that partially block our view of another object as closer.
    d. Proximity refers to the tendency to group items that are near one another.

50. **c.** is the answer.
    a. & b. The Gestalt psychologists did not deal with the origins of perception; they were more concerned with its form.
    d. In fact, they argued just the opposite: Perception is more than mere sensory experience.

51. **c.** is the answer. Humans are able to adjust to upside-down worlds and other visual distortions, fig-

uring out the relationship between the perceived and the actual reality; lower animals, such as chicks, are typically unable to adapt.
    a. Humans are able to adapt quite well to distorted visual environments (and then to readapt).
    b. This answer is incorrect because humans are the most adaptable of creatures.
    d. Humans are able to adapt at any age to distorted visual environments.

52. **a.** is the answer.
    b. Retinal disparity is a binocular depth cue based on the fact that each eye receives a slightly different view of the world.
    c. Interposition is the monocular distance cue in which an object that partially blocks another object is seen as closer.
    d. Kinesthesia is the sense of the position and movement of the parts of the body.

53. **a.** is the answer.
    b. Kant claimed that knowledge is inborn.
    c. & d. Gibson and Walk make no claims about the origins of perception.

54. **b.** is the answer.

55. **c.** is the answer. There appears to be a critical period for perceptual development, in that sensory restriction has severe, even permanent, disruptive effects when it occurs in infancy but not when it occurs later in life.
    a. & d. Sensory restriction does not have the same effects at all ages, and it is more damaging to children than to adults. This is because there is a critical period for perceptual development; whether functional blindness will result depends in part on the nature of the sensory restriction.
    b. Research studies have not indicated that sensory restriction is more damaging to humans than to animals.

56. **d.** is the answer. When we move, stable objects we see also appear to move, and the distance and speed of the apparent motion cue us to the objects' relative distances.
    a., b., & c. These depth cues are unrelated to movement and thus work even when we are stationary.

57. **c.** is the answer.
    a. Many ESP researchers are sincere, reputable researchers.
    b. & d. There have been no reliable demonstrations of ESP.

58. **d.** is the answer. Gestalt means a "form" or "organized whole."

59. **a.** is the answer. Most infants refused to crawl out over the "cliff" even when coaxed, suggesting that much of depth perception is innate. Studies with the young of "lower" animals show the same thing.

60. **d.** is the answer.

61. **a.** is the answer. Proximity is the tendency to group objects near to one another. The diagram is perceived as three distinct units because we tend to group items closest to each to each other.

b. Continuity is the tendency to group stimuli into smooth, uninterrupted patterns. There is no such continuity in the diagram.

c. Closure is the perceptual tendency to fill in gaps in a form. In the diagram, three disconnected units are perceived rather than a single whole.

d. Linear perspective is when parallel lines appear to meet in the distance.

62. **d.** is the answer. Sensorineural hearing loss is caused by destruction of neural tissue as a result of problems with the cochlea's receptors or the auditory nerve.

a. & c. Wax buildup and blockage because of infection are temporary states; sensorineural hearing loss is permanent. Moreover, sensorineural hearing loss involves the inner ear rather than the outer or middle ear.

b. Damage to the eardrum impairs the mechanical system that conducts sound waves; it could therefore cause conduction hearing loss, not sensorineural hearing loss.

63. **a.** is the answer. The Young-Helmholtz theory proposes that there are red-, green-, and blue-sensitive cones.

b. This answer describes Hering's opponent-process theory.

c. The Young-Helmholtz theory proposes that there are three types of cones, not four.

d. The Young-Helmholtz theory concerns only color vision, not the detection of visual detail.

Matching Items

1. i	**6.** b	**11.** j
2. d	**7.** f	
3. g	**8.** e	
4. h	**9.** a	
5. k	**10.** c	

True–False Items

1. F	**5.** F	**9.** T
2. F	**6.** F	**10.** F
3. F	**7.** T	
4. F	**8.** F	

Application Essay 1

The senses that are most important to dancers are vision, hearing, kinesthesia, and the vestibular sense. Your answer should refer to any three of these senses and include, at a minimum, the following information.

Dancers rely on vision to gauge their body position relative to other dancers as they perform specific choreographed movements. Vision also helps dancers assess the audience's reaction to their performance. Whenever dance is set to music, hearing is necessary so that the dancers can detect musical cues for certain parts of their routines. Hearing also helps the dancers keep their movements in time with the music. Kinesthetic receptors in dancers' tendons, joints, and muscles provide their brains with information about the position and movement of body parts to determine if their hands, arms, legs, and heads are in the proper positions. Receptors for the vestibular sense located in the dancers'

inner ears send messages to their brains that help them maintain their balance and determine the correctness of the position and movement of their bodies.

Application Essay 2

1. *Proximity.* We tend to perceive items that are near each other as belonging together. Thus, a small section of dancers or members of a marching band may separate themselves from the larger group in order to form part of a particular image.

2. *Continuity.* Because we perceive smooth, continuous patterns rather than discontinuous ones, dancers or marching musicians moving together (as in a column, for example) are perceived as a separate unit.

3. *Closure.* If a figure has gaps, we complete it, filling in the gaps to create a whole image. Thus, we perceptually fill in the relatively wide spacing between dancers or marching musicians in order to perceive the complete words or forms they are creating.

Summing Up

The Eye

1. Cornea. Light enters the eye through this transparent membrane, which protects the inner structures from the environment.

2. Iris. The colored part of the eye, the iris functions like the aperture of a camera, controlling the size of the pupil to optimize the amount of light that enters the eye.

3. Pupil. The adjustable opening in the iris, the pupil allows light to enter.

4. Lens. This transparent structure behind the pupil changes shape to focus images on the retina.

5. Retina. The light-sensitive inner surface of the eye, the retina contains the rods and cones, which transduce light energy into neural impulses.

6. Blind spot. The region of the retina where the optic nerve leaves the eye, the blind spot contains no rods or cones and so there is no vision here.

7. Optic nerve. This bundle of nerve fibers carries neural impulses from the retina to the brain.

The Ear

1. Outer ear. Hearing begins as sound waves enter the auditory canal of the outer ear.

2. Auditory canal. Sound waves passing through the auditory canal are brought to a point of focus at the eardrum.

3. Eardrum. Lying between the outer and middle ear, this membrane vibrates in response to sound waves.

4. Middle ear. Lying between the outer and inner ear, this air-filled chamber contains the hammer, anvil, and stirrup.

5. Hammer, anvil, and stirrup. These tiny bones of the middle ear concentrate the eardrum's vibrations on the cochlea's oval window.

6. Inner ear. This region of the ear contains the cochlea and the semicircular canals, which play an important role in balance.

7. Cochlea. This fluid-filled multichambered structure contains the hair cell receptors that transduce sound waves into neural impulses.

8. Auditory nerve. This bundle of fibers carries nerve impulses from the inner ear to the brain.

Terms and Concepts to Remember

1. **Sensation** is the process by which our sensory receptors and nervous system receive and represent physical energy from the environment.

2. **Perception** is the process by which we organize and interpret sensory information, enabling us to recognize meaningful objects and events.

3. **Bottom-up processing** is analysis that begins with the sensory receptors and works up to higher levels of processing.

4. **Top-down processing** is information processing guided by higher-level mental processes.

5. **Transduction** refers to the conversion of one form of energy into another. In sensation, it is the process by which receptor cells in the eyes, ears, skin, and nose convert stimulus energies into neural impulses our brain can interpret.

6. The **absolute threshold** is the minimum stimulation needed to detect a stimulus 50 percent of the time.

7. A stimulus that is **subliminal** is one that is below the absolute threshold for conscious awareness.

   Memory aid: Limen is the Latin word for "threshold." A stimulus that is **subliminal** is one that is *sub-* ("below") the *limen*, or threshold.

8. The **difference threshold** (also called the *just noticeable difference,* or *jnd*), is the minimum difference between two stimuli required for detection 50 percent of the time.

9. **Priming** is the activation, often unconsciously, of an association in our mind, thus setting us up to perceive, remember, or respond to objects or events in certain ways.

10. **Weber's law** states that, to be perceived as different, the just noticeable difference between two stimuli must differ by a constant minimum percentage.

    Example: If a difference of 10 percent in weight is noticeable, **Weber's law** predicts that a person could discriminate 10- and 11-pound weights or 50- and 55-pound weights.

11. **Sensory adaptation** refers to the diminished sensitivity that occurs with continued exposure to an unchanging stimulus.

12. **Perceptual set** is a mental predisposition to perceive one thing and not another.

13. **Wavelength,** which refers to the distance from the peak of one light or sound wave to the next, gives rise to the perceptual experiences of **hue,** or color, in vision and **pitch** in hearing.

14. The **intensity,** the amount of energy in a light or sound wave, of light and sound is determined by the amplitude of the waves and is experienced as brightness and loudness, respectively.

Example: Sounds that exceed 85 decibels in amplitude, or **intensity**, will damage the auditory system.

15. The **retina** is the light-sensitive, multilayered inner surface of the eye that contains the rods and cones as well as neurons that form the beginning of the optic nerve.

16. The **rods** and **cones** are visual receptors that convert light energy into neural impulses. The rods are concentrated in the periphery of the retina, the cones in the center (the fovea). The rods have poor sensitivity; detect black, white, and gray; function well in dim light; and are needed for peripheral vision. The cones have excellent sensitivity, enable color vision, and function best in daylight or bright light.

17. Composed of the axons of retinal ganglion cells, the **optic nerve** carries neural impulses from the eye to the brain.

18. The **blind spot** is the region of the retina where the optic nerve leaves the eye. Because there are no rods or cones in this area, there is no vision here.

19. The **Young-Helmholtz trichromatic (three-color) theory** maintains that the retina contains red-, green-, and blue-sensitive color receptors that in combination can produce the perception of any color. This theory explains the first stage of color processing.

20. The **opponent-process theory** maintains that color vision depends on pairs of opposing retinal processes (red-green, yellow-blue, and white-black). This theory explains the second stage of color processing.

21. **Feature detectors**, located in the occipital lobe's visual cortex, are nerve cells that selectively respond to specific visual features, such as edge, line, or angle. Feature detectors are evidently the basis of visual information processing.

22. **Parallel processing** is information processing in which several aspects of a stimulus, such as light or sound, are processed simultaneously.

23. **Gestalt** means organized whole. The Gestalt psychologists emphasized our tendency to integrate pieces of information into meaningful wholes.

24. **Figure-ground** refers to the organization of the visual field into two parts: the figure, which stands out from its surroundings, and the surroundings, or background.

25. **Grouping** is the perceptual tendency to organize stimuli into coherent groups. Gestalt psychologists identified various principles of grouping.

26. **Depth perception** is the ability to see objects in three dimensions although the images that strike the retina are two-dimensional; it allows us to judge distance.

27. The **visual cliff** is a laboratory device for testing depth perception, especially in infants and young animals. In their experiments with the visual cliff, Gibson and Walk found strong evidence that depth perception is at least in part innate.

28. **Binocular cues** are depth cues that depend on information from both eyes.

Memory aid: Bi- indicates "two"; *ocular* means something pertaining to the eye. **Binocular cues** are cues for the "two eyes."

29. **Retinal disparity** refers to the differences between the images received by the left eye and the right eye as a result of viewing the world from slightly different angles. It is a binocular depth cue, since the greater the difference between the two images, the nearer the object.

30. **Monocular cues** are depth cues that depend on information from either eye alone.

    Memory aid: Mono- means one; a monocle is an eyeglass for one eye. A **monocular cue** is one that is available to either the left or the right eye.

31. **Perceptual constancy** is the perception that objects have consistent color, shape, and size, even as illumination and retinal images change.

32. **Color constancy** is the perception that familiar objects have consistent color despite changes in illumination that shift the wavelengths they reflect.

33. In vision, **perceptual adaptation** refers to our ability to adjust to an artificially displaced or even inverted visual field. Given distorting lenses, we perceive things accordingly but soon adjust by learning the relationship between our distorted perceptions and the reality.

34. **Audition** refers to the sense or act of hearing.

35. **Frequency** is directly related to wavelength: longer waves produce lower pitch; shorter waves produce higher pitch. The **pitch** of a sound is determined by its frequency, that is, the number of complete wavelengths that can pass a point in a given time.

36. Lying between the eardrum and the cochlea, the **middle ear** is a chamber containing three small bones (hammer, anvil, and stirrup).

37. The **cochlea** is the coiled, bony, fluid-filled tube of the inner ear through which sound waves trigger neural impulses.

38. The **inner ear** contains the innermost parts of the ear, including the cochlea, semicircular canals, and vestibular sacs.

39. **Sensorineural hearing loss** (nerve deafness) is hearing loss caused by damage to the auditory receptors of the cochlea or to the auditory nerve due to disease, heredity, aging, or prolonged exposure to ear-splitting noise.

40. **Conduction hearing loss** refers to the hearing loss that results from damage in the mechanical system of the outer or middle ear, which impairs the conduction of sound waves to the cochlea.

41. A **cochlear implant** is an electronic device that converts sounds into electrical signals that stimulate the auditory nerve.

42. **Hypnosis** is a social interaction in which one person (the hypnotist) suggests to another (the subject) that certain perceptions, feelings, thoughts, or behaviors will occur without warning.

43. A **posthypnotic suggestion** is a suggestion made during hypnosis, to be carried out after the subject is no longer hypnotized.

44. **Kinesthesia** is the sense of the position and movement of the parts of the body.

45. The sense of your head's (and thus your body's) movement and position, including the sense of balance, is called the **vestibular sense**.

46. **Sensory interaction** is the principle that one sense may influence another.

47. **Embodied cognition** refers to the influence of bodily sensations, gestures, and other states on cognitive preferences and judgments.

48. **Extrasensory perception (ESP)** refers to the controversial claim that perception can occur without sensory input. Supposed ESP powers include telepathy, clairvoyance, and precognition.

    Memory aid: Extra- means "beyond" or "in addition to"; **extrasensory perception** is perception outside or beyond the normal senses.

Learning

Chapter Overview

No topic is closer to the heart of psychology than learning. Chapter 6 covers the basic principles of associative learning, which includes classical conditioning (learning associations between events) and operant conditioning (learning to engage in behaviors that are rewarded and to avoid behaviors that are punished), and cognitive learning, which includes observational learning (learning by observing and imitating others).

The chapter also covers several important issues, including the generality of principles of learning, the role of cognitive processes in learning, and the ways in which learning is constrained by the biological predispositions of different species.

Chapter Review

First, skim each text section, noting headings and boldface items. Review the section by reading the objectives and summaries provided here, then answer the questions that follow. In some cases, STUDY TIPS explain how best to learn a difficult concept and APPLICATIONS help you to know how well you understand the material. Check your understanding of the material by consulting the answers beginning on page 125. Do not continue with the next section until you understand each answer. If you need to, review or reread the section in the textbook before continuing.

How Do We Learn?

Objective 6-1: Identify some basic forms of learning.

Learning is a relatively permanent change in an organism's behavior due to experience. We learn by *association*; our mind naturally links events that occur in sequence. The events linked may be two *stimuli* (as in classical conditioning) or a response and its consequences (as in operant conditioning). In observational learning, one form of *cognitive learning,* we learn by viewing others' experiences and examples.

1. The process of acquiring, through experience, new and relatively enduring information or behaviors is called _____ .

2. Even simple animals, such as the sea slug *Aplysia,* can learn simple _____ between stimuli. This type of learning is called _____ _____ .

3. The type of learning in which we learn to associate two stimuli is _____ conditioning. A stimulus is any event or situation that _____ . When we automatically respond to stimuli we can't control, it is called _____ _____ .

4. The tendency to associate a response and its consequence forms the basis of _____ conditioning. When we learn to repeat acts followed by good results and to avoid acts followed by bad results, it is called _____ .

5. We also acquire mental information that guides our behavior through _____ _____ . In one form of this type of learning, _____ _____ ,we learn from others' experiences.

Classical Conditioning

Objective 6-2: Define *classical conditioning,* and explain how it demonstrates associative learning.

Using what is now known as **classical conditioning,** the Russian physiologist Ivan Pavlov repeatedly presented to a dog a **neutral stimulus (NS),** such as a tone, just before an **unconditioned stimulus (US),** such as food, which triggered the **unconditioned response (UR)** of salivation. After several repetitions, the tone alone (now the **conditioned stimulus [CS]**) began triggering a **conditioned response (CR),** salivation.

6. In Pavlov's classic experiment, a tone, or

_____ _____ ,

is sounded just before food, the

_____ _____ ,

is placed in the animal's mouth.

7. Eventually, the dogs in Pavlov's experiment would salivate on hearing the tone, now called the

_____ _____ .

This salivation is called the

_____ _____ .

STUDY TIP: Students often confuse "stimulus" with "response" and "conditioned" with "unconditioned." The stimulus is the event that causes something else, the response, to happen. Unconditioned means "unlearned"; conditioned means "learned." Thus, an unconditioned response (UR) is an event that occurs naturally in response to some stimulus. An unconditioned stimulus (US) is something that naturally and automatically triggers the unlearned response. A conditioned stimulus (CS) is an originally neutral stimulus that, through learning, comes to be associated with some unlearned response. A conditioned response (CR) is the learned response to the originally neutral but now conditioned stimulus.

Stimulus (event or other trigger) → Response
Unconditioned = unlearned
Conditioned = learned
So, unconditioned stimulus + conditioned stimulus
↓   ↓
unconditioned response   conditioned response

APPLICATION:

Classical conditioning is all around us. It is especially common in the realm of emotional behavior. Test your understanding of the basic elements of classical conditioning in the following example. Then, consider whether there are emotions of your own that might have developed as the product of classical conditioning.

As a child, you were playing in the yard one day when a neighbor's cat wandered over. Your mother (who has a terrible fear of animals) screamed and snatched you into her arms.

Her behavior caused you to cry. You now have a fear of cats.

8. The CS is _____ .

9. The US is _____ .

10. The CR is _____ .

11. The UR is _____ .

Objective 6-3: Describe the parts played by acquisition, extinction, spontaneous recovery, generalization, and discrimination in classical conditoning.

Responses are **acquired** best when the CS is presented half a second before the US. They are **extinguished** when the conditioned stimulus occurs repeatedly without the unconditioned stimulus. If, after a pause, the CR reappears, **spontaneous recovery** has occurred. **Generalization** is the tendency to respond to stimuli that are similar to the conditioned stimulus. **Discrimination** is the learned ability to distinguish between a CS and other irrelevant stimuli.

STUDY TIP: Some students find the terms discrimination and generalization confusing because of their negative social connotations. In the context of classical conditioning, discrimination is a healthy sign that the subject of conditioning has learned the difference between two stimuli, much as a "discriminating coffee lover" can taste subtle variations between two coffee blends. Generalization is apparent when discrimination does not occur.

Use the following graph to answer 12(a), 13(b), and 14(c).

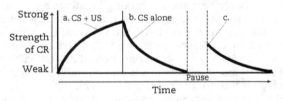

12. The initial learning of a conditioned response is

called (a) _____ . For many conditioning situations, the optimal interval between a neutral stimulus and the US is

_____ _____ .

13. If a CS is repeatedly presented without the US,

(b) _____ soon occurs; that is, the CR diminishes.

14. Following a pause, however, the CR reappears in response to the CS; this is called

(c) _____ .

15. Humans and other animals often respond to a similar stimulus as they would to the original CS. This is

called _____ .

16. Humans and other animals can also be trained not to respond to _____ stimuli. This learned ability is called _____ .

APPLICATION: Bill had an American-made car that was in the shop more than it was out. Since then he will not even consider owning an American-made car.

17. Bill's attitude is an example of _____ .
Bill's friend Andy also had an American-made car with similar problems. Deciding that it was just that brand, Andy decided to try another brand—rather than bunch all American-made cars together, he was a _____ buyer of cars.

Objective 6-4: Explain why Pavlov's work remains important, and describe how his work is being applied.

Pavlov taught us that principles of learning apply across species and that classical conditioning is one way that virtually all organisms learn to adapt to their environment. Pavlov also demonstrated that significant psychological phenomena can be studied objectively. Finally, Pavlov taught us that conditioning principles have important applications, such as how to treat fear.

Classical conditioning principles provide important insights into drug abuse and how it may be overcome. Watson's "Little Albert" study demonstrated how classical conditioning may underlie specific fears. Today, psychologists use extinction procedures to control our less adaptive emotions and condition new responses to emotion-arousing stimuli.

18. Pavlov showed that classical conditioning is one way that virtually all organisms learn to _____ to their environment.

19. Another aspect of Pavlov's legacy is that he showed how a process such as learning could be studied _____ .

20. Through classical conditioning, drug users often develop a _____ when they encounter _____ associated with previous highs.

Describe the Watson and Rayner experiment.

Operant Conditioning

Objective 6-5: Define *operant conditioning,* and describe how operant behavior is reinforced and shaped.

Unlike classical conditioning, which involves automatic *respondent behavior,* **operant conditioning** associates actions with their consequences, and so involves *operant behavior.* Building on Edward Thorndike's *law of effect,* B. F. Skinner developed experiments that would reveal *behavior control.* He created an **operant chamber** (*Skinner box*) for his pioneering studies of operant conditioning with rats and pigeons.

In his experiments, Skinner used **shaping,** a procedure involving **reinforcers** that guide an animal's natural behavior toward a desired behavior. By rewarding responses that are ever closer to the final desired behavior (*successive approximations*) and ignoring all other responses, researchers can gradually shape complex behaviors.

21. Classical conditioning and operant conditioning are both forms of _____ _____ .

22. Through classical conditioning, an organism associates different _____ that it does not _____ and responds _____ .

23. The reflexive responses of classical conditioning are called _____ behavior.

24. The form of learning in which we learn to associate our behavior with its consequences is called _____ _____ .

25. Voluntary behaviors that operate on the environment and produce consequences are called _____ behavior.

26. The principles that rewarded behavior is likely to be repeated is called the _____ _____ _____ and was formulated by _____ .

27. B. F. Skinner designed an apparatus, called the _____ _____ , to investigate learning in animals.

28. Any event that increases the frequency of a preceding response is called _____ .

29. The procedure in which a person teaches an intricate behavior by building up to it in small steps is called _____ . This method involves reinforcing successive _____ of the desired behavior.

Objective 6-6: Discuss the differences between positive and negative reinforcement, and identify the basic types of reinforcers.

Reinforcers can be *positive* (presenting a pleasant stimulus after a response) or *negative* (reducing or removing an unpleasant stimulus). *Primary reinforcers,* such as food when we are hungry, are innately satisfying. *Conditioned reinforcers,* such as cash, are satisfying because we have learned to associate them with more basic rewards. Immediate reinforcers, such as the nicotine addict's cigarette, offer immediate payback. Delayed reinforcers, such as a weekly paycheck, require the ability to delay gratification.

STUDY TIP: Some students have a problem differentiating positive and negative reinforcers because they naturally think "positive" indicates a "good," or desirable, outcome, while "negative" connotes a "bad," or undesirable, outcome. Remember that from the organism's point of view, reinforcement is always a desirable outcome. You may find it useful to think of a photography analogy. A "negative" is a reverse image in which the "positive" photographic image is not present. So too, negative reinforcement involves taking away an event—in this case, one that is undesirable.

---

30. A pleasurable stimulus that, when presented after a response, strengthens that response is a

    _____ _____ .

31. A negative (unpleasant) stimulus that, when removed after a response, strengthens that response is a _____ _____ .

32. Reinforcers, such as food and shock, that are related to basic needs and so do not rely on learning are called _____ _____ . Reinforcers that gain their power through association with basic reinforcers are called

    _____ _____ .

33. As we mature, we learn to _____ gratification rather than opt for the immediate reward.

34. Sometimes, immediate reinforcement _____ (is/is not) more effective than its alternative, _____ reinforcement. This explains in part why many people continue to use the large vehicles that use so much gas, as well as the tendency of some teens to engage in impulsive,

    _____ _____ .

APPLICATIONS:

35. Jack finally takes out the garbage in order to get his father to stop pestering him. Jack's behavior is being influenced by _____ _____ .

36. Your instructor invites you to her home as part of a select group of students to discuss possible careers in psychology. The invitation is an example of a _____

    _____ .

Objective 6-7: Explain how continuous and partial reinforcement schedules affect behavior.

When the desired response is reinforced every time it occurs, *continuous reinforcement* is involved. Learning is rapid but so is extinction if rewards cease. *Partial (intermittent) reinforcement* produces slower acquisition of the target behavior than does continuous reinforcement, but the learning is more resistant to extinction. *Reinforcement schedules* may vary according to the number of responses rewarded (*fixed-ratio* or *variable-ratio*) or the time gap between responses (*fixed-interval* or *variable-interval*).

37. The procedure involving reinforcement of each and every response is called _____ _____ . Under these conditions, learning is _____ (rapid/slow). When this type of reinforcement is discontinued, extinction is _____ (rapid/slow).

38. The procedure in which responses are reinforced only part of the time is called _____ reinforcement. Under these conditions, learning is generally _____ (faster/slower) than it is with continuous reinforcement. Behavior reinforced in this manner is _____ (very/not very) resistant to extinction.

39. When behavior is reinforced after a set number of responses, a _____ - _____ schedule is in effect.

40. When reinforcement occurs after an unpredictable number of responses, a _____ - _____ schedule is being used.

41. Reinforcement of the first response after a set interval of time defines the _____ - _____ schedule. An example of this schedule is _____

    _____ .

42. When the first response after varying amounts of time is reinforced, a _____ - _____ schedule is in effect. An example of this schedule is _____

    _____ .

APPLICATIONS:

43. You are expecting an important letter in the mail. As the regular delivery time approaches you glance more and more frequently out the window, searching for the letter carrier. Your behavior in this situation typifies that associated with which schedule of reinforcement?

   a. fixed-ratio   **c** fixed-interval
   b. variable-ratio   **d.** variable-interval

44. From a casino owner's viewpoint, which of the following jackpot-payout schedules would be the most desirable for reinforcing customer use of a slot machine?

   a. variable-ratio   **c.** variable-interval
   b. fixed-ratio   **d.** fixed-interval

45. Lars, a shoe salesman, is paid every two weeks, whereas Tom receives a commission for each pair of shoes he sells. Evidently, Lars is paid on a _____ schedule of reinforcement, and Tom on a _____ schedule of reinforcement.

   a. fixed-ratio; fixed-interval
   b. continuous; intermittent
   c. fixed-interval; fixed-ratio
   d. variable-interval; variable-ratio

46. Three-year-old Yosef knows that if he cries when he wants a treat, his mother will sometimes give in. Yosef is receiving treats on a _____-_____ schedule.

Objective 6-8: Discuss how punishment and negative reinforcement differ, and explain how punishment affects behavior.

Unlike negative reinforcement, which increases the frequency of a behavior, *punishment* attempts to decrease the frequency of a behavior. Punishment administers an aversive stimulus, for example, spanking or withdrawing something desirable, such as taking away a favorite toy. Punishment can have several undesirable side effects, including suppressing rather than changing unwanted behaviors, creating fear, and teaching aggression.

47. Unlike _____ _____ , which increases the behavior that preceded it, _____ is a negative consequence that decreases the likelihood of the behavior that preceded it. Thus, taking aspirin to relieve a headache is an example of _____ _____ , and a child being sent to his room after spilling his milk is an example of _____ .

48. An aversive consequence that decreases the likelihood of the behavior that preceded it is called _____ . If an aversive stimulus is administered, it is called _____ _____ . If a desirable stimulus is withdrawn, it is called _____ _____ .

49. Because punished behavior is merely _____ , it may reappear. Also, punishment teaches _____ , that behavior that is unacceptable in one context may be acceptable in another. Punishment can also lead to _____ , as well as to the association of the aversive event with _____ .

50. Physical punishment also often increases _____ by _____ violence.

51.

Behavior	Consequence	Which Is Taken Away, Something Good or Bad?	Is This Punishment or Negative Reinforcement?
Driving while intoxicated	Lose driver's license	Good	Punishment
a. Forgetting to give your roommate a phone message			
b. Putting on your coat so that you are no longer cold			
c. Getting a drink when you are thirsty			
d. Using your laptop until the battery dies			
e. Your brother nagging you until you help him with his homework			

Objective 6-9: Discuss why Skinner's ideas were controversial, and describe how his operant conditioning principles might be applied at school, at work, in parenting, and for self-improvement.

Skinner has been criticized for repeatedly insisting that external influences, not internal thoughts and feelings, shape behavior and for urging the use of operant principles to control people's behavior. Critics argue that he dehumanized people by neglecting their personal freedom and by seeking to control their actions. Skinner countered: People's behavior is already controlled by external reinforcers, so why not administer those consequences for human betterment?

Operant principles have been applied in a variety of settings. For example, in schools, online adaptive quizzing systems embody the operant ideal of individualized shaping and immediate feedback. In the workplace, positive reinforcement for jobs well done has boosted employee productivity. At home, parents can reward their children's desirable behaviors and not reward those that are undesirable. To reach our personal goals, we can monitor and reinforce our own desired behaviors and cut back on incentives as the behaviors become habitual.

52. Skinner's critics argued that he _____ people by neglecting their personal _____ and by seeking to _____ their actions.

53. The use of machines and textbooks was an early application of the operant conditioning procedure of _____ to education. Online _____ _____ systems are newer examples of this application of operant principles.

54. In boosting productivity in the workplace, positive reinforcement is _____ (more/less) effective when applied to specific behaviors than when given to reward general merit and when the desired performance is well-defined and _____ . For such behaviors, immediate reinforcement is _____ (more/no more) effective than delayed reinforcement.

55. In parenting, give children attention and other _____ when they are behaving well. When they misbehave or are defiant, explain what they did wrong and give them a _____ - _____ .

56. To improve your own behavior, follow these steps: State a _____ goal and announce it; _____ how, when, and where you'll work toward your goal; _____ how often you engage in your desired behavior; _____ that behavior; then reduce the _____ gradually.

Objective 6-10: Describe how classical conditioning differs from operant conditioning.

Both classical and operant conditioning are forms of *associative learning*. They both involve *acquisition, extinction, spontaneous recovery, generalization,* and *discrimination.* The two forms of learning differ in an important way. In classical conditioning, organisms associate different stimuli that they do not control and respond automatically (*respondent behavior*). In operant conditioning, organisms associate their own behaviors with their consequences (*operant behavior*).

Use the following questions to review your understanding of the similarities and differences between classical and operant conditioning.

57. Classical conditioning and operant conditioning are both forms of _____ learning. Both types of conditioning involve similar processes of _____ , _____ , _____ _____ , _____ , and _____ .

58. Through _____ _____ , an organism associates different stimuli that it doesn't control and responds _____ (called _____ _____).

59. Through _____ _____ , an organism associates its _____ _____ with their _____ .

STUDY TIP/APPLICATION: If you still find yourself confusing classical conditioning and operant conditioning, try the following. Ask yourself two questions: (1) Is the behavior voluntary (operant conditioning) or involuntary (classical conditioning)? (2) Does the learning involve an association between two stimuli (classical conditioning) or between a response and an outcome (operant conditioning)? Test your understanding with the following examples.

60.

Behavior	Is the Behavior Voluntary or Involuntary?	Type of Conditioning
a. After receiving a mild shock from the "invisible fence" surrounding his yard, a dog no longer crosses the boundary.		
b. You flinch when someone yells, "Duck!"		
c. You ask more questions in class after the professor praises you for a good question.		
d. The pupil of your eye dilates (opens wider) after you enter a darkened theater.		

Biology, Cognition, and Learning

Objective 6-11: Describe the limits biology places on conditioning.

Evolutionary theorist Charles Darwin proposed that *natural selection* favors traits that aid survival. In the middle of the twentieth century, researchers (beginning with a discovery by John Garcia and Robert Koelling) showed that there are **biological constraints** on learning. In line with Darwin's theory, each species is biologically prepared to learn associations that enhance its survival.

As with classical conditioning, an animal's natural predispositions constrain its capacity for operant conditioning. Biological constraints predispose organisms to learn associations that are naturally adaptive. Training that attempts to override these tendencies will probably not endure because the animals will revert to their biologically predisposed patterns.

61. Biological _____ predispose organisms to learn associations that are naturally _____ . Garcia and Koelling dis-

covered that rats would associate _____ with taste but not with other stimuli. Garcia found that taste-aversion conditioning _____ (would/would not) occur when the delay between the CS and the US was more than an hour. Results such as these confirm Darwin's principle that _____ _____ favors traits that aid survival.

62. The principle that biological predispositions _____ classical conditioning _____ (does/does not) apply to operant conditioning.

Objective 6-12: Explain how cognitive processes affect classical and operant conditioning.

Pavlov and John B. Watson, who built on Pavlov's work in establishing the school of **behaviorism,** also underestimated the role of cognitive processes in learning.

Research indicates that, for many animals, thoughts, perceptions, and expectations are important to the conditioning process.

With operant conditioning, B. F. Skinner discounted the importance of cognitive influences. But research has shown that rats exploring a maze seem to develop a mental representation (a *cognitive map*) of the maze even in the absence of reward. Their *latent learning* becomes evident only when there is some incentive to demonstrate it.

Research indicates that people may come to see rewards, rather than intrinsic interest, as the motivation for performing a task. Again, this finding demonstrates the importance of cognitive processing in learning. By undermining *intrinsic motivation,* the desire to perform a behavior for its own sake, rewards can carry hidden costs. *Extrinsic motivation* is the desire to perform a behavior because of promised rewards or threats of punishment.

63. The view that psychology should be an objective science based on observable behavior was called

_____ .

64. When a well-learned route in a maze is blocked, rats sometimes choose an alternative route, acting as if they were consulting a _____

_____ .

65. Animals may learn from experience even when reinforcement is not available. When learning is not apparent until reinforcement has been provided, _____ _____ is said to have occurred.

66. Excessive rewards may undermine _____ _____ , which is the desire to perform a behavior for its own sake. The motivation to seek external rewards and avoid punishment is called _____ _____ .

Learning by Observation

Objective 6-13: Discuss how observational learning differs from associative learning, and explain how observational learning may be enabled by mirror neurons.

Among higher animals, especially humans, learning does not occur through direct experience alone (as in associative learning). *Observational learning* also plays a part. The process of observing and imitating a specific behavior is called *modeling*. Albert Bandura was a pioneering researcher of this type of learning. Some researchers believe that *mirror neurons* demonstrate a neural basis for observational learning.

67. Learning by observing and imitating others is called _____ _____ , or _____ when it involves a specific _____ .

68. The psychologist best known for research on observational learning is _____ . Through _____ reinforcement or _____ punishment, we learn to anticipate a behavior's consequences in situations like those we are observing. This is especially true if the models are _____ to ourselves, _____ , and _____ .

69. In one experiment, the child who viewed an adult punch an inflatable doll played _____ (more/less) aggressively than the child who had not observed the adult.

70. Neuroscientists have found _____ neurons in the brain that are thought to provide a neural basis for _____ learning.

Objective 6-14: Discuss the impact of prosocial modeling and of antisocial modeling.

Prosocial models can have prosocial effects. People who show nonviolent, helpful behavior prompt similar behavior in others. Models are most effective when their actions and words are consistent, they are attractive and when they commit seemingly justified violence that goes unpunished and causes no visible pain or harm.

71. Children will model positive, or _____ , behaviors. Models are most effective when their words and actions are _____ .

72. Observational learning may also have _____ effects. These results may help explain why _____ parents might have _____ children. However, _____ factors may also be involved.

APPLICATION: Children—and of course, adults—learn a great deal by watching other people. Depending on the models, the behavior they learn may be good or bad.

73. During holiday breaks Lionel watches wrestling, which _____ his aggressive tendencies. His brother Michael won't watch the wrestling because he feels the pain of the choke hold, for example, as reflected in his brain's _____ _____ . Instead, Michael spends time with Grandma, who cooks for the poor during the holiday season, helping Michael to learn _____ behavior.

Objective 6-15: Describe the violence-viewing effect.

Correlational studies that link viewing violence with violent behavior do not indicate the direction of influence.

Those who behave violently may enjoy watching violence on TV, or some third factor may cause observers both to behave violently and to prefer watching violent programs. To establish cause and effect, researchers have designed experiments in which some participants view violence and others do not. Later, given an opportunity to express violence, the people who viewed violence tend to be more aggressive and less sympathetic. In addition to imitating what they see, observers may become desensitized to brutality, whether on TV or in real life.

74. Correlation does not prove _____ . Most researchers believe that watching violence on television _____ (does/does not) lead to aggressive behavior.

75. Models are most effective when they are perceived as _____ and when their behavior goes _____ and _____ (does/does not) cause visible harm.

76. This violence-viewing effect stems from several factors, including _____ of observed aggression and the tendency of prolonged exposure to violence to _____ viewers.

Progress Test

Multiple-Choice Questions

Circle your answers to the following questions and check them with the answers beginning on page 126. If your answer is incorrect, read the explanation for why it is incorrect and then consult the text.

1. *Learning* is best defined as
   a. any behavior produced by an organism without being provoked.
   b. a change in the behavior of an organism.
   c. the process of acquiring, through experience, new and relatively enduring information or behaviors.
   d. behavior based on operant rather than respondent conditioning.

2. The type of learning associated with B. F. Skinner is
   a. classical conditioning.
   b. operant conditioning.
   c. respondent conditioning.
   d. observational learning.

3. In Pavlov's original experiment with dogs, the tone was initially a(n) _____ stimulus; after it was paired with meat, it became a(n) _____ stimulus.
   a. conditioned; neutral
   b. neutral; conditioned
   c. conditioned; unconditioned
   d. unconditioned; conditioned

4. To obtain a reward a monkey learns to press a lever when a 1000-Hz tone is on but not when a 1200-Hz tone is on. What kind of training is this?
   a. extinction
   b. generalization
   c. classical conditioning
   d. discrimination

5. Which of the following statements concerning reinforcement is correct?
   a. Learning is most rapid with intermittent reinforcement, but continuous reinforcement produces the greatest resistance to extinction.
   b. Learning is most rapid with continuous reinforcement, but intermittent reinforcement produces the greatest resistance to extinction.
   c. Learning is fastest and resistance to extinction is greatest after continuous reinforcement.
   d. Learning is fastest and resistance to extinction is greatest following intermittent reinforcement.

6. When a conditioned stimulus is presented without an accompanying unconditioned stimulus, _____ will soon take place.
   a. generalization   c. extinction
   b. discrimination   d. aversion

7. One difference between classical and operant conditioning is that
   a. in classical conditioning, the responses operate on the environment to produce rewarding or punishing stimuli.
   b. in operant conditioning, the responses are triggered by preceding stimuli.
   c. in classical conditioning, the responses are automatically triggered by stimuli.
   d. in operant conditioning, the responses are reflexive.

8. Learning by imitating others' behaviors is called _____ learning. The researcher best known for studying this type of learning is _____ .
   a. secondary; B. F. Skinner
   b. observational; Albert Bandura
   c. secondary; Ivan Pavlov
   d. observational; John B. Watson

9. Punishment is a controversial way of controlling behavior because
   a. behavior is not forgotten and may return.
   b. punishing stimuli often create fear.
   c. punishment often increases aggressiveness.
   d. of all of these reasons.

10. For the most rapid conditioning, a CS should be presented
   a. after the US.
   b. before the US.
   c. without the US.
   d. at the same time as the US.

11. During extinction, the _____ is omitted; as a result, the _____ seems to disappear.
    a. US; UR
    b. CS; CR
    c. US; CR
    d. CS; UR

12. In Watson and Rayner's experiment, the loud noise was the _____ and the white rat was the _____.
    a. CS; CR
    b. US; CS
    c. CS; US
    d. US; CR

13. In which of the following may classical conditioning play a role?
    a. emotional problems
    b. the nausea a cancer patient experiences upon entering a treatment room.
    c. helping drug addicts
    d. all of these answers

14. Shaping is a(n) _____ technique for _____ a behavior.
    a. operant; establishing
    b. operant; suppressing
    c. respondent; establishing
    d. respondent; suppressing

15. In Pavlov's studies of classical conditioning of a dog's salivary responses, spontaneous recovery occurred
    a. during acquisition, when the CS was first paired with the US.
    b. during extinction, when the CS was first presented by itself.
    c. when the CS was reintroduced following extinction of the CR and a rest period.
    d. during discrimination training, when several conditioned stimuli were introduced.

16. In distinguishing between negative reinforcers and punishment, we note that
    a. punishment, but not negative reinforcement, involves use of a negative stimulus.
    b. in contrast to punishment, negative reinforcement decreases the likelihood of a response by presenting a negative stimulus.
    c. in contrast to punishment, negative reinforcement increases the likelihood of a response by presenting a negative stimulus.
    d. in contrast to punishment, negative reinforcement increases the likelihood of a response by ending a negative stimulus.

17. In promoting observational learning, the most effective models are those we perceive as
    a. similar to ourselves.
    b. admired.
    c. successful.
    d. having all of these attributes.

18. A cognitive map is a
    a. mental representation of one's environment.
    b. sequence of thought processes leading from one idea to another.

c. set of instructions detailing the most effective means of teaching a particular concept.
d. biological predisposition to learn a particular skill.

19. After exploring a complicated maze for several days, a rat subsequently ran the maze with very few errors when food was placed in the goal box for the first time. This performance illustrates
    a. classical conditioning.
    b. discrimination learning.
    c. observational learning.
    d. latent learning.

20. Online adaptive quizzing systems are applications of the operant conditioning principles of
    a. shaping and immediate reinforcement.
    b. immediate reinforcement and punishment.
    c. shaping and primary reinforcement.
    d. continuous reinforcement and punishment.

21. Which of the following is the best example of a conditioned reinforcer?
    a. putting on a coat on a cold day
    b. relief from pain after the dentist stops drilling your teeth
    c. receiving a cool drink after washing your mother's car on a hot day
    d. receiving an approving nod from the boss for a job well done

22. Experiments on taste-aversion learning demonstrate that
    a. for the conditioning of certain stimuli the US need not immediately follow the CS.
    b. any perceivable stimulus can become a CS.
    c. all animals are biologically primed to associate illness with the taste of a tainted food.
    d. all of these findings are true.

23. Regarding the impact of watching television violence on children, most researchers believe that
    a. aggressive children simply prefer violent programs.
    b. television simply reflects, rather than contributes to, violent social trends.
    c. watching violence on television contributes to aggressive behavior.
    d. there is only a weak correlation between exposure to violence and aggressive behavior.

24. You always rattle the box of dog biscuits before giving your dog a treat. As you do so, your dog salivates. Rattling the box is a _____ ; your dog's salivation is a _____ .
    a. CS; CR
    b. CS; UR
    c. US; CR
    d. US; UR

25. You teach your dog to fetch the paper by giving him a cookie each time he does so. This is an example of
    a. operant conditioning.
    b. classical conditioning.

c. conditioned reinforcement.
d. partial reinforcement.

26. A pigeon can easily be taught to flap its wings to avoid shock but not for food reinforcement. According to the text, this is most likely so because
   a. pigeons are biologically predisposed to flap their wings to escape negative events and to use their beaks to obtain food.
   b. shock is a more motivating stimulus for birds than food is.
   c. hungry animals have difficulty delaying their eating long enough to learn *any* new skill.
   d. of all of these reasons.

27. After discovering that her usual route home was closed due to road repairs, Sharetta used her knowledge of the city and sense of direction to find an alternative route. This is an example of
   a. latent learning.
   b. observational learning.
   c. shaping.
   d. using a cognitive map.

28. Cognitive processes are
   a. unimportant in classical and operant conditioning.
   b. important in both classical and operant conditioning.
   c. more important in classical than in operant conditioning.
   d. more important in operant than in classical conditioning.

29. A response that leads to the removal of an unpleasant stimulus is one being
   a. positively reinforced.
   b. negatively reinforced.
   c. punished.
   d. extinguished.

30. Which of the following is an example of reinforcement?
   a. presenting a positive stimulus after a response
   b. removing an unpleasant stimulus after a response
   c. being told that you have done a good job
   d. All of these are examples.

31. For operant conditioning to be MOST effective, when should the reinforcers be presented in relation to the desired response?
   a. immediately before
   b. immediately after
   c. at the same time as
   d. at least a half hour before

32. On an intermittent reinforcement schedule, reinforcement is given
   a. in very small amounts.
   b. randomly.

c. for successive approximations of a desired behavior.
d. only some of the time.

33. After watching coverage of the Olympics on television recently, Lynn and Susan have been staging their own "summer games." Which of the following best accounts for their behavior?
   a. classical conditioning
   b. observational learning
   c. latent learning
   d. shaping

34. Which of the following is an example of shaping?
   a. A dog learns to salivate at the sight of a box of dog biscuits.
   b. A new driver learns to stop at an intersection when the light changes to red.
   c. A parrot is rewarded first for making any sound, then for making a sound similar to "Laura," and then for "speaking" its owner's name.
   d. A psychology student reinforces a laboratory rat only occasionally, to make its behavior more resistant to extinction.

35. Nancy decided to take introductory psychology because she has always been interested in human behavior. Jack enrolled in the same course because he thought it would be easy. Nancy's behavior was motivated by _____ , Jack's by _____ .
   a. extrinsic motivation; intrinsic motivation
   b. intrinsic motivation; extrinsic motivation
   c. drives; incentives
   d. incentives; drives

36. The "piecework," or commission, method of payment is an example of which reinforcement schedule?
   a. fixed-interval
   b. variable-interval
   c. fixed-ratio
   d. variable-ratio

37. Leon's psychology instructor has scheduled an exam every third week of the term. Leon will probably study the most just before an exam and the least just after an exam. This is because the schedule of exams is reinforcing studying according to which schedule?
   a. fixed-ratio
   b. variable-ratio
   c. fixed-interval
   d. variable-interval

38. The highest and most consistent rate of response is produced by a _____ schedule.
   a. fixed-ratio
   b. variable-ratio
   c. fixed-interval
   d. variable-interval

39. Mirror neurons are found in the brain's _____ and are believed by some scientists to be the neural basis for _____ .
   a. frontal lobe; observational learning
   b. frontal lobe; classical conditioning
   a. temporal lobe; operant conditioning
   d. temporal lobe; observational learning

Matching Items

Match each definition or description with the appropriate term.

Definitions or Descriptions

_____ 1. presentation of a desired stimulus
_____ 2. tendency for similar stimuli to evoke a CR
_____ 3. removal of a negative stimulus
_____ 4. an innately reinforcing stimulus
_____ 5. the acquisition of mental information by watching others
_____ 6. an acquired reinforcer
_____ 7. the motivation to perform a behavior for its own sake
_____ 8. reinforcers guide actions closer and closer to a desired behavior
_____ 9. the reappearance of a weakened CR
_____ 10. presentation of a negative stimulus
_____ 11. learning that becomes apparent only after reinforcement is provided
_____ 12. each and every response is reinforced
_____ 13. a desire to perform a behavior due to promised rewards
_____ 14. rewarded behavior becomes more likely

Terms

a. shaping
b. punishment
c. spontaneous recovery
d. latent learning
e. positive reinforcement
f. negative reinforcement
g. primary reinforcer
h. law of effect
i. conditioned reinforcer
j. continuous reinforcement
k. extrinsic motivation
l. intrinsic motivation
m. cognitive learning
n. generalization

Application Essay

Manuel is 9 years old, living in the hills of Guatemala. His school has just received 10 new computers. How might his teachers use operant conditioning to teach him computing basics? (Use the space below to list the points you want to make, and organize them. Then write the essay on a separate piece of paper.)

Summing Up

See pages 126–127.

Terms and Concepts to Remember

Using your own words, on a piece of paper write a brief definition or explanation of each of the following terms.

1. learning
2. associative learning
3. stimulus
4. respondent behavior
5. operant behavior
6. cognitive learning
7. classical conditioning
8. neutral stimulus (NS)
9. unconditioned response (UR)
10. unconditioned stimulus (US)
11. conditioned response (CR)
12. conditioned stimulus (CS)
13. acquisition
14. extinction
15. spontaneous recovery
16. generalization
17. discrimination
18. operant conditioning
19. law of effect
20. operant chamber
21. reinforcement
22. shaping

23. positive reinforcement
24. negative reinforcement
25. primary reinforcer
26. conditioned reinforcer
27. reinforcement schedule
28. continuous reinforcement
29. partial (intermittent) reinforcement
30. fixed-ratio schedule
31. variable-ratio schedule
32. fixed-interval schedule
33. variable-interval schedule
34. punishment
35. biological constraints
36. behaviorism
37. cognitive map
38. latent learning
39. intrinsic motivation
40. extrinsic motivation
41. observational learning
42. modeling
43. mirror neurons
44. prosocial behavior

Answers

Chapter Review

How Do We Learn?

1. learning
2. associations; associative learning
3. classical; evokes a response; respondent behavior
4. operant; operant behavior
5. cognitive learning; observational learning

Classical Conditioning

6. neutral stimulus (NS); unconditioned stimulus (US)
7. conditioned stimulus (CS); conditioned response (CR)
8. Because the cat was associated with your mother's scream, it triggered a fear response, and is thus the CS.
9. Your mother's scream and evident fear, which naturally caused you to cry, was the US.
10. Your fear of cats is the CR. An acquired fear is always a conditioned response.
11. Your crying, automatically triggered by your mother's scream and fear, was the UR.
12. (a) acquisition; one-half second

13. (b) extinction
14. (c) spontaneous recovery
15. generalization
16. similar; discrimination
17. generalization; discriminating. Bill is extending (generalizing) a learned aversion to a specific American-made car to all American-made cars. Andy, on the other hand, looks at each brand of car separately (he is a discriminating buyer).
18. adapt
19. objectively
20. craving; people or places

In Watson and Rayner's experiment, classical conditioning was used to condition fear of a rat in Albert, an 11-month-old infant. When Albert touched the white rat (neutral stimulus), a loud noise (unconditioned stimulus) was sounded. After several pairings of the rat with the noise, Albert began crying at the mere sight of the rat. The rat had become a conditioned stimulus, triggering a conditioned response of fear.

Operant Conditioning

21. associative learning
22. stimuli; control; automatically
23. respondent
24. operant conditioning
25. operant
26. law of effect; Edward Thorndike
27. operant chamber (Skinner box)
28. reinforcement
29. shaping; approximations
30. positive reinforcer
31. negative reinforcer
32. primary reinforcers; conditioned (secondary) reinforcers
33. delay
34. is; delayed; unprotected sex
35. negative reinforcement. By taking out the garbage, Jack terminates a negative stimulus—his father's nagging.
36. conditioned reinforcer. Being invited to your instructor's home as part of a select group is a conditioned reinforcer in that it doesn't satisfy an innate need but has become linked with desirable consequences.
37. continuous reinforcement; rapid; rapid
38. partial (intermittent); slower; very
39. fixed-ratio
40. variable-ratio
41. fixed-interval; checking your e-mail more often as the time for an expected response approaches

Summing Up

CLASSICAL CONDITIONING

| A puff of air to the eye, the _____, | elicits → | an eyeblink, the UR. |

The puff of air is paired with

| a bell ringing, the _____, which becomes a _____, | that elicits → | an eyeblink, a _____ . |

This is the _____ stage of classical conditioning.

Presenting the CS alone for several trials

results in

_____ .

After a period of rest, pairing the _____ and _____

results in

_____ .
_____ .

If a CS similar to the original CS is presented,

| responding with the CR represents | not responding to the similar CS represents |

| _____ ; | _____ . |

OPERANT CONDITIONING

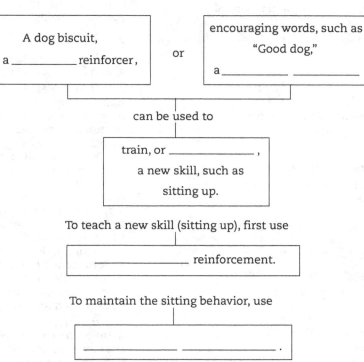

42. variable-interval; rechecking your phone for a longed-for response

43. **c.** is the answer. Reinforcement (the letter) comes after a fixed interval, and as the likely end of the interval approaches, your behavior (glancing out the window) becomes more frequent.
    a. & b. These answers are incorrect because with ratio schedules, reinforcement depends on the number of responses rather than on the passage of time.
    d. Assuming that the mail is delivered at about the same time each day, the interval is fixed rather than variable. Your behavior reflects this, since you glance out the window more often as the delivery time approaches.

44. **a.** is the answer. Ratio schedules maintain higher rates of responding—gambling in this example—than do interval schedules. Furthermore, variable schedules are not associated with the pause in responding following reinforcement that is typical of fixed schedules. The slot machine would therefore be used more often, and more consistently, if jackpots were scheduled according to a variable-ratio schedule.

45. **c.** is the answer. Whereas Lars is paid (reinforced) after a fixed period of time (fixed-interval), Tom is reinforced for each sale (fixed-ratio) he makes.

46. variable-interval

47. negative reinforcement; punishment; negative reinforcement; punishment

48. punishment; positive punishment; negative punishment

49. suppressed; discrimination; fear; the person who administered it

50. aggressiveness; violence

51. **a.** Punishment. You lose something good—conversation with your roommate.
    b. Negative reinforcement. You are no longer cold, which means something bad has been removed.
    c. Negative reinforcement. You are no longer thirsty, so something bad has been removed.
    d. Punishment. You can't use your laptop; certainly, something good has been taken away.
    e. Negative reinforcement. Your brother stops nagging you, so something bad has been removed.

52. dehumanized; freedom; control

53. shaping; adaptive quizzing

54. more; achievable; more

55. reinforce; time-out

56. realistic; plan; monitor; reinforce; rewards

57. associative; acquisition; extinction; spontaneous recovery; generalization; discrimination

58. classical conditioning; automatically; respondent behavior

59. operant conditioning; operant behaviors; consequences

60. **a.** voluntary; operant conditioning
    b. involuntary; classical conditioning
    c. voluntary; operant conditioning
    d. involuntary; classical conditioning

Biology, Cognition, and Learning

61. constraints; adaptive; sickness; would; natural selection

62. constraints (limits); does

63. behaviorism

64. cognitive map

65. latent learning

66. intrinsic motivation; extrinsic motivation

Learning by Observation

67. observational learning; modeling; behavior

68. Albert Bandura; vicarious; vicarious; similar; successful; admirable

69. more

70. mirror; observational

71. prosocial; consistent

72. antisocial; abusive; aggressive; environmental

73. increases; mirror neurons; prosocial

74. causation; does

75. attractive; unpunished; does not

76. imitation; desensitize

Progress Test

Multiple-Choice Questions

1. **c.** is the answer.
   a. This answer is incorrect because it simply describes any behavior that is automatic rather than being triggered by a specific stimulus.
   b. This answer is too general because behaviors can change for reasons other than learning.
   d. Respondently conditioned behavior also satisfies the criteria of our definition of learning.

2. **b.** is the answer.
   a. & c. Classical conditioning is associated with Ivan Pavlov; respondent conditioning is another name for classical conditioning.
   d. Observational learning is most closely associated with Albert Bandura.

3. **b.** is the answer. Prior to its pairing with meat (the US), the tone did not trigger salivation and was therefore a neutral stimulus. Afterward, the tone triggered salivation (the CR) and was therefore a conditioned stimulus (CS).
   c. & d. Unconditioned stimuli, such as meat, innately trigger responding. Pavlov's dogs had to learn to associate the tone with the food.

4. **d.** is the answer. In learning to distinguish between the conditioned stimulus and another, similar stimulus, the monkey has received training in discrimination.
   a. In extinction training, a stimulus and/or response is allowed to go unreinforced.

b. Generalization training involves responding to stimuli similar to the conditioned stimulus; here the monkey is being trained not to respond to a similar stimulus.
   c. This cannot be classical conditioning since the monkey is acting to obtain a reward. Thus, this is an example of operant conditioning.

5. **b.** is the answer. A continuous association will naturally be easier to learn than one that occurs on only some occasions, so learning is most rapid with continuous reinforcement. Yet, once the continuous association is no longer there, as in extinction training, extinction will occur more rapidly than it would have had the organism not always experienced reinforcement.

6. **c.** is the answer. In this situation, the CR will decline, a phenomenon known as extinction.
   a. Generalization occurs when the subject makes a CR to stimuli similar to the original CS.
   b. Discrimination is when the subject does not make a CR to stimuli other than the original CS.
   d. An aversion is a CR to a CS that has been associated with an unpleasant US, such as shock or a nausea-producing drug.

7. **c.** is the answer.
   a. In *operant* conditioning the responses operate on the environment.
   b. In *classical* conditioning responses are triggered by preceding stimuli.
   d. In *classical* conditioning responses are reflexive.

8. **b.** is the answer.
   a. Skinner is best known for studies of *operant* learning. Moreover, there is no such thing as secondary learning.
   c. Pavlov is best known for classical conditioning.
   d. Watson is best known as an early proponent of behaviorism.

9. **d.** is the answer.

10. **b.** is the answer.
   a. Backward conditioning, in which the US precedes the CS, is ineffective.
   c. This interval is longer than is optimum for the most rapid acquisition of a CS-US association.
   d. Simultaneous presentation of CS and US is ineffective because it does not permit the subject to anticipate the US.

11. **c.** is the answer.

12. **b.** is the answer. The loud noise automatically triggered Albert's fear and therefore functioned as a US. After being associated with the US, the white rat acquired the power to trigger fear and thus became a CS.

13. **d.** is the answer.

14. **a.** is the answer. Shaping works on operant behaviors by reinforcing successive approximations to a desired goal.

15. **c.** is the answer.
   a., b., & d. Spontaneous recovery occurs after a CR has been extinguished, and in the absence of the US. The situations described here all involve the

continued presentation of the US and, therefore, the further strengthening of the CR.

16. **d.** is the answer.
  a. Both involve a negative stimulus.
  b. All reinforcers, including negative reinforcers, increase the likelihood of a response.
  c. In negative reinforcement, a negative stimulus is withdrawn following a desirable response.

17. **d.** is the answer.

18. **a.** is the answer.

19. **d.** is the answer. The rat had learned the maze but did not display this learning until reinforcement became available.
  a. Negotiating a maze is clearly operant behavior.
  b. This example does not involve learning to distinguish between stimuli.
  c. This is not observational learning because the rat has no one to observe!

20. **a.** is the answer. Online adaptive quizzing systems apply operant principles such as reinforcement, immediate feedback, and shaping to the teaching of new skills.
  b. & d. Online adaptive quizzing systems provide immediate, and continuous, reinforcement for correct responses, but do not use negative control procedures such as punishment.
  c. Online adaptive quizzing systems are based on feedback for correct responses; this feedback constitutes conditioned, rather than primary, reinforcement.

21. **d.** is the answer. An approving nod from the boss is a conditioned reinforcer in that it doesn't satisfy an innate need but has become linked with desirable consequences. Escape from cold, relief from pain, and a drink are all primary reinforcers, which meet innate needs.

22. **a.** is the answer. Taste-aversion experiments demonstrate conditioning even with CS-US intervals as long as several hours.
  b. Despite being perceivable, a visual or auditory stimulus cannot become a CS for illness in some animals, such as rats.
  c. Some animals, such as birds, are biologically primed to associate the *appearance* of food with illness.

23. **c.** is the answer.

24. **a.** is the answer. Your dog had to learn to associate the rattling sound with the food. Rattling is therefore a conditioned, or learned, stimulus, and salivation in response to this rattling is a learned, or conditioned, response.

25. **a.** is the answer. You are teaching your dog by rewarding him when he produces the desired behavior.
  b. This is not classical conditioning because the cookie is a primary reinforcer presented after the operant behavior of the dog fetching the paper.

  c. Food is a primary reinforcer; it satisfies an innate need.
  d. Rewarding your dog each time he fetches the paper is continuous reinforcement.

26. **a.** is the answer. As in this example, conditioning must be consistent with the particular organism's biological predispositions.
  b. Some behaviors, but certainly not all, are acquired more rapidly than others when shock is used as negative reinforcement.
  c. Pigeons are able to acquire many new behaviors when food is used as reinforcement.

27. **d.** is the answer. Sharetta is guided by her mental representation of the city, or cognitive map.
  a. Latent learning, or learning in the absence of reinforcement that is demonstrated when reinforcement becomes available, has no direct relevance to the example.
  b. Observational learning refers to learning from watching others.
  c. Shaping is the technique of reinforcing successive approximations of a desired behavior.

28. **b.** is the answer.
  c. & d. The text does not present evidence regarding the relative importance of cognitive processes in classical and operant conditioning.

29. **b.** is the answer.
  a. Positive reinforcement involves presenting a favorable stimulus following a response.
  c. Punishment involves presenting an unpleasant stimulus following a response.
  d. In extinction, a previously reinforced response is no longer followed by reinforcement. In this situation, a response causes a stimulus to be terminated or removed.

30. **d.** is the answer. a. is an example of positive reinforcement, b. is an example of negative reinforcement, and c. is an example of conditioned reinforcement.

31. **b.** is the answer.
  a., c., & d. Reinforcement that is delayed, presented before a response, or presented at the same time as a response does not always increase the response's frequency of occurrence.

32. **d.** is the answer.
  a. Intermittent reinforcement refers to the ratio of responses to reinforcers, not the overall quantity of reinforcement delivered.
  b. Unlike intermittent reinforcement, in which the delivery of reinforcement is contingent on responding, random reinforcement is delivered independently of the person's behavior.
  c. This defines the technique of shaping, not intermittent reinforcement.

33. **b.** is the answer. The girls are imitating behavior they have observed.
  a. Because these behaviors are clearly willful rather than involuntary, classical conditioning plays no role.

c. Latent learning plays no role in this example.
d. Shaping is a procedure for teaching the acquisition of a new response by reinforcing successive approximations of the behavior.

34. **c.** is the answer. The parrot is reinforced for making successive approximations of a goal behavior. This defines shaping.
    a. Shaping is an operant conditioning procedure; salivation at the sight of dog biscuits is a classically conditioned response.
    b. Shaping involves the systematic reinforcement of successive approximations of a more complex behavior. In this example there is no indication that the response of stopping at the intersection involved the gradual acquisition of simpler behaviors.
    d. This is an example of the partial reinforcement of an established response, rather than the shaping of a new response.

35. **b.** is the answer. Wanting to do something for its own sake is intrinsic motivation; wanting to do something for a reward (in this case, presumably, a high grade) is extrinsic motivation.
    a. The opposite is true. Nancy was motivated to take the course for its own sake, whereas Jack was evidently motivated by the likelihood of a reward in the form of a good grade.
    c. & d. A good grade, such as the one Jack is expecting, is an incentive. Drives, however, are aroused states that result from physical deprivation; they are not involved in this example.

36. **c.** is the answer. Payment is given after a fixed number of pieces have been completed.
    a. & b. Interval schedules reinforce according to the passage of time, not the amount of work accomplished.
    d. Fortunately for those working on commission, the work ratio is fixed and therefore predictable.

37. **c.** is the answer. Because reinforcement (earning a good grade on the exam) is available according to the passage of time, studying is reinforced on an interval schedule. Because the interval between exams is constant, this is an example of a fixed-interval schedule.

38. **b.** is the answer.
    a. With fixed-ratio schedules, there is a pause following each reinforcement.
    c. & d. Because reinforcement is not contingent on the rate of response, interval schedules, especially fixed-interval schedules, produce lower response rates than ratio schedules.

39. **a.** is the answer.

Matching Items

1. e	**6.** i	**11.** d
2. n	**7.** l	**12.** j
3. f	**8.** a	**13.** k
4. g	**9.** c	**14.** h
5. m	**10.** b	

Application Essay

Principles of operant conditioning are fundamental to all learned voluntary (operant) behaviors, especially those involved in complicated cognitive and motor behaviors such as using a computer. Teaching itself is a form of shaping, and the first step in shaping an operant response, such as teaching a child how to operate a computer, is to find an effective reinforcer. For most children, making a computer work is intrinsically rewarding. Some teachers also use gold stars, check marks, or free time on the computer (to play a game, for instance) to reward successful approximations of more complicated behaviors such as keyboarding, word processing, or spreadsheet use. These types of primary reinforcement should be accompanied by lots of praise (secondary reinforcement) whenever Manuel responds correctly. As success is achieved, the teacher should gradually require closer and closer approximations until the goal response (accurate keyboarding or software use, for example) is attained. When the new response has been established, the teacher should switch from continuous to partial reinforcement in order to strengthen the skill.

Summing Up

Classical Conditioning: A puff of air to the eye, the US, elicits an eyeblink, the UR. The puff of air is paired with a bell ringing, a NS, which becomes a CS that elicits an eyeblink, a CR. This is the *acquisition* stage of classical conditioning. Presenting the CS alone for several trials results in *extinction*. After a period of rest, pairing the CS and US results in *spontaneous recovery*. If a CS similar to the original CS is presented, responding with the CR represents *generalization*; not responding to the similar CS represents *discrimination*.

Operant Conditioning: A dog biscuit, a *primary* reinforcer, or encouraging words, such as "Good dog," a *conditioned reinforcer*, can be used to train, or *shape*, a new skill, such as sitting up. To teach a new skill (sitting up), first use *continuous* reinforcement. To maintain the sitting behavior, use *partial reinforcement*.

Terms and Concepts to Remember

1. **Learning** is the process of acquiring, through experience, new and relatively enduring information or behaviors.

2. **Associative learning** is learning that certain events occur together. Two variations of associative learning are classical conditioning and operant conditioning.

3. A **stimulus** is a situation or an event that evokes a response.

4. **Respondent behavior** is that which occurs as an automatic response to some stimulus.

   Example: In classical conditioning, conditioned and unconditioned responses are examples of **respondent behavior** in that they are automatic responses triggered by specific stimuli.

5. **Operant behavior** is behavior that operates on the environment, producing consequences.

6. **Cognitive learning** is acquiring mental information, whether by observing events, by watching other people, or through language.

7. **Classical conditioning** is a type of learning in which we learn to link two or more stimuli; a neutral stimulus becomes capable of triggering a conditioned response after having become associated with an unconditioned stimulus.

8. In classical conditioning, a **neutral stimulus (NS)** is one that does not elicit a response before conditioning.

9. In classical conditioning, the **unconditioned response (UR)** is the unlearned, naturally occurring response to the unconditioned stimulus (US).

10. In classical conditioning, the **unconditioned stimulus (US)** is the stimulus that naturally and automatically triggers the unconditioned response (UR).

11. In classical conditioning, the **conditioned response (CR)** is the learned response to a previously neutral (but now conditioned) stimulus, which results from the acquired association between the CS and US.

12. In classical conditioning, the **conditioned stimulus (CS)** is an originally neutral stimulus that comes to trigger a CR after association with an unconditioned stimulus (US).

13. In a learning experiment, **acquisition** refers to the initial stage of conditioning in which the new response is established and gradually strengthened. In operant conditioning, it is the strengthening of a reinforced response.

14. **Extinction** refers to the weakening of a CR when the CS is no longer followed by the US; in operant conditioning, extinction occurs when a response is no longer reinforced.

15. **Spontaneous recovery** is the reappearance of an extinguished CR after a pause.

16. **Generalization** refers to the tendency, once a response has been conditioned, to respond similarly to stimuli that resemble the original CS.

17. **Discrimination** in classical conditioning refers to the ability to distinguish the CS from similar stimuli that do not signal a US. In operant conditioning, it refers to responding differently to stimuli that signal a behavior will be reinforced or will not be reinforced.

18. **Operant conditioning** is a type of learning in which behavior is strengthened if followed by a reinforcer or diminished if followed by a punisher.

    Example: Unlike classical conditioning, which works on automatic behaviors, **operant conditioning** works on behaviors that operate on the environment.

19. The **law of effect** is Thorndike's principle that behaviors followed by favorable consequences become more likely and that behaviors followed by unfavorable consequences become less likely.

20. An **operant chamber** (*Skinner box*) is an experimental chamber for the operant conditioning of an animal such as a pigeon or rat. The controlled environment enables the investigator to present visual or auditory stimuli, deliver reinforcement or punishment, and precisely measure simple responses such as bar presses or key pecking.

21. In operant conditioning, **reinforcement** is any event that strengthens the behavior it follows.

22. **Shaping** is the operant conditioning procedure in which reinforcers guide actions closer and closer toward a desired behavior.

23. In operant conditioning, **positive reinforcement** strengthens a response by *presenting* a typically pleasurable stimulus after that response.

24. In operant conditioning, **negative reinforcement** strengthens a response by *stopping* or *reducing* a negative stimulus after that response.

25. The powers of **primary reinforcers** are innate and do not depend on learning; they often satisfy a biological need.

26. **Conditioned reinforcers** are stimuli that acquire their reinforcing power through their association with primary reinforcers; also called *secondary reinforcers*.

27. A **reinforcement schedule** is a pattern that defines how often a desired response will be reinforced.

28. **Continuous reinforcement** is the operant procedure of reinforcing the desired response every time it occurs. In promoting the acquisition of a new response it is best to use continuous reinforcement.

29. **Partial (intermittent) reinforcement** is the operant procedure of reinforcing a response only part of the time. A response that has been partially reinforced is much more resistant to extinction than one that has been continuously reinforced.

30. In operant conditioning, a **fixed-ratio schedule** reinforces a response only after a specified number of responses.

31. In operant conditioning, a **variable-ratio schedule** reinforces a response after an unpredictable number of responses.

32. In operant conditioning, a **fixed-interval schedule** reinforces a response only after a specified time has elapsed.

33. In operant conditioning, a **variable-interval schedule** reinforces a response at unpredictable time intervals.

34. In operant conditioning, **punishment** is an event, such as shock, that decreases the behavior it follows.

    Memory aid: People often confuse negative reinforcement and **punishment**. The former strengthens behavior, while the latter weakens it.

35. **Biological constraints** are evolved biological tendencies that predispose animals' behavior and learning.

36. **Behaviorism** is the view that psychology should be an objective science that studies only observable behaviors without reference to mental processes.

Example: Because he was an early advocate of the study of observable behavior, John Watson is often called the father of behaviorism.

37. A **cognitive map** is a mental image of the layout of your environment.

38. **Latent learning** is learning that occurs in the absence of reinforcement but becomes apparent only when there is an incentive to demonstrate it.

39. **Intrinsic motivation** is the desire to perform a behavior for its own sake, rather than for some external reason.

    Memory aid: Intrinsic means "internal": A person who is **intrinsically motivated** is motivated from within.

40. **Extrinsic motivation** is the desire to perform a behavior in order to gain a reward or avoid a punishment.

Memory aid: Extrinsic means "external": A person who is extrinsically motivated is motivated by some outside factor.

41. **Observational learning** is learning by watching and imitating the behavior of others.

42. **Modeling** is the process of watching and then imitating a specific behavior and is thus an important means through which observational learning occurs.

43. **Mirror neurons** may be the neural basis for observational learning. These neurons fire when certain actions are performed or when another individual who performs those actions is observed.

44. The opposite of antisocial behavior, **prosocial behavior** is positive, helpful, and constructive and is subject to the same principles of observational learning as is undesirable behavior, such as aggression.

Memory

7

Chapter Overview

Chapter 7 explores human memory as a system that processes information in three steps. Encoding refers to the process of putting information into the memory system. Storage is the mechanism by which information is maintained in memory. Retrieval is the process by which information is accessed from memory through recall or recognition.

Chapter 7 also discusses the important role of chunking, mnemonics, spaced study, and self-assessment in encoding new memories; how memory is represented physically in the brain; and how forgetting may result from failure to encode or store information or to find appropriate retrieval cues. The final section of the chapter discusses the issue of memory construction. How "true" are our memories of events? A particularly controversial issue in this area involves suspicious claims of long-repressed memories of sexual abuse and other traumas that are "recovered" with the aid of hypnosis and other techniques. As you study this chapter, try applying some of the memory and studying tips discussed in the text.

Chapter Review

First, skim this section, noting headings and boldface items. After you have read the section, review each objective by completing the sentences and answering the questions that follow it. STUDY TIPS explain how best to learn a difficult concept and APPLICATIONS help you to know how well you understand the material. As you proceed, evaluate your performance by consulting the answers beginning on page 146. Do not continue with the next section until you understand each answer. If you need to, review or reread the section in the textbook before continuing.

Studying Memory

Objective 7-1: Define *memory,* and describe how information-processing models help us study memory.

Memory is the persistence of learning over time. Our memory system does this through the *encoding, storage,* and *retrieval of* information.

1. Memory is your storehouse of _____ _____ .

2. To remember something, we must get it into our brain, a process called _____ , retain it, a process called _____ , and later get it back out, a process called

_____ .

Objective 7-2: Describe the three-stage information-processing model, and discuss how later research has updated this model..

The Atkinson-Shiffrin three-stage processing model states that we first record to-be-remembered information as a fleeting *sensory memory*. From there it is processed into *short-term memory,* where we encode it through *rehearsal* for *long-term memory* and later retrieval. Sometimes we bypass the first two stages and form some memories through *automatic* processing. Short-term memory is actually a *working memory* because it uses and actively maintains information.

3. Atkinson and Shiffrin proposed a memory model involving _____ _____ . According to this model, we first record information as a fleeting

_____ _____ , from which it is processed into _____- _____ memory, where the information is encoded through _____ into _____- _____ memory for later retrieval.

4. Short-term memory has been clarified by the concept of _____ memory, which focuses more on the _____ processing of incoming _____ and _____-_____ information. Short-term memory not only makes sense of new input and links it with

_____-_____ memories, but it also processes _____

_____ .

133

To remember the material in the first half of this chapter, you might find it helpful to use the concept of a *three-part model* as a retrieval cue. In this section, the modified three-stage information-processing model proposes that external events are processed through separate stages of sensory memory, short-term/working memory, and long-term memory. In the next sections, the three processes of (1) getting information into the memory system (encoding), (2) retaining information over time (storage), and (3) getting information out of memory storage (retrieval) are described. Each process (encoding, storage, and retrieval) can occur at each memory stage (sensory memory, short-term memory, long-term memory). The chart below applies what can happen at each stage to the example of getting the written words of a memorable poem in and out of memory. To bolster your understanding of these important concepts, you might try using this type of chart as the basis for an example you create.

Sensory Memory

Encoding: light reflecting from printed words in the poem automatically triggers a response in the eye's receptor cells

Storage: image of each word persists in the visual system for about 1/2 second

Retrieval: visual image is attended to as it passes into working/short-term memory

Working/Short-Term Memory

Encoding: automatic processing of location of words on the page; effortful processing of meaning

Storage: limited capacity and duration of storing words on the page

Retrieval: conscious working memory allows reader to process the meaning of the poem's words

Long-Term Memory

Encoding: memorable passage triggers effortful processing of material from short-term memory to long-term memory

Storage: relatively permanent and limitless; meaningful passage stays with you

Retrieval: recall, recognition, or relearning of memorized passage from the poem

Building Memories: Encoding

Objective 7-3: Distinguish between explicit and implicit memories.

Our mind operates on two tracks. On one track, information goes directly to storage. These **implicit** (unconscious) **memories** are the learned skills or classical conditioning that involve **automatic processing**. On the other track are our **explicit** (conscious) **memories,** the memories of facts and experiences that we can consciously retrieve. They require **effortful processing**.

5. Facts and experiences that we can consciously declare make up _____ memory, which is also called _____ memory. Such memories are processed through conscious, _____ processing. Processing that happens without our awareness, called _____ _____ , produces _____ memories, which are also called _____ _____ .

Objective 7-4: Identify the information we process automatically.

To some extent, encoding occurs automatically. With little or no effort, we encode an enormous amount of information about *space, time,* and *frequency.* For example, we can re-create a sequence of the day's events to guess where we might have left a coat. Automatic processing occurs without our awareness and without interfering with our thinking about other things. Some forms of processing, such as learning to read or drive, require attention and effort when we first perform them but with practice become automatic.

Automatic processing occurs unconsciously; effortful processing requires attention and conscious effort. For example, our memory of the names of researchers mentioned in this chapter will disappear unless we *rehearse* them.

6. Implicit memories include _____ skills and associations among stimuli formed by _____ _____ . Without conscious effort, we also automatically process information about _____ , _____ , and _____ .

Give examples of material that is typically encoded with little or no effort.

7. The first thing Karen did when she discovered that she had misplaced her keys was to re-create in her mind the day's events. That she had little difficulty in doing so illustrates _____ processing.

8. Elderly Mr. Flanagan, a retired electrician, can easily remember how to wire a light switch, but he cannot remember the name of the president of the United States. Evidently, Mr. Flanagan's _____ memory is better than his _____ memory.
  a. implicit; explicit
  b. explicit; implicit
  c. declarative; nondeclarative
  d. explicit; declarative

Objective 7-5: Explain how sensory memory works.

Sensory memory is the first stage in forming explicit memory. It is truly fleeting. Unless our working memory rehearses or meaningfully encodes sensory information, it quickly disappears. Picture-image memory of a scene is referred to as *iconic memory.* Sound memory is called *echoic memory.*

9. Stimuli from the environment enter through the _____ and are first recorded in _____ memory.

10. In one experiment, when people were briefly shown three rows of letters, they could recall _____ (virtually all/about half) of them. When the researcher sounded a tone immediately after a row of letters was flashed to indicate which letters were to be recalled, the participants were much _____ (more/less) accurate. This suggests that people have a brief photographic, or _____ , memory lasting about a few tenths of a second.

11. Sensory memory for sounds is called _____ memory. This memory fades _____ (more/less) rapidly than visual memory, lasting for as long as _____ .

Objective 7-6: Describe the capacity of our short-term memory.

Our short-term memory span for information just presented is very limited—a seconds-long retention of about seven items, give or take two. We know that our capacity for storing information permanently has no real limit.

12. Our short-term memory capacity is about _____ chunks of information. This capacity was discovered by _____ .

13. Researchers found that when _____ was prevented by asking people to count backward, memory for letters was gone after 12 seconds. Without _____ processing, short-term memories have a limited life.

14. Working memory capacity varies, depending on _____ and other factors. We do better and more efficient work when _____ , without _____ , on one task at a time.

15. Brenda has trouble remembering her new five-digit ZIP plus four-digit address code. What is the most likely explanation for the difficulty Brenda is having?
    a. Nine digits are at or above the upper limit of most people's short-term memory capacity.
    b. Nine digits are at or above the upper limit of most people's iconic memory capacity.
    c. The extra four digits cannot be organized into easily remembered chunks.
    d. Brenda evidently has an impaired implicit memory.

Objective 7-7: Describe the effortful processing methods that can help us remember new information.

When we organize information into meaningful units, we recall it more easily. In *chunking,* we cluster information into familiar, manageable units, such as words into sentences. Chunking occurs so naturally that we often take it for granted; in fact, it is often automatic.
Mnemonics are memory aids that often use vivid imagery, because we are particularly good at remembering mental pictures. For example, we remember concrete words that lend themselves to picture images better than we remember abstract, low-imagery words.

16. Memory may be aided by grouping information into meaningful units called _____ .

17. Memory aids, which are known as _____ devices, often rely on _____ imagery.

18. These memory strategies help us form _____ and _____ memories.

Objective 7-8: Explain why cramming is ineffective, define the *testing effect,* and discuss why it is important to make new information meaningful.

The **spacing effect** is our tendency to retain information more easily if we practice it repeatedly than if we practice it in one long session (cram). The **testing effect** refers to the enhanced memory that occurs after retrieving material compared with merely rereading it. It also improves learning if the material is meaningful.

19. Distributed rehearsal is more effective for retention than cramming, or _____ ; this is called the _____ .

20. Repeated self-testing is a good way to _____ practice. Enhanced memory from practicing _____ rather than simply rereading is called the _____ .

21. As memory researcher _____ demonstrated, material that is not _____ is difficult to process.

Memory Storage

Objective 7-9: Describe the capacity of long-term memory, and state whether our long-term memories are processed and stored in specific locations.

Our capacity for storing long-term memories has no limit. We do not store our memories in a single place. Memory requires brain networks, as many parts of the brain interact to encode, store, and retrieve information.

22. In contrast to short-term memory—and contrary to popular belief—the capacity of permanent memory is essentially_____ .

23. Memories are stored _____ (in one place/ in many locations), which requires brain

    _____ .

Objective 7-10: Describe the roles of the hippocampus and frontal lobes in memory processing.

Explicit, conscious memories are either *semantic* (facts and general knowledge) or *episodic* (experienced events). New explicit memories are laid down via the **hippocampus,** a limbic system structure. The hippocampus is not the permanent storehouse, but a loading dock that feeds new information to other brain circuits for permanent storage. This storage process is called **memory consolidation.**

24. A neural center in the limbic system, the

    _____ , is important in the processing and storage of _____ memories. These memories are either

    _____—facts and general knowledge—or _____—experienced events. The storage process is called _____

    _____ .

25. The hippocampus seems to function as a zone where the brain _____ (temporarily/permanently) stores the elements of a memory. However, memories _____ (do/do not) migrate for storage elsewhere. During sleep, the hippocampus and _____ display rhythmic patterns of activity. Researchers suspect that the day's experiences are being transferred for long-term storage.

26. Verbal information is stored in the _____ frontal lobe, while visual images are stored in the _____ frontal lobe.

27. Brad, who suffered accidental damage to his left frontal lobe, has trouble remembering
    a. visual designs.
    b. locations.
    c. all nonverbal information.
    d. verbal information.

28. After suffering damage to the hippocampus, a person would probably
    a. lose memory for skills such as bicycle riding.
    b. be incapable of being classically conditioned.
    c. lose the ability to store new facts.
    d. experience all of these changes.

Objective 7-11: Describe the roles of the cerebellum and basal ganglia in memory processing.

Implicit memories created by classical conditioning are processed by the *cerebellum*. The *basal ganglia*, deep brain structures involved in motor movement, help formation of our memories for physical skills. Our implicit memory system, enabled by the cerebellum and basal ganglia, helps explain why the reactions and skills we learned during infancy reach far into our future. Yet as adults, our conscious memory of our first four years is blank, an experience called *infantile amnesia*.

29. The cerebellum is important in the processing of

    _____ memories. People with a damaged cerebellum are incapable of developing some conditioned _____ .

30. Deep brain structures called the _____

    _____ , which are also involved in

    _____ movement, help us form

    _____ memories for skills.

31. The dual explicit-implicit memory system helps explain _____ amnesia. We do not have explicit memories of our first four years for two reasons: explicit memory requires the use of words that nonspeaking children _____ (have/have not) learned and the _____ is not yet well developed.

Objective 7-12: Discuss how emotions affect our memory processing.

The naturally stimulating hormones that we produce when excited or stressed make more glucose energy available to fuel brain activity, signaling the brain that something important has happened. Stress hormones also focus memory. The amygdala, two emotion-processing clusters in the brain's limbic system, arouses brain areas that process memories. These emotion-triggered hormonal changes help explain our *flashbulb memories* of surprising, significant events. Emotionless events mean weaker memories.

32. Emotions trigger _____ hormones that _____ (influence/do not influence) memory formation by making more _____ available to fuel brain activity.

33. Stress hormones provoke the _____ to boost activity in the brain's memory-forming areas.

34. Memories for surprising, significant moments that are especially clear are called _____ memories. Like other memories, these memories _____ (can/ cannot) err.

APPLICATION:

35. Which of the following is the best example of a flashbulb memory?
   a. suddenly remembering to buy bread while standing in the checkout line at the grocery store
   b. recalling the name of someone from high school while looking at his or her yearbook snapshot
   c. remembering to make an important phone call
   d. remembering what you were doing on September 11, 2001, when terrorists crashed planes into the World Trade Center towers

Objective 7-13: Explain how changes at the synapse level affect our memory processing.

The search for the physical basis of memory has recently focused on the synapses and their neurotransmitters and on the *long-term potentiation (LTP)* of brain circuits. In response to increased activity in neural pathways, neural interconnections form or strengthen. Studies of the California sea slug indicate that when learning occurs, the slug releases more of the neurotransmitter *serotonin* at certain synapses, and these synapses become more sensitive and more efficient at transmitting signals. LTP appears to be a neural basis for learning and remembering.

36. Eric Kandel and James Schwartz have found that when learning occurs in the California sea slug, *Aplysia*, the neurotransmitter _____ is released in greater amounts onto certain neurons, making these cells more efficient.

37. After learning has occurred, a sending neuron needs _____ (more/less) prompting to release its neurotransmitter, and the number of _____ _____ it

stimulates may increase. This phenomenon, called _____-_____ _____ , may be the neural basis for learning and memory. Several lines of evidence confirm this physical basis of memory. _____ that block this process interfere with learning and mice that are unable to produce a specific _____ can't learn their way out of a maze. Rats given a drug that enhances the process of _____ (use abbreviation) will learn a maze _____ (faster/more slowly).

38. After LTP has occurred, an electric current passed through the brain _____ (will/will not) disrupt old memories and _____ (will/will not) wipe out recent experiences.

Retrieval: Getting Information Out

Objective 7-14: Describe how psychologists assess memory with recall, recognition, and relearning.

Recall is memory demonstrated by retrieving information learned earlier, as on a fill-in-the-blank test. *Recognition* is memory demonstrated by identifying items previously learned, as on a multiple-choice test. *Relearning* is memory demonstrated by time saved when relearning previously learned information. Tests of recognition and relearning reveal that we remember more than we recall.

39. The ability to retrieve information not in conscious awareness but that was learned at an earlier time is called _____ . The ability to identify previously learned items is called _____ .

40. If you have learned something and then forgotten it, you will probably be able to _____ it _____ (more/less) quickly than you did originally.

41. Researchers found that 25 years after graduation, people were not able to _____ (recall/recognize) the names of their classmates but were able to _____ (recall/recognize) 90 percent of their names and their yearbook pictures.

42. Using _____ _____ , Hermann Ebbinghaus found that the more frequently he repeated the list aloud on day 1, the fewer repetitions he required to relearn the list on day 2.

APPLICATIONS:

43. Complete this analogy: Fill-in-the-blank test questions are to multiple-choice questions as

    a. encoding is to storage.
    b. storage is to encoding.
    c. recognition is to recall.
    d. recall is to recognition.

44. Matthew wants to be sure that he will ace his chemistry test next week. His best strategy would be to

    a. study the material once every day.
    b. study the material on day 1, then distract himself with a favorite activity on day 2.
    c. study the material on day 1, then try to recall everything on day 2.
    d. study the material a number of times on day 1, so he would have to spend less time relearning on the following days.

Objective 7-15: Describe how external events, internal moods, and order of appearance affect memory retrieval.

We can think of a memory as held in storage by a web of associations. *Retrieval cues* are bits of related information we encode while encoding a target piece of information. They become part of the web. To retrieve a specific memory, we need to identify one of the strands that leads to it. Activating retrieval cues within our web of associations aids memory.

    Memory is sometimes *primed* (activated) by returning to the original context in which we experienced an event or encoded a thought. It can flood our memories with retrieval cues that lead to the target memory.

    Memories are somewhat *mood-congruent*. While in a good or bad mood, we often retrieve memories consistent with that mood. Moods also prime us to interpret others' behavior in ways consistent with our emotions. Mood-congruent memory is part of a larger concept, called *state-dependent memory,* the tendency to recall information best in the same state as when the information was learned.

    Another memory-retrieval quirk is the *serial position effect,* our tendency to remember the last and first items in a long list (for example, a grocery list) better than the middle items. In experiments, immediately after learning, people remembered the last items on a list best; after a delay, they remembered the first items best.

45. Stimuli that are linked to a specific memory are called _____

_____ .

46. The process by which associations can lead to retrieval is called _____ .

47. Studies have shown that retention is best when learning and testing are done in

_____ (the same/different)

contexts.

48. What we learn in one condition is best remembered in that condition, called _____-

_____ memory. For example, we tend to recall experiences that are consistent with our current emotional state, which is called _____-_____ memory.

Describe the effects of mood on memory.

49. People who are currently depressed may recall their parents as _____ and

_____ . People who have recovered from depression typically recall their parents about the same as do people who _____

_____ .

50. The tendency to remember the first and last items in a list best is called the _____

_____ _____ .

51. People briefly recall the _____ (first/last) items in a list quickly and well. This is called the _____ effect. Following a delay, _____ (first/last) items are remembered better. This is called a _____ effect.

APPLICATIONS:

52. Being in a bad mood after a hard day of work, Susan could think of nothing positive in her life. This is best explained as an example of

    a. priming.
    b. the spacing effect.
    c. mood-congruent memory.
    d. a context effect.

53. In an effort to remember the name of the classmate who sat behind her in fifth grade, Martina mentally recited the names of other classmates who sat near her. Martina's effort to refresh her memory by activating related associations is an example of

    a. priming.   **c.** encoding.
    b. mnemonics.   **d.** relearning.

54. Walking through the halls of his high school 10 years after graduation, Tom experienced a flood of old memories. Tom's experience showed the role of

a. state-dependent memory.
b. context effects.
c. implicit memory.
d. echoic memory.

Forgetting

Objective 7-16: Explain why we forget.

The capacity to forget is helpful. Because of his inability to forget, the Russian memory whiz S found it more difficult than others to think abstractly—to generalize, to organize, to evaluate. Without an ability to forget we would be overwhelmed by out-of-date and unimportant information. However, for people who have **amnesia,** memory loss is severe and permanent.

One explanation for forgetting is that we fail to encode information for entry into our memory system. Without effortful processing, much of what we sense we never notice or process. For example, although most people in the United States have seen the Apple logo countless times, they may not be able to draw it accurately. Another explanation, based on Ebbinghaus' *forgetting curve,* is a gradual fading of the physical **memory trace.**

Retrieval failure can occur if we have too few cues to summon information from long-term memory. It may also happen when old and new information compete for retrieval. In some cases, something we learned in the past interferes with our ability to recall information we have recently learned **(proactive interference).** In other cases, something we have recently learned interferes with information we learned in the past **(retroactive interference).** Old and new information do not always compete; instead one type of information may help us learn another, an effect that is called *positive transfer.*

With his concept of **repression,** Sigmund Freud proposed that our memories are self-censoring. To protect our self-concepts and to minimize anxiety, we may block from consciousness anxiety-arousing thoughts, feelings, and memories. In Freud's view, this motivated forgetting submerges memories but leaves them available for later retrieval under the right conditions. Increasing numbers of memory researchers think repression rarely, if ever, occurs. More typically, we have trouble forgetting traumatic experiences.

55. Without the ability to _____ , we would constantly be overwhelmed by information.

56. The disorder called _____ involves a loss of memory.

57. The type of forgetting caused by _____ failure occurs because some of the information that we sense never actually _____ .

58. One reason for age-related memory decline is that the brain areas responsible for _____ new information are _____ (more/less) responsive in older adults.

59. Studies by Hermann Ebbinghaus and others indicate that most forgetting occurs _____ (soon/a long time) after the material is learned. This type of forgetting is known as _____ _____ , which may be caused by a gradual fading of the physical _____ .

60. When information that is stored in memory temporarily cannot be found, _____ failure has occurred.

61. Research suggests that memories are also lost as a result of _____ , which is especially possible if we simultaneously learn similar, new material.

62. The disruptive effect of previous learning on current learning is called _____ _____ . The disruptive effect of learning new material on efforts to recall material previously learned is called _____ _____ .

63. Researchers found that if people went to sleep after learning, their memory for a list of nonsense syllables was _____ (better/worse) than it was if they stayed awake.

64. When learning one subject helps later learning of another subject, _____ _____ has occurred.

65. Freud proposed that motivated forgetting, or _____ , may protect a person from painful memories.

66. Increasing numbers of memory researchers think that motivated forgetting is _____ (less/more) common than Freud believed.

APPLICATIONS:

67. At your high school reunion you cannot remember the last name of your homeroom teacher. Your failure to remember is most likely the result of _____ failure.

68. Which of the following sequences would be best to follow if you wanted to minimize interference-induced forgetting to improve your recall on the psychology midterm?

    a. study, eat, test
    b. study, sleep, test
    c. study, listen to music, test
    d. study, exercise, test

69. When Carlos was promoted, he moved into a new office with a new phone extension. Every time he is asked for his phone number, Carlos first thinks of his old extension, illustrating the effects of

    a. proactive interference.
    b. retroactive interference.
    c. encoding failure.
    d. storage failure.

70. Lewis cannot remember the details of the torture he experienced as a prisoner of war. According to Freud, Lewis' failure to remember these painful memories is an example of

    a. repression.
    b. retrieval failure.
    c. state-dependent memory.
    d. flashbulb memory.

71. After finding her old combination lock, Janice can't remember its combination because she keeps confusing it with the combination of her new lock. She is experiencing

    a. proactive interference.
    b. retroactive interference.
    c. encoding failure.
    d. storage failure.

When We Forget: A Summary

Information bits

Sensory memory
The senses momentarily register amazing detail.

↓

Working (short-term) memory
A few items are both noticed and encoded.

↓

Long-term storage
Some items are altered or lost.

↓

Retrieval from long-term memory
Depending on interference, retrieval cues, moods, and motives, some things get retrieved, some don't.

Memory Construction Errors

Objective 7-17: Explain how misinformation, imagination, and source amnesia influence our memory construction, and describe how we decide whether a memory is real or false.

Memory is not exact. Rather, we construct our memories, using both stored and new information. Researchers call this **reconsolidation**. In many experiments, people have witnessed an event, received or not received misleading information about it, and then taken a memory test. The repeated result is a **misinformation effect:** After exposure to subtle misinformation, many people misremember. Asking leading questions can plant false memories. As people recount an experience, they fill in their memory gaps with plausible guesses. Other vivid retellings may also implant false memories. Even *imagining* nonexistent actions and events can create false memories.

Our memory for the source of an event is particularly frail. In **source amnesia,** we link the wrong source with an event that we have experienced, heard about, read about, or imagined. Thus, we may recognize someone but have no idea where we have seen the person. Or we imagine or dream an event and later are uncertain whether it actually happened. Source amnesia helps explain *déjà vu,* the eerie sense that we are reliving something that we have experienced before. Because the misinformation effect and source amnesia happen outside our awareness, it is hard to separate false memories from real ones.

72. As memories are replayed, they are often modified. This process is called _____ .

73. When witnesses to an event receive misleading information about it, they may experience a _____ _____ and misremember the event. A number of experiments have demonstrated that false memories _____ (can/cannot) be created when people are induced to imagine nonexistent events .

Describe what Loftus' studies have shown about the effects of misleading postevent information.

74. At the heart of many false memories is _____ _____ , which occurs when we _____ an event to the wrong source. This phenomenon helps explain _____ _____ ,

which is the sense that a current situation has already been experienced.

75. Because memory is reconstruction as well as reproduction, we _____ (can/cannot) be sure whether a memory is real by how real it feels.

76. Memory construction explains why memories "refreshed" under _____ are often inaccurate.

APPLICATION:

77. Which of the following illustrates the constructive nature of memory?
    a. Janice keeps calling her new boyfriend by her old boyfriend's name.
    b. After studying all afternoon and then getting drunk in the evening, Don can't remember the material he studied.
    c. After getting some good news, elated Kareem has a flood of good memories from his younger years.
    d. Although Mrs. Harvey, who has Alzheimer's disease, has many gaps in her memory, she invents sensible accounts of her activities so that her family will not worry.

Objective 7-18: Discuss why reports of repressed and recovered memories are so hotly debated.

Innocent people have been falsely convicted of abuse that never happened, and true abusers have used the controversy over recovered memories to avoid punishment. Forgetting of isolated past events, both negative and positive, is an ordinary part of life. Cued by a remark or an experience, we may later recover a memory. Controversy, however, focuses on whether the unconscious mind forcibly *represses* painful experiences and whether they can be retrieved by therapist-aided techniques. Memories "recovered" under hypnosis are especially unreliable, as are memories of things happening before age 4. Traumatic experiences are usually vividly remembered, not banished into an active but inaccessible unconscious.

78. Innocent people are falsely accused, as therapists prompt "_____" memories of childhood abuse. This is in large because of the _____ effect and _____ . The client's image of the threatening person grows vivid with _____ during therapy.

79. Researchers increasingly agree that memories obtained under the influence of hypnosis _____ (are/are not) reliable.

80. Memories of events that happened before age _____ are unreliable. As noted earlier, this phenomenon is called _____ .

Objective 7-19: Describe the reliability of young children's eyewitness descriptions.

Preschool children are particularly sensitive to suggestion, and their memory of sexual abuse may be prone to error. Researchers who have used suggestive interviewing techniques have found that most preschoolers and many older children can be led to report false events. But, even young children can accurately recall events if a neutral person talks to them in words they can understand and uses less suggestive, more effective techniques.

81. Whether a child produces an accurate eyewitness memory depends heavily on how he or she is _____ . Children are most accurate when it is a first interview with a _____ person who asks _____ questions.

Improving Memory

Objective 7-20: Describe how you can use memory research findings to do better in this course and in others.

The psychology of memory suggests several effective study strategies. These include overlearning; using spaced practice; active rehearsal; making new material personally meaningful by relating it to what is already known; mentally re-creating the contexts and moods in which the original learning occurred in order to activate retrieval cues; minimizing interference, for example, by studying just before sleeping; and testing one's knowledge both to rehearse it and to determine what must still be learned.

82. The SQ3R study technique identifies five strategies for boosting memory: _____ , _____ , _____ , _____ , and _____ .

Discuss several specific strategies for improving memory.

Progress Test

Multiple-Choice Questions

Circle your answers to the following questions and check them with the answers beginning on page 148. If your answer is incorrect, read the explanation for why it is incorrect and then consult the text.

1. The three steps in memory information processing are
   a. input, processing, output.
   b. input, storage, output.
   c. input, storage, retrieval.
   d. encoding, storage, retrieval.

2. Visual sensory memory is referred to as
   a. iconic memory.   c. photomemory.
   b. echoic memory.   d. working memory.

3. Echoic memories fade after approximately
   a. 1 hour.   c. 1 second.
   b. 1 minute.   d. 3 to 4 seconds.

4. Which of the following is NOT a measure of retention?
   a. recall   c. relearning
   b. recognition   d. retrieval

5. Our short-term memory span is approximately _____ items.
   a. 2   c. 7
   b. 5   d. 10

6. Memory techniques that involve vivid imagery are called
   a. consolidation devices.
   b. imagery techniques.
   c. encoding strategies.
   d. mnemonic devices.

7. One way to increase the amount of information in memory is to group it into larger, familiar units. This process is referred to as
   a. consolidating.   c. encoding.
   b. organization.   d. chunking.

8. Kandel and Schwartz have found that when learning occurs, more of the neurotransmitter _____ is released into synapses.
   a. ACh   c. serotonin
   b. dopamine   d. noradrenaline

9. Research on memory construction reveals that memories
   a. are stored as exact copies of experience.
   b. reflect a person's biases and assumptions.
   c. may be chemically transferred from one organism to another.
   d. even if long term, usually decay within about five years.

10. In a study on context cues, scuba divers learned words while on land or when they were underwater. In a later test of recall, those with the best retention had
    a. learned the words on land, that is, in the more familiar context.
    b. learned the words underwater, that is, in the more exotic context.
    c. learned the words and been tested on them in different contexts.
    d. learned the words and been tested on them in the same context.

11. The spacing effect means that
    a. distributed study yields better retention than cramming.
    b. retention is improved when encoding and retrieval are separated by no more than 1 hour.
    c. learning causes a reduction in the size of the synaptic gap between certain neurons.
    d. delaying retrieval until memory has consolidated improves recall.

12. Studies demonstrate that learning causes permanent neural changes in the _____ of animals' neurons.
    a. myelin   c. synapses
    b. cell bodies   d. all of these parts

13. In Sperling's memory experiment, research participants were shown three rows of three letters, followed immediately by a low, medium, or high tone. The participants were able to report
    a. all three rows with perfect accuracy.
    b. only the top row of letters.
    c. only the middle row of letters.
    d. any one of the three rows of letters.

14. The basal ganglia of the brain play a critical role in the formation of
    a. iconic memory.
    b. echoic memory.
    c. implicit memory.
    d. explicit memory.

15. Memory for skills is called
    a. explicit memory.   c. prime memory.
    b. declarative memory.   d. implicit memory.

16. The eerie feeling of having been somewhere before is an example of
    a. state dependency.   c. priming.
    b. encoding failure.   d. déjà vu.

17. The three-stage information-processing model of memory was proposed by
    a. Atkinson and Shiffrin.
    b. Hermann Ebbinghaus.
    c. Loftus and Palmer.
    d. George Sperling.

18. "Hypnotically refreshed" memories may prove inaccurate—especially if the hypnotist asks leading questions—because of
    a. encoding failure.
    b. state-dependent memory.
    c. proactive interference.
    d. memory construction.

19. Which area of the brain is most important in the processing of implicit memories?
    a. hippocampus
    b. cerebellum
    c. hypothalamus
    d. amygdala

20. Which of the following best describes the typical forgetting curve?
    a. a steady, slow decline in retention over time
    b. a steady, rapid decline in retention over time
    c. a rapid initial decline in retention, becoming stable thereafter
    d. a slow initial decline in retention, becoming rapid thereafter

21. Researchers found that memory was better in people who were
    a. awake during the retention interval, presumably because decay was reduced.
    b. asleep during the retention interval, presumably because decay was reduced.
    c. awake during the retention interval, presumably because interference was reduced.
    d. asleep during the retention interval, presumably because interference was reduced.

22. Which of the following measures of retention is the least sensitive in triggering retrieval?
    a. recall
    b. recognition
    c. relearning
    d. They are equally sensitive.

23. According to the serial position effect, when recalling a list of words you should have the greatest difficulty with those
    a. at the beginning of the list.
    b. at the end of the list.
    c. at the end and in the middle of the list.
    d. in the middle of the list.

24. Experimenters gave people a list of words to be recalled. When the participants were tested after a delay, the items that were best recalled were those
    a. at the beginning of the list.
    b. in the middle of the list.
    c. at the end of the list.
    d. at the beginning and the end of the list.

25. *Long-term potentiation* refers to
    a. the disruptive influence of old memories on the formation of new memories.
    b. the disruptive influence of recent memories on the retrieval of old memories.
    c. our tendency to recall experiences that are consistent with our current mood.
    d. the increased efficiency of synaptic transmission between certain neurons following learning.

26. Repression is an example of
    a. encoding failure.
    b. memory decay.
    c. motivated forgetting.
    d. all of these things.

27. Studies by Loftus and Palmer, in which people were quizzed about a film of an accident, indicate that
    a. when quizzed immediately, people can recall very little because of the stress of witnessing an accident.
    b. when questioned as little as one day later, their memory was very inaccurate.
    c. most people had very accurate memories as much as 6 months later.
    d. people's recall may easily be affected by misleading information.

28. Which of the following was NOT recommended as a strategy for improving memory?
    a. active rehearsal
    b. distributed study
    c. speed reading
    d. encoding meaningful associations

29. The process of getting information out of memory storage is called
    a. encoding.
    b. retrieval.
    c. rehearsal.
    d. storage.

30. Information is maintained in short-term memory only briefly unless it is
    a. encoded.
    b. rehearsed.
    c. iconic or echoic.
    d. retrieved.

31. Memory researchers are suspicious of long-repressed memories of traumatic events that are "recovered" with the aid of hypnosis because
    a. such experiences usually are vividly remembered.
    b. such memories are unreliable and easily influenced by misinformation.
    c. memories of events happening before about age 4 are especially unreliable.
    d. of all of these reasons.

32. The misinformation effect provides evidence that memory
    a. is constructed during encoding.
    b. is unchanging once established.
    c. may be reconstructed during recall according to how questions are framed.
    d. is highly resistant to misleading information.

Matching Items

Match each definition or description with the appropriate term.

Definitions or Descriptions

_____ 1. sensory memory that decays more slowly than visual sensory memory

_____ 2. the process by which information gets into the memory system

_____ 3. the blocking of painful memories

_____ 4. the phenomenon in which your mood can influence retrieval

_____ 5. memory for a list of words is affected by word order

_____ 6. the work site for conscious, active processing of incoming information

_____ 7. physical basis of memory

_____ 8. new learning interferes with previous knowledge

_____ 9. a measure of memory

_____ 10. old knowledge interferes with new learning

_____ 11. misattributing the origin of an event

_____ 12. sense of having experienced something before

_____ 13. memory loss

_____ 14. stimuli linked to a specific memory

_____ 15. picture-image memory

Terms

a. repression
b. relearning
c. serial position effect
d. amnesia
e. working memory
f. iconic memory
g. proactive interference
h. déjà vu
i. retroactive interference
j. source amnesia
k. retrieval cues
l. mood-congruent memory
m. echoic memory
n. encoding
o. memory trace

Essay Question

Discuss the points of agreement among experts regarding the validity of recovered memories of child abuse. (Use the space below to list the points you want to make, and organize them. Then write the essay on a separate piece of paper.)

Summing Up

See the next page.

Summing Up

INFORMATION PROCESSING

External events are
initially recorded as
_____ _____.

If we pay attention to the information, it is encoded into

memory that holds a few items briefly, or _____-_____
memory. To emphasize the active nature of short-term memory,
psychologists prefer the term _____ memory.

To get information
into storage, we must
_____ it.

To get information
out of storage, we must
_____ it.

The relatively limitless, permanent memory
where information is stored is
_____ -_____ memory.

This type of memory consists of

conscious memory of
facts and events, or
_____ _____,

unconscious memory of
skills and behaviors, or
_____ _____,

which includes

which includes

general knowledge,
or _____,

and personally
experienced events.

_____
skills

and classically
_____
associations.

Terms and Concepts to Remember

Using your own words, on a separate piece of paper write a brief definition or explanation of each of the following terms.

1. memory
2. encoding
3. storage
4. retrieval
5. sensory memory
6. short-term memory
7. long-term memory
8. working memory
9. implicit memory
10. automatic processing
11. explicit memory
12. effortful processing
13. parallel processing
14. chunking
15. mnemonics
16. spacing effect
17. testing effect
18. semantic memory
19. episodic memory
20. hippocampus
21. memory consolidation
22. flashbulb memory
23. long-term potentiation
24. recall
25. recognition
26. relearning
27. retrieval cue
28. priming
29. mood-congruent memory
30. serial position effect
31. amnesia
32. memory trace
33. proactive interference
34. retroactive interference
35. repression
36. reconsolidation
37. misinformation effect
38. source amnesia
39. déjà vu

Answers

Chapter Review

Studying Memory

1. accumulated learning
2. encoding; storage; retrieval
3. three stages; sensory memory; short-term; rehearsal; long-term
4. working; active; auditory; visual-spatial; long-term; already stored information

Building Memories: Encoding

5. explicit; declarative; effortful; automatic processing; implicit; nondeclarative memory
6. automatic; classical conditioning; space; time; frequency

Examples of automatic processing include the encoding of information about when and where you had dinner last night, or where you put your phone before going to bed. It also includes well-learned information, such as words in your native language.

7. automatic
8. **a.** is the answer.
   b., c., & d. Explicit memory, also called declarative memory, is the memory of facts that one can consciously "declare." Nondeclarative memory is what Mr. Flanagan has retained.
9. senses; sensory
10. about half; more; iconic
11. echoic; less; 3 or 4 seconds
12. 7; George Miller
13. rehearsal; active
14. age; focused; distractions
15. **a.** is the answer. Short-term memory capacity is approximately seven bits of information.
   b. Because iconic memory lasts no more than a few tenths of a second, regardless of how much material is experienced, this cannot be the explanation for Brenda's difficulty.
   c. The final four digits should be no more difficult to organize into chunks than the first five digits of the address code.
   d. Memory for digits is an example of explicit, rather than implicit, memory.
16. chunks
17. mnemonic; vivid
18. meaningful; accessible
19. massed practice; spacing effect

20. distribute; retrieval; testing effect

21. Hermann Ebbinghaus; meaningful

Memory Storage

22. unlimited (limitless)

23. in many locations; networks

24. hippocampus; explicit; semantic; episodic; memory consolidation

25. temporarily; do; cortex

26. left; right

27. **d.** is the answer.
    a., b., & c. Damage to the right, not the left, frontal lobe would cause this type of memory deficit.

28. **c.** is the answer. The hippocampus is involved in processing new facts for storage.
    a., b., & d. Neither classical conditioning nor skill memory are impaired with hippocampus damage, indicating that these aspects of memory are controlled by other regions of the brain.

29. implicit; reflexes

30. basal ganglia; motor; implicit

31. infantile; have not; hippocampus

32. stress; influence; glucose

33. amygdala

34. flashbulb; can

35. **d.** is the answer. Flashbulb memories are unusually clear memories of emotionally significant moments in life.

36. serotonin

37. less; receptor sites; long-term potentiation; Drugs; enzyme; LTP; faster

38. will not; will

Retrieval: Getting Information Out

39. recall; recognition

40. relearn; more

41. recall; recognize

42. nonsense syllables

43. **d.** is the answer.
    a. & b. To correctly answer either type of question, the knowledge must have been encoded and stored.
    c. With fill-in-the-blank questions, the answer must be recalled with no retrieval cues other than the question. With multiple-choice questions, the correct answer merely has to be recognized from among several alternatives.

44. **d.** is the answer.
    a., b., & c. None of these strategies would work well for Matthew to achieve his goal.

45. retrieval cues

46. priming

47. the same

48. state-dependent; mood-congruent

When happy, for example, we perceive things in a positive light and recall happy events; these perceptions and memories, in turn, prolong our good mood.

49. rejecting; punishing; have never suffered depression

50. serial position effect

51. last; recency; first; primacy

52. **c.** is the answer. Susan's memories are affected by her bad mood.
    a. Priming refers to the conscious or unconscious activation of particular associations in memory.
    b. The spacing effect is the tendency for distributed study to yield better long-term retention than is achieved through massed study.
    d. Susan has changed contexts, so that is not a factor.

53. **a.** is the answer. Priming is the conscious or unconscious activation of particular associations in memory.
    b. Mnemonics are memory aids.
    c. That Martina is able to retrieve her former classmates' names implies that they already have been encoded.
    d. Relearning is a measure of retention based on how long it takes to relearn something already mastered. Martina is recalling her former classmates' names, not relearning them.

54. **b.** is the answer. Being back in the context in which the original experiences occurred triggered memories of these experiences.
    a. The memories were triggered by similarity of place, not mood.
    c. Implicit memories are procedural memories for automatic skills and classically conditioned associations.
    d. Echoic memory refers to momentary memory of auditory stimuli.

Forgetting

55. forget

56. amnesia

57. encoding; enters the memory system

58. encoding; less

59. soon; storage decay; memory trace

60. retrieval

61. interference

62. proactive interference; retroactive interference

63. better

64. positive transfer

65. repression

66. less

67. retrieval

68. b. is the answer.
a., c., & d. Involvement in other activities, even just eating or listening to music, is more disruptive than sleeping.

69. a. is the answer. Proactive interference occurs when old information makes it difficult to recall new information.
b. If Carlos were having trouble remembering the old extension, this answer would be correct.
c. & d. Carlos has successfully encoded and stored the extension; he's just having problems retrieving it.

70. a. is the answer.
b. Although Lewis' difficulty in recalling these memories could be considered retrieval failure, it is caused by repression, which is therefore the best explanation.
c. This answer is incorrect because it is clear that Lewis fails to remember these experiences because they are painful memories and not because he is in a different emotional or physiological state.
d. Flashbulb memories are especially vivid memories for emotionally significant events. Lewis has no memory at all.

71. b. is the answer. Retroactive interference is the disruption of something you once learned by new information.
a. Proactive interference occurs when old information makes it difficult to correctly remember new information.
c. & d. Interference produces forgetting even when the forgotten material was effectively encoded and stored. Janice's problem is at the level of retrieval.

Memory Construction Errors

72. reconsolidation

73. misinformation effect; can

When people viewed a film of a traffic accident and were quizzed a week later, phrasing of questions affected answers; the word "smashed," for instance, made viewers mistakenly think they had seen broken glass.

74. source amnesia; apply; déjà vu

75. cannot

76. hypnosis

77. d. is the answer.
a. This is an example of proactive interference.
b. This is an example of the disruptive effects of depressant drugs, such as alcohol, on the formation of new memories.
c. This is mood-congruent memory.

78. recovered; misinformation; source amnesia; rehearsal

79. are not

80. 4; infantile amnesia

81. questioned; neutral; nonleading

Improving Memory

82. Survey; Question; Read; Retrieve; Review

Suggestions for improving memory include rehearsing material over many separate and distributed study sessions. Studying should also involve making the material meaningful rather than mindlessly repeating information. Using mnemonic devices that incorporate vivid imagery is helpful, too. Frequent activation of retrieval cues, such as the context and mood in which the original learning occurred, can also help strengthen memory. Studying should also be arranged to minimize potential sources of interference. And, of course, sleep more, so the brain has a chance to organize and consolidate information. Finally, self-tests in the same format (recall or recognition) that will later be used on the actual test are useful.

Progress Test

Multiple-Choice Questions

1. d. is the answer. Information must be encoded, or put into appropriate form; stored, or retained over time; and retrieved, or located and gotten out when needed.

2. a. is the answer. Iconic memory is our fleeting memory of visual stimuli.
b. Echoic memory is auditory sensory memory.
c. There is no such thing as photomemory.
d. Working memory is a term for short-term memory that stresses the active processing that occurs.

3. d. is the answer. Echoic memories last 3 to 4 seconds.

4. d. is the answer. Retrieval refers to the *process* of remembering.

5. c. is the answer.

6. d. is the answer.
a. There is no such term as "consolidation techniques."
b. & c. Imagery and encoding strategies are important in storing new memories, but *mnemonic device* is the general designation of techniques that facilitate memory, such as acronyms and the pegword system.

7. d. is the answer.
a. There is no such process of "consolidating."
b. Organization *does* enhance memory, but it does so through hierarchies, not grouping.
c. Encoding refers to the processing of information into the memory system.

8. c. is the answer. Kandel and Schwartz found that when learning occurred in the sea slug, *Aplysia*, serotonin was released at certain synapses, which then became more efficient at signal transmission.

9. b. is the answer. In essence, we construct our memories, bringing them into line with our biases and assumptions, as well as with our subsequent experiences.

a. If this were true, it would mean that memory construction does not occur. Through memory construction, memories may deviate significantly from the original experiences.
c. There is no evidence that such chemical transfers occur.
d. Many long-term memories are apparently unlimited in duration.

10. **d.** is the answer. In general, being in a context similar to that in which you experienced something will tend to help you recall the experience.
a. & b. The learning environment per se—and its familiarity or exoticness—did not affect retention.

11. **a.** is the answer.
b. & d. The text does not suggest that there is an optimal interval between encoding and retrieval.
c. Learning increases the efficiency of synaptic transmission in certain neurons, but not by altering the size of the synapse.

12. **c.** is the answer.

13. **d.** is the answer. When asked to recall all the letters, participants could recall only about half; however, if immediately after the presentation they were signaled to recall a particular row, their recall was near perfect. This showed that they had a brief photographic memory—so brief that it faded in less time than it would have taken to say all nine letters.

14. **c.** is the answer.
a & b. The basal ganglia are involved in motor movement, not visual or auditory sensory memory.
d. The basal ganglia are involved in the formation of implicit memories, not explicit memories.

15. **d.** is the answer.
a. & b. Explicit memory (also called declarative memory) is memory of facts and experiences that one can consciously know and declare.
c. There is no such thing as prime memory.

16. **d.** is the answer.
a. State-dependent memory is the phenomenon in which information is best retrieved when the person is in the same emotional or physiological state he or she was in when the material was learned.
b. Encoding failure occurs when a person has not processed information sufficiently for it to enter the memory system.
c. Priming is the process by which a memory is activated through retrieval of an associated memory.

17. **a.** is the answer.
b. Hermann Ebbinghaus conducted pioneering studies of verbal learning and memory.
c. Loftus and Palmer conducted influential research studies of eyewitness memory.
d. George Sperling is known for his research studies of iconic memory.

18. **d.** is the answer. It is in both encoding and retrieval that we construct our memories, and as Loftus' studies showed, leading questions affect people's memory construction.

a. The memory encoding occurred at the time of the event in question, not during questioning by the hypnotist.
b. State-dependent memory refers to the influence of one's own emotional or physiological state on encoding and retrieval, and would not apply here.
c. Proactive interference is the interfering effect of prior learning on the recall of new information.

19. **b.** is the answer.
a. The hippocampus is a temporary processing site for *explicit* memories.
c. & d. These areas of the brain are not directly involved in the memory system.

20. **c.** is the answer. As Ebbinghaus showed, most of the forgetting that is going to occur happens soon after learning.

21. **d.** is the answer.
a. & b. This study did not find evidence that memories fade (decay) with time.
c. When one is awake, there are many *more* potential sources of memory interference than when one is asleep.

22. **a.** is the answer. A test of recall presents the fewest retrieval cues and usually produces the most limited retrieval.

23. **d.** is the answer. According to the serial position effect, items at the beginning and end of a list tend to be remembered best.

24. **a.** is the answer.
b. In the serial position effect, the items in the middle of the list always show the *poorest* retention.
c. & d. Delayed recall erases the memory facilitation for items at the end of the list.

25. **d.** is the answer.

26. **c.** is the answer. According to Freud, we repress painful memories to preserve our self-concepts.
a. & b. The fact that repressed memories can sometimes be retrieved suggests that they were encoded and have not decayed with time.

27. **d.** is the answer. When misled by the phrasings of questions, subjects incorrectly recalled details of the film and even "remembered" objects that weren't there.

28. **c.** is the answer. Speed reading, which entails little active rehearsal, yields poor retention.

29. **b.** is the answer.
a. Encoding is the process of getting information *into* memory.
c. Rehearsal is the conscious repetition of information in order to maintain it in memory.
d. Storage is the maintenance of encoded material over time.

30. **b.** is the answer.
a. Information in short-term memory has *already* been encoded.
c. Iconic and echoic are types of *sensory* memory.
d. Retrieval is the process of getting material out of storage and into conscious, short-term memory. Thus, all material in short-term memory has

either already been retrieved or is about to be placed in storage.

31. **d.** is the answer.

32. **c.** is the answer. Loftus and Palmer found that eyewitness testimony could easily be altered when questions were phrased to imply misleading information.

a. Although memories *are* constructed during encoding, the misinformation effect is a retrieval, rather than an encoding, phenomenon.

b. & d. In fact, just the opposite is true.

Matching Items

1. m	**6.** e	**11.** j	
2. n	**7.** o	**12.** h	
3. a	**8.** i	**13.** d	
4. l	**9.** b	**14.** k	
5. c	**10.** g	**15.** f	

Essay Question

Experts agree that child abuse is a real problem that can have long-term adverse effects on individuals. They also acknowledge that forgetting of isolated events, both good and bad, is an ordinary part of life. Although experts all accept the fact that recovered memories are commonplace, they warn that memories "recovered" under hypnosis are unreliable, as are memories of events before age 4. Finally, they agree that memories can be traumatic, whether real or false.

Summing Up

Information Processing

External events are initially recorded as *sensory memory*. If we pay attention to the information, it is encoded into memory that holds a few items briefly, or *short-term* memory. To emphasize the active nature of short-term memory, psychologists prefer the term *working* memory. To get information into storage, we must *encode* it. To get information out of storage, we must *retrieve* it. The relatively limitless, permanent memory where information is stored is *long-term* memory. This type of memory consists of conscious memory of facts and events, or *explicit memory*, which includes general knowledge, or *facts*, and personally experienced events; and unconscious memory of skills and behaviors, or *implicit memory*, which includes *automatic* skills and classically *conditioned* associations.

Terms and Concepts to Remember

1. **Memory** is the persistence of learning over time through the encoding, storage, and retrieval of information.

2. **Encoding** is the first step in memory; the process of getting information into the memory system.

3. **Storage** is the process of retaining encoded information over time.

4. **Retrieval** is the process of getting information out of memory storage.

5. **Sensory memory** is the immediate, very brief recording of sensory information in the memory system.

6. **Short-term memory** is activated memory, which can hold about seven items for a short time.

7. **Long-term memory** is the relatively permanent and unlimited capacity memory system into which information from short-term memory may pass. It includes knowledge, skills, and experiences.

8. **Working memory** is the newer understanding of short-term memory as a work site for the active processing of incoming auditory and visual-spatial information, and of information retrieved from long-term memory.

9. **Implicit memories** are retained learned skills and classically conditioned associations among stimuli, without conscious awareness. These memories are evidently processed, not by the hippocampus, but by the cerebellum and basal ganglia. They are also called *nondeclarative memories*.

10. **Automatic processing** refers to our unconscious encoding of everyday information, such as space, time, and frequency, and of well-learned information.

11. **Explicit memories** are memories of facts and experiences that you can consciously retrieve. They are also called *declarative memories*.

12. **Effortful processing** is encoding that requires attention and conscious effort.

13. **Parallel processing** is the processing of many aspects of a problem at the same time.

14. **Chunking** is the memory technique of organizing material into familiar, manageable units; often occurs automatically.

15. **Mnemonics** are memory aids, which often use vivid imagery and organizational devices.

16. The **spacing effect** is the tendency for distributed study or practice to yield better long-term retention than is achieved through massed study or practice.

17. The **testing effect** is the phenomenon in which memory is enhanced more by retrieval of the information than simply rereading it. Also sometimes referred to as *retrieval practice effect* or *test-enhanced learning*.

18. **Semantic memory** is explicit, conscious memory of facts and general knowledge.

19. **Episodic memory** is the form of explicit memory that stores our personally experienced events.

20. The **hippocampus** is a neural center located in the limbic system that is important in the processing of explicit memories for storage.

21. **Memory consolidation** is the neural storage of a long-term memory.

22. A **flashbulb memory** is an unusually vivid memory of an emotionally important moment or event.

23. **Long-term potentiation (LTP)** is an increase in a synapse's firing potential following brief, rapid stimulation. LTP is believed to be the neural basis for learning and memory.

24. **Recall** is memory demonstrated by retrieving information learned earlier; it has few retrieval cues.

25. **Recognition** is memory demonstrated by identifying previously learned information.

26. **Relearning** is memory demonstrated by time saved when learning material again.

27. A **retrieval cue** is an event, feeling, or other stimulus that is linked to a specific memory.

28. **Priming** is the activation, often unconsciously, of particular associations in memory in order to retrieve a specific memory.

29. **Mood-congruent memory** is the tendency to recall experiences that are consistent with your current mood.

30. The **serial position effect** is the tendency for items at the beginning and end of a list to be more easily retained than those in the middle.

31. **Amnesia** is loss of memory, often due to brain trauma, injury, or disease.

32. A **memory trace** is the lasting physical change in the brain that occurs as a memory is formed.

33. **Proactive** (forward-looking) **interference** is the disruptive effect of something you already have learned on your efforts to learn or recall new information.

34. **Retroactive** (backward-acting) **interference** is the disruptive effect of new learning on the recall of old knowledge.

    Memory aid: Retro means "backward." **Retroactive interference** is "backward-acting" interference.

35. **Repression** is an example of motivated forgetting in that anxiety-arousing thoughts, feelings, and memories are prevented from entering consciousness. In psychoanalytic theory, it is the basic defense mechanism.

36. **Reconsolidation** is the process by which retrieved memories are stored again, after potentially being altered.

37. The **misinformation effect** occurs when a memory has been corrupted by misleading information.

38. At the heart of many false memories (along with the misinformation effect), **source amnesia** refers to faulty memory for how, when, or where information was learned or imagined.

39. **Déjà vu** is the false sense that you have already experienced a current situation.

Thinking, Language, and Intelligence

Chapter Overview

The first part of Chapter 8 deals with thinking, with emphasis on how people logically—or at times illogically—use tools such as algorithms and heuristics when making decisions and solving problems. Also discussed are several common obstacles to problem solving, including our bias to search for information that confirms rather than challenges existing hypotheses and our tendency to base our decisions on what most easily comes to mind. The section also discusses the powers and perils of intuition and the meaning and development of creativity. It concludes with an exploration of the cognitive skills of other species.

The next section is concerned with language, including its development in children, its processing by the brain, our ability to think in images, and the use of language by other species.

The rest of the chapter discusses intelligence, including whether intelligence is a single general ability or several specific ones. It describes the historical origins of intelligence tests and discusses several important issues concerning their use. The chapter also explores the extent of genetic and environmental influences on intelligence.

Chapter Review

First, skim each text section, noting headings and boldface items. Review the section by reading the objectives and summaries provided here, then answer the questions that follow. In some cases, STUDY TIPS explain how best to learn a difficult concept and APPLICATIONS help you to know how well you understand the material. Check your understanding of the material by consulting the answers beginning on page 170. Do not continue with the next section until you understand each answer. If you need to, review or reread the section in the textbook before continuing.

Thinking

Objective 8-1: Define *cognition,* and describe the functions of concepts.

Cognition refers to the mental activities associated with thinking, knowing, remembering, and communicating. To think about the countless events, objects, and people in our world, we organize them into mental groupings called *concepts.* Although we form some concepts by definition—for example, a triangle has three sides—more often we form a concept by developing a *prototype,* a mental image or best example of a particular category. For example, a robin more closely resembles our "bird" category than does a penguin.

1. Cognition can be defined as _____
   _____ .

2. People tend to organize specific items into mental groupings called _____ .

3. Concepts are typically formed through the development of a best example, or
   _____ , of a category. People more easily detect a _____ as a bird than a _____ as a bird.

4. Complete the following analogy: Rose is to flower as
   a. concept is to prototype.
   b. prototype is to concept.
   c. concept is to cognition.
   d. cognition is to concept.

Objective 8-2: Describe the cognitive strategies that help us solve problems, and identify the tendencies that work against us.

Problem solving is one of our most impressive cognitive skills. We approach some problems through *trial and error,* attempting various solutions until stumbling on one that works. For other problems we may follow a methodical rule or step-by-step procedure called an *algorithm.* Because algorithms can be laborious, we often rely instead on simple thinking strategies called *heuristics.* Sometimes, however, we are unaware of using any problem-solving strategy; the answer just comes to us as a sudden flash of *insight.*

Our cognitive tendencies may lead us astray. One obstacle to problem solving is our eagerness to search for information that confirms our ideas, a phenomenon known as *confirmation bias.* This can mean that once we form a wrong idea, we will not budge from our illogic.

Another obstacle to problem solving is *fixation*—the inability to see a problem from a fresh perspective. It may interfere with our taking a fresh approach when faced with problems that demand an entirely new solution.

5. Humans are especially capable of using their reasoning powers for coping with new situations, and thus for _____ _____ .

6. When we try each possible solution to a problem, we are using _____
_____ .

7. Logical, methodical, step-by-step procedures for solving problems are called
_____ .

8. Simple thinking strategies that allow us to solve problems efficiently are referred to as
_____ .

9. When we suddenly realize a problem's solution, _____ has occurred.

10. The tendency of people to look for information that supports their preconceptions is called

_____ _____ .

11. It is human nature to seek evidence that _____ our ideas more eagerly than to seek evidence _____ our ideas.

12. Not being able to take a new perspective when attempting to solve a problem is referred to as

_____ .

STUDY TIP/APPLICATION: We all use any of four techniques for solving problems: trial and error, algorithms, heuristics, and insight. To test your understanding of these approaches, apply them to a problem you might actually face, such as finding a misplaced set of car keys. Using the chart below, see if you can come up with an example of how you could find your keys using each of the four problem-solving approaches.

13. Problem-Solving Approach	How You Would Find Car Keys Using Each Method
a. Trial and error	
b. Algorithm	
c. Heuristics	
d. Insight	

APPLICATIONS:

14. A dessert recipe that gives you the ingredients, their amounts, and the steps to follow is an example of a(n)
_____ .

15. Boris the chess master selects his next move by considering moves that would threaten his opponent's queen. His opponent, a chess-playing computer, selects its next move by considering all possible moves. Boris is using a(n) _____ and the computer is using a(n) _____ .

16. During a televised political debate, the Republican and Democratic candidates each argued that the results of a recent public opinion poll supported their party's platform regarding sexual harassment. Because both candidates saw the information as supporting their belief, it is clear that both were victims of _____
_____ .

Objective 8-3: Define *intuition,* and describe how the availability heuristic can influence our decisions and judgments.

Intuition is our fast, automatic, unreasoned feelings and thoughts. It can be useful or it can lead us astray. A major obstacle to making decisions is the **availability heuristic,** which operates when we base our judgments on the availability of information in our memories. If instances of an event come to mind readily, we presume such events are common. Heuristics enable us to make snap judgments. However, these quick decisions sometimes lead us to ignore important information or to underestimate the chances of something happening.

17. Effortless, immediate, and automatic feelings or thoughts characterize our _____ .

18. When we judge the likelihood of something occurring in terms of how readily it comes to mind, we are using the _____
_____ .

Explain how this heuristic may lead us to make judgmental errors.

Objective 8-4: Identify the factors that exaggerate our fear of unlikely events.

Our intuition about risk can be wrong because of four forces that feed our fears. First, we fear what our ancestral history has prepared us to fear. Also, we fear what we cannot control, what is immediate, and what is most readily available in memory.

19. Many people fear terrorism more than accidents, despite the fact that these fears are not supported by death and injury statistics. This type of faulty thinking occurs because we fear

    a. _____

    b. _____

    c. _____

    d. _____

20. We fear _____ (too much/too little) threats that are less dramatic and _____ and that claim lives one by one.

Objective 8-5: Describe how overconfidence, belief perseverance, and framing affect our decisions and judgments.

Overconfidence, the tendency to overestimate the accuracy of our knowledge and judgments, can have adaptive value. People who err on the side of overconfidence live happily, find it easier to make tough decisions, and seem competent.

We exhibit *belief perseverance,* clinging to our ideas in the face of contrary evidence, because the explanation we accepted as valid lingers in our minds. Once beliefs are formed and justified, it takes more compelling evidence to change them than it did to create them. The best remedy for this form of bias is to make a deliberate effort to consider evidence supporting the opposite position.

The same issue presented in two different but logically equivalent ways can elicit quite different answers. This *framing* effect suggests that our judgments and decisions may not be well reasoned and that those who understand the power of framing can use it to influence important decisions—for example, by wording survey questions to support or reject a particular viewpoint.

21. The tendency of people to overestimate the accuracy of their knowledge results in _____ .

22. Overconfidence may have _____ value because self-confident people tend to live _____ , find it _____ (easier/harder) to make tough decisions, and seem _____ .

23. Research has shown that once we form a belief, it may take more convincing evidence for us to change the belief than it did to create it; this is because of

    _____ _____ .

24. A cure for this is to _____

    _____ _____ .

25. The way an issue is posed is called _____ . This effect _____ (does/does not) influence our decisions about what to buy or who to vote for, for example.

APPLICATIONS:

26. Airline reservations typically decline after a highly publicized plane crash because people overestimate the incidence of such disasters. In such instances, their decisions are being influenced by the _____

    _____ .

27. Dominic is certain that he will be able to finish reading the assigned text chapter over the weekend, even though he also has to write a five-page essay on the U.S. political process and will be going to a party on Saturday night. If he's like most people, Dominic
    a. is accurate in knowing how much he can do over the weekend.
    b. underestimates how much he'll get done over the weekend.
    c. overestimates how much he can get done over the weekend.

28. Which of the following illustrates belief perseverance?
    a. Your belief remains intact even in the face of evidence to the contrary.
    b. You refuse to listen to arguments counter to your beliefs.
    c. You tend to become flustered and angered when your beliefs are refuted.
    d. You tend to search for information that supports your beliefs.

29. In relation to ground beef, consumers respond more positively to an ad describing it as "75 percent lean" than to one referring to its "25 percent fat" content. This is an example of the _____ effect.

Objective 8-6: Describe how smart thinkers use intuition.

Although human intuition is sometimes perilous, it can be remarkably efficient and adaptive. Intuition is born of experience. As we gain expertise in a field, we become better at making quick, adept judgments. Experienced nurses, firefighters, art critics, and car mechanics learn to size up a situation in an eyeblink. Smart thinkers recognize that their gut reactions are terrific at some things, such as knowing that fuzzy-looking objects are far away. Research shows that in making complex decisions, we benefit by letting a problem "incubate" while we attend to other things. Critics remind us that deliberate, conscious thought helps with most complex tasks.

30. Intuitive reactions allow us to react _____ and in ways that are usually _____ .

31. Research suggests that for _____ (simple/complex) decisions, we benefit by letting a problem _____ while we attend to other things. However, after we listen to our intuition, we should_____ evidence, _____ conclusions, and _____ for the future.

Objective 8-7: Define *creativity,* and explain what fosters it.

Creativity requires a certain level of *aptitude,* but it is more than school smarts. Robert Sternberg and his colleagues view creativity as separate from intelligence, which typically requires **convergent thinking**; it requires a different kind of thinking **(divergent thinking)**. Creativity has five necessary parts: expertise, imaginative thinking skills, a venturesome personality, intrinsic motivation, and a creative environment.

32. The ability to produce ideas that are both novel and valuable is called _____ .

33. Aptitude tests, which demand single correct answers to questions, measure _____ thinking. Tests that allow multiple possible answers to problems measure _____ thinking, which is a necessary part of _____ .

Describe five ingredients of creativity other than aptitude.

Describe research findings on how to foster creativity.

34. Vanessa is a very creative sculptress. We would expect that Vanessa also
    a. has an exceptionally high intelligence score.
    b. tries to solve problems in ways that worked before.
    c. has a venturesome personality and is intrinsically motivated.
    d. lacks expertise in most other skills.

Objective 8-8: Describe what we know about thinking in other species.

Other animals show remarkable capacities for thinking. Like humans, they can (1) form concepts, (2) comprehend numbers, (3) display insight, (4) use tools, and (5) transmit cultural patterns. They have other cognitive skills as well, including self-awareness and the ability to learn and remember.

35. Animals are capable of forming _____ . Wolfgang Köhler demonstrated that chimpanzees also exhibit the "Aha!" reaction that characterizes reasoning by _____ .

36. Forest-dwelling chimpanzees learn to use branches, stones, and other objects as _____ . These behaviors, along with behaviors related to grooming and courtship, _____ (vary/ do not vary) from one group to another, suggesting the transmission of _____ customs.

37. Animals _____ (do/do not) have many other cognitive skills. For example, elephants have shown _____ and chimpanzees have demonstrated _____ , _____ , and group aggression.

Language

Objective 8-9: Name the milestones in language development, and identify the critical period for learning language.

Children's **language** development moves from simplicity to complexity. Their *receptive language* abilities mature before their *productive language.* Beginning at about 4 months, infants enter a **babbling stage** in which they spontaneously utter various sounds at first unrelated to the household language. By about age 10 months, a trained ear can identify the language of the household by listening to an infant's babbling. Around the first birthday, most children enter the **one-word stage,** and by their second birthday, they are uttering two-word sentences. This **two-word stage** is characterized by **telegraphic speech**. This soon leads to their uttering longer phrases, and by early elementary school, they understand complex sentences.

Childhood does seem to represent a *critical* (or "sensitive") *period* for certain aspects of learning. Research indicates that children who have not been exposed to either a spoken or signed language by about age 7 gradually lose their ability to master any language. Learning a second language also becomes more difficult after the window of opportunity closes.

Noam Chomsky notes that children are born with a built-in readiness to learn grammar rules. He argues that children acquire untaught words and grammar so well that it can't be explained solely by training. Moreover, there is a *universal grammar* that underlies all human language.

No matter what language we speak (we are not born with a built-in *specific* language), we start speaking in nouns. Then, whatever language we experience as children, we readily learn its specific *grammar* and vocabulary.

38. Language is defined as _____
_____ .

39. By _____ months of age, babies can read lips and sort out speech sounds. This marks the beginning of their _____
_____ , their ability to understand what is said to them. This ability begins to mature before their _____ _____ ,
or ability to produce words.

40. The first stage of language development, in which children spontaneously utter different sounds, is the _____ stage. This stage typically begins at about _____
months of age. The sounds children make during this stage _____ (do/do not) include only the sounds of the language they hear.

41. Deaf infants who observe their deaf parents _____ begin to babble more with their hands.

42. As infant babbling begins to resemble the household language, the ability to discriminate and produce speech sounds outside the infant's native language is _____ (lost/acquired).

43. During the second stage, called the _____-_____ stage, children convey complete thoughts using single words. This stage begins at about _____ year(s) of age.

44. During the _____-_____ stage, children speak in sentences containing mostly

nouns and verbs. This type of speech is called _____ speech, and it follows the rules of _____ .

45. After this stage, children quickly begin to utter longer phrases and by early elementary school, they are able to understand _____ sentences.

46. Childhood seems to represent a _____
_____ for mastering certain aspects of language. Those who learn a second language as adults _____ (do/do not) understand the grammar of that language as well as native speakers do.

47. The window for learning language gradually begins to close after age _____ . When a young brain doesn't learn any language, its language-learning capacity _____ (never/may still) fully develop(s).

48. The theorist who believes that humans are born with a built-in readiness to learn grammar rules is _____ . This theorist argues that all human languages have the same grammatical building blocks, which suggests that there is a _____ _____ .

49. Although all children begin speaking mostly in _____ , they do not come prepared to learn a specific language. However, they readily learn their language's vocabulary and _____ , the system of rules that allow us to communicate with and understand others.

APPLICATIONS:

50. A listener hearing a recording of Japanese, Spanish, and North American infants babbling would
   a. not be able to tell them apart at any age.
   b. be able to tell them apart if they were older than 6 months.
   c. be able to tell them apart if they were older than 10 months.
   d. be able to tell them apart at any age.

51. The child who says "Milk gone" is engaging in _____ _____ . This type of "sentence" demonstrates that children are actively experimenting with the rules of _____ .

Objective 8-10: Identify the brain areas involved in language processing and speech.

Broca's area, an area in the left frontal lobe, controls language expression by directing the muscle movements involved in speech. *Wernicke's area,* an area in the left temporal lobe, controls language reception. Language functions are distributed across other brain areas as well. Thus, in processing language, as in other forms of information processing, the brain operates by dividing its mental functions, but your conscious experience seems indivisible.

52. Studies of people with language and speech impairments have shown that

    (a) _____

    is involved in producing speech

    and (b) _____

    _____ is involved

    in understanding speech.

(a)
Speaking words
(_____ and
the motor cortex)

53. Although our conscious experience of language seems indivisible, functional MRI scans show that different _____

    _____ are activated

    by nouns and verbs, or objects and actions, for example.

(b)
Hearing words
(auditory cortex and
_____)

54. As in other forms of information processing, the brain operates by dividing its mental functions into _____ .

APPLICATION:

55. In a soccer game, Laura suffered damage to her left temporal lobe. As a result, she is unable to speak in meaningful sentences. The damage affected
    a. Wernicke's area.
    b. Broca's area.
    c. the hypothalamus.
    d. the hippoccampus.

Objective 8-11: Explain how thinking in images can be useful.

We often think in images. In remembering how we do things, for example, turning on the water in the bathroom, we use a mental picture of how we do it. Imagining a physical activity triggers action in the same brain areas that are triggered when actually performing that activity. Researchers have found that thinking in images is especially useful for mentally practicing upcoming events (*process simulation*) and can actually increase our skills.

56. It appears that thinking _____ (can/cannot) occur without the use of language.

57. Athletes often supplement physical practice with _____ practice.

58. Research studies have shown that imagining or watching an event activates _____

(the same/different) areas of the brain that are active when the skill is actually performed.

59. In one study of psychology students preparing for a midterm exam, the greatest benefits were achieved by those who visualized themselves _____ (receiving a high grade/ studying effectively), a process called

    _____ _____ .

APPLICATION:

60. Luke is the backup quarterback for his high school football team. The starting quarterback has been injured, so Luke will play on Saturday. In addition to physical practice, Luke should visualize throwing the ball, a technique called _____ _____ , rather than seeing a touchdown noted on the scoreboard, called _____ _____ .

Objective 8-12: Describe what we know about other species' capacity for language.

Other animals obviously communicate. Vervet monkeys display different alarm cries for different predators. Several teams of psychologists have taught various species of apes, including a number of chimpanzees, to communicate with humans by signing or by pushing buttons. Apes have developed considerable vocabularies. They string words together to form sentences and have taught their skills to younger animals. Skeptics point out important differences between apes' and humans' facilities with language, especially in their respective abilities to master the verbal or signed expression of complex rules of grammar. Nevertheless, studies reveal that apes have considerable ability to think and communicate.

61. Other animals definitely _____ (do/do not) communicate.

62. The Gardners attempted to communicate with the chimpanzee Washoe by teaching her

    _____ _____ .

63. Skeptics believe that interpreting chimpanzees' signs may be little more than the trainers' wishful thinking, an example of _____

    _____ .

64. Most now agree that humans _____ (alone/along with primates) possess language that involves complex grammar.

Summarize some of the arguments of skeptics of animal language research and some responses of believers.

Intelligence

Objective 8-13: Give psychologists' definition of *intelligence,* and discuss the arguments for general intelligence *(g).*

Intelligence varies from context to context. Thus, most psychologists now define *intelligence* as the ability to learn from experience, solve problems, and use knowledge to adapt to new situations.

Charles Spearman granted that people have specific abilities, such as verbal and mathematical aptitudes, but he believed that a *general intelligence (g)* factor runs through all our intelligent behavior. Spearman's position stemmed in part from *factor analysis,* a statistical tool that searches for clusters of related items.

65. In any context, intelligence can be defined as

    _____

    _____ .

66. Charles Spearman, based in part on his work with the statistical tool _____

    _____ , believed that a factor called *g,* or _____

    _____ , runs through the more specific aspects of intelligence.

67. One controversy regarding the nature of intelligence centers on whether intelligence is one

    _____ ability or several

    _____ abilities.

Objective 8-14: Describe how Gardner's and Sternberg's theories of multiple intelligences differ, and discuss the criticisms they have faced.

Evidence that brain damage may diminish one ability but not others, as well as studies of *savant syndrome,* led Howard Gardner to propose a theory of multiple intelligences. These include linguistic, logical-mathematical, musical, spatial, bodily-kinesthetic, intrapersonal, interpersonal, and naturalist.

Robert Sternberg also proposes a *triarchic* theory of multiple intelligences in which he distinguishes among analytical (academic problem solving), practical, and creative intelligences.

Recent research has confirmed that there is a general intelligence factor. But intelligence alone doesn't predict success. *Grit* (your motivation and drive) is also important.

68. People with _____ _____

    score at the low end of intelligence tests but possess exceptional specific skills. Many such people also have the developmental disorder _____

    _____ _____ .

69. Howard Gardner proposes that there are

    _____ _____ ,

    each relatively independent of the others. He first proposed _____ (how many?) such

intelligences. He has also proposed another intelligence, _____ intelligence, the ability to think in depth about deep questions in life.

70. Sternberg's _____ theory distinguishes three types of intelligence:

    _____ intelligence,

    _____ intelligence, and

    _____ intelligence.

71. Critics of theories of multiple intelligences point out that the world is not so just: Using factor analysis, research has _____ (confirmed/ refuted) the idea that there is a general intelligence factor that predicts performance on various complex tasks and in various jobs. Even so, success requires a combination of talent and _____ , as noted in the _____-

    _____ rule.

APPLICATIONS:

72. Melvin is limited in mental ability but has an exceptional ability to play complex music on the piano after hearing it only once. He has been diagnosed as having

    _____ _____ .

73. Don's intelligence scores were only average, but he has been enormously successful as a corporate manager. Robert Sternberg would probably suggest that

    a. Don's verbal intelligence exceeds his performance intelligence.

    b. Don's performance intelligence exceeds his verbal intelligence.

    c. Don's academic intelligence exceeds his practical intelligence.

    d. Don's practical intelligence exceeds his academic intelligence.

Objective 8-15: Describe the four abilities that make up emotional intelligence.

The four abilities of *emotional intelligence,* a critical part of *social intelligence,* are the abilities to (1) *perceive* emotions (to recognize them in faces, music, and stories), (2) *understand* emotions (to predict them and how they change and blend), (3) *manage* emotions (to know how to express them in varied situations), and (4) *use* emotions to enable adaptive or creative thinking. Those who are emotionally smart often succeed in careers, marriages, and parenting where other academically smarter (but emotionally less intelligent) people fail.

74. Social intelligence is defined as _____

    _____ .

75. A critical part of social intelligence is

    _____ _____—

    the ability to _____ ,

    _____ , _____ ,

    and _____ emotions.

Briefly describe emotionally intelligent people.

APPLICATION:

76. Gerardeen has superb social skills, manages conflicts well, and has great empathy for her friends and co-workers. Researchers would probably say that Gerardeen possesses a high degree of _____ _____ .

Objective 8-16: Define *intelligence test,* and describe how achievement and aptitude tests differ.

Psychologists define an **intelligence test** as a method for assessing an individual's mental aptitudes and comparing them with those of others, using numerical scores. **Achievement tests** are designed to measure what people have learned. **Aptitude tests** are designed to assess what people will be able to learn.

77. Tests that assess a person's mental capacities and compare them to those of others, using numerical scores, are called _____ tests. Tests designed to predict your ability to learn something new are called _____ tests. Tests designed to measure what you have already learned are called _____ tests.

Objective 8-17: Describe when and why intelligence tests were created, and discuss how today's tests differ from early intelligence tests.

The modern intelligence-testing movement started when French psychologist Alfred Binet began assessing intellectual abilities. Together with Théodore Simon, Binet developed an intelligence test containing questions that assessed **mental age** and helped predict children's future progress in the Paris school system. The test sought to identify French schoolchildren needing special attention.
  Lewis Terman of Stanford University adapted Binet's test as the *Stanford-Binet;* he had found that the Paris-developed age norms did not work well with California schoolchildren. William Stern derived the **intelligence quotient,** or **IQ,** for Terman's test. The IQ was simply a person's mental age divided by chronological age multiplied by 100. Today, we refer to intelligence test scores, which represent the test-taker's performance relative to the average performance (assigned a score of 100) of others the same age.
  The *Wechsler Adult Intelligence Test (WAIS),* created by David Wechsler, is the most widely used intelligence test. It consists of 15

subtests and yields not only an overall intelligence score but also separate verbal comprehension, perceptual organization, working memory, and processing speed scores. Striking differences among these scores can provide clues to cognitive strengths or weaknesses that teachers or therapists might build upon.

78. The French psychologist who devised a test to predict the success of children in school was _____ . Predictions were made by comparing children's chronological age with their _____ age, which was determined by the test.

79. Lewis Terman's revision of Binet's test is referred to as the _____-_____ . Terman assumed that intelligence tests revealed a _____ mental capacity present from birth and that some ethnic groups were more intelligent than others. He supported the controversial _____ movement, which promoted selective breeding and sterilization.

80. William Stern developed the formula for computing a test-taker's performance on Terman's test. The term for the person's score was _____ _____ .

Give the original formula for computing IQ, and explain any items used in the formula.

81. Today's tests _____ (do/do not) compute an IQ score. They represent the test-taker's performance relative to the average performance of others of _____ (the same/different) age(s). These tests are designed so that a score of _____ is considered average.

82. The most widely used intelligence test is the _____ _____ _____ _____ . Consisting of 15 subtests, it provides not only a general intelligence score but also separate scores for _____ _____ , _____ _____ , _____ _____ , and _____ _____ .

APPLICATIONS:

83. Before becoming attorneys, law students must pass a special licensing exam, which is an _____ test. Before entering college, high school students must take the SAT®, which is an _____ test.

84. Benito was born in 1937. In 1947, he scored 130 on an intelligence test. Benito's mental age when he took the test was _____ .

85. If asked to guess the intelligence score of a stranger, your best guess would be _____ .

Objective 8-18: Describe a normal curve, and explain what it means to say that a test has been standardized and is reliable and valid.

Because scores become meaningful only when they can be compared with others' performance, they must be defined relative to a pretested group, a process called *standardization*. Obviously, the group on which a test is standardized must be representative of those who will be taking the test in the future. Standardized test results typically form a bell-shaped pattern of scores that forms the *normal curve*. Most scores cluster around average, and increasingly fewer are distributed at the extremes.

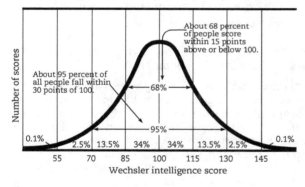

Reliability refers to the extent to which a test yields consistent scores. Consistency may be assessed by comparing scores on two halves of the test or on retesting. A test can be reliable but not valid.

Validity refers to the extent to which a test measures or predicts what it is supposed to. Intelligence tests have *content validity*—they measure what they are supposed to measure—and they have *predictive validity*: They can predict future performance.

86. One requirement of a good test is the process of defining meaningful scores by comparison with the performance of a pretested group, which is called _____ .

87. When scores on a test are compiled, they generally result in a bell-shaped pattern, or _____ _____ .

Describe this bell-shaped pattern, and explain its significance in the standardization process.

88. If a test yields consistent results, it is said to be _____ . To determine a test's reliability, researchers may retest people using _____ (the same/a different) test or they may _____ _____ . If the two sets of scores generally agree—if they _____ —the test is reliable. The Stanford-Binet, WAIS, and WISC _____ (are/are not) reliable.

89. The degree to which a test measures or predicts what it is supposed to is referred to as the test's _____ .

90. The degree to which a test measures what it is supposed to measure is referred to as the test's _____ _____ .

91. The degree to which a test predicts future performance of a particular behavior is referred to as the test's _____ _____ .

APPLICATIONS:

92. If you wanted to develop a test of musical aptitude in North American children, which would be the appropriate standardization group?
    a. children all over the world
    b. North American children
    c. children of musical parents
    d. children with known musical ability

93. Jack takes the same test of mechanical reasoning on several different days and gets virtually identical scores. This suggests that the test has high _____ .

94. You would not use a test of hearing ability as an intelligence test because it would lack _____ .

Objective 8-19: Describe the traits of those who score at the low and high extremes on intelligence tests.

To be labeled as having an *intellectual disability,* a child must have both a low test score (70 or below) and difficulty adapting to the normal demands of living independently. Intellectual disability sometimes results from known physical causes, such as *Down syndrome,* a disorder of varying intellectual and physical severity that is attributed to an extra copy of chromosome 21.

Contrary to the popular myth that "gifted" children are frequently maladjusted, research suggests that these high-scoring children are healthy, well adjusted, and unusually academically successful. Most children with extraordinary academic gifts thrive.

95. Individuals whose intelligence scores fall below 70 and who have difficulty adapting to the demands of life may be labeled _____

_____ .

96. An intellectual disability sometimes has a physical basis, such as _____

_____ , a disorder caused by an

extra copy of chromosome _____ .

97. At the high extreme, Lewis Terman's "gifted children" turned out to be _____ ,

well-_____ , and unusually successful

_____ . More recent research

_____ (confirms/refutes)

Terman's conclusions.

APPLICATION:

98. Twenty-two-year-old Dan has an intelligence score of 63 and the academic skills of a fourth-grader and is unable to live independently. Dan probably
   a. is in the middle of the normal curve for intelligence test scores.
   b. has savant syndrome.
   c. is intellectually disabled.
   d. will eventually achieve self-supporting social and vocational skills.

Objective 8-20: Explain what we mean when we say that a trait is heritable, and discuss what twin and adoption studies tell us about the nature and nurture of intelligence.

Studies of twins, family members, and adopted children together point to a significant genetic contribution to intelligence scores. For example, even when identical twins are reared separately, their test scores are similar. Furthermore, the most genetically similar people have the most similar scores. However, shared environment also matters. *Heritability* refers to the extent to which differences among people are attributable to genes. To say that the heritability of intelligence is 50 percent does not mean that half of an individual's intelligence is inherited. Rather, it means that we can attribute to heredity 50 percent of the variation of intelligence among those studied. Intelligence appears to involve many genes.

99. The intelligence scores of identical twins raised together are _____ (more/no more) similar than those of fraternal twins.

100. The intelligence test scores of fraternal twins are _____ (more alike/no more alike) than the intelligence test scores of other

siblings. This provides evidence of a(n)

_____ (genetic/environmental)

effect because fraternal twins, being the same

_____ , are treated more alike.

101. Studies of adopted children and their adoptive and biological families demonstrate that with age, genetic influences on intelligence become

_____ (more/less) apparent.

Thus, children's intelligence scores are more like

those of their _____ (biological/

adoptive) parents than those of their

_____ (biological/adoptive)

parents.

102. The amount of variation in a trait within a group that is attributed to genetic factors is called its

_____ . For intelligence, this has

been estimated as _____ per-

cent or more.

103. If we know a trait has perfect heritability, this

knowledge _____ (does/does

not) enable us to rule out environmental factors in explaining differences between groups.

Objective 8-21: Describe how environmental influences can affect cognitive development.

With mental abilities, as with physical abilities, our genes shape the experiences that shape us. Studies of children raised in extremely neglectful or enriched environments also indicate that life experiences significantly influence intelligence test scores. However, although extreme deprivation can retard normal brain development, there is no environmental recipe for creating a genius out of a normal infant.

104. Studies indicate that neglected children

_____ (do/do not) show signs of

recovery in intelligence and behavior when placed in more nurturing environments. Although normal brain development can be retarded by

_____ , _____

deprivation, and _____

_____ , there is no sure environment that will produce a "superbaby."

STUDY TIP: Heritability is a difficult concept to grasp in part because it is often confused with genetic determination, which refers to what causes a characteristic to develop. The number of toes on your feet is genetically determined because your genes cause five toes to develop on each foot. Heritability, on the other hand, is what causes differences in a characteristic. As explained in the text, to say that the heritability of intelligence is 50 percent does not mean that half of an individual's intelligence is inherited. Rather, it means that we can attribute to heredity 50 percent of the variation of intelligence among those studied. A good way to keep the two concepts straight is to remember that while the concept of genetic determination makes sense in the case of a single person, heritability does not. Genetic determination is biological; heritability is a statistical measure. Heritability only makes sense relative to differences among groups of people. It doesn't make sense to ask, "What's the heritability of my intelligence?"

APPLICATION:

105. Raoul and Fidel are identical twins separated at birth. Because they have similar heredity and different environments, heritability for their intelligence is likely to be _____ (high/low). Ramona was adopted by Francesa's parents when she was 2 months old. The heritability for their intelligence is likely to be _____ (high/low).

Objective 8-22: Discuss the stability of intelligence scores over the life span, and describe how psychologists study this issue.

By age 4, children's intelligence test scores begin to predict their adolescent and adult scores. By late adolescence, intelligence and other aptitude scores are quite stable. Psychologists use the results of **cross-sectional** and **longitudinal studies** to demonstrate that intelligence is stable over the life span and that high scores predict health and a long life.

106. Intelligence becomes _____ (more/less) stable with age.

107. A research study in which people of various ages are compared with one another is called a _____-_____ study.

108. A research study in which the same people are retested over a period of years is called a _____ study.

109. A famous Scottish study found that the longest-living adults had intelligence test scores that were _____ (lower/higher) than their shorter-lived counterparts.

State several possible explanations for this finding.

Objective 8-23: Define *crystallized* and *fluid intelligence*, and describe how they are affected by aging.

Crystallized intelligence—one's accumulated knowledge and verbal skills as reflected in vocabulary and word-power tests—increases into middle age. *Fluid intelligence*—one's ability to reason speedily and abstractly, as when solving unfamiliar logic problems—declines slowly up to age 75, then more rapidly, especially after age 85. Thus, while we lose recall memory and processing speed, we gain vocabulary knowledge and we are less affected by negative emotions.

110. The accumulation of knowledge and verbal skills is referred to as _____ intelligence.

111. The ability to reason speedily and abstractly is referred to as _____ intelligence.

112. During adulthood, _____ intelligence declines gradually until about age _____ , and then more rapidly, especially after about age _____ .

113. With age, older adults' _____ and _____ increases. Also, their _____ reasoning skills increase and decisions become less distorted by _____ _____ .

APPLICATIONS:

114. Deborah is a mathematician and Willie is a philosopher. Considering their professions, Deborah will make her most significant career accomplishments _____ (at about the same time as/at an earlier age than/at a later age than) Willie will.

115. Sixty-five-year-old Jordan cannot reason as well as he could when he was younger. Most likely, Jordan's _____ intelligence has declined.

Objective 8-24: Describe how and why the genders differ in mental ability scores.

Although gender similarities far outnumber gender differences, we find the differences in abilities more interesting. Research indicates that, compared with boys, girls are better spellers, are more verbally fluent, are better at locating objects, and are more sensitive to touch, taste, and color. Boys outperform girls in spatial ability and complex math problem solving. Males' mental ability scores vary more than females'. Worldwide, boys outnumber girls at both the low extreme and the high extreme. Women detect emotions more easily than do men.

116. Females tend to outscore males on
_____ tests and are more
_____ fluent. They also have an
edge in locating objects; are more sensitive to odor,
_____ , and _____ ;
and are better _____ detectors.

117. The gender gap in math achievement
_____ (varies/does not vary)
across countries. _____-
_____ cultures exhibit little
of the gender math gap. Males tend to outscore
females on tests of _____
_____ .

118. Working from an _____ per-
spective, some theorists speculate that these gender differences in spatial manipulation helped our
ancestors survive.

Objective 8-25: Describe how and why racial and ethnic
groups differ in mental ability scores.

White Americans have outscored Black Americans on
intelligence tests. New Zealanders of European descent
outscore native Maori New Zealanders, Israeli Jews
outscore Israeli Arabs, and most Japanese outscore the
stigmatized Japanese minority. Research suggests that
environmental differences are largely responsible for
these group differences. Consider: (1) Genetics research
indicates that the races are remarkably alike under the
skin; (2) race is not a neatly defined biological category;
(3) intelligence test performance of today's better-fed,
better-educated, and more test-prepared population
exceeds that of the 1930s population by the same margin
that the score of the average White today exceeds that
of the average Black; (4) given the same information,
Whites and Blacks show similar information-processing skills; (5) Asian students, who outperform North
American students on math achievement and aptitude
tests, have also spent 30 percent more time in school
and much more time in and out of school studying math;
and (6) in different eras, different ethnic groups have
experienced periods of remarkable achievement.

119. Research evidence suggests that group differences
in intelligence are mainly _____
(genetic/environmental).

120. Group differences in intelligence scores
_____ (do/do not) provide an
accurate basis for judging individuals. Individual
differences within a race are _____
(greater than/less than) between-race differences.
Furthermore, race _____ (is/is
not) a neatly defined biological category.

121. The test scores of today's better-educated population are _____ (higher/lower)
than those of earlier populations, and in different
eras, different _____ groups
have experienced golden ages.

122. Differences in access to _____
may account for differences in intelligence test
performance.

123. Although Asian students on the average score
_____ (higher/lower) than North
American students on math tests, this difference
may be due to the fact that _____
_____ .

APPLICATION:

124. Hiroko, who goes to school in Osaka, Japan, has a math
achievement score that is considerably higher than that
of most American students her age. Explain this difference between Asian and North American students.

_____

_____

Objective 8-26: Discuss whether intelligence tests are
biased and discriminatory, and describe how stereotype
threat affects test-takers' performance.

Intelligence tests are "biased" in the sense that they are
sensitive to performance differences caused by cultural
experience. However, tests are not biased in that they
predict as accurately for one group as they do for another. For example, the predictive validity is roughly the
same for women and men, for various races, and for rich
and poor. *Stereotype threat* is a self-confirming concern
that one will be evaluated based on a negative stereotype. The phenomenon sometimes appears in intelligence testing among Blacks and among women.
  Believing that intelligence is changeable, rather than
biologically fixed, can foster a *growth mind-set*—a focus
on learning and growing.

125. In the sense that they detect differences caused by
cultural experiences, intelligence tests probably
_____ (are/are not) biased.

126. Most psychologists agree that, in terms of predictive validity, the major aptitude tests
_____ (are/are not) biased in the
scientific meaning of the term.

127. When women and members of ethnic minorities
are led to expect that they won't do well on a test,
a _____ _____
may result, and their scores may actually be lower.

128. In programs fostering a _____
_____-_____ ,
young teens learn that the brain is like a muscle
that grows stronger with use as neuron connections grow.

Progress Test

Multiple-Choice Questions

Circle your answers to the following questions and check them with the answers beginning on page 173. If your answer is incorrect, read the explanation for why it is incorrect and then consult the text.

1. The text defines *cognition* as
   a. silent speech.
   b. all mental activity.
   c. mental activity associated with thinking, knowing, remembering, and communicating information.
   d. logical reasoning.

2. Confirmation bias refers to the tendency to
   a. overestimate the accuracy of your beliefs.
   b. cling to your initial conceptions after the basis on which they were formed has been discredited.
   c. search randomly through alternative solutions when problem solving.
   d. look for information that is consistent with your beliefs.

3. Which of the following is NOT true of babbling?
   a. It is imitation of adult speech.
   b. It is the same in all cultures.
   c. It typically occurs from about age 4 months to 1 year.
   d. Babbling increasingly comes to resemble a particular language.

4. Which of the following has been argued by critics of ape language research?
   a. Ape language is merely imitation of the trainer's behavior.
   b. Ape vocabularies and sentences are simple, like those of a 2-year-old child.
   c. Interpreting chimpanzee signs as language may be little more than the trainers' wishful thinking.
   d. All of these points have been argued.

5. Which of the following best describes Chomsky's view of language development?
   a. Humans are born with a built-in specific language.
   b. Language is an innate ability.
   c. Humans have a biological predisposition to acquire language.
   d. There are no social influences on the development of language.

6. Which of the following is an example of the use of heuristics?
   a. trying every possible letter ordering when unscrambling a word
   b. considering each possible move when playing chess
   c. using the formula "area = length x width" to find the area of a rectangle

d. playing chess using a defensive strategy that has often been successful for you

7. The chimpanzee Sultan used a short stick to pull a longer stick that was out of reach into his cage. He then used the longer stick to reach a piece of fruit. Researchers hypothesized that Sultan's discovery of the solution to his problem was the result of
   a. trial and error.   c. fixation.
   b. heuristics.   d. insight.

8. Researchers who are convinced that animals can think point to evidence that
   a. monkeys can learn to classify dogs and cats.
   b. chimpanzees regularly use branches, stones, and other objects as tools in their natural habitats.
   c. chimps invent grooming and courtship customs and pass them on to their peers.
   d. all of these are true.

9. Deaf children who are NOT exposed to sign language until they are teenagers
   a. are unable to master the basic words of sign language.
   b. learn the basic words but not how to order them.
   c. are unable to master either the basic words or syntax of sign language.
   d. never become as fluent as those who learned to sign at a younger age.

10. A 6-year-old child has a mental age of 9. Using the original formula, the child's IQ would be
    a. 96.   c. 125.
    b. 100.   d. 150.

11. Which of the following is NOT true?
    a. In spatial ability, males have an edge over females.
    b. In science and math achievement, males always surpass females.
    c. Women are better than men at detecting emotions.
    d. Males score higher than females on tests of spatial abilities.

12. One reason psychologists give for their belief that racial gaps in test scores are environmental is that
    a. the differences are too large to be explained biologically.
    b. the heritability of intelligence is increasing.
    c. race is primarily a social category, not a neatly defined biological category.
    d. the gap is increasing as environment changes.

13. Standardization refers to the process of
    a. determining the portion of test-score variation that can be assigned to genes.
    b. defining meaningful scores relative to a representative pretested group.
    c. determining the consistency of test scores obtained by retesting people.
    d. measuring the success with which a test predicts the behavior it is designed to predict.

14. Which of the following is NOT a requirement of a good test?
    a. reliability   c. fixation
    b. standardization   d. validity

15. First-time parents Geena and Brad want to give their baby's intellectual abilities a jumpstart by providing a super-enriched learning environment. Experts would suggest that the new parents should
    a. pipe stimulating classical music into the baby's room.
    b. hang colorful mobiles and artwork over the baby's crib.
    c. take the child to one of the new "superbaby" preschools that specialize in infant enrichment.
    d. relax, since there is no surefire environmental recipe for giving a child a superior intellect.

16. Which of the following statements is true?
    a. The predictive validity of intelligence tests is not as high as their reliability.
    b. The reliability of intelligence tests is not as high as their predictive validity.
    c. Modern intelligence tests have extremely high predictive validity and reliability.
    d. The predictive validity and reliability of most intelligence tests is very low.

17. Which of the following best describes the relationship between creativity and aptitude?
    a. Creativity appears to depend on the ability to think imaginatively and has little if any relationship to the ability to learn.
    b. Creativity is best understood as a certain kind of aptitude.
    c. The more intelligent a person is, the greater his or her creativity.
    d. A certain level of aptitude is necessary but not sufficient for creativity.

18. The existence of _____ reinforces the generally accepted notion that intelligence is a multidimensional quality.
    a. adaptive skills   c. general intelligence
    b. stereotype threat   d. savant syndrome

19. Current estimates are that _____ percent of the total variation among intelligence scores can be attributed to genetic factors.
    a. less than 10   c. 50
    b. 25   d. 75

20. Reported racial gaps in average intelligence scores are most likely due to
    a. the use of biased tests of intelligence.
    b. the use of unreliable tests of intelligence.
    c. genetic factors.
    d. environmental factors.

21. The bell-shaped pattern of intelligence scores in the general population is called a
    a. *g* distribution.
    b. standardization curve.
    c. intelligence quotient.
    d. normal curve.

22. A common problem in everyday reasoning is our tendency to
    a. cling to our beliefs in the face of evidence that proves us wrong.
    b. accept as logical those conclusions that disagree with our own opinions.
    c. underestimate the accuracy of our knowledge.
    d. accept as logical conclusions that involve unfamiliar concepts.

23. Many psychologists are skeptical of claims that chimpanzees can acquire language because the chimps have not shown the ability to
    a. use symbols meaningfully.
    b. acquire speech.
    c. acquire even a limited vocabulary.
    d. use syntax in communicating.

24. Assume that Congress is considering revising its approach to welfare and so is hearing a range of testimony. A member of Congress who uses the availability heuristic would be most likely to
    a. want to experiment with numerous possible approaches to see which of these seems to work best.
    b. want to find the best solution by systematically examining every possibility.
    c. refuse to be budged from his or her beliefs despite persuasive testimony to the contrary.
    d. base his or her ideas on the most memorable testimony given, even though many of the statistics presented run counter to this testimony.

25. If you want to be absolutely certain that you will find the solution to a problem you know is solvable, you should use
    a. a heuristic.   c. insight.
    b. an algorithm.   d. trial and error.

26. Telegraphic speech is typical of the _____ stage.
    a. babbling   c. two-word
    b. one-word   d. three-word

27. Children first demonstrate a rudimentary understanding of syntax during the _____ stage.
    a. babbling   c. two-word
    b. one-word   d. three-word

28. The study in which people who immigrated to the United States at various ages were compared in terms of their ability to understand English grammar found that
    a. age of arrival had no effect on mastery of grammar.
    b. those who immigrated as children understood grammar as well as native speakers.
    c. those who immigrated as adults understood grammar as well as native speakers.
    d. whether English was spoken in the home was the most important factor in mastering the rules of grammar.

29. Researchers taught the chimpanzee Washoe to communicate by using
    a. various sounds.
    b. plastic symbols of various shapes and colors.
    c. sign language.
    d. all of these things.

30. The test created by Alfred Binet was designed specifically to
    a. measure inborn intelligence in adults.
    b. measure inborn intelligence in children.
    c. predict school performance in children.
    d. identify children who are mentally slow so that they could be institutionalized.

31. Which of the following provides the strongest evidence of environment's role in intelligence?
    a. Adopted children's intelligence test scores are more like their adoptive parents' scores than their biological parents'.
    b. Children's intelligence test scores are more strongly related to their mothers' scores than to their fathers'.
    c. Children moved from a deprived environment into an intellectually enriched one show gains in intellectual development.
    d. The intelligence test scores of identical twins raised separately are no more alike than those of siblings.

32. If a test designed to indicate which applicants are likely to perform the best on the job fails to do so, the test has
    a. low reliability.
    b. low validity.
    c. low predictive validity.
    d. not been standardized.

33. The formula for the intelligence quotient was devised by
    a. Robert Sternberg.   c. Lewis Terman.
    b. Alfred Binet.   d. William Stern.

34. Current intelligence tests compute an individual's intelligence score as
    a. the ratio of mental age to chronological age multiplied by 100.
    b. the ratio of chronological age to mental age multiplied by 100.
    c. the test-taker's performance relative to the average performance of others the same age.
    d. the ratio of the test-taker's verbal intelligence score to his or her nonverbal intelligence score.

35. The concept of a g factor implies that intelligence
    a. is a single overall ability.
    b. is several specific abilities.
    c. cannot be defined.
    d. cannot be measured.

36. Most experts view intelligence as a person's
    a. ability to perform well on intelligence tests.
    b. innate mental capacity.

    c. ability to learn from experience, solve problems, and adapt to new situations.
    d. diverse skills acquired throughout life.

37. Originally, IQ was defined as
    a. mental age divided by chronological age and multiplied by 100.
    b. chronological age divided by mental age and multiplied by 100.
    c. mental age subtracted from chronological age and multiplied by 100.
    d. chronological age subtracted from mental age and multiplied by 100.

38. Which of the following statements most accurately reflects the text's position regarding the relative contribution of genes and environment in determining intelligence?
    a. Except in cases of a neglectful early environment, each individual's basic intelligence is largely the product of heredity.
    b. Intelligence is primarily the product of environmental experiences.
    c. Both genes and life experiences significantly influence performance on intelligence tests.
    d. Because intelligence tests have such low predictive validity, the question cannot be addressed until psychologists agree on a more valid test of intelligence.

39. The contribution of environmental factors to racial gaps in intelligence scores is indicated by
    a. evidence that individual differences within a race are much greater than differences between races.
    b. the fact that Whites and Blacks given the same information display similar information-processing skills.
    c. the fact that Asian students outperform North American students on math achievement and aptitude tests.
    d. all of these facts.

40. Tests of _____ measure what an individual can do now, whereas tests of _____ predict what an individual will be able to do later.
    a. aptitude; achievement
    b. achievement; aptitude
    c. reliability; validity
    d. validity; reliability

41. Damage to _____ will usually cause a person to lose the ability to understand language.
    a. the hypothalamus
    b. Broca's area
    c. Wernicke's area
    d. the frontal lobe

42. A person's general ability to think abstractly is called _____ intelligence. This ability generally _____ with age.
    a. fluid; increases   c. crystallized; decreases
    b. fluid; decreases   d. crystallized; increases

43. A person's accumulation of stored information, called _____ intelligence, generally _____ with age.
   a. fluid; decreases
   b. fluid; increases
   c. crystallized; decreases
   d. crystallized; increases

44. Longitudinal research
   a. compares people of different ages.
   b. studies the same people at different times.
   c. usually involves a larger sample than does cross-sectional research.
   d. usually involves a smaller sample than does cross-sectional research.

45. Cross-sectional research
   a. compares people of different ages with one another.
   b. studies the same group of people at different times.
   c. is used for studying cognitive development during infancy.
   d. is used for studying social development during infancy.

Matching Items

Match each definition or description with the appropriate term.

Definitions or Descriptions

_____ **1.** the consistency with which a test measures performance
_____ **2.** the way an issue or question is posed
_____ **3.** the process of defining meaningful scores relative to a pretested group
_____ **4.** the degree to which a test measures what it is designed to measure
_____ **5.** presuming that something is likely if it comes readily to mind
_____ **6.** the tendency to overestimate the accuracy of one's judgments
_____ **7.** being unable to see a problem from a different angle
_____ **8.** haphazard problem solving by trying one solution after another
_____ **9.** the sudden realization of the solution to a problem
_____**10.** Terman's revision of Binet's original intelligence test
_____ **11.** an underlying, general intelligence factor
_____ **12.** the proportion of variation among individuals that we can attribute to genes
_____**13.** a very low intelligence score accompanied by one extraordinary skill

Terms

   a. standardization
   b. heritability
   c. *g*
   d. trial and error
   e. availability heuristic
   f. savant syndrome
   g. insight
   h. framing
   i. overconfidence
   j. fixation
   k. Stanford-Binet
   l. predictive validity
   m. reliability

Application Essay

You have been asked to devise a Psychology Achievement Test (PAT) that will be administered to freshmen who declare psychology as their major. What steps will you take to ensure that the PAT is a good intelligence test? (Use the space below to list the points you want to make, and organize them. Then write the essay on a separate sheet of paper.)

Summing Up

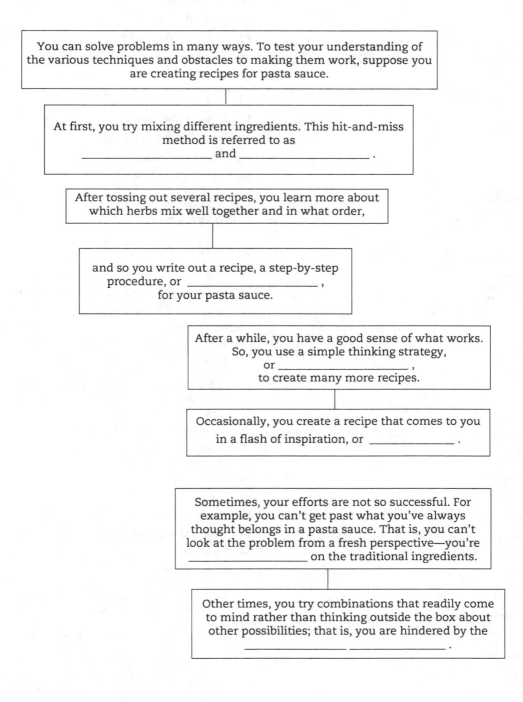

You can solve problems in many ways. To test your understanding of the various techniques and obstacles to making them work, suppose you are creating recipes for pasta sauce.

At first, you try mixing different ingredients. This hit-and-miss method is referred to as _____ and _____ .

After tossing out several recipes, you learn more about which herbs mix well together and in what order,

and so you write out a recipe, a step-by-step procedure, or _____ , for your pasta sauce.

After a while, you have a good sense of what works. So, you use a simple thinking strategy, or _____ , to create many more recipes.

Occasionally, you create a recipe that comes to you in a flash of inspiration, or _____ .

Sometimes, your efforts are not so successful. For example, you can't get past what you've always thought belongs in a pasta sauce. That is, you can't look at the problem from a fresh perspective—you're _____ on the traditional ingredients.

Other times, you try combinations that readily come to mind rather than thinking outside the box about other possibilities; that is, you are hindered by the _____ _____ .

Terms and Concepts to Remember

Using your own words, on a piece of paper write a brief definition or explanation of each of the following terms.

1. cognition
2. concept
3. prototype
4. algorithm
5. heuristic
6. insight
7. confirmation bias
8. fixation
9. intuition
10. availability heuristic
11. overconfidence
12. belief perseverance
13. framing
14. creativity
15. convergent thinking
16. divergent thinking
17. language
18. babbling stage
19. one-word stage
20. two-word stage
21. telegraphic speech
22. grammar
23. Broca's area
24. Wernicke's area
25. intelligence
26. general intelligence (*g*)
27. savant syndrome
28. emotional intelligence
29. intelligence test
30. achievement test
31. aptitude test
32. mental age
33. Stanford-Binet
34. intelligence quotient (IQ)
35. Wechsler Adult Intelligence Scale (WAIS)
36. standardization
37. normal curve
38. reliability
39. validity
40. content validity
41. predictive validity
42. intellectual disability
43. Down syndrome
44. heritability
45. cross-sectional study
46. longitudinal study
47. crystallized intelligence
48. fluid intelligence
49. stereotype threat

Answers

Chapter Review

Thinking

1. all the mental activity associated with thinking, knowing, remembering, and communicating
2. concepts
3. prototype; robin; penguin
4. **b.** is the answer. A rose is a prototypical example of the concept *flower*.
   c. & d. Cognition is the overall term for thinking. This example is more specific, dealing with a prototype of a concept.
5. problem solving
6. trial and error
7. algorithms
8. heuristics
9. insight
10. confirmation bias
11. supports; against
12. fixation
13. **a.** Trial and error: randomly looking everywhere in the house
    b. Algorithm: methodically checking every possible location in the house as well as all the pockets in your clothes
    c. Heuristics: thinking about the most logical place for you to have left your keys
    d. Insight: suddenly realizing that you left your keys in the car when you took the groceries out
14. algorithm. Follow the recipe precisely and you can't miss!
15. heuristic; algorithm. Boris is using a simple, more efficient thinking strategy. The computer is programmed to check every possible move.
16. confirmation bias. The confirmation bias is the tendency to search for information that confirms your preconceptions. In this example, the politicians' preconceptions are biasing their interpretations of the survey results.

17. intuition

18. availability heuristic

The availability heuristic leads us to estimate the likelihood of events based on how readily they come to mind. Thus, we may think certain ethnic groups are more likely to be terrorists because of the vividness of recent attacks.

19. **a.** what our ancestral history has prepared us to fear.
   b. what we cannot control.
   c. what is immediate.
   d. what is most readily available in memory.

20. too little; ongoing

21. overconfidence

22. adaptive; happily; easier; competent

23. belief perseverance

24. consider the opposite

25. framing; does

26. availability heuristic. The publicity surrounding disasters makes such events vivid and seem more probable than they actually are.

27. **c.** is the answer. Most people are more confident than correct in estimating their knowledge and the amount of time a task will take.

28. **a.** is the answer. Although b. and c. may be true, they do not describe belief perseverance. The d. answer is the confirmation bias.

29. framing. How a question or statement is worded can have a major effect on how people respond.

30. quickly; adaptive

31. complex; incubate' evaluate; test; plan

32. creativity

33. convergent; divergent; creativity

Creative people tend to have expertise, or a solid base of knowledge; imaginative thinking skills, which allow them to see things in new ways, to recognize patterns, and to make connections; intrinsic motivation, or the tendency to focus on the pleasure and challenge of their work; and a venturesome personality that tolerates gray areas and risk and seeks new experiences. Creative people also have generally benefited from living in creative environments.

Research suggests that you can boost your creativity by developing your expertise in an area you care about and enjoy; allow time for a problem to hatch (sleep on it!); set aside time for your mind to roam freely; and experience other cultures and ways of thinking, which will expose you to multiple perspectives and foster flexible thinking.

34. **c.** is the answer.
   a. She is more likely than average to create something special, but creativity is more than school smarts.
   b. Just the opposite is true of creative people.
   d. This may or may not be true, but most likely it isn't.

35. concepts; insight

36. tools; vary; cultural

37. do; self-awareness; altruism; cooperation

Language

38. our spoken, written, or signed words and the ways we combine them to communicate meaning

39. 4; receptive language; productive language

40. babbling; 4; do not

41. signing

42. lost

43. one-word; 1

44. two-word; telegraphic; syntax

45. complex

46. critical period; do not

47. 7; never

48. Noam Chomsky; universal grammar

49. nouns; grammar

50. **c.** is the answer. Before 10 months of age, infants babble sounds from all languages.

51. telegraphic speech; syntax. These "sentences," characteristic of a child of about 2 years, are like telegrams, in that they consist mainly of nouns and verbs and show use of syntax.

52. Broca's area; Wernicke's area

53. neural networks

54. smaller tasks

55. **b.** is the answer.
   a. Wernicke's area is involved in understanding speech.
   c. & d. The hypothalamus and the hippocampus have nothing to do with language.

56. can

57. mental

58. the same

59. studying effectively; process simulation

60. process simulation; outcome simulation. Imagining the procedure activates the brain areas involved in actually performing the activity, so process simulation produces better results than outcome simulation.

61. do

62. sign language

63. perceptual set

64. alone

Chimps have gained only limited vocabularies and—in contrast to children—have gained these vocabularies only with great difficulty. Also in contrast to children, it's unclear that chimps can use syntax to express meaning. The signing of chimps is often nothing more than imitation of the trainer's actions. People tend to interpret such unclear behavior in terms of what they want to see. Believers argue that although animals do not have our facility for language, they have the abilities to communicate. For example, Washoe and Loulis sign spontaneously. Also, bonobos can learn to understand English syntax.

Intelligence

65. the ability to learn from experience, solve problems, and use knowledge to adapt to new situations

66. factor analysis; general intelligence

67. general; specific

68. savant syndrome; autism spectrum disorder (ASD)

69. multiple intelligences; eight; existential

70. triarchic; analytical (school smarts); practical (street smarts); creative (trailblazing smarts)

71. confirmed; grit; 10-year

72. savant syndrome. People with savant syndrome tend to score low on intelligence tests but have one exceptional ability.

73. **d.** is the answer.

74. the know-how involved in understanding social situations and managing yourself successfully

75. emotional intelligence; perceive; understand; manage; use

Emotionally intelligent people are socially aware and self-aware. They enjoy higher-quality interactions with friends. They can manage their emotions and they can delay gratification. They handle others' emotions skillfully. They also perform modestly better on the job.

76. emotional intelligence. Emotionally intelligent people are able to perceive, manage, understand, and use emotions.

77. intelligence; aptitude; achievement

78. Alfred Binet; mental

79. Stanford-Binet; fixed; eugenics

80. intelligence quotient

In the original formula for IQ, measured mental age is divided by chronological age and multiplied by 100. "Mental age" refers to the chronological age that most typically corresponds to a given level of performance. Multiplying by 100 gets rid of the decimal point.

81. do not; the same; 100

82. Wechsler Adult Intelligence Scale; verbal comprehension; perceptual organization; working memory; processing speed

83. achievement; aptitude. An exam for a professional license is intended to measure whether you have gained the overall knowledge and skill to practice the profession. The SAT® is designed to predict ability, or aptitude, for learning a new skill.

84. 13. At the time he took the test, Benito's chronological age (CA) was 10. Knowing that IQ = 130 and CA = 10, solving the equation for mental age yields a value of 13.

85. 100. Standard intelligence tests today set 100 as the average score for a given age.

86. standardization

87. normal curve

The normal curve describes the pattern of scores for many physical and psychological attributes (including mental aptitudes), with most scores falling near the average and fewer near the extremes. When a test is standardized on a normal curve, individual scores are assigned according to how far they are above or below the average.

88. reliable; the same; split the test in half; correlate; are

89. validity

90. content validity

91. predictive validity

92. **b.** is the answer. A standardization group provides a representative comparison for the trait being measured by a test. Because this test will measure musical aptitude in North American children, the standardization group should be limited to North American children but should include children of all degrees of musical aptitude.

93. reliability. Reliability is the extent to which a test produces the same results each time.

94. validity. A test is not valid if it does not measure what it is designed to measure. Obviously, a hearing test would not measure intelligence.

95. intellectually disabled

96. Down syndrome; 21

97. healthy; adjusted; academically; confirms

98. **c.** is the answer. To be labeled intellectually disabled a person must have a test score of 70 or below and experience difficulty adapting to the normal demands of living.

    a. Dan's score is well below the middle of the normal curve for intelligence.

    b. There is no indication that Dan possesses one extraordinary skill, as do people with savant syndrome.

    d. The text does not suggest that intellectually disabled people eventually become self-supporting.

99. more

100. more alike; environmental; age

101. more; biological; adoptive

102. heritability; 50

103. does not

104. do; malnutrition; sensory; social isolation

105. low; high. When people are genetically similar, heritability is low (in this case, 0, because they are identical twins). When environments are similar but not necessarily identical (as in the case of Ramona and Francesa), heritability is high (closer to 100 percent).

106. more

107. cross-sectional

108. longitudinal

109. higher

Intelligence gives people better access to education, better jobs, and a healthier environment. It also encourages people to live healthier lives. Prenatal events or childhood illnesses could influence both intelligence and health.

110. crystallized

111. fluid

112. fluid; 75; 85

113. vocabulary; knowledge; social; negative emotions

114. at an earlier age than. Mathematical and philosophical reasoning involve fluid and crystallized intelligence, respectively. Because fluid intelligence generally declines with age while crystallized intelligence increases, it is likely that significant mathematical accomplishments will occur at an earlier age than philosophical accomplishments.

115. fluid. Fluid intelligence refers to a person's ability to reason speedily and abstractly, an ability that declines with age.

116. spelling; verbally; touch; taste; emotion

117. varies; Gender-equal; mental rotation

118. evolutionary

119. environmental

120. do not; greater than; is not

121. higher; ethnic

122. information

123. higher; Asian students have a longer school year and spend more time studying math

124. Asian students have a longer school year, and they spend more time at home and in school studying math

125. are

126. are not

127. stereotype threat

128. growth mind-set

Progress Test

Multiple-Choice Questions

1. **c.** is the answer.

2. **d.** is the answer. It is a major obstacle to problem solving.
   a. & b. These refer to overconfidence and belief perseverance, respectively.
   c. This is trial-and-error problem solving.

3. **a.** is the answer. Babbling is not the imitation of adult speech because babbling infants produce sounds from languages they have not heard and could not be imitating.

4. **d.** is the answer.

5. **c.** is the answer.
   a. Chomsky did not believe this.
   b. According to Chomsky, although we are born with a readiness to learn language, we only acquire language in association with others.
   d. Social influences are an important example of the influence of learning on language development.

6. **d.** is the answer. Heuristics are simple thinking strategies—such as playing chess defensively—that are based on past successes in similar situations.
   a., b., & c. These are all algorithms.

7. **d.** is the answer. Sultan suddenly arrived at a novel solution to his problem, thus displaying apparent insight.
   a. Sultan did not randomly try various strategies of reaching the fruit; he demonstrated the "light bulb" reaction that is the hallmark of insight.
   b. Heuristics are simple thinking strategies.
   c. Fixation hinders problem solving. Sultan obviously solved his problem.

8. **d.** is the answer.

9. **d.** is the answer. Compared with deaf children exposed to sign language from birth, those who learn to sign as teens have the same grammatical difficulties as do hearing adults trying to learn a second spoken language.

10. **d.** is the answer. If we divide 9, the measured mental age, by 6, the chronological age, and multiply the result by 100, we obtain 150.

11. **b.** is the answer. The stronger a culture's male-science stereotype, the greater its gender difference in math and science achievement. So, in some countries, females may achieve more in these fields.

12. **c.** is the answer.
    a. On the contrary, many *group* differences are highly significant, even though they tell us nothing about specific *individuals*.
    b. Although heredity contributes to individual differences in intelligence, it does not necessarily contribute to group differences.
    d. In fact, the difference has weakened somewhat in recent years.

13. **b.** is the answer.
    a. This answer refers to heritability.
    c. This answer refers to test-retest reliability.
    d. This answer refers to predictive validity.

14. **c.** is the answer. Fixation is an obstacle to problem solving.

15. **d.** is the answer.

16. **a.** is the answer. As the text indicates, intelligence tests predict future performance *to some extent,* but they are *very reliable.*
    c. & d. Most modern tests have very high reliabilities; their predictive validity is not as high.

17. **d.** is the answer. Factors other than aptitude are involved in creativity.
    a. The ability to think imaginatively and aptitude are *both* components of creativity.
    b. Creativity, the capacity to produce ideas that are novel and valuable, is related to and depends in part on aptitude but cannot be considered simply a kind of aptitude.
    c. Greater intelligence does not necessarily mean a more creative person.

18. **d.** is the answer. That people with savant syndrome excel in one area but are intellectually slow in others suggests that there are multiple intelligences.
    a. The ability to adapt defines the capacity we call intelligence.
    b. Stereotype threat is the concept that the fear of being evaluated negatively may result in a poorer performance.

c. A general intelligence factor was hypothesized by Spearman to underlie each specific factor of intelligent behavior, but its existence is controversial and remains to be proved.

19. **c.** is the answer.

20. **d.** is the answer. Findings from a range of studies have led experts to focus on the influence of environmental factors.
a. Most experts believe that in terms of predictive validity, the major tests are not racially biased.
b. The reliability of the major tests is actually very high.
c. The bulk of the evidence on which experts base their findings points to the influence of environmental factors.

21. **d.** is the answer.
a. *g* is Spearman's term for "general intelligence"; there is no such thing as a "*g* distribution."
b. There is no such thing.
c. IQ is Terman's original term for an individual's score on the Stanford-Binet.

22. **a.** is the answer. Reasoning in daily life is often distorted by our beliefs, which may lead us, for example, to accept conclusions that haven't been arrived at logically.
b., c., & d. These are just the opposite of what we tend to do.

23. **d.** is the answer. Syntax is one of the fundamental aspects of language, and chimps seem unable, for example, to use word order to convey differences in meaning.
a. & c. Chimps' use of sign language demonstrates that they can use symbols and can have fairly large vocabularies.
b. No psychologist would require the use of speech as evidence of language; significantly, all the research and arguments focus on what chimps are and are not able to do in learning other aspects of language.

24. **d.** is the answer. If we use the availability heuristic, we base judgments on the availability of information in our memories, and more vivid information is often the most readily available.
a. This would be an example of the use of the trial-and-error approach to problem solving.
b. This would be an example of the use of an algorithm.
c. This would be an example of belief perseverance.

25. **b.** is the answer. Because they involve the systematic examination of all possible solutions to a problem, algorithms guarantee that a solution will be found.
a., c., & d. None of these methods guarantees that a problem's solution will be found.

26. **c.** is the answer.

27. **c.** is the answer. Although the child says only two words as a sentence, the words are placed in a sensible order. In English, for example, adjectives are placed before nouns.
a. & b. Syntax specifies rules for *combining* two or more units in speech.
d. There is no three-word stage.

28. **b.** is the answer.

29. **c.** is the answer.

30. **c.** is the answer. A new French law brought more children into the school system, and the government didn't want to rely on teachers' biases to determine which children would require special help.
a. & b. Binet's test was intended for children; there is nothing in the text to indicate that Binet's test was intended to measure inborn intelligence.
d. This was not a purpose of the test, which dealt with children in the school system.

31. **c.** is the answer.
a., b., & d. None of these is true.

32. **c.** is the answer. Predictive validity is the extent to which tests predict future performance.
a. Reliability is the consistency with which a test samples the particular behavior of interest.
b. This is too general a term.
d. Standardization is the process of defining meaningful test scores based on the performance of a representative group.

33. **d.** is the answer.

34. **c.** is the answer.
a. This is William Stern's original formula for the intelligence quotient.
b. & d. Neither of these formulas is used to compute the score on current intelligence tests.

35. **a.** is the answer.

36. **c.** is the answer.
a. Performance ability and intellectual ability are separate traits.
b. This has been argued by some, but certainly not most, experts.
d. Although many experts believe that there are multiple intelligences, this would not be the same thing as diverse acquired skills.

37. **a.** is the answer.

38. **c.** is the answer.
a. & b. Studies of twins, family members, and adopted children point to a significant hereditary contribution to intelligence scores. These same studies, plus others comparing children raised in neglectful or enriched environments, indicate that life experiences also significantly influence test performance.
d. Although the issue of how intelligence should be defined is controversial, intelligence tests generally have some predictive validity, especially in the early years.

39. **d.** is the answer.

40. **b.** is the answer.
c. & d. Reliability and validity are characteristics of good tests.

41. **c.** is the answer. Wernicke's area is involved in comprehension, and people who have damage to Wernicke's area are unable to understand what is said to them.
a. The hypothalamus plays no role in language.

b. Broca's area is involved in the physical production of speech; damage would result in the inability to speak fluently.
d. The frontal lobe is the location of Broca's area.

42. **b.** is the answer.
    a. Fluid intelligence tends to decrease with age.
    c. & d. Crystallized intelligence refers to the accumulation of facts and general knowledge that takes place during a person's life. Crystallized intelligence generally increases with age.

43. **d.** is the answer.
    a. & b. Fluid intelligence, which decreases with age, refers to the ability to reason abstractly.
    c. Crystallized intelligence increases with age.

44. **b.** is the answer.
    a. This is cross-sectional research.
    c. & d. Sample size is not a factor in the type of research.

45. **a.** is the answer.
    b. This answer describes the longitudinal research method.
    c. Cross-sectional studies compare people of different ages throughout the life span, generally beginning after the person is able to verbalize.
    d. Cross-sectional studies do not deal with social development.

Matching Items

1. m	6. i	11. c
2. h	7. j	12. b
3. a	8. d	13. f
4. l	9. g	
5. e	10. k	

Application Essay

The first step in constructing the test is to create a valid set of questions that measure psychological knowledge and therefore give the test overall validity. If your objective is to predict students' future achievement in psychology courses, the test questions should be selected to measure, for example, information faculty members expect all psychology majors to master before they graduate.

To enable meaningful comparisons, the test must be standardized. That is, the test should be administered to a representative sample of incoming freshmen at the time they declare psychology to be their major. From the scores of your pretested sample you will then be able to assign an average score and evaluate any individual score according to how much it deviates above or below the average.

To check your test's reliability you might retest a sample of people using the same test or another version of it. If the two scores are correlated, your test is reliable. Alternatively, you might split the test in half and determine whether scores on the two halves are correlated.

Summing Up

You can solve problems in many ways. To test your understanding of the various techniques and obstacles to making them work, suppose you are creating recipes for pasta sauces. At first, you try mixing different ingredients. This hit-and-miss method is referred to as *trial and error*. After tossing out several recipes, you learn more about which herbs mix well together and in what order, and so you write out a recipe, a step-by-step procedure, or *algorithm*, for your pasta sauce. After a while, you have a good sense of what works. So, you use a simple thinking strategy, or *heuristic*, to create many more recipes. Occasionally, you create a recipe that comes to you in a flash of inspiration, or *insight*.

Sometimes, your efforts are not so successful. For example, you can't get past what you've always thought belongs in a pasta sauce. That is, you can't look at the problem from a fresh perspective—you're *fixated* on the traditional ingredients. Other times, you try combinations that readily come to mind rather than thinking outside the box about other possibilities. That is, you are hindered by the *availability heuristic*.

Terms and Concepts to Remember

1. **Cognition** refers to all the mental activities associated with thinking, knowing, remembering, and communicating information.
2. A **concept** is a mental grouping of similar objects, events, ideas, or people.
3. A **prototype** is a mental image or best example of a category.
4. An **algorithm** is a methodical, logical rule or procedure that, while sometimes slow, guarantees success.
5. A **heuristic** is a simple thinking strategy that often allows us to make judgments and solve problems efficiently. Although heuristics are more efficient than algorithms, they do not guarantee success and are more error-prone.
6. **Insight** is a sudden and often novel realization of the solution to a problem.
7. The **confirmation bias** is an obstacle to problem solving in which we tend to search for information that confirms our preconceptions and to ignore or distort evidence that contradicts them.
8. **Fixation** is an inability to see a problem from a new perspective; it is an obstacle to problem solving.
9. **Intuition** is an immediate, automatic, and effortless feeling or thought.
10. The **availability heuristic** is based on estimating the likelihood of certain events based on how readily they come to mind.
11. Another obstacle to problem solving, **overconfidence** refers to the tendency to overestimate the accuracy of our beliefs and judgments.
12. **Belief perseverance** is the tendency for people to cling to a particular belief even after the information that led to the formation of the belief is proven wrong.
13. **Framing** refers to the way an issue or question is posed. It can affect people's perception of the issue or answer to the question.

14. Most experts agree that **creativity** refers to an ability to produce novel and valuable ideas. Aptitude is only one component of creativity.

15. **Convergent thinking** involves the ability to provide a single correct answer.

16. **Divergent thinking** involves the ability to consider many different options and to think in novel ways.

17. **Language** refers to spoken, written, or signed words and how we combine them to communicate meaning.

18. The **babbling stage** of speech development, which begins around 4 months, is the stage in which the infant spontaneously utters various sounds at first unrelated to the household language. During the babbling stage, children the world over sound alike.

19. Between 1 and 2 years of age children speak mostly in single words; they are therefore in the **one-word stage** of speech development.

20. Beginning about age 2, children are in the **two-word stage** and speak mostly in two-word sentences.

21. **Telegraphic speech** is the telegram-like speech of children in the two-word stage. Speech consists mostly of nouns and verbs; however, words occur in the correct order, showing that the child has learned some of the language's syntactic rules.

22. In a specific language, **grammar** is a system of rules that enables us to communicate with and understand others.

23. **Broca's area,** located in the left frontal lobe, is involved in controlling the muscle movements to produce speech.

24. **Wernicke's area,** located in the left temporal lobe, is involved in language comprehension and expression.

25. Most experts define **intelligence** as the ability to learn from experience, solve problems, and use knowledge to adapt to new situations.

26. **General intelligence** (*g*), according to Spearman and others, is a general factor that underlies specific mental abilities and is therefore measured by every task on an intelligence test.

27. A person with **savant syndrome** has limited mental ability, yet possesses one exceptional ability, for example, in music or drawing.

28. **Emotional intelligence** is the ability to perceive, manage, understand, and use emotions.

29. **Intelligence tests** measure people's mental aptitudes and compare them with those of others through numerical scores.

30. **Achievement tests** measure a person's current knowledge.

31. **Aptitude tests** are designed to predict future performance. They measure your capacity to learn new information, rather than measuring what you already know.

32. A concept introduced by Binet, **mental age** is the chronological age that most typically corresponds to a given level of performance.

33. The **Stanford-Binet** is Lewis Terman's widely used revision of Binet's original intelligence test.

34. The **intelligence quotient (IQ)** was defined originally as the ratio of mental age to chronological age multiplied by 100. Contemporary intelligence tests assign a score of 100 to the average performance for a given age.

35. The **Wechsler Adult Intelligence Scale (WAIS)** is the most widely used intelligence test. It is individually administered and contains 15 subtests broken into verbal and performance areas.

36. **Standardization** is the process of defining meaningful scores by comparison with the performance of a pretested standardization group.

37. The **normal curve** is a symmetrical bell-shaped curve that represents the distribution (frequency of occurrence) of many physical and psychological attributes. The curve is symmetrical, with most scores near the average and fewer near the extremes.

38. **Reliability** is the extent to which a test produces consistent results.

39. **Validity** is the degree to which a test measures or predicts what it is supposed to.

40. **Content validity** is the extent to which a test samples the behavior of interest.

41. **Predictive validity** is the success with which a test predicts the behavior it is designed to predict.

42. The two criteria that designate **intellectual disability** are an IQ of 70 or below and difficulty adapting to the normal demands of independent living; formerly called *mental retardation*.

43. A condition of mild to severe intellectual disability and associated physical disorders, **Down syndrome** is usually the result of an extra copy of chromosome 21.

44. **Heritability** is the proportion of variation in a trait among individuals that we can attribute to genes.

45. A **cross-sectional study** compares people of different ages with one another.

46. A **longitudinal study** restudies and retests the same people over a long period.

47. **Crystallized intelligence** is the accumulated knowledge and verbal skills that come with education and experience.

48. **Fluid intelligence** is the ability to reason speedily and abstractly.

49. **Stereotype threat** is a self-confirming concern that we will be evaluated based on a negative stereotype (as on an aptitude test, for example).

Motivation and Emotion

9

Chapter Overview

Motivation is a need or desire that energizes and directs our behavior. Chapter 9 discusses various motivational concepts and looks closely at two motives: hunger and the need to belong. Research on hunger points to the fact that our biological drive to eat is strongly influenced by psychological and social-cultural factors. Research on the need to belong and social networking reveals that social networking tends to increase self-disclosure and strengthen relationships with people we already know.

Chapter 9 also discusses the nature of emotion. Emotions are responses of the whole individual, involving physiological arousal, expressive behaviors, and conscious experience. The chapter first discusses several theoretical controversies concerning the relationship and sequence of the components of emotion, primarily regarding whether the body's response to a stimulus causes the emotion and whether thinking is necessary to and must precede the experience of emotion. After describing the physiology of emotion, the chapter examines how we communicate emotions, as well as the differences in emotional expression among different groups. The chapter concludes with a discussion of the effects of facial expressions and behavior on emotion.

Chapter Review

First, skim each text section, noting headings and boldface items. Review the section by reading the objectives and summaries provided here, then answer the questions that follow. In some cases, STUDY TIPS explain how best to learn a difficult concept and APPLICATIONS help you to know how well you understand the material. Check your understanding of the material by consulting the answers beginning on page 192. Do not continue with the next section until you understand each answer. If you need to, review or reread the section in the textbook before continuing.

Motivational Concepts

Objective 9-1: Define *motivation,* and identify three key perspectives that help us understand motivated behaviors.

Motivation is a need or desire that energizes and directs behavior. The perspectives useful for studying motivated behavior include (1) drive-reduction theory, (2) arousal theory, and (3) Abraham Maslow's hierarchy of needs.

    Drive-reduction theory proposes that unmet **physiological needs** create aroused states that translate into a psychological drive to reduce those needs. The goal of drive reduction is **homeostasis.** We are also pulled by **incentives.** Whether the incentive is toasted bread or toasted ants depends on our culture and experience.

    Arousal theory states that rather than reducing our feelings of arousal, some motivated behaviors increase arousal. Curiosity-driven behaviors, for example, suggest that too little or too much stimulation can motivate people to seek just the right level of arousal. According to the the **Yerkes-Dodson law,** moderate arousal leads to optimal performance.

    Abraham Maslow's **hierarchy of needs** expresses the idea that, until satisfied, some motives are more compelling than others. At the base of the hierarchy are our physiological needs, such as for food and water. Only if these are met are we prompted to meet our need for safety, and then to meet the uniquely human needs to give and receive love and to enjoy self-esteem. Beyond this, said Maslow, lies the highest human needs. At the *self-actualization* level, people seek to realize their own potential. At the *self-transcendence* level, people strive for "transpersonal" meaning, purpose, and identity that is beyond (*trans*) the self.

1. Motivation is defined as _____ _____ _____ .

2. Three perspectives on motivation are _____-_____ theory, _____ theory, and the _____ of needs proposed by _____ .

3. According to one view of motivation, an unmet physiological _____

creates an aroused, motivated state called a
_____ , which pushes us
to reduce the need. The physiological aim of drive
reduction is to maintain a constant internal state,
called _____ .

4. Behavior is often not so much pushed by our
   drives as it is pulled by _____
   in the environment.

5. Rather than reduce a physiological need, some motivated behaviors actually _____
   arousal. This demonstrates that human motives
   _____ (do/do not) always
   satisfy some biological need. Too much stimulation,
   however, brings _____ .

6. According to the _____-
   _____ _____ ,
   arousal levels that are _____
   (low/moderate/high) are associated with optimal
   performance.

7. Starting from the idea that some needs are more
   important than others, Maslow constructed a
   _____ of needs.

8. According to Maslow, the _____
   needs are the most pressing. These are followed
   by _____ needs,
   _____ and love needs, and
   _____ needs. The highest-
   order needs relate to the need to live up to your full
   potential, or _____ , fol-
   lowed by the need for meaning and purpose beyond
   the self, called _____ .

9. In poorer nations, feelings of well-being are best predicted by satisfaction of the need for
   _____ , and the food and
   shelter it buys; in wealthy nations,
   _____-_____
   satisfaction matters more.

APPLICATIONS:

10. Mary loves hang gliding. It would be most difficult to
    explain Mary's behavior according to
    _____-_____ theory.

11. For two weeks, Orlando has been on a hunger strike to
    protest his country's involvement in what he perceives as
    an immoral war. Orlando's willingness to starve himself
    to make a political statement conflicts with the theory of
    motivation advanced by _____ .

Hunger

Objective 9-2: Describe the physiological factors that
cause us to feel hungry.

Although the stomach's pangs contribute to hunger,
variations in body chemistry are more important. A
major source of energy in your body is the blood sugar
glucose. We do not
consciously feel
changes in blood
chemistry. Rather,
our body's internal
state is monitored
by the *hypothalamus,*
which regulates the
body's weight as it
influences our feel-
ings of hunger and
fullness. Other hor-
mones monitored
by the hypothala-
mus include *ghrelin*
(which is secreted by
an empty stomach),
leptin (secreted by fat
cells), and *PYY* (a
digestive tract hor-
mone). *Insulin,* a hormone secreted by the pancreas,
controls blood glucose. *Orexin* is a hunger-triggering
hormone secreted by the hypothalamus. One neural
area (called the *arcuate nucleus*) has a center that secretes
appetite-stimulating hormones and another center that
secretes appetite-suppressing hormones. Some researchers have abandoned the idea that the body has a precise
set point—the stable weight at which our body's "weight
thermostat" is set—preferring the term *settling point* to
indicate an environmentally and biologically influenced
level at which weight settles in response to caloric input
and expenditure. Human bodies regulate weight through
the control of food intake, energy output, and **basal metabolic rate**—a measure of the body's resting rate of energy
expenditure.

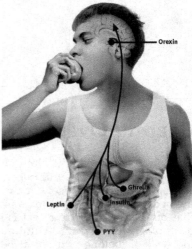

12. Ancel Keys observed that men became preoccupied
    with thoughts of food when they underwent
    _____ .

13. Cannon and Washburn's experiment using a balloon
    indicated that there is an association between hun-
    ger and _____
    _____ .

14. When an animal has had its stomach removed, hun-
    ger _____ (does/does not)
    continue.

15. A major source of energy in the body is the blood
    sugar _____ . Decreases in
    the level of this sugar cause hunger to
    _____ (increase/decrease).

16. The brain's monitoring of hunger occurs in several neural areas, some housed deep in the brain within the _____ . Animals will begin eating when a center of the neural area called the _____ _____ is electrically stimulated. When a different center in this neural area is electrically stimulated, hunger _____ (increases/decreases).

17. The hunger-arousing hormone secreted by an empty stomach is _____

18. When a portion of an obese person's stomach is surgically sealed off, the remaining stomach produces _____ (more/less) of this hormone.

For questions 19–23, identify the appetite hormone that is described (see Figure 9.7):

19. Hunger-triggering hormone: _____ .

20. Hormone secreted by empty stomach: _____ .

21. Hormone secreted by pancreas: _____ .

22. Protein hormone secreted by fat cells: _____ .

23. Digestive tract hormone that signals fullness:

_____ .

24. The weight level at which an individual's body is programmed to stay is referred to as the body's

_____ _____ .
A person whose weight goes beyond this level will tend to feel _____
(more/less) hungry than usual and expend _____ (more/less) energy.

25. The rate of energy expenditure in maintaining basic functions when the body is at rest is the

_____ _____
rate. When food intake is reduced, the body compensates by _____
(raising/ lowering) this rate.

26. The concept of a precise body set point that drives hunger _____ (is accepted/is not accepted) by all researchers. Some researchers believe that set point is too rigid to explain some things. Support for this idea comes from evidence that set point can be altered by

_____ .

Also, when people and other animals are given unlimited access to tasty foods, they tend to

_____ and _____

_____ . For these reasons, some researchers prefer to use the term

_____ _____

as an alternative to the idea that there is a fixed set point.

STUDY TIP: Memory strategies such as chunking and mnemonics can help you learn hard-to-remember material by associating it with easy-to-remember ideas that are personally meaningful. Medical students often use these devices to memorize details of anatomy, chemistry, and physiology. For instance, to remember the colors of the rainbow in order, the first letters in the made-up name Roy G Biv or the sentence "Richard Of York Gave Battle in Vain" will trigger the answer: Red, orange, yellow, Green, Blue, indigo, and violet. You might find these devices helpful in learning some of the physiological terms in this chapter. See if you can find a way to chunk the first letters of the five appetite hormones— insulin, leptin, orexin, ghrelin, and PYY—that will help you to remember them.* You might want to think of other ways to use these devices to learn important terms in psychology and other subjects— for example, HOMES will help you to learn the names of the Great Lakes (Huron, Ontario, Michigan, Erie, and Superior).

APPLICATIONS:

27. A lab technician needs your help in explaining why one well-fed rat begins to eat while a starving rat has no interest in food. You explain that the the appetite-enhancing center of the well-fed rat's _____

_____ has been electrically stimulated, while the appetite-suppressing area of that same _____ area has been stimulated in the starving rat.

28. Kenny and his brother have nearly identical eating and exercise habits, yet Kenny is obese and his brother is very thin. The most likely explanation for the difference in their body weights is that they differ in their

_____ _____ .

29. Lucille has been sticking to a strict diet but can't seem to lose weight. What is the most likely explanation for her difficulty?
   a. Her body has a very low set point.
   b. Her prediet weight was near her body's set point.
   c. Her weight problem is actually caused by low glucose levels in the blood.
   d. Lucille is influenced primarily by external factors.

Objective 9-3: Explain how cultural and situational factors affect our taste preferences and eating habits.

Part of knowing when to eat is our memory of our last meal. As time passes, we anticipate eating again and feel hungry.

Although some taste preferences are genetic (for example, sweet and salty tastes), learning and culture also affect taste. For example, Bedouins enjoy eating the eye of a camel, which most North Americans would find repulsive. Most North Americans and Europeans also shun dog, rat, and horse meat, all of which are prized elsewhere. We avoid unfamiliar foods, especially those that are animal-based. We may learn to prefer some tastes because they are adaptive.

We eat more when eating with others (through social facilitation). In addition, the size of food portions and even of bowls, plates, and eating utensils affects how much we eat. Food variety also stimulates eating.

30. Research with patients who do not remember events occurring more than a minute ago indicates that part of knowing when to eat is our
    _____ of our last meal.

31. Carbohydrates boost levels of the neurotransmitter
    _____ , which
    _____ (calms/arouses) the body.

32. Taste preferences for sweet and salty are
    _____ (genetic/learned) and universal. Other influences on taste include
    _____ and
    _____ . We have a natural dislike of foods that are _____ ;
    this was probably adaptive for our ancestors and protected them from toxic substances.

33. Because of _____ facilitation, people tend to eat _____ (less/more) when they are with other people. People tend to mindlessly eat _____ (more/less) when portions are larger. Another factor that stimulates eating is food _____ .

APPLICATIONS:

34. Randy, who has been under a lot of stress lately, has intense cravings for sugary junk foods, which tend to make him feel more relaxed. Which of the following is the most likely explanation for his craving?
    a. Randy feels that he deserves to pamper himself with sweets because of the stress he is under.
    b. The extra sugar gives Randy the energy he needs to cope with the demands of daily life.
    c. Carbohydrates boost levels of serotonin, which has a calming effect.
    d. The extra sugar tends to lower blood insulin level, which promotes relaxation.

35. Ali's parents have tried hard to minimize their son's exposure to sweet, fattening foods. If Ali has the occasion to taste sweet foods in the future, which of the following is likely?
    a. He will have a strong aversion to such foods.
    b. He will have a neutral reaction to sweet foods.
    c. He will display a preference for sweet tastes.
    d. It is impossible to predict Ali's reaction.

Objective 9-4: Discuss the factors that predispose some people to become and remain obese.

Fat is stored energy. It is a fuel reserve that can carry us through times when food is scarce. In fact, where people face famine, obesity signals wealth and social status. However, the tendency to eat energy-rich fat or sugar works against us in a world where food and sweets are abundant. Significant obesity can shorten your life, greatly reduce your quality of life, and increase your health care costs. It increases the risk of diabetes and heart disease, for example.

Obesity affects both how you are treated and how you feel about yourself. Obese 6- to 9-year-olds are 60 percent more likely to suffer bullying. Adult obesity is linked with lower psychological well-being, increased depression, and discrimination in employment.

People differ in their resting metabolic rates, and once someone gains fat tissue, less energy is needed to maintain that tissue than is needed to maintain other tissue. Unquestionably, environmental factors such as sleep loss, social influence, often eating high-calorie foods, and living an inactive lifestyle also matter. Genes also have a lot to do with our weight.

Research indicates that most people who succeed on a weight-loss program eventually regain most of the weight. Those who wish to diet should feel motivated and self-disciplined, minimize exposure to tempting food cues, boost energy expenditure through exercise, get enough sleep, limit variety and eat healthy foods spaced throughout the day, reduce portion sizes, be aware of social influences, beware of the binge, and connect to a support group.

36. Obesity has been associated with lower
    _____ well-being, increased
    _____ , and increased risk of
    _____ in employment.

37. Clinical obesity is defined as a BMI
    of _____ or more. In the United States, _____ percent of adults are obese. Significant obesity increases the risk of _____
    _____
    _____ .

38. Obesity has also been linked in women to their risk of late-life cognitive decline, including
    _____ disease and brain tissue loss.

39. Fat tissue has a _____ (higher/lower) metabolic rate than lean tissue. The result is that fat tissue requires _____ (more/less) food energy to be maintained.

Explain why, metabolically, many obese people find it so difficult to become and stay thin.

40. Studies of adoptees and twins _____ (do/do not) provide evidence of a genetic influence on obesity.

41. Also contributing to the problem of obesity are _____ factors. For example, adults who suffer from _____ _____ are more vulnerable to obesity. Also, people are _____ (less/more) likely to become obese when a friend becomes obese, thus demonstrating a _____ influence as a factor in obesity.

42. Two reasons for the global increase in weight are changing _____ _____ and _____ _____ .

State several pieces of advice for those who want to lose weight.

APPLICATIONS:

43. Owen is on a diet. His weight has dropped below his body's _____ _____ , so his hunger _____ (increases/ decreases) and his metabolic rate has _____ (increases/decreases).

44. Which of the following would be the WORST piece of advice to offer to someone trying to lose weight?
   a. "To treat yourself to one 'normal' meal each day, eat very little until the evening meal."
   b. "Reduce your consumption of saturated fats."
   c. "Boost your metabolism by exercising regularly."
   d. "Before eating with friends, decide how much you want to eat."

The Need to Belong

Objective 9-5: Discuss the evidence that points to our human need to belong.

Social bonds boosted our ancestors' chances of survival. Adults who formed attachments were more likely to come together to reproduce and to stay together to nurture their offspring to maturity. Cooperation in groups also enhanced survival. When our need for relatedness is satisfied in balance with two other basic psychological needs—*autonomy* (a sense of personal control) and *competence*—the result is a deep sense of well-being. Even our *self-esteem* is a measure of how valued and accepted we feel.

When something threatens our social ties, negative emotions overwhelm us. When **ostracized,** people may engage in self-defeating behavior and to underperform on aptitude tests. They are also likely to act in mean or aggressive ways.

45. The Greek philosopher _____ referred to humans as the _____ animal. From an evolutionary standpoint, social bonds in humans boosted our ancestors' _____ rates. Those who felt this need to _____ survived and reproduced more successfully, and so their _____ now rule.

46. Feeling included, accepted, and loved by others boosts our _____ . Satisfaction of our relatedness need, along with the other psychological needs of _____ and _____ , gives us a strong feeling of well-being.

47. Much of our _____ behavior aims to increase our belonging.

48. After years of placing individual refugee and immigrant families in _____ communities, U.S. policies today encourage _____ _____ .

49. _____ (Throughout the world/ Only in certain cultures do) people use social exclusion, or _____ , to control social behavior.

50. Researchers have found that people who are rejected are more likely to engage in _____
behaviors and may act in _____
or _____ ways. They are also
more likely to underperform on

_____ _____ .

Objective 9-6: Describe how social networking
influences us.

The growth of the Internet has in many ways changed
the way we connect with people. The Internet is diver-
sifying our social networks and enhancing our existing
real-world friendships. Electronic communication makes
us less self-conscious and less inhibited, resulting in
increased self-disclosure, which deepens friendships. In
general, social networks reveal people's real personalities. People with high *narcissism* scores are especially
active on social networking sites. It is important that we
find a healthy balance between our real-world time with
people and our online sharing.

51. Social networking is mostly _____
(strengthening/weakening) our connections with
people we already know.

52. By connecting like-minded people, the Internet
serves as a social _____ . In
times of social crisis or personal stress, it provides
information and _____ con-
nections.

53. When communicating electronically rather than
face to face, we often are less focused on others'
reactions, less _____ , and
thus less _____ . The result
is increased _____ , which
serves to deepen friendships.

54. Generally, social networks _____
(do/do not) reveal people's real personalities.

55. Those who score high on items reflecting
self-importance and self-promotion, or
_____ , are more active on
social networking sites.

List some suggestions proposed by experts for maintaining a healthy balance of online connecting with friends
and meeting your real-world responsibilities.

APPLICATIONS:

56. Summarizing her report on the need to belong, Rolanda
states that
    a. "Cooperation amongst our ancestors was
    uncommon."
    b. "Social bonding is not in our nature; it is a learned
    human trait."
    c. "Because bonding with others increased our ances-
    tors' success at reproduction and survival, it became
    part of our biological nature."
    d. "Some cultures encourage people to separate from
    their families."

57. Right after dinner, Dennis goes to his room, turns on his
computer, and begins chatting with friends on Facebook.
Which of the following is true, according to the most
recent research?
    a. His connections with friends have been strengthened.
    b. He is more willing to disclose personal thoughts and
    feelings, which deepens his friendships.
    c. He reveals his true personality to friends and others
    online.
    d. All of these statements are true.

Emotion: Arousal, Behavior, and Cognition

Objective 9-7: Identify the three parts of an emotion,
and discuss the theories that help us to understand our
emotions.

An *emotion* is a response of the whole organism that
involves an interplay among (1) bodily arousal, (2)
expressive behaviors, and (3) conscious experience.

The *James-Lange theory* states that our experience
of an emotion is a consequence of our physiological
responses to emotion-arousing stimuli; we are afraid
because our heart pounds (say, in response to an
approaching stranger). The *Cannon-Bard theory,* on the
other hand, proposes that the physiological response
and subjective experience of emotion occur simultaneously. Heart pounding and fear occur at the same
time—one does not cause the other. In the Schachter
and Singer *two-factor theory* of emotion, to experience
emotion, one must (1) be physically aroused and (2) cognitively label the arousal.

The *spillover effect* occurs when arousal from one
event affects our response to other events. Dozens of
experiments show that a stirred-up state can
be experienced as different emotions, depending on how
we interpret and label it. Arousal fuels emotion and
cognition channels it.

Because of our two-track mind, some emotion-
provoking stimuli can follow a pathway that leads via
the thalamus to the amygdala, bypassing the cortex and
triggering a rapid reaction that is outside our conscious
awareness. Other, more complex emotions, including
hatred and love, require interpretation and are routed
along the slower route to the cortex for analysis.

58. Emotions have three components: _____
_____ , _____
_____ , and _____
_____ .

Identify two major questions in understanding emotions.

59. According to the James-Lange theory, emotional states _____ (come before/ follow) body arousal.

Describe two problems that Walter Cannon identified with the James-Lange theory.

60. Cannon proposed that emotional stimuli in the environment travel at the same time to the _____ , which results in awareness of the emotion, and to the _____ nervous system, which causes the body's arousal. Because another scientist proposed similar ideas, this theory has come to be known as the _____-_____ theory.

61. The two-factor theory of emotion proposes that emotion has two components: _____ arousal and _____ appraisal. This theory was proposed by _____ and _____ .

62. The *spillover effect* refers to occasions when our _____ response to one event carries over into our response to another event.

63. Schachter and Singer found that physically aroused college men told that an injection would cause arousal _____ (did/did not) become emotional in response to an accomplice's aroused behavior. Physically aroused volunteers not expecting arousal _____ (did/ did not) become emotional in response to an accomplice's behavior.

64. Arousal _____ emotion; cognition _____ emotion.

65. Robert Zajonc believes that the feeling of emotion _____ (can/cannot) precede our cognitive labeling of that emotion.

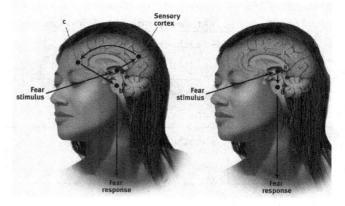

66. (Use art above to answer the following.) Sometimes emotions take what Joseph LeDoux has called the " _____ _____ ": A pathway from the _____ via the (a) _____ to the (b) _____ enables us to experience emotion before _____ . For more complex emotions, sensory input is routed through the (c) _____ for interpretation.

67. The researcher who disagrees with Zajonc and argues that most emotions require cognitive processing, whether or not it is _____ , is _____ . According to this view, emotions arise when we _____ an event as beneficial or harmful to our well-being.

68. Complex emotions are affected by our _____ , _____ , and _____ .

Express some general conclusions that can be drawn about cognition and emotion.

STUDY TIP/APPLICATION: The theories of emotion discussed in this chapter seem so similar that it's often hard to tell them apart. As you think about the theories, remember: The theories differ in the order of importance they assign to the three components of emotions: physical arousal (increased heart rate, for example), the expression of the emotion (feeling angry, for example), and the importance of cognitive appraisal of the situation in which the emotion has occurred. To help ensure your understanding of the theories, see if you can fill in the missing information in the chart below for a common emotional experience: Hearing the screeching of a car's tires. For example, the first response might be a physical reaction such as increased heartbeat or an emotional expression of fear, or it might be the opposite.

69.

Theory	Stimulus Event	First Response	Second Response	Third Response
James-Lange	Screeching tires			
Cannon-Bard	Screeching tires			
Two-factor	Screeching tires			

APPLICATIONS:

70. You are on your way to school to take a big exam. Suddenly, you feel nervous and you notice that your pulse is racing and you are sweating. This fits with the

_____-_____

theory of emotion.

71. Two years ago, Maria was in an automobile accident in which her spinal cord was severed, leaving her paralyzed from the neck down. Today, Maria finds that she experiences emotions less intensely than she did before her accident. This tends to support the

_____-_____

theory of emotion.

72. After hitting a grand-slam home run, Mike noticed that his heart was pounding. Later that evening, after nearly having a collision while driving on the freeway, Mike again noticed that his heart was pounding. That he interpreted this reaction as fear, rather than as ecstasy, can best be explained by the _____-

_____ theory of emotion.

Embodied Emotion

Objective 9-8: Identify some basic emotions.

Carroll Izard identified 10 basic emotions: joy, interest-excitement, surprise, sadness, anger, disgust, contempt, fear, shame, and guilt. Although other researchers argue for additional emotions, Izard contends that other emotions are combinations of these 10.

73. Carroll Izard believes that there are

_____ basic emotions, most of which _____ (are/are not) present in infancy. Although others claim that

_____ emotions such as pride and love should be added to the list, Izard contends that they are _____ of the basic emotions.

Objective 9-9: Describe the link between emotional arousal and the autonomic nervous system.

The *autonomic nervous system (ANS)* controls arousal. In an emergency, the *sympathetic division* mobilizes the body for action, directing the adrenal glands to release stress hormones. Your heart rate, blood pressure, and blood sugar level increase, your pupils dilate, digestion slows, and sweating increases. The parasympathetic division calms the body after a crisis has passed, although arousal diminishes gradually.

74. Describe the major physiological changes that each of the following undergoes during emotional arousal.

a. heart: _____

b. liver: _____

c. respiration: _____

d. digestion: _____

e. salivation: _____

f. pupils: _____

g. blood: _____

h. skin: _____

i. immune system: _____

75. The responses of arousal are activated by the

_____ nervous system. The

_____ division arouses;

the _____ division calms.

76. When the need for arousal has passed, the body is calmed through activation of the _____ nervous system.

Objective 9-10: Describe how our body states relate to specific emotions.

Similar physiological arousal occurs during fear, anger, and sexual arousal. Nonetheless, these emotions feel different. And, despite similar arousal, sometimes our facial expressions differ during these three states.

Some emotions sometimes differ in the finger temperatures and hormone secretions that accompany them. Other emotions differ in the facial muscles they stimulate. Emotions also differ in the brain circuits they use. For example, the right prefrontal cortex becomes more electrically active as people experience negative emotions, such as disgust. The left frontal lobe shows more activity with positive emotions.

Polygraph is the technical name for a lie detector.

77. The various emotions are associated with _____ (similar/different) bodily responses. In particular, the emotions of _____ , _____ , and _____ _____ are difficult to spot by measuring perspiration, breathing, and heart rate.

78. The emotions of fear and rage are accompanied by differing _____ temperatures and _____ secretions.

79. The emotions of fear and joy stimulate different _____ _____ .

80. The brain circuits underlying different emotions _____ (are/are not) different. For example, people who have generally negative personalities, and those who are prone to _____ , show more _____ _____ lobe activity.

81. When people experience positive moods, brain scans reveal more activity in the _____ _____ _____ .

82. Individuals with more active _____ (right/left) _____ lobes tend to be more cheerful than those in whom this pattern of brain activity is reversed.

83. The technical name for the "lie detector" is the _____ .

APPLICATIONS:

84. A student participating in an experiment concerned with physical responses that indicate emotions reports that her mouth is dry, her heart is racing, and she feels flushed. Can the emotion she is experiencing be determined?
  a. Yes, it is anger.
  b. Yes, it is fear.
  c. Yes, it is ecstasy.
  d. No, it cannot be determined from the information given.

85. Nine-month-old Nicole's left frontal cortex is generally more active than her right frontal cortex. This would indicate that she probably has a _____ (positive/negative) personality.

86. Julio was extremely angry when he came in for a routine EEG of his brain activity. When he later told this to the doctor, she was no longer concerned about the _____ electrical activity in Julio's _____ _____ lobe.

Objective 9-11: Discuss the effectiveness of polygraphs in using body states to detect lies.

The polygraph measures several physiological indicators of emotion—for example, changes in breathing, heart rate, and perspiration. Research suggests that if polygraph experts were the judges, more than one-third of the innocent would be declared guilty and one-quarter of the guilty would be declared innocent, percentages that are too high to justify its widespread use in business and government. A more effective approach is the guilty knowledge test.

87. The polygraph measures several of the physiological responses that accompany emotion, such as changes in _____ , _____ , and _____ . The assumption is that lying is _____ , so a person who is lying will become physiologically aroused.

88. How well the lie detector works depends on how a person responds to _____ questions as compared with _____ questions.

89. Those who criticize lie detectors feel that the tests are particularly likely to err in the case of the _____ (innocent/guilty) because different _____ all register as _____ .

90. By and large, experts _____
(agree/do not agree) that lie detector tests are NOT
highly accurate.

91. A test that assesses a suspect's knowledge of details
of a crime that only the guilty person should know is
the _____ _____
_____ .

APPLICATION:

92. As part of her job interview, Jan is asked to take a lie-
detector test. Jan politely refuses and points out the problems with the test, which are that
   a. _____
   b. _____

Expressed and Experienced Emotion

Objective 9-12: Describe how we communicate nonverbally, and discuss how women and men differ in these
abilities.

All of us communicate nonverbally as well as verbally.
For example, Westerners "read" a firm handshake as
evidence of an outgoing, expressive personality. A glance
can communicate intimacy,while darting eyes may signal anxiety. Most people can detect nonverbal cues, and
we are especially sensitive to nonverbal threats.

Women generally surpass men at reading people's
emotional cues. Women's skill at decoding others' emotions may explain why women tend to respond with and
express greater emotion. When surveyed, women are far
more likely than men to describe themselves as *empathic*.
Women also tend to experience emotional events more
deeply with greater brain activation in areas sensitive to
emotion.

93. Most people are especially good at interpreting nonverbal _____ . Although we are
good at detecting emotions, we find it difficult to
detect _____ expressions.

94. Women are generally _____
(better/worse) than men at detecting nonverbal
signs of emotion, a skill that emerges early in development. Women tend to _____
with and _____ greater emotion
than men. Although women are _____
(more/less) likely than men to describe themselves
as empathic, physiological measures reveal a much
_____ (smaller/larger) gender
difference. Women are _____
(more/less) likely than men to express empathy.

APPLICATION:

95. Pat is very accurate at reading others' nonverbal behavior
and is more likely to express empathy. Based on body
responses, Alex seems to feel almost as much empathy.
Pat is _____ (male/female); Alex is
_____ (male/female).

Objective 9-13: Discuss how nonverbal expressions of
emotion are understood within and across cultures.

Although the meaning of gestures varies with culture,
facial expressions, such as those of happiness and anger,
are common the world over. Cultures and languages also
tend to categorize emotions as anger, fear, and so on
in similar ways. Charles Darwin suggested that before
our ancestors communicated in words, their ability to
convey threats, greetings, and submissions with facial
expressions helped them survive. Emotional expressions may also enhance our survival in other ways. For
example, surprise widens the eyes, enabling us to take in
more information. Disgust wrinkles the nose, closing it
from foul odors.

96. Gestures have _____ (the
same/different) meanings in different cultures.

97. Studies of adults indicate that in different cultures
facial expressions have _____
(the same/different) meanings.

98. According to _____ , human
emotional expressions evolved because they
helped our ancestors communicate before language developed. They also may enhance our
_____ in other ways, such as
by widening our eyes in surprise so we can take in
more information.

99. Smiles are _____ as well as
emotional events. Natively blind athletes, when
they win an event, display _____
(the same/different) smiles as seeing athletes in
the same situation.

100. Although our facial language is universal, it has
been adaptive for us to interpret faces in particular
_____ .

APPLICATION:

101. Children in New York, Nigeria, and New Zealand smile
when they are happy and frown when they are sad. This
suggests that
   a. the Cannon-Bard theory is correct.
   b. some emotional expressions are learned at a very
   early age.
   c. the two-factor theory is correct.
   d. facial expressions of emotion are universal and
   biologically determined.

Objective 9-14: Describe how facial expressions influence our feelings.

The *facial feedback effect* indicates that facial muscle states tend to trigger corresponding feelings, such as fear or anger. For example, students induced to make a frowning expression reported feeling a little angry. Similarly, the *behavior feedback effect* shows that if we move our body as we would when experiencing some emotion (shuffling along with downcast eyes, as when sad), we are likely to feel that emotion to some degree.

102. In one study, students who were tricked into mak-
     ing a _____ reported feeling a
     little angry. Thus, the _____
     _____ effect occurs when
     expressions amplify our emotions by activating
     muscles associated with specific states.

103. Studies have found that imitating another person's
     facial expressions _____
     (leads/does not lead) to greater empathy with that
     person's feelings.

104. Similarly, moving our body as we would when
     experiencing a particular emotion causes us to feel
     that emotion. This is the _____
     _____ effect.

APPLICATION:

105. The candidate stepped before the hostile audience,
     panic written all over his face. It is likely that the candi-
     date's facial expression caused him to experience
     a. a lessening of his fear.
     b. an intensification of his fear.
     c. a surge of digestive enzymes in his body.
     d. increased body temperature.

Progress Test

Multiple-Choice Questions

Circle your answers to the following questions and check them with the answers beginning on page 194. If your answer is incorrect, read the explanation for why it is incorrect and then consult the text.

1. Motivation is best understood as a state that
   a. reduces a drive.
   b. aims at satisfying a biological need.
   c. energizes an organism to act.
   d. energizes and directs behavior.

2. Which of the following is a difference between a drive and a need?
   a. Needs are learned; drives are inherited.
   b. Needs are physiological states; drives are psychological states.
   c. Drives are generally stronger than needs.
   d. Needs are generally stronger than drives.

3. One problem with the idea of motivation as drive reduction is that
   a. because some motivated behaviors do not seem to be based on physiological needs, they cannot be explained in terms of drive reduction.
   b. it fails to explain any human motivation.
   c. it cannot account for metabolic rates.
   d. it does not explain the hunger drive.

4. Electrical stimulation of the arcuate nucleus of the hypothalamus will cause an animal to
   a. begin eating.
   b. lose weight.
   c. become obese.
   d. begin having sex.

5. The text suggests that the tendency to avoid unfamiliar tastes
   a. is more common in children than in adults.
   b. protected our ancestors from potentially toxic substances.
   c. may be an early warning sign of an eating problem.
   d. only grows stronger with repeated exposure to those tastes.

6. I am a protein hormone produced by fat cells and monitored by the hypothalamus. When in abundance, I cause the brain to increase metabolism. What am I?
   a. PYY   c. orexin
   b. ghrelin   d. leptin

7. Drive-reduction theory emphasizes _____ factors in motivation.
   a. environmental   c. psychological
   b. cognitive   d. biological

8. In his study of men on a semistarvation diet, Ancel Keys found that
   a. the metabolic rate of the men increased.
   b. the men eventually lost interest in food.
   c. the men became obsessed with food.
   d. the men's behavior directly contradicted predictions made by Maslow's hierarchy of needs.

9. As the Greek philosopher Aristotle noted, we all
   a. behave in ways that allow us to maintain good health.
   b. need challenging work.
   c. are social animals.
   d. want to serve others.

10. Research on genetic influences on obesity reveals that
    a. the body weights of adoptees most closely resemble those of their biological parents.
    b. the body weights of adoptees most closely resemble those of their adoptive parents.
    c. identical twins usually have very different body weights.
    d. the body weights of identical twin women are more similar than those of identical twin men.

11. Research on obesity indicates that
    a. pound for pound, fat tissue requires more calories to maintain than lean tissue.
    b. it increases the risk of diabetes and gallstones.
    c. one pound of weight is lost for every 3500-calorie reduction in diet.
    d. when weight drops below the set point, hunger and metabolism also decrease.

12. Which of the following influences on hunger motivation does NOT belong with the others?
    a. set/settling point
    b. attraction to sweet and salty tastes
    c. reduced production of ghrelin after stomach bypass surgery
    d. memory of time elapsed since your last meal

13. The tendency to overeat when food is plentiful
    a. is a recent occurrence that is related to the luxury of having ample food.
    b. emerged in our prehistoric ancestors as an adaptive response to alternating periods of feast and famine.
    c. is greater in developed, than in developing, societies.
    d. is stronger in women than in men.

14. The brain area that when stimulated secretes appetite-suppressing hormones is the
    a. hippocampus.
    b. arcuate nucleus.
    c. thalamus.
    d. amygdala.

15. According to Maslow's theory
    a. the most basic motives are based on physiological needs.
    b. needs are satisfied in a specified order.
    c. the highest motives relate to self-transcendence.
    d. all of these are true.

16. The digestive tract hormone that sends "I'm not hungry" signals to the brain is.
    a. leptin.   c. insulin.
    b. PYY.   d. glucose.

17. Which of the following is NOT necessarily a reason that obese people have trouble losing weight?
    a. Fat tissue has a lower metabolic rate than lean tissue.
    b. Once a person has lost weight, it takes fewer calories to maintain his or her current weight.

    c. The tendency toward obesity may be genetically based.
    d. Obese people are often sleep-deprived, resulting in high levels of leptin in their bodies.

18. Beginning with the most basic needs, which of the following represents the correct sequence of needs in the hierarchy described by Maslow?
    a. safety; physiological; esteem; belongingness and love; self-fulfillment; self-transcendence
    b. safety; physiological; belongingness and love; self-transcendence; esteem; self-fulfillment
    c. physiological; safety; esteem; belongingness and love; self-transcendence; self-fulfillment
    d. physiological; safety; belongingness and love; esteem; self-fulfillment; self-transcendence

19. Which division of the nervous system is especially involved in bringing about emotional arousal?
    a. somatic nervous system
    b. peripheral nervous system
    c. sympathetic nervous system
    d. parasympathetic nervous system

20. Concerning emotions and their accompanying body responses, which of the following appears to be true?
    a. Each emotion has its own body response and underlying brain circuit.
    b. All emotions involve the same body response as a result of the same underlying brain circuit.
    c. Many emotions involve similar body responses but have different underlying brain circuits.
    d. All emotions have the same underlying brain circuits but different body responses.

21. The Cannon-Bard theory of emotion states that
    a. emotions have two ingredients: physical arousal and a cognitive label.
    b. the conscious experience of an emotion occurs at the same time as the body's physical reaction.
    c. emotional experiences are based on an awareness of the body's responses to an emotion-arousing stimulus.
    d. emotional ups and downs tend to balance in the long run.

22. Which of the following was NOT raised as a criticism of the James-Lange theory of emotion?
    a. The body's responses are too similar to trigger the various emotions.
    b. Emotional reactions occur before the body's responses can take place.
    c. The cognitive activity of the cortex plays a role in the emotions we experience.
    d. People with spinal cord injuries at the neck typically experience less emotion.

23. Current estimates are that the polygraph is inaccurate approximately _____ of the time.
    a. three-fourths   c. one-third
    b. one-half   d. one-fourth

24. In one experiment, college men were injected with the hormone epinephrine. Which participants reported feeling an emotional change in the presence of the experimenter's highly emotional confederate?
   a. those receiving epinephrine and expecting to feel physical arousal
   b. those receiving a placebo and expecting to feel physical arousal
   c. those receiving epinephrine and not expecting to feel physical arousal
   d. those receiving a placebo and not expecting to feel physical arousal

25. Emotions consist of which of the following components?
   a. physiological reactions
   b. behavioral expressions
   c. conscious feelings
   d. all of these components

26. Law enforcement officials sometimes use a lie detector to assess a suspect's responses to details of the crime believed to be known only to the perpetrator. This is known as the
   a. inductive approach.
   b. deductive approach.
   c. guilty knowledge test.
   d. screening examination.

27. In laboratory experiments, fear and joy
   a. result in an increase in heart rate.
   b. stimulate different facial muscles.
   c. increase heart rate and stimulate different facial muscles.
   d. result in a decrease in heart rate.

28. With regard to emotions, Darwin believed that
   a. the expression of emotions helped our ancestors to survive.
   b. our ancestors communicated threats, greetings, and submission with facial expressions.
   c. human facial expressions of emotion retain elements of animals' emotional displays.
   d. all of these are true.

29. The Schachter and Singer two-factor theory emphasizes that emotion involves both
   a. the sympathetic and parasympathetic divisions of the nervous system.
   b. verbal and nonverbal expression.
   c. physical arousal and cognitive appraisal.
   d. universal and culture-specific aspects.

30. Which theory of emotion emphasizes the simultaneous experience of body response and emotional feeling?
   a. James-Lange
   b. Cannon-Bard
   c. two-factor
   d. Schachter-Singer

31. Izard believes that there are _____ basic emotions.
   a. 3   **c.** 7
   b. 5   **d.** 10

32. The polygraph measures
   a. lying.
   b. brain rhythms.
   c. chemical changes in the body.
   d. physiological responses accompanying emotion.

33. People who are exuberant and persistently cheerful show increased activity in the brain's
   a. right frontal lobe.
   b. left frontal lobe.
   c. amygdala.
   d. thalamus.

34. Which of the following is true regarding gestures and facial expressions?
   a. Gestures are universal; facial expressions, culture-specific.
   b. Facial expressions are universal; gestures, culture-specific.
   c. Both gestures and facial expressions are universal.
   d. Both gestures and facial expressions are culture-specific.

35. Which theory of emotion implies that every emotion is associated with a unique physiological reaction?
   a. James-Lange
   b. Cannon-Bard
   c. two-factor
   d. Zajonc

36. In an emergency situation, emotional arousal will result in
   a. increased rate of respiration.
   b. increased blood sugar.
   c. a slowing of digestion.
   d. all of these actions.

37. Many psychologists are opposed to the use of lie detectors because
   a. they represent an invasion of a person's privacy and could easily be used for unethical purposes.
   b. there are often serious discrepancies among the various indicators such as perspiration and heart rate.
   c. polygraphs cannot distinguish among the various possible causes of arousal.
   d. they are accurate only about 50 percent of the time.

Matching Items

Match each definition or description with its term

Definitions or Descriptions

_____ **1.** the body's weight-maintenance setting

_____ **2.** the body's tendency to maintain a balanced internal state

_____ **3.** a form of sugar in the blood

_____ **4.** emotions consist of physical arousal and a cognitive label

_____ **5.** an emotion-arousing stimulus triggers cognitive and body responses simultaneously

_____ **6.** the division of the nervous system that calms the body following arousal

_____ **7.** the division of the nervous system that activates arousal

_____ **8.** a device that measures the physiological correlates of emotion

_____ **9.** environmental stimulus that motivates behavior

_____ **10.** we are sad because we cry

Terms

a. set point
b. two-factor theory
c. incentive
d. sympathetic nervous system
e. James-Lange theory
f. polygraph
g. Cannon-Bard theory
h. parasympathetic nervous system
i. homeostasis
j. glucose

Application Essays

1. Explain how the three major theories of motivation differ and why each one separately cannot fully account for human behavior. (Use the space below to list the points you want to make, and organize them. Then write the essay on a separate sheet of paper.)

2. Discuss biological and cultural influences on emotions. (Use the space below to list the points you want to make, and organize them. Then write the essay on a separate sheet of paper.)

Summing Up

See p. 191.

Terms and Concepts to Remember

Using your own words, write on a separate piece of paper a brief definition or explanation of each of the following terms.

1. motivation
2. drive-reduction theory
3. physiological needs
4. homeostasis
5. incentive
6. Yerkes-Dodson law
7. hierarchy of needs
8. glucose
9. set point
10. basal metabolic rate
11. ostracism
12. narcissism
13. emotion
14. James-Lange theory
15. Cannon-Bard theory
16. two-factor theory
17. polygraph
18. facial feedback effect

Summing Up

Walking home from school after the basketball game, Jesse takes a shortcut through an area with no street lights. He sees a shadow of a person with something glistening in his hand, which causes him to experience the three parts of a distinct emotion.

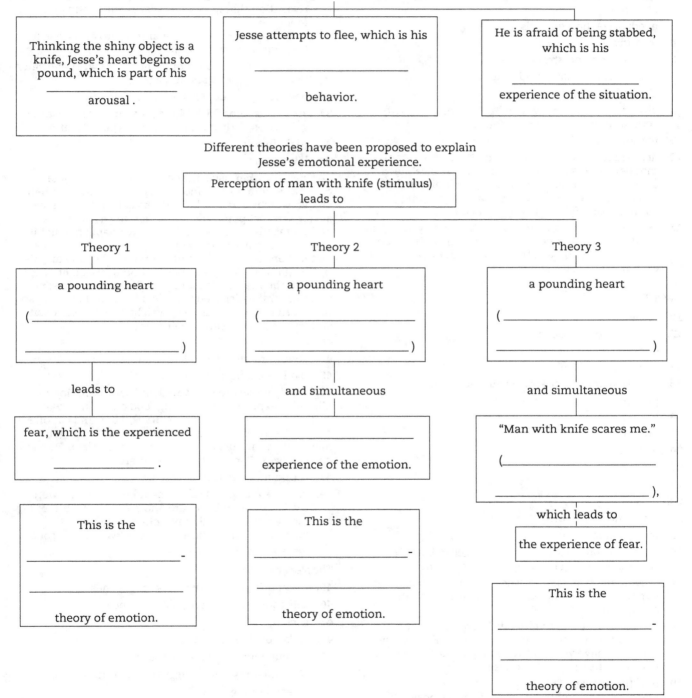

Thinking the shiny object is a knife, Jesse's heart begins to pound, which is part of his _____ arousal .

Jesse attempts to flee, which is his _____ behavior.

He is afraid of being stabbed, which is his _____ experience of the situation.

Different theories have been proposed to explain Jesse's emotional experience.

Perception of man with knife (stimulus) leads to

Theory 1

a pounding heart

(_____

_____)

leads to

fear, which is the experienced _____ .

This is the _____ - _____ theory of emotion.

Theory 2

a pounding heart

(_____

_____)

and simultaneous

_____ experience of the emotion.

This is the _____ - _____ theory of emotion.

Theory 3

a pounding heart

(_____

_____)

and simultaneous

"Man with knife scares me."

(_____

_____),

which leads to

the experience of fear.

This is the _____ - _____ theory of emotion.

Answers

Chapter Review

Motivational Concepts

1. a need or desire that energizes and directs behavior
2. drive-reduction; arousal; hierarchy; Abraham Maslow
3. need; drive; homeostasis
4. incentives
5. increase; do not; stress
6. Yerkes-Dodson law; moderate
7. hierarchy
8. physiological; safety; belongingness, esteem; self-actualization; self-transcendence
9. money; home-life
10. drive-reduction. Drive-reduction theory maintains that behavior is motivated when a biological need creates an aroused state, driving the individual to satisfy the need. It's unlikely that Mary's hang gliding is satisfying a biological need.
11. Maslow. According to Maslow's theory, physiological needs, such as the need to satisfy hunger, must be satisfied before a person pursues loftier needs, such as making political statements.

Hunger

12. semistarvation
13. stomach contractions
14. does
15. glucose; increase
16. hypothalamus; arcuate nucleus; decreases
17. ghrelin
18. less
19. orexin
20. ghrelin
21. insulin
22. leptin
23. PYY
24. set point; less; more
25. basal metabolic; lowering
26. is not accepted; slow, steady changes in body weight; overeat; gain weight; settling point
27. arcuate nucleus; neural. The arcuate nucleus in the hypothalamus includes centers that either enhance or suppress eating behavior.
28. metabolic rates. Individual differences in metabolism and set point explain why it is possible for two people to have very different weights despite similar patterns of eating and exercise.
29. b. is the answer. The body acts to defend its set point, or the weight to which it is predisposed. If Lucille was already near her set point, weight loss would prove difficult.

30. memory
31. serotonin; calms
32. genetic; learning; culture; unfamiliar
33. social; more; more; variety
34. c. is the answer. Serotonin is a neurotransmitter that is elevated by the consumption of carbohydrates and has a calming effect.
    a. & b. These answers do not explain the feelings of relaxation that Randy associates with eating junk food.
    d. The consumption of sugar tends to elevate insulin level rather than lower it.
35. c. is the answer. Our preferences for sweet and salty tastes are genetic and universal.
36. psychological; depression; discrimination
37. 30; 36; diabetes, high blood pressure, heart disease, gallstones, arthritis, and certain types of cancer
38. Alzheimer's
39. lower; less

Compared with muscle tissue, fat has a lower metabolic rate—it takes less food energy to maintain. When an overweight person's body drops below its previous set (or settling) point, the person's hunger increases and metabolism decreases. The body adapts to what it perceives as starvation by burning fewer calories. The dieter therefore finds it hard to progress beyond an initial weight loss. Also, lean people and overweight people differ in their rates of resting metabolism. Lean people seem naturally disposed to move about, and in doing so, they burn more calories. Overweight people tend to sit still longer and conserve their energy.

40. do
41. environmental; sleep loss; more; social
42. food consumption; activity levels

Begin only if you are motivated and self-disciplined. Minimize exposure to tempting food cues. Limit variety and eat healthy foods. Don't starve all day and eat one big meal at night. Beware of binge eating. Boost your metabolism through exercise. Get enough sleep. Reduce portion sizes. Connect to a support group.

43. set point; increases; decreases
44. a. is the answer. Dieting, including fasting, lowers the body's metabolic rate and reduces the amount of food energy needed to maintain body weight.
    b., c. & d. Each of these strategies would be a good piece of advice to a dieter.

The Need to Belong

45. Aristotle; social; survival; belong; genes
46. self-esteem; autonomy; competence
47. social
48. isolated; chain migration
49. Throughout the world; ostracism
50. self-defeating; mean; aggressive; aptitude tests
51. strengthening
52. amplifier; supportive

53. self-conscious; inhibited; self-disclosure
54. do
55. narcissism

Experts suggest that you monitor your time, noting whether your time online is interfering with school or work performance; monitor your feelings; "hide" your more distracting online friends; try turning off your handheld devices or leaving them elsewhere; try a Facebook fast or a time-controlled Facebook diet; and refocus by taking a nature walk.

56. **c.** is the answer.
57. **d.** is the answer.

Emotion: Arousal, Behavior, and Cognition

58. bodily arousal; expressive behaviors; conscious experience

Does bodily arousal come before or after emotional feeling? How do thinking and feeling interact?

59. follow

Cannon argued that the body's responses were not sufficiently distinct to trigger the different emotions and, furthermore, that bodily changes occur too slowly to trigger sudden emotion.

60. cortex; sympathetic; Cannon-Bard
61. physical; cognitive; Stanley Schachter; Jerome Singer
62. arousal
63. did not; did
64. fuels; channels
65. can
66. low road; eye or ear; thalamus; amygdala; cognition; cortex
67. conscious; Richard Lazarus; appraise
68. interpretations; expectations; memories

It seems that some emotional responses—especially simple likes, dislikes, and fears—involve no conscious thinking. Other emotions—more complex emotions such as love and hate—are greatly affected by our interpretations, expectations, and memories.

69. Answers are given in order: first response, second response, third response.
    James-Lange theory: physical arousal, expressed emotion, cognitive appraisal is unimportant
    Cannon-Bard theory: physical arousal and cognitive appraisal occur simultaneously, expressed emotion
    Two-factor theory: physical arousal, cognitive appraisal, expressed emotion
70. James-Lange. The James-Lange theory proposes that the experienced emotion is an awareness of a prior body response: Your pulse races, and so you feel nervous.
71. James-Lange. According to the James-Lange theory, Maria's emotions should be greatly diminished because her brain is unable to sense physical arousal.
72. two-factor. According to the two-factor theory, it is cognitive interpretation of the same general physiological arousal that distinguishes the two emotions.

Embodied Emotion

73. 10; are; complex; combinations
74. **a.** Heart rate speeds up.
    b. The liver pours extra sugar into the bloodstream.
    c. Respiration rate increases.
    d. Digestion slows.
    e. Salivation decreases.
    f. Pupils open wider.
    g. If wounded, blood tends to clot more quickly.
    h. Skin perspires.
    i. Immune system functioning is reduced.
75. autonomic; sympathetic; parasympathetic
76. parasympathetic
77. similar; fear; anger; sexual arousal
78. finger; hormone
79. facial muscles
80. are; depression; right frontal
81. left frontal lobe
82. left; frontal
83. polygraph
84. **d.** is the answer.
85. positive. Individuals with more active left frontal lobes tend to be more cheerful and are less likely to be depressed.
86. increased; right hemisphere. As people experience negative emotions, such as anger, the right hemisphere becomes more electrically active.
87. breathing; heart rate; perspiration; stressful
88. critical; control
89. innocent; emotions; arousal
90. agree
91. guilty knowledge test
92. **a.** Our physiological arousal is much the same from one emotion to another.
    b. Many innocent people respond with heightened tension to the accusations implied by the critical questions.

Expressed and Experienced Emotion

93. threats, deceiving
94. better; respond; express; more; smaller; more
95. female; male
96. different
97. the same
98. Charles Darwin; survival
99. social; the same
100. contexts
101. **d.** is the answer.
    a. & c. The Cannon-Bard and two-factor theories of emotion do not address the universality of emotional expressions.
    b. Even if it is true that emotional expressions are acquired at an early age, this would not necessarily account for the common facial expressions of

children from around the world. If anything, the different cultural experiences of the children might lead them to express their feelings in very *different* ways.

102. frown; facial feedback
103. leads
104. behavior feedback
105. **b.** is the answer. Expressions may amplify the associated emotions.
    a. Laboratory studies have shown that facial expressions intensify emotions.
    c. Arousal of the sympathetic nervous system, such as occurs when one is afraid, slows digestive function.
    d. Increased body temperature accompanies anger but not fear.

Progress Test

Multiple-Choice Questions

1. **d.** is the answer.
   a. & b. Although motivation is often aimed at reducing drives and satisfying biological needs, this is by no means always the case.
   c. Motivated behavior not only is energized but also is directed at a goal.

2. **b.** is the answer. A drive is the psychological consequence of a physiological need.
   a. Needs are unlearned states of deprivation.
   c. & d. Because needs are physical and drives psychological, their strengths cannot be compared directly.

3. **a.** is the answer. The curiosity of a child or a scientist is an example of behavior apparently motivated by something other than a physiological need.
   b. & d. Some behaviors, such as thirst and hunger, are partially explained by drive reduction.
   c. Metabolic rate is unrelated to drive reduction.

4. **a.** is the answer. This area of the hypothalamus seems to elevate hunger.
   b. If the animal begins eating, it will most likely gain weight.
   c. Obesity may be a long-term effect but is not the first result of such stimulation.
   d. The hypothalamus is involved in sexual motivation, but not in this way.

5. **b.** is the answer.
   a. The tendency to avoid food based on taste is typical of all age groups.
   c. The tendency to avoid food based on taste is *not* an indicator of an eating problem.
   d. With repeated exposure, our appreciation for a new taste typically *increases*.

6. **d.** is the answer.
   a. PYY signals fullness, which is associated with decreased metabolism.
   b. Ghrelin is a hormone secreted by the empty stomach that sends hunger signals.

c. Orexin is a hormone secreted by the hypothalamus.

7. **d.** is the answer.

8. **c.** is the answer. The food-deprived men focused on food almost to the exclusion of anything else.
   a. To conserve energy, the men's metabolic rate actually *decreased*.
   b. & d. Far from losing interest in food, the men came to care only about food—a finding consistent with Maslow's hierarchy, in which physiological needs are at the base.

9. **c.** is the answer.

10. **a.** is the answer.

11. **b.** is the answer.

12. **d.** is the answer. Memory of the time of the last meal is an example of a psychological influence on hunger motivation.
    a., b., & c. Each of these is a biological influence on hunger motivation.

13. **b.** is the answer.
    c. If anything, just the opposite is true.
    d. Men and women do not differ in the tendency to overeat.

14. **b.** is the answer.
    a. The hippocampus is involved in memory.
    c. The thalamus is a sensory control center; stimulation of it has no effect on eating.
    d. The amygdala is involved in emotions, especially fear and rage.

15. **d.** is the answer.

16. **b.** is the answer.
    a. Leptin is secreted by fat cells.
    c. & d. Insulin is secreted by the pancreas and regulates the amount of glucose in the bloodstream.

17. **d.** is the answer. The text does not suggest that obese people frequently suffer sleep deprivation. Moreover, sleep deprivation, which is associated with a greater tendency toward obesity, results in LOWER levels of leptin.

18. **d.** is the answer.

19. **c.** is the answer.
    a. The somatic division of the peripheral nervous system carries sensory and motor signals to and from the central nervous system.
    b. The peripheral nervous system is too general an answer, since it includes the sympathetic and parasympathetic divisions, as well as the somatic division.
    d. The parasympathetic nervous system restores the body to its unaroused state.

20. **c.** is the answer. Although many emotions have the same general body arousal, resulting from activation of the sympathetic nervous system, they appear to be associated with different brain circuits.

21. **b.** is the answer.
    a. This expresses the two-factor theory.
    c. This expresses the James-Lange theory.
    d. This theory was not discussed.

22. **d.** is the answer. The finding that people whose brains can't sense the body's responses experience considerably less emotion in fact supports the James-Lange theory, which claims that experienced emotion follows from body responses.
a., b., & c. All these statements go counter to the theory's claim that experienced emotion is essentially just an awareness of the body's response.

23. **c.** is the answer.

24. **c.** is the answer. As proof of the spillover effect, the men who received epinephrine without an explanation felt arousal and experienced this arousal as whatever emotion the experimental confederate in the room with them was displaying.
a. Epinephrine recipients who expected arousal attributed their arousal to the drug and reported no emotional change in reaction to the confederate's behavior.
b. & d. In addition to the two groups discussed in the text, the experiment involved placebo recipients; these men were not physically aroused and did not experience an emotional change.

25. **d.** is the answer. These are the three components of emotions identified in the text.

26. **c.** is the answer. If the suspect becomes physically aroused while answering questions about details only the guilty person could know, the test-giver can assume that he or she committed the crime.

27. **c.** is the answer. Both fear and joy increase heart rate but stimulate different facial muscles.

28. **d.** is the answer.

29. **c.** is the answer. According to Schachter and Singer, the two factors in emotion are (1) physical arousal and (2) conscious interpretation of the arousal.

30. **b.** is the answer.
a. The James-Lange theory states that the experience of an emotion is an awareness of one's physical response to an emotion-arousing stimulus.
c. & d. The two-factor theory (Schachter-Singer theory) states that to experience emotion one must be physically aroused and cognitively label the arousal.

31. **d.** is the answer.

32. **d.** is the answer. No device can literally measure lying. The polygraph measures breathing, blood pressure, and perspiration for changes indicative of physiological arousal.

33. **b.** is the answer.

34. **b.** is the answer. The meanings of gestures vary from culture to culture; facial expressions seem to have the same meanings around the world.

35. **a.** is the answer. If, as the theory claims, emotions are triggered by physiological reactions, then each emotion must be associated with a unique physiological reaction.
b. According to the Cannon-Bard theory, the same general body response accompanies many emotions.
c. The two-factor theory states that the cognitive interpretation of a general state of physical arousal determines different emotions.

d. Zajonc believed that some emotions occur before we have a chance to interpret a situation.

36. **d.** is the answer.

37. **c.** is the answer. As heightened arousal may reflect feelings of anxiety or irritation rather than of guilt, the polygraph, which simply measures arousal, may easily err.
a. Misuse and invasion of privacy are valid issues, but researchers primarily object to the use of lie detectors because of their inaccuracy.
b. Although there are discrepancies among the various measures of arousal, this was not what researchers objected to.
d. The lie detector errs about one-third of the time.

Matching Items

1.	a	**6.**	h
2.	i	**7.**	d
3.	j	**8.**	f
4.	b	**9.**	c
5.	g	**10.**	e

Application Essays

1. Drive-reduction is the idea that biological needs create aroused drive states that motivate the individual to satisfy these needs. Drive-reduction theory failed as a complete account of human motivation because many human motives do not satisfy any obvious biological need. Instead, such behaviors are motivated by environmental incentives.
   Arousal theory emerged in response to evidence that some motivated behaviors *increase*, rather than decrease, arousal. This doesn't explain why some behaviors decrease arousal.
   Maslow's hierarchy of needs suggests that we are motivated to satisfy basic needs, such as the need for food and water, first. We then look to satisfy needs for self-esteem, love and belongingness, and so on until we reach the highest-level needs of self-actualization and self-transcendence. The problem with Maslow's hierarchy is that some people will sacrifice their need for food, for example, to make a philosophical statement.

2. All emotions involve some degree of physiological arousal of the sympathetic nervous system. Although the arousal that occurs with different emotions is in most ways undifferentiated, there may be subtle differences in the brain pathways and hormones associated with different emotions. Other examples of the influence of biological factors on emotion are the universality of facial expressions of emotion. Unlike facial expressions of emotion, the meaning of many gestures is culturally determined. Culture also influences how people express their feelings.

Summing Up

Walking home from school after the basketball game, Jesse takes a shortcut through an area with no street lights. He sees a shadow of a person with something glistening in his hand, which causes him to experience the three parts of a distinct emotion. Thinking the shiny object is a knife, Jesse's heart begins to pound, which is part of his *physical* arousal. Jesse attempts to flee, which is his *expressive* behavior. He is afraid of being stabbed, which is his *conscious* experience of the situation.

Different theories have been proposed to explain Jesse's emotional experience. Perception of man with knife (stimulus) leads to Theory 1: a pounding heart (*physical arousal*) leads to fear, which is the experienced *emotion*. This is the *James-Lange* theory of emotion. Theory 2: a pounding heart (*physical arousal*) and simultaneous *subjective* experience of the emotion. This is the *Cannon-Bard* theory of emotion. Theory 3: a pounding heart (*physical arousal*) and simultaneous "Man with knife scares me" (*cognitive appraisal*), which leads to the experience of fear. This is the *two-factor* theory of emotion.

Terms and Concepts to Remember

1. **Motivation** is a need or desire that energizes and directs behavior.

2. **Drive-reduction theory** attempts to explain behavior as arising from a physiological need that creates an aroused state (a drive) that motivates us to satisfy the need.

3. **Physiological needs** include our basic bodily requirements, such as thirst and hunger.

4. **Homeostasis** refers to the body's tendency to maintain a balanced or constant internal state.

5. **Incentives** are positive or negative environmental stimuli that motivate behavior.

6. The **Yerkes-Dodson law** states that performance increases with arousal up to a certain point, beyond which performance declines.

7. Maslow's **hierarchy of needs** proposes that human motives may be ranked from the basic, physiological level through higher-level needs for safety, belongingness and love, esteem, self-actualization, and self-transcendence; until they are satisfied, the more basic needs are more compelling than the higher-level ones.

8. **Glucose**, or blood sugar, is the major source of energy for the body's tissues. Elevating the level of glucose in the body will reduce hunger.

9. **Set point** is the point at which your "weight thermostat" is supposedly set, which is maintained by adjusting food intake and energy output.

10. **Basal metabolic rate** is the body's resting rate of energy output.

11. **Ostracism** is the deliberate social exclusion of individuals or groups.

12. **Narcissism** is excessive self-absorption.

13. **Emotion** is a response of the whole organism, involving three components: (1) physical arousal, (2) expressive behaviors, and (3) conscious experience.

14. The **James-Lange theory** states that emotional experiences are based on an awareness of the body's responses to emotion-arousing stimuli. A stimulus triggers the body's responses that in turn trigger the experienced emotion.

15. The **Cannon-Bard theory** states that the subjective experience of an emotion occurs at the same time as the body's physical reaction.

16. The **two-factor theory** of emotion proposes that emotions have two ingredients: physical arousal and cognitive appraisal. Thus, physical arousal is a necessary, but not a sufficient, component of emotional change. For an emotion to be experienced, arousal must be attributed to an emotional cause.

17. The **polygraph**, or lie detector, is a device that measures several of the physiological responses accompanying emotion.

18. The **facial feedback effect** occurs when making an emotional facial expression (such as smiling) triggers the corresponding emotional feeling (happiness).

Stress, Health, and Human Flourishing

10

Chapter Overview

Behavioral factors play a major role in maintaining health and causing illness. The effort to understand this role more fully focuses on questions such as: How do our perceptions of a situation determine the stress we feel? How do our emotions and personality influence our risk of disease? How can psychology contribute to the prevention of illness? Chapter 10 addresses key topics in this area. First and foremost is stress—its nature, its effects on the body, psychological factors that determine how it affects us, and how stress contributes to infectious diseases, cancer, and heart disease. The chapter then looks at physical and psychological factors that promote good health, including exercise and social support.

The last section is a discussion of happiness, the goal of all people everywhere. It begins with a discussion of resilience, or how people effectively cope with negative events. The chapter concludes with suggestions for improving your happiness.

Chapter Review

First, skim each text section, noting headings and boldface items. Review the section by reading the objectives and summaries provided here, then answer the questions that follow. In some cases, STUDY TIPS explain how best to learn a difficult concept and APPLICATIONS help you to know how well you understand the material. Check your understanding of the material by consulting the answers on page 208. Do not continue with the next section until you understand each answer. If you need to, review or reread the section in the textbook before continuing.

Stress: Some Basic Concepts

Objective 10-1: Discuss how our appraisal of an event affects our stress reaction, and identify the three main types of stressors.

Stress is the process by which we appraise and cope with environmental events. When perceived as challenges, *stressors* can arouse and motivate us to conquer problems. When perceived as threats, stressors can lead to severe stress. Three main types of stressors are catastrophes, significant life changes, and daily hassles.

1. Stress is the _____ by which we perceive and respond to environmental threats and challenges.

2. This definition highlights the fact that stressful events, or _____ , can have _____ (only negative/both positive and negative) effects, depending on how they are perceived. Three categories of stressors are

   _____ , _____

   _____ _____ ,

   and _____ _____ .

3. Long-term studies have found that people who have recently been widowed, fired, or divorced are _____ (more/no more) disease-prone.

Objective 10-2: Describe how the body responds to stress.

Walter Cannon observed that, in response to stress, the sympathetic nervous system activates the secretion of stress hormones, triggers increased heart rate and respiration, diverts blood to skeletal muscles, dulls our feelings of pain, and releases sugar and fat from the body's stores, all to prepare the body for the *fight-or-flight response.*

In Hans Selye's *general adaptation syndrome (GAS),* the body's adaptive response to stress is a three-stage process. In Phase 1, we experience an *alarm reaction* due to the sudden activation of our sympathetic nervous system. Heart rate increases, blood flows to our skeletal muscles, and we feel the faintness of shock. With our resources mobilized, we then fight the challenge during Phase 2, *resistance.* Temperature, blood pressure, and respiration remain high, and stress hormones pour out from our adrenal glands. If the stress is persistent, it may eventually deplete our body's reserves during Phase 3, *exhaustion.* With exhaustion, we are more vulnerable to illness or even, in extreme cases, collapse and death.

There are other options for dealing with stress. One is to withdraw, pull back, and so conserve energy. Another option, found especially among women, is to *tend and befriend,* that is, to provide or seek support from others.

4. In the 1920s, physiologist Walter _____ began studying the effect of stress on the body. He discovered that stress _____ are released by the _____ _____ into the bloodstream in response to stress. This and the response of your _____ nervous system prepare your body for the _____-_____-_____ .

5. In studying animals' reactions to stressors, Hans Selye referred to the body's adaptive response to stress as the _____ _____ _____ .

6. During the first phase of the GAS—the _____ reaction—the person is in a state of shock due to the sudden arousal of the _____ nervous system.

7. This is followed by Phase 2, _____ , in which the body's resources are mobilized to cope with the stressor.

8. If stress continues, the person enters Phase 3, _____ . During this phase, a person is _____ (more/less) vulnerable to disease.

9. Another common response to stress among women has been called the _____-_____-_____ response, which refers to the increased tendency to _____ . This response may be due to the hormone _____ .

The words *stress* and *stressor* are so similar it's easy to think that they mean the same thing. To understand the difference, remember that *stress* is the process by which we appraise and cope with challenging environmental events (the *stressors*). But they are different concepts describing different aspects of a behavior. It may help you to see the difference between these concepts if you realize that stressors can be external events, such as having your flight cancelled, or internal events, such as worrying about an upcoming term paper assignment, and that stress includes those events plus your response to them. To make sure you understand the differences between stress and stressors, see if you can come up with examples of each in the following chart. The first example has already been filled in.

10. Stressor (Stressful Event)	Appraisal		Response	
	Threat	Challenge	Threat	Challenge
Getting cut off by a driver on the freeway	"I'm going to be in an accident"	"I need to watch more carefully"	Heart races; hit the brakes hard	Heart races; swerve out of the way

APPLICATIONS:

11. Cristina complains to the campus psychologist that she has too much stress in her life. The psychologist tells her that the level of stress people experience depends primarily on
   a. how many activities they are trying to do at the same time.
   b. how they appraise the events of life.
   c. their physical hardiness.
   d. how predictable stressful events are.

12. Each semester, Jin does not start studying until just before midterms. Then he is forced to work around the clock until after final exams, which makes him sick, probably because he is in the _____ phase of the _____ _____ _____ .

Stress Effects and Health

Objective 10-3: Explain how stress influences our immune system.

Our understanding of the impact of stress on resistance to disease has fostered the development of the field of **psychoneuroimmunology,** which studies how psychological, neural, and endocrine processes together affect our immune system and health.

The immune system has four types of cells that work to keep us healthy. *B lymphocytes* are important in fighting bacterial infections, and *T lymphocytes* fight cancer cells, viruses, and foreign substances. *Macrophage cells* ingest harmful invaders and worn-out cells, and *natural killer cells* (NK cells) attack diseased cells. When animals are physically restrained, given unavoidable electric shocks, or subjected to noise, crowding, cold water, social defeat, or maternal separation, their immune system functioning is suppressed. Studies suggest that stress similarly depresses the human immune system, making us more vulnerable to illness.

Stress and negative emotions speed the progression of HIV infection to AIDS and predict a faster decline in those infected. Efforts to reduce stress also help somewhat to control the disease. Educational programs, grief support groups, talk therapy, relaxation training, and exercise programs that reduce distress have all had good results for HIV-positive individuals.

Although stress does not produce cancer cells, some researchers have reported that people are at risk for cancer a year or so after experiencing depression, helplessness, or grief. A large study found that people with a history of workplace stress had a 5.5 times greater risk of colon cancer than those who reported no such problems. Although a relaxed, hopeful attitude may enhance the body's natural defenses against a few growing cancer cells, merely maintaining a determined attitude is not likely to derail the powerful biological forces at work in advanced cancer or AIDS.

13. The field of _____ studies how psychological, neural, and endocrine processes together affect the immune system and health.

14. The body's system of fighting disease is the _____ system. This system includes four types of cells: the _____ _____ , which fight bacterial infections; the _____ _____ , which attack viruses, cancer cells, and foreign substances; _____ cells, which identify, pursue, and ingest foreign substances and worn-out cells, and _____ _____ cells, which pursue diseased cells.

15. Our immune system's activity is influenced by our age, _____ , genetics, body _____ , and stress.

16. Responding too strongly, the immune system may attack the body's tissues and cause _____ or an _____ reaction. Or it may _____ , allowing a dormant herpes virus to erupt, a _____ infection to flare, or _____ cells to multiply.

17. Stress responses draw energy away from the disease-fighting _____ _____ and send it to the _____ and _____ , mobilizing the body for action.

18. Stress suppresses immune functioning. People with AIDS already have a damaged immune system, as indicated by the name of the virus that causes it, the _____ _____ _____ . Stressful events _____ (have/have not) been shown to speed the transition from infection to full-blown AIDS.

19. Educational programs, support groups, and other efforts to control stress _____ (have/have not) been shown to have positive consequences on HIV-positive individuals.

20. Stress _____ (does/does not) create cancer cells.

21. When _____ cells were implanted in rodents, the rodents that were also exposed to _____ stress developed cancer more often, experienced tumor growth _____ , and grew _____ tumors.

22. In some studies, experiencing depression, _____ , or grief _____ (has/has not) been linked to increased risk for cancer. Other studies _____ (have/have not) found elevated cancer rates in former prisoners of war.

APPLICATIONS:

23. A cell in the immune system that attacks cancer cells is a _____ _____ .

24. When would you expect that your immune responses would be weakest?
    a. during summer vacation
    b. during exam weeks
    c. just after receiving good news
    d. Immune activity would probably remain constant during these times.

Objective 10-4: Describe how stress increases coronary heart disease risk.

Stress can increase the risk of **coronary heart disease,** the leading cause of death in the United States today. It has been linked with the competitive, hard-driving, and impatient **Type A** personality. The toxic core of Type A is negative emotions, especially anger. Under stress, the sympathetic nervous system of the Type A person redistributes bloodflow to the muscles and away from internal organs such as the liver, which removes cholesterol and fat from the blood. The resulting excess cholesterol later gets deposited around the heart. The more easygoing **Type B** personality is less likely to suffer coronary heart disease. Depression also can be lethal. While Type A individuals direct their negative emotion toward dominating others, *Type D* individuals suppress their negative emotion to avoid social disapproval.

25. The leading cause of death in the United States and many other countries today is _____ _____ _____ .

List several risk factors for developing this condition: _____ _____ _____ .

26. Stress and personality also play a big role in heart disease. The more psychological trauma people experience, the more their bodies generate _____ , which is associated with heart disease and other health problems, as well as _____ .

27. Researchers discovered that tax accountants experience an increase in blood _____ level and blood-_____ speed during tax season. This showed there was a link between heart attack risk and _____ .

Friedman and Rosenman, in a nine-year study, grouped people into Type A and Type B personality types. Characterize these types, and indicate how they differed over the course of this study.

28. The Type A characteristic that is most strongly linked with coronary heart disease is _____ _____ , especially _____ .

29. When a _____ (Type A/Type B) person is angered, bloodflow is pulled away from the internal organs, including the liver, which normally removes _____ and fat from the blood. Thus, such people have high levels of these substances in the blood.

30. More recently, researchers have found that those who suppress negative emotions to avoid _____ _____ , called _____ _____ individuals, are at significant risk for mortality and nonfatal heart attack.

APPLICATION:

31. Jill is an easygoing, noncompetitive person who is happy in her job and enjoys her leisure time. She would probably be classified as _____ _____ .

Objective 10-5: Discuss whether stress *causes* illness.

Stress may not directly cause illness, but it does make us more vulnerable by influencing our behaviors and our physiology. For example, anger or depression and unhealthy behaviors can contribute to illness.

32. Anger or depression and persistent _____ can lead to the release of _____ _____ , which can result in high _____ , headaches, and _____ , as well as _____ suppression and _____ disease. _____ also contribute to illness and disease.

APPLICATION:

33. Martin is a lawyer, who smokes two packs of cigarettes a day, has several drinks every day after work, and gets very little sleep. It is likely that, among other things, his behavior will suppress his _____ _____ , making him more vulnerable to disease.

Coping With Stress

Objective 10-6: Identify two basic ways that people cope with stress.

People *cope* with stress in one of two ways. Through *problem-focused coping* we attempt to reduce stress by changing the stressor or the way we interact with that stressor. We tend to use problem-focused strategies when we think we can change the situation, or at least change ourselves to more capably deal with the situation. We tend to use *emotion-focused coping* when we believe we cannot change a situation. For example, we may confide in friends when we cannot get along with a family member.

34. When we cope directly with a stressor, we are using _____-_____ coping. When we attempt to reduce stress by avoiding or ignoring it and attending to emotional needs, we are using _____-_____ coping.

35. People tend to use _____-_____ coping when they feel a sense of _____ over a situation. They turn to _____-_____ coping when they cannot or believe they cannot _____ a situation.

STUDY TIP/APPLICATION: Two basic strategies for coping with stressors are problem-focused coping and emotion-focused coping. *Problem-focused coping* is an action-oriented strategy in which we attempt to reduce stress by changing the stressor or the way we interact with that stressor. In contrast, with *emotion-focused coping* we focus on our feelings and try to change how we think about stressors. Think about how you typically cope with stress. Do you more often rely on problem-focused coping or emotion-focused coping? Now complete the chart below. For each stressor, write down one example of a problem-focused strategy and one example of an emotion-focused strategy.

36. Stressor	Emotion-Focused Strategy	Problem-Focused Strategy
You are worried about the amount of reading needed to prepare for an exam.	To take your mind off things, you go to a movie.	You divide the reading into manageable, daily sessions and get started!
a. You get into an argument with your roommate.		
b. Your car muffler falls off.		
c. You develop a cold sore on your lip the day of an important dance.		

APPLICATIONS:

37. Ricardo has been unable to resolve a stressful relationship with a family member. To cope, he turns to a close friend for social support. Ricardo's strategy is an example of _____-_____ coping.

38. To help him deal with a stressful schedule of classes, work, and studying, Randy turns to a regular program of exercise and relaxation training. Randy's strategy is an example of _____-_____ coping.

Objective 10-7: Describe how our sense of control influences stress and health.

Both animal and human studies show that loss of perceived *personal control* can trigger physical symptoms. Facing an ongoing series of events beyond our control can lead to feelings of hopelessness and passive resignation, which is called *learned helplessness.*

As compared to those with an *external locus of control,* those with an *internal locus of control* have achieved more in school and work, acted more independently, enjoyed better health, and felt less depressed. Although some freedom and control is better than none, ever-increasing choice (the *tyranny of choice*) brings information overload and may decrease happiness.

One way to actively manage our behavior is to increase our *self-control,* which is linked to health and well-being. Self-control weakens after use, recovers after rest, and grows stronger with exercise.

39. Personal control refers to our sense of either controlling our _____ or feeling _____ by it.

40. The state of passive resignation called _____ _____ occurs when we experience no control over repeated negative events. For some animals and people, sudden lack of control is followed by a drop in immune responses, a(n) _____ (increase/decrease) in blood pressure, and a rise in the levels of _____ _____.

41. Too much choice, however, may bring information overload and regret over some of the things we left behind. This is called the _____ _____.

42. The perception that outside forces beyond our control determine our fate is called _____ _____.

The perception that we control our own fate is called _____ _____.

State several behavioral and health differences between people with an internal locus of control and those with an external locus of control.

43. A person with the ability to control impulses and delay immediate gratification is said to have _____ , which has been linked to health and well-being. People with more self-control get better _____ , earn higher _____ , and enjoy good health.

APPLICATIONS:

44. Genji is in love with Chen but wants to wait until they are married to have sex with him. Genji's ability to delay gratification suggests an _____ locus of control.

45. Pilar says that she hasn't been promoted at work because her boss doesn't think women should be in management. Pilar's reasoning indicates an _____ locus of control.

Objective 10-8: Discuss how optimists and pessimists differ, and explain why our outlook on life matters.

In comparison to *pessimists, optimists* enjoy better health and better moods, and they respond to stress with smaller increases in blood pressure. Research suggests that optimism may relate to a longer life. Excessive optimism can blind us to real risks, however.

46. People who expect the best and therefore are _____ are more likely than those who are _____ to enjoy good health. They also expect to have _____ and cope well with _____

_____ .

47. Excessive or _____ optimism often blinds students to risky behaviors. They view themselves as less likely than their average classmate to _____

_____ .

Objective 10-9: Discuss how social support and finding meaning in life influence health.

Feeling liked and encouraged by intimate friends and family promotes both happiness and health. It helps you cope with stress. Compared to those with few social ties, people supported by close relationships are less likely to

die early. Social support strengthens immune functioning and calms the cardiovascular system, lowering blood pressure and stress hormone levels. A strong sense of meaning in life can have positive health consequences.

48. Besides control and optimism, another buffer against the effects of stress is _____ support. This helps fight illness by calming our _____ system and strengthening _____ functioning.

49. Longitudinal research reveals that a _____ _____ at age 50 predicts healthy aging better than _____ _____ at the same age.

50. For many people, an important part of coping with stress is having a strong sense of _____ , giving them a purpose for which to live.

51. Close relationships allow us to _____ painful feelings.

52. In one study, researchers contacted surviving spouses of people who had committed suicide or died in car accidents. If they bore their grief alone, they were _____ (more/less) likely to have health problems.

Managing Stress Effects

Objective 10-10: Describe how well aerobic exercise helps to manage stress and improve well-being.

Many studies suggest that *aerobic exercise,* sustained activity that increases heart and lung fitness, can reduce stress, depression, and anxiety. It strengthens the heart, increases bloodflow, keeps blood vessels open, and lowers both blood pressure and the blood pressure reaction to stress. Research has linked aerobic exercise to increased arousal and increases in serotonin activity in the brain.

53. Sustained exercise that increases heart and lung fitness is known as _____ exercise.

54. Experiments _____ (have/have not) been able to demonstrate conclusively that such exercise reduces anxiety, depression, and stress.

State two ways aerobic exercise reduces depression and anxiety.

Objective 10-11: Describe the ways in which relaxation and meditation might influence stress and health.

Research indicates that relaxation procedures provide relief from headaches, high blood pressure, anxiety, and insomnia. They have also been used to help heart attack survivors reduce their risk of future attacks.

Those experienced in *mindfulness meditation* relax and attend to their inner state, without judging it. They focus on certain body parts and responses, and remain aware and accepting. They also pay attention to their breathing. Mindfulness meditation reduces levels of anxiety and depression, and improves immune system functioning. These practices have also been linked with reducing sleep problems, cigarette use, binge eating, and alcohol and other substance abuse.

55. Like aerobic exercise, _____ can improve your well-being, including providing relief from headaches, high _____ _____ , anxiety, and insomnia. It also has been used to help _____ _____ heart attack survivors reduce the risk of another attack.

56. A key component of many stress management programs is _____ _____ , in which a person relaxes, attends to his or her inner state, without _____ it. This practice has been linked with many benefits, including improved functioning of the body's _____ system, better _____ , and reduced _____ _____ .

57. Brain scans of people practicing mindfulness meditation have found reduced activation of the _____ , a brain region associated with _____ , and increased activation in the _____ _____ , which improves the regulation of _____ . Also, it strengthens connections among the brain regions associated with _____ _____ .

Objective 10-12: Discuss whether religious involvement relates to health.

Investigators who attempt to explain the *faith factor* have isolated three intervening variables. (1) Religiously active people have healthier lifestyles; for example, they smoke and drink less. (2) Faith communities provide social support networks and often encourage marriage, which, when happy, is linked with better health and a longer life span. (3) Religious attendance is often accompanied by a stable worldview, sense of hope for the long-term

future, feelings of ultimate acceptance, and a relaxed meditative state.

58. Several recent studies demonstrate that religious involvement _____ (predicts/does not predict) health and longevity.

State three possible reasons for the "faith factor" in health.

59. You have just transferred to a new campus and find yourself in a potentially stressful environment. According to the text, which of the following would help you cope with the stress?
    a. believing that you have some control over your environment
    b. having a friend to confide in
    c. feeling optimistic that you will eventually adjust to your new surroundings
    d. All of these behaviors would help.

60. Concluding her presentation on spirituality and health, Maja notes that
    a. religiously active people have feelings of ultimate acceptance.
    b. religious involvement predicts health and longevity.
    c. religiously active people have healthier lifestyles.
    d. all of these statements are true.

Happiness

Objective 10-13: Identify the causes and consequences of happiness.

A good mood boosts people's perceptions of the world and their willingness to help others (the *feel-good, do-good phenomenon*). Mood-boosting experiences make us more likely to give money, pick up someone's dropped papers, volunteer time, and do other good deeds. After decades of focusing on negative emotions, psychologists are now actively exploring the causes and consequences of *subjective well-being* (self-perceived happiness or satisfaction with life).

Positive emotion rises over the early to middle part of most days. Although stressful events trigger bad moods, the gloom nearly always lifts by the next day. Times of elation are similarly hard to sustain and, over the long run, our emotional ups and downs tend to balance. Even significant bad events, such as a serious illness, seldom destroy happiness for long. The surprising reality is that we overestimate the duration of emotions and underestimate our *resilience*.

At a basic level, money helps us to avoid misery, but having it is no guarantee of happiness. Sudden increases in wealth such as winning a state lottery only increase happiness in the short term. In the long run, increased wealth hardly affects happiness. For example, during the last four decades, the average U.S. citizen's buying power almost tripled, yet the average American is no happier. More generally, research indicates that economic growth in wealthy countries has not boosted morale or social well-being. What matters more is how we feel about what we have.

The *adaptation-level phenomenon* describes our tendency to judge events relative to a neutral level defined by our past experiences. If our income or social prestige increases, we may feel initial pleasure. However, we then adapt to this new level of achievement, come to see it as normal, and require something better to give us another surge of happiness.

Relative deprivation is the perception that we are worse off relative to those with whom we compare ourself. As people climb the ladder of success, they mostly compare themselves with those who are at or above their current level. This explains why increases in income may do little to increase happiness.

High self-esteem, close friendships or a satisfying marriage, and meaningful religious faith are among the predictors of happiness. Age, gender, educational level, and parenthood are among the factors unrelated to happiness.

61. Difficult challenges, especially those that occur _____ (early/late) in life, can foster personal growth and emotional _____ .

62. Happy people tend to perceive the world as _____ and live _____ and more energized and satisfied lives.

63. Happy people are also _____ (more/less) willing to help others. This is called the _____-_____ , _____-_____ phenomenon. The reverse is also true: _____ good promotes _____ good.

64. An individual's self-perceived happiness or satisfaction with life is called his or her _____ _____ , which is the focus of the field of _____ _____ .

65. Positive emotions _____ (rise/fall) early in the day and _____ (rise/fall) during the later hours. The gloom of stressful events usually _____ (is gone by/continues into) the next day.

66. After experiencing tragedy or dramatically positive events, people generally _____ (regain/do not regain) their previous degree of near-normal happiness.

67. Most people tend to _____ (underestimate/overestimate) the duration of emotions and _____ (underestimate/overestimate) their resilience.

68. During the last four decades, spendable income in the United States has almost tripled; personal happiness has _____ (increased/decreased/remained almost unchanged).

69. The idea that happiness is relative to our recent experience is stated by the _____-_____ phenomenon.

Explain how this principle accounts for the fact that, for some people, material desires can never be satisfied.

70. The principle that we feel worse off than others is known as _____ _____ . This helps to explain why comparing ourselves with those who are less well off _____ (does/does not) boost our contentment.

71. List six factors that have been shown to be positively correlated with feelings of happiness.

_____
_____
_____
_____
_____
_____

72. List at least three factors that are evidently unrelated to happiness.

_____
_____
_____

73. Research studies of identical and fraternal twins have led to the estimate that about _____ percent of the variation in people's happiness ratings is due to heredity.

State several research-based suggestions for increasing your satisfaction with life.

APPLICATIONS:

74. As elderly Mr. Hooper crosses the busy intersection, he stumbles and drops the packages he is carrying. Which passerby is most likely to help Mr. Hooper?
    a. Drew, who has been laid off from work for three months
    b. Leon, who is on his way to work
    c. Bonnie, who graduated from college the day before
    d. Nancy, whose father recently passed away

75. Cindy was happy with her promotion until she found out that Janice, who has the same amount of experience, receives a higher salary. Cindy's feelings are best explained by which principle? _____

    _____

76. When Professor Simon acquired a spacious new office, he was overjoyed. Six months later, however, he was taking the office for granted. His behavior illustrates which principle? _____

    _____ _____

Progress Test

Multiple-Choice Questions

Circle your answers to the following questions and check them with the answers on page 209. If your answer is incorrect, read the explanation for why it is incorrect and then consult the text.

1. Researchers Friedman and Rosenman refer to individuals who are very time-conscious, supermotivated, verbally aggressive, and easily angered as
    a. ulcer-prone personalities.
    b. cancer-prone personalities.
    c. Type A.
    d. Type B.

2. During which phase of the general adaptation syndrome is a person especially vulnerable to disease?
    a. alarm reaction   c. exhaustion
    b. resistance   d. adaptation

3. The leading cause of death in the United States and many other countries is
    a. lung cancer.
    b. AIDS.
    c. coronary heart disease.
    d. alcohol-related accidents.

4. Stress has been demonstrated to place a person at increased risk of
    a. cancer.
    b. progressing from HIV infection to AIDS.
    c. bacterial infections.
    d. all of these problems.

5. *Stress* is defined as
    a. unpleasant or aversive events that cannot be controlled.
    b. situations that threaten health.
    c. the process by which we perceive and respond to challenging or threatening events.
    d. anything that decreases immune responses.

6. Attempting to reduce stress directly by changing a stressor or how we interact with it is an example of
    a. problem-focused coping.
    b. emotion-focused coping.
    c. managing rather than coping with stress.
    d. mindfulness meditation.

7. Researchers have found that social support helps us fight illness by fostering stronger immune functioning and by
    a. increasing our ability to control muscle tension.
    b. controlling the activity of our autonomic nervous system.
    c. calming our cardiovascular system.
    d. promoting the relaxation response.

8. Which of the following was NOT mentioned in the text as a potential health benefit of exercise?
    a. Exercise can increase the ability to cope with stress.
    b. Exercise can lower blood pressure.
    c. Exercise can reduce stress, depression, and anxiety.
    d. Exercise improves immune system functioning.

9. Social support _____ our ability to cope with stressful events.
    a. has no effect on
    b. usually increases
    c. usually decreases
    d. has an unpredictable effect on

10. Research has demonstrated that as a predictor of health and longevity, religious involvement
    a. has a small, insignificant effect.
    b. is more accurate for women than men.
    c. is more accurate for men than women.
    d. equals nonsmoking and exercise.

11. In order, the sequence of phases in the general adaptation syndrome is
    a. alarm reaction, resistance, exhaustion.
    b. resistance, alarm reaction, exhaustion.
    c. exhaustion, resistance, alarm reaction.
    d. alarm reaction, exhaustion, resistance.

12. AIDS causes a breakdown in the body's
    a. endocrine system.   c. immune system.
    b. circulatory system.   d. respiratory system.

13. The tend-and-befriend response refers to
   a. the final phase of the general adaptation syndrome.
   b. the health-promoting impact of having a strong system of social support.
   c. an alternative to the fight-or-flight response that may be more common in women.
   d. the fact that spiritual people typically are not socially isolated.

14. Which of the following statements concerning Type A and B persons is true?
   a. Even when relaxed, Type A persons have higher blood pressure than Type B persons.
   b. When stressed, Type A persons redistribute bloodflow to the muscles and away from internal organs.
   c. Type B persons tend to suppress anger more than Type A persons.
   d. Type A persons tend to be more outgoing than Type B persons.

15. The disease- and infection-fighting cells of the immune system include
   a. B lymphocytes.
   b. T lymphocytes.
   c. NK cells.
   d. all of these types of cells.

16. One effect of stress on the body is to
   a. weaken the immune system.
   b. facilitate the immune system response.
   c. increase disease resistance.
   d. increase the growth of B and T lymphocytes.

17. Allergic reactions and arthritis are caused by
   a. an overreactive immune system.
   b. an underreactive immune system.
   c. the presence of B lymphocytes.
   d. the presence of T lymphocytes.

18. Some research on cancer patients reveals that
   a. stress affects the growth of cancer cells by weakening the body's natural resources.
   b. avoiding stress is not likely to derail the biological processes of advanced cancer.
   c. cancer occurs slightly more often than usual among those experiencing depression, helplessness, or grief.
   d. all of these facts are true.

19. The toxic core of Type A behavior that is the most predictive of coronary disease is
   a. time urgency.   c. high motivation.
   b. competitiveness.   d. anger.

20. Which of the following was NOT suggested as a possible explanation of the faith factor in health?
   a. Having a stable worldview is a buffer against stress.
   b. Religious people tend to have healthier lifestyles.

   c. Those who are religious have stronger networks of social support.
   d. Because they are wealthier, religiously active people receive better health care.

21. Which of the following is true regarding happiness?
   a. People with more education tend to be happier.
   b. Beautiful people tend to be happier than plain people.
   c. Women tend to be happier than men.
   d. People who are socially outgoing or who exercise regularly tend to be happier.

22. Research indicates that a person is most likely to be helpful to others if he or she
   a. is feeling guilty about something.
   b. is happy.
   c. recently received help from another person.
   d. recently offered help to another person.

23. When students studied others who were worse off than themselves, they felt greater satisfaction with their own lives. This is an example of the principle of
   a. relative deprivation.
   b. adaptation level.
   c. behavioral contrast.
   d. opponent processes.

24. Which of these factors have researchers NOT found to relate to happiness?
   a. close, positive, and lasting relationships
   b. high self-esteem
   c. religious faith
   d. physical attractiveness

25. Type D individuals are at significant risk for mortality and nonfatal heart attack because they
   a. are easily angered and impatient.
   b. supress their negative emotion to avoid social disapproval.
   c. direct their negative emotion toward dominating others.
   d. are too relaxed and don't exercise enough to strengthen their heart muscles.

Application Essay

Discuss several factors that enhance a person's ability to cope with stress. (Use the space below to list the points you want to make, and organize them. Then write the essay on a separate sheet of paper.)

Summing Up

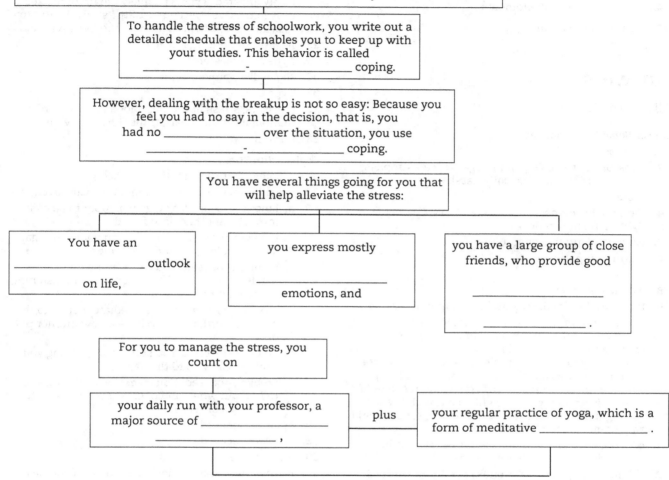

Consider your first year at college. The courses are tough. You are away from home and away from your steady girl/boyfriend, who has suddenly found a new love.

To handle the stress of schoolwork, you write out a detailed schedule that enables you to keep up with your studies. This behavior is called _____-_____ coping.

However, dealing with the breakup is not so easy: Because you feel you had no say in the decision, that is, you had no _____ over the situation, you use _____-_____ coping.

You have several things going for you that will help alleviate the stress:

You have an _____ outlook on life,

you express mostly _____ emotions, and

you have a large group of close friends, who provide good _____ _____.

For you to manage the stress, you count on

your daily run with your professor, a major source of _____ _____ ,

plus

your regular practice of yoga, which is a form of meditative _____ .

Terms and Concepts to Remember

Using your own words, on a separate piece of paper write a brief definition or explanation of each of the following terms.

1. stress
2. fight-or-flight response
3. general adaptation syndrome (GAS)
4. tend-and-befriend response
5. psychoneuroimmunology
6. coronary heart disease
7. Type A
8. Type B
9. coping
10. problem-focused coping
11. emotion-focused coping
12. personal control
13. learned helplessness
14. external locus of control
15. internal locus of control
16. self-control
17. optimism
18. pessimism
19. aerobic exercise
20. mindfulness meditation

21. resilience

22. feel-good, do-good phenomenon

23. subjective well-being

24. adaptation-level phenomenon

25. relative deprivation

Answers

Chapter Review

Stress: Some Basic Concepts

1. process

2. stressors; both positive and negative; catastrophes; significant life changes; daily hassles

3. more

4. Cannon; hormones; adrenal glands; sympathetic; fight-or-flight response

5. general adaptation syndrome

6. alarm; sympathetic

7. resistance

8. exhaustion; more

9. tend-and-befriend; seek and give support; oxytocin

10. Many answers will complete the table. Just think about stressful events in your life—an upcoming exam, a first date, a job interview. For each one, consider how you would appraise it (as a subject beyond your ability or as a task to be completed with extra work), then ask yourself how you would respond (if beyond your ability, you might go out with friends the night before the exam; as a challenge, you would stay home and study hard).

11. **b.** is the answer. How an event is *perceived* is important in deciding whether it is stressful.

12. exhaustion; general adaptation syndrome. According to Selye's GAS, diseases are most likely to occur during this final stage.

Stress Effects and Health

13. psychoneuroimmunology

14. immune; B lymphocytes; T lymphocytes; macrophage; natural killer (NK)

15. nutrition; temperature

16. arthritis; allergic; underreact; bacterial; cancer

17. immune system; brain; muscles

18. human immunodeficiency virus (HIV); have

19. have

20. does not

21. tumor; uncontrollable; sooner; larger

22. helplessness; has; have not

23. T lymphocyte

24. **b.** is the answer. Stressful situations, such as exam weeks, decrease immune responses.

25. coronary heart disease; smoking, obesity, an unhealthy diet, physical inactivity, high cholesterol level

26. inflammation; depression

27. cholesterol; clotting; stress

Type A people were competitive, hard-driving, supermotivated, impatient, time-conscious, verbally aggressive, and easily angered. Type B people were more relaxed and easygoing. Over the course of the study, heart attack victims came overwhelmingly from the Type A group.

28. negative emotions; anger

29. Type A; cholesterol

30. social disapproval; Type D

31. Type B

32. stressors; stress hormones; blood pressure; inflammation; immune; heart; Unhealthy behaviors

33. immune system

Coping With Stress

34. problem-focused; emotion-focused

35. problem-focused; control; emotion-focused; change

36. **a.** Emotion-focused: You go next door to be comforted by another close friend.

    Problem-focused: You talk with your roommate about resolving your disagreement.

    b. Emotion-focused: You call a friend but keep driving, leaving the muffler where it is and listening to the loud noises of the car.

    Problem-focused: You immediately drive to the nearest muffler shop to have a new muffler put on.

    c. Emotion-focused: You start crying, saying you can't possibly go to the dance.

    Problem-focused: You go to the local drug store to find out what kind of cream you can buy to get rid of the cold sore.

37. emotion-focused

38. problem-focused

39. environment; controlled

40. learned helplessness; increase; stress hormones

41. tyrany of choice

42. external locus of control; internal locus of control

"Internals" have achieved more in school and work, acted more independently, enjoyed better health, and felt less depressed than "externals." In one study, those who had expressed a more internal locus of control at age 10 exhibited less obesity, lower blood pressure, and less distress at age 30.

43. self-control; grades; incomes

44. internal

45. external

46. optimists; pessimists; control; stressful events

47. unrealistic; drink excessively, drop out of school, or have a heart attack

48. social; cardiovascular; immune

49. good marriage; low cholesterol

50. meaning

51. confide

52. more

Managing Stress Effects

53. aerobic

54. have

Aerobic exercise reduces depression and anxiety by increasing arousal and by doing naturally what some prescription drugs do chemically—increasing serotonin activity in the brain.

55. relaxation; blood pressure; Type A

56. mindfulness meditation; judging; immune; sleep; cigarette smoking, binge eating, and substance use

57. amygdala; fear; prefrontal cortex; emotions; focused attention

58. predicts

Religiously active people have healthier lifestyles. They also tend to have stronger networks of social support and are more likely to be married. They also have a stable worldview, a sense of hope for the long-term future.

59. d. is the answer.

60. d. is the answer.

Happiness

61. early; resilience

62. safer; healthier

63. more; feel-good, do-good; doing; feeling

64. subjective well-being; positive psychology

65. rise; fall; is gone by

66. regain

67. overestimate; underestimate

68. remained almost unchanged

69. adaptation-level

If we acquire new possessions, we feel an initial surge of pleasure. But we then adapt to having these new possessions, come to see them as normal, and require other things to give us another surge of happiness.

70. relative deprivation; does

71. high self-esteem; close, positive, and lasting relationships; active religious faith; optimistic, outgoing, and agreeable personality; good sleeping habits and regular exercise; having work and leisure that engage our skills

72. age; gender; physical attractiveness

73. 50

Take control of your time. Act happy. Seek work and leisure that engage your skills. Buy shared experiences rather than things. Engage in regular aerobic exercise. Get plenty of sleep. Give priority to close relationships. Focus beyond self. Be grateful. Nurture your spiritual self.

74. c. is the answer. People who are in a good mood are more likely to help others. Bonnie, who is probably pleased with herself following her graduation from college, is likely to be in a better mood than Drew, Leon, or Nancy.

75. relative deprivation. Cindy is unhappy with her promotion because she feels deprived relative to Janice.

76. adaptation-level phenomenon. Professor Simon's judgment of his office is affected by his recent experience: When that experience was of a smaller office, his new office seemed terrific; now, however, it is commonplace.

Progress Test

Multiple-Choice Questions

1. c. is the answer.
a. & b. Researchers have not identified such personality types.
d. Individuals who are more easygoing are labeled Type B.

2. c. is the answer.
a. & b. During these phases, the body's defensive mechanisms are at peak function.
d. This is not a phase of the GAS.

3. c. is the answer.

4. d. is the answer. Because stress depresses the immune system, stressed individuals are prone to all of these conditions.

5. c. is the answer.
a., b., & d. Whether an event is stressful depends on how it is appraised.

6. a. is the answer.
b. In emotion-focused coping, we attempt to alleviate stress by avoiding or ignoring it.
c. This is an example of coping rather than managing stress because it involves an attempt to actually alleviate a stressor.
d. Mindfulness meditation is a way of managing stress by sitting quietly and focusing on current experiences in a nonjudgmental and accepting manner.

7. c. is the answer. In calming our cardiovascular system, social support lowers blood pressure and stress hormones.
a. & b. The autonomic nervous system has no effect on immune responses.
d. Social support may help us relax, but research has not found this effect specifically.

8. d. is the answer. Regular aerobic exercise has been shown to increase the ability to cope with stress, lower blood pressure, and reduce depression and anxiety. The text does not cite evidence that exercise enhances immune function.

9. b. is the answer.

10. d. is the answer.
b. & c. The text does not indicate that a gender difference exists in the faith factor in health.

11. a. is the answer.

12. c. is the answer.

13. c. is the answer.
a. The final stage of the general adaptation syndrome is exhaustion.
b. & d. Although both of these are true, neither has anything to do with tend and befriend.

14. b. is the answer. The result is that their blood may contain excess cholesterol and fat.
a. Under relaxed situations, there is no difference in blood pressure.
c. Anger, both expressed and suppressed, is more characteristic of Type A people.

d. The text doesn't indicate that Type A persons are more outgoing than Type B persons.

15. **d.** is the answer. B lymphocytes fight bacterial infections; T lymphocytes attack cancer cells, viruses, and foreign substances; and NK cells pursue diseased cells.

16. **a.** is the answer. A variety of studies have shown that stress depresses the immune system, increasing the risk and potential severity of many diseases.

17. **a.** is the answer.
   b. An *under*reactive immune system would make an individual more susceptible to infectious diseases or the growth of cancer cells.
   c. & d. Lymphocytes are disease- and infection-fighting white blood cells in the immune system.

18. **d.** is the answer.

19. **d.** is the answer. The crucial characteristic of Type A behavior seems to be a tendency to react with negative emotions, especially anger. Other aspects of Type A behavior appear not to predict heart disease, and some appear to be helpful to the individual.

20. **d.** is the answer. As a group, religiously active people are not wealthier than other people.

21. **d.** is the answer. Education level, parenthood, gender, and physical attractiveness seem unrelated to happiness.

22. **b.** is the answer.
   a., c., & d. Research studies have not found these factors to be related to helpful behavior.

23. **a.** is the answer. The principle of relative deprivation states that happiness is relative to others' attainments. This helps explain why those who are relatively well off tend to be slightly more satisfied than the relatively poor, with whom the better-off can compare themselves.
   b. Adaptation level is the tendency for our judgments to be relative to our prior experience.
   c. This phenomenon has nothing to do with the interpretation of emotion.
   d. Opponent processes are not discussed in the text in relation to emotion.

24. **d.** is the answer.

25. **b.** is the answer.
   a. & c. These refer to Type A individuals
   d. This is not true of anyone.

Application Essay

When potentially stressful events occur, a person's appraisal is a major factor in determining their impact. Catastrophes, significant life events, and daily hassles are especially stressful when appraised as negative and uncontrollable and when the person has a pessimistic outlook on life. Under these circumstances, stressful events may suppress immune responses and make the person more vulnerable to disease. If stressors cannot be eliminated, aerobic exercise, relaxation, and spirituality can help the person cope. Aerobic exercise can reduce stress, depression, and anxiety, perhaps by increasing production of mood-boosting serotonin. Research demonstrates that people who regularly practice mindfulness meditation show less activation in the amygdala, a brain region associated with fear, and more activation in the prefrontal cortex, which aids emotion regulation. People with strong social ties have lower blood pressure and stronger immune functioning. Religiously active people enjoy a better lifestyle, smoking and drinking less.

Summing Up

Consider your first year at college. The courses are tough. You are away from home and away from your steady girl/boyfriend, who has suddenly found a new love. To handle the stress of schoolwork, you write out a detailed schedule that enables you to keep up with your studies. This behavior is called *problem-focused* coping. However, dealing with the breakup is not so easy: Because you feel you had no say in the decision, that is, you had no *control* over the situation, you use *emotion-focused* coping.

You have several things going for you that will help alleviate the stress: You have an *optimistic* outlook on life, you express mostly *positive* emotions, and you have a large group of close friends, who provide good *social support.* For you to manage the stress, you count on your daily run with your professor, a major source of *aerobic exercise,* plus your regular practice of yoga, which is a form of meditative *relaxation.*

Terms and Concepts to Remember

1. **Stress** refers to the process by which we perceive and react to events, called *stressors,* that we appraise as threatening or challenging.

2. The **fight-or-flight response** refers to the body's response to an emergency, including activity of the sympathetic nervous system to mobilize energy for attacking or escaping a threat.

3. The **general adaptation syndrome (GAS)** is the three-stage sequence of the body's adaptive reaction to stress outlined by Hans Selye.

4. The **tend-and-befriend response** is the stress response in which people (especially women) offer support (tend) and bond with and seek support from others (befriend).

5. **Psychoneuroimmunology (PNI)** is the study of how psychological, neural, and endocrine processes combine to affect the immune system and resulting health.

6. The leading cause of death in the United States, **coronary heart disease** results from the clogging of the vessels that nourish the heart muscle.

7. **Type A** personality is Friedman and Rosenman's term for the coronary-prone behavior pattern of competitive, hard-driving, impatient, verbally aggressive, and anger-prone people.

8. **Type B** personality is Friedman and Rosenman's term for the coronary-resistant behavior pattern of easygoing, relaxed people.

9. **Coping** is the use of cognitive, emotional, or behavioral methods to reduce stress.

10. **Problem-focused coping** is the strategy of attempting to reduce stress directly by changing the stressor itself or the way we interact with it.

11. **Emotion-focused coping** is the strategy of attempting to reduce stress indirectly by avoiding or ignoring a stressor and attending to emotional needs.

12. **Personal control** is our sense of controlling our environment rather than feeling helpless.

13. **Learned helplessness** is the hopelessness and passive resignation that a person or animal learns when unable to avoid repeated aversive events.

14. **External locus of control** is the perception that chance or another outside force determines our fate.

15. **Internal locus of control** is the perception that we control our own fate.

16. **Self-control** is the ability to control impulses and delay short-term gratification for greater long-term rewards.

17. **Optimism** is the tendency to expect positive outcomes.

18. **Pessimism** is the tendency to expect negative outcomes.

19. **Aerobic exercise** is any sustained activity that promotes heart and lung fitness and may help reduce depression and anxiety.

20. **Mindfulness meditation** is attending to current experiences in an accepting, nonjudgmental manner.

21. **Resilience** is the personal strength that helps people cope with stress and recover from adversity and even trauma.

22. The **feel-good, do-good phenomenon** is our tendency to be helpful when we are in a good mood.

23. **Subjective well-being** refers to a our sense of satisfaction with our life.

24. The **adaptation-level phenomenon** refers to our tendency to judge things relative to a neutral level defined by our past experiences.

25. **Relative deprivation** is the perception that we are worse off relative to those with whom we compare ourselves.

Social Psychology

Chapter Overview

Chapter 11 demonstrates the powerful influences of social situations on the behavior of individuals. The social principles that emerge help us understand how individuals are influenced by advertising, political candidates, and the various groups to which they belong. Although social influences are powerful, we need to remember the significant role of individuals in choosing and creating the social situations that influence them.

    The chapter also discusses how people relate to one another, from the negative—developing prejudice and behaving aggressively—to the positive—being attracted to people who are nearby and/or similar and behaving altruistically. The chapter concludes with a discussion of situations that provoke conflict and techniques that have been shown to promote conflict resolution.

Chapter Review

First, skim each text section, noting headings and bold-face items. Review the section by reading the objectives and summaries provided here, then answer the questions that follow. In some cases, STUDY TIPS explain how best to learn a difficult concept and THINK ABOUT IT and APPLICATIONS help you to know how well you understand the material. Check your understanding of the material by consulting the answers beginning on page 228. Do not continue with the next section until you understand each answer. If you need to, review or reread the section in the textbook before continuing.

What Is Social Psychology's Focus?

Objective 11-1: Identify the three main focuses of social psychology.

Social psychology scientifically studies how (1) we *think about*, (2) *influence*, and (3) *relate to* one another.

1. Psychologists who scientifically study how we think about, influence, and relate to one another are called

_____ _____ .

Social Thinking

Objective 11-2: Explain how the fundamental attribution error describes how we tend to explain others' behavior compared with our own.

We may explain people's behavior in terms of internal traits or in terms of the external situation. For example, a teacher may explain a child's hostility in terms of an aggressive personality or as a reaction to stress or abuse. The *fundamental attribution error*—our tendency to underestimate situational influences and to overestimate the influence of personal traits—can lead us to unwarranted conclusions about other people's behavior. For example, we may blame the poor and the unemployed for their own misfortune.

2. Most people tend to_____ (overestimate/underestimate) the extent to which people's actions are influenced by social situations and _____ (overestimate/underestimate) the influence of personality. This tendency is called the _____

_____ _____ .

When explaining our own behavior, or that of someone we know well, this tendency is _____ (stronger/weaker). This tendency also is found more often in _____ (Western/East Asian) cultures than in _____ (Western/East Asian) cultures.

Give an example of the practical consequences of attributions.

STUDY TIP: To drive home the concept of the fundamental attribution error, think about a recent embarrassing moment. Perhaps you made an unkind remark that you later regretted. In explaining your behavior, you likely would say, "I was caught up in the moment," or "It was the people I was with." These are *external* (situational) attributions. Now think about how you would explain the same type of behavior in another person, especially someone you have just met. If you committed the fundamental attribution error, you would be less likely to "forgive" the person by making an external attribution. Instead, you would attribute it to personality and expect the person to behave similarly in the future.

APPLICATION:

3. Professor Vargas' students did very poorly on the last exam. The tendency to make the fundamental attribution error might lead her to conclude that the class did poorly because
   a. the test was unfair.
   b. students didn't have enough time to complete the test.
   c. students were distracted by some social function on campus.
   d. students were unmotivated.

Objective 11-3: Define *attitude*, and discuss how attitudes and actions affect each other.

Attitudes are feelings, often based on our beliefs, that predispose us to respond in a particular way to objects, people, and events. For example, we may *feel* dislike for a person because we *believe* he or she is mean, and so *act* unfriendly toward that person. *Peripheral route persuasion* uses unimportant cues to trigger speedy, emotion-based judgments. *Central route persuasion* offers evidence and arguments in hopes of motivating careful thinking.

Attitudes have a strong impact on actions when (1) outside influences on what we say and do are minimal; (2) the attitude is stable and specific to the behavior; and (3) the attitude is easily recalled. Attitudes also follow behavior. For example, the *foot-in-the-door phenomenon* is the tendency for people who have first agreed to a small request to comply later with a larger request. Because doing becomes believing, a trivial act makes the next act easier. Similarly, the behaviors associated with a new *role* may at first feel phony. However, play-acting soon becomes real as we adopt attitudes in keeping with our roles, as demonstrated in a study by Philip Zimbardo. *Cognitive dissonance theory,* proposed by Leon Festinger, argues that we feel discomfort when two of our thoughts (cognitions) clash. For example, when our actions conflict with our feelings and beliefs, we reduce the discomfort by bringing our attitudes more in line with our actions.

4. Feelings, often based on our beliefs, that predispose our responses are called _____ .

5. Persuasion based on unimportant cues such as a speaker's appearance is called _____

   _____ .

   Persuasion based on the evidence and arguments a speaker offers is called _____

   _____ _____ .

List four conditions under which our attitudes do predict our actions. Give examples.

6. Many research studies demonstrate that our attitudes are strongly influenced by our

   _____ . One example of this is the tendency for people who agree to a small request to comply later with a larger one. This is the

   _____-_____-

   _____-_____

   phenomenon.

7. When you follow society's expectations for how you should act as, say, a student, you are adopting a

   _____ . Taking on a set of behaviors, or acting in a certain way, generally

   _____ (changes/does not change) people's attitudes.

8. According to _____

   _____ theory, thoughts and feelings change because people are motivated to justify actions that would otherwise not match their attitudes. This theory was proposed by

   _____ .

9. Dissonance theory predicts that people made to feel responsible for behavior that clashes with their attitudes will be motivated to reduce the resulting

   _____ by changing their

   _____ .

STUDY TIP/APPLICATION: Cognitive dissonance theory and the foot-in-the-door phenomenon are two powerful examples of our attitudes following our actions. Think about these examples as you complete the following exercises.

10. a. Using the foot-in-the-door technique, how might you persuade a friend to take on an important, time-consuming task such as becoming treasurer of a ski club?

    b. Suppose your roommate thinks climate change is nothing more than a hoax promoted by politicians to a gullible public. Using cognitive dissonance theory, how might you go about changing your roommate's attitude?

APPLICATIONS:

11. Which of the following is an example of the foot-in-the-door phenomenon?

    a. To persuade a customer to buy a product a store owner offers a small gift.

    b. After agreeing to wear a small "Enforce Recycling" lapel pin, a woman agrees to collect signatures on a petition to make recycling required by law.

    c. After offering to sell a car at a ridiculously low price, a car salesperson is forced to tell the customer the car will cost $1000 more.

    d. All of these are examples.

12. Which of the following situations should produce the greatest cognitive dissonance?

    a. A soldier is forced to carry out orders he finds disagreeable.

    b. A student who loves animals has to dissect a cat in order to pass biology.

    c. As part of an experiment, a participant is directed to deliver electric shocks to another person.

    d. A student volunteers to debate an issue, taking the side he personally disagrees with.

Social Influence

Objective 11-4: Explain how experiments on conformity and obedience reveal the power of social influence.

We all have a natural tendency to mimic others, called the *chameleon effect.* Unconsciously mimicking others' expressions, postures, and voice tones helps us to *empathize* with others. Research participants in an experiment tend to rub their own face when confederates rub their face; similarly, the participants shake their own foot when they are with a foot-shaking person. The most empathic people mimic and are liked the most.

    Conformity is adjusting our behavior or thinking toward some group standard, or *norm.* Solomon Asch found that under certain conditions, people will conform to a group's judgment, even when it is clearly incorrect. Experiments indicate that conformity increases when we feel incompetent or insecure, admire the group's status and attractiveness, have made no prior commitment to a response, are being observed by other group members, come from a culture that encourages respect for social standards, and are in a group with at least three people who all agree. People conform for two possible reasons: *normative social influence,* in which we are sensitive to social norms, or *informational social influence,* in which we conform because we want to be correct.

    In the Milgram studies, the experimenter ordered "teachers" to deliver shocks to a "learner" for wrong answers. Torn between obeying the experimenter and responding to the learner's pleas, the people usually chose to obey orders, even though it supposedly meant harming the learner. Obedience was highest when the person giving the orders was close at hand and was perceived to be a legitimate authority; when the authority figure was supported by a respected, well-known institution; when the victim was depersonalized or at a distance; and when there were no role models for defiance.

13. The chameleon effect refers to our natural tendency to unconsciously _____ others' expressions, postures, and voice tones. This helps us to feel what they are feeling, referred to as _____ .

14. The term that refers to the tendency to adjust one's behavior to coincide with an assumed group standard is _____ .

15. The psychologist who first studied the effects of group pressure on conformity is

_____ .

16. In this study, when the opinion of other group members was contradicted by objective evidence, research participants _____ (were/were not) willing to conform to the group opinion.

List some of the conditions under which people are more likely to conform.

17. People conform for two reasons: to gain social approval or avoid disapproval, called

_____ _____

_____ , or to accept other people's view of reality, called _____

_____ _____ .

18. The classic social psychology studies of obedience were conducted by _____ . When ordered by the experimenter to electrically shock the "learner," the majority of participants (the "teachers") in these studies _____ (complied/refused). More recent studies have found that women's compliance rates in similar situations were _____ (higher than/lower than/similar to) men's.

List the conditions under which obedience was highest in Milgram's studies.

APPLICATIONS:

19. José is the one student member on the board of trustees. At the board's first meeting, José wants to disagree with the others on several issues but in each case decides to say nothing. Studies on conformity suggest all except one of the following are factors in José's not speaking up. Which one is NOT a factor?
   a. The board is a large group.
   b. The board is respected and most of its members are well known.
   c. The board members are already aware that José and the student body disagree with them on these issues.
   d. Because this is the first meeting José has attended, he feels insecure and not fully competent.

20. Twenty-year-old Marge belonged to a sorority. During pledge week, she was ordered to force potential members to strip in front of their friends. Although Marge disapproved of asking fellow students to embarrass themselves, she did it anyway. She respected the sorority officers, and all her fellow sisters were also hazing the pledges. How would Milgram explain Marge's behavior?

Objective 11-5: Describe what the social influence studies teach us about ourselves, and discuss how much power we have as individuals.

The Asch and Milgram experiments demonstrate that social influences can be strong enough to make people conform to falsehoods or give in to cruelty. The studies, because of their design, also illustrate how great evil sometimes grows out of people's acceptance of lesser evils. Evil does not require devilish villains but ordinary people corrupted by an evil situation.

In studying the power of the individual, social psychologists have learned that *social control* and *personal control* interact. A minority that consistently holds to its position can sway the majority (*minority influence*). This is especially true if the minority's self-confidence stimulates others to consider why the minority reacts as it does. Even when a minority's influence is not yet visible, it may be convincing members of the majority to rethink their views.

21. In getting people to administer increasingly larger shocks, Milgram was in effect applying the

_____-_____

_____-_____ technique.

22. The Asch and Milgram studies demonstrate that strong _____ influences can make people _____ to falsehoods and _____ orders to commit cruel acts.

23. In considering the power of social influence, we cannot overlook the interaction of

_____ _____ (the power of the situation) and

_____ _____ (the power of the individual).

24. The power of one or two individuals to sway the opinion of the majority is called

_____ _____ .

You are far more likely to sway the majority if you _____ (hold firmly to/are flexible in) your position. This tactic will make you influential, especially if your _____ stimulates others to consider why you react as you do.

Objective 11-6: Describe how the presence of others influences our actions, via social facilitation, social loafing, or deindividuation.

Experiments on *social facilitation* reveal that the presence of observers can arouse individuals, strengthening the most likely response and so boosting their performance on easy or well-learned tasks but hindering it on difficult or newly learned ones. When people pool their efforts toward a group goal, *social loafing* may occur as individuals free ride on others' efforts. When a group experience arouses people and makes them anonymous, they become less self-aware and self-restrained, a psychological state known as *deindividuation*.

25. The tendency to perform a task better when other people are present is called _____ _____ , as _____ found when observing adolescents wind a fishing reel. Later studies revealed that people become aroused in the presence of others, and arousal strengthens the correct response on _____ (easy/difficult) or well-learned tasks and the incorrect response on _____ (easy/difficult) tasks.

26. Researchers have found that the reactions of people in crowded situations are often _____ (lessened/amplified).

27. Researchers found that people worked _____ (harder/less hard) in a team tug-of-war than they had in an individual contest. This phenomenon has been called

_____ _____ .

28. The feeling of anonymity and loss of self-restraint that an individual may develop when in a group is called _____ .

THINK ABOUT IT: To help solidify the idea of social facilitation in your mind, think about sports you play–or don't play (because you do not do well). Think about your friends in similar situations, your children if you are a parent. Then think about professional athletes. Does the same hold true for the performing arts (acting, dancing, etc.)? What about your everyday activities? How well do you (or they) perform in front of an audience?

APPLICATIONS:

29. Which of the following would MOST likely be subject to social facilitation?
    a. proofreading a page for spelling errors
    b. typing a letter with accuracy
    c. playing a difficult piece on a musical instrument
    d. running quickly around a track

30. Concluding her presentation on deindividuation, Renée notes that deindividuation is less likely in situations that make a person feel aroused and _____.

Objective 11-7: Explain how group interaction can enable group polarization.

Within groups, discussions among like-minded members often produce *group polarization,* a strengthening of the group's preexisting attitudes. Group polarization can have positive results, as when low-prejudice students become even more accepting while discussing racial issues. But it can also have negative results, as it can strengthen a terrorist mentality.

31. Over time, the initial differences between groups usually _____ (increase/decrease).

32. The strengthening of each group's preexisting attitudes over time is called _____.

APPLICATION:

33. Jane and Sandy were best friends as freshmen. Jane joined a sorority; Sandy didn't. By the end of their senior year, they found that they had less in common with each other than with the other members of their respective circles of friends. Their change in feelings is most likely due to _____.

Objective 11-8 Describe the role the Internet plays in group polarization.

The Internet connects like-minded people and strengthens their ideas. Electronic communication and social networking encourage people to isolate themselves from those with different opinions. While White supremacists become more racist, the good news is that cancer survivors and bereaved parents strengthen shared perspectives of resilience.

34. A current source for like-minded individuals to strengthen their opinions is the _____. For example, _____ sites encourage people to isolate themselves from those with _____ (the same/different) opinions.

Objective 11-9 Explain how group interaction enables groupthink.

Sometimes, group interaction distorts important decisions. In *groupthink,* the desire for harmony overrides a realistic appraisal of alternatives.

35. When the desire for group harmony overrides realistic thinking in individuals, the phenomenon known as _____ has occurred. Several factors contribute to this phenomenon, including _____ , conformity, self-justification, and _____ .

THINK ABOUT IT: Have you ever served in a leadership role in a group of people? Perhaps you have been a club president, or other officer, who had to lead group discussions. Based on the information in this section, how might a group leader in such a situation promote groupthink? What steps could a leader take to discourage groupthink from developing?

Social Relations

Objective 11-10: Identify the three parts of prejudice, and describe how prejudice has changed over time.

Prejudice is a mixture of *beliefs* (often overgeneralized and called *stereotypes*), *emotions* (hostility, envy, or fear), and predispositions to *action* (to discriminate). Prejudice is a negative attitude; *discrimination* is a negative behavior.

As *open* racial prejudice has waned, *subtle* prejudice lingers. Prejudice is often *implicit,* an automatic attitude that does not involve thought. Expectations also influence perceptions.

Gender prejudice and discrimination also persist. Prejudice against gays and lesbians, although rapidly declining in Western countries, persists worldwide, especially among men, older adults, and those who are less educated.

36. Prejudice is an _____ and usually _____ attitude toward a group that involves overgeneralized beliefs known as _____ .

37. Like all attitudes, prejudice is a mixture of _____ , _____ , and predispositions to _____ .

38. Prejudice is a negative _____ , and _____ is a negative _____ .

39. Americans today express _____ (less/the same/more) racial prejudice than they did a half-century ago. As overt prejudice _____ (increases/decreases/remains), subtle prejudice _____ (increases/decreases/remains).

40. Even people who deny holding prejudiced attitudes may carry negative _____ . Studies of prejudice indicate that it is often automatic and unthinking, or _____ .

41. Our perceptions are also influenced by our _____ . In one study, people (Blacks and Whites) perceived Blacks to be the most threatening.

42. Despite gender equality in intelligence scores, people have tended to perceive their _____ (mothers/fathers) as more intelligent than their _____ (mothers/fathers).

43. Many places in the world have laws criminalizing _____-_____ relationships.

APPLICATION:

44. Alexis believes that all male athletes are self-centered and sexist. Her beliefs are an example of _____ .

Objective 11-11: Identify the factors that contribute to the social roots of prejudice, and describe how scapegoating illustrates the emotional roots of prejudice.

Prejudice often arises as those who enjoy social and economic superiority attempt to justify the status quo by the *just-world phenomenon,* the idea that good is rewarded and evil is punished. Through our *social identities* we also associate ourselves with some groups and contrast ourselves with others. Mentally drawing a circle that defines "us" (the *ingroup*) also excludes "them" (the *outgroup*). Such group identifications promote an *ingroup bias,* that is, a favoring of one's own group. Even creating an "us-them" distinction by the toss of a coin leads people to show ingroup bias.

Facing the fear of death tends to heighten patriotism and produce anger and aggression toward those who threaten one's world. *Scapegoat theory* suggests that prejudice offers an outlet for anger by providing someone to blame.

45. For those with money, power, and prestige, prejudice often serves as a means of _____ social inequalities.

46. The view that good is rewarded and evil is punished is called the _____-_____ _____ .

Victims of discrimination may react in ways that feed prejudice through the classic _____-_____-_____ dynamic.

47. Through our _____ _____ , we associate ourselves with certain groups.

48. Prejudice is also fostered by the _____ _____ , a tendency to favor the group to which one belongs—called the _____—while excluding others, or the _____ .

49. That prejudice derives from attempts to blame others for one's frustration is proposed by the _____ theory.

50. Prejudice levels tends to be high among people who are _____ frustrated.

51. People who feel loved and supported become more _____ to and _____ of those who differ from them.

52. The terror of facing death tends to produce anger and _____ toward people who threaten our _____ .

APPLICATIONS:

53. Students at State University are convinced that their school is better than any other; this most directly illustrates an _____ _____ .

54. Ever since their cabin lost the camp softball competition, the campers have become increasingly hostile toward one camper in their cabin, blaming her for every problem in the cabin. This behavior is best explained by _____ _____ .

Objective 11-12: Describe the cognitive roots of prejudice.

One way we simplify the world is to *form categories.* In categorizing others, we often stereotype them, overestimating the similarity of those within another group. The **other-race effect** (or *cross-race effect* or *own-race bias*) is the tendency to recall faces of one's own race more accurately than faces of other races. It emerges during infancy, between 3 and 9 months of age. We also estimate the frequency of events by *vivid cases* (violence, for example) that come to mind more readily than the less vivid events involving the same group. Third, we can believe the *world is just* and that people get what they deserve and deserve what they get (as noted earlier, the just-world phenomenon).

104. In Mozafer Sherif's study, two conflicting groups of campers were able to resolve their conflicts by working together on projects in which they shared _____ goals. Shared _____ breed solidarity. What reduced conflict was not mere contact, but _____ contact.

APPLICATIONS:

105. Mr. and Mrs. Samuels are constantly fighting, and each perceives the other as hard-headed and insensitive. Their conflict is being fueled by _____- _____ _____ .

106. Which of the following strategies would be most likely to foster positive feelings between two conflicting groups?
    a. Take steps to reduce the likelihood of mirror-image perceptions.
    b. Separate the groups so that tensions diminish.
    c. Increase the amount of contact between the two conflicting groups.
    d. Have the groups work on a superordinate goal.

Progress Test

Multiple-Choice Questions

Circle your answers to the following questions and check them with the answers beginning on page 230. If your answer is incorrect, read the explanation for why it is incorrect and then consult the text.

1. In his study of obedience, Stanley Milgram found that the majority of participants
    a. refused to shock the learner even once.
    b. complied with the experiment until the "learner" first indicated pain.
    c. complied with the experiment until the "learner" began screaming in agony.
    d. complied with all the demands of the experiment.

2. According to cognitive dissonance theory, dissonance is most likely to occur when
    a. a person's behavior is not based on strongly held attitudes.
    b. two people have conflicting attitudes and find themselves in disagreement.
    c. an individual does something that is personally disagreeable.
    d. an individual is coerced into doing something that he or she does not want to do.

3. Which of the following statements is true?
    a. Groups are almost never swayed by minority opinions.
    b. Group polarization is most likely to occur when group members frequently disagree with one another.
    c. Groupthink provides the consensus needed for effective decision making.
    d. A group that is like-minded will probably not change its opinions through discussion.

4. Conformity increased under which of the following conditions in Asch's studies of conformity?
    a. The group had three or more people.
    b. The group had high status.
    c. Individuals were made to feel insecure.
    d. All of these situations increased conformity.

5. Violent criminals often have diminished activity in the _____ of the brain, which play(s) an important role in _____ .
    a. occipital lobes; aggression
    b. hypothalamus; hostility
    c. frontal lobes; controlling impulses
    d. temporal lobes; patience

6. The phenomenon in which individuals lose their identity and relinquish normal restraints when they are part of a group is called
    a. groupthink.   c. empathy.
    b. cognitive dissonance.   d. deindividuation.

7. Participants in Asch's line-judgment experiment gave the same answers as the rest of the group, even when they knew the answers were wrong. This behavior is referred to as
    a. social facilitation.
    b. social loafing.
    c. scapegoating.
    d. conformity.

8. Based on findings from Milgram's obedience studies, participants would be LESS likely to follow the experimenter's orders when
    a. they hear the "learner" cry out in pain.
    b. they merely administer the test while someone else delivers the shocks.
    c. the "learner" is an older person or mentions having some physical problem.
    d. they see another person disobey instructions.

9. *Aggression* is defined as behavior that
    a. hurts another person.
    b. is intended to hurt another person.
    c. is hostile, passionate, and produces physical injury.
    d. has all of these characteristics.

10. Which of the following is true about aggression?
    a. It varies too much to be instinctive in humans.
    b. It is just one instinct among many.
    c. It is instinctive but shaped by learning.
    d. It is the most important human instinct.

11. Research studies have found a positive correlation between aggressive tendencies in animals and levels of the hormone
    a. estrogen.   c. noradrenaline.
    b. adrenaline.   d. testosterone.

12. Research studies have indicated that the tendency of viewers to see sexual aggression as less serious is
    a. increased by exposure to pornography.
    b. not changed after exposure to pornography.
    c. decreased in men by exposure to pornography.
    d. decreased in both men and women by exposure to pornography.

13. Increasing the number of people who are present during an emergency tends to
    a. increase the likelihood that people will cooperate in rendering assistance.
    b. decrease the empathy that people feel for the victim.
    c. increase the role that social norms governing helping will play.
    d. decrease the likelihood that anyone will help.

14. Which of the following was NOT mentioned in the text discussion of the roots of prejudice?
    a. people's tendency to overestimate the similarity of people within groups
    b. people's tendency to assume that exceptional, or especially memorable, individuals are unlike the majority of members of a group
    c. people's tendency to assume that the world is just and that people get what they deserve
    d. people's tendency to discriminate against those they view as "outsiders"

15. The mere exposure effect demonstrates that
    a. familiarity breeds contempt.
    b. opposites attract.
    c. birds of a feather flock together.
    d. familiarity breeds fondness.

16. In one experiment, men were physically aroused and then introduced to an attractive woman. Compared with men who had not been aroused, these men
    a. reported more positive feelings toward the woman.
    b. reported more negative feelings toward the woman.
    c. were ambiguous about their feelings toward the woman.
    d. were more likely to feel that the woman was "out of their league" in terms of attractiveness.

17. The deep affection that is felt in long-lasting relationships is called _____ love; this feeling is fostered in relationships in which _____ .
    a. passionate; there is equity between the partners
    b. passionate; traditional roles are maintained
    c. companionate; there is equity between the partners
    d. companionate; traditional roles are maintained

18. Which of the following is associated with an increased tendency on the part of a bystander to offer help in an emergency situation?
    a. being in a good mood

    b. having recently needed help and not received it
    c. observing someone as he or she refuses to offer help
    d. being a female

19. The belief that those who suffer deserve their fate is expressed in the
    a. just-world phenomenon.
    b. phenomenon of ingroup bias.
    c. fundamental attribution error.
    d. mirror-image perception principle.

20. Which of the following phenomena is best explained by cognitive dissonance theory?
    a. group polarization
    b. the foot-in-the-door phenomenon
    c. ingroup bias
    d. scapegoating

21. Which of the following is an example of implicit prejudice?
    a. Jake, who is White, gives higher evaluations to essays he believes to be written by Blacks than to White-authored essays.
    b. Carol believes that White people are arrogant.
    c. Brad earns more than Jane, despite having the same job skills, performance level, and seniority.
    d. In certain countries, women are not allowed to drive.

22. We tend to perceive the members of an ingroup as _____ and the members of an outgroup as _____ .
    a. similar to one another; different from one another
    b. different from one another; similar to one another
    c. above average in ability; below average in ability
    d. below average in ability; above average in ability

23. Regarding the influence of alcohol and testosterone on aggressive behavior, which of the following is true?
    a. Drinking alcohol increases aggressive behavior; injections of testosterone reduce aggressive behavior.
    b. Drinking alcohol reduces aggressive behavior; injections of testosterone increase aggressive behavior.
    c. Drinking alcohol and injections of testosterone both promote aggressive behavior.
    d. Drinking alcohol and injections of testosterone both reduce aggressive behavior.

24. Most people prefer mirror-image photographs of their faces. This is best explained by
    a. the principle of equity.
    b. the principle of self-disclosure.
    c. the mere exposure effect.
    d. mirror-image perceptions.

25. The tendency to overestimate the influence of personal traits and underestimate the effects of the situation is called
    a. cognitive dissonance theory.
    b. two-factor theory.
    c. peripheral route persuasion.
    d. the fundamental attribution error.

26. Research studies indicate that in an emergency situation, the presence of others often
    a. prevents people from even noticing the situation.
    b. prevents people from interpreting an unusual event as an emergency.
    c. prevents people from assuming responsibility for assisting.
    d. leads to all of these situations.

27. Two neighboring nations are each stockpiling weapons. Each sees its neighbor's actions as an act of aggression and its own actions as self-defense. Evidently, these nations are victims of
    a. prejudice.
    b. groupthink.
    c. group polarization.
    d. mirror-image perceptions.

28. Which of the following factors is the MOST powerful predictor of friendship?
    a. similarity in age
    b. common racial and religious background
    c. similarity in physical attractiveness
    d. physical proximity

29. Most researchers agree that media violence
    a. is a factor in aggression.
    b. and aggressiveness are negatively correlated.
    c. ultimately diminishes an individual's aggressive tendencies.
    d. is too unreal to promote aggression in viewers.

30. When male students in an experiment were told that a woman to whom they would be speaking had been instructed to act in a friendly or unfriendly way, most of them subsequently attributed her behavior to
    a. the situation.
    b. the situation *and* her personal traits.
    c. her personal traits.
    d. their own skill or lack of skill in a social situation.

31. Which of the following is true?
    a. Attitudes and actions rarely correspond.
    b. Attitudes predict behavior about half the time.
    c. Attitudes are excellent predictors of behavior.
    d. Attitudes predict behavior under certain conditions.

32. People with power and status may become prejudiced because
    a. they tend to justify the social inequalities between themselves and others.
    b. those with less status and power tend to resent them.
    c. those with less status and power appear less capable.
    d. they feel proud and are boastful of their achievements.

33. Which of the following most accurately states the effects of crowding on behavior?
    a. Crowding makes people irritable.
    b. Crowding sometimes intensifies people's reactions.
    c. Crowding promotes altruistic behavior.
    d. Crowding usually weakens the intensity of people's reactions.

34. Research has found that for a minority to succeed in swaying a majority, the minority must
    a. make up a sizable portion of the group.
    b. express its position as consistently as possible.
    c. express its position in the most extreme terms possible.
    d. be able to convince a key majority leader.

35. Which of the following conclusions did Milgram reach as a result of his studies of obedience?
    a. Even ordinary people, without any particular hostility, can become agents in a destructive process.
    b. Most people are able, under the proper circumstances, to suppress their natural aggressiveness.
    c. The need to be accepted by others is a powerful motivating force.
    d. He reached all of these conclusions.

36. Which of the following is important in promoting conformity in individuals?
    a. whether an individual's behavior will be observed by others in the group
    b. whether the individual is male or female
    c. the size of the room in which a group is meeting
    d. whether the individual is of a higher status than other group members

37. Which of the following is MOST likely to promote groupthink?
    a. The group's leader fails to take a firm stance on an issue.
    b. A minority faction holds to its position.
    c. The group consults with various experts.
    d. Group polarization is evident.

Matching Items

Match each term with the appropriate definition or description.

Terms

_____ **1.** social facilitation
_____ **2.** social loafing
_____ **3.** bystander effect
_____ **4.** conformity
_____ **5.** ingroup bias
_____ **6.** group polarization
_____ **7.** stereotype
_____ **8.** altruism
_____ **9.** mere exposure effect
_____ **10.** reciprocity norm
_____ **11.** norm
_____ **12.** social-responsibility norm
_____ **13.** self-fulfilling prophecy

Definitions or Descriptions

a. a generalized belief about a group of people
b. a set of expected behaviors
c. performance is improved by an audience
d. the tendency to favor one's own group
e. expectation that people will help those who depend on them
f. group discussion enhances prevailing tendencies
g. unselfish concern for others
h. the tendency that a person is less likely to help someone in need when others are present
i. the increased liking of a stimulus that results from repeated exposure to it
j. beliefs that confirm themselves
k. people work less hard in a group
l. the expectation that people will help those who have helped them
m. adjusting one's behavior to coincide with a group standard

Application Essay

The Panhellenic Council on your campus has asked you to make a presentation on the topic of social psychology to all freshmen who have signed up to "rush" a fraternity or sorority. In a fit of cynicism following your rejection last year by a popular fraternity or sorority, you decide to speak about the negative influences of groups on the behavior of individuals. What will you discuss? (Use the space below to list the points you want to make, and organize them. Then write the essay on a separate sheet of paper.)

Summing Up

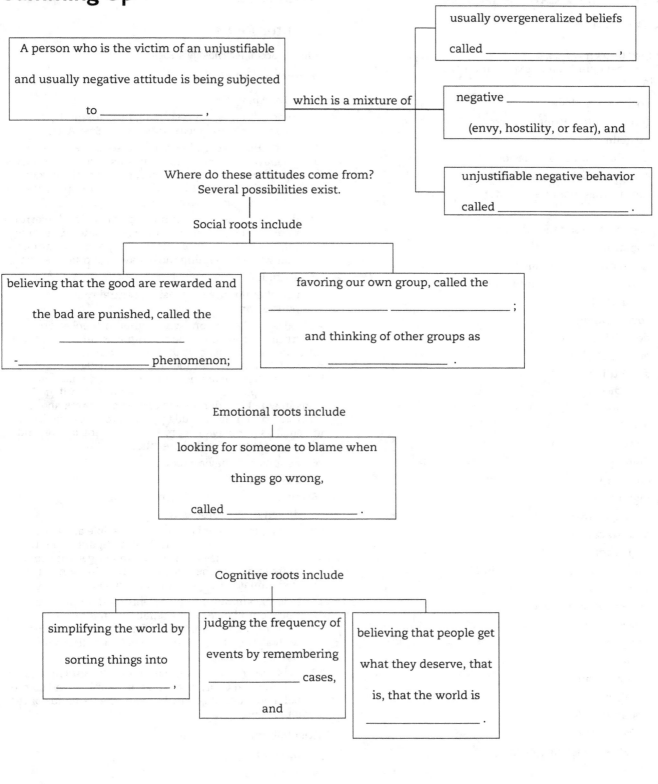

A person who is the victim of an unjustifiable and usually negative attitude is being subjected to _____ ,

which is a mixture of

usually overgeneralized beliefs called _____ ,

negative _____ (envy, hostility, or fear), and

unjustifiable negative behavior called _____ .

Where do these attitudes come from? Several possibilities exist.

Social roots include

believing that the good are rewarded and the bad are punished, called the _____ -_____ phenomenon;

favoring our own group, called the _____ _____ ; and thinking of other groups as _____ .

Emotional roots include

looking for someone to blame when things go wrong, called _____ .

Cognitive roots include

simplifying the world by sorting things into _____ ,

judging the frequency of events by remembering _____ cases, and

believing that people get what they deserve, that is, that the world is _____ .

Terms and Concepts to Remember

Using your own words, on a separate piece of paper write a brief definition or explanation of each of the following terms.

1. social psychology
2. fundamental attribution error
3. attitude
4. peripheral route persuasion
5. central route persuasion
6. foot-in-the-door phenomenon
7. role
8. cognitive dissonance theory
9. conformity
10. normative social influence
11. informational social influence
12. social facilitation
13. social loafing
14. deindividuation
15. group polarization
16. groupthink
17. prejudice
18. stereotype
19. discrimination
20. just-world phenomenon
21. ingroup
22. outgroup
23. ingroup bias
24. scapegoat theory
25. other-race effect
26. aggression
27. frustration-aggression principle
28. social script
29. mere exposure effect
30. passionate love
31. companionate love
32. equity
33. self-disclosure
34. altruism
35. bystander effect
36. reciprocity norm
37. social-responsibility norm
38. conflict
39. mirror-image perceptions
40. self-fulfilling prophecy
41. superordinate goals

Answers

Chapter Review

What Is Social Psychology's Focus?

1. social psychologists

Social Thinking

2. underestimate; overestimate; fundamental attribution error; weaker; Western; East Asian

Our attributions—to individuals' personalities or to situations—have important practical consequences. A hurtful remark from an acquaintance, for example, is more likely to be forgiven if it is attributed to a temporary situation than to a mean personality.

3. **d.** is the answer. The fundamental attribution error refers to the tendency to underestimate situational influences in favor of this type of personal attribution when explaining the behavior of other people.

4. attitudes

5. peripheral route persuasion; central route persuasion

Attitudes predict actions when other influences on the attitudes and actions are minimized and when the attitude is stable, specific to the behavior, and easily recalled. Thus, our attitudes are more likely to predict behavior when we are not attempting to adjust our behavior to please others, when we are in familiar situations in which we don't have to stop and think about our attitudes, when the attitude pertains to a specific behavior, such as purchasing a product or casting a vote, and when the attitude is easily recalled.

6. actions or behavior; foot-in-the-door

7. role; changes

8. cognitive dissonance; Leon Festinger

9. dissonance; attitudes

10. No single answer is correct. A possible answer for a. is to ask the friend to check some figures from the monthly expenses. For b., you might get your roommate to debate the issue and have him or her argue that climate change is a major concern.

11. **b.** is the answer. In the foot-in-the-door phenomenon, compliance with a small initial request, such as wearing a lapel pin, later is followed by compliance with a much larger request, such as collecting petition signatures.

12. **d.** is the answer. In this situation, the student has volunteered to argue against his opinion, and so the behavior cannot be attributed to the demands of the situation.

Social Influence

13. mimic; empathy

14. conformity

15. Solomon Asch

16. were

People are most likely to conform when they are made to feel incompetent or insecure, they are in a group with at least three people, they are in a group in which everyone else agrees, they admire the group's status and attractiveness, they have not already committed to any response, they know that others in the group are observing them, and they are from a culture that encourages respect for social standards.

17. normative social influence; informational social influence

18. Stanley Milgram; complied; similar to

Obedience was highest when the person giving the orders was close at hand and perceived to be a legitimate authority figure; the authority figure was supported by a respected, well-known institution; the victim was depersonalized or at a distance; and there were no role models for defiance.

19. **c.** is the answer. Prior commitment to an opposing view generally tends to work against conformity. In contrast, large group size, respect for the group, and an individual's feelings of incompetence and insecurity all strengthen the tendency to conform.

20. Milgram would say that Marge's behavior was a product of the situation, not her personal traits. She respected the officers of the sorority and everyone else was participating in the hazing.

21. foot-in-the-door

22. social; conform; obey

23. social control; personal control

24. minority influence; hold firmly to; self-confidence

25. social facilitation; Norman Triplett; easy; difficult

26. amplified

27. less hard; social loafing

28. deindividuation

29. **d.** is the answer. Social facilitation, or better performance in the presence of others, occurs for easy tasks but not for more difficult ones. For tasks such as proofreading, typing, or playing an instrument, the arousal resulting from the presence of others can lead to mistakes.

30. anonymous. Deindividuation refers to the loss of self-restraint and self-awareness that sometimes occurs in group situations where people are aroused and feel anonymous.

31. increase

32. group polarization

33. group polarization. Group polarization means that the tendencies within a group—and therefore the differences among groups—grow stronger over time. Thus, because the differences between the sorority and nonsorority students have increased, Jane and Sandy are likely to have little in common.

34. Internet; social networking; different

35. groupthink; overconfidence; group polarization

Social Relations

36. unfair; negative; stereotypes

37. beliefs; emotions; action

38. attitude; discrimination; behavior

39. less; decreases; remains

40. associations; implicit

41. expectations

42. fathers; mothers

43. same-sex

44. stereotyping. This is an often overgeneralized belief about a group of people, which describes Alexis' view of male athletes.

45. justifying

46. just-world phenomenon; blame-the-victim

47. social identities

48. ingroup bias; ingroup; outgroup

49. scapegoat

50. economically

51. open; accepting

52. aggression; world

53. ingroup bias. In viewing students from other schools as the outgroup, State University students have formed an ingroup and are exhibiting the ingroup bias by favoring their own group.

54. scapegoat theory. According to the scapegoat theory, when things go wrong, people look for someone on whom to take out their frustration and anger.

55. categorizing; overestimate; other-race effect (cross-race effect; own-race bias)

56. overestimate; just-world

57. **c.** is the answer. People tend to overestimate the similarity of people within groups other than their own. Thus, Juan is not likely to form stereotypes of fitness enthusiasts (a.), political liberals (b.), or older adults (c.), which are groups to which he belongs.

58. any act intended to harm someone physically or emotionally

59. biology; experience

60. do not

61. varies

62. bred; do

63. neural; hormones

64. testosterone; decreased; irritability; assertiveness; impulsivity; low tolerance

65. alcohol

66. amygdala; frontal lobes; impulses

67. **c.** is the answer. Just the opposite is true of a., b., and d.

68. frustration-aggression

69. hot temperatures, physical pain, personal insults, foul odors, cigarette smoke, and crowding

70. rewards (reinforcement); observation (or imitation)

71. model; reinforce

72. rich; poor; father care

73. sensitive; prime

74. social scripts

The research study found that after viewing sexually explicit films for several weeks, undergraduates were more likely to recommend a lighter prison sentence for a convicted rapist than were those who viewed nonerotic films.

75. does; can
76. aggressive thoughts; empathy; aggression
77. hostile; arguments; fights; grades
78. biological; psychological; social-cultural
79. frustration-aggression principle. According to this principle, the blocking of an attempt to achieve some goal—in Teresa's case, buying concert tickets—creates anger and can generate aggression.
80. proximity; increases; mere exposure
81. happier, less; speed dating
82. appearance
83. Attractive people are perceived as healthier, happier, more sensitive, more successful, and more socially skilled.
84. is not
85. youthful; fertile; mature; dominant; masculine; wealthy
86. attitudes, beliefs, interests, religion, race, education, intelligence, smoking behavior, economic status, age

A reward theory of attraction says that we are attracted to, and continue relationships with, those people whose behavior is rewarding to us, including those who are both able and willing to help us achieve our goals. Proximity makes it easy to enjoy the benefits of friendship at little cost, attractiveness is pleasing, and similarity rewards us by confirming our beliefs.

87. d. is the answer. Hundreds of experiments indicate that first impressions are most influenced by physical appearance.
88. a. is the answer. Friends and couples are much more likely than randomly paired people to be similar in views, interests, and a range of other factors.
89. passionate
90. arousal; appraisal
91. were
92. companionate; equity; self-disclosure
93. a. is the answer. According to the two-factor theory, physical arousal can intensify whatever emotion is currently felt. Only in the situation described in a. is Joan likely to be physically aroused.
94. altruism
95. notice; interpret; responsibility
96. less
97. less; bystander effect

People are most likely to help someone when they have just observed someone else being helpful, when they are not in a hurry, when the victim appears to need and deserve help, when the person is a woman, when they are in some way similar to the victim, when in a small town or rural area, when feeling guilty, when not preoccupied, and when in a good mood.

98. is; reward

99. reciprocity
100. social-responsibility
101. conflict; cultural groups
102. mirror-image
103. noncompetitive; is not
104. superordinate; predicaments; cooperative
105. mirror-image perceptions. The couple's similar, and presumably distorted, feelings toward each other fuel their conflict.
106. d. is the answer. Sherif found that hostility between two groups could be eliminated by giving the groups superordinate, or shared, goals.

Progress Test

Multiple-Choice Questions

1. d. is the answer. In Milgram's initial experiments, 63 percent of the subjects fully complied with the experiment.
2. c. is the answer. Cognitive dissonance is the tension we feel when we are aware of a discrepancy between our thoughts and actions, as would occur when we do something we find distasteful.
   a. Dissonance requires strongly held attitudes, which must be perceived as not fitting behavior.
   b. Dissonance is a personal cognitive process.
   d. In such a situation the person is less likely to experience dissonance, since the action can be attributed to "having no choice."
3. d. is the answer. In such groups, discussion usually strengthens prevailing opinion; this phenomenon is known as group polarization.
   a. Minority opinions, especially if consistently and firmly stated, can sway the majority in a group.
   b. Group polarization, or the strengthening of a group's prevailing tendencies, is most likely in groups where members agree.
   c. When groupthink occurs, there is so much consensus that decision making becomes less effective.
4. d. is the answer.
5. c. is the answer.
6. d. is the answer.
   a. Groupthink refers to the mode of thinking that occurs when the desire for group harmony overrides realistic and critical thinking.
   b. Cognitive dissonance refers to the discomfort we feel when two thoughts (which include the knowledge of our *behavior*) are inconsistent.
   c. Empathy is feeling what another person feels.
7. d. is the answer. People are most likely to conform when they are unsure of themselves, are in a group of three or more, and have no models for defiance.
   a. Social facilitation involves performing simple or well-learned tasks better or faster in the presence of others.
   b. Social loafing refers to the tendency for people in a group to exert less effort.

c. Scapegoating is finding someone to blame as an outlet for your anger when things go wrong.

8. **d.** is the answer. Role models for defiance reduce levels of obedience.
   a. & c. These did not result in diminished obedience.
   b. This "depersonalization" of the victim resulted in increased obedience.

9. **b.** is the answer. Aggression is any act intended to harm someone physically or emotionally
   a. A person may accidentally be hurt in a nonaggressive incident; aggression does not necessarily prove hurtful.
   c. Verbal behavior, which does not result in physical injury, may also be aggressive. Moreover, acts of aggression may be cool and calculated, rather than hostile and passionate.

10. **a.** is the answer. The very wide variations in aggressiveness from culture to culture indicate that aggression cannot be considered an unlearned instinct.

11. **d.** is the answer.

12. **a.** is the answer.

13. **d.** is the answer. This phenomenon is known as the bystander effect.
    a. This answer is incorrect because individuals are less likely to render assistance at all if others are present.
    b. Although people are less likely to assume responsibility for helping, this does not mean that they are less empathic.
    c. This answer is incorrect because norms tend to encourage helping others, yet people are less likely to help with others around.

14. **b.** is the answer. In fact, people tend to overestimate the similarity among members of a group.
    a., c., & d. Each of these is an example of a cognitive (a. & c.) or a social (d.) root of prejudice.

15. **d.** is the answer. Being repeatedly exposed to novel stimuli increases our liking for them.
    a. For the most part, the opposite is true.
    b. & c. The mere exposure effect concerns our tendency to develop likings on the basis, not of similarities or differences, but simply of familiarity, or repeated exposure.

16. **a.** is the answer. This result supports the two-factor theory of emotion and passionate attraction, according to which arousal from any source can facilitate an emotion, depending on how we label the arousal.

17. **c.** is the answer. Deep affection is typical of companionate love, rather than passionate love, and is promoted by equity. Traditional roles may be characterized by the dominance of one sex.

18. **a.** is the answer.
    b. & c. These factors would most likely decrease a person's altruistic tendencies.
    d. There is no evidence that one sex is more altruistic than the other.

19. **a.** is the answer.

b. Ingroup bias is the tendency of people to favor their own group.
c. The fundamental attribution error is the tendency of people to underestimate situational influences when observing the behavior of other people.
d. The mirror-image perception principle is the tendency of conflicting parties to form similar, diabolical images of each other.

20. **b.** is the answer.
    a. Group polarization involves group opinions.
    c. Ingroup bias is the tendency to favor groups to which you belong.
    d. Scapegoating is finding someone to blame as an outlet for your anger.

21. **a.** is the answer.
    b. This is an example of overt prejudice.
    c. & d. These are examples of discrimination.

22. **b.** is the answer.
    a. We are keenly sensitive to differences within our group, less so to differences within other groups.
    c. & d. Although we tend to look more favorably on members of the ingroup, the text does not suggest that ingroup bias extends to evaluations of abilities.

23. **c.** is the answer.

24. **c.** is the answer. The mere exposure effect refers to our tendency to like what we're used to, and we're used to seeing mirror images of ourselves.
    a. Equity refers to equality in giving and taking between the partners in a relationship.
    b. Self-disclosure is the sharing of intimate feelings with a partner in a loving relationship.
    d. Although people prefer mirror images of their faces, mirror-image perceptions are often held by parties in conflict. Each party views itself favorably and the other negatively.

25. **d.** is the answer.
    a. According to cognitive dissonance theory, we act to reduce the discomfort we feel when two conflicting thoughts clash.
    b. The two-factor theory is the idea that emotions involve both arousal and cognitive appraisal.
    c. Peripheral route persuasion refers to the influence of unimportant cues on decision making.

26. **d.** is the answer.

27. **d.** is the answer. Each nation sees itself as ethical and peaceful and views the other side as evil and aggressive.

28. **d.** is the answer. Because it provides people with an opportunity to meet, proximity is the most powerful predictor of friendship, even though, once a friendship is established, the other factors mentioned become more important.

29. **a.** is the answer.

30. **c.** is the answer. In this example of the fundamental attribution error, even when given the situational explanation for the woman's behavior, students ignored it and attributed her behavior to her personal traits.

31. **d.** is the answer. Our attitudes are more likely to guide our actions when other influences are minimal, when there's a specific connection between the two, and when we're keenly aware of our beliefs. The presence of other people would more likely be an outside factor that would lessen the likelihood of actions being guided by attitude.

32. **a.** is the answer. Such justifications arise as a way to preserve inequalities. The just-world phenomenon presumes that people get what they deserve. According to this view, someone who has less must deserve less.

33. **b.** is the answer.
    a. & c. Crowding may amplify irritability or altruistic tendencies that are already present. Crowding does not, however, produce these reactions as a general effect.
    d. In fact, just the opposite is true. Crowding often intensifies people's reactions.

34. **b.** is the answer.
    a. Even if they made up a sizable portion of the group, although still a minority, their numbers would not be as important as their consistency.
    c. & d. These aspects of minority influence were not discussed in the text; however, they are not likely to help a minority sway a majority.

35. **a.** is the answer.

36. **a.** is the answer. As Solomon Asch's experiments demonstrated, individuals are more likely to conform when they are being observed by others in the group. The other factors were not discussed in the text and probably would not promote conformity.

37. **d.** is the answer. Group polarization, or the enhancement of a group's prevailing attitudes, promotes groupthink, which leads to the disintegration of critical thinking.
    a. Groupthink is more likely when a leader highly favors an idea, which may make members reluctant to disagree.
    b. A strong minority faction would probably have the opposite effect: It would diminish group harmony while promoting critical thinking.
    c. Consulting experts would discourage groupthink by exposing the group to other opinions.

Matching Items

1. c	7. a	13. j
2. k	8. g	
3. h	9. i	
4. m	10. l	
5. d	11. b	
6. f	12. e	

Application Essay

Your discussion might focus on some of the following topics: conformity, obedience, group polarization, and groupthink.

   As a member of any group with established social norms, individuals will often act in ways that enable them to avoid rejection or gain social approval. Thus, a fraternity or sorority pledge would be likely to conform to the attitudes and norms projected by the group—or be rejected socially. In extreme cases of pledge hazing, acute social pressures may lead to atypical and antisocial individual behaviors—for example, on the part of pledges complying with the demands of senior members of the fraternity or sorority. Over time, meetings and discussions will probably enhance the group's prevailing attitudes (group polarization). This may lead to the unrealistic and irrational decision making that is groupthink. The potentially negative consequences of groupthink depend on the issues being discussed, but may include a variety of socially destructive behaviors.

Summing Up

A person who is the victim of an unjustifiable and usually negative attitude is being subjected to *prejudice,* which is a mixture of usually overgeneralized beliefs called *stereotypes,* negative *emotions* (envy, hostility, or fear), and unjustifiable negative behavior called *discrimination.* Where do these attitudes come from? Several possibilities exist. Social roots include believing that the good are rewarded and the bad are punished, called the *just-world* phenomenon; favoring our own group, called the *ingroup bias;* and thinking of other groups as *outgroups.* Emotional roots include looking for someone to blame when things go wrong, called *scapegoating.* Cognitive roots include simplifying the world by sorting things into *categories,* judging the frequency of events by remembering *vivid* cases, and believing that people get what they deserve, that is, that the world is *just.*

Terms and Concepts to Remember

1. **Social psychology** is the scientific study of how we think about, influence, and relate to one another.

2. The **fundamental attribution error** is our tendency to underestimate the impact of situations and overestimate the impact of personal traits on the behavior of others.

3. **Attitudes** are feelings, often based on our beliefs, that predispose us to respond in particular ways to objects, people, and events.

4. **Peripheral route persuasion** occurs when a person's judgment is influenced by unimportant cues, such as a speaker's attractiveness.

5. **Central route persuasion** occurs when a person is persuaded directly by the evidence provided in an argument.

6. The **foot-in-the-door phenomenon** is the tendency for people who have first agreed to a small request to comply later with a larger request.

7. A **role** is a set of expectations about how people in a specific social position ought to behave.

8. **Cognitive dissonance theory** refers to the theory that we act to reduce the psychological discomfort (dissonance) we experience when two of our thoughts (cognitions) clash. This is often done by changing our attitude rather than our behavior.

Memory aid: *Dissonance* means "lack of harmony." **Cognitive dissonance** occurs when two thoughts, or cognitions, are at variance with one another.

9. **Conformity** is the tendency to adjust our thinking or behavior to coincide with a group standard.

10. **Normative social influence** occurs when a person conforms to gain approval or avoid disapproval.

11. **Informational social influence** occurs when a person accepts other people's opinions about reality.

12. **Social facilitation** is improved performance on simple or well-learned tasks that occurs when other people are present.

13. **Social loafing** is the tendency for individual effort to be diminished when a person is part of a group working toward a common goal.

14. **Deindividuation** refers to the loss of self-restraint and self-awareness that sometimes occurs in group situations that foster arousal and anonymity.

Memory aid: As a prefix, *de-* indicates reversal or undoing. To **deindividuate** is to undo one's individuality.

15. **Group polarization** refers to the strengthening of a group's preexisting attitudes through discussion within the group, which often has the effect of emphasizing the group's differences from other groups.

Memory aid: To *polarize* is to "cause thinking to concentrate about two poles, or contrasting positions."

16. **Groupthink** refers to the unrealistic thought processes and decision making that occur within groups when the desire for group harmony overrides a realistic appraisal of alternatives.

Example: The psychological tendencies of conformity and group polarization foster the development of the "team spirit" mentality known as **groupthink**.

17. **Prejudice** is an unjustifiable and usually negative attitude toward a group and its members.

18. A **stereotype** is a generalized (sometimes accurate but often overgeneralized) belief about a group of people.

19. **Discrimination** is unjustifiable negative behavior toward a group and its members.

20. The **just-world phenomenon** is people's tendency to believe that good is rewarded and evil is punished. The logic is indisputable: "If I am rewarded, I must be good."

21. The **ingroup** refers to the people with whom we share a common identity.

22. The **outgroup** refers to the people and groups perceived as different or apart from our group.

23. The **ingroup bias** is the tendency to favor our own group.

24. The **scapegoat theory** proposes that prejudice provides an outlet for anger by finding someone to blame.

25. The **other-race effect** is the tendency to recall faces of one's own race more accurately than faces of other races; also called the *cross-race effect* or *own-race bias*.

26. **Aggression** is any act intended to harm someone physically or emotionally.

27. The **frustration-aggression principle** states that aggression is triggered when people become angry because their efforts to achieve a goal have been blocked (they are frustrated).

28. A **social script** is a culturally modeled guide for how to act in a particular situation.

29. The **mere exposure effect** refers to the fact that repeated exposure to an unfamiliar stimulus increases our liking of it.

30. **Passionate love** refers to an aroused state of intense positive absorption in another person, especially at the beginning of a love relationship.

31. **Companionate love** refers to a deep, affectionate attachment we feel for those with whom our lives are intertwined.

32. **Equity** refers to the condition in which there is mutual giving and receiving between the partners in a relationship.

33. **Self-disclosure** refers to revealing intimate aspects of ourselves to another.

34. **Altruism** is unselfish concern for the welfare of others.

35. The **bystander effect** is the tendency of a person to be less likely to offer help to someone if there are other people present.

36. The **reciprocity norm** is the expectation that people will help, not hurt, those who have helped them.

37. The **social-responsibility norm** is the expectation that people will help those who depend on them.

38. **Conflict** is a perceived incompatibility of actions, goals, or ideas between individuals or groups.

39. **Mirror-image perceptions** are mutual views of each other often held by people in conflict.

40. A **self-fulfilling prophecy** is a belief that leads to its own fulfillment.

41. **Superordinate goals** are shared goals that override differences among people and require their cooperation.

Personality

12

Chapter Overview

Personality refers to each individual's characteristic pattern of thinking, feeling, and acting. Chapter 12 examines four perspectives on personality. Psychodynamic theories emphasize the unconscious and irrational aspects of personality. Humanistic theories draw attention to the self-concept and to the human potential for growth. Trait theory led to advances in techniques for evaluating and describing personality. The social-cognitive perspective emphasizes the effects of our interactions with the environment. The text first describes and then evaluates the contributions, shortcomings, and historical significance of the psychoanalytic and humanistic perspectives. Next, the text turns to today's more scientific study of personality, focusing on how the trait and social-cognitive perspectives explore and assess traits and the focus of many contemporary researchers on the concept of self.

Chapter Review

First, skim each text section, noting headings and boldface items. Review the section by reading the objectives and summaries provided here, then answer the questions that follow. In some cases, STUDY TIPS explain how best to learn a difficult concept and APPLICATIONS help you to know how well you understand the material. Check your understanding of the material by consulting the answers beginning on page 252. Do not continue with the next section until you understand each answer. If you need to, review or reread the section in the textbook before continuing.

What Is Personality?

Objective 12-1: Define *personality*, and identify the theories that inform our understanding of personality.

Psychologists consider **personality** to be an individual's characteristic pattern of thinking, feeling, and acting. Four categories of personality theories are *psychodynamic* (including Freud's *psychoanalysis*), *humanistic, trait,* and *social-cognitive.*

1. Personality is defined as an individual's characteristic pattern of _____ , _____ , and _____ .

2. The psychoanalytic perspective on personality was proposed by _____ ; this theory inspired today's _____ theories. Another, historically significant perspective was the _____ approach, which focused on people's capacities for _____ and _____ . Today's perspectives include _____ theory, which examines characteristic patterns of behavior, and _____-_____ theory, which explores the interaction between people and their social context.

Psychodynamic Theories

Objective 12-2: Explain how Freud's treatment of psychological disorders led to his study of the unconscious mind.

Psychodynamic theories of personality view human behavior as a dynamic interaction between the conscious and unconscious minds, including their associated motives and conflicts.

In his private practice, Freud found that nervous disorders often made no medical sense. Piecing together his patients' accounts of their lives, he concluded that their disorders had psychological causes. His effort to understand these causes led to his "discovery" of the **unconscious.**

At first, Freud thought hypnosis might unlock the door to the unconscious. However, hypnosis did not do the job, so Freud turned to *free association,* which he believed produced a chain of thoughts in the patient's unconscious. He called his treatment and the underlying theory of personality **psychoanalysis.**

Freud believed the mind is mostly hidden. Below the surface is this large unconscious region, which contains unacceptable passions and thoughts. Freud believed we *repress* these unconscious ideas and feelings.

3. Freud's theory is an example of a _____ theory in that it views human behavior as an interaction between the _____ and _____ minds.

4. Sigmund Freud was a medical doctor who special-ized in _____ disorders.

5. Freud developed his theory in response to his obser-vation that many patients had disorders that did not make _____ sense.

6. At first, Freud tried using _____ to uncover his patients' thoughts, wishes, feelings, and memories. The technique later used by Freud, in which the patient relaxes and says whatever comes to mind, is called _____

_____ .

7. Freud called his theory and associated treatment techniques, whereby the therapist seeks to expose and interpret painful unconscious tensions,

_____ .

8. According to this theory, many of a person's thoughts, wishes, and feelings are hidden in a large _____ region. Many of the memories of this region are blocked, or _____ , from consciousness.

9. Freud believed that nothing was accidental. He saw the unconscious appearing not only in symptoms, but also in _____ habits, _____ , and daily habits, as well as in _____ of the tongue and pen, _____ , and _____ .

Objective 12-3: Describe Freud's view of personality.

Freud believed that personality arises from our efforts to resolve the conflict between our impulses and the social restraints against them. He theorized that the conflict centers on three interacting systems: the *id*, which oper-ates on the *pleasure principle*; the **ego**, which functions on the *reality principle*; and the **superego**, an internalized set of ideals. The superego's demands often oppose the id's, and the ego, as the "executive" part of personality, seeks to reconcile the two. Although the modern iceberg image is useful, it is a simplification and doesn't show the interactive nature of the three systems.

10. Freud believed that human personality arises from a conflict between _____

and _____

.

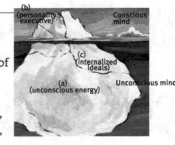

11. According to Freud, personality consists of three interacting structures: the

(a) _____ ,

(b) _____ ,

and the

(c) _____ .

12. The id is a reservoir of psychic energy that is primarily _____ (conscious/unconscious) and operates according to the _____ principle.

13. The ego is the _____ (conscious/unconscious) part of personality that tries to satisfy the id's impulses according to the _____ principle. It tries to sat-isfy the id's desires in realistic ways that will bring long-term _____ rather than _____ or destruction.

14. The personality structure that reflects moral values is the _____ , which Freud believed began emerging at about age

_____ .

Explain why the ego is considered the "executive" of personality.

15. Conflict	The Id's Response	The Ego's Response	The Superego's Response
a. The driver ahead of you is driving 10 miles/hour below the speed limit.			
b. You have pledged a charitable donation but now need money to buy a new sweater.			
c. You've put off doing a term paper and a friend suggests buying one online.			

Objective 12-4: Identify the developmental stages proposed by Freud.

Freud maintained that children pass through a series of *psychosexual stages* during which the id's pleasure-seeking energies focus on distinct pleasure-sensitive areas of the body called *erogenous zones*. During the *oral stage* (0–18 months) pleasure centers on the mouth, and during the *anal stage* (18–36 months) the focus is on bowel/bladder elimination.

During the critical *phallic stage* (3–6 years), pleasure centers on the genitals. Boys experience the *Oedipus complex,* with unconscious sexual desires toward their mother and hatred of their father. They cope with these threatening feelings through *identification* with their father, thereby incorporating many of his values and developing a sense of what psychologists now call *gender identity*. *Latency* stage (6 years to puberty), in which sexuality is dormant, gives way to the *genital stage* (from puberty on) as sexual interests mature.

In Freud's view, conflicts unresolved during any one of the stages may cause trouble in adulthood. At any point, conflict can lock, or *fixate,* the person's pleasure-seeking energies in that stage.

16. According to Freud, personality is formed as the child passes through a series of _____ stages, each of which is focused on a distinct body area called an _____ _____ .

17. The first stage is the _____ stage, which takes place during the first 18 months of life. During this stage, the id's energies are focused on behaviors such as _____ .

18. The second stage is the _____ stage, where energies are focused on bowel and bladder elimination, which lasts from about age _____ months to _____ months.

19. The third stage is the _____ stage, which last roughly from ages _____ to _____ years. During this stage, the id's energies are focused on the _____ . Freud also believed that during this stage boys develop sexual desires for their _____ . Freud referred to these feelings as the _____ _____ . Some psychoanalysts of Freud's era identified for girls a parallel _____ _____ .

20. Freud believed that _____ with the same-sex parent is the basis for what psychologists now call _____ _____ .

Explain how this conflict is resolved through the process of identification.

21. During the next stage, sexual feelings are repressed. This phase is called the _____ stage and lasts until puberty.

22. During the final stage of development, sexual interests _____ ; this is called the _____ stage.

23. According to Freud, it is possible for a person's development to become blocked in any of the stages; in such an instance, the person is said to be

_____ .

APPLICATION:

24. Song Yi works in a smoke-free office. So, she frequently has to leave work and go outside to smoke a cigarette. Freud would probably say that Song Yi is _____ at the _____ stage of development.

Objective 12-5: Describe how Freud thought people defended themselves against anxiety.

Defense mechanisms reduce or redirect anxiety in various ways, but always by unconsciously distorting reality. *Repression,* which underlies the other defense mechanisms, banishes anxiety-arousing thoughts from consciousness; *regression* involves retreat to a more infantile stage of development; and *reaction formation* makes unacceptable impulses look like their opposites. *Projection* attributes our own threatening impulses to others, *rationalization* offers self-justifying explanations for behavior, *displacement* shifts sexual or aggressive impulses to a more acceptable object or person, and *denial* involves refusal to believe or even perceive painful realities.

25. The ego attempts to protect itself against anxiety through the use of _____

_____ . The process underlying each of these mechanisms is

_____ .

26. All defense mechanisms function _____ and _____ .

27. Dealing with anxiety by returning to an earlier stage of development is called _____ .

28. When a person reacts in a manner opposite that of his or her true feelings, _____

_____ is said to have occurred.

29. When a person assigns his or her own feelings to another person, _____ has occurred.

30. When a person offers a false, self-justifying explanation of his or her actions, _____ has occurred.

31. When impulses are directed toward an object other than the one that caused arousal,

_____ has occurred.

32. When a person refuses to believe or even perceive a painful realty, he or she is experiencing

_____ .

APPLICATIONS:

33. According to the psychoanalytic perspective, a child who frequently "slips" and calls her teacher "Mom" probably
    a. has some unresolved conflicts concerning her mother.
    b. is fixated in the oral stage of development.
    c. is ruled by the pleasure principle.
    d. has a superego that overrides her id.

34. Match each defense mechanism in the following list with the proper example of how it could show itself.

Defense Mechanisms

_____ 1. displacement
_____ 2. projection
_____ 3. reaction formation
_____ 4. rationalization
_____ 5. regression
_____ 6. denial

Example

a. nail biting or thumb sucking in an anxiety-producing situation
b. overzealous crusaders against "immoral behaviors" who don't want to admit to their own sexual desires
c. saying you drink "just to be sociable" when in reality you have a drinking problem
d. a parent will not admit that his child could cheat on a test
e. thinking someone hates you when in reality you hate that person
f. a child who is angry at his parents and vents this anger on the family pet, a less threatening target

35. Suzy bought a used, high-mileage automobile because it was all she could afford. Attempting to justify her purchase, she raves to her friends about the car's attractiveness, good acceleration, and stereo. According to Freud, Suzy is using the defense mechanism of

    a. displacement.
    b. reaction formation.
    c. rationalization.
    d. projection.

Objective 12-6: Identify which of Freud's ideas were accepted or rejected by his followers.

Neo-Freudians such as Alfred Adler, Karen Horney, and Carl Jung accepted Freud's basic ideas regarding personality structures, the importance of the unconscious, the shaping of personality in children, and the use of defense mechanisms to ward off anxiety. However, in contrast to Freud, the neo-Freudians generally placed more emphasis on the conscious mind, and they emphasized loftier motives and social interactions over sex and aggression. Modern psychodynamic theorists and clinicians reject the notion that sex is the basis of personality but agree with Freud that much of our mental life is unconscious, that we struggle with inner conflicts, and that childhood shapes our personalities and attachment styles.

36. The theorists who established their own, modified versions of psychoanalytic theory are called

    _____-_____ .

    These theorists typically place _____ (more/less) emphasis on the conscious mind than Freud did and _____ (more/less) emphasis on sex and aggression. Included in this group were Karen _____ , Alfred _____ , and Carl _____ .

Briefly summarize how each of the following theorists departed from Freud.

    a. Adler _____

    _____

    b. Horney _____

    _____

    c. Jung _____

    _____

37. More recently, some of Freud's ideas have been incorporated into _____ theory. Unlike Freud, the theorists who study personality from this perspective do not believe that _____ is the basis of personality. They do agree, however, that much of mental life is _____ , that _____ shapes personality, and that we often struggle with _____ .

Objective 12-7: Describe projective tests and how they are used, and discuss how they are criticized.

Projective tests provide unclear images designed to trigger projection of the test-taker's unconscious thoughts or feelings. In the *Thematic Apperception Test (TAT)*, people view images and then make up stories about them. The *Rorschach inkblot test* seeks to identify people's inner feelings and conflicts by analyzing their interpretations of 10 inkblots. Rorschach has neither much reliability nor great validity.

38. Tests that provide test-takers with unclear images for interpretation are called _____ tests.

39. The test that requires people to make up stories about images, the _____

    _____ _____ ,

    has been used to measure _____ motivation.

40. The most famous projective test is the _____ , in which people are shown a series of _____ . Critics contend that these tests have _____ (little/significant) validity and reliability.

APPLICATION:

41. Teresa is taking a personality test that asks her to describe random patterns of dots. This is a _____ test.

Objective 12-8: Discuss how today's psychologists view Freud's psychoanalysis.

Critics contend that new research has made many of Freud's specific ideas out of date and that his theory offers only after-the-fact explanations. Developmental psychologists question the overriding importance of childhood experiences, the degree of parental influence, the timing of gender-identity formation, the significance of childhood sexuality, and the existence of hidden content in dreams. Many researchers now believe that repression rarely, if ever, occurs. Nevertheless, Freud drew psychology's attention to the unconscious and the irrational.

42. Contrary to Freud's theory, research indicates that human development is _____ (fixed in childhood/lifelong), that children gain their gender identity at a(n) _____ (earlier/later) age, and that the presence of a same-sex parent _____ (is/is not) necessary for the child to become strongly masculine or feminine.

43. Research also disputes Freud's belief that dreams disguise unfulfilled _____ .

44. Criticism of psychoanalysis as a scientific theory centers on the fact that it provides

_____-_____-_____ explanations and does

not offer _____ _____ .

45. Psychoanalytic theory rests on the assumption that the human mind often _____ painful experiences. Many of today's researchers think that this process is much _____ (more common/rarer) than Freud believed. They also believe that when it does occur, it is a reaction to terrible _____ .

State several of Freud's ideas that have endured.

Objective 12-9: Discuss how modern research has developed our understanding of the unconscious.

Although the current view of the unconscious differs from Freud's view, research does confirm the reality of unconscious information processing. Recent research provides some support for his idea of defense mechanisms. For example, his idea of projection is what researchers now call the *false consensus effect*. Freud also focused attention on the importance of human sexuality and the tension between biological impulses and our social well-being. Unquestionably, his cultural impact has been enormous.

46. Today's psychologists agree with Freud that we have limited access to all that goes on in our minds. However, they believe that the unconscious involves the _____ and _____ that automatically influence how we process information, the _____ processing of different aspects of vision and thinking, the _____ we experience instantly, and our _____ memories, for example.

47. An example of the defense mechanism that Freud called _____ is what researchers today call the _____ _____ effect. This refers to our tendency to _____ the extent to which others share our beliefs and behaviors.

48. Another Freudian idea that has received support is that people have unconscious mechanisms that trade unacceptable impulses for their opposite, called _____ _____ .

Humanistic Theories

Objective 12-10: Describe how humanistic psychologists viewed personality, and explain their goal in studying personality.

Humanistic psychologists view personality with a focus on the ways healthy people strive for self-determination and self-realization. According to Maslow, human motivations form a *hierarchy of needs.* At the top are *self-actualization* and *self-transcendence,* the ultimate psychological needs that arise after basic physical and psychological needs are met and self-esteem is achieved. Maslow focused on healthy, creative people.

Carl Rogers agreed with Maslow that people have self-actualizing tendencies. Rogers' *person-centered perspective* held that people are basically good. To nurture growth in others, Rogers advised being *genuine, empathic,* and *accepting* (offering **unconditional positive regard**). In such a climate, people can develop a deeper self-awareness and a more realistic and positive *self-concept.*

49. Humanistic psychology began as a reaction to Freud's _____ views and the mechanical aspects of Watson's and Skinner's _____ .

50. Two influential theories of humanistic psychology were proposed by _____ and _____ . These theorists focused on the ways people strive for _____ and _____ .

51. According to Maslow, humans are motivated by needs that are organized into a _____ _____ . Maslow refers to the process of fulfilling our potential as _____ and the striving for meaning beyond the self as _____ . Many people who fulfill their potential have been moved by _____ _____ that were beyond normal consciousness.

List some of the characteristics Maslow associated with those who fulfilled their potential.

52. According to Rogers, a person nurtures growth in a relationship by being _____ , _____ , and _____ . People who are accepting of others offer them _____ _____ _____ . By so doing, they free others to be _____ without fearing what others will think.

53. For both Maslow and Rogers, an important feature of personality is how an individual perceives himself or herself; this is the person's _____ . If it is negative—if in our own eyes we fall far short of our _____ _____ —we feel dissatisfied and unhappy.

APPLICATIONS:

54. Professor Choi believes that people are basically good and are endowed with self-actualizing tendencies. Evidently, Professor Choi is a proponent of _____ hierarchy of needs.

55. Javier's grandfather, who has lived a rich and productive life, is a spontaneous, loving, and self-accepting person. Maslow might say that he is a _____ person.

56. The school psychologist works within the humanistic perspective. She believes that having a positive _____ is necessary before students can achieve their potential.

57. Wanda wishes to instill in her children an accepting attitude toward other people. Maslow and Rogers would probably recommend that she
  a. teach her children first to accept themselves.
  b. use discipline sparingly.
  c. be affectionate with her children only when they behave as she wishes.
  d. do all of these things.

Objective 12-11: Explain how humanistic psychologists assessed a person's sense of self.

Humanistic psychologists sometimes assessed personality through questionnaires on which people reported their self-concept. One questionnaire asked people to compare their *actual* self with their *ideal* self. Other humanistic psychologists maintained that we can only understand each person's unique experience through interviews and intimate conversations.

58. Humanistic psychologists sometimes use _____ to assess personality, that is, to evaluate the _____ .

59. One questionnaire, inspired by Carl Rogers, asked people to describe themselves both as they would _____ like to be and as they _____ are. When these

two selves are alike, the self-concept is _____ .

60. Some humanistic psychologists feel that questionnaires are _____ and prefer to use _____ to assess personality.

Objective 12-12: Describe how humanistic theories have influenced psychology, and discuss the criticisms they have faced.

Maslow's and Rogers' ideas have influenced counseling, education, child raising, and management. They also laid the groundwork for today's scientific positive psychology.

Critics complain that the humanistic perspective's concepts are vague and based on the theorists' personal opinions. For example, the description of self-actualizing people seems more a reflection of Maslow's personal values than a scientific description. Critics also argue that the attitudes promoted by humanistic psychology may promote self-indulgence, selfishness, and a lack of moral restraint. A final complaint is that humanistic psychology fails to appreciate the reality of our human capacity for evil.

61. Humanistic psychologists have influenced such diverse areas as _____ , _____ , _____ , and _____ . They have also had a major impact on today's scientific _____ psychology.

62. Critics contend that the concepts of humanistic theory are _____ and based on the theorists' personal _____ .

63. Another criticism of humanistic theory is that it encourages attitudes that can lead to _____ _____ .

64. A third criticism of humanistic theory is that it fails to appreciate the human capacity for _____ .

Trait Theories

Objective 12-13: Explain how psychologists use traits to describe personality.

Trait theorists attempt to describe personality in terms of stable and enduring behavior patterns, or tendencies to feel and act in a certain way.

One strategy that psychologists have used to identify a person's personality has been to identify *factors,* clusters of behavior tendencies that occur together. For example, using this approach Hans and Sybil Eysenck reduced

normal variations to two basic dimensions, extraversion–introversion and emotional stability–instability.

Research has shown that our genes, by influencing autonomic nervous system arousal, also affect our temperament and behavioral style, which help define our personality. Brain activity scans suggest that extraverts and introverts differ in their level of arousal.

65. Gordon Allport developed trait theory, which defines personality in terms of people's characteristic pattern of _____ or a tendency to _____ and _____ in a certain way. Unlike Freud, he was less interested in _____ individual traits than in _____ them.

66. Clusters of behavior tendencies that occur together are called _____ .

67. The Eysencks think that two basic factors are sufficient; these are _____– _____ and emotional _____–_____ .

68. Research increasingly reveals that our _____ play an important role in defining our _____ and _____ style. Some researchers believe that extraverts seek stimulation because their level of _____ _____ is relatively low. Also, an area of the brain's _____ lobe is less active in _____ (extraverts/introverts) than in _____ (extraverts/introverts).

69. Personality differences among dogs, birds, and other animals _____ (are/are not) stable.

APPLICATIONS:

70. Dr. Gonzalez observes that Lili is outgoing and likes excitement and practical jokes. He believes that this cluster of behaviors, or _____ , reflects what the Eysencks referred to as _____ .

71. Because you have a relatively low level of brain arousal, a trait theorist would suggest that you are an _____ who would naturally seek _____ .

72. Nadine has a relatively high level of brain arousal. Trait theorists would probably predict that she is an _____ .

Objective 12-14. Identify some common misunderstandings about introversion.

Superheroes and attractive, successful people are presumed to be extraverts. Being introverted seems to imply that we don't have the "right stuff." However, introverted leaders outperform extraverted leaders in some contexts, such as encouraging employees to voice their opinions.

Explain why Western cultures prize extraversion over introversion.

73. People who are quiet because they fear others will evaluate them negatively are _____ , not introverted.

74. Some researchers believe that introverts seek low levels of stimulation because they are _____ .

Objective 12-15. Describe personality inventories.

Psychologists assess several traits at once by administering *personality inventories* on which people respond to items designed to measure a wide range of feelings and behaviors. Although the **Minnesota Multiphasic Personality Inventory (MMPI)** was designed to assess emotional disorders, it also assesses people's personality traits. The objective scoring of the test does not guarantee its validity. For example, those taking the MMPI for employment screening may give socially desirable responses that create a good impression.

75. Questionnaires that categorize personality traits are called _____ _____ .

76. The most widely used of all such personality tests is the _____ _____ _____ _____ . Although it was originally developed to identify emotional _____ , it also assesses people's _____ _____ .

APPLICATION:

77. A psychologist at the campus mental health center administered a personality test to diagnose an emotionally troubled student. Which test did the psychologist most likely administer?
    a. the MMPI
    b. the Big Five Index
    c. the Rorschach
    d. the Eysenck Personality Questionnaire

Objective 12-16: Identify the traits that seem to provide the most useful information about personality variation.

Researchers have isolated five distinct personality dimensions, called the Big Five: conscientiousness, agreeableness, neuroticism (emotional stability versus instability), openness, and extraversion. These traits appear to be stable in adulthood, are about 50 percent heritable, correlate with different brain regions, and are relatively common to all cultures. Locating an individual on these five dimensions provides a comprehensive picture of personality.

78. Researchers have arrived at a cluster of five factors that seem to describe the major features of personality. List the Big Five, which cover a range of traits between two extremes. (Hint: Remember that the first letters of these traits spell CANOE.)

a. _____

b. _____

c. _____

d. _____

e. _____

79. By adulthood, the Big Five have become fairly stable, although _____ ,

_____ , _____ ,

and _____ continue to increase over the life span, and _____ decreases.

80. Our genes are credited for roughly _____ percent or more for each dimension. Moreover, these traits _____ (do/do not) describe personality in various cultures reasonably well, and _____ (do/do not) predict our actual behavior.

APPLICATION:

81. For his class presentation, Bruce plans to discuss the Big Five personality factors used by people throughout the world to describe others or themselves. Which of the following is not a factor that Bruce will discuss?

a. extraversion   c. independence
b. openness   d. conscientiousness

Objective 12-17: Discuss whether research supports the consistency of personality traits over time and across situations.

Although people's traits seem to persist over time, critics of the trait perspective note that human behavior varies widely from situation to situation. Defenders of the trait perspective note that, despite these variations, a person's average behavior across different situations is fairly consistent.

82. Human behavior is influenced both by our inner _____ and by the external _____ . The issue of which of these is the more important influence on personality is called the _____-_____ controversy.

83. To be considered a personality trait, a characteristic must persist over _____ and across _____ . Research studies reveal that personality trait scores _____ (correlate/do not correlate) with scores obtained seven years later; the correlation was strongest for comparisons done in _____ (childhood/adolescence/adulthood). The consistency of specific behaviors from one situation to the next is _____ (predictably consistent/not predictably consistent).

84. An individual's score on a personality test _____ (is/is not) very predictive of his or her behavior in any given situation.

Explain the apparent contradiction between behavior in specific situations and average behavior patterns.

85. People's expressive styles, which include their _____ , manner of _____ , and _____ , are quite _____ (consistent/inconsistent), which_____ (does/does not) reveal distinct personality traits.

APPLICATION:

86. Dayna is not very consistent in showing up for class and turning in assignments when they are due. Research studies would suggest that Dayna's inconsistent behavior
a. indicates that she is troubled and may need professional counseling.
b. is a sign of emotional instability.
c. is not necessarily unusual.
d. probably reflects a temporary problem in another area of her life.

Social-Cognitive Theories

Objective 12-18: Describe how social-cognitive theorists view personality development, and explain how they explore behavior.

The *social-cognitive perspective* views behavior as influenced by the interaction between persons (and their thinking) and their social context. *Reciprocal determinism* is Albert Bandura's term for the interacting influences of behavior, internal personal factors, and environment. Our behavior in any social situation is influenced by our past learning, our *self-efficacy,* and our thinking about the situation. Differences in behavior occur because different people choose different environments, people's personalities shape how they interpret and react to events, and their personalities help create situations to which they react.

87. Personality is shaped by the mutual influence of our _____ , internal _____ factors, and _____ influences. This is the principle of _____ _____ , a concept described by _____ .

88. Social-cognitive theories of personality view behavior as influenced by the interaction between persons (and their _____) and their _____ _____ .

89. To every situation we bring our past _____ ; our sense of competence on a task, or our _____ ; and our way of thinking about that situation.

Describe three different ways in which the environment and personality interact.

90. In addition to the interaction of internal personal factors with the environment, we also experience _____ - _____ interaction.

91. At every moment, our behavior is influenced by our biology, our social and cultural experiences, and our thought processes and traits, according to the _____ approach.

92. It follows from the social-cognitive perspective that the best means of predicting people's future behavior is their _____ _____ .

APPLICATIONS:

93. Ramona identifies with her politically conservative parents. At college, most of her friends also held conservative views. After four years in this environment Ramona's politics have become even more conservative. According to the social-cognitive perspective, in this case

Ramona's parents (_____ factor) helped shape her political beliefs (_____ factor), which influenced her choice of a college (also a _____ factor) and created an _____ that fostered her already formed political attitudes.

94. In high school, Chella and Nari were best friends. They thought they were a lot alike, as did everyone else who knew them. After high school, they went on to very different colleges, careers, and life courses. Now, at their twenty-fifth reunion, they are shocked at how little they have in common. Bandura would suggest that their differences reflect the interactive effects of environment, personality, and behavior, which he refers to as _____ _____ .

Objective 12-19: Discuss the criticisms social-cognitive theorists have faced.

95. The major criticism of the social-cognitive perspective is that it fails to appreciate a person's _____ _____ .

Exploring the Self

Objective 12-20: Explain why psychology has generated so much research on the self, and discuss the importance of self-esteem to our well-being.

The *self* is organizer of our thoughts, feelings, and actions, and as such is the center of personality. The concept of *possible selves* includes people's visions of the self they dream of becoming and the person they fear becoming. Such possible selves motivate us by laying out specific goals and calling forth the energy to work toward them. Carried too far, a self-focused perspective can lead to a *spotlight effect,* which is our tendency to overestimate others' noticing and evaluating our appearance, performance, and blunders.

People who have high *self-esteem* have fewer sleepless nights, are less conforming, are more persistent at difficult tasks, are less shy, anxious, and lonely, are more successful, and are just plain happier. Some research shows a destructive effect of low self-esteem. For example, temporarily deflating people's self-esteem can lead them to insult others and express racial prejudice. But inflated self-esteem can also cause problems. *Narcissistic* men and women forgive others less, take a game-playing approach to their romantic relationships, and engage in sexually forceful behavior.

96. One of Western psychology's most vigorously researched topics today is the organizer of our thoughts, feelings, and actions—the center of our personality—that is, the _____ .

97. The concept of an individual's _____ _____ emphasizes how our specific goals direct our energy effectively and efficiently.

98. Our tendency to overestimate the extent to which others are noticing and evaluating us is called the _____ _____ .

99. According to self theorists, personality development hinges on our feelings of self-worth, or _____ . People who feel good about themselves are _____ (dependent on/independent of) outside pressures.

100. In a series of experiments, researchers found that people whose self-images were deflated were _____ (more/less) likely to insult other persons or tended to express _____ _____ .

101. Excessive self-love and self-absorption is referred to as _____ . People with this trait are _____ (more/less) forgiving.

APPLICATION:

102. The behavior of many people has been described in terms of a spotlight effect. This means that they
    a. tend to see themselves as being above average in ability.
    b. perceive that their fate is determined by forces not under their personal control.
    c. overestimate the extent to which other people are noticing them.
    d. do all of these things.

Objective 12-21: Identify the evidence that reveals self-serving bias, and explain how defensive and secure self-esteem differ.

Self-serving bias is our readiness to perceive ourselves favorably. This bias is evident in our tendency to accept more responsibility for good deeds than for bad and for successes than for failures. Most people also see themselves as better than average. Self-serving bias underlies conflicts. It is very common, even though people tend to put themselves down. There are four reasons for these put-downs: People are protecting themselves from repeating mistakes, they are prompting positive feedback, they are preparing themselves for possible failure, and they are really criticizing past selves.

Some researchers have separated self-esteem into two categories. *Defensive self-esteem* is fragile and correlates with aggressive and antisocial behaviors. *Secure self-esteem* relies less on other people's evaluations and leads to greater quality of life. Feeling accepted for who we are enables us to lose ourselves in relationships and purposes larger than self.

103. Research has shown that most people tend to have _____ (high/low) self-esteem.

104. The tendency of people to judge themselves favorably is called the _____ bias.

105. Responsibility for success is generally accepted _____ (more/less) readily than responsibility for failure.

106. Most people perceive their own behavior and traits as being _____ (above/below) average.

107. Researchers distinguish _____ self-esteem, which is fragile and makes failures and _____ feel threatening, from _____ self-esteem, which is less focused on _____ evaluations.

APPLICATION:

108. James attributes his failing grade in chemistry to an unfair final exam. His attitude is an example of the _____ _____ .

Objective 12-22: Describe how individualist and collectivist cultures differ in their values and goals.

Individualists give priority to personal goals; they have an *independent* sense of self. They define their identity mostly in terms of personal traits, and they strive for personal control and individual achievement. *Collectivists* give priority to group identity, which provides a sense of belonging and a set of values; they have an *interdependent* sense of self. Preserving group spirit and avoiding social embarrassment are important goals. People in individualist cultures have more personal freedom but at the cost of more loneliness, divorce, homicide, and stress-related disease.

109. Cultures and people who give higher priority to personal goals are called _____ . People in such cultures have more personal _____ , but they also suffer more often from _____ _____ .

110. Cultures and people who give higher priority to group goals are called _____ . They avoid direct _____ , blunt honesty, and uncomfortable topics. They value _____ , not self-importance.

APPLICATION:

111. Chad, who grew up in the United States, is more likely to encourage _____ in his future children than Hidiyaki from Japan, who is more likely to encourage _____ in his future children.
    a. obedience; independence
    b. independence; emotional closeness
    c. emotional closeness; obedience
    d. loyalty; emotional closeness

Progress Test

Multiple-Choice Questions

Circle your answers to the following questions and check them with the answers beginning on page 254. If your answer is incorrect, read the explanation for why it is incorrect and then consult the text.

1. The text defines *personality* as
   a. the set of personal attitudes that characterizes a person.
   b. an individual's characteristic pattern of thinking, feeling, and acting.
   c. a predictable set of responses to environmental situations.
   d. an unpredictable set of responses to environmental situations.

2. Which of the following places the greatest emphasis on the unconscious mind?
   a. the humanistic perspective
   b. the social-cognitive perspective
   c. the trait perspective
   d. the psychoanalytic perspective

3. Which of the following is the correct order of psychosexual stages proposed by Freud?
   a. oral, anal, phallic, latency, genital
   b. anal, oral, phallic, latency, genital
   c. oral, anal, genital, latency, phallic
   d. anal, oral, genital, latency, phallic

4. According to Freud, defense mechanisms are methods of reducing
   a. anger.   c. anxiety.
   b. fear.   d. lust.

5. Neo-Freudians such as Alfred Adler and Karen Horney believed that
   a. Freud placed too great an emphasis on the conscious mind.
   b. Freud placed too great an emphasis on sexual and aggressive instincts.
   c. the years of childhood were more important in the formation of personality than Freud had indicated.
   d. Freud's ideas about the id, ego, and superego as personality structures were incorrect.

6. Collectivist cultures
   a. give priority to the goals of their groups.
   b. value the maintenance of social harmony.
   c. foster social interdependence.
   d. have all of these characteristics.

7. Which two dimensions of personality have the Eysencks emphasized?
   a. extraversion–introversion and emotional stability–instability
   b. ego–superego and extraversion–introversion
   c. ego–superego and emotional stability–instability
   d. identification–fixation and individualism–collectivism

8. With regard to personality, it appears that
   a. there is little consistency of behavior from one situation to the next and little consistency of traits over the life span.
   b. there is little consistency of behavior from one situation to the next but significant consistency of traits over the life span.
   c. there is significant consistency of behavior from one situation to the next but little consistency of traits over the life span.
   d. there is significant consistency of behavior from one situation to the next and significant consistency of traits over the life span.

9. Humanistic theories of personality
   a. emphasize the driving force of unconscious motivations in personality.
   b. emphasize the growth potential of individuals.
   c. emphasize the importance of interaction with the environment in shaping personality.
   d. describe rather than explain personality traits.

10. According to Carl Rogers, three conditions are necessary to promote growth in personality. These are
    a. honesty, sincerity, and empathy.
    b. high self-esteem, honesty, and empathy.
    c. high self-esteem, genuineness, and acceptance.
    d. genuineness, acceptance, and empathy.

11. Psychologists who study the self have found that high self-esteem
    a. is generally maladaptive to the individual because it distorts reality by overinflating self-esteem.
    b. is generally adaptive to the individual because it reduces shyness, anxiety, and loneliness.
    c. tends to prevent the individual from viewing others with compassion and understanding.
    d. tends *not* to characterize people who have experienced unconditional positive regard.

12. Which of Freud's ideas would NOT be accepted by most contemporary psychologists?
    a. Development is essentially fixed in childhood.
    b. Sexuality is a potent drive in humans.
    c. Many of our thoughts and feelings are unconscious.
    d. Reaction formation is one way we defend ourselves against anxiety.

13. Projective tests such as the Rorschach inkblot test have been criticized because
    a. their scoring system is too rigid and leads to unfair labeling.
    b. they were standardized with unrepresentative samples.
    c. they have low reliability and low validity.
    d. it is easy for people to fake answers in order to appear healthy.

14. A major criticism of trait theory is that it
    a. places too great an emphasis on early childhood.
    b. overestimates the consistency of behavior in different situations.

c. underestimates the importance of heredity in personality development.

d. places too great an emphasis on positive traits.

15. For humanistic psychologists, many of our behaviors and perceptions are ultimately shaped by whether our _____ is _____ or _____ .
   a. ego; strong; weak
   b. self-esteem; internal; external
   c. personality structure; introverted; extraverted
   d. self-concept; positive; negative

16. In studying personality, a trait theorist would MOST LIKELY
   a. use a projective test.
   b. observe a person in a variety of situations.
   c. use a personality inventory.
   d. use the method of free association.

17. Id is to ego as _____ is to _____ .
   a. reality principle; pleasure principle
   b. pleasure principle; reality principle
   c. conscious forces; unconscious forces
   d. conscience; "personality executive"

18. Which of the following is the major criticism of the social-cognitive perspective?
   a. It focuses too much on early childhood experiences.
   b. It focuses too little on the inner traits of a person.
   c. It provides descriptions but not explanations.
   d. It lacks appropriate assessment techniques.

19. Research has provided more support for defense mechanisms such as _____ than for defense mechanisms such as _____ .
   a. projection; reaction formation
   b. reaction formation; projection
   c. displacement; regression
   d. displacement; repression

20. Free association is a key technique in
   a. self-actualization.   c. psychoanalysis.
   b. humanistic theory.   d. projective testing.

21. Which personality theories emphasize the interaction between the individual and the environment in shaping personality?
   a. psychoanalytic   c. humanistic
   b. trait   d. social-cognitive

22. According to Freud's theory, personality arises in response to conflicts between
   a. our unacceptable urges and our tendency to become self-actualized.
   b. the process of identification and the ego's defense mechanisms.
   c. our projections and our individual desires.
   d. our biological impulses and the social restraints against them.

23. Compared with people in collectivist societies, people in individualist societies

a. have a stronger sense of family.
b. exhibit greater shyness toward strangers.
c. exhibit greater concern for loyalty and social harmony.
d. have a stronger sense of self.

24. Research has shown that individuals who are made to feel insecure are subsequently
   a. more critical of others.
   b. less critical of others.
   c. more likely to display self-serving bias.
   d. less likely to display self-serving bias.

25. An example of the self-serving bias described in the text is the tendency of people to
   a. see themselves as better than average on nearly any desirable dimension.
   b. accept less responsibility for successes than failures.
   c. be overly critical of other people.
   d. conform to what most people expect of them.

26. The Minnesota Multiphasic Personality Inventory (MMPI) is a
   a. projective personality test.
   b. personality test that covers a wide range of feelings and behaviors.
   c. personality test developed mainly to assess job applicants.
   d. personality test used primarily to assess unconscious beliefs.

27. Trait theory attempts to
   a. show how personality development is lifelong.
   b. describe and classify people in terms of their tendency to behave in certain ways.
   c. determine which traits are most likely to lead to individual self-actualization.
   d. explain how behavior is shaped by the interaction between traits, behavior, and the environment.

28. The spotlight effect refers to
   a. the tendency of people to overestimate the extent to which others are evaluating them.
   b. an individual's feeling of self-worth.
   c. the interaction of personal factors and the environment.
   d. a person's sense of competence on a task.

29. Which of the following statements about self-esteem is NOT correct?
   a. People with low self-esteem tend to be negative about others.
   b. People with high self-esteem are more persistent at difficult tasks.
   c. People with low self-esteem tend to be nonconformists.
   d. People with high self-esteem suffer less from insomnia.

30. The Oedipus complex has its roots in the
   a. anal stage.   c. latency stage.
   b. oral stage.   d. phallic stage.

31. Which of the following is a common criticism of the humanistic perspective?
    a. Its concepts are vague.
    b. The emphasis on the self encourages selfishness in individuals.
    c. The humanistic perspective fails to appreciate the reality of evil in human behavior.
    d. All of these are common criticisms.

32. In studying personality, a social-cognitive theorist would MOST likely make use of
    a. personality inventories.
    b. projective tests.
    c. observing behavior in different situations.
    d. the Rorschach inkblot test.

33. A major difference between the psychoanalytic and trait perspectives is that
    a. trait theory defines personality in terms of behavior; psychoanalytic theory, in terms of its underlying dynamics.
    b. trait theory describes behavior but does not attempt to explain it.
    c. psychoanalytic theory emphasizes the origins of personality in childhood sexuality.
    d. all of these answers give differences.

34. The Big Five personality factors are
    a. emotional stability, openness, introversion, sociability, projection.
    b. neuroticism, extraversion, openness, emotional stability, sensitivity.
    c. neuroticism, displacement, extraversion, impulsiveness, conscientiousness.
    d. neuroticism, extraversion, openness, agreeableness, conscientiousness.

35. Which of the following was NOT mentioned in the text as a criticism of Freud's theory?
    a. The theory rests on few observations.
    b. It offers few testable hypotheses.
    c. There is no evidence of anything like an unconscious.
    d. The theory ignores the fact that human development is lifelong.

36. According to Freud, _____ is the process by which children incorporate their parents' values into their

    _____ .
    a. reaction formation; superegos
    b. reaction formation; egos
    c. identification; superegos
    d. identification; egos

37. Which of the following refers to the tendency to overestimate the extent to which others share our beliefs?
    a. the spotlight effect   c. rationalization
    b. displacement   d. the false consensus effect

38. In promoting personality growth, Rogers emphasized all but
    a. empathy.   c. genuineness.
    b. acceptance.   d. altruism.

39. Research on the Big Five personality factors provides evidence that
    a. some tendencies decrease during adulthood, while others increase.
    b. these traits only describe personality in Western, individualist cultures.
    c. the genetic contribution to individual differences in these traits generally runs about 25 percent or less.
    d. all of these facts are true.

Matching Items 1

Match each definition or description with the appropriate term.

Definitions or Descriptions

_____ 1. redirecting impulses to a less threatening object

_____ 2. test consisting of a series of inkblots

_____ 3. the conscious executive of personality

_____ 4. personality inventory

_____ 5. disguising an impulse by imputing it to another person

_____ 6. switching an unacceptable impulse into its opposite

_____ 7. the unconscious repository of instinctual drives

_____ 8. cluster of personality traits

_____ 9. personality structure that corresponds to a person's conscience

_____ 10. providing self-justifying explanations for an action

Terms

a. id
b. ego
c. superego
d. reaction formation
e. rationalization
f. displacement
g. factor
h. projection
i. Rorschach
j. MMPI

Matching Items 2

Match each term with the appropriate definition or description.

Terms

_____ **1.** projective test
_____ **2.** identification
_____ **3.** reality principle
_____ **4.** psychosexual stages
_____ **5.** pleasure principle
_____ **6.** reciprocal determinism
_____ **7.** personality inventory
_____ **8.** Oedipus complex
_____ **9.** collectivism
_____ **10.** individualism
_____ **11.** self-efficacy
_____ **12.** narcissism

Definitions or Descriptions

a. the id's demand for immediate gratification
b. a boy's sexual desires toward the opposite-sex parent
c. giving priority to one's own goals
d. stages of development proposed by Freud
e. questionnaire used to assess personality traits
f. the two-way interactions of behavior with personal and environmental factors
g. excessive self-love and self-absorption
h. giving priority to group goals
i. personality test that provides unclear images
j. the process by which children incorporate their parents' values into their developing superegos
k. the process by which the ego seeks to gratify impulses of the id in nondestructive ways
l. sense of competence and effectiveness

Application Essay

You are an honest, open, and responsible person. Discuss how these characteristics would be explained according to the major perspectives on personality. (Use the space below to list points you want to make, and organize them. Then write the essay on a separate piece of paper.)

Summing Up

See pages 250 and 251.

Summing Up

1. Klaus is 18 years old and, like all adolescents, is trying to figure out who he is.

He wants to know why he thinks, feels, and acts the way he does; that is, he wants to define his _____ .

Klaus decides to read about the various personality theorists, beginning with

Sigmund _____ , who believed that most of the mind is hidden from view, and is therefore _____ ,

and that

personalty is a product of the _____ between our basic sexual and aggressive impulses, directed by the _____ , and the social restraints derived from the _____ .

After reading about psychoanalytic theory, Klaus decided that his long-standing aggressive behavior toward his younger brother

could have been the result of _____ his anger with his parents for being so strict,

and that this

protects him from the _____ he might feel if he were to express that anger.

Perhaps

the part of his personality called the _____ redirects his anger, and so the hitting of his brother is a _____ mechanism called _____ .

Klaus also thought that perhaps he had _____ his behavior by saying that his brother needed the discipline.

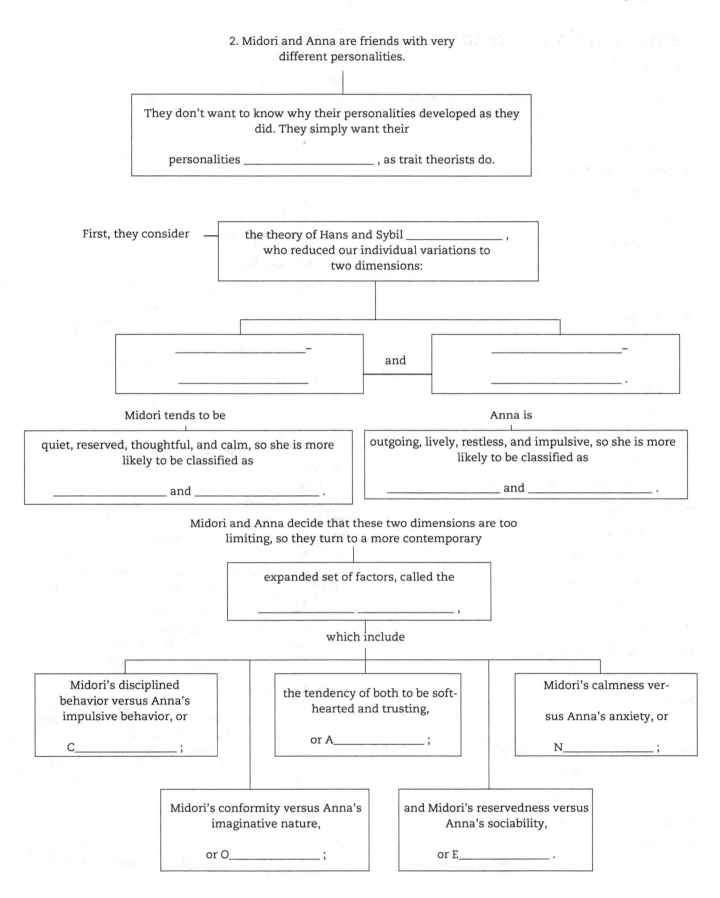

2. Midori and Anna are friends with very different personalities.

They don't want to know why their personalities developed as they did. They simply want their

personalities _____ , as trait theorists do.

First, they consider — the theory of Hans and Sybil _____ , who reduced our individual variations to two dimensions:

_____-
_____

and

_____-
_____ .

Midori tends to be

quiet, reserved, thoughtful, and calm, so she is more likely to be classified as

_____ and _____ .

Anna is

outgoing, lively, restless, and impulsive, so she is more likely to be classified as

_____ and _____ .

Midori and Anna decide that these two dimensions are too limiting, so they turn to a more contemporary

expanded set of factors, called the

_____ _____ ,

which include

Midori's disciplined behavior versus Anna's impulsive behavior, or

C_____ ;

the tendency of both to be soft-hearted and trusting,

or A_____ ;

Midori's calmness ver-

sus Anna's anxiety, or

N_____ ;

Midori's conformity versus Anna's imaginative nature,

or O_____ ;

and Midori's reservedness versus Anna's sociability,

or E_____ .

Terms and Concepts to Remember

Using your own words, on a separate piece of paper write a brief definition or explanation of each of the following terms.

1. personality
2. psychodynamic theories
3. psychoanalysis
4. unconscious
5. free association
6. id
7. ego
8. superego
9. psychosexual stages
10. Oedipus complex
11. identification
12. fixation
13. defense mechanisms
14. repression
15. collective unconscious
16. projective test
17. Thematic Apperception Test (TAT)
18. Rorschach inkblot test
19. hierarchy of needs
20. self-actualization
21. self-transcendence
22. unconditional positive regard
23. self-concept
24. trait
25. factor
26. Minnesota Multiphasic Personality Inventory (MMPI)
27. personality inventory
28. reciprocal determinism
29. social-cognitive perspective
30. self-efficacy
31. self
32. spotlight effect
33. self-esteem
34. narcissism
35. self-serving bias
36. individualism
37. collectivism

Answers

Chapter Review

What Is Personality?

1. thinking; feeling; acting
2. Sigmund Freud; psychodynamic; humanistic; growth; self-fulfillment; trait; social-cognitive

Psychodynamic Theories

3. psychodynamic; conscious; unconscious
4. nervous
5. medical
6. hypnosis; free association
7. psychoanalysis
8. unconscious; repressed
9. work; beliefs; slips; jokes; dreams
10. impulse; restraint
11. id; ego; superego
12. unconscious; pleasure
13. conscious; reality; benefits; pain
14. superego; 4 or 5

The ego is considered the executive of personality because it directs our actions as it reconciles the impulsive demands of the id, the reality of the external world, and the restraining demands of the superego.

15. There are no right or wrong answers. Here's a sample answer to a. Complete b. and c. on your own.

    a. The id's response: "I'm so angry; the driver is extremely thoughtless. So, I think I'll speed up and tailgate."

    The ego's response: "I'll relieve my frustration by mentioning the other driver to my friend in the car, then wait for a safe opportunity to pass."

    The superego's response: "The driver may be going way below the speed limit because he or she is an elderly person or is sick or having car trouble."

16. psychosexual; erogenous zone
17. oral; sucking (also biting, chewing)
18. anal; 18; 36
19. phallic; 3; 6; genitals; mother; Oedipus complex; Electra complex

20. identification; gender identity

Children eventually cope with their feelings for the opposite-sex parent by repressing them and by identifying with the rival (same-sex) parent. Through this process children take on many of their parents' values, thereby strengthening the superego.

21. latency

22. mature; genital

23. fixated

24. fixated; oral. Song Yi was probably orally deprived (weaned too early) as an infant, so she is fixated at the oral stage. Smoking satisfies her id's needs.

25. defense mechanisms; repression

26. indirectly; unconsciously

27. regression

28. reaction formation

29. projection

30. rationalization

31. displacement

32. denial

33. **a.** is the answer. Freud believed that dreams and such slips of the tongue reveal unconscious conflicts.

34. *Matching Items*

  1. f   **4.** c

  2. e   **5.** a

  3. b   **6.** d

35. **c.** is the answer. Suzy is trying to justify her purchase by generating (inaccurate) explanations for her behavior.

  a. Displacement is the redirecting of impulses toward an object other than the one responsible for them.

  b. Reaction formation is the transformation of unacceptable impulses into their opposites.

  d. Projection is the attribution of one's own unacceptable thoughts and feelings to others.

36. neo-Freudians; more; less; Horney; Adler; Jung

  a. Adler emphasized that much of behavior is driven by the need to overcome feelings of inferiority.

  b. Horney questioned the male bias in Freud's theory. She proposed that children's feelings of dependency give rise to feelings of helplessness and anxiety, which trigger adult desires for love and security.

  c. Jung emphasized an inherited collective unconscious.

37. psychodynamic; sex; unconscious; childhood; inner conflicts

38. projective

39. Thematic Apperception Test (TAT); achievement

40. Rorschach; inkblots; little

41. projective

42. lifelong; earlier; is not

43. wishes

44. after-the-fact; testable predictions

45. represses; rarer; trauma

Freud drew attention to the unconscious and the irrational, to human defenses against anxiety, to the importance of human sexuality, and to the tension between our biological impulses and our social well-being. He challenged our self-righteousness, pointed out our self-protective defenses, and reminded us of our potential for evil.

46. self-concept; stereotypes; parallel; emotions; implicit

47. projection; false consensus; overestimate

48. reaction formation

Humanistic Theories

49. negative; behaviorism

50. Abraham Maslow; Carl Rogers; self-determination; self-realization

51. hierarchy of needs; self-actualization; self-transcendence; peak experiences

For Maslow, such people were self-aware, open, self-accepting, spontaneous, loving, caring, and not paralyzed by others' opinions, and they embraced uncertainties and stretched themselves to seek out new experiences.

52. genuine; accepting; empathic; unconditional positive regard; themselves

53. self-concept; ideal self

54. Maslow's. As a humanistic theorist, Maslow believed that people are basically good and that at their best they strive for self-actualization and self-transcendence.

55. self-actualizing. Maslow studied healthy people and found that they had all the characteristics of Javier's grandfather, as well as being self-aware and unconcerned about other people's opinions.

56. self-concept. Humanistic psychologists believed that the self-concept is central to our personality. A positive self-concept allows us to act and perceive the world positively.

57. **a.** is the answer. Humanistic psychologists believe that to love and accept others, we must first love and accept ourselves.

58. questionnaires; self-concept

59. ideally; actually; positive

60. depersonalizing; interviews

61. counseling; education; child raising; management; positive

62. vague; opinions

63. self-indulgence; selfishness, and a lack of moral restraint

64. evil

Trait Theories

65. behaviors; feel; act; explaining; describing

66. factors

67. extraversion–introversion; stability–instability

68. genes; temperament; behavioral; brain arousal; frontal; extraverts; introverts

69. are

70. factors; extraversion. Factors are clusters of behavior tendencies that occur together. Lili's characteristic behaviors indicate she is an extravert.

71. extravert; stimulation. The relatively low level of brain arousal causes extraverts to seek stimulation.

72. introvert. This situation is the reverse of that described in 71.

Extraversion is prized by Western cultures for several reasons. One reason is that superheroes, as well as attractive, successful people are presumed to be extraverts. Another is that people mistakenly equate introversion with shyness. Finally, people hold the false belief that introversion is a barrier to success.

73. shy

74. sensitive

75. personality inventories

76. Minnesota Multiphasic Personality Inventory; disorders; personality traits

77. **a.** is the answer.
    b. There is no such test.
    c. The Rorschach is a projective test that is not considered valid or reliable.
    d. A personality test that measures only the Eysencks' basic personality dimensions would not be helpful in identifying troubled behaviors.

78. **a. C**onscientiousness
    b. Agreeableness
    c. Neuroticism (emotional instability)
    d. Openness
    e. Extraversion

79. conscientiousness; agreeableness; openness; extraversion; neuroticism

80. 40; do; do

81. **c.** is the answer.

82. traits; situation (or environment); person-situation

83. time; situations; correlate; adulthood; not predictably consistent

84. is not

At any given moment a person's behavior is powerfully influenced by the immediate situation, so that it may appear that the person does not have a consistent personality. But averaged over many situations a person's outgoingness, happiness, and carelessness, for instance, are more predictable.

85. animation; speaking; gestures; consistent; does

86. **c.** is the answer.

Social-Cognitive Theories

87. behavior; personal; environmental; reciprocal determinism; Albert Bandura

88. thinking; social context

89. learning; self-efficacy

Different people choose different environments partly on the basis of their traits. Our personality shapes how we interpret and react to events. It also helps create the situations to which we react.

90. gene; environment

91. biopsychosocial

92. behavior in past similar situations

93. situational; internal; situational; environment. This shows the interaction of internal and situational factors, using the social-cognitive view of how personality develops.

94. reciprocal determinism. This shows how the interaction of behavior, internal personal factors, and environment can change behavior.

95. inner traits

Exploring the Self

96. self

97. possible selves

98. spotlight effect

99. self-esteem; independent of

100. more; racial prejudice

101. narcissism; less

102. **c.** is the answer.
     a. This describes self-serving bias.
     b. This describes an external locus of control.

103. high

104. self-serving

105. more

106. above

107. defensive; criticism; secure; external

108. self-serving bias

109. individualists; freedom; loneliness, divorce, homicide, and stress-related disease

110. collectivists; confrontation; humility

111. **b.** is the answer. Westerners value independence and achievement, and so they would want their children to think for themselves, while people from Asian countries such as Japan place greater value on emotional closeness.
     a. Both of these values are more typical of Western than Asian cultures.
     c. & d. These values are more typical of Asian than Western cultures.

Progress Test

Multiple-Choice Questions

1. **b.** is the answer. Personality is defined as patterns of response—of thinking, feeling, and acting—that are relatively consistent across a variety of situations.

2. **d.** is the answer.
   a. & b. Conscious processes are the focus of these perspectives.
   c. The trait perspective focuses on the description of behaviors.

3. **a.** is the answer.

4. **c.** is the answer. According to Freud, defense mechanisms reduce anxiety unconsciously, by disguising our threatening impulses.
a., b., & d. Unlike these specific emotions, anxiety need not be focused. Defense mechanisms help us cope when we are unsettled but are not sure why.

5. **b.** is the answer.
a. According to most neo-Freudians, Freud placed too great an emphasis on the *unconscious* mind.
c. Freud placed great emphasis on early childhood, and the neo-Freudians basically agreed with him.
d. The neo-Freudians accepted Freud's ideas about the basic personality structures.

6. **d.** is the answer.

7. **a.** is the answer.
b., c., & d. Ego, superego, identification, and fixation are Freudian concepts.

8. **b.** is the answer. Studies have shown that people do not act with predictable consistency from one situation to the next. But, over a number of situations, consistent patterns emerge, and this basic consistency of traits persists over the life span.

9. **b.** is the answer.
a. This is true of the psychoanalytic perspective.
c. This is true of the social-cognitive perspective.
d. This is true of the trait perspective.

10. **d.** is the answer.

11. **b.** is the answer. Psychologists who study the self emphasize that for the individual, high self-esteem is generally adaptive (therefore, not a.); that such thinking maintains self-confidence, minimizes depression, and enables us to view others with compassion and understanding (therefore, not c.); and that unconditional positive regard tends to promote self-esteem (therefore, not d.).

12. **a.** is the answer. Developmental research indicates that development is lifelong.
b., c., & d. To varying degrees, research has partially supported these Freudian ideas. The modern view of the unconscious is that routine information processing occurs there.

13. **c.** is the answer. As scoring is largely subjective and the tests have not been very successful in predicting behavior, their reliability and validity have been called into question.
a. This is untrue.
b. Unlike empirically derived personality tests, projective tests are not standardized.
d. Although this may be true, it was not mentioned as a criticism of projective tests.

14. **b.** is the answer. In doing so, it underestimates the influence of the environment.
a. The trait perspective does not emphasize early childhood experiences.
c. This criticism is unlikely because trait theory does not seek to explain personality development.
d. Trait theory does not look on traits as being "positive" or "negative."

15. **d.** is the answer.
a. & c. Personality structure is a concern of the psychoanalytic perspective.
b. Self-esteem is a major focus of research on the self.

16. **c.** is the answer.
a. & d. A psychoanalytic theorist would be most likely to use a projective test or free association.
b. This would most likely be the approach taken by a social-cognitive theorist.

17. **b.** is the answer. In Freud's theory, the id operates according to the pleasure principle; the ego operates according to the reality principle.
c. The id is presumed to be unconscious.
d. The superego is, according to Freud, the equivalent of a conscience; the ego is the "personality executive."

18. **b.** is the answer. The social-cognitive theory has been accused of putting so much emphasis on the situation that inner traits are neglected.
a. Such a criticism has been made of the psychodynamic perspective but is not relevant to the social-cognitive perspective.
c. Such a criticism might be more relevant to the trait perspective; the social-cognitive perspective offers an explanation in the form of reciprocal determinism.
d. There are assessment techniques appropriate to the theory, namely, questionnaires and observations of behavior in situations.

19. **b.** is the answer. Today's researchers call projection the false consensus effect.
c. & d. The evidence supports defenses that defend self-esteem, rather than those that are tied to instinctual energy.

20. **c.** is the answer.

21. **d.** is the answer.
a. This perspective emphasizes unconscious dynamics in personality.
b. This perspective is more concerned with *describing* than *explaining* personality.
c. This perspective emphasizes the self-actualizing tendencies of personality.

22. **d.** is the answer.

23. **d.** is the answer.
a., b., & c. These are characteristic of people in collectivist societies.

24. **a.** is the answer. Feelings of insecurity reduce self-esteem, and those who feel negative about themselves tend to feel negative about others as well.

25. **a.** is the answer.
b., c., & d. Just the opposite is true.

26. **b.** is the answer. The MMPI is an objective test that can be scored by computer.
a. Projective tests present unclear images for people to interpret; the MMPI is a questionnaire.
c. Although sometimes used to assess job applicants, the MMPI was developed to assess emotional disorders.
d. The MMPI does not focus on unconscious beliefs but, rather, measures various aspects of personality.

27. **b.** is the answer. Trait theory attempts to describe behavior and not to develop explanations or applications. The emphasis is more on consistency than on change.

28. **a.** is the answer.
    b. This is self-esteem.
    c. This is reciprocal determinism.
    d. This is self-efficacy.

29. **c.** is the answer. In actuality, people with *high* self-esteem are generally more independent of pressures to conform.

30. **d.** is the answer.

31. **d.** is the answer.

32. **c.** is the answer. In keeping with their emphasis on interactions between people and situations, social-cognitive theorists would most likely make use of observations of behavior in relevant situations.
    a. Personality inventories and the analysis of factors would more likely be used by a trait theorist.
    b. & d. Projective tests, including the Rorschach would more likely be used by a psychologist working within the psychodynamic perspective.

33. **d.** is the answer. Trait theory defines personality in terms of behavior and is therefore interested in describing behavior; psychoanalytic theory defines personality as dynamics underlying behavior and therefore is interested in explaining behavior in terms of these dynamics.

34. **d.** is the answer.

35. **c.** is the answer. Although many researchers think of the unconscious as information processing without awareness rather than as a reservoir of repressed information, they agree with Freud that we do indeed have limited access to all that goes on in our minds.

36. **c.** is the answer.
    a. & b. Reaction formation is the defense mechanism by which people transform unacceptable impulses into their opposites.
    d. It is the superego, rather than the ego, that represents parental values.

37. **d.** is the answer.

38. **d.** is the answer.

39. **a.** is the answer. Conscientiousness, extraversion, agreeableness, and openness tend to increase, while neuroticism tends to decrease.
    b. The Big Five dimensions describe personality in various cultures reasonably well.
    c. Heritability generally runs 50 percent or more for each dimension.

Matching Items 1

1. f		**5.** h		**9.** c
2. i		**6.** d		**10.** e
3. b		**7.** a		
4. j		**8.** g		

Matching Items 2

1. i		**6.** f		**11.** l
2. j		**7.** e		**12.** g
3. k		**8.** b		
4. d		**9.** h		
5. a		**10.** c		

Application Essay

Because you are apparently in good psychological health, according to the psychoanalytic perspective you must have experienced a healthy childhood and successfully passed through Freud's stages of psychosexual development. Freud would also say that your ego is functioning well in balancing the demands of your id with the restraining demands of your superego and reality. Freud might also say that your honest nature reflects a well-developed superego.

According to the humanistic perspective, your open and honest nature indicates that your basic needs have been met and that you are in the process of self-actualization (Maslow). Furthermore, your openness indicates that you have a healthy self-concept and were likely nurtured by genuine, accepting, and empathic caregivers (Rogers). More recently, researchers who emphasize the self would also focus on the importance of a high self-esteem.

Trait theorists would be less concerned with explaining these specific characteristics than with describing them. Some trait theorists attribute certain trait differences to biological factors such as autonomic reactivity and heredity.

According to the social-cognitive perspective, your internal personal factors, behavior, and environmental influences interacted in shaping your personality and behaviors.

Summing Up

1. Klaus is 18 years old and, like all adolescents, is trying to figure out who he is. He wants to know why he thinks, feels, and acts the way he does; that is, he wants to define his *personality*. Klaus decides to read about the various personality theorists, beginning with Sigmund *Freud*, who believed that most of the mind is hidden from view, and is therefore *unconscious*, and that personality is a product of the *conflict* between our basic sexual and aggressive impulses, directed by the *id*, and the social restraints derived from the *superego*. After reading about psychoanalytic theory, Klaus decided that his long-standing aggressive behavior toward his younger brother could have been the result of *repressing* his anger with his parents for being so strict, and that this protects him from the *anxiety* he might feel if he were to express that anger. Perhaps the part of his personality called the *ego* redirects his anger, and so the hitting of his brother is a *defense* mechanism called *displacement*. Klaus also thought that perhaps he had

rationalized his behavior by saying that his brother needed the discipline.

2. Midori and Anna are friends with very different personalities. They don't want to know why their personalities developed as they did. They simply want their personalities *described*, as trait theorists do. First, they consider the theory of Hans and Sybil *Eysenck,* who reduced our individual variations to two dimensions: *extraversion–introversion* and *emotional stability–instability.* Midori tends to be quiet, reserved, thoughtful, and calm, so she is more likely to be classified as *introverted* and *stable.* Anna is outgoing, lively, restless, and impulsive, so she is more likely to be classified as *extraverted* and *unstable.* Midori and Anna decide that these two dimensions are too limiting, so they turn to a more contemporary expanded set of factors, called the *Big Five,* which include Midori's disciplined behavior versus Anna's impulsive behavior, or *Conscientiousness;* the tendency of both to be soft-hearted and trusting, or *Agreeableness;* Midori's calmness versus Anna's anxiety, or *Neuroticism;* Midori's conformity versus Anna's imaginative nature, or *Openness;* and Midori's reservedness versus Anna's sociability, or *Extraversion.*

Terms and Concepts to Remember

1. **Personality** is an individual's characteristic pattern of thinking, feeling, and acting.

2. **Psychodynamic theories** view human behavior as a dynamic interaction between the conscious and unconscious minds. They stress the importance of childhood experiences.

3. **Psychoanalysis** is Freud's theory of personality that attributes thoughts and actions to unconscious motives and conflicts; also, the techniques used in treating psychological disorders by seeking to expose and interpret the tensions within a patient's unconscious.

4. In Freud's theory, the **unconscious** is the repository of mostly unacceptable thoughts, wishes, feelings, and memories. According to contemporary psychologists, it is a level of information processing of which we are unaware.

5. **Free association** is the Freudian technique in which the person is encouraged to say whatever comes to mind as a means of exploring the unconscious.

6. In Freud's theory, the **id** is a reservoir of unconscious psychic energy that strives to satisfy basic sexual and aggressive drives. It operates on the *pleasure principle.*

7. In psychoanalytic theory, the **ego** is the largely conscious, "executive" division of personality that attempts to mediate among the demands of the id, the superego, and reality. It operates on the *reality principle.*

8. In Freud's theory, the **superego** is the division of personality that represents internalized ideals and provides standards for judgment (the conscience) and for future goals.

9. Freud's **psychosexual stages** are developmental periods children pass through during which the id's pleasure-seeking energies are focused on different erogenous zones.

10. According to Freud, boys in the phallic stage develop a collection of feelings, known as the **Oedipus complex,** that center on sexual desires for the mother and jealousy of and hatred for the rival father.

11. In Freud's theory, **identification** is the process by which the child's superego develops and incorporates the parents' values. Freud saw identification as crucial, not only to resolution of the Oedipus complex but also to the development of what is now called *gender identity*.

12. In Freud's theory, **fixation** occurs when development becomes arrested, due to unresolved conflicts, in an earlier psychosexual stage.

13. In Freud's theory, **defense mechanisms** are the ego's methods of protecting itself against anxiety by unconsciously distorting reality.

14. The basis of all defense mechanisms, **repression** banishes from consciousness the thoughts, feelings, and memories that arouse anxiety.

15. The **collective unconscious** is Carl Jung's concept of a shared, inherited group of species' memories.

16. **Projective tests**, such as the TAT and the Rorschach, present unclear images onto which people supposedly *project* their own inner feelings.

17. The **Thematic Apperception Test (TAT)** is a projective test in which people express their inner feelings and interests through the stories they make up about ambiguous scenes.

18. The **Rorschach inkblot test,** a famous projective test, consists of 10 inkblots that people are asked to interpret; it seeks to identify people's inner feelings by analyzing their interpretations of the blots.

19. In Maslow's theory, physiological needs, safety needs, and psychological needs are organized into a **hierarchy of needs** that must be met in that order.

20. In Maslow's theory, **self-actualization** describes the process of fulfilling our potential and becoming spontaneous, loving, creative, and self-accepting. Self-actualization becomes active only after the more basic physical and psychological needs have been met.

21. In Maslow's theory, **self-transcendence** describes the process of striving for identity, meaning, and purpose beyond the self.

22. **Unconditional positive regard** is, according to Rogers, an attitude of total acceptance toward another person.

23. **Self-concept** refers to all our thoughts and feelings about ourselves, in answer to the question, "Who am I?" In the humanistic perspective, the self-concept is a central feature of personality; life happiness is significantly affected by whether the self-concept is positive or negative.

24. A **trait** is a characteristic pattern of behavior or a tendency to feel and act in a certain way, as assessed by self-reports on a personality test.

25. A **factor** is a cluster of traits that occur together.

26. The **Minnesota Multiphasic Personality Inventory (MMPI)** is the most widely researched and clinically used personality inventory.

27. **Personality inventories**, associated with the trait perspective, are questionnaires used to gauge a wide range of feelings and behaviors.

28. According to Albert Bandura, personality is shaped through **reciprocal determinism,** or the interacting influences of behavior, internal personal factors, and environment.

29. According to the **social-cognitive perspective,** behavior is the result of interactions between people (and their thinking) and their social context.

30. **Self-efficacy** is our sense of competence and effectiveness.

31. The **self** refers to your understanding of who you are.

32. The **spotlight effect** is the tendency of people to overestimate the extent to which other people are noticing and evaluating them.

33. **Self-esteem** refers to an individual's sense of high or low self-worth.

34. **Narcissism** is excessive self-love and self-absorption.

35. The **self-serving bias** is the tendency to perceive oneself favorably.

36. **Individualism** is giving priority to our own goals over group goals and defining our identity in terms of personal traits rather than group membership.

37. **Collectivism** is giving priority to the goals of our group and defining our identity accordingly.

Psychological Disorders

13

Chapter Overview

Although there is no clear-cut line between normal and abnormal behavior, we can define a psychological disorder as a syndrome involving a clinically significant disturbance in a person's thoughts, feelings, or behaviors. Chapter 13 discusses types of anxiety disorders; obsessive-compulsive disorder; posttraumatic stress disorder; substance use disorders and addictive behaviors; major depressive disorder and bipolar disorder; schizophrenia; and eating, dissociative, and personality disorders, as classified by the Diagnostic and Statistical Manual of Mental Disorders (DSM-5). Although this classification system follows a medical model, in which disorders are viewed as illnesses, the chapter discusses psychological and social-cultural factors, as well as physiological factors, as advocated by the current biopsychosocial approach.

The chapter concludes with a discussion of whether people with disorders are dangerous.

Chapter Review

First, skim each text section, noting headings and bold-face items. Review the section by reading the objectives and summaries provided here, then answer the questions that follow. In some cases, STUDY TIPS explain how best to learn a difficult concept and APPLICATIONS help you to know how well you understand the material. Check your understanding of the material by consulting the answers beginning on page 279. Do not continue with the next section until you understand each answer. If you need to, review or reread the section in the textbook before continuing.

What Is a Psychological Disorder?

Objective 13-1: Discuss how we draw the line between normal behavior and psychological disorder.

A *psychological disorder* is a syndrome marked by a clinically significant disturbance in a person's thoughts, feelings, or behaviors. Standards of behavior vary by culture, the situation, and even time.

1. A psychological disorder is a _____ (a collection of symptoms) marked by a _____ _____ disturbance in a person's _____ , _____ , or _____ . To be classified as disordered, the symptoms must interfere with everyday life; that is, they must be _____ or _____ . The symptoms are often accompanied by _____ .

2. This definition emphasizes that standards for determining whether behavior is considered disordered are _____ (constant/variable).

3. These standards depend on the situation, the _____ , and time.

4. High-energy children once regarded as normal children running wild are now being diagnosed with _____ . The key symptoms of this disorder are _____ , _____ , and/or _____ .

Objective 13-2: Discuss the controversy over attention-deficit/hyperactivity disorder.

5. ADHD is diagnosed more often in _____ (boys/girls) than in _____ (boys/girls), and mostly in _____ (children and adolescents/adults).

6. Skeptics think ADHD is _____ (over/under)diagnosed. They also maintain that the real problem lies in the _____ in which children are forced to sit for hours in chairs inside. Supporters point to increased _____ and abnormal _____ _____ patterns.

7. ADHD is often accompanied by a _____ _____ or _____ _____ . ADHD _____ (is/is not) genetic.

8. Drugs used to treat ADHD are classified as

_____ . The distress of ADHD

may be helped by _____

_____ .

Objective 13-3: Discuss how the medical model and the biopsychosocial approach influence our understanding of psychological disorders.

Resulting in part from Philippe Pinel's work to improve the treatment of the mentally ill, the *medical model* assumes that psychological disorders are mental illnesses that need to be *diagnosed* on the basis of their *symptoms* and *cured* through *therapy,* which may include *treatment* in a psychiatric *hospital.* Psychologists who reject the "sickness" idea typically note that all behavior arises from the interaction of our biology, our psychology, and our social-cultural environment. As research on *epigenetics* shows and the biopsychosocial approach confirms, disorders are influenced by genes, physiology, inner psychological dynamics, and social and cultural circumstances, that is, that mind and body are inseparable.

9. The view that psychological disorders are sicknesses is the basis of the _____ model. According to this view, psychological disorders are viewed as mental _____ , diagnosed on the basis of _____ , treated and cured through _____ .

10. To call psychological disorders "sicknesses" tilts research heavily toward the influence of _____ . However, behavior also is influenced by our _____ histories and _____ and _____ surroundings. This is a _____ approach to disordered behavior.

11. Psychological disorders such as _____ and _____ have appeared more consistently worldwide; others, such as _____ _____ , are culture-bound. These culture-bound disorders may be responses to the same underlying cause, such as _____ , yet differ in their _____ .

12. As research on _____ shows, DNA and our environment interact. In one environment, a gene will be expressed, but in another it will lie dormant.

STUDY TIP: Think about the implications of the medical model and biopsychosocial approach to psychological disorders. If a behavior pattern that represents a clinically signifi-

cant disturbance in a person's cognition is caused by a brain abnormality, for example, how would you answer the following questions?

1. How should this behavior be diagnosed?
2. How should this behavior be treated in efforts to cure it?
3. How will people view people who are diagnosed with this disorder? For example, are they to blame for their plight?

Now think about a disordered behavior that is caused by a person's environment, thinking patterns, and habits. Would your answers to these questions change for this type of behavior? Why or why not?

APPLICATION:

13. Haya, who suffers from *taijin-kyofusho,* is afraid of direct eye contact with another person. A therapist who believes in the medical model would say that her problem has a _____ basis. A biopsychosocial therapist would want to look into the interaction of her

_____ , _____ ,

and _____ - _____

environment.

Objective 13-4: Describe how and why clinicians classify psychological disorders, and explain why some psychologists criticize the use of diagnostic labels.

DSM-5 is a current authoritative scheme for classifying psychological disorders. This volume is the American Psychiatric Association's *Diagnostic and Statistical Manual of Mental Disorders,* fully revised in 2013. Physicians and mental health workers use the detailed listings in the DSM-5 to guide medical diagnoses and treatment. This new edition has changed some diagnostic labels and added others, some of which are controversial.

Critics point out that labels can create preconceptions that bias our perceptions of people's past and present behavior and unfairly stigmatize these individuals. Labels can also serve as self-fulfilling prophecies. However, diagnostic labels help not only to describe a psychological disorder but also to enable mental health professionals to communicate about their cases and to study the causes and treatments of disorders.

14. The current best scheme for classifying psychological disorders is the American Psychiatric Association manual, commonly known by its abbreviation, _____ . This manual _____ (does/does not) explain the cause of a disorder; rather, it _____ the disorder and estimates how often it occurs.

15. Classification attempts to _____ the disorder's future course and to suggest treatment. It also prompts _____ into the causes.

16. In DSM-5, conditions formerly called "autism" and "Asperger's syndrome" have been combined under the label _____

    _____ _____ .

    New categories in DSM-5 include _____ disorder, _____

    _____ , and

    _____-_____ disorder.

17. Real-world tests, called _____

    _____ , of independent diagnoses made by different clinicians show _____ (high/low/varied) agreement across categories. Clinician agreement on adult _____ _____ disorder and childhood autism spectrum disorder, for example, was near 70 percent. But for

    _____ _____ disorder and generalized anxiety disorder, agreement was closer to 20 percent.

18. One criticism of DSM-5 is that as the number of disorder categories has _____ (increased/decreased), the number of adults who meet the criteria for at least one disorder has _____ (increased/decreased).

19. Studies have shown that labeling has _____ (little/a significant) effect on our interpretation of individuals and their behavior.

Outline the pros and cons of labeling psychological disorders.

Anxiety Disorders, OCD, and PTSD

Objective 13-5: Describe how generalized anxiety disorder, panic disorder, and phobias differ, and explain how the anxiety disorders differ from the ordinary worries and fears we all experience.

Many everyday experiences—public speaking, preparing to play in a big game, looking down from a high ledge—may elicit anxiety. In contrast, *anxiety disorders* are characterized by distressing, persistent anxiety or maladaptive behaviors that reduce anxiety. For example, *social anxiety disorder,* an intense fear of being scrutinized by others, is shyness taken to an extreme.

Generalized anxiety disorder is an anxiety disorder in which a person is continually tense, fearful, and in a state of autonomic nervous system arousal. *Panic disorder* is an anxiety disorder in which the anxiety may at times suddenly escalate into a terrifying panic attack, a minutes-long feeling of intense fear in which a person experiences terror and accompanying chest pain, choking, or other frightening sensations. The constant fear of another attack can lead people with panic disorder to avoid situations where panic might strike, which might lead to a further diagnosis of *agoraphobia*.

A *phobia* is an anxiety disorder marked by a persistent, irrational fear of a specific object, activity, or situation. *Specific phobias* may focus on particular animals, insects, heights, blood, or enclosed spaces.

20. Anxiety disorders are psychological disorders characterized by _____

    _____ .

    For example, when a person has an intense fear of being scrutinized by others, the diagnosis is a

    _____ _____ disorder.

21. When a person is continually tense, fearful, and physiologically aroused for no apparent reason, he or she is diagnosed as suffering from a

    _____ _____ disorder. In Freud's term, the anxiety is

    _____-_____ .

22. Generalized anxiety disorder can lead to physical problems, such as _____

    _____ _____ .

    Also, it is often accompanied by

    _____ .

23. In some instances, anxiety may intensify dramatically and unpredictably and be accompanied by chest pain or choking, for example; people with these symptoms are said to have _____

    _____ . This anxiety may escalate into a minutes-long episode of intense fear, or a

    _____ _____ .

24. People who smoke have at least a doubled risk of a first-time _____ _____ because _____ is a stimulant.

25. People who fear situations in which escape or help might not be possible when panic strikes suffer from

    _____ .

26. When a person has an irrational fear of a specific object, event, or situation, the diagnosis is a _____ . Although in many situations, the person can live with the problem, some

    _____ _____ , such as a fear of thunderstorms, are incapacitating.

Objective 13-6: Describe OCD.

An *obsessive-compulsive disorder (OCD)* is a disorder characterized by unwanted repetitive thoughts (obsessions) and/or actions (compulsions). The repetitive thoughts and behaviors become so haunting and senselessly time-consuming that they interfere with everyday living.

27. When a person cannot control repetitive thoughts and actions, an _____-_____ disorder is diagnosed.

28. Obsessive thoughts are _____ and _____ . Responses to such thoughts are classified as _____ _____ .

Objective 13-7: Describe PTSD.

Posttraumatic stress disorder (PTSD) is characterized by haunting memories, nightmares, social withdrawal, jumpy anxiety, a numb feeling, and/or insomnia that last for four weeks or more after a traumatic experience. Many combat veterans, accident and disaster survivors, and violent and sexual assault victims have experienced the symptoms of PTSD. Most of us, however, display an impressive *survivor resiliency*. About half of adults experience at least one traumatic event in their lifetime but only about 5 to 10 percent of people develop PTSD symptoms. For some, suffering can lead to *posttraumatic growth*.

29. Traumatic stress, such as that associated with witnessing atrocities or combat, can produce

    _____ _____
    disorder. The symptoms of this disorder include ____
    _____
    _____ .
    People who have a sensitive emotion-producing
    _____ _____
    are more vulnerable to this disorder. And, the higher the _____ , the greater the risk for symptoms.

30. After stress, most people display an impressive

    _____ _____ .
    Also, researchers have pointed out that suffering can lead to _____
    _____ . Some psychologists believe that this disorder has been stretched to include normal _____-related bad memories and dreams.

APPLICATIONS:

31. Han has an intense, irrational fear of snakes. He is suffering from a _____ .

32. Isabela is continually tense, jittery, and fearful for no specific reason. She would probably be diagnosed as suffering from _____ _____ disorder.

33. Jason is so preoccupied with staying clean that he showers as many as 10 times a day. Jason would be diagnosed as suffering from _____-_____ disorder.

34. Although she escaped from an ISIL-controlled area of Afghanistan two years ago, Zheina still has haunting memories and nightmares. Because she is also severely depressed, her therapist diagnoses her condition as _____ _____ disorder.

35. Song Yi occasionally experiences unpredictable episodes of intense dread accompanied by chest pains and a sensation of smothering. Because her symptoms have no apparent cause, they would probably be classified as indicative of _____ _____ .

Objective 13-8: Describe how conditioning, cognition, and biology contribute to the feelings and thoughts that mark anxiety disorders, OCD, and PTSD.

The learning perspective views anxiety disorders as a product of fear conditioning, stimulus generalization, reinforcement of fearful behaviors, and observational learning of others' fear. The biological perspective helps explain why we learn some fears more readily and why some individuals are more vulnerable. It emphasizes genetic, physiological, and evolutionary influences.

36. Freud's _____ theory proposed that anxiety disorders are symptoms of submerged mental energy that occurs because impulses that were _____ during childhood leak out in odd ways.

37. Drawing on experiments in which rats are given unpredictable shocks, researchers link general anxiety with _____ conditioning of _____ .

38. Some fears arise from _____ _____ , such as when a person who fears heights after a fall also comes to fear riding in a plane.

39. Avoiding or escaping the object of a phobia and compulsive behaviors reduce anxiety and thereby are _____ . Through _____ learning, someone might also learn fear by seeing others display their own fears.

40. The anxiety response probably _____ (is/is not) genetically influenced. Whether a gene will be expressed is affected by _____ .

41. People with generalized anxiety disorder, panic attacks, phobias, OCD, and PTSD show overarousal in brain areas involved in _____ control and _____ behaviors.

42. Humans probably _____ (are/ are not) biologically prepared to develop certain fears. Compulsive acts typically are exaggerations of behaviors that contributed to our species'

_____ .

STUDY TIP: Phobias are persistent fears of certain objects, activities, or situations. They are irrational because they are much stronger than the actual danger. Also, many *specific phobias* may be unrelated to a direct, negative experience with the feared object. Are there any specific objects, activities, or situations that you find particularly frightening? How do you think you acquired these fears? Can you remember a bad experience? Did you see someone else have a problem? Does your fear ever interfere with your daily life?

APPLICATIONS:

43. Julia's psychologist believes that Julia's fear of heights can be traced to a conditioned fear she developed after falling from a ladder. This explanation reflects a _____ perspective.

44. After being scratched by a wild cat, Joseph is afraid of tame, house cats. This demonstrates that some fears arise from _____ _____ .

45. Before he can study, Rashid must arrange his books, pencils, paper, and other items on his desk so that they are "just so." The campus counselor suggests that Rashid's compulsive behavior may result from higher-than-normal activity in the brain area that controls habitual behavior. This explanation of obsessive-compulsive behavior is most consistent with the _____ perspective.

46. To which of the following is a person most likely to acquire a phobia?
   a. heights
   b. being in public
   c. being dirty
   d. All of these are equally likely to become phobias.

Substance Use Disorders and Addictive Behaviors

Objective 13-9: Describe substance use disorders, and explain the roles that tolerance, withdrawal, and addiction play in these disorders.

Substance use disorders are characterized by continued substance craving and use despite significant life disruption and/or physical risk. Drugs that can lead to abuse, *psychoactive drugs,* are chemicals that change perceptions and moods. Continued use of a psychoactive drug produces *tolerance.* The ever-increasing doses required as a result of tolerance may lead to addiction, a craving for drugs or certain behaviors despite harmful consequences. Discontinuing use may produce the undesirable side effects of *withdrawal.*

A drug's overall effect depends not only on its *biological* effects but also on the *psychology* of the user's expectations, which vary with *cultures.*

Psychoactive drugs operate at the brain's synapses by stimulating, inhibiting, or mimicking the activity of neurotransmitters, the brain's chemical messengers.

47. Drugs that alter moods and perceptions are called _____ drugs.

48. Continued craving and use of a substance despite significant life disruption and/or physical risk describes a _____ _____ disorder.

49. The overall effect of a drug depends on its _____ effects and the user's _____ , which vary from one _____ to another.

50. The diminishing effect that occurs with regular use of the same dose of a drug is called _____ . This may lead to craving of the drug, or _____ . Sometimes, even _____ become compulsive and dysfunctional. Abruptly stopping the drug or behavior can lead to the discomfort and distress of _____ .

51. The three broad categories of drugs discussed in the text include _____ , which tend to slow body functions; _____ , which speed body functions; and _____ , which alter perception. These drugs all work by mimicking, stimulating, or inhibiting the activity of the brain's

_____ .

APPLICATION:

52. Dan has recently begun using an addictive, euphoria-producing drug. Which of the following will probably occur if he repeatedly uses this drug?
   a. As tolerance to the drug develops, Dan will experience increasingly pleasurable "highs."
   b. The dosage needed to produce the desired effect will increase.
   c. After each use, he will become more and more elated.
   d. Tolerance will become less of a problem.

Objective 13-10: Define *depressants,* and describe their effects.

Depressants such as alcohol, the barbiturates, and the opiates act by calming neural activity and slowing body functions. Each offers its own pleasures, but at the cost of impaired memory and self-awareness or other physical consequences. Alcohol is a *disinhibitor* and thus increases the likelihood that we will act on both helpful and harmful impulses. It also impairs judgment, lowers inhibitions, and disrupts memory processes by suppressing REM sleep. In those with *alcohol use disorder,* prolonged and excessive drinking can shrink the brain. Research indicates that when people believe that alcohol affects social behavior in specific ways, and believe that they have been drinking alcohol, they will behave accordingly.

The **barbiturates,** or tranquilizers, may be prescribed to induce sleep or reduce anxiety. They can impair memory and judgment.

When the brain is repeatedly flooded with artificial **opiates,** it stops producing its own opiates, the *endorphins*.

53. Depressants _____ neural activity and _____ body function. Alcohol, which acts as a _____ , slows brain activity that controls _____ and _____ .

54. Cognitively, alcohol disrupts the processing of recent experiences into _____-_____ memory in part because alcohol suppresses _____ _____ . Prolonged and excessive drinking may cause the brain to actually _____ . Binge drinking contributes to the death of _____ _____ and impairs the growth of _____ connections.

55. Low doses relax the drinker by slowing _____ nervous system activity. With larger doses, speech slurs, _____ slow, and skilled performance declines.

Describe how a person's expectations can influence the behavioral effects of alcohol.

56. Tolerance, withdrawal, and a drive to continue problematic use are symptoms of _____ _____ disorder. Girls and young women are especially vulnerable because they have less of a stomach _____ that digest alcohol.

57. Tranquilizers, which are also known as _____ , have effects similar to those of alcohol. They are sometimes prescribed to induce sleep or reduce _____ .

58. Opium, heroin, and the medically prescribed pain-

relief narcotics, such as codeine, morphine, and _____ all _____ (excite/depress) neural functioning. Together, these drugs are called the _____ . When they are present, the brain eventually stops producing _____ .

APPLICATION:

59. Roberto is moderately intoxicated by alcohol. Which of the following changes in his behavior is likely to occur?
    a. If angered, he is more likely to become aggressive than when he is sober.
    b. He will be less self-conscious about his behavior.
    c. If sexually aroused, he will be less inhibited about engaging in sexual activity.
    d. All of these changes are likely.

Objective 13-11: Define *stimulants*, and describe their effects.

Stimulants, such as caffeine, **nicotine, cocaine,** the **amphetamines,** and the even more powerful Ecstasy, and **methamphetamine,** excite neural activity and speed up body functions. As with nearly all psychoactive drugs, they act at the synapses by influencing the brain's neurotransmitters. Nicotine triggers the release of epinephrine and norepinephrine, which in turn diminish appetite and boost alertness and mental efficiency. Regular users become addicted. Cocaine produces a euphoric rush that depletes the brain's supply of the neurotransmitters dopamine, serotonin, and norepinephrine. A crash of agitated depression follows as the drug's effects wear off. Its effects depend on dosage and the user's personality and expectations. Methamphetamine is highly addictive; over time, it appears to reduce the brain's normal output of dopamine. **Ecstasy (MDMA)** is both a stimulant and a mild hallucinogen. By releasing serotonin and blocking its reuptake, it produces euphoria and feelings of intimacy. Its repeated use may suppress the immune system, destroy serotonin-producing neurons, and permanently damage mood and memory.

60. Types of stimulants include _____ _____ _____ . Stimulants, which _____ (excite/depress) neural activity and _____ (speed up/slow down) body functions, _____ (can be/cannot be) addictive.

61. Cigarette smokers _____ (do/do not) become addicted to the drug _____ . This drug quickly stimulates the _____ system to release _____ and _____ , two neurotransmitters that diminish _____ and boost _____ and _____ . Nicotine also stimulates the release of _____ and _____ , neurotransmitters that calm

_____ and reduce sensitivity to

_____ .

62. Cocaine enters the bloodstream quickly, producing a rush of _____ until the brain's supply of the neurotransmitters

_____ , _____ , and

_____ are depleted. Cocaine use may heighten reactions and may also lead to

_____ _____ , suspiciousness, convulsions, cardiac arrest, or

_____ failure. Its psychological effects depend on the _____ and form consumed, as well as the situation and the user's _____ and _____ .

63. _____ are the parent drug for the powerfully addictive stimulant

_____ , which triggers the release of the neurotransmitter _____ . This neurotransmitter stimulates brain cells that enhance _____ and _____ .

64. The drug _____ , or MDMA, is both a _____ and a mild

_____ . About a half-hour after taking it, users experience high _____ and _____ elevation. This drug triggers the release of the neurotransmitter

_____ . It also releases stored _____ and blocks its reuptake, thus interfering with its regulation of body _____ (including sleep), our disease-fighting _____

_____ , and our memory and other _____ functions.

APPLICATION:

65. I am a synthetic stimulant and mild hallucinogen that produces euphoria and social intimacy by triggering the release of dopamine and serotonin. What am I?

_____

Objective 13-12: Define *hallucinogens,* and describe their effects.

Hallucinogens distort perceptions and evoke sensory images in the absence of sensory input. People who have had a ***near-death experience*** have reported sensations that resemble the hallucinations caused by these drugs, loss of oxygen, or extreme sensory deprivation. Like Ecstasy, *LSD* interfers with the serotonin neurotransmitter system. An LSD "trip" may include hallucinations and emotions ranging from euphoria to panic. Marijuana's main active ingredient, *THC,* produces a variety of effects, including disinhibition, a euphoric high, feelings of relaxation, relief from pain, and intense sensitivity to

colors, sounds, tastes, and smells. It may also increase anxiety or depression, impair motor coordination, perceptual skills, and reaction time, and disrupt memory formation. Because THC lingers in the body for a month or more, regular users may achieve a high with smaller amounts of the drug than do occasional users.

66. Hallucinogens are also referred to as

_____ . The best-known synthetic hallucinogens are _____ and LSD.

67. The _____-_____ experiences reported by some people who survive a brush with death are similar to those that result from _____ deprivation or other insults to the brain.

68. LSD works by interfering with the _____ neurotransmitter system. An LSD "trip" may involve emotions ranging from _____ to detachment to _____ , depending in part on the person's current _____ and _____ .

69. The active ingredient in marijuana is abbreviated

_____ . This drug lingers in the body _____ (about as long as/much longer than) alcohol, which means regular users may experience a _____ (more/less) abrupt withdrawal.

Describe some of the physical and psychological effects of marijuana.

APPLICATIONS:

70. Lyndall was in a car accident that required critical surgery to repair her damaged internal organs. During surgery, she had a sense of being outside her body, floating above the operating room. These _____-

_____ experiences are similar to the hallucinations from psychedelic drug use.

71. Which of the following is true of marijuana?
   a. The by-products of marijuana are cleared from the body more slowly than are the by-products of alcohol.
   b. Regular users may need a larger dose of the drug to achieve a high than occasional users would need to get the same effect.
   c. Marijuana is as addictive as nicotine or cocaine.
   d. Even small doses of marijuana hasten the loss of brain cells.

Objective 13-13: Discuss the biological, psychological, and social-cultural factors that help explain why some people abuse mind-altering drugs.

Substance use by North American youth increased during the 1970s. Then, with increased drug education, substance use declined sharply. After the early 1990s, drugs have again been glamorized in some music and films. Since then, drug use has been holding fairly steady. Some people are biologically vulnerable to particular drugs. For example, researchers have identified genes that are more common among people predisposed to alcohol use disorder. These genes may produce deficiencies in the brain's natural dopamine reward system. One psychological factor that contributes to drug use is the feeling that one's life is meaningless and directionless. Studies reveal that heavy drug users often have experienced significant stress or failure and are depressed. Substance use can also have social roots, evident in differing rates of drug use across cultural and ethnic groups. Substance addiction rates are very low among the Amish, Mennonites, Mormons, and Orthodox Jews. Peer pressure may lead people, especially teen-agers, to experiment with—and become dependent on—drugs. Possible avenues for treatment and prevention involve education, boosting people's self-esteem and purpose in life, and inoculation against peer pressure.

72. Having an identical twin with alcohol use disorder _____ (does/does not) put one at increased risk for alcohol problems. Genes that are more common among people predisposed to alcohol use disorder may cause deficiencies in the brain's _____ _____ system. A study of adopted people found that environment _____ (does/does not) have an influence.

Identify some of the psychological and social-cultural roots of substance use disorder.

73. Rates of substance use _____ (vary/are about the same) across _____ and _____ groups.

74. Among African-American teens, rates of drinking, smoking, and cocaine use are _____ (higher/lower) than among other U.S. teens.

75. State three possible channels of influence for drug prevention and treatment programs.
    a. _____
    b. _____
    c. _____

STUDY TIP: This chapter discusses three major categories of psychoactive drugs, drugs that when abused may lead to clinically significant impairment or distress. Information about their psychological effects and their actions on the nervous system is best organized in the form of a chart. To help you review this material, complete the missing information in the chart below. To get you started, the first drug category has already been filled in. In combination with text Table 13.5, you should have a useful summary of substance use disorders.

76. Psychoactive Drug Category	Specific Drugs in This Category	Psychological Effects of These Drugs	How These Drugs Affect the Nervous System
Depressants	alcohol, barbiturates, opiates	disrupt judgment and inhibition, induce sleep, reduce anxiety	decrease neural activity, slow body functions
Stimulants			
Hallucinogens			

Major Depressive Disorder and Bipolar Disorder

Objective 13-14: Explain how major depressive disorder and bipolar disorder differ.

In *major depressive disorder,* a person experiences two or more weeks of at least five signs of depression, minimally including depressed mood or reduced interest or pleasure. A milder form of depression is *persistent depressive disorder.* In *bipolar disorder,* a person alternates between the hopelessness and lethargy of depression and overexcited *manic* episodes (euphoric, hyperactive, wildly optimistic states). Major depressive disorder is much more common than is bipolar disorder.

77. The experience of prolonged depression with no discernible cause is called _____ _____ disorder. When a person's mood alternates between depression and the hyperactive state of _____ , a _____ disorder is diagnosed.

78. Although _____ are more common, _____ is the number one reason that people seek mental health services in the United States. Depression trails only low back pain as the leading cause of disability.

79. According to the DSM-5, the minimal symptoms of major depressive disorder are _____ _____ or reduced _____ . Other possible symptoms of major depressive disorder include _____ _____ _____ .

80. Major depressive disorder occurs when its signs last _____ _____ or more with no apparent cause. A mildly depressed mood more often than not for at least two years is called _____ _____ _____ , or _____ .

81. Mania is characterized by _____ _____ .

82. Bipolar disorder is less common among creative professionals who rely on _____ and _____ than among those who rely on _____ expression and vivid _____ .

APPLICATIONS:

83. As a child, Monica was criticized severely by her mother for not living up to her expectations. This criticism was always followed by a beating with a whip. As an adult, Monica is generally introverted and extremely shy. Sometimes, however, she acts more like a young child, throwing tantrums if she doesn't get her way. At other times, she is a flirting, happy-go-lucky young lady. Most likely, Monica is suffering from _____ _____ .

84. For the past six months, Haeji has complained of feeling isolated from others, dissatisfied with life, and discouraged about the future. Haeji could be diagnosed as suffering from _____ _____ _____ .

85. On Monday, Delon felt optimistic, energetic, and on top of the world. On Tuesday, he felt hopeless and lethargic, and thought that the future looked very grim. Delon would most likely be diagnosed as having _____ _____ .

Objective 13-15: Discuss how the biological and social-cognitive perspectives can help us understand major depressive disorder and bipolar disorder.

Researchers have suggested that any theory of depression must explain the many behavioral and cognitive changes that accompany the disorder, its widespread occurrence, women's greater vulnerability to depression, the tendency for most major depressive episodes to self-terminate, the link between stressful events and the onset of depression, and the disorder's increasing rate and earlier age of onset.

The biological perspective emphasizes the importance of genetic and biochemical influences. Depressive disorders run in families. Certain neurotransmitters, including norepinephrine and serotonin, seem to be scarce in depression. Finally, the brain's left frontal lobe, which is active during positive emotions, is less active during depression.

The *social-cognitive perspective* suggests that self-defeating beliefs, arising in part from *learned helplessness,* and a negative explanatory style feed depression. Depressed people explain bad events in terms that are *global, stable,* and *internal.* This perspective sees the disorder as a vicious cycle in which (1) negative, stressful events are interpreted though (2) a brooding, pessimistic explanatory style, creating (3) a hopeless, depressed state that (4) hampers the way a person thinks and acts. This, in turn, fuels (1) more negative experiences.

86. Depression is accompanied by many changes in _____ and _____ .

87. Depression is _____ .

88. Compared with men, women are _____ (more/less) vulnerable to major depression. In general, women are most vulnerable to disorders involving _____ states, such as _____ .

89. Men's disorders tend to be more _____ and include _____ _____ .

90. Depressed persons usually _____ (can/cannot) recover without therapy.

91. It often _____ (is/is not) the case that a depressive episode has been triggered by a stressful event. An individual's risk of depression also increases following, for example, _____ .

92. With each new generation, the rate of depression is _____ (increasing/decreasing) and the disorder is striking _____ (earlier/later). In North America today, young adults are _____ times (how many?) more likely than their grandparents to suffer depression.

93. Major depressive disorder and bipolar disorder _____ (do/do not) run in families. Studies of _____ also reveal that genetic influences on major depressive disorder are _____ (weak/strong). Some researchers have used _____ _____ to discover the genes that put people at risk for depression.

94. During depression, the brain is _____ (more/less) active, especially in the _____ _____ .

95. Depression may also be caused by _____ (high/low) levels of two neurotransmitters, _____ and _____ .

96. Drugs that relieve depression tend to make more _____ or _____ available to the depressed brain. A similar effect can be obtained from repetitive _____ _____ .

97. Animal studies suggest that long-lasting _____ influences, such as diet, drugs, and stress, may play a role in depression.

98. According to the social-cognitive perspective, depression may be linked with _____ beliefs and a _____ _____ style.

99. Such beliefs may arise from _____ _____ , the feeling that can arise when the individual repeatedly experiences uncontrollable, painful events.

100. Gender differences in responding to _____ help explain why women have been twice as vulnerable to depression. When trouble strikes, women tend to _____ .

Describe how depressed people differ from others in their explanations of failure and how such explanations tend to feed depression.

101. Being withdrawn, self-focused, and complaining tends to elicit social _____ (empathy/rejection).

Outline the vicious cycle of depression.

APPLICATION:

102. Complete the following flow chart comparing how a depressed person and a person who is not depressed would deal with this situation.

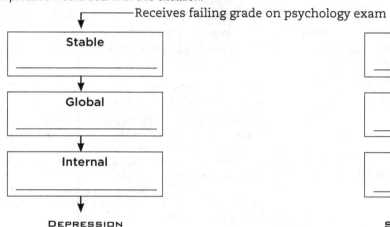

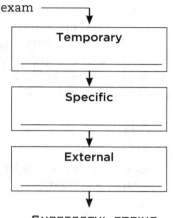

Objective 13-16: Identify the factors that increase the risk of suicide, and explore why some people injure themselves.

The risk of suicide is at least five times greater for those who have been depressed than for the general population. People are most at risk when they begin to rebound from depression and become capable of following through. The elderly sometimes choose death as an alternative to current or future suffering. Suicidal urges typically arise when people feel disconnected from others and a burden to them, or when they feel defeated and trapped by a situation they believe they cannot escape. Warning signs include verbal hints, giving possessions away, self-inflicted injuries, or withdrawal and preoccupation with death.

Some people, especially adolescents and young adults, engage in *nonsuicidal self-injury (NSSI)* as a way to ask for help and gain attention or to gain relief from intense negative thoughts, for example.

103. The risk of suicide is at least _____ times (how many?) greater for those who have been _____ than for the general population.

104. Suicide _____ (is/is not) always an act of hostility or revenge.

105. Cutting or burning the skin, hitting oneself, and self-tattooing are examples of _____ _____ . Such behaviors are especially common in _____ and among _____ . These behaviors usually _____ (do/ do not) lead to suicide.

State several reasons people may engage in nonsuicidal self-injury.

Schizophrenia

Objective 13-17: Describe the patterns of thinking, perceiving, and feeling that characterize schizophrenia.

Schizophrenia, a chief example of a *psychotic disorder,* is a disorder characterized by delusions, hallucinations, disorganized speech, and/or diminished, inappropriate emotional expression. Literally, schizophrenia means "split mind," which refers to a split from reality rather than multiple personality. The thinking of people with schizophrenia may be marked by *delusions,* that is, false beliefs—often of persecution or grandeur. Sometimes, they also experience *hallucinations,* sensory experiences without sensory stimulation. Hallucinations are usually auditory and often take the form of voices making insulting statements or giving orders.

Schizophrenia patients who are disorganized and deluded in their talk or tend toward inappropriate laughter, tears, or rage are said to have positive symptoms. When appropriate behaviors are absent—for example, patients may be mute or rigid—symptoms are said to be negative. Other people with schizophrenia show a *flat affect,* a zombielike state. *Chronic,* or *process, schizophrenia* develops gradually, emerging from a long history of social inadequacy. Recovery is doubtful. *Acute,* or *reactive, schizophrenia* develops rapidly in response to particular life stresses. Recovery is much more likely.

106. Schizophrenia, or "split mind," refers not to a split personality but rather to a split from

_____ .

107. Characteristics of schizophrenia are disturbed
_____ and _____ ,
disorganized _____ , and
diminished, inappropriate _____
_____ . People with schizophrenia
who have hallucinations or talk in disorganized
and deluded ways are said to have _____
symptoms, while those with toneless voices and
expressionless faces are said to have _____
symptoms.

108. The distorted, false beliefs of schizophrenia
patients are called _____ .

109. Disorganized thinking may appear as jumbled
ideas that make no sense, called _____
_____ .

110. The disturbed perceptions of people suffering from
schizophrenia may take the form of
_____ , which usually are
_____ (visual/auditory).

111. Some victims of schizophrenia lapse into a zombielike state of no apparent feeling, or
_____ _____ .

112. Most people with schizophrenia have difficulty
reading other people's facial expressions and state
of mind; that is, they have an impaired
_____ _____
_____ .

APPLICATIONS:

113. Claiming that she heard a voice commanding her to
warn other people that eating is harmful, Kelly attempts
to convince others in a restaurant not to eat. The psychiatrist to whom she is referred finds that Kelly's thinking and speech are often fragmented and distorted. In
addition, Kelly has an unreasonable fear that someone
is "out to get her" and consequently trusts no one. Her
condition is most indicative of _____
symptoms of schizophrenia.

114. Shawn hears voices; this symptom is a(n)
_____ ; Pierre believes that he is
Napoleon; this is a(n) _____ .

Objective 13-18: Explain how *acute schizophrenia* and
chronic schizophrenia differ.

115. When schizophrenia develops slowly (called
_____ schizophrenia), recovery
is _____ (more/less) likely than
when it develops rapidly in reaction to particular
life stresses (called _____
schizophrenia).

116. Social withdrawal, a negative symptom, is often
found among those with _____
schizophrenia. _____ (Men/
Women), whose schizophrenia develops on
average four years earlier than _____
(men's/women's), more often exhibit negative
symptoms and _____ schizophrenia.

Objective 13-19: Identify the brain abnormalities that are
associated with schizophrenia.

Researchers have linked certain forms of schizophrenia with brain abnormalities such as an excess number
of receptors for the neurotransmitter dopamine. Brain
scans indicate that some people with schizophrenia
have abnormally low brain activity in the frontal lobes or
enlarged, fluid-filled areas and a corresponding shrinkage of cerebral tissue. One area that becomes active during hallucinations is the thalamus.

117. The brain tissue of schizophrenia patients has
been found to have an excess of receptors for the
neurotransmitter _____ .
Drugs that block these receptors have been found
to _____ (increase/decrease)
positive symptoms of schizophrenia.

118. Brain scans have shown that many people suffering from schizophrenia have abnormally
_____ (high/low) brain activity in the _____ lobes. Others
have an unusual _____
_____ .

119. Enlarged, _____-filled areas
and a corresponding _____ of
cerebral tissue is also characteristic of schizophrenia. When schizophrenia patients are hal-
lucinating, PET scans show unusual activity in
the _____ , which filters
incoming _____ signals and
transmits them to the cortex. Another PET scan
study of people with paranoia found increased
activity in the _____ , a fear-
processing center.

Objective 13-20: Identify the prenatal events that are
associated with increased risk of developing
schizophrenia.

Prenatal risk factors for schizophrenia include low birth
weight, mother's diabetes, father's older age, or lack
of oxygen during delivery. Another possible cause of
schizophrenia is a midpregnancy viral infection that
impairs fetal brain development. For example, people are
at increased risk of schizophrenia if, during the middle
of their fetal development, their country experienced a
flu epidemic. People born in densely populated areas,
where viral diseases spread more readily, also seem at
greater risk for schizophrenia.

120. Some scientists contend that the brain abnormalities of schizophrenia may be caused by a prenatal problem, such as _____ _____ _____ ; birth complications, such as lack of _____ during delivery; or a midpregnancy _____ _____ contracted by the mother.

List several pieces of evidence for the idea that a midpregnancy viral infection could impair fetal brain development.

Objective 13-21: Explain how genes influence schizophrenia.

The nearly 1-in-100 odds of any person developing schizophrenia become about 1 in 10 if a family member has it and about 1 in 2 if an identical twin has the disorder. Adoption studies confirm the genetic contribution to schizophrenia. An adopted child's probability of developing the disorder is greater if one of their biological parents has schizophrenia.

The search for specific genes that underlie schizophrenia-inducing brain abnormalities continues. Schizophrenia is a group of disorders, influenced by many genes, each with very small effects. A variety of environmental factors such as prenatal viral infections, nutritional deficiencies, and maternal stress may activate the genes (epigenetics) that make some people more susceptible to the disease.

121. Twin studies _____ (support/do not support) the belief that heredity plays a role in schizophrenia.

122. The role of the prenatal environment in schizophrenia is demonstrated by the fact that identical twins who share the same _____ , and are therefore more likely to experience the same prenatal _____ , are more likely to share the disorder.

123. Adoption studies _____ (confirm/do not confirm) a genetic link in the development of schizophrenia.

124. It appears that for schizophrenia to develop there must be both a _____ predisposition and other (_____) factors such as those listed earlier that turn on the _____ that predispose this disease.

APPLICATIONS:

125. Wayne has been diagnosed with schizophrenia. His doctor attempts to help Wayne by prescribing a drug that blocks receptors for _____ .

126. Lolita, whose class presentation is titled "Current Views on the Causes of Schizophrenia," concludes her talk with the statement
   a. "Schizophrenia is caused by intolerable stress."
   b. "Schizophrenia is inherited."
   c. "Genes may predispose some people to react to particular experiences by developing schizophrenia."
   d. "As of this date, schizophrenia is completely unpredictable and its causes are unknown."

Other Disorders

Objective 13-22: Describe the three main eating disorders, and discuss how biological, psychological, and social-cultural influences make people more vulnerable to them.

Anorexia nervosa is an eating disorder in which a normal-weight person (usually an adolescent female) diets to become significantly underweight, yet feels fat and is obsessed with losing weight.

Bulimia nervosa is an eating disorder characterized by a binge-purge cycle of overeating, followed by vomiting, laxative use, fasting, or excessive exercise.

With *binge-eating disorder,* significant binge eating is followed by remorse but not by attempts to get rid of the excess food.

People with anorexia often come from competitive, high-achieving, and protective families. People with eating disorders tend to have low self-esteem, set impossible standards, fret about falling short of expectations, and worry about how others perceive them. Although twin studies suggest that eating disorders may also have a genetic component, environment also matters, especially in weight-obsessed cultures.

127. The disorder in which a person, usually a female adolescent, becomes significantly underweight and yet feels fat is known as _____ _____ . Many people with this disorder come from _____ , _____-_____ , and protective families.

128. A more common disorder is _____ _____ , which is characterized by repeated _____-_____ episodes and by feelings of guilt, depression, and anxiety. When bouts

of excessive eating followed by remorse are not accompanied by purging or fasting, the

_____-_____

_____ is diagnosed.

129. Genetic factors _____ (may/do not) influence susceptibility to eating disorders.

130. Vulnerability to eating disorders _____ (increases/does not increase) with greater body dissatisfaction.

131. In impoverished areas of the world, where thinness can signal poverty, _____ is better. In _____ cultures, however, the rise in eating disorders has coincided with an increasing number of women having a poor _____ _____ .

132. When young women were shown pictures of unnaturally thin models, they felt more

_____ , _____ ,

and _____ with their own bodies.

APPLICATION:

133. Of the following individuals, who might be most prone to developing an eating disorder?
    a. Jason, an adolescent boy who is somewhat overweight and is unpopular with his peers
    b. Jennifer, a teenage girl who has a poor self-image and a fear of not being able to live up to her parents' high standards
    c. Susan, a 35-year-old woman who is a "workaholic" and devotes most of her energies to her high-pressured career
    d. Bill, a 40-year-old man who has had problems with alcohol use disorder and is seriously depressed after losing his job of 20 years

Objective 13-23: Describe the dissociative disorders, and discuss why they are controversial.

In *dissociative disorders,* the person's conscious awareness is said to *dissociate* from painful memories. In this state, the person may experience a sudden loss of memory or change in identity. **Dissociative identity disorder (DID)** is a rare disorder in which a person exhibits two or more distinct and alternating personalities, with the original personality typically denying awareness of the other(s).

Skeptics find it suspicious that the disorder became so popular in the late twentieth century and that it is not found in many countries and is very rare in others. Some argue that the condition is either role playing by fantasy-prone people or constructed out of the therapist-patient interaction. Those who believe it is a real disorder find evidence of distinct brain and body states associated with differing personalities.

Psychodynamic theorists see DID as a defense against the anxiety caused by unacceptable impulses. Learning theorists see dissociative disorders as behaviors reinforced by anxiety reduction. Still others view dissociative disorders as posttraumatic disorders—a natural protective response to traumatic childhood experiences. Many people with DID recall suffering physical, sexual, or emotional abuse as children.

134. In _____ disorders, a person experiences a sudden loss of _____ or change in _____ .

135. A person who develops two or more distinct personalities is experiencing _____ _____ disorder.

136. Those who accept this as a genuine disorder point to evidence that differing personalities may be associated with distinct _____ and _____ states.

Identify two pieces of evidence cited by those who do not accept dissociative identity disorder as a genuine disorder.

137. The psychodynamic and learning perspectives view dissociative disorders as ways of dealing with _____ . Others include them under the umbrella of _____ _____ disorder, viewing DID as a natural, protective response to _____ _____ . Skeptics claim these disorders are sometimes created by _____-prone people and are sometimes constructed out of the _____-_____ interaction.

APPLICATION:

138. Multiple personalities have long been a popular subject of films and novels. For example, Dr. Jekyll, whose second personality was Mr. Hyde, had _____ _____ disorder.

Objective 13-24: Identify the characteristics that are typical of personality disorders in general, and describe the biological and psychological factors that are associated with antisocial personality disorder.

Personality disorders are psychological disorders characterized by inflexible and enduring behavior patterns that impair social functioning. The most troubling of these disorders is the *antisocial personality disorder,* in which a person (usually a man) exhibits a lack of conscience for wrongdoing, even toward friends and family members. This person may be aggressive and ruthless or a clever con artist. Those with antisocial personality disorder have a genetic tendency toward an uninhibited approach to life and low levels of arousal, which may interact with environmental influences to produce this disorder. Brain scans of murderers with this disorder have revealed reduced activity in the frontal lobes, an area of the cortex that helps control impulses. Violent repeat offenders also have less frontal lobe tissue, which may help explain why people with antisocial personality disorder show impaired planning, organization, and inhibition.

139. Personality disorders exist when an individual has character traits that are enduring and impair

    _____ _____ .

140. Some people with these disorders are anxious and _____ , and they avoid social contact. Some behave in _____ or odd ways, or interact without engaging emotionally. Others seem overly dramatic or

    _____ .

141. An individual who seems to have no conscience, lies, steals, is generally irresponsible, shows lower _____ intelligence, and may be criminal is said to have an _____ personality. This person is sometimes labeled a _____ .

142. Studies of biological relatives of those with antisocial and unemotional tendencies suggest that there _____ (is/is not) a biological predisposition to such traits.

143. Some studies have detected early signs of antisocial behavior in children, including low levels of _____ and lower levels of _____ hormones.

144. PET scans of murderers' brains reveal reduced activity in the _____ _____ , an area of the brain that helps control _____ . People with antisocial criminal tendencies also have a smaller-than-normal _____ , an emotion-controlling part of the brain.

145. As in other disorders, in antisocial personality, genetics _____ (is/is not) the whole story. Genetic influences, in combination with negative environmental factors such as

    _____ _____ , help wire the brain.

APPLICATION:

146. Ming has never been able to keep a job. He's been in and out of jail for charges such as theft, sexual assault, and spousal abuse. Ming would most likely be diagnosed as having _____ _____ disorder.

Does "Disorder" Equal "Danger"?

Objective 13-25: Discuss whether people with psychological disorders are likely to commit violent acts.

The majority of violent crimes are committed by those with no diagnosed disorder. Moreover, mental disorders seldom lead to violence, and clinical prediction of violence is unreliable. People with disorders also are more likely to be victims than perpetrators of violence.

147. In real life, people with psychological disorders are _____ (more/less) likely than those with no diagnosed disorder to commit a violent crime. They are _____ (more/less) likely to be victims of violence.

SUMMARY STUDY TIP: This chapter discusses a number of psychological disorders. To help organize your study of this material, complete the table on the next page. For each category, list the specific disorders discussed. Then, for each disorder, give a description and a brief explanation of possible causes of the disorders. To get you started, portions of the first category of disorders, plus some random information, has been provided.

Category or Disorder	Specific Disorders as Appropriate	Description of the Disorder	Possible Explanations of Causes
Anxiety disorders	Generalized anxiety disorder Panic disorder Phobias	Distressing, persistent anxiety or maladaptive behaviors that reduce anxiety	Conditioning and reinforcement of fears. For example, stimulus generalization. Also, observational learning. Pairing of a traumatic event with a genetic predisposition.
Obsessive-compulsive disorder			
Posttraumatic stress disorder			
Dissociative disorders			
Personality disorders			
Substance use disorders			
Major depressive disorder and bipolar disorder			
Schizophrenia			
Eating disorders			
Dissociative disorders			
Personality disorders			

Progress Test

Multiple-Choice Questions

Circle your answers to the following questions and check them with the answers beginning on page 282. If your answer is incorrect, read the explanation for why it is incorrect and then consult the text.

1. Gender differences in the widespread occurrence of depression may be partly due to the fact that when stressful experiences occur
   a. women tend to act, while men tend to think.
   b. women tend to think, while men tend to act.
   c. women tend to distract themselves by drinking, while men tend to lose themselves in their work.
   d. women tend to lose themselves in their work, while men tend to distract themselves by drinking.

2. The view that all behavior arises from the interaction of heredity and environment is referred to as the _____ approach.
   a. biopsychosocial
   b. psychoanalytic
   c. medical
   d. conditioning

3. Which of the following is NOT true concerning depression?
   a. Depression is more common in females than in males.
   b. Most depressive episodes appear not to be preceded by any particular factor or event.
   c. Most depressive episodes last for only a few weeks or months.
   d. Most people recover from depression without professional therapy.

4. Which of the following is NOT true regarding schizophrenia?
   a. It occurs more frequently in people born in winter and spring months.
   b. It occurs less frequently as infectious disease rates have declined.
   c. It occurs more frequently in lightly populated areas.
   d. It usually appears during adolescence or early adulthood.

5. Evidence of environmental effects on psychological disorders is seen in the fact that certain disorders, such as _____ , have appeared more consistently worldwide; others, such as _____ , are culture-bound.
   a. schizophrenia; depression
   b. depression; schizophrenia
   c. antisocial personality; bulimia nervosa
   d. depression; bulimia nervosa

6. The effect of drugs that block receptors for dopamine is to
   a. lessen schizophrenia symptoms.
   b. reduce feelings of depression.
   c. increase schizophrenia symptoms.
   d. increase feelings of depression.

7. Phobias and panic disorders are classified as
   a. anxiety disorders.
   b. depressive disorders.
   c. dissociative disorders.
   d. personality disorders.

8. According to the social-cognitive perspective, a person who experiences unexpected negative events may develop helplessness and
   a. obsessive-compulsive disorder.
   b. a dissociative disorder.
   c. a personality disorder.
   d. major depressive disorder.

9. Which of the following was presented in the text as evidence of biological influences on anxiety disorders, OCD, and PTSD?
   a. Identical twins often develop similar phobias.
   b. Brain scans of persons with obsessive-compulsive disorder reveal unusually high activity in brain areas involved in impulse control and habitual behavior.
   c. Brain pathways resulting from fear-learning experiences create easy inroads for more fear experiences.
   d. All of these facts were presented.

10. Most of the hallucinations of schizophrenia patients involve the sense of
    a. smell.   c. hearing.
    b. vision.   d. touch.

11. When expecting to be electrically shocked, people with an antisocial personality disorder, as compared with normal people, show
    a. greater bodily arousal and higher levels of stress hormones.
    b. little bodily arousal and lower levels of stress hormones.
    c. greater fear and greater bodily arousal.
    d. greater fear and less bodily arousal.

12. In treating depression, a psychiatrist would probably prescribe a drug that would
    a. increase levels of acetylcholine.
    b. decrease levels of dopamine.
    c. increase levels of norepinephrine.
    d. decrease levels of serotonin.

13. When schizophrenia is slow to develop, called _____ schizophrenia, recovery is _____ .
    a. acute; unlikely   c. chronic; unlikely
    b. chronic; likely   d. acute; likely

14. Which of the following is true concerning disordered behavior?
    a. Definitions of disordered behavior are culture-dependent.
    b. A behavior cannot be defined as disordered unless it is considered harmful to society.
    c. Disordered behavior can be defined as any behavior that is distressful.
    d. Definitions of disordered behavior are based on physiological factors.

15. Research evidence links the brain abnormalities of schizophrenia to _____ during prenatal development.
    a. maternal stress
    b. a viral infection contracted
    c. abnormal levels of certain hormones
    d. the weight of the unborn child

16. Disorders such as schizophrenia have appeared more consistently worldwide and are influenced by heredity. Other disorders such as anorexia nervosa are culture-bound. These facts provide evidence for the _____ model of psychological disorders.
    a. medical   c. social-cultural
    b. biopsychosocial   d. psychodynamic

17. In general, women are more vulnerable than men to
    a. external disorders such as anxiety.
    b. internal disorders such as depression.
    c. external disorders such as antisocial conduct.
    d. internal disorders such as alcohol abuse.

18. Which of the following statements concerning the labeling of disordered behaviors is NOT true?
    a. Labels interfere with effective treatment of psychological disorders.
    b. Labels promote research studies of psychological disorders.
    c. Labels may create preconceptions that bias people's perceptions.
    d. Labels may be self-fulfilling.

19. Which neurotransmitter is present in overabundant amounts during the manic phase of bipolar disorder?
    a. dopamine   c. epinephrine
    b. serotonin   d. norepinephrine

20. Which of the following provides evidence that human fears have been subjected to the evolutionary process?
    a. Compulsive acts typically exaggerate behaviors that contributed to our species' survival.
    b. Most phobias focus on objects that our ancestors also feared.
    c. It is easier to condition some fears than others.
    d. All of these facts provide evidence.

21. Which of the following is true of the medical model?
    a. In recent years, it has been in large part discredited.
    b. It views psychological disorders as sicknesses that are diagnosable and treatable.
    c. It emphasizes the role of psychological factors in disorders over that of physiological factors.
    d. It focuses on cognitive factors.

22. Psychodynamic and learning theorists both agree that the symptoms of dissociative identity disorder are the person's attempt to deal with
    a. unconscious conflicts.
    b. anxiety.
    c. unfulfilled wishes.
    d. unpleasant responsibilities.

23. Women in _____ consider "bigger" to be the ideal body shape.
    a. Western cultures
    b. areas with high rates of poverty
    c. the United States
    d. Australia, New Zealand, and England

24. Many psychologists worry that the DSM-5
    a. will fail to emphasize observable behaviors in the diagnostic process.
    b. has too strong a learning theory bias.
    c. will extend the pathologizing of everyday life.
    d. will prove to be unreliable.

25. Which of the following is NOT a symptom of schizophrenia?
    a. diminished, inappropriate emotions
    b. disturbed perceptions
    c. panic attacks
    d. disorganized thinking

26. Social-cognitive theorists believe that depression is linked with
    a. negative moods.
    b. maladaptive explanations of failure.
    c. self-defeating beliefs.
    d. all of these symptoms.

27. Among the following, which is generally accepted as a possible cause of schizophrenia?
    a. an excess of endorphins in the brain
    b. being a twin
    c. extensive learned helplessness
    d. a genetic predisposition

28. Psychoactive drugs affect behavior and perception through
    a. the power of suggestion.
    b. the placebo effect.
    c. altering neural activity in the brain.
    d. psychological, not physiological, influences.

29. Alcohol has its strongest effect on
    a. the transfer of experiences to long-term memory.
    b. immediate memory.
    c. previously established long-term memories.
    d. all of these answers.

30. A person who requires increasing amounts of a drug in order to feel its effect is said to have developed
    a. tolerance.
    b. an addiction.
    c. a genetic predisposition.
    d. withdrawal symptoms.

31. Which of the following is NOT a stimulant?
    a. amphetamines   **c.** nicotine
    b. caffeine   **d.** alcohol

32. THC is the major active ingredient in
    a. nicotine.   **c.** marijuana.
    b. MDMA.   **d.** cocaine.

33. How a particular psychoactive drug affects a person depends on
    a. the dosage and form in which the drug is taken.
    b. the user's expectations and personality.
    c. the situation in which the drug is taken.
    d. all of these factors.

Matching Items

Match each term with the appropriate definition or description.

Terms

_____ **1.** dissociative disorder
_____ **2.** medical model
_____ **3.** major depressive disorder
_____ **4.** phobia
_____ **5.** withdrawal
_____ **6.** mania
_____ **7.** obsessive-compulsive disorder
_____ **8.** schizophrenia
_____ **9.** hallucination
_____ **10.** panic attack
_____ **11.** antisocial personality
_____ **12.** delusion
_____ **13.** tolerance
_____ **14.** bipolar disorder
_____ **15.** bulimia nervosa
_____ **16.** anorexia nervosa
_____ **17.** ADHD

Definitions or Descriptions

a. a disorder in which a person experiences, at a minimum, depressed mood or loss of interest
b. an eating disorder marked by binge eating and purging
c. an individual who seems to have no conscience
d. a false sensory experience
e. an eating disorder marked by self-starvation
f. a sudden escalation of anxiety often accompanied by a sensation of choking or other physical symptoms
g. a disorder in which the person alternates between depression and mania
h. a psychological disorder marked by extreme inattention and/or hyperactivity and impulsivity
i. the discomfort and distress that follow ending the use of an addictive drug or behavior
j. the diminishing of a psychoactive drug's effect with repeated use
k. a false belief
l. a disorder marked by disorganized thinking and speech, disturbed perceptions, and/or diminished, inappropriate emotional expression
m. a disorder characterized by repetitive thoughts and actions
n. an anxiety disorder marked by a persistent, irrational fear of a specific object or situation
o. an approach that considers behavior disorders as illnesses that can be diagnosed, treated, and, in most cases, cured
p. an extremely elevated mood
q. a disorder in which conscious awareness becomes separated from previous memories, feelings, and thoughts

Application Essay

Discuss the potential benefits and dangers of using diagnostic labels.

Summing Up

Soo-Mee often feels tense and uneasy for no apparent reason. She has trouble concentrating on her studies, and her thoughts wander from problem to problem. This suggests that

she may suffer from a _____ _____ disorder,	which	may lead to physical problems, such as high _____ _____ .

Because Soo-Mee cannot identify the cause of her tension,

it would be described by Sigmund _____ as _____-_____ ,	while	learning theorists would link her anxiety with _____ _____ of fear, and biological psychologists might link it to an overarousal of _____ areas involved in _____ control.

Soo-Mee's friend Shayna complains of similar feelings, but she also

experiences unexpected episodes of intense dread, indicating _____ attacks,	which	are accompanied by physical symptoms such as irregular _____ , shortness of breath, and choking sensations.

Fearing that she might be having a heart attack when these episodes occur, Shayna avoids situations in which

she fears _____ may be difficult.	So,	Shayna refuses to leave her house, a sure sign that she suffers from _____ .

Soo-Mee and Shayna's friend Randal laughs at their inability to identify the source of their anxiety. He says,

"I know exactly what I fear: snakes. I have a _____ ,	which	I know is _____ , but at least I can deal with it by avoiding areas where snakes are known to be, for example.

My problem may result from my _____ a friend being bitten by a snake."

Terms and Concepts to Remember

Using your own words, on a separate piece of paper write a brief definition or explanation of each of the following terms.

1. psychological disorder
2. attention-deficit/hyperactivity disorder (ADHD)
3. medical model
4. epigenetics
5. DSM-5
6. anxiety disorders
7. generalized anxiety disorder
8. panic disorder
9. phobia
10. obsessive-compulsive disorder (OCD)
11. posttraumatic stress disorder (PTSD)
12. psychoactive drug
13. substance use disorder
14. tolerance
15. withdrawal
16. depressants
17. alcohol use disorder
18. barbiturates
19. opiates
20. stimulants
21. nicotine
22. cocaine
23. amphetamines
24. methamphetamine
25. Ecstasy (MDMA)
26. hallucinogens
27. near-death experience
28. LSD
29. THC
30. major depressive disorder
31. bipolar disorder
32. mania
33. schizophrenia
34. psychotic disorders
35. delusions
36. acute schizophrenia
37. chronic schizophrenia
38. anorexia nervosa
39. bulimia nervosa
40. binge-eating disorder
41. dissociative disorder
42. dissociative identity disorder
43. personality disorder
44. antisocial personality disorder

Answers

Chapter Review

What Is a Psychological Disorder?

1. syndrome; clinically significant; thoughts; feelings; behaviors; dysfunctional; maladaptive; distress
2. variable
3. culture
4. attention-deficit/hyperactivity disorder (ADHD); extreme inattention, hyperactivity, and impulsivity
5. boys; girls; children and adolescents
6. over; environment; awareness; brain activity
7. learning disorder; defiant and temper-prone behavior; is
8. stimulants; psychological therapies
9. medical; illnesses; symptoms; therapy
10. biology; personal; social; cultural; biopsychosocial
11. depression; schizophrenia; bulimia nervosa; anxiety; symptoms
12. epigenetics
13. biological; biology; psychology; social-cultural. Haya's behavior is directed by a specific situation. Because it does not interfere with her everyday life, it is not considered disordered.
14. DSM-5; does not; describes
15. predict; research
16. autism spectrum disorder; hoarding; intellectual disability; binge-eating
17. field trials; varied; posttraumatic stress; antisocial personality
18. increased; increased
19. a significant

Psychological labels may be arbitrary. They can create preconceptions that bias our perceptions and interpretations and they can affect people's self-images. Moreover, labels can change reality by being self-fulfilling. Despite these drawbacks, labels are useful in describing, treating, and researching the causes of psychological disorders.

Anxiety Disorders, OCD, and PTSD

20. distressing, persistent anxiety or maladaptive behaviors that reduce anxiety; social anxiety
21. generalized anxiety; free-floating
22. high blood pressure; depression
23. panic disorder; panic attack
24. panic attack; nicotine
25. agoraphobia
26. phobia; specific phobias

27. obsessive-compulsive
28. unwanted; repetitive; compulsive behaviors
29. posttraumatic stress; haunting memories, nightmares, social withdrawal, jumpy anxiety, and insomnia; limbic system; distress
30. survivor resiliency; posttraumatic growth; stress
31. phobia. Phobias are intense fears of objects or situations that result either from experience or from observing another person's experience.
32. generalized anxiety. The key to identifying this disorder is the fact that the anxiety occurs for no apparent reason.
33. obsessive-compulsive. Showering a couple of times a day could be normal, depending on the situation. Showering 10 times a day is a compulsion resulting from an obsession with dirt and/or germs.
34. posttraumatic stress. Zheina's behavior is a direct result of the traumatic events she experienced during the attacks.
35. panic attack. These are unpredictable, exaggerated fears that something bad is about to happen.
36. psychoanalytic; repressed
37. classical; fears
38. stimulus generalization
39. reinforced; observational
40. is; experience
41. impulse; habitual
42. are; survival
43. conditioning. In the conditioning perspective, a phobia such as Julia's is seen as a conditioned fear.
44. stimulus generalization. Joseph's fear has generalized from a wild cat to all house cats.
45. biological. According to the biological perspective, increased activity in areas of the brain involved in impulse control and habitual behavior is a factor in compulsive behavior.
46. a. is the answer. Humans seem biologically prepared to develop a fear of heights and other dangers that our ancestors feared.

Substance Use Disorders and Addictive Behaviors

47. psychoactive
48. substance use
49. biological; expectations; culture
50. tolerance; addiction; behaviors; withdrawal
51. depressants; stimulants; hallucinogens; neurotransmitters
52. b. is the answer. Continued use of a drug produces tolerance; to experience the same "high," Dan will have to use larger and larger doses.
53. reduce; slow; disinhibitor; judgment; inhibitions
54. long-term; REM sleep; shrink; nerve cells; synaptic connections
55. sympathetic; reactions

Studies have found that if people believe that alcohol affects social behavior in certain ways, then, when they drink alcohol (or even mistakenly think that they have been drinking alcohol), they will behave according to their expectations, which vary by culture. For example, if people believe alcohol promotes sexual feeling, on drinking they are likely to behave in a sexually aroused way.

56. alcohol use; enzyme
57. barbiturates; anxiety
58. methadone; depress; opiates; endorphins
59. d. is the answer. Alcohol loosens inhibitions and reduces self-awareness, making people more likely to act on their feelings of anger or sexual arousal. It also disrupts the processing of experiences into long-term memory.
60. caffeine, nicotine, cocaine, amphetamines, methamphetamine, and Ecstasy; excite; speed up; can be
61. do; nicotine; central nervous; epinephrine; norepinephrine; appetite; alertness; mental efficiency; dopamine; opioids; anxiety; pain
62. euphoria; dopamine; serotonin; norepinephrine; emotional disturbances; respiratory; dosage; expectations; personality
63. Amphetamines; methamphetamine; dopamine; energy; mood
64. Ecstasy; stimulant; hallucinogen; energy; emotional; dopamine; serotonin; rhythms; immune system; cognitive
65. MDMA (Ecstasy). As an amphetamine derivative, MDMA releases serotonin and blocks its reuptake, prolonging its feel-good flood. As a mild hallucinogen, it distorts perceptions.
66. psychedelics; MDMA (Ecstasy)
67. near-death; oxygen
68. serotonin; euphoria; panic; mood; expectations
69. THC; much longer than; less

Like alcohol, marijuana relaxes, disinhibits, and may produce a euphoric feeling, depending on the situaiton. Also like alcohol, marijuana impairs perceptual and motor skills. Marijuana is a mild hallucinogen; it can increase sensitivity to colors, sounds, tastes, and smells. Marijuana also interrupts memory formation.

70. near-death
71. a. is the answer. Alcohol is eliminated from the body within hours. Marijuana and its by-products may stay in the body for more than a week.
72. does; dopamine reward; does

A psychological factor in substance use disorder is the feeling that one's life is meaningless and lacks direction. Regular users of psychoactive drugs often have experienced stress or failure and are somewhat depressed. Drug use often begins as a way to cope with depression, anger, anxiety, or insomnia. A powerful social factor in drug use, especially among adolescents, is peer influence. Peers shape attitudes about drugs, provide drugs, and establish the social context for their use.

73. vary; cultural; ethnic
74. lower

75. **a.** education about the long-term costs of a drug's temporary pleasures
   b. efforts to boost people's self-esteem and purpose in life
   c. attempts to "inoculate" youth against peer pressures

76. Stimulants include caffeine, nicotine, cocaine, amphetamines, methamphetamines, and Ecstasy. They enhance energy and mood and can be addictive. They excite neural activity and speed up body functions.
   Hallucinogens include Ecstasy, LSD, and marijuana. They distort perceptions and evoke sensory images in the absence of sensory input. They produce their effects by interfering with the serotonin neurotransmitter system.

Major Depressive Disorder and Bipolar Disorder

77. major depressive; mania; bipolar

78. phobias; depression

79. depressed mood; interest; lethargy, feelings of worthlessness, challenges regulating appetite, weight, and sleep, problems in thinking, concentrating, or making decisions, and thinking of death and suicide

80. two weeks; persistent depressive disorder; dysthymia

81. a euphoric, wildly energetic, and extremely optimistic state

82. precision; logic; emotional; imagery

83. bipolar disorder. Bipolar disorder is marked by emotional extremes, as seen in Monica's varying behavior.

84. major depressive disorder. Haeji's symptoms are classic symptoms of this disorder. The fact that they have lasted for six months makes them clinically significant.

85. bipolar disorder

86. behavior; thoughts

87. widespread

88. more; internal; depression, anxiety, and inhibited sexual desire

89. external; alcohol use disorder, antisocial conduct, and lack of impulse control

90. can

91. is; a loved one's death, loss of a job, a marriage break-up, or a physical assault

92. increasing; earlier; three

93. do; twins; strong; linkage analysis

94. less; reward centers

95. low; norepinephrine; serotonin

96. norepinephrine; serotonin; physical exercise

97. epigenetic

98. self-defeating; negative explanatory

99. learned helplessness

100. stress; overthink (ruminate)

Depressed people are more likely than others to explain failures or bad events in terms that are stable (it's going to last forever), global (it will affect everything), and internal (it's my fault). Such explanations lead to feelings of hopelessness, which in turn feed depression.

101. rejection

Depression is often brought on by stressful experiences. Depressed people brood over such experiences with a negative explanatory style that creates a hopeless, depressed state that hampers the way the person thinks and acts. These thoughts and actions fuel social rejection and other negative experiences.

102. There are no right or wrong answers to this. Possible responses of a depressed person might be "I'll never be able to pass this course (stable)," "I'm never going to do well in any college courses (global)," and "It's my fault; I didn't study hard enough (internal)."

103. five; depressed

104. is not

105. nonsuicidal self-injury (NSSI); adolescence; females; do not

People may engage in NSSI to gain relief from intense negative thoughts through the distraction of pain, as a way of asking for help and gaining attention, to relieve guilt through self punishment, to get others to change their negative behavior, or to fit in with a peer group.

Schizophrenia

106. reality

107. perceptions; beliefs; speech; emotional expression; positive; negative

108. delusions

109. word salad

110. hallucinations; auditory

111. flat affect

112. theory of mind

113. positive. Kelly's hallucinations (hearing voices), delusions (fearing someone is "out to get her"), and fragmented speech indicate positive symptoms.

114. hallucination; delusion. Hallucinations are false perceptions. Delusions are false beliefs.

115. chronic (or process); less; acute (or reactive)

116. chronic; Men; women's; chronic

117. dopamine; decrease

118. low; frontal; corpus callosum

119. fluid; shrinkage; thalamus; sensory; amygdala

120. low birth weight; oxygen; viral infection

Risk of schizophrenia increases for those who undergo fetal development during a flu epidemic, or simply during the flu season. People born in densely populated areas and those born during winter and spring months are at increased risk. The months of excess schizophrenia births are reversed in the Southern Hemisphere, where the seasons are the reverse of the Northern Hemisphere's. Mothers who were sick with influenza during their pregnancy may be more likely to have children who develop schizophrenia. Blood drawn from pregnant women whose children develop schizophrenia has higher-than-normal levels of viral infection antibodies.

121. support
122. placenta; viruses
123. confirm
124. genetic; epigenetic; genes
125. dopamine. Schizophrenia patients sometimes have an excess of receptors for dopamine. Drugs that block these receptors can therefore reduce symptoms of schizophrenia.
126. **c.** is the answer. Risk for schizophrenia increases for individuals who are related to a person with schizophrenia, and the greater the genetic relatedness, the greater the risk.

Other Disorders

127. anorexia nervosa; competitive; high-achieving
128. bulimia nervosa; binge-purge; binge-eating disorder
129. may
130. increases
131. bigger; Western; body image
132. ashamed; depressed; dissatisfied
133. **b.** is the answer. Adolescent females with low self-esteem and high-achieving families seem especially prone to eating disorders such as anorexia nervosa.
     a. & d. Eating disorders occur much more frequently in women than in men.
     c. Eating disorders usually develop during adolescence, rather than during adulthood.
134. dissociative; memory; identity
135. dissociative identity
136. brain; body

Skeptics point out that the recent increase in the number of reported cases of dissociative identity disorder indicates that it has become a fad. The fact that the disorder is almost nonexistent outside North America also causes skeptics to doubt the disorder's genuineness. Another possible answer is that some think that DID could be an extension of the way we vary the "selves" we present.

137. anxiety; posttraumatic stress; childhood trauma; fantasy; therapist-patient
138. dissociative identity. Unlike schizophrenia, which is a split from reality, dissociative identity disorder involves the existence of multiple personalities.
139. social functioning
140. withdrawn; eccentric; impulsive
141. emotional; antisocial; psychopath (or sociopath)
142. is
143. arousal; stress
144. frontal lobe; impulses; amygdala
145. is not; childhood abuse
146. antisocial personality. Repeated wrongdoing and aggressive behavior are part of the pattern associated with the antisocial personality disorder, which may also include marital problems and an inability to keep a job.

Does "Disorder" Equal "Danger"?
147. less; more

Summary Study Tip: Using the text discussion and tables to complete this chart will enhance your understanding of the material in this chapter.

Progress Test

Multiple-Choice Questions

1. **b.** is the answer.
   c. & d. Men are more likely than women to cope with stress in these ways.
2. **a.** is the answer.
3. **b.** is the answer. Depression is often preceded by a stressful event related to work, marriage, or a close relationship.
4. **c.** is the answer.
5. **d.** is the answer. Although depression appears more consistently worldwide, anorexia nervosa and bulimia nervosa are rare outside Western culture.
   a. & b. Schizophrenia and depression are both universal.
   c. Although anorexia is mentioned as a culture-bound disorder, antisocial personality is not mentioned as a universal disorder.
6. **a.** is the answer.
   b. & d. Thus far, only norepinephrine and serotonin have been implicated in depression and bipolar disorder.
   c. Schizophrenia has been associated with an excess of dopamine receptors. Blocking them alleviates, rather than increases, schizophrenia symptoms.
7. **a.** is the answer.
   b. The depressive disorders include major depressive disorder and persistent depressive disorder.
   c. Dissociative identity disorder is the only dissociative disorder discussed in the text.
   d. Antisocial personality disorder is the only personality disorder discussed in the text.
8. **d.** is the answer. Learned helplessness may lead to self-defeating beliefs, which in turn are linked with depression.
9. **d.** is the answer.
10. **c.** is the answer.
11. **b.** is the answer. Those with antisocial personality disorders show less autonomic arousal in such situations, and emotions, such as fear, are tied to arousal.
12. **c.** is the answer. Drugs that relieve depression tend to increase levels of norepinephrine.
    a. Acetylcholine is a neurotransmitter involved in muscle contractions.
    b. It is in certain types of schizophrenia that decreasing dopamine levels is known to be helpful.
    d. On the contrary, it appears that a particular type of depression may be related to *low* levels of serotonin.

13. **c.** is the answer.

14. **a.** is the answer. Different cultures have different standards for behaviors that are considered acceptable and normal.
    b. Most people with disorders are not harmful to society.
    c. Many behaviors may be temporarily distressful; they are disordered only if they interfere with the person's day-to-day life.
    d. Although physiological factors play a role in the various disorders, they do not define disordered behavior. Rather, behavior is said to be disordered if it is marked by a clinically significant disturbance in a person's cognition, emotion regulation, or behavior.

15. **b.** is the answer.

16. **b.** is the answer. The fact that some disorders have appeared more consistently worldwide and are at least partly genetic in origin implicates biological factors in their origin. The fact that other disorders appear only in certain parts of the world implicates social-cultural and psychological factors in their origin.

17. **b.** is the answer.
    a. Anxiety is an internal disorder.
    d. Alcohol abuse is an external disorder.

18. **a.** is the answer. In fact, just the opposite is true. Labels are useful in promoting effective treatment of psychological disorders.

19. **d.** is the answer. In bipolar disorder, norepinephrine appears to be overabundant during mania and in short supply during depression.
    a. There is an overabundance of dopamine receptors in some schizophrenia patients.
    b. Serotonin sometimes appears to be scarce during depression.
    c. Epinephrine has not been implicated in psychological disorders.

20. **d.** is the answer.

21. **b.** is the answer.
    a. This isn't the case; in fact, the medical model has gained credibility from recent discoveries of genetic and biochemical links to some disorders.
    c. & d. The medical perspective tends to place more emphasis on physiological factors.

22. **b.** is the answer. The psychoanalytic explanation is that DID symptoms are defenses against the anxiety caused by unacceptable impulses. According to the learning perspective, the troubled behaviors that result from this disorder have been reinforced by anxiety reduction.
    a. & c. These are true of the psychoanalytic, but not the learning, perspective.

23. **b.** is the answer.

24. **c.** is the answer.
    a. & d. In fact, just the opposite is true. the DSM was revised to improve reliability by basing diagnoses on observable behaviors.

b. DSM-5 does not reflect a learning or a psychoanalytic bias.

25. **c.** is the answer. Panic attacks are characteristic of certain anxiety disorders, not of schizophrenia.

26. **d.** is the answer.

27. **d.** is the answer. Risk for schizophrenia increases for individuals who are related to a schizophrenia victim, and the greater the genetic relatedness, the greater the risk.
    a. Schizophrenia victims have an overabundance of the neurotransmitter dopamine, not endorphins.
    b. Being a twin is, in itself, irrelevant to developing schizophrenia.
    c. Although learned helplessness has been suggested by social-cognitive theorists as a cause of self-defeating depressive behaviors, it has not been suggested as a cause of schizophrenia.

28. **c.** is the answer. Such drugs work primarily at synapses, altering neural transmission.
    a. What people believe will happen after taking a drug will likely have some effect on their individual reactions, but psychoactive drugs actually work by altering neural transmission.
    b. Since a placebo is a substance without active properties, this answer is incorrect.
    d. This answer is incorrect because the effects of psychoactive drugs on behavior, perception, and so forth have a physiological basis.

29. **a.** is the answer. Alcohol disrupts the processing of experiences into long-term memory but has little effect on either immediate or previously established memories.

30. **a.** is the answer.
    b. Addiction is a compulsive craving of drugs or certain behaviors despite known harmful consequences.
    c. A genetic predisposition is an inherited tendency toward a particular characteristic.
    d. Withdrawal refers to the discomfort and distress that follow discontinuing an addictive drug or behavior.

31. **d.** is the answer. Alcohol is a depressant.

32. **c.** is the answer.

33. **d.** is the answer.

Matching Items

1. q	6. p	11. c	16. b
2. o	7. m	12. k	17. h
3. a	8. l	13. j	
4. n	9. d	14. g	
5. i	10. f	15. e	

Application Essay

One of the benefits of labeling psychological disorders is improved communication among mental health professionals. A label such as "ADHD" is a quick way of describing a complex set of behaviors. Classification also stimulates research, and attempts to predict the course and treatment of a disorder. Labels can also benefit clients, who may be relieved to find that they are not alone in experiencing a collection of symptoms. According to critics, however, labels are value judgments that often lead to overdiagnosis and bias in misinterpreting normal behaviors as symptoms.

Summing Up

Soo-Mee often feels tense and uneasy for no apparent reason. She has trouble concentrating on her studies, and her thoughts wander from problem to problem. This suggests that she may suffer from a *generalized anxiety* disorder, which may lead to physical problems, such as high *blood pressure.* Because Soo-Mee cannot identify the cause of her tension, it would be described by Sigmund Freud as *free-floating,* while learning theorists would link her anxiety with *classical conditioning* of fear, and biological psychologists might link it to an overarousal of *brain* areas involved in *impulse* control.

Soo-Mee's friend Shayna complains of similar feelings, but she also experiences unexpected episodes of intense dread, indicating *panic* attacks, which are accompanied by physical symptoms such as irregular *heartbeat,* shortness of breath, and choking sensations. Fearing that she might be having a heart attack when these episodes occur, Shayna avoids situations in which she fears *escape* may be difficult. So, Shayna refuses to leave her house, a sure sign that she suffers from *agoraphobia.*

Soo-Mee and Shayna's friend Randal laughs at their inability to identify the source of their anxiety. He says, "I know exactly what I fear: snakes. I have a *phobia,* which I know is *irrational,* but at least I can deal with it by avoiding areas where snakes are known to be, for example. My problem may result from my *observing* a friend being bitten by a snake."

Terms and Concepts to Remember

1. A **psychological disorder** is a syndrome marked by a clinically significant disturbance in a person's cognition, emotion regulation, or behavior.
2. **Attention-deficit/hyperactivity disorder** *(ADHD)* is a psychological disorder marked by extreme inattention and/or hyperactivity and impulsivity.
3. The **medical model** holds that psychological disorders are illnesses that can be diagnosed, treated, and, in most cases, cured, often through treatment in a psychiatric hospital.
4. **Epigenetics** is the study of environmental influences on gene expression that occur without a DNA change.
5. The **DSM-5** is a short name for the American Psychiatric Association's *Diagnostic and Statistical Manual of Mental Disorders,* Fifth Edition, which provides a widely used system of classifying psychological disorders.
6. **Anxiety disorders** involve distressing, persistent anxiety or maladaptive behaviors that reduce anxiety.
7. In the **generalized anxiety disorder,** the person is continually tense, fearful, and in a state of autonomic nervous system arousal for no apparent reason.

8. A **panic disorder** is an unpredictable episode of intense dread accompanied by chest pain, dizziness, or choking. It is essentially an increase of the anxiety associated with generalized anxiety disorder.
9. A **phobia** is an anxiety disorder in which a person has a persistent, irrational fear and avoidance of a specific object or situation.
10. **Obsessive-compulsive disorder (OCD)** is a disorder in which the person experiences uncontrollable and repetitive thoughts (obsessions) and/or actions (compulsions).
11. **Posttraumatic stress disorder (PTSD)** is a disorder characterized by haunting memories, nightmares, social withdrawal, jumpy anxiety, and/or insomnia lasting four weeks or more after a traumatic experience.
12. **Psychoactive drugs**—which include stimulants, depressants, and hallucinogens—are chemical substances that alter mood and perceptions. They work by stimulating, inhibiting, or mimicking the activity of neurotransmitters.
13. A **substance use disorder** is continued substance craving and use despite significant life disruption and/or physical risk.
14. **Tolerance** is the diminishing of a psychoactive drug's effect that occurs with repeated use, requiring larger and larger doses in order to produce the same effect.
15. **Withdrawal** refers to the discomfort and distress that follow the discontinued use of an addictive drug or behavior.
16. **Depressants** are psychoactive drugs, such as alcohol, opiates, and barbiturates, that reduce neural activity and slow body functions.
17. Popularly known as alcoholism, **alcohol use disorder** is characterized by the development of alcohol tolerance, withdrawal, and a drive to continue use.
18. **Barbiturates** are depressants, sometimes used to induce sleep or reduce anxiety; they depress central nervous system activity and impair memory and judgment.
19. **Opiates** are depressants derived from the opium poppy, such as opium, morphine, and heroin; they reduce neural activity and temporarily lessen pain and anxiety.
20. **Stimulants** are psychoactive drugs, such as caffeine, nicotine, cocaine, the amphetamines, methamphetamine, and Ecstasy, that excite neural activity and speed up body functions.
21. **Nicotine** is the stimulant drug found in tobacco; it is highly addictive. It diminishes appetite and boosts alertness and mental efficiency.
22. **Cocaine,** a powerful and addictive stimulant derived from the coca plant, temporarily increases alertness and produces feelings of euphoria.
23. **Amphetamines** are a type of stimulant and, as such, stimulate neural activity, causing speeded-up body functions and associated energy and mood changes.

24. **Methamphetamine** is a powerfully addictive stimulant that speeds up body functions and is associated with energy and mood changes.

25. Classified as both a (synthetic) stimulant and mild hallucinogen, **Ecstasy (MDMA)** produces short-term euphoria and social intimacy. Repeated use may permanently damage serotonin neurons, suppressing immunity and disrupting memory and other cognitive functions.

26. **Hallucinogens** are psychedelic drugs, such as LSD and marijuana, that distort perception and evoke sensory images in the absence of sensory input.

27. The **near-death experience** is an altered state of consciousness that has been reported by some people who have had a close brush with death.

28. **LSD** *(lysergic acid diethylamide)* is a powerful hallucinogen capable of producing perceptual distortions and hallucinations and extreme emotions. LSD produces its unpredictable effects partially because it blocks the action of the neurotransmitter serotonin.

29. The major active ingredient in marijuana, **THC** is classified as a mild hallucinogen.

30. **Major depressive disorder** is the mood disorder that occurs when a person exhibits five or more symptoms, at least one of which must be either a depressed mood or loss of interest or pleasure for more than a two-week period and for no obvious reason.

31. **Bipolar disorder** is the mood disorder in which a person alternates between depression and the euphoria of a manic state; formerly called *manic-depressive disorder*.

    Memory aid: *Bipolar* means having two poles, that is, two opposite qualities. In **bipolar disorder,** the opposing states are mania and depression.

32. **Mania** is the wildly optimistic, euphoric, hyperactive state that alternates with depression in the bipolar disorder.

33. **Schizophrenia** is a psychological disorder characterized by delusions, hallucinations, disorganized thinking and speech, and/or diminished, inappropriate emotional expression.

34. **Psychotic disorders** are a group of disorders marked by distorted perceptions, irrational ideas, and loss of contact with reality.

35. **Delusions** are false beliefs that may accompany schizophrenia and other disorders.

36. **Acute schizophrenia** is a psychotic disorder that frequently occurs in response to an emotionally traumatic event; it can occur at any age and has extended recovery periods. Also called *reactive schizophrenia.*

37. **Chronic schizophrenia** is a slow-developing psychotic disorder in which recovery is doubtful; symptoms usually occur by late adolescence or early adulthood. Also called *process schizophrenia.*

38. **Anorexia nervosa** is an eating disorder, most common in adolescent females, in which a person maintains a starvation diet despite being significantly underweight.

39. **Bulimia nervosa** is an eating disorder characterized by episodes of overeating followed by purging (by vomiting or laxative use), fasting, or excessive exercise.

40. **Binge-eating disorder** is characterized by episodes of overeating, followed by remorse, but without the purging or fasting that marks bulimia nervosa.

41. **Dissociative disorders** involve a separation of conscious awareness from previous memories, thoughts, and feelings.

    Memory aid: To *dissociate* is to separate or pull apart. In the **dissociative disorders** a person becomes dissociated from his or her memories and identity.

42. The **dissociative identity disorder** is a dissociative disorder in which a person exhibits two or more distinct and alternating personalities; formerly called *multiple personality disorder.*

43. A **personality disorder** is characterized by inflexible and enduring maladaptive character traits that impair social functioning.

44. The **antisocial personality disorder** is a personality disorder in which the person (usually a man) shows no sign of a conscience that would inhibit wrongdoing, even toward friends and family members. May be ruthless and aggressive or a clever con artist.

14

Therapy

Chapter Overview

Chapter 14 discusses the major psychotherapies and biomedical therapies for maladaptive behaviors. The various psychotherapies all derive from the personality theories discussed earlier, namely, the psychoanalytic and psychodynamic, humanistic, behavioral, and cognitive theories. The chapter groups the therapies by perspective but also emphasizes the common threads that run through them. In evaluating the psychotherapies, the chapter points out that, although people who are untreated often improve, those receiving psychotherapy tend to improve somewhat more, regardless of the type of psychotherapy.

The chapter includes in the discussion of the biomedical therapies a description of therapeutic lifestyle change because everything psychological is also biological. Other biomedical therapies are drug therapies, electroconvulsive therapy and other forms of brain stimulation, and psychosurgery, which is seldom used. By far the most important of these, drug therapies are being used in the treatment of psychotic, anxiety, and mood disorders.

Chapter Review

First, skim each text section, noting headings and boldface items. Review the section by reading the objectives and summaries provided here, then answer the questions that follow. In some cases, STUDY TIPS explain how best to learn a difficult concept and APPLICATIONS help you to know how well you understand the material. Check your understanding of the material by consulting the answers beginning on page 304. Do not continue with the next section until you understand each answer. If you need to, review or reread the section in the textbook before continuing.

Treating Psychological Disorders

Objective 14-1: Explain how psychotherapy and the biomedical therapies differ.

In *psychotherapy,* a trained therapist uses psychological techniques to assist someone seeking to overcome psychological difficulties or achieve personal growth. The *biomedical therapies* use prescribed medications or medi-

cal procedures. Psychotherapists often combine multiple methods, describing their approach as *eclectic.*

1. Mental health therapies are classified as either _____ therapies or _____ therapies.

2. Psychological therapy is more commonly called _____ .

3. Biomedical therapies include the use of _____ _____ and medical procedures.

4. Some psychotherapists blend several techniques and so are said to take an _____ approach.

The Psychological Therapies

Objective 14-2: Discuss the goals and techniques of psychoanalysis, and explain how they have been adapted in psychodynamic therapy.

Psychoanalysis is Sigmund Freud's therapeutic approach to help the person release repressed feelings and gain self-insight. The goal of psychoanalysis is to help people gain insight into the unconscious origins of their disorders, to work through the accompanying feelings, and to take responsibility for their own growth.

Psychoanalysts emphasize the power of childhood experiences to mold us. Their therapy draws on techniques such as *free association* (saying aloud anything that comes to mind), *resistances* (the blocking from consciousness of anxiety-laden material) and their *interpretation,* dream interpretation, and other behaviors such as *transference* (transferring to the therapist long-repressed feelings). Psychoanalysis is criticized because its interpretations are hard to prove or disprove and because it is time-consuming and costly.

Those using *psychodynamic therapy* techniques try to understand patients' current symptoms by focusing on themes across important relationships, including childhood experiences and the therapist relationship. They may also help the person explore and gain perspective on defended-against thoughts and feelings. However, they talk with the patient face-to-face, once a week, and for only a few weeks or months.

5. The goal of Freud's psychoanalysis is to help the patient gain _____ .

6. Freud assumed that many psychological problems originate in childhood impulses and conflicts that have been _____ .

7. Psychoanalysts attempt to bring _____ feelings into _____ awareness where they can be dealt with.

8. Freud's technique in which a patient says whatever comes to mind is called _____ _____ .

9. When, in the course of therapy, a person omits shameful or embarrassing material, _____ is occurring. Insight is enabled by the analyst's _____ of the meaning of such omissions, of dreams, and of other information revealed during therapy sessions.

10. When strong feelings, similar to those experienced in other important relationships, are developed toward the therapist, _____ has occurred.

11. Critics point out that psychoanalysts' interpretations are hard to _____ and that therapy takes a long time and is very _____ .

12. Therapists who are influenced by Freud's psychoanalysis but who talk to the patient face-to-face are using _____ therapy techniques. These therapists try to understand a patient's current symptoms by focusing on _____ across important _____ . In addition, they work with patients only once or twice a week and for only a few weeks or months.

13. While this approach aims to help people gain _____ into their difficulties, it focuses on _____ _____ rather than on past hurts.

Objective 14-3: Identify the basic themes of humanistic therapy, and describe the goals and techniques of Rogers' person-centered approach.

Humanistic therapies focus on the present and the future instead of the past, on clients' conscious thoughts, and on clients' taking responsibility for their own growth. In emphasizing people's inherent potential for self-fulfillment, they aim to promote growth rather than to cure illness. In his nondirective **person-centered therapy,** Rogers used **active listening** to express *genuineness, acceptance,* and *empathy.* This **unconditional positive regard,** he believed, would help clients to increase their self-understanding and self-acceptance. The therapist interrupts only to echo, restate, and clarify the client's feelings and to accept what the client is expressing. The person-centered counselor seeks to provide a psychological mirror that helps clients see themselves more clearly.

14. Humanistic and psychodynamic therapies are often called _____ therapies. Humanistic therapies attempt to help people meet their potential for _____ .

List several ways that humanistic therapy differs from psychoanalysis.

15. The humanistic therapy based on Rogers' theory is called _____-_____ therapy, which is described as _____ therapy because the therapist _____ (interprets/does not interpret) the person's problems.

16. To promote growth in clients, therapists using Rogers' approach exhibit _____ , _____ , and _____ .

17. Rogers' technique of echoing, restating, and clarifying what a person is saying is called _____ _____ .

18. Given a nonjudgmental environment that provides _____ _____ _____ , patients are better able to accept themselves as they are and to feel valued and whole.

19. Three tips for listening more actively in your own relationships are to _____ , _____ _____ , and _____ _____ .

Objective 14-4: Explain how the basic assumption of behavior therapy differs from the assumptions of psychodynamic and humanistic therapies, and describe the techniques used in exposure therapies and aversive conditioning.

Traditional psychoanalysis attempts to help people gain insight into their unresolved and unconscious conflicts. Humanistic therapies help clients to get in touch with their feelings. In contrast, *behavior therapies* question the healing power of self-awareness. They assume problem behaviors *are* the problems and thus do not look for inner causes. Instead, they apply learning principles to eliminate a troubling behavior.

Counterconditioning is based on classical conditioning, and it involves conditioning new responses to stimuli that trigger unwanted behaviors. Two types are exposure therapies and aversive conditioning. *Exposure therapies* treat anxieties by exposing people to the things they fear and avoid. In *systematic desensitization,* a widely used exposure therapy, a pleasant, relaxed state is associated with gradually increasing anxiety-triggering stimuli. *Virtual reality exposure therapy* equips patients with a head-mounted display unit that provides vivid simulations of feared stimuli, such as a plane's takeoff. In *aversive conditioning,* an unpleasant state (such as nausea) is associated with an unwanted behavior (such as drinking alcohol). This method works in the short run, but for long-term effectiveness it is combined with other methods.

20. Behavior therapy applies principles of _____ to eliminate troubling behaviors.

Contrast the assumption of the behavior therapies with the assumptions of psychodynamic and humanistic therapies.

21. One cluster of behavior therapies is based on the principles of _____ _____ , as developed in the experiments of _____ .

22. The technique, in which a new, incompatible response is substituted for a maladaptive one, is called _____ . Two examples of this technique are _____ _____ and _____ _____ .

23. The idea behind exposure therapy was first developed in experiments by _____ , who eliminated a young boy's fear of rabbits by _____ , or replacing, it with a relaxed state.

24. One widely used exposure therapy is _____ _____ . The idea behind this technique is that a person cannot simultaneously be _____ and relaxed.

25. The first step in systematic desensitization is to make a list of anxiety-arousing stimuli. The second step involves training in _____ _____ . In the final step, the person is trained to associate the _____ state with the _____ -arousing stimuli.

26. A newer option, involving a head-mounted display unit, is _____ _____ therapy. This method is used when the actual situation is too expensive, embarrassing, or difficult to re-create.

27. In aversive conditioning, the therapist attempts to substitute a _____ (positive/negative) response to a harmful stimulus for one that is currently _____ (positive/negative). In this technique, a person's unwanted behaviors become associated with _____ feelings. Because this technique usually works only in the _____ _____ , therapists often combine it with other treatments.

Objective 14-5: State the basic idea of operant conditioning therapies.

Operant conditioning therapies are based on the concept that our behaviors are strongly influenced by their consequences. They apply operant conditioning principles by reinforcing desired behaviors while failing to reinforce or punishing undesired behaviors. The rewards used to modify behavior vary from attention or praise to more concrete rewards such as food. In institutional settings, therapists may create a **token economy,** in which a patient exchanges a token of some sort, earned for displaying appropriate behavior, for rewards, such as candy or TV time.

28. Reinforcing desired behaviors and withholding reinforcement for or punishing undesired behaviors are key aspects of _____ _____ .

29. Therapies that influence behavior by controlling its consequences are based on principles of _____ conditioning. One application of this form of therapy to institutional settings is the _____ _____ , in which desired behaviors are rewarded.

STUDY TIP/APPLICATION: Each type of behavior therapy discussed is derived from principles of either classical conditioning or operant conditioning. Recall from Chapter 6 that classical conditioning is based on the formation of a learned association between two stimulus situations or events. Operant conditioning is based on the use of reinforcement and punishment to modify the future likelihood of behaviors.

Several problem behaviors are described in the chart below. Test your understanding of behavior therapy by completing the chart and explaining how you would treat the problem behavior using one of the behavior therapies. Be sure to identify any reinforcers, conditioned stimuli, and unconditioned stimuli that you would use. The first example is completed for you.

30.

Situation	Type of Conditioning	Procedure
A friend is trying to quit smoking	Aversive conditioning, a type of counterconditioning (classical conditioning)	Each time your friend puffs the cigarette, the taste of the cigarette (conditioned stimulus) is paired with a blast of hot air delivered to his/her face (unconditioned stimulus).
a. A relative has a fear of flying (Hint: use imagined situations)		
b. The parents of a sloppy teenager want to get him to clean up his room		
c. A child is terrified of dogs (Hint: use real situations)		

Objective 14-6: Describe the goals and techniques of the cognitive therapies and of cognitive-behavioral therapy.

Like psychodynamic approaches, the *cognitive therapies* assume that our thinking colors our feelings, and so they try to teach people who suffer psychological disorders new, more adaptive ways of thinking.

In treating depression, Aaron Beck seeks to reverse clients' negative thinking about themselves, their situations, and their futures. His technique is a gentle questioning that aims to help people discover their irrationalities.

Cognitive-behavioral therapy combines cognitive therapy (changing self-defeating thinking) with behavior therapy (changing behavior). It aims to make people aware of their irrational negative thinking, to replace it with new ways of thinking and talking, and to practice the more positive approach in everyday settings.

31. Therapists who teach people new, more constructive ways of thinking are using _____ therapy. It is used to modify the behaviors associated with _____ and those associated with _____ _____ .

32. One variety of cognitive therapy attempts to reverse the _____ themes often associ-

ated with _____ by helping clients see their irrationalities. This therapy was developed by _____ . Psychologists call the overgeneralized, self-blaming thinking of depressed people _____ .

33. Children, teens, and college students trained to " _____ _____ " to their negative thoughts showed a modestly reduced rate of future depression.

34. Treatment that combines an attack on negative thinking with efforts to modify behavior is known as _____-_____ therapy. This therapy has been particularly effective in treating people with _____-_____ disorder.

35. A type of CBT therapy that attempts to make peace between two opposing forces—acceptance and change—is called _____ _____ therapy.

APPLICATIONS FOR ALL PSYCHOTHERAPIES:

36. Given that Don Carlos' therapist attempts to help him by offering genuineness, acceptance, and empathy, she is probably practicing _____ therapy.

37. To help Sam lose weight by eating fewer sweets, his therapist laced a batch of cookies with a nausea-producing drug. Which technique is the therapist using?

_____ _____

38. B.J.'s therapist interprets her psychological problems in terms of repressed impulses. Which type(s) of therapy is she using? _____

39. Ben is a therapist who takes a cognitive-behavioral approach. Compared with Rachel, who applies operant conditioning techniques in her therapy, Ben is more likely to
  a. base his therapy on principles of operant conditioning.
  b. base his therapy on principles of classical conditioning.
  c. address clients' attitudes as well as behaviors.
  d. focus on clients' unconscious urges.

40. To help him overcome his fear of heights, Duane's therapist has him construct a list of anxiety-triggering stimuli and then learn to associate each with a state of deep relaxation. Duane's therapist is using the technique called

_____ _____ .

41. A patient in a hospital receives poker chips for making her bed, being punctual at meal times, and maintaining her physical appearance. The poker chips can be exchanged for privileges, such as television viewing, snacks, and magazines. This is an example of the
  a. psychodynamic therapy technique called systematic desensitization.
  b. behavior therapy technique called token economy.
  c. cognitive therapy technique called token economy.
  d. humanistic therapy technique called systematic desensitization.

42. After Darnel dropped a pass in an important football game, he became depressed and vowed to quit the team because of his athletic incompetence. The campus psychologist used gentle questioning to reveal to Darnel that his thinking was irrational: His "incompetence" had earned him an athletic scholarship. The psychologist's response was most typical of a therapist taking a

_____ approach.

43. Leota is startled when her therapist says that she needs to focus on eliminating her problem behavior rather than gaining insight into its underlying cause. Most likely, Leota has consulted a therapist taking a

_____ approach.

Objective 14-7: Discuss the aims and benefits of group and family therapies.

The social context provided by *group therapy* allows people to discover that others have problems similar to their own and to try out new ways of behaving. Receiving honest feedback can be very helpful, and it can be reassuring to find that you are not alone. *Family therapy* assumes that we live and grow in relation to others. This type of therapy views an individual's unwanted behaviors as influenced by or directed at other family members. In an effort to heal relationships, therapists attempt to guide family members toward positive relationships and improved communication.

List several advantages of group therapy.

44. The type of group interaction that focuses on the fact that we live and grow in relation to others is

_____ _____ .

45. In this type of group, therapists focus on improving _____ within the family.

STUDY TIP/APPLICATION: To organize your thinking about the psychological therapies discussed in this chapter, complete the following chart. For each category of therapy, state the assumed underlying cause of psychological disorders, the overall goal of therapy, and the role of the therapist. To help you get started, the first example is already filled in.

46. Type of Psychotherapy	Assumed Cause of Psychological Disorder	Goal of Therapy	Role of Therapist
Psychoanalysis	Repression of forbidden impulses and childhood conflicts	Self-insight	Interpreting dreams, free associations, resistances, and transferences
Psychodynamic therapies			
Humanistic Therapies			
Behavior Therapies			
Cognitive Therapies			
Group and Family Therapies			

Evaluating Psychotherapies

Objective 14-8: Discuss whether psychotherapy works, and describe how we know.

Clients tend to overestimate the effectiveness of psychotherapy because they enter therapy in crisis. With the normal ebb and flow of events, the crisis passes and people say the therapy helped them. Clients may also need to believe that the investment of time and money has been worth it. Finally, clients generally speak positively of therapists who have been understanding and who have helped them gain a new perspective.

Clients enter therapy when they are extremely unhappy, usually leave when they are less unhappy, and stay in touch only if satisfied. Thus, therapists, like most clients, testify to therapy's success. Clinicians are mostly aware of other therapists' failures as clients seek new therapists for their recurring problems.

Randomized clinical trials assign people on a waiting list to therapy or no therapy. Statistical methods that combine the results of these studies reveal that people who remain untreated often improve, but those who receive psychotherapy are more likely to improve.

47. A majority of psychotherapy clients express _____ (satisfaction/dissatisfaction) with their therapy.

Give three reasons that client testimonials are not persuasive evidence for psychotherapy's effectiveness.

48. Clinicians tend to _____ (overestimate/underestimate) the effectiveness of psychotherapy.

49. One reason clinicians' perceptions of the effectiveness of psychotherapy are inaccurate is that clients justify entering therapy by emphasizing their _____ and justify leaving therapy by emphasizing their _____ .

50. In hopes of better assessing psychotherapy's effectiveness, psychologists have turned to _____ research.

51. The debate over the effectiveness of psychotherapy began with a study by _____ ; it showed that the rate of improvement for those who received therapy _____ (was/was not) higher than the rate for those who did not.

52. In response to these findings, hundreds of studies were conducted. The best of these were

_____ _____

trials.

53. When researchers used statistical methods to combine the results of outcome studies, they found that psychotherapy is _____ (somewhat effective/ineffective). They found that the outcome for the average therapy client was better than that for _____ (what percentage?) of the untreated clients.

Objective 14-9: Discuss whether some psychotherapies are more effective than others for specific disorders.

No one psychotherapy has been shown to be best in all cases, nor is there any relationship between clinicians' experience, training, supervision, and licensing and their clients' outcomes. Some therapies are, however, well suited to particular disorders, such as behavioral conditioning therapies for treating specific problems such as phobias, compulsions, and sexual dysfunctions and cognitive therapy for coping with anxiety, posttraumatic stress disorder, and depression. Unsupported psychotherapies that should be avoided include energy therapies, recovered-memory therapies, rebirthing therapies, and conversion therapies.

Who should decide which psychotherapies should be used? Science-oriented clinicians call for *evidence-based practice.* Thus, they make decisions based on research evidence, clinical expertise, and knowledge of the patient.

54. Comparisons of the effectiveness of different forms of psychotherapy reveal _____ (clear/no clear) differences, that the type of therapy provider _____ (matters greatly/does not matter), and that whether therapy is provided by an individual therapist or within a group _____ (makes a difference/does not make a difference).

55. With phobias, compulsions, and other specific behavior problems, _____ _____ therapies have been the most effective. Depression and anxiety have been helped by_____ , and _____-_____ counseling often helps people with mild to moderate depression. And many studies have demonstrated that anxiety, depression, and posttraumatic stress disorder may be effectively treated with _____ therapy.

56. There _____ (is/is no) scientific support for psychotherapies such as energy therapies and rebirthing therapies.

57. To determine which psychotherapies are acceptable, science-oriented clinicians call for

_____-_____

_____ .

APPLICATION:

58. Your best friend Armand wants to know which type of therapy works best. You should tell him that
   a. psychotherapy does not work.
   b. behavior therapy is the most effective.
   c. cognitive therapy is the most effective.
   d. no one type of therapy is consistently the most successful.

Objective 14-10: Describe the three elements shared by all forms of psychotherapy.

Despite their differences, all therapies offer at least three benefits. First, they all offer the expectation that, with commitment from the person, things can and will get better. Second, every therapy offers people an explanation of their symptoms and new experiences. Third, no matter what technique they use, effective therapists are empathic people who seek to understand another's experience, whose care and concern the client feels, and who earn the client's trust and respect. As a result, a *therapeutic alliance* forms between therapist and client. In short, all therapies offer hope for demoralized people, a new perspective on oneself and the world, and an empathic, trusting, caring relationship.

59. All forms of effective therapy offer three benefits: _____ for demoralized people; a new _____ on oneself and the world; and a relationship that is _____ , _____ , and _____ .

60. The emotional bond between therapist and client—the _____ _____— is a key aspect of effective therapy.

61. The importance of a fresh perspective by a caring person is why paraprofessionals _____ (are/are not) able to assist so many troubled people so effectively.

62. In summary, those who do not seek help improve _____ (more than/less than/as much as) those who undergo psychotherapy. And, people with _____-_____ , specific problems tend to improve the most.

Objective 14-11: Discuss how culture and values influence the client-therapist relationship.

Therapists' personal beliefs and values influence their therapy. While nearly all agree on the importance of encouraging clients' sensitivity, openness, personal responsibility, and sense of purpose, they differ in cultural and moral matters. Value differences also become important when a client from one culture meets a therapist from another. For example, clients from a *collectivist* culture may have difficulty with a therapist from an *individualist* culture, who requires them to think only of their own well-being. Such differences may help explain the reluctance of some minorities to use mental health services. Another area of potential value conflict is religion.

63. Clients and therapists often differ from one another in matters of _____ and _____ .

64. Generally speaking, therapists' personal values _____ (do/do not) influence their therapy. This is particularly significant when the therapist and client are from _____ (the same/different) cultures.

65. Cultures that give priority to personal desires and identity reflect _____ . Three examples of such cultures are those found in _____ , _____ , and _____ .

66. Cultures that place more emphasis on others' expectations reflect _____ . Many _____ cultures fall into this category.

67. Differences in values may help explain the reluctance of some _____ populations to use mental health services.

Objective 14-12. Identify what a person should look for when selecting a therapist.

In choosing a therapist, a potential client may wish to have a consultation with two or three. After describing the problem, you can learn the therapist's specific treatment approach. Moreover, you can ask questions about the therapist's values, credentials, state license, and fees. Finally, recognizing the significance of the emotional bond between therapist and client, you can sense the appropriateness of the match.

Identify some of the common trouble signals that indicate a person should seek help from a mental health professional.

68. Clinical psychologists who hold the _____ (what degree?) have completed research training supplemented by a supervised internship. Those with a

_____ (what degree?) received training more focused on therapy.

69. Medical doctors who specialize in treating psychological disorders are _____ . As M.D.s or D.O.s, they can prescribe _____ .

70. Clinical and psychiatric _____ have completed a two-year master's degree program that prepares them to offer psychotherapy, mostly to people with everyday problems.

71. Marriage and family _____ specialize in family relations problems.

The Biomedical Therapies

Objective 14-13: Explain why therapeutic lifestyle change is considered an effective biomedical therapy, and explain how it works.

Everything psychological is also biological. Stress affects body chemistry and health. And chemical imbalances can produce schizophrenia and depression. This suggests that it is no longer valid to treat mind and body separately. Researchers are promoting *therapeutic lifestyle change,* which involves aerobic exercise, adequate sleep, light exposure, social connection, reducing rumination, and nutritional supplements. Research suggests that their program provides relief from depressive symptoms. Future research will suggest which parts of the program produce the therapeutic effect.

72. When considering the effectiveness of therapy, it is important to remember that everything psychological is also _____ . The neat separation of _____ and _____ that prevailed in the past no longer is valid. We were designed for _____ _____ and _____ engagement.

73. Researchers have developed training seminars that promote _____ _____ change. The elements of this program include _____ _____ .

74. Research reveals that regular _____ _____ rivals the healing power of antidepressant drugs. Regular _____ improves mood and energy. Positive thinking is enhanced by _____ _____ and _____ supplements enhance brain functioning.

Objective 14-14: Describe the drug therapies, and explain how double-blind studies help researchers evaluate a drug's effectiveness.

To control for normal recovery and the *placebo effect,* researchers use the *double-blind technique:* Neither staff nor patients know who gets a drug and who gets a placebo. Using this approach, several types of drugs have proven effective in treating psychological disorders.

Antipsychotic drugs, such as chlorpromazine (sold as Thorazine), provide help to people experiencing the positive symptoms of auditory hallucinations and paranoia by reducing their overreaction to irrelevant stimuli. Antipsychotic drugs are not equally effective in changing the schizophrenia symptoms of apathy and withdrawal. Antipsychotics work by mimicking certain neurotransmitters. Some block the activity of dopamine by occupying its receptor sites. Long-term use of some of these drugs can produce *tardive dyskinesia,* which is marked by involuntary movements of facial muscles, tongue, and limbs. Many of the newer antipsychotics work best who have severe symptoms and have fewer such side effects, but they may increase the risk of obesity and diabetes.

Antianxiety drugs such as Xanax and Ativan depress central nervous system activity. Used with psychological therapy, they can help people learn to cope with frightening stimuli. Antianxiety drugs can produce both psychological and physiological dependence.

Antidepressant drugs aim to lift people up. Typically, they work by increasing the availability of the neurotransmitters norepinephrine or serotonin. For example, Prozac slows the reuptake of serotonin, and so Prozac and its cousins Zoloft and Paxil are called *selective serotonin reuptake inhibitors (SSRIs).* They also are increasingly being used to treat anxiety disorders, obsessive-compulsive disorder, and posttraumatic stress disorder. Although antidepressants influence neurotransmitter systems within hours, their full psychological effects may take four weeks. Depression may also be helped by aerobic exercise and cognitive therapy in combination with drugs.

The simple salt *lithium* is often an effective *mood stabilizer* for those suffering the manic-depressive swings of bipolar disorder. Although lithium significantly lowers the risk of suicide, we do not fully understand how it works.

75. The most widely used biomedical treatments are the _____ therapies. Most drugs for anxiety and depression are prescribed by _____ _____ providers, followed by _____ and, in some states, _____ . Thanks to these therapies and support from community _____ _____ programs, the number of residents in mental hospitals has _____ (increased/decreased) sharply.

76. To guard against the _____ effect and normal _____ , neither the patients nor the staff involved in a study may be aware of which condition a given individual is in; this is called the _____-_____ technique.

77. One effect of chlorpromazine (Thorazine), a type of _____ drug, is to decrease people's responsiveness to _____ _____ . Thus, they are most helpful to people experiencing _____ hallucinations and _____ . These drugs work by _____ certain neurotransmitters. Some block the activity of _____ by occupying its receptor sites.

78. Long-term use of antipsychotic drugs can produce _____ _____ , which involves involuntary movements of the muscles of the _____ , _____ , and _____ .

79. Antipsychotics, combined with _____-_____ programs and family support, have given new hope to many people with schizophrenia.

80. Xanax and Ativan are classified as _____ drugs. These drugs depress activity in the _____ _____ .

81. When used in combination with _____ _____ , these drugs have been used successfully in treating not only anxiety disorders but also _____-_____ disorder and _____ disorder by helping people cope with frightening situations and fear-triggering stimuli.

82. Antianxiety drugs have been criticized for merely reducing _____ , rather than resolving underlying _____ . These drugs may also be _____ .

83. Drugs that are prescribed to alleviate depression are called _____ drugs. These drugs work by increasing levels of the neurotransmitters _____ or _____ .

84. One example of this type of drug is
_____ , which works by
slowing the vacuuming up of _____
from synapses and is therefore called a
_____ _____
_____ _____ .

85. These drugs are now also used to treat
_____ _____ ,
_____-_____
_____ , and _____
_____ _____ .

86. Equally effective in calming anxious people and
energizing depressed people is
_____ _____ ,
which has positive side effects. Even better is to use
antidepressant drugs, which work from the
_____ (bottom up/top down), in
conjunction with _____-
_____ therapy, which works
from the _____ (bottom up/top
down).

87. Although people with depression often improve
after one month on antidepressants, studies demonstrate that a large percentage of the effectiveness is
due to _____
_____ or a _____
_____ .

88. The mood-stabilizing drug _____ ,
which was originally used to treat epilepsy, was
found effective in controlling the _____
episodes associated with bipolar disorder.

89. To stabilize the mood swings of a bipolar disorder,
the simple salt _____
is often prescribed.

APPLICATIONS:

90. In an experiment testing the effects of a new antipsychotic drug, neither Dr. Vargas nor her patients know whether
the patients are in the experimental or the control group.
This is an example of the _____-
_____ technique.

91. Zuza's doctor prescribes medication that blocks the activity of dopamine in her nervous system. Evidently, Zuza is
being treated with an _____
drug.

92. Donovan's doctor prescribes medication that increases
the availability of norepinephrine or serotonin in his nervous system. Evidently, Donovan is being treated with an
_____ drug.

93. A psychiatrist has diagnosed a patient as having bipolar
disorder. It is likely that she will prescribe
_____ .

Objective 14-15: Describe the use of brain stimulation
and psychosurgery in treating specific disorders.

Electroconvulsive therapy (ECT), or shock treatment, is
used for severely depressed patients. A brief electric
current is sent through the brain of an anesthetized
patient. Although ECT is credited with saving many from
suicide, no one knows for sure how it works. *Repetitive
transcranial magnetic stimulation (rTMS)* is performed on
wide-awake patients. Magnetic energy penetrates only
to the brain's surface. Unlike ECT, the rTMS procedure
produces no memory loss or other side effects. Initial
studies have found a small antidepressant effect. A new
experimental procedure is *deep brain stimulation,* which is
administered by a pacemaker. .

Psychosurgery removes or destroys brain tissue in an
effort to change behavior. For example, the *lobotomy* was
once used to calm uncontrollably emotional or violent
patients. The nerves that connect the frontal lobes to
the emotion-controlling centers of the inner brain are
cut. The lobotomy usually produced a permanently list-
less, immature, impulsive personality. Because of these
effects and the introduction of drug treatments in the
1950s, the procedure has been abandoned. Other psychosurgery is used only in extreme cases. For example,
for patients who suffer uncontrollable seizures, surgeons
may deactivate the specific nerve clusters that cause or
transmit the convulsions. MRI-guided precision surgery
may also be used to cut the circuits involved in severe
obsessive-compulsive disorder.

94. The therapeutic technique in which the patient
receives an electric shock to the brain is referred to
as _____ therapy, abbreviated
as _____ .

95. ECT is most often used with patients suffering from
severe _____ . Research evi-
dence _____ (confirms/does
not confirm) ECT's effectiveness with such patients.
However, the mechanism by which ECT works is
_____ .

96. A painless procedure called _____
_____ _____
_____ aims to treat depression
by presenting pulses through a magnetic coil held
close to a person's skull. Unlike ECT, this procedure
produces no _____ loss or other
side effects. This procedure may work by
energizing the brain's left _____
_____ , which is relatively inactive
during depression.

97. Implanted electrodes are controlled by a pacemaker in an experimental procedure called

_____ _____

stimulation.

98. The biomedical therapy in which a portion of brain tissue is removed or destroyed is called

_____ .

99. In the 1930s, Moniz developed an operation called the _____ . In this procedure, the _____ lobe of the brain is disconnected from the _____-controlling centers of the brain.

100. Today, most psychosurgery has been replaced by the use of _____ or some other form of treatment.

Preventing Psychological Disorders and Building Resilience

Objective 14-16: Describe what may help prevent psychological orders, and explain why it is important to develop resilience.

Preventive mental health workers, including *community psychologists,* view many psychological disorders as an understandable response to a disturbing and stressful society. It is not only the person who needs treatment but also the person's social context. Thus, the aim of preventive mental health is to identify and wipe out the conditions that cause the problem, the situations that undermine a person's sense of competence, personal control, and self-esteem.

Faced with unforeseen trauma, most adults exhibit **resilience.** Research has shown that those who suffer often develop a greater-than-usual sensitivity to suffering, greater empathy for those who suffer, an increased sense of responsibility, and enlarged capacity for caring. Other evidence shows that struggling with challenging crises can lead to *posttraumatic growth.*

101. Psychotherapies and biomedical therapies locate the cause of psychological disorders within the

_____ .

102. An alternative viewpoint is that many psychological disorders are responses to _____

_____ .

103. According to this viewpoint, it is not just the

_____ who needs treatment, but also the person's _____

_____ .

104. Preventive mental health seeks to wipe out the social stresses that undermine people's sense of

_____ , _____

_____ , and _____ .

These stresses include _____ ,

work that is _____ , constant

_____ , _____ ,

_____ , and _____ .

105. One group of psychologists who focus on creating environments that support psychological health are _____ _____ .

106. One way to prevent some disorders is by building individuals' _____ , their ability to cope with stress and recover from adversity. _____ (Most/Few) adults exhibit this ability.

107. Research indicates that those who have suffered develop, among other things, a greater _____ for life, more meaningful _____ , changed _____ , and increased personal _____ . Taken together, these indicate _____

_____ .

Progress Test

Multiple-Choice Questions

Circle your answers to the following questions and check them with the answers beginning on page 306. If your answer is incorrect, read the explanation for why it is incorrect and then consult the text.

1. Electroconvulsive therapy is most useful in the treatment of
   a. schizophrenia.
   b. depression.
   c. personality disorders.
   d. anxiety disorders.

2. The technique in which a person is asked to report everything that comes to his or her mind is called _____ ; it is favored by_____ therapy.
   a. active listening; cognitive
   b. natural recovery; humanistic
   c. free association; psychoanalytic
   d. systematic desensitization; behavior

3. Of the following categories of psychotherapy, which is known for its nondirective nature?
   a. psychoanalysis   c. behavior therapy
   b. humanistic therapy   d. cognitive therapy

4. Which of the following is NOT a common criticism of psychoanalysis?
   a. It emphasizes the existence of repressed memories.
   b. It provides interpretations that are hard to disprove.
   c. It is generally a very expensive process.
   d. It gives therapists too much control over patients.

5. Which of the following types of therapy does NOT belong with the others?
   a. cognitive therapy
   b. family therapy
   c. behavior therapy
   d. psychosurgery

6. Which of the following is NOT necessarily an advantage of group therapies over individual therapies?
   a. They tend to take less time for the therapist.
   b. They tend to cost less money for the client.
   c. They are more effective.
   d. They allow the client to test new behaviors in a social context.

7. Which biomedical therapy is MOST likely to be practiced today?
   a. psychosurgery
   b. electroconvulsive therapy
   c. drug therapy
   d. counterconditioning

8. The effectiveness of psychotherapy has been assessed both through clients' perspectives and through controlled research studies. What have such assessments found?
   a. Clients' perceptions and controlled studies alike strongly affirm the effectiveness of psychotherapy.
   b. Clients' perceptions strongly affirm the effectiveness of psychotherapy, but studies point to more modest results.
   c. Studies strongly affirm the effectiveness of psychotherapy, but many clients feel dissatisfied with their progress.
   d. Clients' perceptions and controlled studies alike paint a very mixed picture of the effectiveness of psychotherapy.

9. Cognitive-behavioral therapy aims to
   a. alter the way people act.
   b. make people more aware of their irrational negative thinking.
   c. alter the way people think and act.
   d. countercondition anxiety-provoking stimuli.

10. The results of outcome research on the effectiveness of different psychotherapies reveal that
   a. no single type of therapy is consistently superior.
   b. behavior therapies are most effective in treating specific problems, such as phobias.

   c. cognitive therapies are most effective in treating depressed emotions.
   d. all of these answers are correct.

11. The antipsychotic drugs appear to produce their effects by blocking the receptor sites for
   a. dopamine.   c. norepinephrine.
   b. epinephrine.   d. serotonin.

12. Psychologists who believe in a _____ approach to mental health contend that many psychological disorders could be prevented by changing the disturbed individual's _____ .
   a. biomedical; diet
   b. family; behavior
   c. humanistic; feelings
   d. preventive; environment

13. A therapist who describes his or her approach as eclectic is one who
   a. takes a nondirective approach in helping clients solve their problems.
   b. views psychological disorders as usually stemming from one cause, such as a biological abnormality.
   c. uses one particular technique, such as psychoanalysis or counterconditioning, in treating disorders.
   d. uses a variety of techniques, depending on the client and the problem.

14. The technique in which a therapist echoes, restates, and clarifies what a person says in a nondirective manner is called
   a. active listening.
   b. free association.
   c. systematic desensitization.
   d. transference.

15. One reason that aversive conditioning may only be temporarily effective is that
   a. for ethical reasons, therapists cannot use sufficiently intense unconditioned stimuli to sustain classical conditioning.
   b. patients are often unable to become sufficiently relaxed for conditioning to take place.
   c. patients know that outside the therapist's office they can engage in the undesirable behavior without fear of aversive consequences.
   d. most conditioned responses are elicited by many nonspecific stimuli and it is impossible to countercondition them all.

16. The technique of systematic desensitization is based on the concept that maladaptive symptoms are
   a. a reflection of irrational thinking.
   b. conditioned responses.
   c. expressions of unfulfilled wishes.
   d. all of these things.

17. The operant conditioning technique in which desired behaviors are rewarded with points or poker chips that can later be exchanged for various rewards is called
    a. counterconditioning.
    b. systematic desensitization.
    c. a token economy.
    d. exposure therapy.

18. One variety of _____ therapy is based on the finding that depressed people often attribute their failures to _____ .
    a. humanistic; themselves
    b. behavior; external circumstances
    c. cognitive; external circumstances
    d. cognitive; themselves

19. A person can benefit from psychotherapy simply by believing in it. This illustrates the importance of
    a. natural recovery.
    b. the placebo effect.
    c. transference.
    d. interpretation.

20. Believing that the mind and body are a unit, therapeutic lifestyle change promotes
    a. an empathic, caring, trusting relationship between therapist and client.
    b. changing self-defeating thinking and behavior.
    c. aerobic exercise, adequate sleep, and social connection, for example, to relieve depressive symptoms.
    d. reforming the social context and developing people's coping skills.

21. Carl Rogers developed the _____ technique of _____ .
    a. behavior; systematic desensitization
    b. psychoanalytic; insight therapy
    c. humanistic; person-centered therapy
    d. cognitive; cognitive therapy for depression

22. Using techniques of classical conditioning to develop an association between unwanted behavior and an unpleasant experience is known as
    a. aversive conditioning.
    b. systematic desensitization.
    c. transference.
    d. electroconvulsive therapy.

23. Which type of psychotherapy emphasizes the individual's inherent potential for self-fulfillment?
    a. behavior therapy
    b. psychoanalysis
    c. humanistic therapy
    d. biomedical therapy

24. Which type of psychotherapy focuses on changing unwanted behaviors rather than on discovering their underlying causes?
    a. behavior therapy
    b. cognitive therapy
    c. humanistic therapy
    d. psychoanalysis

25. The techniques of counterconditioning are based on principles of
    a. observational learning.
    b. classical conditioning.
    c. operant conditioning.
    d. behavior modification.

26. In which of the following does the client learn to associate a relaxed state with a hierarchy of anxiety-arousing situations?
    a. cognitive therapy
    b. aversive conditioning
    c. counterconditioning
    d. systematic desensitization

27. Principles of operant conditioning underlie which of the following techniques?
    a. counterconditioning
    b. systematic desensitization
    c. aversive conditioning
    d. the token economy

28. Which type of therapy focuses on eliminating irrational thinking?
    a. rTMS
    b. person-centered therapy
    c. cognitive therapy
    d. behavior therapy

29. Some antidepressant drugs are believed to work by affecting serotonin and
    a. dopamine.
    b. lithium.
    c. norepinephrine.
    d. acetylcholine.

30. Long-term use of antipsychotic drugs can result in a condition in which facial muscles sometimes twitch involuntarily. This condition is called
    a. tardive dyskinesia.
    b. a double blind.
    c. repetitive transcranial magnetic stimulation.
    d. the placebo effect.

31. Which of the following is the mood-stabilizing drug most commonly used to treat bipolar disorder?
    a. Ativan
    b. chlorpromazine
    c. Xanax
    d. lithium

32. The type of drugs criticized for reducing symptoms without resolving underlying problems are the
    a. antianxiety drugs.
    b. antipsychotic drugs.
    c. antidepressant drugs.
    d. amphetamines.

33. Which form of therapy is MOST likely to be successful in treating depression?
    a. behavior modification
    b. psychoanalysis
    c. cognitive therapy
    d. humanistic therapy

34. The lobotomy procedure is not widely used today because
    a. it produces a listless, immature personality.
    b. it is irreversible.
    c. calming drugs became available in the 1950s.
    d. of all of these reasons.

35. Among the common ingredients of the psychotherapies is/are
    a. the offer of a therapeutic relationship.
    b. the expectation among clients that the therapy will prove helpful.
    c. the chance to develop a fresh perspective on oneself and the world.
    d. all of these answers.

36. Family therapy differs from other forms of psycho-therapy because it focuses on
    a. using a variety of treatment techniques.
    b. conscious rather than unconscious processes.
    c. the present instead of the past.
    d. how family tensions may cause individual problems.

37. The idea that mind and body are inseparable is the basis for
    a. person-centered therapy.
    b. evidence-based practice.
    c. therapeutic lifestyle change.
    d. resilience.

38. Having to cope with extremely challenging circum-stances and life crises may result in
    a. posttraumatic growth.
    b. the placebo effect.
    c. therapeutic lifestyle change.
    d. resilience.

Matching Items 1

Match each term with the appropriate definition or description.

Terms

_____ **1.** cognitive therapy
_____ **2.** behavior therapy
_____ **3.** systematic desensitization
_____ **4.** cognitive-behavioral therapy
_____ **5.** person-centered therapy
_____ **6.** exposure therapy
_____ **7.** aversive conditioning
_____ **8.** psychoanalysis
_____ **9.** preventive mental health
_____ **10.** biomedical therapy
_____ **11.** counterconditioning

Definitions or Descriptions

a. associates unwanted behavior with unpleasant experiences
b. associates a relaxed state with anxiety-arousing stimuli
c. emphasizes the social context of psychological disorders
d. integrated therapy that focuses on changing self-defeating thinking and unwanted behavior
e. category of therapies that teach people more adaptive ways of thinking
f. a widely used method of behavior therapy
g. therapy developed by Carl Rogers
h. therapy based on Freud's theory of personality
i. treatment with psychosurgery, electroconvulsive therapy, or drugs
j. classical conditioning procedure in which new responses are conditioned to stimuli that trigger unwanted behaviors
k. category of therapies based on learning principles

Matching Items 2

Match each term with the appropriate definition or description.

Terms

_____ 1. active listening
_____ 2. token economy
_____ 3. placebo effect
_____ 4. lobotomy
_____ 5. lithium
_____ 6. double-blind technique
_____ 7. Xanax
_____ 8. free association
_____ 9. therapeutic lifestyle change
_____ 10. resilience
_____ 11. therapeutic alliance

Definitions or Descriptions

a. type of psychosurgery
b. mood-stabilizing drug
c. empathic technique used in person-centered therapy
d. ability to cope with stress
e. antianxiety drug
f. technique of psychoanalytic therapy
g. an operant conditioning procedure
h. an emotional bond between therapist and client
i. experimental procedure in which both the patient and staff are unaware of a patient's treatment condition
j. intervention focusing on regular exercise, sleep, social interaction, and healthy patterns of thinking
k. the beneficial effect of a person's expecting that treatment will be effective

Application Essay

Willie has been diagnosed as suffering from major depressive disorder. Describe the treatment he might receive if he were to undergo psychoanalysis, cognitive therapy, and one of the biomedical therapies. (Use the space below to list points you want to make, and organize them. Then write the essay on a separate sheet of paper.)

Summing Up

See pp. 302–303

Terms and Concepts to Remember

Using your own words, on a separate piece of paper write a brief definition or explanation of each of the following terms.

1. psychotherapy
2. biomedical therapy
3. eclectic approach

4. psychoanalysis
5. resistance
6. interpretation
7. transference
8. psychodynamic therapy
9. insight therapies
10. person-centered therapy
11. active listening
12. unconditional positive regard
13. behavior therapy
14. counterconditioning
15. exposure therapies
16. systematic desensitization
17. virtual reality exposure therapy
18. aversive conditioning
19. token economy
20. cognitive therapy
21. cognitive-behavioral therapy (CBT)
22. group therapy
23. family therapy
24. evidence-based practice
25. therapeutic alliance
26. antipsychotic drugs
27. antianxiety drugs
28. antidepressant drugs
29. electroconvulsive therapy (ECT)
30. repetitive transcranial magnetic stimulation (rTMS)
31. psychosurgery
32. lobotomy
33. resilience
34. posttraumatic growth

Summing Up

BEHAVIOR THERAPY

Trish, who lives in Canada, is so afraid of flying that she can never visit her closest friend, who lives 3000 miles away. Because this fear interferes with her life,

| it is considered a _____, | and so | Trish seeks a therapist trained in _____, |

which

uses _____ conditioning to pair new responses with the stimuli that trigger her fear.

The therapy shown to be most effective in treating Trish's problem is

a technique called systematic _____,

which is

| a type of _____ therapy that pairs _____ | with | gradually increasing _____-triggering stimuli (going to the airport, going to the gate, getting on the plane, learning about flight procedures, actually taking a flight). |

Because of her limited time, Trish decides to try another route to curing her problem.

| She decides that vivid simulation through _____ _____ _____ therapy would work just as well | because | within the confines of a room, she can experience her fears through _____ sensors that adjust the scene as she turns her head. |

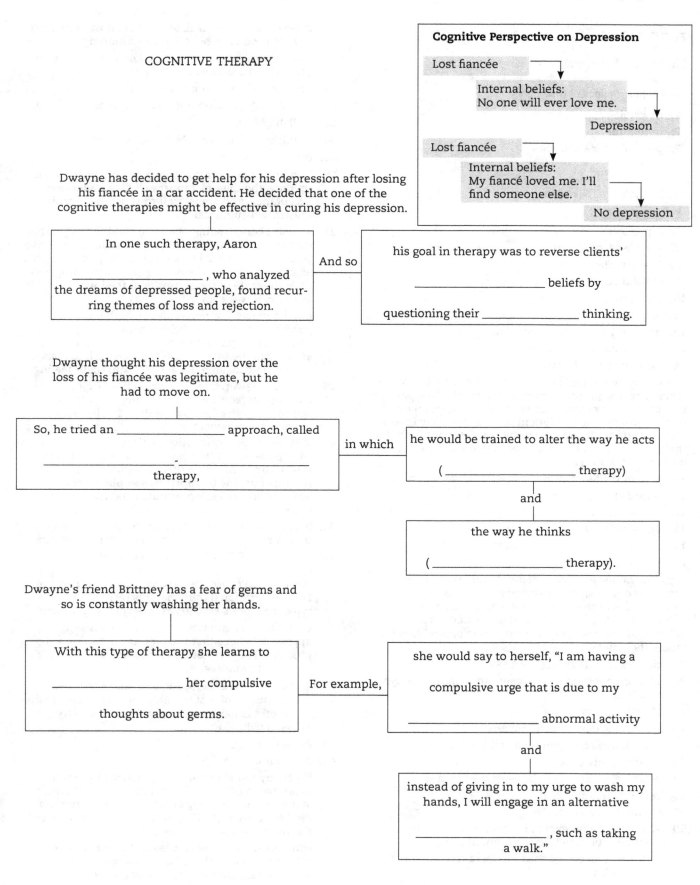

COGNITIVE THERAPY

Cognitive Perspective on Depression

Lost fiancée → Internal beliefs:
No one will ever love me. → Depression

Lost fiancée → Internal beliefs:
My fiancé loved me. I'll find someone else. → No depression

Dwayne has decided to get help for his depression after losing his fiancée in a car accident. He decided that one of the cognitive therapies might be effective in curing his depression.

In one such therapy, Aaron
_____ , who analyzed the dreams of depressed people, found recurring themes of loss and rejection.

And so

his goal in therapy was to reverse clients'
_____ beliefs by questioning their _____ thinking.

Dwayne thought his depression over the loss of his fiancée was legitimate, but he had to move on.

So, he tried an _____ approach, called
_____-_____ therapy,

in which

he would be trained to alter the way he acts
(_____ therapy)

and

the way he thinks
(_____ therapy).

Dwayne's friend Brittney has a fear of germs and so is constantly washing her hands.

With this type of therapy she learns to
_____ her compulsive
thoughts about germs.

For example,

she would say to herself, "I am having a compulsive urge that is due to my
_____ abnormal activity

and

instead of giving in to my urge to wash my hands, I will engage in an alternative
_____ , such as taking a walk."

Answers

Chapter Review

Treating Psychological Disorders

1. psychological; biomedical
2. psychotherapy
3. prescribed medications
4. eclectic

The Psychological Therapies

5. insight
6. repressed
7. repressed; conscious
8. free association
9. resistance; interpretation
10. transference
11. disprove; expensive
12. psychodynamic; themes; relationships
13. insight; current relationships
14. insight; self-fulfillment

Unlike psychodynamic therapies, humanistic therapy is focused on the present and future instead of the past, on conscious rather than unconscious processes, on promoting growth and fulfillment instead of curing illness, and on helping clients take immediate responsibility for their feelings and actions rather than on uncovering the obstacles to doing so.

15. person-centered; nondirective; does not interpret
16. genuineness; acceptance; empathy
17. active listening
18. unconditional positive regard
19. summarize; invite clarification; reflect feelings
20. learning

Psychodynamic and humanistic therapies assume that problems diminish as self-awareness grows. Behavior therapies doubt that self-awareness is the key. Instead of looking for the inner cause of unwanted behavior, behavior therapies apply learning principles to directly attack the unwanted behavior itself.

21. classical conditioning; Ivan Pavlov
22. counterconditioning; exposure therapies; aversive conditioning
23. Mary Cover Jones; countering
24. systematic desensitization; anxious
25. progressive relaxation; relaxed; anxiety
26. virtual reality exposure
27. negative; positive; unpleasant; short run
28. behavior modification
29. operant; token economy
30. **a.** Virtual reality exposure therapy, a type of counterconditioning (classical conditioning).
    b. Token economy, based on operant conditioning principles.

c. Systematic desensitization, an exposure therapy, which is a form of counterconditioning.
Specific procedures may vary. Refer to the text for general descriptions.

31. cognitive; depression; unfocused anxiety
32. negative; depression; Aaron Beck; catastrophizing
33. "talk back"
34. cognitive-behavioral; obsessive-compulsive
35. dialectical behavior
36. humanistic. According to Rogers' person-centered therapy, the therapist must exhibit genuineness, acceptance, and empathy if the client is to move toward self-fulfillment.
37. aversive conditioning. Aversive conditioning is the classical conditioning technique in which a positive response is replaced by a negative response. (In this example, the US is the nausea-producing drug, the CS is the taste of the sweets, and the intended CR is aversion to sweets.)
38. psychoanalysis or psychodynamic therapy. Both psychoanalysis and psychodynamic therapy seek insight into a patient's unconscious feelings. The analysis of dreams, slips of the tongue, and resistances are considered a window into these feelings.
39. **c.** is the answer. Cognitive therapies attempt to change a person's way of thinking about themselves. Cognitive-behavioral therapy also tries to change the behaviors that result from that thinking.
40. systematic desensitization. This type of exposure therapy assumes that you cannot be simultaneously relaxed and anxious. Whenever Duane begins to feel anxious, the therapist moves him back to a less anxiety-triggering stimulus and focuses on relaxation.
41. **b.** is the answer. The token economy is an application of operant conditioning principles. Rewarding desired behavior gets the person to repeat that behavior.
42. cognitive. Because the psychologist is focusing on Darnel's irrational thinking, this response is most typical of Beck's cognitive therapy for depression.
43. behavioral. Therapists who take a behavioral approach believe that the problem behavior is the problem. They do not try to uncover unconscious, repressed impulses.

Group therapy saves therapists time and clients money. The social context of group therapy allows people to discover that others have similar problems and to try out new ways of behaving.

44. family therapy
45. communication
46. Psychodynamic therapies, influenced by Freud's ideas, try to help people understand their current symptoms by focusing on themes across important relationships, including childhood experiences and the therapist-client relationship.

Humanistic therapies focus on the present and future, conscious thoughts, and having the person take responsibility for his or her feelings and actions. The goal is self-fulfillment. The therapist is genuine, accepting, and empathic and uses active listening in this nondirective therapy.

Behavior therapies focus on the problem behavior. The goal is to change undesirable behaviors to desirable behaviors. Therapists use techniques based on classical and operant conditioning principles—for example, exposure therapies, aversive conditioning, and token economies.

Cognitive therapies focus on the person's way of thinking about himself or herself. Self-blaming and overgeneralized explanations of bad events cause the problem. The goal is to change the person's negative thinking. Therapists use gentle questioning to reveal the patient's irrational thinking and persuade a depressed person, for example, to adopt a more positive attitude.

Group and family therapies assume that problems arise from social interactions. They help people to see that others have similar problems and that communication can resolve most problems. During sessions, for example, therapists try to guide family members toward positive relationships and improved communication.

Evaluating Psychotherapies

47. satisfaction

People often enter therapy in crisis. When the crisis passes, they may attribute their improvement to the therapy. Clients, who may need to believe the therapy was worth the cost and effort, may overestimate its effectiveness. Clients generally find positive things to say about their therapists, even if their problems remain.

48. overestimate
49. unhappiness; well-being
50. controlled
51. Hans Eysenck; was not
52. randomized clinical
53. somewhat effective; 80
54. no clear; does not matter; does not make a difference
55. behavioral conditioning; psychodynamic; person-centered; cognitive
56. is no
57. evidence-based practice
58. d. is the answer. Behavioral conditioning therapies work best with specific problems, and cognitive therapy is effective in treating depression. But no one therapy is consistently superior.
59. hope; perspective; caring; trusting; empathic
60. therapeutic alliance
61. are
62. less than; clear-cut
63. culture; values
64. do; different
65. individualism; North America; Australia; Europe
66. collectivism; Asian

67. minority

Some of the common trouble signals include feelings of hopelessness; deep and lasting depression, self-destructive behavior, disruptive fears, sudden mood shifts, thoughts of suicide, compulsive rituals, sexual difficulties, and hearing voices or seeing things.

68. Ph.D.; Psy.D.
69. psychiatrists; medications
70. social workers
71. counselors

The Biomedical Therapies

72. biological; body; mind; physical activity; social
73. therapeutic lifestyle; aerobic exercise, adequate sleep, light exposure, social connection, reducing rumination, and nutritional supplements
74. aerobic exercise; sleep; reducing rumination; nutritional
75. drug; primary care; psychiatrists; psychologists; mental health; decreased
76. placebo; recovery; double-blind
77. antipsychotic; irrelevant stimuli; auditory; paranoia; mimicking; dopamine
78. tardive dyskinesia; face; tongue; limbs
79. life-skills
80. antianxiety; central nervous system
81. psychological therapy; obsessive-compulsive; post-traumatic stress
82. symptoms; problems; addictive
83. antidepressant; norepinephrine; serotonin
84. fluoxetine (Prozac); serotonin; selective serotonin reuptake inhibitor
85. anxiety disorders; obsessive-compulsive disorder; posttraumatic stress disorder
86. aerobic exercise; bottom up; cognitive-behavioral; top down
87. natural recovery; placebo effect
88. Depakote; manic
89. lithium
90. double-blind. To control for the influences of the placebo effect and normal recovery rates, researchers give half the patients the drug and half a similar-appearing placebo. The double-blind technique prevents the researchers' biases from affecting the results.
91. antipsychotic. These drugs are used in treating severe disorders such as schizophrenia.
92. antidepressant. SSRI drugs increase the availability of the neurotransmitters norepinephrine and serotonin, which increase more positive moods.
93. lithium. This simple salt seems to act as a mood stabilizer in people with bipolar disorder.
94. electroconvulsive; ECT
95. depression; confirms; unknown
96. repetitive transcranial magnetic stimulation (rTMS); memory; frontal lobe
97. deep brain

98. psychosurgery
99. lobotomy; frontal; emotion
100. drugs

Preventing Psychological Disorders and Building Resilience

101. person
102. a disturbing and stressful society
103. person; social context
104. competence; personal control; self-esteem; poverty; meaningless; criticism; unemployment; racism; sexism
105. community psychologists
106. resilience; Most
107. appreciation; relationships; priorities; strength; posttraumatic growth

Progress Test

Multiple-Choice Questions

1. **b.** is the answer. Although no one is sure how ECT works, one possible explanation is that it weakens connections in a "hyperconnected" neural hub in the left frontal lobe.

2. **c.** is the answer.
    a. Active listening is a Rogerian technique in which the therapist echoes, restates, and clarifies the client's statements.
    b. Natural recovery refers to improvement without treatment.
    d. Systematic desensitization is a process in which a person is conditioned to associate a relaxed state with anxiety-triggering stimuli.

3. **b.** is the answer.

4. **d.** is the answer. This is not among the criticisms commonly made of psychoanalysis. (It would more likely be made of behavior therapies.)

5. **d.** is the answer.
    a., b., & c. Each of these is a type of psychological therapy.

6. **c.** is the answer. Outcome research on the relative effectiveness of different therapies reveals no clear winner; the other factors mentioned are advantages of group therapies.

7. **c.** is the answer.
    a. The fact that its effects are irreversible makes psychosurgery a drastic procedure, and with advances in drug research, psychosurgery was largely abandoned.
    b. ECT is still widely used as a treatment of severe depression, but in general it is not used as frequently as drug therapy.
    d. Counterconditioning is not a biomedical therapy.

8. **b.** is the answer. Clients' testimonials regarding psychotherapy are generally very positive. The research, in contrast, seems to show that therapy is only *somewhat* effective.

9. **c.** is the answer.

10. **d.** is the answer.

11. **a.** is the answer. By occupying receptor sites for dopamine, these drugs block its activity and reduce its production.

12. **d.** is the answer.

13. **d.** is the answer. Today, many therapists describe themselves as eclectic—as using a blend of therapies.
    a. A therapist who uses a blend of therapies may use a nondirective approach with certain behaviors; however, a more directive approach might be chosen for other clients and problems.
    b. In fact, just the opposite is true. Therapists who take an eclectic approach generally view disorders as stemming from many influences.
    c. Therapists who take an eclectic approach, in contrast to this example, use a combination of treatments.

14. **a.** is the answer.

15. **c.** is the answer. Although aversive conditioning may work in the short run, the person's ability to discriminate between the situation in which the aversive conditioning occurs and other situations can limit the treatment's effectiveness.
    a., b., & d. These were not offered in the text as limitations of the effectiveness of aversive conditioning.

16. **b.** is the answer.
    a. This reflects a cognitive perspective.
    c. This reflects a psychoanalytic perspective.

17. **c.** is the answer.
    a. & b. Counterconditioning is the replacement of an undesired response with a desired one by means of aversive conditioning or systematic desensitization.
    d. Exposure therapy exposes a person, in imagination or in actuality, to a feared situation.

18. **d.** is the answer.

19. **b.** is the answer.
    a. Natural recovery refers to improvement without any treatment.
    c. Transference is the psychoanalytic phenomenon in which a client transfers feelings from other relationships onto his or her analyst.
    d. Interpretation is the psychoanalytic procedure through which the analyst helps the client become aware of resistances and understand their meaning.

20. **c.** is the answer. This approach also promotes light exposure, reducing rumination, and nutritional supplements.
    a. This is one of the three elements common to all forms of psychotherapy.
    b. This is the view of cognitive-behavioral therapy.
    d. This is the view of preventive mental health workers.

21. **c.** is the answer.
    a. This answer would be a correct description of behavior therapy.

b. Humanistic therapy is an insight therapy, but Rogers does not take a psychoanalytic approach.
d. This answer would be a correct description of Aaron Beck.

22. **a.** is the answer.
b. In systematic desensitization, a hierarchy of anxiety-provoking stimuli is gradually associated with a relaxed state.
c. Transference refers to a patient's transferring of feelings from other relationships onto his or her psychoanalyst.
d. Electroconvulsive therapy is a biomedical shock treatment.

23. **c.** is the answer.
a. Behavior therapy focuses on behavior, not self-awareness.
b. Psychoanalysis focuses on bringing repressed feelings into awareness.
d. Biomedical therapy focuses on physical treatment through drugs, ECT, or psychosurgery.

24. **a.** is the answer. For behavior therapy, the problem behaviors *are* the problems.
b. Cognitive therapy teaches people to think and act in more adaptive ways.
c. Humanistic therapy promotes growth and self-fulfillment by providing an empathic, genuine, and accepting environment.
d. Psychoanalytic therapy focuses on uncovering and interpreting repressed feelings.

25. **b.** is the answer. Counterconditioning techniques involve taking an established stimulus, which triggers an undesirable response, and pairing it with a new stimulus in order to condition a new, and more adaptive, response.
a. As indicated by the name, counterconditioning techniques are a form of conditioning; they do not involve learning by observation.
c. & d. The principles of operant conditioning are the basis of behavior modification, which, in contrast to counterconditioning techniques, involves use of reinforcement.

26. **d.** is the answer.
a. This is a confrontational therapy, which is aimed at teaching people to think and act in more adaptive ways.
b. Aversive conditioning is a form of counterconditioning in which unwanted behavior is associated with unpleasant feelings.
c. Counterconditioning is a general term, including not only systematic desensitization, in which a hierarchy of fears is desensitized, but also other techniques, such as aversive conditioning.

27. **d.** is the answer.
a. & b. These techniques are based on classical conditioning.
c. Aversive conditioning is a form of counterconditioning in which unwanted behavior is associated with unpleasant feelings. It is based on principles of classical conditioning.

28. **c.** is the answer.
a. rTMS is a gentler method of brain stimulation for treating people who are depressed.
b. In this humanistic therapy, the therapist facilitates the client's growth by offering a genuine, accepting, and empathic environment.
d. Behavior therapy concentrates on modifying the actual symptoms of psychological problems.

29. **c.** is the answer.

30. **a.** is the answer.

31. **d.** is the answer. Lithium works as a mood stabilizer.
a. & c. Ativan and Xanax are antianxiety drugs.
b. Chlorpromazine is an antipsychotic drug.

32. **a.** is the answer.

33. **c.** is the answer.
a. Behavior modification is most likely to be successful in treating specific behavior problems, such as bed wetting.
b. & d. The text does not single out particular disorders for which these therapies tend to be most effective.

34. **d.** is the answer.

35. **d.** is the answer.

36. **d.** is the answer.
a. This is true of most forms of psychotherapy.
b. & c. This is true of humanistic, cognitive, and behavior therapies.

37. **c.** is the answer. Therapeutic lifestyle change involves treating both mind and body through aerobic exercise, plentiful sleep, and nutritional supplements, for example.
a. Person-centered therapy is Rogers' nondirective form of therapy.
b. Evidence-based practice is suggested by science-oriented clinicians as the most appropriate way of selecting acceptable therapies.
d. Resilience is the ability to cope with stress.

38. **a.** is the answer.
b. The placebo effect is the healing power of positive expectations.
c. Therapeutic lifestyle change is a biomedical therapy that believes that the mind and body are a unit.
d. Resilience is the personal strength that helps most people cope with stress; it can be a forerunner of posttraumatic growth.

Matching Items 1

1. e	**5.** g	**9.** c
2. k	**6.** f	**10.** i
3. b	**7.** a	**11.** j
4. d	**8.** h	

Matching Items 2

1. c	**5.** b	**9.** j
2. g	**6.** i	**10.** d
3. k	**7.** e	**11.** h
4. a	**8.** f	

Application Essay

Psychoanalysts assume that psychological problems such as depression are caused by unresolved, repressed, and unconscious impulses and conflicts from childhood. A psychoanalyst would probably attempt to bring these repressed feelings into Willie's conscious awareness and help him gain insight into them. He or she would likely try to interpret Willie's resistance during free association, his dreams, and any emotional feelings he might transfer to the analyst.

Therapists who take a cognitive approach assume that a person's emotional reactions are influenced by the person's thoughts in response to the event in question. A cognitive therapist would probably try to teach Willie new and more constructive ways of thinking in order to reverse his negative beliefs about himself, his situation, and his future.

In one form of biomedical therapy, the therapist would consider mind and body as one and would recommend lifestyle changes, such as aerobic exercise, adequate sleep, and improved social connections. In other biomedical therapies, the primary care provider (or maybe psychiatrist or, in some states, psychologist) attempts to treat disorders by altering the functioning of the patient's brain. This therapist would probably prescribe an antidepressant drug such as Prozac, which lifts spirits by increasing the availability of norepinephrine and serotonin. If Willie's depression is especially severe, electroconvulsive therapy might be performed.

Summing Up

Behavior Therapy

Trish, who lives in Canada, is so afraid of flying that she can never visit her closest friend, who lives 3000 miles away. Because this fear interferes with her life, it is considered a *phobia,* and so Trish seeks a therapist trained in *counterconditioning,* which uses *classical* conditioning to pair new responses with the stimuli that trigger her fear. The therapy shown to be most effective in treating Trish's problem is a technique called systematic *desensitization,* which is a type of *exposure* therapy that pairs *relaxation* with gradually increasing *anxiety*-triggering stimuli (going to the airport, going to the gate, getting on the plane, learning about flight procedures, actually taking a flight). Because of her limited time, Trish decides to try another route to curing her problem. She decides that vivid simulation through *virtual reality exposure* therapy would work just as well because within the confines of a room, she can experience her fears through *motion* sensors that adjust the scene as she turns her head.

Cognitive Therapy

Dwayne has decided to get help for his depression after losing his fiancée in a car accident. He decided that one of the cognitive therapies might be effective in curing his depression. In one such therapy, Aaron *Beck,* who analyzed the dreams of depressed people, found recurring themes of loss and rejection. And so his goal in therapy was to reverse clients' *catastrophizing* beliefs by questioning their *irrational* thinking. Dwayne thought his depression over the loss of his fiancée was legitimate, but he had to move on. So, he tried an *integrated* approach, called *cognitive-behavioral* therapy, in which he would be trained to alter the way he acts (*behavior* therapy) and the way he thinks (*cognitive* therapy).

Dwayne's friend Brittney has a fear of germs, and so is constantly washing her hands. With this type of therapy, she learns to *relabel* her compulsive thoughts about germs. For example, she would say to herself, "I am having a compulsive urge that is due to my *brain's* abnormal activity and instead of giving in to my urge to wash my hands, I will engage in an alternative *behavior,* such as taking a walk."

Terms and Concepts to Remember

1. **Psychotherapy** is an interaction between a trained therapist and someone who is seeking to overcome psychological difficulties or wants to achieve personal growth.

2. **Biomedical therapy** is the use of prescribed medications or medical procedures that act directly on a person's physiology to treat psychological disorders.

3. With an **eclectic approach,** therapists are not locked into one form of psychotherapy, but draw on whatever combination seems best suited to a client's needs.

4. **Psychoanalysis,** the therapy developed by Sigmund Freud, attempts to give clients self-insight by bringing into awareness and interpreting previously repressed feelings.

   Example: The tools of the **psychoanalyst** include free association, the analysis of dreams and transferences, and the interpretation of repressed impulses.

5. **Resistance** is the psychoanalytic term for the blocking from consciousness of anxiety-laden memories. Hesitation during free association may reflect resistance.

6. **Interpretation** is the psychoanalytic term for the analyst's helping the client to understand resistances and other aspects of behavior, so that the client may gain deeper insights.

7. **Transference** is the psychoanalytic term for a patient's redirecting to the analyst emotions from other relationships.

8. **Psychodynamic therapy** is a therapy derived from the psychoanalytic tradition that sees behavior, thinking, and emotions in terms of unconscious motives but focuses on a patient's current symptoms and relationships.

9. **Insight therapies,** including psychodynamic and humanistic therapies, focus on increasing a person's awareness of underlying motives and defenses.

10. **Person-centered therapy** is a humanistic nondirective therapy developed by Carl Rogers, in which growth and self-awareness are promoted in an environment that offers genuineness, acceptance, and empathy. (Also called *client-centered therapy.*)

11. **Active listening** is a nondirective technique of Rogers' person-centered therapy, in which the listener echoes, restates, and clarifies, but does not interpret, clients' remarks.

12. **Unconditional positive regard** is a caring, accepting, nonjudgmental attitude toward others, which Carl Rogers believed would help clients develop self-acceptance and self-awareness.

13. **Behavior therapy** is therapy that applies learning principles to the elimination of unwanted behaviors.

14. **Counterconditioning** is a category of behavior therapy in which new responses are classically conditioned to stimuli that trigger unwanted behaviors.

15. **Exposure therapies** treat anxiety by exposing people to things they normally fear and avoid. Among these therapies are systematic desensitization and virtual reality exposure therapy.

16. **Systematic desensitization** is a type of exposure therapy in which a pleasant, relaxed state is classically conditioned to a hierarchy of gradually increasing anxiety-provoking stimuli.

    Memory aid: This is a form of **counterconditioning** in which sensitive, anxiety-triggering stimuli are *desensitized* in a progressive, or **systematic,** fashion.

17. **Virtual reality exposure therapy** is a counterconditioning technique that progressively exposes people to electronic simulations of feared situations to treat their anxiety.

18. **Aversive conditioning** is a type of counterconditioning in which an unpleasant state becomes associated with an unwanted behavior.

19. A **token economy** is an operant conditioning procedure in which desirable behaviors are promoted in people by rewarding them with tokens, or positive reinforcers, which can be exchanged for privileges or treats. For the most part, token economies are used in hospitals, schools, and other institutional settings.

20. **Cognitive therapy** focuses on teaching people new and more adaptive ways of thinking. The therapy is based on the idea that thoughts intervene between events and our emotional reactions.

21. **Cognitive-behavioral therapy** is an integrated therapy that focuses on changing self-defeating thinking (cognitive therapy) and unwanted behaviors (behavior therapy).

22. **Group therapy** is therapy conducted with groups rather than individuals, providing benefits from group interaction.

23. **Family therapy** views problem behavior as influenced by, or directed at, other family members. Therapy treats the family as a system.

24. **Evidence-based practice** refers to clinical decision making that integrates the best available research evidence with clinical expertise and patient characteristics and preferences.

25. The **therapeutic alliance** is the bond of mutual trust and understanding between a therapist and a client.

26. **Antipsychotic drugs,** such as chlorpromazine, are used to treat schizophrenia and other severe thought disorders.

27. **Antianxiety drugs,** such as Xanax, help control anxiety and agitation by reducing central nervous system activity.

28. **Antidepressant drugs,** such as Prozac, treat depression, anxiety disorders, obsessive-compulsive disorder, and posttraumatic stress disorder by altering the availability of norepinephrine and serotonin.

29. In **electroconvulsive therapy (ECT)**, a biomedical therapy often used to treat severe depression, electric shock is passed through the brain.

30. **Repetitive transcranial magnetic stimulation (rTMS)** is the delivery of repeated pulses of magnetic energy to stimulate or suppress brain activity.

31. **Psychosurgery** is a biomedical therapy that attempts to change behavior by removing or destroying brain tissue. Since drug therapy became widely available in the 1950s, psychosurgery has been infrequently used.

32. Once used to control violent patients, the **lobotomy** is a form of psychosurgery in which the nerves linking the emotion centers of the brain to the frontal lobes are severed.

33. **Resilience** is the personal strength that helps people cope with stress and recover from traumatic events.

34. **Posttraumatic growth** refers to positive psychological changes that may develop following challenging life crises.

Statistical Reasoning in Everyday Life

Appendix Overview

A basic understanding of statistical reasoning has become a necessity in everyday life. Statistics are tools that help the psychologist and layperson to interpret the vast quantities of information they are confronted with on a daily basis. Appendix A discusses how statistics are used to describe data and to generalize from instances.

In studying this appendix, you must concentrate on learning a number of procedures and understanding some underlying principles in the science of statistics. The graphic and computational procedures in the section called "Describing Data" include how data are distributed in a sample; measures of central tendency such as the mean, median, and mode; variation measures such as the range and standard deviation; and correlation, or the degree to which two variables are related. Most of the conceptual material is then covered in the section titled "Significant Differences." You should be able to discuss three important principles concerning populations and samples, as well as the concept of significance in testing differences. The ultimate goal is to make yourself a better consumer of statistical research by improving your critical thinking skills.

Appendix Review

First, skim each section, noting headings and boldface items. After you have read the section, review each Objective By answering the fill-in and essay-type questions that follow it. APPLICATIONS help you to know how well you understand the material. As you proceed, evaluate your performance by consulting the answers on page 318. Do not continue with the next section until you understand each answer. If you need to, review or reread the section in the textbook before continuing.

Describing Data

Objective A-1: Explain how we describe data using three measures of central tendency, and discuss the relative usefulness of the two measures of variation.

We use *descriptive statistics* to organize data, sometimes depicting it as a *bar graph*.

The *mode* is the most frequently occurring score in a distribution. The *mean* is the arithmetic average of a distribution, obtained by adding the scores and then dividing by the number of scores. If the distribution is *skewed* by even a few extreme scores, the mean will be biased. The *median* is the middle score in a distribution; half the scores are above it and half are below it.

The *range* of scores—the gap between the lowest and highest score—provides only a rough estimate of variation. The more standard measure of how scores deviate from one another is the **standard deviation**. It better gauges whether scores are packed together or dispersed because it uses information from each score. Many types of scores are distributed along a bell-shaped curve, or a **normal curve** (normal distribution). Roughly 68 percent of the cases fall within one standard deviation of the mean. About 95 percent fall within two standard deviations.

1. We should be skeptical when presented with numbers that are _____ , _____ , and _____ .

2. The first step in describing data is to _____ it in some meaningful way, such as by displaying it as a _____ _____ . When reading these, it's important to read the scale _____ and note their _____ .

3. The three measures of central tendency are the _____ , the _____ , and the _____ .

4. The most frequently occurring score in a distribution is called the _____ .

5. The mean is computed as the _____ of all the scores divided by the _____ of scores.

6. The median is the score at the _____ percentile.

7. When a distribution is lopsided, or
_____ , the _____
(mean/median/mode) can be biased by a few
extreme scores.

8. Averages derived from scores with
_____ (high/low) variability are
more reliable than those with
_____ (high/low) variability.

9. The measures of variation include the
_____ and the
_____ _____ .

10. The range is computed as the _____
_____ .

11. The range provides a(n) _____
(crude/accurate) estimate of variation because it
_____ (is/is not) influenced by
extreme scores.

12. The standard deviation is a _____
(more accurate/less accurate) measure of variation than the range. Unlike the range, the standard
deviation _____ (uses/does not
use) information from each score in the distribution.
The standard deviation is calculated as the square
root of the sum of _____ from the
means squared divided by the _____
_____ _____ .

13. The bell-shaped distribution that often describes
large amounts of data is called the
_____ _____ .

14. In this distribution, approximately
_____ percent of the individual
scores fall within 1 standard deviation on either side
of the mean. Within 2 standard deviations on either
side of the mean fall _____
percent of the individual scores.

Explain what it means to score 116 on the normally distributed Wechsler IQ test. (Recall that the mean is 100;
the standard deviation is ±15 points. Hint: You might
find it helpful to draw the normal curve first.)

15. The football team's punter wants to determine how consistent his punting distances have been during the past
season. He should compute the
   a. mean.   c. mode.
   b. median.   d. standard deviation.

16. Esteban refuses to be persuaded by an advertiser's claim
that people using their brand of gasoline average 50
miles per gallon. His decision probably is based on
   a. the possibility that the average is the mean, which
could be artificially inflated by a few extreme scores.
   b. the absence of information about the size of the
sample studied.
   c. the absence of information about the variation in
sample scores.
   d. all of these statements.

17. Bob scored 43 out of 70 points on his psychology exam.
He was worried until he discovered that most of the class
earned the same score. Bob's score was equal to the
   a. mean.   c. mode.
   b. median.   d. range.

18. The four families on your block all have annual household incomes of $25,000. If a new family with an annual
income of $75,000 moved in, which measure of central
tendency would be most affected?
   a. mean   c. mode
   b. median   d. standard deviation

Objective A-2: Explain what it means when we say two
things are correlated.

The **correlation coefficient** is a statistical measure of how
strongly related any two sets of scores are. It can range
from +1 (a perfect positive correlation) through 0.00
(the scores are unrelated) to –1 (a perfect negative correlation). Scores with a positive correlation increase
and decrease together. A negative correlation coefficient indicates that one score falls as the other rises.
Scatterplots reveal patterns of relationships between two
sets of scores. Like other statistical measures, the correlation coefficient can help us see what the naked eye
misses. However, it does not tell us about cause and
effect.

19. A measure of the direction and extent of relationship between two sets of scores is called the
_____ _____ .
Numerically, this measure can range from _
_____ to _____ .

20. To depict a correlation, researchers create a graph
called a _____ , which uses dots to
represent the values of the two variables.

21. When there is no relationship at all between two sets of scores, the correlation coefficient is

    _____ . The strongest possible correlation between two sets of scores is either

    _____ or _____ .

    When the correlation between two sets of scores is negative, as one increases, the other

    _____ .

Cite an example of a positive correlation and a negative correlation. Your examples can be drawn from previous chapters of the text or can be based on observations from daily life.

An example of a positive correlation is

An example of a negative correlation is

22. The correlation coefficient _____ (gives/does not give) information about cause-effect relationships. It does, however, tell how well one factor _____ the other related factor.

APPLICATIONS:

23. Meagan has found a positive correlation between the height and body weight of students at her school. Which of the following is true?

    a. There is a cause-effect relationship between height and weight.
    b. As height increases, weight decreases.
    c. Knowing a person's height, one can predict his or her weight.
    d. All of these statements are true.

24. Given the positive correlation found by Meagan, how should she depict the relationship on a scatterplot?

    a. All the points should fall on a straight line.
    b. The points should be spread randomly about the plot.
    c. All the points should fall on a curved line.
    d. It is impossible to determine from the information given.

Objective A-3: Define *regression toward the mean*.

Illusory correlation often occurs because our belief that a relationship exists leads us to notice and recall confirm-

ing instances of our belief and to disregard disconfirming ones. Illusory correlation sometimes feeds the illusion that chance events are subject to our personal control. For example, gamblers, remembering their lucky rolls, may come to believe that they can influence the roll of the dice by again, say, throwing gently for low numbers and hard for high numbers.

Regression toward the mean can also fuel the illusion that uncontrollable events correlate with our actions. After an unusual event, things tend to return toward their average level. However, we readily attribute this normal statistical regression to something we have done.

25. A correlation that is perceived but doesn't really exist is called an _____

    _____ .

26. When we believe that a relationship exists between two things, we are most likely to recall instances that _____ (confirm/disconfirm) our belief.

27. This type of correlation feeds the illusion of _____—that we can control events that actually are due to _____ .

    It is also fed by a statistical phenomenon called

    _____ _____

    _____ _____ ,

    the idea that extreme or unusual results tend to fall back toward the average.

APPLICATIONS:

28. Which of the following exemplifies regression toward the mean?

    a. In his second season of varsity basketball, Edward averaged 5 points more per game than in his first season.
    b. A gambler rolls 5 consecutive "sevens" using her favorite dice.
    c. After earning an unusually low score on the first exam in a class, a "B student" scores much higher on the second exam.
    d. A student who usually gets Bs earns grades of A, C, C, and A on four exams, thus maintaining a B average overall for the class.

29. Joe believes that his basketball game is always best when he wears his old gray athletic socks. Joe is a victim of the phenomenon called

    a. regression toward the mean.
    b. the availability heuristic.
    c. illusory correlation.
    d. skewed scoring.

Significant Differences

Objective A-4: Explain how we know whether an observed difference can be generalized to other populations.

Important principles to remember in making generalizations include the following:

a. Representative samples are better than biased samples. We are particularly prone to overgeneralize from vivid cases at the extremes.

b. Less-variable observations are better than those that are more variable. Averages are more reliable when derived from scores with low variability.

c. More cases are better than fewer. Small samples provide less reliable estimates of the average than do large samples.

Psychologists use tests of statistical significance to help them determine whether differences between two groups are reliable. When the averages of the samples drawn from the groups are reliable, and the difference between them is relatively large, we say the difference has **statistical significance.** This means that the difference very likely reflects a real difference and is not due to chance variation between the samples. Given large enough samples, a difference between them may be statistically significant yet have little practical significance.

30. The best basis for generalizing is not from _____ cases but from a _____ sample of cases.

31. Observations are more reliable when they are based on scores with _____ (high/low) variability.

32. Averages based on a large number of cases are _____ (more/less) reliable than those based on a few cases.

33. Tests of statistical _____ are used to estimate whether observed differences are real, that is, to make sure they are not simply the result of _____ variation. The differences are probably real if the sample averages are _____ and the difference between them is _____ .

APPLICATION:

34. Dr. Salazar recently completed an experiment in which she compared reasoning ability in a sample of women and a sample of men. The means of the female and male samples equaled 21 and 19, respectively, on a 25-point scale. A statistical test revealed that her results were not statistically significant. What can Dr. Salazar conclude?

a. Women have superior reasoning ability.
b. The difference in the means of the two samples is probably due to chance variation.
c. The difference in the means of the two samples is reliable.

d. She cannot reach any of these conclusions.

Objective A-5: Define *cross-sectional studies* and *longitudinal studies,* and discuss why it is important to know which method was used.

In **cross-sectional studies,** people of different ages are compared with one another at the same time. In **longitudinal studies,** the same people are restudied and retested at different times in their life span. Knowing which method was used helps us to know whether we should be considering the effects of cultural generation differences (in cross-sectional studies, which show a decline in intelligence) or factoring in contributors to longevity (in longitudinal studies, which show stability).

35. Researchers use _____- _____ studies to investigate a randomly sampled group of people of _____ (the same/different) age(s). This type of study generally extends over a very _____ (long/short) time.

36. Researchers use _____ studies to study, test, and re-test _____ (the same/different) group(s) over a _____ (long/short) time.

37. The first kind of study found evidence of intellectual (stability/ decline) during adulthood; the second found evidence of intellectual _____ (stability/decline).

Explain why the conflicting results of these two types of studies point to the importance of knowing how researchers reached their conclusions.

Progress Test

Multiple-Choice Questions

Circle your answers to the following questions and check them with the answers beginning on page 319. If your answer is incorrect, read the explanation for why it is incorrect and then consult the text. Use the page margins if you need extra space for your computations.

1. What is the mean of the following distribution of scores: 2, 3, 7, 6, 1, 4, 9, 5, 8, 2?

a. 5   c. 4.7
b. 4   d. 3.7

2. What is the median of the following distribution of scores: 1, 3, 7, 7, 2, 8, 4?
   a. 1   c. 3
   b. 2   d. 4

3. What is the mode of the following distribution: 8, 2, 1, 1, 3, 7, 6, 2, 0, 2?
   a. 1   c. 3
   b. 2   d. 7

4. Compute the range of the following distribution: 9, 14, 2, 8, 1, 6, 8, 9, 1, 3.
   a. 10   c. 8
   b. 9   d. 13

5. Which of the following is true of the longitudinal method?
   a. It compares people of different ages.
   b. It studies the same people at different times.
   c. It usually involves a larger sample than does the cross-sectional method.
   d. It usually involves a smaller sample than does the cross-sectional method.

6. If two sets of scores are negatively correlated, it means that
   a. as one set of scores increases, the other decreases.
   b. as one set of scores increases, the other increases.
   c. there is only a weak relationship between the sets of scores.
   d. there is no relationship at all between the sets of scores.

7. Regression toward the mean is the
   a. tendency for unusual scores to fall back toward a distribution's average.
   b. basis for all tests of statistical significance.
   c. reason the range is a more accurate measure of variation than the standard deviation.
   d. reason the standard deviation is a more accurate measure of variation than the range.

8. In a normal distribution, what percentage of scores fall between +2 and –2 standard deviations of the mean?
   a. 50 percent   c. 95 percent
   b. 68 percent   d. 99.7 percent

9. Which of the following statistics must fall on or between –1.00 and +1.00?
   a. the mean
   b. the standard deviation
   c. the correlation coefficient
   d. none of these statistics

10. In generalizing from a sample to the population, it is important that
    a. the sample is representative of the population.
    b. the sample is large.
    c. the scores in the sample have low variability.
    d. all of these conditions are observed.

11. When a difference between two groups is "statistically significant," this means that
    a. the difference is statistically real but of little practical significance.
    b. the difference is probably the result of sampling variation.
    c. the difference is not likely to be due to chance variation.
    d. all of these differences exist.

12. A lopsided set of scores that includes a number of extreme or unusual values is said to be
    a. symmetrical.   c. skewed.
    b. normal.   d. dispersed.

13. Which of the following is NOT a measure of central tendency?
    a. mean   c. median
    b. range   d. mode

14. Which of the following is the measure of central tendency that would be most affected by a few extreme scores?
    a. mean   c. median
    b. range   d. mode

15. The symmetrical, bell-shaped distribution in which most scores are near the mean and fewer near the extremes forms a
    a. skewed curve.   c. normal curve.
    b. bimodal curve.   d. bar graph.

16. A sample with little variation in scores will have a(n) _____ standard deviation.
    a. small
    b. moderate
    c. large
    d. unknown (It is impossible to determine.)

17. If there is no relationship between two sets of scores, the correlation coefficient equals
    a. 0.00   c. +1.00
    b. –1.00   d. 0.50

18. Illusory correlation refers to
    a. the perception that two negatively correlated variables are positively correlated.
    b. the perception of a relationship between two unrelated variables.
    c. an insignificant correlation coefficient.
    d. a correlation coefficient that equals –1.00.

19. Gamblers who blow on their dice "for luck" are victims of
    a. regression toward the mean.
    b. the illusion of control.
    c. chance variation.
    d. the decline effect.

20. What is the mode of the following distribution of scores: 2, 2, 4, 4, 4, 14?
   a. 2   c. 5
   b. 4   d. 6

21. What is the mean of the following distribution of scores: 2, 5, 8, 10, 11, 4, 6, 9, 1, 4?
   a. 2   c. 6
   b. 10   d. 15

22. What is the median of the following distribution: 10, 7, 5, 11, 8, 6, 9?
   a. 6   c. 8
   b. 7   d. 9

23. Which statistic is the average amount by which the scores in a distribution vary from the average?
   a. standard deviation   c. median
   b. range   d. mode

24. The most frequently occurring score in a distribution is the
   a. mean.   c. mode.
   b. median.   d. range.

25. In the following distribution, the mean is _____ the mode and _____ the median: 4, 6, 1, 4, 5.
   a. less than; less than
   b. less than; greater than
   c. equal to; equal to
   d. greater than; equal to

26. In which type of study are the same people tested and retested over a period of years?
   a. cross-sectional   c. longitudinal
   b. correlational   d. scatterplot

27. Which of the following is true of the cross-sectional method?
   a. It compares people of different ages with one another.
   b. It studies the same group of people at different times.
   c. It tends to paint too favorable a picture of the effects of aging on intelligence.
   d. It is more appropriate than the longitudinal method for studying intellectual change over the life span.

28. Which of the following sets of scores would likely be most representative of the population from which it was drawn?
   a. a sample with a relatively large standard deviation
   b. a sample with a relatively small standard deviation
   c. a sample with a relatively large range
   d. a sample with a relatively small range

29. The *value* of the correlation coefficient indicates the _____ of the relationship between two variables, and the *sign* (positive or negative) indicates the _____ of the relationship.
   a. direction; strength   c. direction; reliability
   b. strength; direction   d. reliability; strength

30. If a difference between two samples is NOT statistically significant, which of the following can be concluded?
   a. The difference is probably not a true one.
   b. The difference is probably not reliable.
   c. The difference could be due to sampling variation.
   d. All of these statements are true.

31. The first step in constructing a bar graph is to
   a. measure the standard deviation.
   b. organize the data.
   c. calculate a correlation coefficient.
   d. determine the range.

32. Why is the median at times a better measure of central tendency than the mean?
   a. It is more sensitive to extreme scores.
   b. It is less sensitive to extreme scores.
   c. It is based on more of the scores in the distribution than the mean.
   d. Both a. and c. explain why.

33. Standard deviation is to mode as _____ is to _____ .
   a. mean; median
   b. variation; central tendency
   c. median; mean
   d. central tendency; variation

34. In a normal distribution, what percentage of scores fall between −1 and +1 standard deviation units of the mean?
   a. 50 percent   c. 95 percent
   b. 68 percent   d. 99.7 percent

35. The precision with which sample statistics reflect the population is greater when the sample is
   a. large.
   b. characterized by high variability.
   c. small in number but consists of vivid cases.
   d. statistically significant.

36. The following scatterplot depicts a correlation coefficient that would be close to

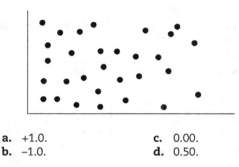

    a. +1.0.   **c.** 0.00.
    b. −1.0.   **d.** 0.50.

37. Which of the following correlation coefficients indicates the strongest relationship between two variables?
    a. −.73   **c.** 0.00
    b. +.66   **d.** −.50

38. A correlation coefficient
    a. indicates the direction of relationship between two variables.
    b. indicates the strength of the relationship between two variables.
    c. does *not* indicate whether there is a cause-effect relationship between two variables.
    d. does all of these things.

Matching Items

Match each term with the appropriate definition or description.

Terms

_____ **1.** bar graph
_____ **2.** median
_____ **3.** normal curve
_____ **4.** regression toward the mean
_____ **5.** mode
_____ **6.** range
_____ **7.** standard deviation
_____ **8.** skewed
_____ **9.** mean
_____ **10.** measures of central tendency
_____ **11.** measures of variation
_____ **12.** cross-sectional study
_____ **13.** longitudinal study
_____ **14.** correlation coefficient
_____ **15.** scatterplot

Definitions or Descriptions

a. the mean, median, and mode
b. the difference between the highest and lowest scores
c. a graphed cluster of dots, each of which represents the values of two variables.
d. the arithmetic average of a distribution
e. the range and standard deviation
f. a statistical index of the relationship between two things
g. a symmetrical, bell-shaped distribution
h. the most frequently occurring score
i. the tendency for extremes of unusual scores to fall back toward the average
j. research in which people of different ages are compared
k. a graph depicting a table of data
l. the middle score in a distribution
m. research in which the same people are tested and retested over a long period of time.
n. an asymmetrical distribution
o. the square root of the average squared deviation of scores from the mean

True–False Items

Indicate whether each statement is true or false by placing a *T* or *F* in the blank next to the item.

_____ **1.** The first step in describing raw data is to organize it.
_____ **2.** In almost all distributions, the mean, the median, and the mode will be the same.
_____ **3.** When a distribution has a few extreme scores, the range is more misleading than the standard deviation.
_____ **4.** If increases in the value of variable *x* are accompanied by decreases in the value of variable *y*, the two variables are negatively correlated.
_____ **5.** Over time, extreme results tend to fall back toward the average.
_____ **6.** If a sample has low variability, it cannot be representative of the population from which it was drawn.
_____ **7.** The mean is always the most precise measure of central tendency.
_____ **8.** Averages that have been derived from scores with low variability are more reliable than those derived from scores that are more variable.
_____ **9.** A relationship between two variables is depicted on a scatterplot.
_____ **10.** Small samples are less reliable than large samples for generalizing to the population.

Application Essay

Discuss several ways in which statistical reasoning can improve your own everyday thinking. (Use the space below to list the points you want to make, and organize them. Then write the essay on a separate sheet of paper.)

Terms and Concepts to Remember

Using your own words, on a separate piece of paper write a brief definition or explanation of each of the following terms.

1. mode
2. mean
3. median
4. range
5. standard deviation
6. normal curve
7. correlation coefficient
8. scatterplot
9. regression toward the mean
10. cross-sectional study
11. longitudinal study
12. statistical significance

Answers

Chapter Review

Describing Data

1. big; round; undocumented
2. organize; bar graph; labels; range
3. mean; median; mode
4. mode
5. sum; number
6. 50th

7. skewed; mean
8. low; high
9. range; standard deviation
10. difference between the lowest and highest scores in a distribution
11. crude; is
12. more accurate; uses; deviations; number of scores
13. normal curve
14. 68; 95

Because the mean equals 100 and the standard deviation is 15 points, a score of 116 is just over one standard deviation unit above the mean. Because 68 percent of the population's scores fall within one standard deviation on either side of the mean, 34 percent fall between 0 and +1 standard deviation unit. By definition, 50 percent of the scores fall below the mean. Therefore, a score at or above 115 is higher than that obtained by 84 percent of the population (50 percent + 34 percent = 84 percent).

15. **d.** is the answer. A small or large standard deviation indicates whether a distribution involves similar or variable scores.
    a., b., & c. These statistics would not give any information regarding the consistency of performance.
16. **d.** is the answer.
17. **c.** is the answer.
    a. The mean is computed as the sum of the scores divided by the number of scores.
    b. The median is the midmost score in a distribution.
    d. The range is the difference between the highest and lowest scores in a distribution.
18. **a.** is the answer. The mean is strongly influenced by extreme scores. In this example, the mean would change from $25,000 to (75,000 + 25,000 + 25,000 + 25,000 + 25,000)/5 = $35,000.
    b. & c. Both the median and the mode would remain $25,000, even with the addition of the fifth family's income.
    d. The standard deviation is a measure of variation, not central tendency.
19. correlation coefficient; +1.00; –1.00
20. scatterplot
21. 0.00; +1.00; –1.00; decreases

An example of a positive correlation is the relationship between air temperature and ice cream sales: As one increases so does the other.

An example of a negative correlation is the relationship between good health and the amount of stress a person is under: As stress increases, the odds of good health decrease.

22. does not give; predicts
23. **c.** is the answer. If height and weight are positively correlated, increased height is associated with increased weight. Thus, one can predict a person's weight from his or her height.
    a. Correlation does not imply causality.
    b. This situation depicts a negative correlation between height and weight.

24. **a.** is the answer. Because the two variables—height and weight—correlate perfectly, they would vary together perfectly and form a straight line.

25. illusory correlation

26. confirm

27. control; chance; regression toward the mean

28. **c.** is the answer. Regression toward the mean is the phenomenon that average results are more typical than extreme results. Thus, after an unusual event (the low exam score in this example) things tend to return toward their average level (in this case, the higher score on the second exam).
    a. Edward's improved average indicates only that, perhaps as a result of an additional season's experience, he is a better player.
    b. Because the probability of rolling 5 consecutive "sevens" is very low, the gambler's "luck" will probably prove on subsequent rolls to be atypical and things will return toward their average level. This answer is incorrect, however, because it states only that 5 consecutive "sevens" were rolled.
    d. In this example, although the average of the student's exam grades is her usual grade of B, they are all extreme grades and do not regress toward the mean.

29. **c.** is the answer. A correlation that is perceived but doesn't actually exist, as in the example, is known as an illusory correlation.
    a. Regression toward the mean is the tendency for extreme scores to fall back toward the average.
    b. The availability heuristic is the tendency of people to estimate the likelihood of something in terms of how readily it comes to mind (see Chapter 9).
    d. There is no such thing as skewed scoring.

Significant Differences

30. exceptional (memorable); representative

31. low

32. more

33. significance; chance; reliable; large

34. **b.** is the answer.
    a. If the difference between the sample means is not significant, then the groups probably do not differ in the measured ability.
    c. When a result is not significant it means that the observed difference is unreliable.

35. cross-sectional; different; short

36. longitudinal; the same; long

37. decline; stability
    Because cross-sectional studies compare people not only of different ages but also of different eras, education levels, family size, and affluence, it is not surprising that such studies reveal cognitive decline with age. In contrast, longitudinal studies test and retest one group over a span of years. However, because those who survive to the end of longitudinal studies may be the brightest and healthiest, these studies may underestimate the average decline in intelligence. It is therefore important to know which method was used and whether the sample was truly representative of the population being studied.

Progress Test

Multiple-Choice Questions

1. **c.** is the answer. The mean is the sum of scores divided by the number of scores. [(2 + 3 + 7 + 6 + 1 + 4 + 9 + 5 + 8 + 2)/10 = 4.7.]

2. **d.** is the answer. When the scores are put in order (1, 2, 3, 4, 7, 7, 8), 4 is at the 50th percentile, splitting the distribution in half.

3. **b.** is the answer. The mode is the most frequently occurring score. Since there are more "twos" than any other number in the distribution, 2 is the mode.

4. **d.** is the answer. The range is the gap between the highest and lowest scores in a distribution. (14 − 1 = 13.)

5. **b.** is the answer.
   a. This answer describes cross-sectional research.
   c. & d. Sample size does not distinguish cross-sectional from longitudinal research.

6. **a.** is the answer.
   b. This situation indicates that the two sets of scores are positively correlated.
   c. Whether a correlation is positive or negative does not indicate the strength of the relationship, only its direction.
   d. In negative correlations, there is a relationship; the correlation is negative because the relationship is an inverse one.

7. **a.** is the answer.
   b. Regression toward the mean has nothing to do with tests of statistical significance.
   c. In fact, just the opposite is true.
   d. This is true, but not because of regression toward the mean.

8. **c.** is the answer.
   a. 50 percent of the normal curve falls on either side of its mean.
   b. 68 percent of the scores fall between −1 and +1 standard deviation units.
   d. 99.7 percent fall between −3 and +3 standard deviations.

9. **c.** is the answer.

10. **d.** is the answer.

11. **c.** is the answer.
    a. A statistically significant difference may or may not be of practical importance.
    b. This is often the case when a difference is *not* statistically significant.

12. **c.** is the answer.

13. **b.** is the answer.

14. **a.** is the answer. As an average, calculated by adding all scores and dividing by the number of scores, the mean could easily be affected by the inclusion of a few extreme scores.
    b. The range is not a measure of central tendency.
    c. & d. The median and mode give equal weight to all scores; each counts only once and its numerical value is unimportant.

15. **c.** is the answer.

a. A skewed curve is formed from an asymmetrical distribution.
b. A bimodal curve has two modes; a normal curve has only one.
d. A bar graph depicts a distribution of scores.

16. a. is the answer. The standard deviation is the average deviation in a distribution; therefore, if variation (deviation) is small, the standard deviation will also be small.

17. a. is the answer.
b. & c. These are "perfect" correlations of equal strength.
d. This indicates a much stronger relationship between two sets of scores than does a coefficient of 0.00.

18. b. is the answer.

19. b. is the answer.

20. b. is the answer.

21. c. is the answer. The mean is the sum of the scores divided by the number of scores. (60/10 = 6.)

22. c. is the answer. When the scores are put in order (5, 6, 7, 8, 9, 10, 11), 8 is at the 50th percentile, splitting the distribution in half.

23. a. is the answer.
b. The range is the difference between the highest and lowest scores in a distribution.
c. The median is the score that falls at the 50th percentile.
d. The mode is the most frequently occurring score.

24. c. is the answer.
a. The mean is the arithmetic average.
b. The median is the score that splits the distribution in half.
d. The range is the difference between the highest and lowest scores.

25. c. is the answer. The mean, median, and mode are equal to 4.

26. c. is the answer.
a. In a cross-sectional study, people of different ages are compared with one another.
b. Correlational studies deal with the relationship between two variables.
d. A scatterplot is a type of graph.

27. a. is the answer.
b. This answer describes the longitudinal research method.
c. & d. Cross-sectional studies have tended to exaggerate the negative effects of aging on intellectual functioning; for this reason they may not be the most appropriate method for studying life-span development.

28. b. is the answer. Averages derived from scores with low variability tend to be more reliable estimates of the populations from which they are drawn. Thus, a. and c. are incorrect. Because the standard deviation is a more accurate estimate of variability than the range, d. is incorrect.

29. b. is the answer.

30. d. is the answer. A difference that is statistically significant is a true difference, rather than an apparent difference due to factors such as sampling variation, and it is reliable.

31. b. is the answer. A bar graph is based on a data distribution.

32. b. is the answer.
a. In fact, just the opposite is true.
c. Both the mean and the median are based on all the scores in a distribution. The median is based on the number of scores, while the mean is based on the average of their sum.
d. The mean is the arithmetic average.

33. b. is the answer. Just as the standard deviation is a measure of variation, so the mode is a measure of central tendency.

34. b. is the answer.
a. 50 percent of the scores in a normal distribution fall on one side of the mean.
c. 95 percent fall between –2 and +2 standard deviations.
d. 99.7 percent fall between –3 and +3 standard deviations.

35. a. is the answer. Figures based on larger samples are more reliable.
b. & c. These sample characteristics would tend to lower precision.
d. A test of significance is a determination of the likelihood that an obtained result is real.

36. c. is the answer.

37. a. is the answer. The closer the correlation coefficient is to either +1 or –1, the stronger the relationship between the variables.

38. d. is the answer.

Matching Items

1. k		**6.** b		**11.** e	
2. h		**7.** o		**12.** j	
3. g		**8.** n		**13.** m	
4. i		**9.** d		**14.** f	
5. l		**10.** a		**15.** c	

True–False Items

1. T		**6.** F	
2. F		**7.** F	
3. T		**8.** T	
4. T		**9.** T	
5. T		**10.** T	

Application Essay

The use of tables and bar graphs is helpful in accurately organizing, describing, and interpreting events, especially when there is too much information to remember and one wishes to avoid conclusions based on general impressions. Computing an appropriate measure of central tendency provides an index of the overall average of a set of scores. Knowing that the mean is the most common measure of central tendency, but that it is very sensitive to unusually high or low scores, can help one avoid being misled by claims based on misleading averages.

Being able to compute the range or standard deviation of a set of scores allows one to determine how similar the scores in a distribution are and provides a basis for realistically generalizing from samples to populations. Understanding the correlation coefficient can help us to see the world more clearly by revealing the extent to which two things relate. Being aware that unusual results tend to return to more typical results (regression toward the mean) helps us to avoid the practical pitfalls associated with illusory correlation. Finally, understanding the basis for tests of statistical significance can make us more discerning consumers of research reported in the media.

Terms and Concepts to Remember

1. The **mode** is the most frequently occurring score in a distribution; it is the simplest measure of central tendency to determine.

2. The **mean** is the arithmetic average, the measure of central tendency computed by adding together the scores in a distribution and dividing by the number of scores.

3. The **median**, another measure of central tendency, is the score that falls at the 50th percentile, cutting a distribution in half.

   Example: When the *mean* of a distribution is affected by a few extreme scores, the **median** is the more appropriate measure of central tendency.

4. The **range** is a measure of variation computed as the difference between the highest and lowest scores in a distribution.

5. The **standard deviation** is the average amount by which the scores in a distribution deviate from the mean. Because it is based on every score in the distribution, it is a more precise measure of variation than the range.

6. The **normal curve** is the symmetrical, bell-shaped curve that describes many types of data, with most scores centering around the mean and progressively fewer scores occurring toward the extremes.

7. The **correlation coefficient** is a statistical index of the relationship between two variables, and thus measures how well either predicts the other.

   Example: When the **correlation coefficient** is positive, the two sets of scores increase together. When it is negative, increases in one set are accompanied by decreases in the other.

8. A **scatterplot** is a graph consisting of dots, each of which represents the value of two variables.

9. **Regression toward the mean** is the tendency for extreme or unusual scores to return back, or regress, toward the average.

10. In a **cross-sectional study**, people of different ages are compared with one another.

11. In a **longitudinal study**, the same people are tested and retested over a period of years.

12. **Statistical significance** means that an obtained result, such as the difference between the averages for two samples, very likely reflects a real difference rather than sampling variation or chance factors. Tests of statistical significance help researchers decide when they can justifiably generalize from an observed instance.

Psychology at Work

Appendix Overview

Research on worker motivation reveals that workers who view their careers as a meaningful calling, those working in jobs that optimize their skills, and those who become absorbed in activities that result in flow find work satisfying and enriching. Effective leaders recognize this and develop management styles that focus on workers' strengths and adapt their leadership style to the situation. Research on achievement motivation underscores the importance of self-discipline and persistence in achieving one's goals.

Appendix Review

First, skim each text section, noting headings and bold-face items. Review the section by reading the objectives and summaries provided here, then answer the questions that follow. In some cases, STUDY TIPS explain how best to learn a difficult concept. Check your understanding of the material by consulting the answers on page 326. Do not continue with the next section until you understand each answer. If you need to, review or reread the section in the textbook before continuing.

Work and Life Satisfaction

Objective B-1: Define *flow*.

Work supports us, connects us to others, and helps define us. People may view their work as a *job*, a *career*, or a *calling*. When work fully engages our skills, we experience *flow*. We are completely involved and have a diminished awareness of self and time. Flow experiences boost our sense of self-esteem, competence, and well-being.

1. Most people _____ (have/do not have) a predictable career path. People who work to make money for other activities see work as a _____ , those who see their present position as a rung on the ladder to a better position view it as a _____ , and those

view work as a fulfilling and socially useful activity see it as a _____ .

2. Psychologist Mihaly Csikszentmihalyi formulated the concept of _____ , which is defined as an intense, _____ state and diminished awareness of _____ and time. People who experience this state also experience increased feelings of _____ , _____ , and _____ .

3. Buckingham and Clifton suggest answering four questions to find your own strengths and interests:

   (a) _____

   (b) _____

   (c) _____

   (d) _____

4. Satisfied and successful people devote less time to _____ _____ than to _____ _____ .

STUDY TIP: Think about relatives and other people you know who have been employed for a period of years. Of these, which person's attitude toward work best represents the concept of a calling? A career? A job?

Industrial-Organizational Psychology

Objective B-2: Identify the key fields and subfields related to industrial-organizational psychology.

Industrial-organizational (I/O) psychology applies psychology's principles to the workplace through its primary subfields of human factors psychology, personnel psychology, and organizational psychology. *Human factors psychology,* a field of psychology allied with I/O psychology, explores how machines and environments can be made safe and easy to use. *Personnel psychology* is a subfield of I/O psychology that applies the discipline's methods and principles to selecting, placing, training, and evaluating workers. *Organizational psychology,* an I/O psychology subfield, considers how an organization's goals, work environments, and management styles influence worker motivation, satisfaction, and productivity.

5. The nature of work has changed, from _____ to _____ to _____ _____ .

6. The field of _____- _____ psychology applies psychology's concepts and methods to human behavior in workplaces. The distinct field allied with I/O psychology, _____ _____ psychology, focuses on how machines and work environments can be made safe and easy to use. The subfield of

_____ _____ focuses on selecting, placing, training, and evaluating workers. Another subfield,

_____ _____ ,

examines how work environments and _____ styles influence worker motivation, satisfaction, and productivity.

Motivating Achievement

Objective B-3: Explain why it is important to motivate achievement.

People who score high in *achievement motivation* have a desire for significant accomplishment; for mastering things, people, or ideas; for control; and for meeting a high standard. Researchers refer to passionate dedication to a long-term goal as *grit.* Employee satisfaction contributes to successful organizations. Positive moods at work foster creativity, persistence, and helpfulness. Engaged workers know what's expected of them, have what they need to do their work, feel fulfilled in their work, have regular opportunities to do what they do best, perceive that they are part of something significant, and have opportunities to learn and to develop. Worker satisfaction and engagement are associated with less employee turnover, higher productivity, and greater profits.

7. A desire for significant accomplishment; for mastery of things, people, or ideas; and for attaining a high standard is called _____

_____ .

8. The best predictor of school performance, attendance, and graduation honors among high school and college students is _____ rather than _____

_____ . This motivation also _____ talent.

9. Passionate dedication to an ambitious long-term goal has been called _____ .

10. Training students in resilience under stress, or _____ , leads to better grades.

11. Positive moods at work contribute to worker _____ , _____ , and _____ . Researchers have also found a positive correlation between measures of organizational success and employee _____ , or the extent of workers' involvement, identification, and enthusiasm.

Identify the characteristics of engaged workers.

12. A longitudinal study found that employee _____ predicted success rather than the other way around.

STUDY TIP: Research studies have shown that people who possess a low need for achievement tend to prefer situations and tasks that are either very easy or impossibly hard. Conversely, people with a high need for achievement tend to prefer tasks that are moderately difficult. Why do you think this might be? Which types of tasks (e.g., college courses) do you prefer?

Leadership

Objective B-4: Describe how leaders can be most effective.

Effective leaders engage their employees' interests and loyalty, figure out their natural talents and adjust their work roles to suit those talents, and develop those talents into great strengths. They care about how their people feel about their work and reinforce positive behaviors through recognition and reward. To improve productivity, managers work with people to define specific, challenging goals; make a plan to achieve those goals; and provide feedback on progress.

Some managers excel at *task leadership*—setting standards, organizing work, and focusing attention on goals. They keep a group centered on its mission. Task leaders typically have a directive style, which can work well if they are bright enough to give good orders. Other managers excel at *social leadership*—solving conflicts, building high-achieving teams, and offering support. Social leaders often delegate authority and welcome the participation of team members. Research suggests that effective managers exhibit a high degree of both task and social leadership.

13. The best managers help people to
_____ and _____
their talents, match tasks to their
_____ , care how their people feel
about their work, and _____
positive behaviors.

14. Higher worker achievement is motivated by a leader
who sets _____ ,
_____ goals. People best sustain
their mood and motivation when they focus on
_____ goals (such as daily study).

15. The most effective style of leadership
_____ (varies/does not vary) with the
situation and/or the person. In some situations, the
_____ style of a commanding leader
may be needed. In other situations, a
_____ style that shares power is
best.

16. Managers who are directive, set clear standards,
organize work, and focus attention on specific goals
are said to employ _____
_____ . More democratic
managers who aim to build teamwork and mediate
conflicts in the work force employ

_____ _____ .

17. Effective leaders tend to exude a self-confident
_____ that is a mix of a
_____ of some goal, an ability to
_____ the goal clearly, and
enough optimism to _____ others
to follow. Leadership that inspires others to tran-
scend their own self-interests for the sake of the
group is called _____ leadership.
_____ (Women/Men) more than
_____ (women/men) tend to be
this type of leader.

18. Effective managers _____
(rarely/often) exhibit a high degree of both task and
social leadership. Giving workers a chance to voice
their opinion before a decision is made
_____ them in the process. This
_____ decision making takes longer but increases worker _____
to the decision.

STUDY TIP: Think about several leaders you know. These
might be group leaders, employers, teachers, and relatives.
Of these people, whose leadership skills do you admire the
most? Why? What type of leadership style (e.g., social leadership, task leadership) best characterizes this person?

Progress Test

Multiple-Choice Questions

Circle your answers to the following questions and check
them with the answers beginning on page 327. If your
answer is incorrect, read the explanation for why it is
incorrect and then consult the appropriate pages of the
text (in parentheses following the correct answer).

1. Alycia spends most days perfecting her writing style
to achieve her goal of being a published author.
Alycia would be described as
   a. having grit.
   b. having a career.
   c. being an engaged worker.
   d. experiencing reinforcement.

2. To increase employee productivity, managers should
   a. adopt a directive leadership style.
   b. adopt a democratic leadership style.
   c. instill competitiveness in each employee.
   d. deal with employees according to their
      individual motives.

3. Because Brent helps group members solve their
conflicts, Brent would be described as a _____
manager.
   a. directive   c. task-oriented
   b. social-oriented   d. charismatic

4. Which of the following individuals would be characterized as experiencing flow?
   a. Sheila, who, despite viewing her work as merely
      a job, performs her work conscientiously
   b. Larry, who sees his work as an artist as a calling
   c. Arnie, who views his present job as merely a
      stepping stone in his career
   d. Montel, who often becomes so immersed in his
      writing that he loses all sense of self and time

5. Darren, a sales clerk at a tire store, enjoys his job,
not so much for the money as for its challenge and
the opportunity to interact with a variety of people.
The store manager asks you to recommend a strategy for increasing Darren's motivation. Which of the
following is most likely to be effective?
   a. Create a competition among the salespeople so
      that whoever has the highest sales each week
      receives a bonus.
   b. Put Darren on a week-by-week employment
      contract, promising him continued employment
      only if his sales increase each week.
   c. Leave Darren alone unless his sales drop and
      then threaten to fire him if his performance
      doesn't improve.
   d. Involve Darren as much as possible in company
      decision making and use rewards to inform him
      of his successful performance.

6. For as long as she has been the plant manager, Juanita has welcomed input from employees and has delegated authority. Bill, in managing his department, takes a more authoritarian, iron-fisted approach. Juanita's style is one of _____ leadership, whereas Bill's is one of _____ leadership.
   a. task; social
   b. social; task
   c. directive; democratic
   d. democratic; participative

7. Dr. Iverson conducts research focusing on how management styles influence worker motivation. Dr. Iverson would most accurately be described as a(n)
   a. motivation psychologist.
   b. personnel psychologist.
   c. organizational psychologist.
   d. human factors psychologist.

Matching Items

Match each term with its definition or description.

Terms

_____ 1. transformational leadership
_____ 2. personnel psychology
_____ 3. organizational psychology
_____ 4. human factors psychology
_____ 5. task leadership
_____ 6. social leadership
_____ 7. flow
_____ 8. industrial-organizational (I/O) psychology

Definitions or Descriptions

a. an intense, focused state
b. applies psychological concepts and methods to human behavior in the workplace
c. applies psychological methods and principles to selecting, placing, training, and evaluating workers
d. goal-oriented leadership that sets standards, organizes work, and focuses attention on goals
e. group-oriented leadership that builds teamwork, solves conflict, and offers support
f. examines organizational influences on worker satisfaction and productivity
g. motivates others to commit themselves to the group's mission
h. explores how people and machines interact

Terms and Concepts to Remember

Using your own words, write on a separate piece of paper a brief definition or explanation of each of the following terms.

1. flow
2. industrial-organizational (I/O) psychology
3. human factors psychology
4. personnel psychology
5. organizational psychology
6. achievement motivation
7. grit
8. task leadership
9. social leadership

Answers

Chapter Review

Work and Life Satisfaction

1. do not have; job; career; calling
2. flow; focused; self; self-esteem, competence, well-being
3. (a) What activities give me pleasure?
   (b) What activities leave me eager to do them again?
   (c) What sorts of challenges do I relish?
   (d) What sorts of tasks do I learn easily?
4. correcting weaknesses; sharpening skills

Industrial-Organizational Psychology

5. farming; manufacturing; knowledge work
6. industrial-organizational; human factors; personnel psychology; organizational psychology; management

Motivating Achievement

7. achievement motivation
8. self-discipline; intelligence score; refines
9. grit

10. hardiness
11. creativity; persistence; helpfulness; engagement

Researchers found that engaged workers know what's expected of them, have what they need to do their work, feel fulfilled in their work, have regular opportunities to do what they do best, perceive that they are part of something significant, and have opportunities to learn and develop.

12. attitude

Leadership

13. identify; measure; talents; reinforce
14. specific; challenging; immediate
15. varies; directive; democratic
16. task leadership; social leadership
17. charisma; vision; communicate; inspire; transformational; Women; men
18. often; engages; shared; commitment

Progress Test

Multiple-Choice Questions

1. **a.** is the answer.
2. **d.** is the answer. As different people are motivated by different things, to increase motivation and thus productivity, managers are advised to learn what motivates individual employees and to challenge and reward them accordingly.
   a. & b. The most effective management style will depend on the situation.
   c. This might be an effective strategy with some, but not all, employees.
3. **b.** is the answer.
   a. & c. Directive, or task-oriented, managers are likely to assume that worker motivation is low.
   d. The most effective leaders are generally charismatic, which has nothing to do with whether they are directive or democratic leaders.
4. **d.** is the answer.
5. **d.** is the answer. Because Darren appears to resonate with the principle that people are intrinsically motivated to work for reasons beyond money, giving him feedback about his work and involving him in decision making are probably all he needs to be very satisfied with his situation.
   a., b., & c. Creating competitions and using controlling, rather than informing, rewards may have the opposite effect and actually undermine Darren's motivation.

6. **b.** is the answer.
   a. Bill's style is one of task leadership, whereas Juanita's is one of social leadership.
   c. Juanita's style is democratic, whereas Bill's is directive.
   d. Participative is another term used to refer to the social or group-oriented style of leadership.
7. **c.** is the answer.

Matching Items

1. g		5. d	
2. c		6. e	
3. f		7. a	
4. h		8. b	

Terms and Concepts to Remember

1. **Flow** is a completely involved, focused state that engages a person's skills, often accompanied by a diminished awareness of self and time.
2. **Industrial-organizational (I/O) psychology** applies psychological concepts and methods to human behavior in the workplace.
3. **Human factors psychology** is a field of psychology allied with I/O psychology that explores how people and machines interact and how machines and physical environments can be made safe and easy to use.
4. **Personnel psychology** is a subfield of I/O psychology that focuses on employee selection, placement, training, and appraisal.
5. **Organizational psychology** is a subfield of I/O psychology that examines organizational influences on worker satisfaction and productivity and facilitates organizational change.
6. **Achievement motivation** is the desire for significant accomplishment; mastery of things, people, or ideas; and for attaining a high standard.
7. In psychology, **grit** is passion and perseverance in the pursuit of long-term goals.
8. **Task leadership** is goal-oriented leadership that sets standards, organizes work, and focuses attention on goals.
9. **Social leadership** is group-oriented leadership that builds teamwork, mediates conflict, and offers support.